THE POLITICAL ECONOMY OF REGULATION
Creating, Designing, and Removing Regulatory Forms

THE
POLITICAL ECONOMY
OF
REGULATION

Creating, Designing, and Removing Regulatory Forms

Barry M. Mitnick

Columbia University Press
New York 1980

Permission to quote material from the following previously published works has been granted
and is appreciated:

Cushman, Robert E. *The Independent Regulatory Commissions*. New York: Oxford University
    Press, 1941; reprinted by Octagon Books, 1972.

Fainsod, Merle. "Some Reflections on the Nature of the Regulatory Process." In C. J. Fried-
    rich and Edward S. Mason, eds., *Public Policy*. Cambridge, Mass.: Harvard University Press
    (1940), 1:297–323. Copyright 1940 by the President and Fellows of Harvard College.

Herring, E. Pendleton. *Federal Commissioners: A Study of Their Careers and Qualifications*.
    Cambridge, Mass.: Harvard University Press, 1936. Copyright 1936 by the President and
    Fellows of Harvard College.

Short, Lloyd M. *The Development of National Administrative Organization in the United
    States*. Baltimore, Md.: Johns Hopkins University Press, 1923. Copyright 1923 by the Insti-
    tute for Government Research (The Brookings Institution, 1775 Massachusetts Avenue,
    N.W., Washington, D.C.).

Library of Congress Cataloging in Publication Data

Mitnick, Barry M
    The political economy of regulation.

    Bibliography: p.
    Includes index.
    1. Industry and state—United States.   2. Trade
regulation—United States.   I. Title.
HD3616.U46M57   338.973   79-26172
ISBN 0-231-04023-7

Columbia University Press
New York   Guildford, Surrey

To My Parents

Contents

Acknowledgments

I WOULD LIKE to acknowledge a great many debts that cannot be adequately repaid. Perhaps the strongest influence visible in these pages is that of my former teacher, Robert W. Backoff, who, as friend and collaborator, remains my teacher. The basic incentive systems model of organizations summarized in chapters 3 and 6 was developed in collaboration with him.

Russell Hardin and Charles Levine contributed greatly in direct and indirect ways to any logic and lucidity that resides in this work.

For certain perspectives, ways of thinking, or introductions, all of which have quite noticeably found their way into this book, I wish to thank Edward C. Banfield, Steven J. Brams, Stephen Elkin, Charles D. Elder, Ruth Ginsberg, Edwin T. Haefele, Herbert Kaufman, David T. Stanley, and Charles Weiss, Jr.

For a number of generous specific comments, criticisms, and suggestions, I am grateful to Robert Backoff, Mel Dubnick, James M. Graham, Russell Hardin, Douglas Jones, Charles Levine, Alfred Marcus, Margery M. Mitnick, William Morrison, Paul Quirk, Hal G. Rainey, Bert Rockman, David T. Stanley, Martha Stratton, and William P. Welch.

For help in obtaining data and background information and in performing the questionnaire study on state reclamation inspectors (the results of which are partly summarized in chapter 3), I would like to thank Robert Backoff, Charles Call, Steven Cover, Rohit Deshpande, Lori Hunter, Hal Rainey, Rebecca Roberts and, especially, Jeffrey L. Wilson.

Over the four and one-half years during which I worked on this book, I benefited from the help of a number of able research assistants, including Daniel Beck, Vivian Witkind Davis, Rohit Deshpande, William Morrison, Timothy Murphy, Hal G. Rainey, Scott Solsman, and James D. Sorg.

For skillfully converting forest products into typed copy I am grateful to Lorraine Carlat, Kevin Duffy, Molly Miller, Margery M. Mitnick, Carl Myer, Rebecca Roberts, Michelle Whetzel-Newton, and

Roy Vromer's word processing unit in the College of Administrative Science, Ohio State University.

Versions of sections of the book have been published as articles, presented at conferences, and issued in working paper series. Versions of parts of chapters 1 and 9 appeared in the *Bulletin of Business Research*,[1] versions of parts of chapter 3 in *Public Choice* and in the *Journal of Environmental Economics and Management*,[2] a version of part of chapter 4 in *Administration and Society*,[3] and a version of part of chapter 9 in *Public Administration Review*.[4] I am grateful to these journals for permitting the published material to appear in this book, and to the editors and reviewers for the journals for comments that improved these papers.

Versions of part of chapter 2 were delivered at the 1978 Annual Meeting of the Public Choice Society[5] and were included in a report for a National Regulatory Research Institute (Columbus, Ohio) study funded by the U.S. Department of Energy.[6] A version of part of chapter 3 was presented at the 1979 National Conference of the American Society for Public Administration.[7] Versions of parts of chapter 6 were presented at the 1977 Annual Meeting of the Public Choice Society[8] and the 1978 Annual Meeting of the American Political Science Association.[9] Short sections scattered through the book have also been part of papers delivered at other conferences and of other published articles cited in the text of the book. I am grateful to a number of discussants on the panels at which these papers were presented for their comments, criticisms, and suggestions.

Versions of parts of chapters 2 and 9 were presented at seminars at Duke University, Michigan State University, Rice University, SUNY-Albany, SUNY-Binghamton, SUNY-Buffalo, Tulane Univer-

[1] "The Concept of Regulation" (May 1978), 53(5):1–8; "Deregulation as a Process of Organizational Reduction" (October 1977), 52(10):1–10.

[2] Mitnick (1975b). Mitnick and Weiss (1974), by permission of Academic Press, Inc.

[3] "A Typology of Conceptions of the Public Interest" (May 1976), 8(1):5–28. Parts reprinted by permission of the publisher, Sage Publications, Inc.

[4] "Deregulation as a Process of Organizational Reduction" (July/August 1978), 38(4):350–57. Copyright 1978 by the American Society for Public Administration, 1225 Connecticut Avenue, N.W., Washington, D.C. All rights reserved.

[5] "A Critique of Life Cycle Theories of Regulation" (New Orleans, La.).

[6] "Understanding Trends and Change in Regulation" (May 1979).

[7] Mitnick (1979).

[8] "Organizing Regulation: Considerations in Regulation by Incentive and by Directive" (New Orleans, La.).

[9] "A Comparison of Regulation by Incentive and by Directive" (New York, N.Y.). In *Proceedings of the American Political Science Association, 1978* (Xerox University Microfilms).

sity, the University of Connecticut, the University of Illinois at Chicago Circle, the University of Pittsburgh, the Urban Institute (Washington, D.C.), and Vanderbilt University. I wish to thank the participants at these seminars for their helpful comments.

For support during work on projects, some of whose parts are in this book, I would like to thank the College of Administrative Science, Ohio State University, where I held the Dean's Research Professorship during Spring Quarter 1978; and The Brookings Institution (Washington, D.C.), where I began work on the book in 1974 as a Research Fellow, after completing my dissertation there.

While writing this book, I have enjoyed the comments and critical insights of students at Ohio State University and the University of Pittsburgh in classes for which parts of the book served as lecture notes and/or readings.

I am especially grateful for the patience and encouragement of my editor, Bernard Gronert, and the staff at Columbia University Press.

I am sure that there are others I have accidentally overlooked who deserve my thanks.

The person most thankful that this book is finally done should be my wife, Margy; the book was a thief of time that was hers as well as mine. For her help, *I* am most thankful.

Pittsburgh, Pa.   B.M.M.
August 1978 and May 1979

Introduction

THE STORY is told of the physicist, the chemist, the mathematician, and the economist marooned together on a tiny desert isle. Starving, they despaired of ever seeing a classroom again. One day the economist, alert to the values of things from the earth, spotted a silver gleam in the sand. It was a can of beans, apparently left by a political scientist who had been marooned there some years before but had somehow got away. Excitedly, the four planned how to get at the beans.

The physicist, after much elegant figuring employing abstruse formulae named after his teachers and arcane statistics named after his friends, announced that the method of release of the beans from the can was intuitively obvious to the most casual observer. Merely launch the can from a bent palm tree with a force sufficient so that the can on reentry would attain a terminal velocity high enough to insure that it would split apart on impact.

The chemist praised the physicist for his ingenuity but noted that the can would fall into the sea and immediately sink, making the can and its released beans somewhat inaccessible. Observing the nature of the metal in the can and the properties of seawater, the chemist proposed that the beans might be freed by simply allowing the can to corrode.

Rather testily, the economist pointed out that the value of the beans to him, discounted for the intervening corrosion years, was rather small, and suggested that perhaps the chemist was proposing an intergenerational transfer of value with which he, the economist, was not in total accord.

Meanwhile, the mathematician had been squatting on the beach, absorbed in a series of elaborate Archimedean geometries in the sand. Suddenly, he sprang up and declared, excitedly, "A solution exists!"

And walked away.

"Well," said the chemist to the economist, somewhat exasperated, "what do *you* propose?"

"It's easy," the economist replied, arching both his voice and his manner. *"Assume* we have a can opener." [1]

To a large extent, this is a book about assumptions—assumptions regarding the nature of public and, in particular, regulatory organizations and their occupants and beginnings; assumptions about the rationales for public action and the forms in which they are commonly offered and analyzed; assumptions about the design of regulatory means that are too often assumed to require given and traditional forms.

As a result, this work pays a great deal of attention to conceptual analysis. I have tried in many areas to integrate, organize, and extend existing analyses, often presenting the results through typologies; or to devise perhaps new and more systematic ways of organizing concepts and phenomena, displaying the logic, again, through typology.

There is much confusion in social-scientific analysis, a confusion which I hope this work might diminish in small ways. Many concepts—more so than are acknowledged—are employed with multiple or imprecise meanings. Too often, researchers assume they are using the "common" meaning. The concept of the "public interest" is of course the most notorious and most cautioned against, but the literature discussing "public interest" theories of regulation is nevertheless shot through with differing usages for the term and consequently different "theories."

My analysis does not always stop with taxonomy, though I hope the taxonomies themselves constitute a useful contribution of this book. Typologies may be employed as tools to organize concepts so that theories may be generated more systematically. Systematic typologies, generated through a systematic factoring of a set of (key) dimensions, can help identify the range of (at least) the logical possibilities within the concept and theories using the concept. For example, in chapter 2, Anthony Downs's classification of bureaucrats is shown to be a subset of a systematically generated typology. The systematic typology permits identification of a potentially important type not noticed by Downs, the "loyalist." The augmented Downs typology is then used in several places in the book to (speculatively) predict behavior.

Useful typologies of the kind we seek (and do not always obtain) employ a few "natural" or realistic and theoretically interesting vari-

[1] This story is based on two similar ones related to me by Wilpen Gorr, an operations researcher who has never had any trouble getting beans out of cans.

able dimensions to generate inclusive, mutually exclusive categories. Parsimony is desirable and usually exists for the number of dimensions used if not the number of categories produced; the typology is a tool to understanding and overly complex ones may not help us that much, especially if simpler, "better" ones are available.[2]

But, and this may well be another theme of this book, the social world is complex. Development of a field in social science seems so often to consist of succeeding scholars taking conceptual slices that present the phenomena from alternative single-factor perspectives. These perspectives, much as light as waves and light as particles were integrated in physics, seem to join in mature analyses. Parsimony as a criterion can be stultifying; it is ultimately an editor's, not a social theorist's, tool. The reviewer, looking back, typically points out that all the researchers have, in effect, been speaking prose all along, and that the twists and turns that produced "counterintuitive" surprises were all along merely exits on a superhighway. There is perhaps some of this in chapter 3's analysis of theories of regulatory origin, though I do not provide the reader with the final road map he or she probably deserves from puzzling through all the variants in this area.

The book is, broadly speaking, a systems analysis (with the double meaning that the work hopes in places to be systematic, or more systematic than is current in the area). Regulatory rationales are specified, and alternative regulatory means are assessed. But the analysis is limited and nondeterminative. Some of the arguments present the joys known fondly to social scientists of landing on both sides of the fence.

But knowledge in comparative regulatory design, both theoretical and empirical, is severely limited today. I have tried to develop a useful, organized compendium of claimed and/or reasonable advantages and disadvantages of major forms of hierarchical regulatory means. No listing of this type and extensiveness is currently available in the literature. Selected criteria or rationales for public action and conditional/situational factors can then serve to choose and array advantages and disadvantages of the given means for the particular case. In effect, a trade-off is set up through array of the particular

---

[2] More complex typological forms—"polythetic" rather than "monothetic"—can be employed as well. On typologies, see, e.g., Altman (1968); Bailey (1973, 1975); Deutsch (1966); Sokal (1974). On parsimony and typology construction, cf. Humphrey Bogart in *The Maltese Falcon:* "The cheaper the crook, the gaudier the patter."

advantages and disadvantages—a trade-off that may not have a determinative solution, given existing knowledge in the field (including any added by this book).

But governments will design and implement regulation anyway. Thus, this work aims to facilitate that design. Perhaps it can help to build the molding forms, if not lay the foundations, of an adequate future prescriptive design capability. In this sense, the efforts of this work at theory-building and explanation can be servants to the goal of choice of future institutions. I have elsewhere called one part of this, "prescriptive explanation"—the study and evaluation of the principles of societal operation that produce differently valued future states (Mitnick 1973a). We may value certain institutional structures differently because, if implemented, they would perform differently, i.e., we would value their behaviors and impacts differently. This leads us to *choose* institutions on this basis and to study institutions (prescriptive explanation) in order to facilitate choice.

I would not limit justification of theoretical inquiry, however, to this base alone. It is entirely sufficient, in my view, to justify inquiry simply because we seek to understand the phenomena in question, whether they are aspects of evolution and change in regulatory agencies, processes by which regulators come to act in the interest of the regulated industry, the effects produced by alternative means of regulation, or anything else. Theory-building and explanation are sufficiently—and perhaps ultimately—the servants of understanding alone.

The book, therefore, is a mixture of hopefully clarifying conceptualization, suggestive theory, and applied design. It is also a mixture in that it is interdisciplinary, linking materials in several of the social sciences. As a result, I rather suspect it will not please disciplinary purists. The elegance of design and closure of microeconomic theory is not always here. The sensitivity to variation, flexibility, and bargaining in political settings characteristic of good political analyses may perhaps be found lacking; regulatory agency behavior in the real world may have more lines, creases, and pimples than we are presenting. The professional organizational theorist may find the theoretical treatment of organizations simplistic; in many places, in fact, I point out such problems with existing approaches but do not proceed to fill in the gaps.[3] But the value of this work is, I hope, in the juxtapositions and integrations achieved.

[3] On organizational design, see, e.g., Backoff (1974a); Galbraith (1973, 1977); Kilmann, Pondy, and Slevin (1976); Khandwalla (1977); Levine et al. (1975); Pfeffer (1978).

It is time to bring organizations and institutions back in. Hence the emphasis on organizations in this work. There can be an aridity in those elegant formal models of political behavior that collapse away many variables of interest. They can demonstrate formal relationships of great theoretical import, but they often leave gaps. This is not a criticism of formalism in general, just an observation that most existing models need to build on the foundations established. Public choice and formal or analytic "positive" theory models have, indeed, made significant contributions to advancing understanding of political behavior. But many need more realistic assumptions and better reflection of real people and organizations. This will lead to complexity. But, as we have already noted, the social world is complex, too.

I feel this book is inadequate in realizing fully the sense of these remarks. But perhaps it, along with other works, makes a start in this direction. In many cases, I have provided copious citations to the literature so that my work can be used as a reference and a starting point for others.

One point of deliberate ambiguity in this book is the title; "political economy" is an overworked concept with multiple meanings. But many of them are relevant to this work. Fundamentally, it is a book about choice, e.g., rational choice by individuals and macro-choice among alternative regulatory means. It is about optimal or efficient choices in political settings largely made by *agents*, and about *processes* of choice, with optimality and efficiency determined with respect to guiding preferences and institutional opportunities and constraints. Hence, "political economy." The book also deals, in places or in varying degrees, with the application of economic models to political behavior, with the explanation and prediction of political behavior on the basis of the behavior's "effects on the distribution of income and wealth" (Noll 1971a:40), and with the study of the impact of the public sector on private activity.[4]

The structure of the book follows its subtitle: creating, designing, and removing regulatory forms. In chapter 1, we establish some of the conceptual framework for the succeeding analysis by considering the concept of "regulation." In the published literature today (outside government reports trying to identify regulatory agencies), there is little recognition and discussion of the definitional problems with "regulation." The chapter specifies a perhaps fundamental and pre-

---

[4] On the concept of political economy, see, e.g., Ilchman and Uphoff (1969); Uphoff and Ilchman (1972); Liebhafsky (1971, ch. 1); and Smith (1975).

viously unnoticed parallelism between regulation and externalities, and offers several definitional perspectives on regulation. Regulation is viewed as a generic relation extending outside the traditional context of public control of private economic activities. The scope and objects of regulation are briefly discussed.

Chapters 2 and 3 constitute the "creating" part of the book. Chapter 2 begins with a historical look at the creation of administrative departments from committees of Congress during the American Revolution. This is used to develop some generalizations regarding delegation from legislatures (developed further in chapter 6) and the creation of regulatory agencies. Some historical forms of regulation, their advantages and disadvantages in comparison to the administrative agency, and some trends in regulation in this country are reviewed. The major part of chapter 2—a review, critique, and extension of models of evolution, change, and rigidification in regulation—follows. In the literature, there has been no careful, extensive analysis and critique of "life cycle" models of regulation. The discussion emphasizes an organizational perspective on change and includes a typology of bureaucrats (of which Anthony Downs's typology is a subset) and an adaptation of Downs's arguments in the form of a theory of prevention of rigidification.

Chapter 3 is probably the key part of the book. The stages of the public policy-making process—access, decision, implementation, administration, effects—are offered as a means of organizing the phenomena that theories of regulatory origin seek to explain. Public and private interest theories of regulatory origin are identified and critically reviewed. Through consideration of the policy process stages that the theories cover, I show how a number of recent theories are only partial theories and are, in some cases, potentially complements to one another rather than substitutes. No such extensive critical analysis of general theories of regulatory origin has been available in the published literature (but see Posner 1974; Owen and Braeutigam 1978).

Following this review, I identify four simple interest theories of regulatory origin, including what I have termed the bureaucratic behavior theory; introduce an incentive systems approach to organizations useful in analyzing regulatory agency behavior; argue the central role of the regulatory agency as organization and the importance of its environmental control capabilities; and discuss aspects of the access stage in regulatory origin. Emphasized here is a major theme of this book: the importance and utility of introducing organizational factors to the consideration of regulatory behavior.

A case study of the origins of regulation by the ICC follows, showing how evidence for each of the four simple interest theories exists at a number of points in the ICC's development. In this case study, I add the bureaucratic behavior theory to the theories discussed previously by others: consumer (shippers, farmers, merchants, etc.), industry (railroads, trucks), and public (national social goals) protection theories (for related bureaucratic or organizational approaches, see Huntington 1952; Hoogenboom and Hoogenboom 1976). After some general observations on regulatory origin, I apply the incentive systems model to develop a partial theory of regulatory capture. This theory integrates and extends the literature in the area. To ground and support some of the assumptions and propositions in the theory, I then review the empirical literature on regulatory agency personnel.

Chapter 4 begins the "designing" part of the book. Together with chapter 5, it constitutes the discussion of the objective function in the book's general systems analysis framework. Chapter 4 begins with a brief look at some forerunners of the public interest concept (as the ultimate justification for public regulatory action) and then shows that no clear notion of the "public interest" is available from the history of legal analysis of regulation by the courts. Lacking legal indicators, I turn to the political philosophical literature and find many conceptions but no systematic framework for categorizing or ordering them. This I endeavor to supply. The chapter ends with an explanation for the occurrence of public interest rhetoric, an explanation which employs some concepts from the theory of agency.

Chapter 5 presents a description and discussion of the rationale for regulation. Given that conceptions of the ultimate goal, the public interest, are uninformative or abstract, we need to specify intermediate goals. A typology of such goals is developed. The discussion of the rationale covers regulation introduced to correct or alter intentional market activities (e.g., natural monopoly) and that introduced to correct or alter unintentional by-products of activities (e.g., externalities).

Chapters 6, 7, and 8 are concerned with the comparative analysis of regulatory means, i.e., the design of appropriate means given the objective function and rationale. In chapter 6, the analysis is placed squarely in the context of general institutional choice. Regulatory bodies are seen as *agents*, and delegation from legislatures to administrative agencies is examined within the framework of the creation of agents. Reasons for delegation are deduced loosely from initial definitions and common conditions. Types of social choice processes are identified. Incentives and directives are seen as alternative regulatory means used in the hierarchical social choice process to create agents in the regulated entity. Incentives are identified as basically relational in character, i.e., as "incentive relations." Finally, the relative advantages of incentive and directive means are listed and are discussed in the context of a hypothetical case of environmental pollution. The discussion of incentives and directives is meant, however, to be generalizable to common agency relationships, since incentives and directives are seen as basic means used by principals to control agents. No such compilation of incentive/directive advantages is currently available in the literature.

In chapters 7 and 8, the advantages and disadvantages of major forms of incentive means (chapter 7) and of directive means (chapter 8) are listed and discussed. Much of the discussion proceeds in the context of regulation of environmental pollution, but is meant to be generalizable to other regulatory areas. Included under incentive means are tax incentives, effluent charges, and subsidies. Also discussed is a basically market (as against hierarchical) alternative, auctions of pollution rights. Included under directive means are rules and standards and an extreme case, public enterprise. Although discussions of alternative regulatory means in pollution control are common in the literature, I do not believe that a similar, extensive compilation of claims, tendencies, or propositions has been available.

Finally, in chapter 9, we come to the "removing" part. Deregulation is analyzed in an organizational and strategic perspective. Previous discussions in the book of regulatory agency environmental control, types of bureaucrats, and other conceptual material are applied to the deregulatory case. The likely strategies of industries and of agencies in deregulation controversies are identified and discussed.

Perhaps the central analytical concept in the book is that of *agency:* Regulatory bodies are seen as agents, and as creators of agents. The use of incentive system models suggests the fundamental problem in agent-principal relationships of insuring agent behavior desired by the principal (see, e.g., Ross 1973, 1974; Mitnick 1973b, 1974). These models are used to examine both control of regulators (at the individual or micro level) and the control of regulated parties, which are usually organizations (macro level choice among regulatory means).

The problems of creating, designing, and removing regulation are centrally the problems of agency.

In closing, I wish to note that this book was begun in 1974 and written over four and one-half years. Sections of it were, in revised form, given at professional meetings, issued as working papers, and published as articles. But the book was planned and, hopefully, written as an integral work rather than a collection of smaller pieces. Much of the book has not, in fact, appeared in any other form. Where possible I have updated my original writing as newer works appeared in what is a fast-changing literature. The original version of the section on "four simple interest theories of regulatory origin" in chapter 3, for example, was done before much of the origin literature appeared, including Posner's (1974) insightful review. I am sure that I will have overlooked some recent works that deserve mention in these pages.

With that caveat, let me return to the story with which this introduction begins and, with deference to the economists among us, begin to spill the beans.

THE POLITICAL ECONOMY OF REGULATION
Creating, Designing, and Removing Regulatory Forms

I

Concept and Objects of Regulation

THE CONCEPT of regulation is not often defined; indeed, it is not often discussed as a concept. It has no accepted definition, yet it is frequently used in the apparent context of economic regulation, or regulation of economic activities. But what may be considered governmental regulation under broader usages includes much more. In this chapter, we shall take a brief look at the concept of regulation, defining it and offering several of what may be termed definitional perspectives. A few functional problems of the regulatory process that are consequent on the definition will then be identified, and the chapter will conclude with some remarks on the scope and objects of regulation.

Before developing a definition, it is interesting to examine one employed by the Congressional Budget Office (CBO 1976) in the practical task of counting the number of federal employees engaged in regulatory activities. The CBO report noted the absence of an accepted definition and observed that "a 'traditional' definition would include those activities which impact major aspects of private enterprise operations, such as market entry and exit; rate, price, and profit structures; and competitive environment." Beyond this, however,

> many activities of the federal government in the areas of health, safety, environmental and consumer protection, and employment standards have significant regulatory impact on private enterprise operations. The broadest definition of federal regulation would include all governmental activities which somehow affect the operations of private industry or the lives of private citizens. Such a definition would result in the identification of most federal activities as regulatory. (Congressional Budget Office 1976:1)

The Congressional Budget Office therefore adopted as its working definition the following, which they said would offer a "reasonable" basis for identifying regulators. Included are activities which

Impact on the operating business environment of broad sectors of private enterprise, including market entry and exit; rate, price, and profit structures; and competition;

Impact on specific commodities, products, or services through permit, certification, or licensing requirements; and

Involve the development, administration, and enforcement of national standards, violations of which could result in civil or criminal penalties, or which result in the types of impact described above. (Congressional Budget Office 1976:1–2)

Regulation is here defined essentially through a listing of regulatory *targets* and regulatory *tools,* rather than through consideration of the generic nature of the activity itself. Such a listing may "work" very well as far as the purposes of the CBO researchers are concerned, since it provides operationalization of the concept and thus permits easier counting of regulators (see also the descriptive listing by Comptroller General of the United States, U.S. General Accounting Office 1978). But it may not directly resolve concerns regarding the basic concept of "regulation."

1.0 Concept of Regulation

1.1 INTERFERENCES

Perhaps the central element of the class of behaviors that might be termed "regulation" is an *interference* of some sort in the activity subject to regulation—it is to be governed, altered, controlled, guided, *regulated* in some way. Interference involves a diversion from what otherwise would occur, a blocking off, restriction, or alteration in the alternatives open to the subject. Note, however, that the activity itself is not to be replaced, but, rather, regulated—the regulation is not directly part of, or involved in, the activity that is regulated.

Now consider the general class of things called "interferences," including the possible relationships between the interferer and the party interfered with. These possibilities are depicted in figure 1.1, which can be consulted to sort out the following discussion.[1]

When I interfere with what you are doing, I can hurt your performance of the activity, help your performance, or affect it in some way which you would neither oppose nor favor. Thus my interven-

---

[1] For a depiction of the possibilities inherent in exchange relationships, where we may consider the class of interferences to be a subclass of "exchanges," see Wallace (1969:33).

Figure 1.1. Interferences

Act of interference by itself makes a difference to interferer	Act of interference by itself makes a difference to subject of interference		
	Yes		No
↓	+	−	O

			+	I	I	D	Regulatory effect region
Intentional	Yes						
			−	I	I	D	
	No	O		D	D	S	
			+	I	I	D	Externality effect region
By-product	Yes						
			−	I	I	D	
	No	O		D	D	S	

+ = Positive "difference" (benefit).   I = Region of interdependence.
− = Negative "difference" (hurt).   D = Region of dependence.
O = Indifference.   S = Region of separability.

tion may or may not make a difference to you; if it does, I may harm you or help you.

My act of interference with you may or may not also by itself make a difference to *me*. My act of interference may be a side effect or by-product of some other activity I myself am performing, and I may not care about the interference with you. Even if I did care positively or negatively about the interference with you, considered by itself, I might continue to behave in a way contrary to that feeling if the interference was linked to another activity I valued more highly. My interference may not only be a by-product; I may also, of course, intentionally perform the act of interference. Since that intention could also relate to some other valued activity, it is possible that the act of interference by itself may be again viewed positively, negatively, or indifferently.

An example is the archetypical industry whose production of widgets leads to pollution of the air, which dirties clothes hung out to dry. The widget makers may not intend to pollute and dirty clothes, and they may not like to do it (people keep calling up to complain; or the widget makers may genuinely not like to hurt their neighbors), but the profitability of the widget business outweighs such concerns.

Here one must be careful to distinguish any acts that may lead to interferences (e.g., industrial production) from the act of interference itself (e.g., pollution dirtying clothes). Such a distinction may not always be easy, or even relevant. The contrast drawn here in speaking of "performing an act" is between the state occurring if the act is performed, and the state occurring if the act of interference is not performed.

All effects from interferences with your activity that make a difference to you and that are a by-product of my activity are termed "externalities" in the economic literature. They are effects "external" to the performance of my activity; they are not intentional. Two regions may then be distinguished in figure 1.1, interpreting "externality" broadly to include also effects from by-product acts of interference that are indifferent to the subject of interference: the regulatory effect region, involving intentional acts of interference, and the externality effect region, involving by-product acts of interference. Ironically, regulation is often undertaken as an intentional interference to correct a by-product interference, i.e., to remove an externality.

With respect to differential effects on interferer and interfered-with, one can identify: regions of interdependence (I) where both are affected, i.e., the act of interference makes a difference to both; regions of dependence (D) where only one is affected; and regions of separability (S) where both are indifferent. In regions of interdependence where both interferer and interfered-with are either helped or hurt, they have a common interest in keeping—or working to eliminate—the interference. In regions where one is helped, and the other hurt, there is of course a conflict of interest. As noted above, an interferer may, however, seek to keep performing an intentional act that by itself hurts himself because it may be instrumental, for example, to other acts that yield offsetting benefits. Thus, it is important to remember that figure 1.1 maps out possible interactions in isolation from any further consequences. The situation of common interest described above may no longer obtain when further consequences are admitted.

1.2 DEFINITIONS OF REGULATION

Whether my interference with you is intentional or a by-product, it affects the performance of your activity; in particular, it restricts your *choice* of how to do that activity. Choice may be affected whether or not the restriction makes a difference to you. For example, assume that you have five alternatives and prefer 1 over 2, 2 over 3, 3 over 4 and 4 over 5. Thus you will pick number 1. I interfere, removing alternative 5. This makes no difference to you, though removal of alternative 5 may for some reason make a difference to me. At any rate, the set of alternatives available for choice was affected by my interference, though the outcome of choice remained the same.[2]

Intuitively, regulation implies governed, guided, controlled interference—in the broadest sense, deliberate or intentional interference. The effect of regulation is not an "externality"; it is intended. Provisionally, then, as a *broad* definition:

1. Regulation is the intentional restriction of a subject's choice of activity, by an entity not directly party to or involved in that activity.

This basic definition contains the fundamental elements of intentionality, restriction of choice, and removal from direct performance of the regulated activity. What is missing in this definition? What may be added to increase the specificity of the broad definition, tying it closer to empirical referents in public regulation? For one thing, the notion of a concrete purpose, goal, or objective—i.e., the source of the regulator's "intention"—is missing. "Intention" with respect to—what? The regulator has a goal with respect to which the subject regulated is supposed to perform. In other words, the subject is to be *policed* (emphasizing in addition the corrective nature of the regulation) with respect to the regulator's objective. There is, however, no implication intended here that the policing does or does not involve coercion. If the subject's choice would fall outside the bounds implied by the regulator's goal, the regulator interferes by some means to restrict choice to within those bounds.[3]

Thus, as a second definition—including the notion of policing with respect to a goal (which implies and extends the "intention" of our first definition)—we have:

2. Regulation is the policing, with respect to a goal, of a subject's choice of activity, by an entity not directly party to or involved in that activity.

[2] For a broader notion of regulation which includes restriction of alternatives open to choice, cf. William Riker's treatment in Riker and Ordeshook (1973, ch. 10).

[3] Cf. Ashby's concept of regulation in a system (1956). The author wishes to acknowledge the suggestiveness of Dubnick (1979) in helping to improve the quality of some aspects of the succeeding discussion of regulatory definition. Dubnick's work should be consulted for a penetrating and more extended, but contrasting, view.

What else is missing? Regulation is generally an ongoing process or relation. It occurs over, or at different points in, time. The regulator's goal remains consistent over time, which was not necessarily implied in the previous definitions. The regulator's goal clearly involves, or implies, or enables the regulator to deduce, a specification of the subject's choices of activities that are acceptable to the regulator; it is a guideline or standard. Thus regulation implies policing with respect to a *rule,* a value directive consistent and persistent over time, that specifies objectives and enables consistent policing of the subject's range of choice. Although it specifies the consistent nature of the choice restriction, introduction of "rule" into the definition does not fully capture the sense of regulation as "process;" we shall return to this point in the next section.

It is important to note that the *means* of regulation need not be a directive or rule. As we discuss in chapter 6, it is possible to distinguish both directive and incentive means, e.g., administrative standards vs. effluent charges or subsidies as means of regulation. But the basic decision criteria for regulation tend to take, or be conceived of in, rulelike form. An example would be an instruction in legislation to regulate in the public convenience and necessity.

The third definition is then:

3. Regulation is the policing, according to a rule, of a subject's choice of activity, by an entity not directly party to or involved in that activity.

Given this definition, the following still needs to be specified:

1. The identities of regulator and regulatee (i.e., subject). The regulator, in this work, is most often the government and, more specifically, it is generally the administrative component of government. The regulatee is a nongovernment, or private, party. Intra-governmental regulation, however, is also possible (see figure 1.2).

2. The nature of the activity regulated—most generally, the social or economic activity of a private party.

3. The rationale of regulation; the "rule" for which regulative policing is effected. The ultimate formal rule—the "public interest"—will be discussed in chapter 4; intermediate-level goals, such as efficiency, safety, or equity, and the rationale for regulation, are discussed in chapter 5.

4. The specific means of policing employed by the regulator. The advantages and disadvantages of some basic means of regulation will be examined in chapters 6 to 8.

Then a more restrictive, but still very broad, definition of regulation is:

4. Regulation is the public administrative policing of a private activity with respect to a rule prescribed in the public interest.

The contrast of public-administrative with private satisfies the requirement that the regulator entity not be a direct party to or involved in the activity of the regulatee, or subject (cf. Domestic Council Review Group 1977). Note that this restrictive definition applies only to regulation of private by public, the perhaps traditional usage of "regulation." In general, we would have to employ the first, and broadest, definition.

In the literature, most usages of the term "regulation" assume that the private activity regulated is economic in nature. This is not required here, though most of the discussions in this work will involve regulation of economic activity. Some examples of the range of private activities that are regulated will be given below.

1.3 PERSPECTIVES ON REGULATION: REGULATION AS PROCESS

Although regulation was defined broadly above as intentional restriction of choice, it is possible to emphasize certain features of the definitionally described behavior as being more or less characteristic of regulation in practice. In particular, a focus on *practice* exposes the essentially static character of the behavioral restriction specified in the definition. This suggests an emphasis on the definitional behavior *in process,* and leads to identification (in the next section) of several functional problems of regulation. Consider first the dictionary definitions of "to regulate":

1. To govern or direct according to rule. This implies regulation as *guided direction,* as orders and the giving of orders, where these orders may be held as authoritative, i.e., accepted as legitimate, or "rightful" or "proper."

2. To reduce to order, method, or uniformity; to regularize. This is regulation as *regularization.*

3. To fix or adjust the time, amount, degree or rate of. This implies regulation as a *dynamic process of correction.*

W. G. Shepherd argues in effect that the second dictionary definition is probably closest to what really happens; he says, "Regulation . . . legitimizes, reinforces and smooths interest group compromises'' (Shepherd 1973:99). Often, however, he says, a fourth dictionary definition is applicable:

4. To make regulations. This implies regulation as *busywork,* with no real or substantive effect. Regulation may then be essentially *symbolic*.

Robert E. Cushman began his study of the independent regulatory commissions with a definition of "regulatory": "A commission is regulatory when it exercises governmental control or discipline over private conduct or property interests. This control may take different forms and use different methods, but there is always present an element of coercion" (Cushman 1941:3):

5. Regulation as *coercion*.

Marver Bernstein in effect contrasts the perspectives of regulation as direction and regulation as dynamic process: He contrasts a conception of regulation as static and determinant rule application with regulation as a dynamic, indeterminant process—a process of adjustment of interests, public and private, with the outcomes not determined in advance:

6. Regulation as a *political process*. Rules are not rigidly applied to reach the regulatory outcome of restriction of private activity. Any restriction that results is, rather, the resultant of interaction and adjustment processes between contending parties (Bernstein 1955, ch. 9).

Finally, Fainsod argues that regulation can only be understood in a wider context than that of the parties directly involved, public and private; regulation can only be understood in the context of the environment in which it is embedded:

7. Regulation is therefore the *resultant* of the actions of regulator and regulatee constrained by, and in interaction with, their environment (Fainsod 1940).

We shall not take a given limited perspective on regulation, i.e., consciously emphasize some limited aspect of regulation. The foregoing review suggests that regulation may be viewed *in practice,* however, not as a static policing of choice according to some decision rule, but as an ongoing dynamic process. Regulation is not merely outcome, but process. As a process affecting choice, regulating may be seen as:

1. Prohibitive policing—as saying no; as guarding against deviation from regulatory goals and derived rules. Regulating as controlling, influencing, persuading, advocating, advising.

2. Mediating—as filter, buffer, or modifier between public and private and perhaps protecting each;[4] as mutual control process, where regulatee and regulator try to control one another; regulating as process of exchange through a mediating body.
3. Promoting—as saying yes; as creating and fostering.

Any of these three aspects may be emphasized by decision rules consistent with them. A statute that specifies that a regulatory commission guarantee a utility some rate of return on investment may lead to actions by the commission consistent with promotion.

With regulation viewed as a process, its *broad* definition simply becomes:

Regulation is a process consisting of the intentional restriction of a subject's choice of activity, by an entity not directly party to or involved in that activity.

The other, more restrictive definitions can then be similarly modified to explicitly include the concept of regulation as *process*.

A definition of regulation as a process of intentional restriction of choice suggests that we can characterize or model the process by examining the structure and dynamics of choice restriction. In particular, regulation may be viewed as a form of *agency relation,* i.e., a relation in which an *agent* is acting for a *principal* (see Mitnick 1974, 1975b; Goldberg 1973, 1976). The principal as regulator faces the basic problem of regulating his agent's behavior so that the agent will behave in a manner consistent with the principal's preferences (see Ross 1973). In order to regulate the agent—restrict his choice of activities—the principal can employ *incentives* or *directives*. Relevant here, of course, is the contrast in regulatory process between promoting and prohibiting, though either incentives or directives can be designed to promote, prohibit, or mediate.

As we shall discuss in chapter 6, the relation between agent (regulated party) and principal (regulator) in regulation can be modeled as an *incentive relation.* In this relation, the *incentive sender* (regulator) attempts to control the *incentive receiver* (regulated party) through messages and rewards structured and transmitted through the *sender-receiver relation.* A directive can be viewed broadly as a form of incentive relation involving negative incentives.

Regulation can be classified according to aspects of the incentive relation. Thus we could classify regulation according to aspects of the

---

[4] Cf. Bernstein (1955:277–78) on regulation as a two-way process.

sender (e.g., procedures, structure, or resources of the regulatory agency), aspects of the receiver (e.g., the regulatory *target,* including structure or resources of the regulated firms; nature of activity being regulated), and aspects of the sender-receiver relation (e.g., aspects of regulatory *tools,* such as a schedule of effluent charges or subsidies or penalties) (cf. Dubnick 1979). We shall consider the advantages and disadvantages of basic (incentive vs. directive) and of particular means of regulation in chapters 6 to 8.

The incentive systems model can also be used to explain the behavior of regulators, who are themselves in a complex incentive relation with various components of their environment (see chapters 2, 3). In this relation, the regulators are agents, with the regulated party, the general public, particular groups, and other government institutions as incentive-sending principals.

Having identified "regulation" both as static restriction and as process, we may ask what, then, is *not* regulation in either sense? Actions which do not satisfy one or more of the conditions in the definition employed would, of course, constitute nonregulatory actions. For the *broad* definition, this refers to actions that are either not intentional, not a restriction of choice, or (and) are undertaken by a party involved in performing the subject activity. Legislating, itself, is not regulating, although in the *broad* sense almost all laws are regulations. Some administration—i.e., governmental management—is not regulation; the government is viewed as undertaking an activity itself, rather than regulating the activity of another (for example: administering national parks and lands, except as administration involves restrictions on private activities, such as lumbering in national forests; making foreign policy; defending the country; managing and servicing the operation of the government itself). Most of the judicial process does involve aspects of regulation—enforcing and adjudicating rules relating to private activity. Police departments are regulatory agencies, in the *broad* sense. Thus regulation is immensely broad in scope.

Distinction of regulatory from nonregulatory actions can often be difficult, however, in applying the definitional concepts to governmental actions. Just about anything, for example, can be taken as a restriction of choice. The administration of national parks may in some sense restrict one's vacation choices merely by permitting existence and operation of the parks. Such administration, except as it involves restriction of private activities within the parks is, however, not "normally" considered regulation. This does not destroy the utility of the *broad* definition. Analytically, some activities not "normally" considered as regulation *can* be viewed from the regulatory perspective of restriction of choice, depending on the purposes of study.

Specification of additional conditions, such as those in the additional definitions developed above, and/or consistent operationalization of the definitional concepts, may be helpful, however, in identifying particular kinds of regulatory cases for study. The Congressional Budget Office definition cited at the beginning of this chapter may be a useful one because it consists largely of lists of what are to be included in regulation. But, as noted above, it does not tell one much about the concept itself.

Even given an easily operationalizable definition in the pure form, however, it is often hard to specify whether some given governmental activity is essentially regulatory or nonregulatory; many agencies perform activities that have aspects of both. The CBO report noted that even according to its applied definition of regulation there were a number of "gray area" activities. The CBO excluded regulations which determine eligibility requirements and benefit levels in programs providing assistance and transfer payments, and regulations on grantees and contractors who must conform with them as a requirement of doing business with the government. The CBO argued that such regulations "deal primarily with the *administration* of programs whose primary objectives are not to regulate private sector operations but to achieve different public policy goals" (Congressional Budget Office 1976:7). The CBO also excluded programs for managing public lands, national parks, and similar resources, public enterprises like the Tennessee Valley Authority, and information-gathering activities, "even though they may place a 'paperwork' requirement on an industry, State or local government, or private individual" (Congressional Budget Office 1976:7). There are many activities in some of the above programs (e.g., restrictions on access and use of public lands) which satisfy the broad definition (and the more restrictive definitions) we developed, and which do seem entirely similar to programs that are more completely of a regulatory nature. Thus there may be a considerable problem in characterizing and subsequently studying governmental programs that are "regulatory."

1.4 PROBLEMS OF REGULATION

Several basic functional problems in the conduct of regulation may be deduced from the broad definition of regulation, given the likely conditions under which the regulation would proceed. The regulatory mechanism must be established (possibly against opposition from those whose choice would be restricted, though there are many cases in which regulation was apparently sought by the subject parties); the regulation will probably have to respond to change in its environment, and may be designed or adjusted to cause or encourage various kinds of changes in that environment; the choice of specific regulatory decision criteria is not automatic or determinant and must be made, the restriction of choice that is specified must be interpreted in a variety of circumstances and when information is poor, and that restriction must be maintained in operation; and the restriction of choice must be enforced and compliance assured. These points follow from an assumption that the regulators are rational and desire to choose and then pursue certain regulatory goals in a changing and possibly uncertain environment. In practice, of course, regulatory decision-making may not be so systematically rational, though the formal structure will probably exhibit these elements. At any rate, these conceptually identified, functional problems arise because regulation is viewed as a *restriction of choice over time,* i.e., a process operating under extant participant and environmental constraints.

Additional ''problems'' of regulation may, of course, be identified once the nature of the regulatory organization, its relationship to the regulated parties, the nature of its environment, and so on, are specified. Many of these may be instrumental to the basic functional problems. Problems in obtaining, distributing, and employing information within the regulatory body, for example, may contribute to difficulties in administering and enforcing the regulatory restriction of choice.

Brief descriptions of the kinds of factors that may be considered in understanding the basic functional problems are given below:

1.4.1   Establishment

Factors included under the establishment problem consist of those relating to the creation of the regulatory mechanism, including sources of support or opposition to its establishment, the precedents established by it, and establishment costs such as the information cost in ascertaining the preferences of the regulated parties.

1.4.2   Change

Factors included under the change problem consist of factors relevant both to change in the regulated party that affects or is affected by regulation, and to change in the regulation that affects or adjusts to the regulated party or the environment. Examples of factors covered here include, on the one hand, the occurrence of innovation and research and development in the regulated industry, and the flexibility in application and cost of change in, say, administrative rules and standards, on the other.

1.4.3 Administration

Factors included under the administration problem consist, for example, of factors related to the process and static impact of regulation, including such aspects as the cost of the process, coordination and planning in the process, flexibility in design of the regulation, and the differential impact of the regulation.

As a function, administration will be considered to include the process of deciding on the specific nature and scope of the restriction of choice involved in the regulation, interpreting the restriction under conditions of risk or uncertainty, and maintaining or operating the restriction.

In terms of the process of decision, administration may involve creation, modification, and destruction of specific decision criteria and regulatory means. Regulatory actions in the specific case must be deduced from the wider basic regulatory mandate or goal; instrumental objectives must be deduced from the general and basic ones.

In terms of interpreting the restriction of choice, administration generally involves, for specific cases, either: 1) rule adjudication, which includes interpretation of the existing rules or criteria which govern the decision so that application to the specific case may then follow directly and easily; or 2) adjudication of cases with respect to the existing rules or criteria so that decisions on consequences of the rules or criteria in particular matters are made.

In terms of maintaining or operating the restriction of choice, administration generally involves providing resources or support, such as necessary expertise, in the functioning of the regulation.

1.4.4 Enforcement

Factors included under the enforcement problem consist of factors related to the methods and difficulties of policing as well as variables affecting the likelihood of compliance to the regulatory restriction of choice. One important question here is whether the regulator has the power of coercion over the regulatee. Riker (Riker and Ordeshook 1973:296–303) distinguishes people who are benefited by regulation

(and would not otherwise benefit) and people who are hurt by regulation (and would otherwise benefit). He argues that the latter case,
where regulation "hurts," would be more "intractable" to successful
regulation—it is not to the benefit of the regulatee to obey.

2.0 Scope and Objects of Regulation

The scope of regulatory possibilities in the context of public policy
concerns (as against more general social scientific considerations of
regulation of social relationships) is considerable. It extends, in fact,
somewhat beyond the common perception of public control of private

Figure 1.2. Typology of Regulation

		Regulatee	
		Public Regulatee	Private Regulatee
Regulator	Public Regulator	Government Self-Regulation III	Traditional Regulation I
	Private Regulator	"Capture" II	Private Self-Regulation IV

social and market–related activities. It is only recently, of course,
that regulation of social as well as market–related activities has been
accorded major public recognition (see, e.g., Lilley and Miller 1977;
Dominguez 1978). In figure 1.2 are depicted the four possibilities of
regulation *among* public and private parties.

"Traditional" regulation (category I), e.g., the alphabet federal independent regulatory commissions, involves controls directed by a
public regulator on the private sector. Criticism of regulatory performance has often included the observation that, *in practice,* the direction of interference or control is opposite (category II); regulatory outputs tend to correspond to the interests of the regulated party rather
than those specified in the formal regulatory authorization, e.g., legislation. Thus such "capture" could be understood as a kind of reverse regulation.

Public agencies often regulate other public agencies (category III), such as when they monitor affirmative action compliance or performance under grant programs. Here the (admittedly sometimes problematic) distinction between definitional "regulation" and direct programmatic authority or control must be observed. Wilson and Rachal (1977) have recently commented on the problems attending what we have called "government self-regulation" (see also Mitnick 1978).

Finally, "private self-regulation" (category IV), which would seem to be a paradoxically titled form given traditional areas of focus, is actually extremely common. Private as well as public legal systems exist (see, e.g., Evan 1976) and private agreements in such areas as product specification standardization (e.g., stereophonic recordings and equipment) can be viewed as regulatory in character. Analyti-

Figure 1.3. Typology of Regulatory Object Areas

Level of Regulation

		Intra-Organizational	Inter-Organizational
Behavior Objects	"Social": Activities with direct impacts on people	OSHA EEO	Income redistribution
	"Economic": Instrumental market activities	Production process controls Management audits Rate regulation	Anti-trust Entry controls Some macroeconomic policies

cally, some component of the private sector area is distinguished as the "regulator," and is then not directly party to, or involved in performance of, the activity. In practice, of course, self-regulation often fails because this definitional distinction is not recognized in regulatory performance by practitioners.

These categories can be further subdivided (see Mitnick 1978), e.g., identifying whether regulation occurs at the same or cross-level, and the cross-level direction of regulation. In addition to distinctions based on the nature of the actor and direction of control, regulation can be characterized by the *objects* of regulation and the *levels of analysis* at which regulatory controls are directed.

In figure 1.3, regulatory types are identified by level of analysis (intra- versus inter-organizational) and by activities or behaviors at which regulatory interferences are directed. These interferences then involve control of individual behavior or of activities with direct impacts on people (e.g., "social" regulation such as safety standards and EEO) versus control of instrumental market activities (e.g., "economic" regulation such as entry or price controls). Under the intra-organizational level we include controls directed at individual organizations or activities within them in contrast to those controls directed at relations between organizations or the overall structure of an inter-organizational set or industry. Figure 1.3 also offers one or two examples of the controls or regulated areas in each category.[5]

What kinds of things can be regulated? Just about any activity that could be subject to the conditions of the definition, e.g., activities whose choice by the regulated party may be restricted. Clearly, activities that are more easily measured and controlled are more easily regulated. This follows, given that the activity will occur in a possibly risky or uncertain world in which the regulator is not directly involved in the subject activity. Consequently, it may be hypothesized that activities that are relatively easily measured and controlled are more likely to have regulation, and to have formally established regulation. The relative ease of measurement and control may perhaps be due to low information costs or an easily manipulable technology in the regulated activity—or to a relatively simple technology of control.

Thus, one cannot regulate the number of angels that can stand on a pin, an old philosophical issue; one cannot measure angel size and capabilities to make, for example, a rule regarding it, and one could not enforce such a rule, i.e., actually restrict angel activity in this regard. On the other hand, air pollution from power generation is often controlled not by directly restricting emissions, but by specifying the fuel input mix. Such regulation is probably cheaper to administer and police.

In addition to ease of restriction, other conditions that may facilitate regulation can be derived from the definitional attributes and simple assumptions about the regulator, the regulated party, and the environment in which the regulation is to occur. For example, the requirement that regulation be intentional, or a policing according to a rule, suggests that ease of specification of the intention or rule can facilitate regulation. If the regulation is to be rationalized in the "public interest" or some such conception, and cannot be, then one would not *formally* expect regulation. Ease of specification of the rule

[5] The author wishes to thank Alfred Marcus for remarks helpful in constructing the typology of figure 1.3.

may involve such factors as consensus among those people specifying the rule and the costs involved in adding clarity and specificity to the rule statement (as well as the possibility of attaining such clarity and specificity at all). Due to uncertainty in the environment, it may not be possible to specify rules with content sufficient to guide the choice restriction in all situations (cf. J. Q. Wilson 1974:167). An aspect of this, delegation to administrative agencies, is discussed in chapter 6. The need to decide on the objective and means of choice restriction may imply a need to build support around the prospective regulation. As noted above, regulation in which the restriction of choice is favored by (helps) the parties subject to it may be more likely to be instituted. Such regulation may be more readily adopted, more readily implemented, and more readily abided by.

In general:

1. Regulatory objects may vary by *level:* individuals, groups, organizations, systems.

2. Regulation may apply to *relations* between subjects or to *characteristics of the subjects* themselves, including activities they engage in; and these relations and characteristics may cover a broad range of subject areas.

Some objects are not considered, in our society, to be fit objects for regulation. For example, the number of children a couple may have is not in general regulated, though there have been regulations attempted restricting the having of children in welfare-assisted families. Clearly, however, the having of children by inmates of prisons *is* regulated. The Bill of Rights of the U.S. Constitution in effect forbids regulation in certain areas. We shall consider the range of regulatory goals later in this work.

The regulatory establishment in the U.S. government is broad in scope and substantial in size, though in comparison with the rest of the government and with certain very large private organizations, it is not so large. In recent years much controversy has surrounded the perceived impact of this establishment. According to Louis Kohlmeier's now dated count (1969, Appendix), there were already over one hundred administrative units, including agencies and offices, with "the authority to write regulations which apply with the force of law to private obligations and privileges" (1969:307). According to the Congressional Budget Office's definition of regulation (1976), thirty-three departments and agencies were identified. A General Accounting Office study identified 116 agencies (Comptroller General of the United States, U.S. General Accounting Office 1978); a Domestic Council study, 90 (Domestic Council Review Group 1977). The federal independent regulatory agencies alone cover such diverse areas as communication, transportation, commerce, banking, labor relations, and so on (see, e.g., Belonzi, D'Antonio, and Helfand 1977; Dominguez 1978). Approximate fiscal 1976 budget outlays for some of these agencies, together with estimated man-years devoted to regulation, are listed in table 1.1. Of course, as discussed above, there are many more governmental bodies (perhaps almost all) that have as some feature of their activities an aspect of regulation.

Overall, the Congressional Budget Office study found, however, that only about two percent of federal workers (computed in man-years) were involved directly in regulation. Even after subtracting the military from the total of government workers and allowing for variation in the number of regulators due to different definitions of what is to be considered under "regulation," the percentage is probably around four or less. The actual number of workers is probably under 100,000. The same report estimated the budgetary outlays for regulation under its definition as $2.9 billion for fiscal 1976, or less than one percent of the total budget. Though the absolute numbers seem

TABLE 1.1. APPROXIMATE FISCAL 1976 BUDGET OUTLAYS AND 1976 REGULATORY MAN-YEARS, SELECTED FEDERAL INDEPENDENT REGULATORY AGENCIES

Agency	1976 Man-Years	1976 Budget Outlays ($ million)
Civil Aeronautics Board	708	19
Consumer Product Safety Commission	935	48
Equal Employment Opportunity Commission	2,584	63
Federal Communications Commission	2,018	51
Federal Maritime Commission	321	8
Federal Power Commission [a]	1,398	38
Federal Trade Commission	1,678	47
Interstate Commerce Commission	2,142	52
National Labor Relations Board	2,570	72
Nuclear Regulatory Commission	2,335	200
Securities and Exchange Commission	2,030	12

SOURCE: Congressional Budget Office, "The Number of Federal Employees Engaged in Regulatory Activities." The table reflects the "general definition" of regulation cited in the report.

[a] Now Federal Energy Regulatory Commission in Department of Energy.

large, the relative numbers, the percentages, are quite small. According to the definition of regulation used in that study, the number of federal regulators is less than one-eighth the number of workers on General Motors' payroll.[6]

Why, then, the substantial apparent impact of federal regulation? The number of regulators and direct cost of regulation may not be directly related, of course, to the cost imposed on regulated industries. Industries adversely affected by regulation may publicize the impact on them; some have led campaigns for deregulation. The resultant visibility of the regulation in question may contribute to the perception of regulatory impact in general. The rate of growth in regulation has probably been high in recent years, though some of the new federal regulatory agencies, such as the Consumer Product Safety Commission, were created in large part through mergers of preexisting units. Such a rapid growth rate could also add to the impression of pervasive regulation. Finally, and perhaps of significant importance, is what may be called the multiplier effect in regulation. Federal regulations often implicitly require the creation of state and local government agencies by requiring the creation, implementation, or enforcement of certain regulations. An example is the requirement of creation of sulfur dioxide regulations (or substitution of federally specified ones) by state environmental protection agencies. Thus the federal regulators may be only the tip of a rather large ice cube, if not iceberg, in absolute size. In addition, adherence to regulations by private firms may require the establishment of regulation-processing and responding bureaucracies within the firms. Anthony Downs (1967:152) notes that, since reports can be read faster than written, this response bureaucracy may be large indeed.[7]

These speculations on the size of the regulatory community suggest that the interests of the regulators and those who deal directly with them could indeed play a major role in explaining the origin and growth of regulation. We shall examine some aspects of this in later chapters.

The pervasiveness of regulation is well illustrated in the case of occupational licensing. Every state requires the licensing of some occupations. The median number of licensed occupations in each jurisdiction in a 1968 study that included forty-six states, Puerto Rico,

[6] These figures appear in or are derived from Congressional Budget Office (1976).

[7] On recent growth in regulation, and costs or impacts of regulation, see, e.g., Lilley and Miller (1977); DeFina (1977); Weidenbaum (1977); and Leone (1977).

and the Virgin Islands was thirty-seven.[8] Sixty-seven occupations were licensed in five or more jurisdictions. Occupations licensed ranged from attorney and physician in all jurisdictions to egg grader in eleven, well digger in thirteen, weather modifier in Louisiana, and tattoo artist in Hawaii. The degree of intervention represented by licensing may vary from simple registration, through certification by test of competency, to licensing by an authority that sets entry requirements to practice (which generally include certification).[9]

3.0 Conclusion

In this chapter the concept of regulation was defined, in a broad sense, as *the intentional restriction of a subject's choice of activity, by an entity not directly party to or involved in that activity.* Additional, more restrictive definitions were also developed. Perspectives on the definition of regulation that emphasize certain features of the definitionally described behavior as being more or less characteristic of regulation in practice were reviewed. We noted that we shall consider regulation in practice as a dynamic process rather than a static outcome. Some basic functional problems of regulation that may be deduced from the broad definition, given the likely conditions under which the regulation would proceed, were listed: establishment, change, administration, and enforcement problems. And, finally, we took a brief look at the very broad scope of regulation and its objects, noting especially the potentially large role that the interests of the regulators and those who deal with them could play in explaining the origin and growth of regulation. In subsequent chapters we shall elaborate some of the distinctions and themes outlined above.

[8] Council of State Governments (1968). For data on licensing, see also Council of State Governments (1952); U.S. Department of Commerce (1942); Shimberg, Esser, and Kruger (1972, 1973); and W. Gellhorn (1956).

[9] See Friedman (1962):144–45. Also see, e.g., Council of State Governments (1952); Shimberg (1976b); and Shimberg, Esser, and Kruger (1972, 1973). On the effects of licensing, see, e.g., Davis and North (1971:203–8); H. S. Cohen (1973, 1975); Plott (1965); Benham and Benham (1975).

II

Problems and Trends in the Creation and Life of Administrative/Regulatory Organizations

WE HAVE DEFINED "regulation." We now ask: What is the historical experience with regulation in this country—how has regulation developed over time? Why are special units established for the purpose of regulation—why not have existing institutions perform the regulation? How are regulatory units established and why do they persist? In partial answer to the second question, we begin by looking at how national executive government began in this country. That experience provides to some extent a model for the creation of an executive body from a legislative one, which is developed in chapter 6. Next we discuss some earlier forms of regulation, and describe some general trends in the evolution of regulation. We end the chapter with a description of the life cycles of regulatory agencies and regulated industries. In the following chapter, we shall consider theories of regulatory origin, using the development of the Interstate Commerce Commission as illustration, and offer some generalizations about the regulatory experience in the United States.

1.0 Experience during the American Revolution as an Example of the Problem of the Creation of Administrative Organization

One would think that a government getting started would attempt at least some minimal plan—identifying objectives and establishing a range of structural means to reach them. At least, we might expect a careful and conscious patterning after existing mechanisms of government at lower levels or in other countries. But this was largely not the case during the American Revolution,[1] although names and some general forms were lifted from other contexts, including temporary devices that had been used at the colony level; at the start, no really close patterning or copying of existing permanent forms occurred. Lessons were generally learned from scratch by trial and error— remember, at first the objective was independence, not common government. So administrative forms were initially established to obtain and protect that independence rather than to effect some set of longer-range *governmental* goals. The experience of the Continental Congress is revealing in that it illustrates a few recurring problems in the creation of administration, including regulation.

With the prospect, and later the outbreak, of war, the Continental Congress, as the only body acting in the interests of the colonies as a whole, found it necessary in 1775 to act to defend the positions it had taken. It did this by creating, as needed, a number of ad hoc committees of members of Congress to actually perform the work needed. Thus it created, in rapid succession, a committee to consider ways to secure ammunition and military stores; a committee to borrow money to buy gunpowder; a committee to draw up rules for the government of the army; a committee to devise ways to bring the militia to readiness; a committee to devise ways of supplying the army with medicine; a committee to secure or provide for the manufacture of gunpowder, arms, and cannon; and a committee to estimate the number of cannon needed for the defense of the United Colonies and to devise ways of obtaining the cannon. Guggenheimer (1889:120) comments that "the management of military affairs had been entrusted to a legion of small boards, who neither took pains to render mutual assistance to each other, nor to preserve peace within their own ranks."

After complaints about the efficiency of this random group of committees, a single Board of War and Ordnance, composed of five members of Congress, was established. Something of a model existed in the Councils of Safety and Committees of Observation that had been formed earlier in some of the colonies on the recommendation of the Continental Congress. The members of Congress found that the duties of overseeing war preparations and performing their legislative tasks were too strenuous and that skilled, full-time attention to the details of the matters was required. A three- and then five-man Board of War, composed of nonmembers of Congress, was es-

---

[1] The discussion of the experience during the American Revolution is based mostly on Short (1923, ch. 2); Guggenheimer (1889); and Learned (1912).

tablished, with the old Board of War and Ordnance continuing in existence to supervise the Board of War. Later, two of the five commissioners of the Board of War were required to be members of Congress. This pattern, in which committees of Congress gradually gave way to delegation to nonmember boards and commissions, was followed in other areas as the need arose, including finance and naval administration.

In response to a letter from George Washington, who was apparently frustrated at the lack of use to which the Continental navy was being put, John Jay wrote the following regarding the Marine Committee in April 1779:

> While the maritime affairs of the continent continue under the direction of a committee, they will be exposed to all the consequences of want of system, attention, and knowledge. The marine committee consists of a delegate from each state. It fluctuates; new members constantly coming in and old ones going out. Three or four indeed have remained in it from the beginning and have a proportionable influence, or more properly *interest* in it. Very few of the members understand even the state of our naval affairs or have time or inclination to attend to them. . . . The commercial committee is equally useless.[2] (U.S. George Washington Bicentennial Commission 1936, 14:436 n. 89)

Guggenheimer (1889:149) concluded that,

> There was, in short, no element of permanency to be found anywhere in the entire system. Worse than all, petty jealousies and local prejudices frequently distracted the otherwise peaceable councils of the boards, and any wise and patriotic intentions on the part of some were sure to be neutralized by the selfish and personal biases of others. The result was, that where peremptory and decisive action was most essential, there was only childlish hesitancy and delay.

Thus, Congress at first tried to administer the task itself through committees of its members. It turned to delegation, i.e., the creation of agents to perform an act or task heretofore performed by the delegating party, when it found that: 1) self-administration was physically impossible because of time constraints and work loads on double-functioning members; 2) consolidation of committees along

---

[2] It is interesting to note that Washington's letter was in the handwriting of his aide, Alexander Hamilton (U.S. George Washington Bicentennial Commission 1936, 14:437 n. 91). Hamilton, of course, became a strong advocate of the single-headed department system (see below) and both he and Jay played major roles in the adoption of the Constitution and the establishment of the governmental system that succeeded the Confederation. We might speculate that such direct exposure to the failings of the committee system as that indicated by this exchange might have contributed to the positions on governmental organization they later took.

functional lines was necessary to reduce inefficiency by shortening the time for action and allowing better coordination; 3) expertise in the technical matters of such areas as war materiel, finance, and naval administration was lacking among the members of Congress, necessitating delegation to skilled personnel; in addition, the average competence of members of a changing Congress could not be maintained consistently at a high level and was, in fact, decreasing; 4) partisanship and politics on the committees composed of members of Congress delayed and diluted decision; change to impartial, expert decision mechanisms could remedy this; and 5) relatively high turnover among representatives interfered with consistent policy-making and administration, which suggested the need for permanent officials to perform these tasks.

The trend to delegation was opposed because of: 1) reluctance to part with complete power over the disposition of the matter in question (this was especially true in finance); and 2) reaction against their experience with the British colonial administration—some leaders of the revolution, such as Samuel Adams, opposed any measures looking toward concentration of authority in executives. Robert Morris, whose position in this controversy is obvious from the following, wrote in 1776:

> If the Congress mean to succeed in this contest, they must pay good executive men to do their business as it ought to be, and not lavish millions away by their own mismanagement. I say mismanagement, because no man living can attend the daily deliberations of Congress and do executive parts of business at the same time.

And

> . . . So long as that respectable body (Congress) persist in the attempt to execute, as well as to deliberate on their business, it never will be done as it ought, and this has been urged many and many a time, by myself and others, but some of them do not like to part with power, or to pay others for doing what they cannot do themselves. (Short 1923:48)

In 1779, however, Congress finally decided to investigate how other countries administered their affairs, and asked all its representatives in Europe to obtain information on the forms of their treasury, war, and marine departments. The popularity of French institutions after the alliance contributed to the subsequent influence of the centralized French departmental scheme. But that influence, and all other foreign influences, were probably peripheral to the establishment, in

1781, of departments of Foreign Affairs, War, Finance, and Marine, each to be headed by a single "secretary" or, in the case of Finance, a Superintendent of Finance. The major influence toward single-headed departments had been Congress's earlier experience with committee executives. Washington observed in a 1780 letter that:

> If Congress suppose that boards composed of their body, and always fluctuating, are competent to the great business of war (which requires not only close application but a constant uniform train of thinking and acting) they will most assuredly deceive themselves. Many, many instances might be deduced in proof of this. . . . (Short 1923:54)

And Alexander Hamilton foreshadowed recent self-interest models of bureaucratic behavior (see chapter 3), when he wrote to Robert Morris in 1780:

> Congress have too long neglected to organize a good scheme of administration, and throw public business into proper executive departments. For Commerce, I prefer a Board; but for most other things, single men. We want a Minister of War, a Minister of Foreign Affairs, a Minister of Finance, and a Minister of Marine. There is always more decision, more dispatch, more secrecy, more responsibility, where single men, than where bodies are concerned. By a plan of this kind, we should blend the advantages of a Monarchy and of a Republic, in a happy and beneficial union. Men will only devote their lives and attentions to the mastering a profession, on which they can build reputation and consequence which they do not share with others. (Short 1923:53)

Writing to James Duane later in 1780 Hamilton developed his arguments for single-headed departments:

> Congress have kept the power too much in their own hands, and have meddled too much with details of every sort. Congress is, properly, a deliberative corps; and it forgets itself when it attempts to play the executive. . . . The variety of business must distract; and the proneness of every assembly to debate, must at all times delay. (Short 1923:53)

Administrative boards would not help, since they

> partake of a part of the inconveniences of larger assemblies. Their decisions are slower, their energy less, their responsibility more diffused. They will not have the same abilities and knowledge as an administration by single men. (Short 1923:53)

Further reorganizations in the 1780s restored a board to control in the Department of Finance and put naval matters, which were of decreasing importance, under control of Finance. But the government formed in 1789 under the authority of the new Constitution returned to the single-headed form, as a matter of demonstrated superiority; the only objection, to the finance department, was easily defeated.[3]

Some characteristics of the experience during the Revolution that are illustrative of recurring problems in the administration of regulation are summarized below (cf. Sam Rayburn's remarks, cited by Bernstein 1955:67). Note that these factors may be included under the establishment and administration problem categories identified in chapter 1:

1. Process of, and rationale for, the establishment of the administrative body: Establishment reflected a basically incremental decision; there was no comprehensive overview; the administrative body was established in response to a crisis or specific problem; a narrow view was taken of the problem, e.g., narrowly defined committees were abandoned only after they did not work. Establishment reflected the influence of an ideological view of how things ought to be organized, rather than how they should be organized to meet certain objectives efficiently, e.g., the opposition to giving strong power to the executive contributed to the persistence of the committee form.

2. Structure and composition of the administrative body: A need for expertise, including full-time and permanent specialization within the administrative body, was discovered, not recognized in advance. The committee executive, or commission form, was found to produce inefficiencies (cf. President's Advisory Council on Executive Organization 1971).

An example of trial-and-error discovery of the need for full-time specialization is the administration of the early Federal Power Commission. Almost like the legislative committee that tries to implement by itself, a quasi-representative body was set up under the Federal Water Power Act of 1920. This Water Power Commission consisted of the Secretaries of War, Interior, and Agriculture. Its full-time staff was one executive secretary; other work was to be done by the commissioners and their respective departmental staffs. Representative Celler of New York commented in 1930 in the *Congressional Record* on this group's performance: "With all due respect to them, Congress might just as well have put the King of England, Mussolini, and Albert Einstein on the commission as far as any spontaneous, decisive action originating with the commissioners is concerned" (72 Cong. Rec. 8199; cited by Cushman 1941:288).

[3] On the creation of the federal departments under the Constitution, see, e.g., Short (1923); L. D. White (1948); and Learned (1912).

3. Relation of the administrative body to its authorizing organization (in this case a legislature, Congress): Political, partisan committees who could not, or would not, decide expeditiously delegated solution of their problem to a nonpolitical expert, who supposedly could decide. But the political body was reluctant to yield power through delegation, and continued meddling in the affairs of the administrative body after it was established (as evidenced during the Revolutionary years by continual changes in structure). Continuity in policy and planning capability suffered. Issues of the "independence" of the executive became relevant.

The Revolutionary experience exemplifies the general problem of delegation, i.e., the creation of substituting agents, where the agents are formally supposed to act *for,* not merely *instead of,* the delegating party.[4] In particular, it illustrates delegation by a legislature. We shall develop the general rationale for delegation in chapter 6.

2.0 Earlier Forms of Regulation and Their Inadequacies; Historical Trends in Regulation

Regulation of economic life was the norm in the Middle Ages (for examples of regulation in ancient times, see Johns 1903). Merchant, craft, and professional guilds dominated not only industry and occupations, but also the political life of towns. Regulation by towns in such areas as licensing traders, controlling markets or fairs, and protecting guild monopolies, was accompanied by regulation by the Church against such activities as charging interest, and was backed by the authority of feudal lords. Because these detailed regulations were based on existing technology, they tended to inhibit innovation. The guild system largely dissolved, however, under the impact of the Commercial Revolution, which changed industrial processes and practices, and the rise of nation states, which superseded town control. The nation states practiced mercantilism, involving regulation of trade in the national interest (see, e.g., Kemmerer and Jones 1959:54–59). The rise of laissez faire in the late eighteenth century, which argued the material benefits of permitting the operation of unrestricted individual self-interest, and thus minimized the state's role in the economy, was the final blow for the guilds and led to a

---

[4] We include under "acting for" the case where the delegating party refuses to decide and designates another to act. See the analysis of delegation in chapter 6.

lessening of regulation in general. The guilds did, however, linger in the professions, such as medicine.[5] Note the influence of the extant ideological view of the way political and economic institutions ought to be organized on the form of regulation as feudalism was followed by mercantilism, and then by laissez faire.

By the early nineteenth century, regulation in general in the United States, as described by Phillips (1965:86–89) and others,[6] was limited to the following means:

1. *The common law.* This is a nonlegislated body of principles created by court decisions and consequently developed from case to case. Its limitations as a regulatory device include: 1) Litigation is costly; an individual might lack both funds and information to sue and thus participate effectively. 2) Courts lack necessary expertise to decide the questions brought to them. 3) The courts can only take action after the fact and can only deal with those cases brought to them for decision. Oversight of the regulated area is, obviously, not fulltime. Courts cannot plan and so cannot develop continuous coherent policy. By being linked to precedents, court decisions cannot easily take into account changing economic and technological conditions. 4) Courts cannot handle the large number of cases that require adjudication under regulation. As a result, regulation involving the courts is slow. These limitations apply to any scheme of regulation involving judicial decision-making.[7]

It can be argued, however, that these are not necessary limitations: financial support can be offered litigants; courts routinely decide complicated cases in nonregulatory areas and, at any rate, may acquire necessary expertise; courts can establish consistent policy in a string of cases, and some courts may decide which cases they want to hear, thus permitting some choice in issues to be addressed; methods can be developed to expedite decision-making where the case load is heavy. Thus the criticisms by Phillips and others may be seen as effective only in the absence of remedies such as those we list.

2. *Direct statutory control.* A legislature or local government

---

[5] On the historical development of regulation, see, e.g., Loevinger (1949, ch. 1); Dimock (1949:19–25); Council of State Governments (1952:10–13); Steiner (1953, ch. 3); Koontz and Gable (1956:5–10); Glaeser (1957); Levy and Sampson (1962); Loevinger (1966:110–11, 123 n. 24); Corley and Black (1968:335–39).

[6] On the development of regulation in the United States see, e.g., the brief description by Smead (1969:3–7); Glaeser (1957); Levy and Sampson (1962); and the other works cited below.

[7] On these points see also Barnes (1942:170–71); Koontz and Gable (1956:52–53); Glaeser (1957:31–32); Wilcox (1966:18–19); and Farris and Sampson (1973:60–61).

passes a law providing for detailed direct regulation of some activity. Limitations here include arguments that can be offered in general in support of delegation by a legislature, e.g., the lack of expertise (see chapter 6). In addition, changing economic and technological conditions would require continual adjustments in the law. Since legislatures were in session for a relatively short time in those days, laws could often not be amended when needed; there was no continuous oversight and planning was difficult. The legislative process necessary for changes in the law can be cumbersome, i.e., slow moving; it can be difficult and costly to gain access to the process and to operate it. And members of legislatures, according to some views (e.g., Barnes 1942:172), may be overly subject to short-term political considerations in their regulatory decision-making.[8]

3. *Franchises*. State or local governments, e.g., cities, granted franchises, or rights to perform certain services for varying time periods (short-term, long-term, perpetual, indeterminate). The franchise is a contract that contains regulatory specifications of service, rates, and so on. But: 1) The franchises were often drafted poorly due to the lack of expertise of city or other officials. 2) Franchises had the status of a contract[9] and so could not be altered except by mutual consent. Thus standards and rates could not be changed easily, though economic and technological conditions might change. 3) Service tended to worsen as the franchise's termination date neared. The company would try to hedge against nonrenewal of the franchise. Similarly, fixed termination dates could interfere with long-range planning. And corruption frequently accompanied renewal controversies. 4) Service often fell below the level indicated in the franchise because administrative mechanisms to monitor the franchised company's performance were lacking; full-time oversight was absent, and public access difficult. 5) Economies of scale soon made it more economical for a single company in some types of service to serve more than one locality.[10] Thus regulation at a higher level became necessary.

Regulation by each of these means (common law, statutory control, franchises) persists today, though the major regulatory means

[8] See also Barnes (1942:172–73); Koontz and Gable (1956:53–54); Wilcox (1966:19–20); Farris and Sampson (1973:61–62). On this area in conjunction with consideration of franchises, see Glaeser (1957).

[9] According to *Trustees of Dartmouth College v. Woodward*, 4 Wheaton 518, 643 (1819).

[10] Also on franchises, see Barnes (1942:171–72, 218–241); Koontz and Gable (1956:50–52); Glaeser (1957); Wilcox (1966:21–22); Farris and Sampson (1973:62–63).

now encountered are largely of other types. Beginning in chapter 6, some major means of regulation will be discussed and compared.

Regulation by administrative agency, with the regulatory commission as the most notable form, may be seen as having developed to meet the criticisms directed at these earlier types (see figure 2.1). At least, the rationales given for institution of agency regulation often cite correction of these problems as expected advantages (see, e.g., Koontz and Gable 1956:57–58; Barnes 1942:173; J. Anderson 1962:145–54). The bureau form of administrative regulation, consisting basically of a hierarchical organization with a single head, may be an office or division of a larger government division or depart-

Figure 2.1. Comparison of Administrative/Regulatory Means

Reputed Problem:	Means				
	Legislative Committee	Common Law	Direct Statutory Control	Franchise	Administrative Agency
Lack of expertise	X	X	X	X	
Inability to plan and to develop continuous, coherent policy	X	X	X	X	
Inability to handle large number of cases; slow	X	X	X	X	
Lack of full-time oversight	X	X	X	X	
Inflexible response to changing economic and technological conditions	X	X	X	X	
Subject to political/partisan influences	X		X	X	
Access/participation difficult and costly		X		X	

ment, or constitute a separate organization. The commission form, consisting also most often of a hierarchical organization but with a usually appointed group or "commission" head, is generally a separate organization. Unlike the regulatory means described above, the administrative agency—whether bureau or commission—is supposed to be characterized by expertise in its managers/heads and staff, who are able to give full-time attention to oversight of the regulated area; capability to handle large numbers of cases rapidly and relatively economically through specialization of function; continuity of policy through continuity of personnel and institutional existence and actions, and ability to plan; flexibility in its ability to respond to changing environmental and technological conditions; absence of political distortions through independence and judicialization of its procedures; and representation of the public and other interested parties through procedures like public hearings and staff representation of the public interest. In practice, as many critics have noted (see, e.g., B. Schwartz 1959; Landis 1960; Cary 1967; Kohlmeier 1969; Freedman 1975; Cutler and Johnson 1975) administrative agencies have frequently exhibited a lack of any or all of these attributes.

In addition, as discussed below, the rise in administrative regulation has seen a shift from regulation "after" to regulation "before," and has seen a rise in affirmative and active, as against passive, means of regulation. The regulators have been expected to behave more like agents who regulate prospectively in the interests of given parties, than avengers who correct for past misdeeds. And with respect to the definition of regulation, the growth of administrative agencies has seen an increase in interference before the performance of the regulated activity rather than after, and a steady closing of the definitional gap of being not directly involved in performance of the activity.[11]

As Hurst (1950) notes, there has been a continual increase in adjudication by executives, i.e., administrators, rather than by specialized adjudicatory mechanisms, i.e., judges. Under regulation by statute in the nineteenth century, e.g., the criminal law, the prosecutor could perform regulation by simply deciding who to prosecute, who not to prosecute, or who to allow to plead guilty to a lesser charge. Similarly, the police could decide who to arrest. With the growth of urbanization after industrialization came the growth of large police

---

[11] For observations regarding trends in regulation, see Hurst (1950:387–395).

departments, and so more opportunities for adjudication by the police. But such regulation involved enforcement after the activity had
occurred. Administrative agencies, however, could plan, promulgate,
and adjudicate regulation in addition to enforce it. Their rise as a
technique of regulation therefore meant a shift in the time focus of
regulation from after to before the activity.[12]

Where regulation by common law and by statute often placed a
burden on private parties to carry their cases to and in court, administrative agencies sometimes provided mechanisms to support or substitute for private activity. This "extension of the prosecutor's role," as
Hurst terms it, is particularly active today with proposals for consumer and public interest advocates. Such advocates may help solve
the collective action dilemmas faced by individuals for whom, for example, direct action or protest is too costly, or at least has net costs to
an isolated individual. While not reducing the gap between regulator
and regulatee in the sense that government performs the regulated activity, this development has at least meant that some of those affected
by regulated activities may receive governmental prosecution of their
grievances, i.e., a governmental agent to act for them. This may be
related to what we will argue in a later chapter is a basic aspect of
regulation: that regulation may be understood as the creation of government agents to solve such collective action dilemmas.

The growth of regulation by administration has also seen growth in
the investigative functions of government and of affirmative action to
assure certain conditions obtain in the regulated sector. Unlike the
court that passively oversees the amassing of evidence by contesting
parties, administrative agencies have perhaps increasingly stepped in
to ascertain conditions and then regulated to restore or attain certain
standards.[13] This may involve varying degrees of interference in the
performance of the regulated activity, and may through close supervision verge on public performance of that activity. Thus governments engage in health and safety inspections, regulating closely, for
example, certain food-handling practices.

Rather than perform a desired public service itself, such as electric

[12] With the recent increased emphasis on participation in administrative proceedings resulting
from activism and devices like special counsels and financial support for public interest groups,
one wonders whether we shall see a renaissance of formalized adjudication, only this time
within agencies, as a way of resolving conflicting interests.

[13] Recently, on occasion they have been warned by the courts that they must investigate actively. On this "investigative caveat," see Mitnick and Weiss (1974:153), but see Justice
Rehnquist's opinion in *Vermont Yankee Nuclear Power Corp.* v. *Natural Resources Defense
Council, Inc.; Consumers Power Co.* v. *Nelson Aeschliman,* 435 U.S. 519(1978), 46 LW
4301(1978).

power generation, government attempted to assure provision of the service in a specified manner by regulating private provision of that service. But as the complexity of the regulated enterprises grew, so did the complexity of the regulation. Administrative agencies required increasingly detailed regulations; control extended from rates and services to financial practices and capital expansion. Regulator and regulatee worked in a partnership that often made the regulated activity often little different from a public enterprise. Thus, as Hurst (1950:396) writes, "through the back door of regulation, twentieth-century government moved toward the direct rendering of services for fees." The definitional gap between regulator and regulatee has in many areas been closing in practice. As William Orton wrote regarding the increase in governmental intervention during the Depression, "To whatever strange ports we are wafted on the warm breeze of the New Deal, we shall not see the lotus land of laissez-faire again. That is probably the major historical fact of our generation" (Orton 1935; cited by Funigiello 1973:xi).

Because of the increasing complexity of society in general, and the rapidity of change, extension of regulation has often, paradoxically, increased the discretion with which it is administered. Thus, both extension of regulation to new areas and delegation of decision-making on important areas of regulatory content, has occurred. Lowi (1969, ch. 5) has argued, in part, that, as regulation has expanded in scope of coverage (in terms of the number and variety of objects of regulation), the categories of objects subject to regulation have become more general and more abstract. Similarly, the regulatory standards or criteria to which those objects are subject have become more general and abstract (cf. Friendly 1962; Jaffe 1973). Thus, for example, regulation of specific abuses by the railroads (see chapter 3) expanded to cover several modes of surface transport (trucks, barges) and was directed broadly at regulating features of the transport market using such abstract criteria as "just and reasonable." This development has raised questions of "quo warranto," e.g., according to what authority are the regulations under a given apparent delegation really made. The rationale for delegation itself will be discussed in chapter 6. The quo warranto question (see Haefele 1973a, 1973b) remains a basic one. We shall argue that a design perspective involving evaluative comparison of alternative regulatory means could, when fully developed, reduce quo warranto objections by permitting more explicit linkage of regulatory goals to desired impacts.

In conclusion, consider the inadequacies noted above for the earlier forms of U.S. regulation in the light of the previous discussion of the creation of administrative organization. Common law, direct statutory, and franchise regulation each exhibit some or all of the following potentially problematic characteristics observed in the administration by committee attempted by the Continental Congress: lack of expertise; lack of full-time, permanent personnel able to provide intensive and continuous attention; inability to provide consistent policy and to plan; partisanship and politics in decision-making, often leading to delay; the influence of a particular ideological view of the way the relevant institutions ought to be organized. Both administration by legislative committee, and regulation through common law, statutes, and franchises (the latter two, like the administration by committee case, frequently requiring legislative action), seem therefore to have been superseded by the administrative agency for at least some of the same reasons (see figure 2.1). But, as we shall see, administrative regulation (and, in fact, regulation in general) possesses some characteristics that make it different in important ways from other administration. In particular, the ability of regulators to control their environment leads, for example, to important consequences for the establishment, and disestablishment, of regulatory means. We shall discuss these consequences for regulatory origin in chapter 3, and for deregulation in chapter 9.

3.0   The Life Cycles of Regulatory Agencies and Regulated Industries

We have discussed reasons for the historical shift to the administrative regulatory form, including some of the supposed advantages of that form, and noted some overall trends in regulatory development in the United States. We now turn to consideration of the individual evolutionary patterns of the administrative regulatory form and elements of its environment. Before this is done, it is necessary to describe the components of the regulatory system.

3.1   THE REGULATORY SYSTEM

In figure 2.2, the common regulatory system for regulation by administrative agency is depicted in simplified form. Here we assume the regulated party is some industry. Among the relationships displayed are the following: Legislatures typically create regulatory

Figure 2.2. The Regulatory System[a]

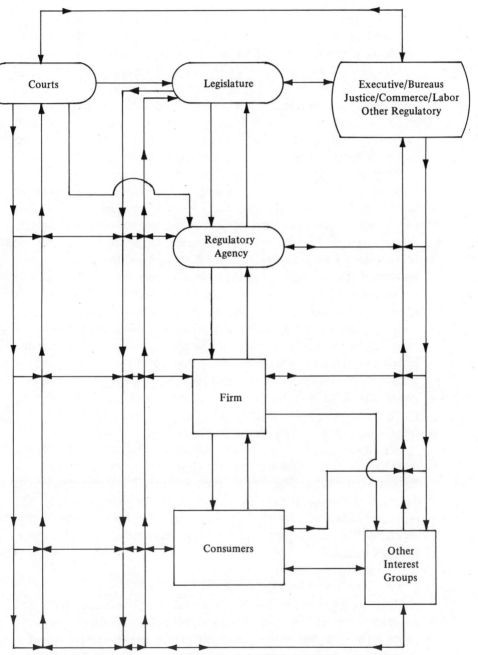

[a] For other depictions of the regulatory system, see, e.g., Krasnow and Longley (1978: 97) on exchanges in the system and Sabatier (1977:457) on regulatory policy-making. Some relationships are depicted redundantly (e.g., courts and legislature to regulatory agency) to pictorially emphasize their importance.

agencies through delegation, for reasons such as those discussed earlier (and to be discussed more formally in chapter 6). The agency regulates some industry, whose activities impact some group of consumers as well as, perhaps, other groups interested in the effects of the industry's production. The activities of the regulated industry may be protested and/or affected in various ways by the relevant consumer and other interest groups, who, along with the industry, may also suggest or request actions by the agency, as well as suggest changes in (including creation of) the regulatory mandate to the legislature. Agency actions may also be appealed in the courts (and court decisions appealed by the agency and the participant interest groups to higher courts), who may direct the agency to alter its behavior, and may interpret and even disallow aspects of the legislature's mandate to the agency. The agency may request changes in its mandate or support level from the legislature. Actions by other administrative units may also be included in the system. These may consist, for example, of requests to the legislature for changes in or creation of a regulatory mandate or structure, appointments of officials in the regulatory agency by the agency's administrative sovereign (see Downs 1967, ch. 5) as well as requests to the agency for regulatory actions, activities (including other regulation) that affect the industry and interest groups, and prosecutions and appeals of actions in the courts.

Scholars have at various times proposed that elements or groups of elements in this system undergo characteristic paths of evolution, or even "life cycles" (on development, change, evolution, and life cycles in organizations generally, see, e.g., Backoff 1974b; Davis and North 1971; Kaufman 1971, 1973, 1975, 1976; Meyer and Brown 1977; Rosengren 1970; Starbuck 1965; Stinchcombe 1965; Tansik and Radnor 1971). These include the regulatory agency, the regulated industry (particularly utilities), and the industry and agency together. We shall review some of these evolutionary and life cycle theories below.

3.2 THE EVOLUTION OF PUBLIC UTILITIES

Glaeser (1957) and Farris and Sampson (1973) have each identified a series of stages in the evolution of public utilities. Shepherd (1973, 1974, 1975; Wilcox and Shepherd 1975) has presented a model of the linked evolution of utilities and regulatory agencies.

3.2.1 The Four Epochs of Martin G. Glaeser

Martin G. Glaeser (1957) specifies four overlapping "epochs" in the development of public utilities in the United States. In the first, the "promotional epoch" (colonial times until about the Civil War), public utilities were tools for developing the country and had to be encouraged. Glaeser (1957:15) notes that "it was in most respects a period of beginnings in the establishment of facilities, in the exploration of their techniques, in understanding the economic principles of operation, and in adapting to them an inherited system of social control." Regulatory forms included common law, statutes, and franchises and charters. Franchises encouraged development through exclusive grants of service rights. Examples of utilities in this period include turnpikes, canals, and the early railways.

The second period, the "competitive epoch" (about 1850 to 1900) was characterized by intensive technological development that supplied markets able to support several competitors. Exclusive franchises gave way to general and permissive grants. Examples of utilities developing in this period include railroads, who embarked on a great wave of expansion, and electric power production.

The third era, the "monopolistic epoch" (1880s to Great Depression), came, according to Glaeser (1957:16), "after the competitive urge had done its worst by generating in turn all the evils of cutthroat competition, such as discrimination and rebating and the corruption of legislative bodies" and saw "a rebirth of regulation." A new regulatory form, the administrative commission, was created to control these abuses. But it soon became evident that, because the public utilities were "natural" monopolies, it might be wiser to change the emphasis from enforcing and controlling competition to one of recognizing and regulating monopolies. The progressive movement led the change, and the railroads were subject to it.

The fourth period, that of "national coordination and planning" (Depression to the present), has involved, according to Glaeser, the development of national policies that join or integrate heretofore separate regulated industries (e.g., the bringing together of railroads, trucks, and barges in the Interstate Commerce Commission). Frequently, both public regulation and public ownership are employed to reach the national policy goals.

Glaeser's description of the stages of utility development is intuitively appealing in the depiction of a steady progress in industrial de-

velopment accompanied by regulation established in the public interest. But it can be subject to serious criticism, not the least of which is
the question of whether his interpretation of historical events is sup-
portable. Much relatively recent research has argued that regulation
was often *sought* by industries for their own protection, rather than
being imposed in some "public interest" (see chapter 3). Although
the distinction is not always made clear in this recent literature, we
may add that regulation which is not directly sought at the outset is
generally "captured" later on so it behaves with consistency to the
industry's major interests, or at least has been observed to behave in
this manner (see, e.g., Hilton 1966; Kolko 1965; MacAvoy 1965).
And it does not really appear that a period of national coordination
and planning in regulation has occurred. The regulatory literature, for
example, is full of cases and criticisms of the lack of coordination
among the federal transportation regulatory agencies (see, e.g.,
Burby 1971).

The degree of overlap in Glaeser's epochs suggests that they could
be used to characterize the life cycle of given utilities, as well as the
development of utilities in general. The railroads may be the easiest
example we could take here, advancing as they did from promotion
in their early days, to competition in the post–Civil War era, to monopolistic supervision under the ICC by the early twentieth century,
and to coordination (at least in pricing and services) with motor carriers and barges by the end of the Depression. Because the railroad
example is so prominent, the danger exists that it will be generalized
to apply to all utilities. It is, usually, the case that best fits models
like those discussed here. In chapter 3 we shall suggest that there is at
least some evidence in the railroad case to support each of several
normally conflicting theories of regulatory origin. It is difficult and
risky to confine complex processes like regulation and economic development into a very few, simplified categories or stages.

3.2.2 The Five Stages of Farris and Sampson

Martin T. Farris and Roy J. Sampson (1973) have developed a
related model of utility development. They specify five stages in the
evolution of a utility, with some amount of overlapping of stages and
with utilities of recent origin possibly skipping an earlier stage. For
each stage, Farris and Sampson (1973:10) discuss the utility's "public image," the "degree of social control," and the "sophistication
of service."

In the first or "promotional" stage, which is similar to Glaeser's, the utilities were viewed favorably and "highly sought," given tax advantages and gifts including grants of land, subsidies, and other incentives. They were subjected to little restrictive regulation, "a minimum of social control" and even in some cases "a willingness to look the other way when abuses occurred." They had crude technology, gave erratic service, and displayed primitive management and rate setting. Examples include canal facilities during the "Canal Era" and early manufactured gas and communication utilities. (Farris and Sampson 1973:10–11)

The abuses and poor performance of the promotional stage created a negative public image for the utilities in the next period, the "competitive" stage. As a result, social control was increased, with the control taking the form of sponsorship of competing franchises as checks against one another. Evidence is apparent in the development of manufactured gas, transit, telephones and power utilities, for example. Like the promotional era, service and management were poor and although pricing practices improved, firms had not learned the advantages of economies of scale and remained small. The increased competition, in fact, led to economies that hurt service further. (Farris and Sampson 1973:11–12)

In the "monopolistic" stage, the benefits of economies of scale and monopoly were recognized and successfully sought despite initial attempts by government to promote competition. Beginning with transportation, however, "society" decided "reluctantly" that "the monopolistic form . . . was inevitable in utilities." Since "the key to maximizing the economic benefits of a monopoly was effective regulation," many state regulatory commissions were established, for the most part in the early twentieth century, to "secure the benefits of monopoly" while sparing the public its abuses. Regulation was held to be a "substitute for competition." Under regulation, the public image of utilities was good as service improved and prices fell due to regulation and economies of scale. Social control through regulatory commissions was, for a while, relatively effective. Sophistication of technology and management was relatively high; modern pricing methods were developed. But utilities discovered ways to get around regulation and maintained effective public relations. Abuses in such areas as speculation and intercorporate dealing developed. As the period ended, "public disillusionment," "frustration and doubt" were apparent. (Farris and Sampson 1973:12–14)

The fourth period, the "regional stage," saw expansion of utilities to cover states and even regions. Sometimes holding companies linked several utilities. The public image was one of "exploitation, frustration, fear, and distrust." Social control responded with extensive investigation and publicity, federal regulation in the form of new commissions (in the 1930s) which could deal better than the state commissions with regional utilities, and the sponsorship of federal competition, including public enterprises in such areas as power production. Utilities grew more efficient, service quality improved, and a new and favorable public image developed. (Farris and Sampson 1973:14–15)

In the fifth stage, "cooperation," which utilities such as power, gas, and telephone have recently entered, utilities have developed several means of cooperating with other utilities in the same field. For example, public and private power producers have developed interconnections and "power pools." National power and energy planning has been increasing. One infers from Farris and Sampson's comments about the fourth stage that the public image of the fifth stage is good. The restrictive social controls of the previous era are questioned in a period in which the emphasis is on cooperation. And "service levels are highly sophisticated, pricing forms highly advanced, and management very efficient." (Farris and Sampson 1973:15–16).

Farris and Sampson's model is obviously very close to Glaeser's, though they are more explicit about the characteristics that distinguish the levels and permit comparisons (i.e., public image, social control, sophistication of service and management). Farris and Sampson substitute "regional" and "cooperation" periods for Glaeser's "national coordination and planning period." Increased coordination or cooperation, and planning, does seem to occur in both models, if in possibly different areas and beginning at possibly different times.

But Farris and Sampson may be subject to the same criticisms as Glaeser. They present regulation largely as a public-spirited means of social control continually directed at and adopted to the abuses of the industry. On the contrary, as noted above, many recent writers have viewed regulation as something which is actually desired and even acquired by the industry for its protection. Such a perspective would view a period designated as "cooperation" or "coordination" as possibly one in which the industry's partiality to the regulation is simply more public, and its ability to consort or even collude with other members of the industry or other utilities or other firms in related industries is simply more blatant. "Cooperation" between public and private, or among private, would then merely be evidence perhaps of "capture." Or cooperation may be merely a facade to legitimize actions of the industry. We do not need to accept these contrary views uncritically. But the support for this and other views (see chapter 3) suggests, at best, an oversimplification in the model. Perhaps both public protection, and industry protection, have characterized utility regulation at different times and/or different locations.

Farris and Sampson's praise of the efficiency of the modern utility takes no account of the concerns of recent writers that regulation may lead to distortions from efficiency in the operation of the regulated firm[14] as well as the disagreement over whether or not innovation is sparked or slowed.[15] In addition, it is not at all clear that the management of utilities has been as efficient as Farris and Sampson claim. These are really empirical questions that have only recently begun to receive study, and are likely to see a great deal more in the future.

Note that both the Glaeser and Farris-and-Sampson models imply a path for the evolution of regulation in their description of how utilities have evolved. These implied models are extracted in figure 2.3. Since the original stages focus on the utility rather than the regulation, we of course run the risk that the respective authors would not be satisfied with these stages as adequate descriptions of the regulatory evolutionary pattern.

3.2.3 The Four Stages of William G. Shepherd

William G. Shepherd's model (1973, 1974, 1975; and Wilcox and Shepherd 1975) discusses the utility evolutionary pattern as a "life cycle." Regulation in this life cycle is seen "as part of a Basic Social Contract: a monopoly is officially granted, in exchange for a degree of public control" (Wilcox and Shepherd 1975:348). In Stage I, invention of the system is often accompanied by control through pat-

---

[14] See, e.g., Shepherd (1975). A frequently cited distortion is the "A-J-W" effect. If the rate of return on investment allowed by the regulatory agency is greater than the cost of capital, total profit may be increased through overinvestment in capital. Thus the firm may select a technology which is relatively capital-intensive and/or attempt to expand its output. For a discussion of possible consequences of the effect, see Kahn (1971, 2:49–59, 106–8). For recent empirical support of the effect, see Spann (1974); Courville (1974); Petersen (1975); and Hayashi and Trapani (1976); but cf. Boyes (1976).

[15] On technological change and innovation in regulated firms see, e.g., Capron (1971); Noll (1971a:23–27).

Figure 2.3. The Evolution of Utility Regulation According to Glaeser, Farris and Sampson, and Shepherd

Glaeser (1957)	Farris and Sampson (1973)	Shepherd (1973–75)
Promotional Epoch: common law statutes franchises and charters (exclusive grants)	*Promotional Stage:* positive incentives including tax advantages, grants of land, subsidies.	*Stage I:* patents
Competitive Epoch: exclusive franchises → general and permissive grants (freer entry)	*Competitive Stage:* competing franchises – established to try to control abuses	*Stage II:* regulation by commission is sought to achieve market control, legitimize the industry, constrain interest groups
Monopolistic Epoch: administrative commission: enforcing competition → recognizing and regulating monopolies	*Monopolistic Stage:* state regulatory commissions – tried to control abuses while getting benefits of monopoly – initially successful, but utilities found ways to get around them	*Stage III:* defense: regulatory mechanisms protect firm from new competition, technologies regulatory agency has inadequate funds, talent to perform review process
National Coordination and Planning: administrative commission with integrated policies toward several related industries public ownership	*Regional Stage:* investigation and publicity federal regulatory commissions federally sponsored competition, including public enterprise	*Stage IV:* new competition and new technology threaten to overwhelm the regulated situation results: – reversion to competition – public ownership – extended survival of highly nonoptimal regulation
	Cooperation Stage: restrictive controls questioned	

ents. After this brief period, Stage II sees growth of the system, which may replace an existing system, as buses superseded trolleys. The price structure comes to reflect cross-subsidies among system users as well as to distinguish the lucrative (creamy) and barely profitable (skim) markets. The utility actually seeks to become regulated "in order to achieve permanence, legitimacy, and market control" (Wilcox and Shepherd 1975:349), whereupon the regulators promote the service, making it universally available. Thus regulation begins "in harmony" with the regulated interest. In fact, "the structure of mutual interests, the profit expectations, and the basic terms of exchange (especially the supplier's rate level and structure) . . . *precede* regulation" (Wilcox and Shepherd 1975:349–50). Regulation then merely legitimizes and smooths interest-group compromises (see Shepherd's definition in our chapter 1).

In Stage III, the utility has saturated its market and developed its technology. It now goes on the defensive. It fights competing new technologies or tries to modify the new technologies to fit the utility's own interests. Rate and physical structures do not fit as well, and the utility is confronted with challenges from users in creamy markets who are charged more than they think they ought to pay, and from parties who may be subject to negative externalities produced by the utility (on externalities, see chapter 5). Regulation, meanwhile, enjoys inadequate funds and talent, and cannot perform the review process it has accepted in exchange for granting the monopoly. Since the utility is not sanctioned, responsibility for service quality ends up with the regulators. Since "the only penalties are political," such as "open criticism," which can "hurt the regulators as much as the utilities," the utility and the regulators develop a shared objective of simply minimizing "political repercussions," avoiding "redressing inequities," and glossing over (Shepherd 1975:230; Wilcox and Shepherd 1975:351).

In Stage IV the utility finally yields to the pressures of technology and competition and may revert to a component of a competitive system. Or if externalities or other social effects are particularly important, it may become a public enterprise. But the regulation has followed a path of evolution reversed from that of the utility, a path that may shield the regulated firms and freeze their markets. Inefficiencies result. And " 'better' regulation of rates—by hiring more brilliant commissioners or staffs, giving them bigger budgets, etc.—does not correct the basic structural problems or the inefficiencies" (Shepherd

1975:232–33). Thus regulation may survive indefinitely, far beyond the point at which it ceases to be socially optimal.[16]

Shepherd explicitly recognizes the life cycle aspects of utility evolution, freeing his model more from the historical period ties that heavily influence the Glaeser and Farris and Sampson approaches. And he tries to integrate more explicitly the parallel (and "reversed") cycle through which the regulation passes. He recognizes inefficiencies in regulation and describes regulation as being essentially industry protective in character, since it is sought by the utility and then protects the utility from competitors. Shepherd may, of course, be going too far the other way; there may be utilities that are relatively more efficient and utilities which do not seek and prefer regulation. This is really an empirical question that deserves further study, though there is evidence accumulating that utility regulation does in fact suffer from at least some of the criticisms that theorists have directed at it.[17] Furthermore, it is not at all clear that utilities in all areas follow this pattern. "Natural" monopoly may be necessary in the interest of efficiency for very long periods of time. This may be the case, for example, in some areas of electric power production.

Shepherd's categories, like those of Glaeser and Farris and Sampson, are really only sketched, not fully described and developed. He acknowledges this, calling his stages "only crude summaries of complex interactions" that "await a complete formal analysis" (Shepherd 1975:227 n. 3). In Shepherd's model, the utility really does not go through much of an evolution once it is established; it is the environment which changes (i.e., new competing technologies appear) and which a fairly static utility tries to control through the instrumentality of regulation. But there is a growing literature on aging in organizations and the processes of change which accompany and govern it (e.g., Kaufman 1971, 1976; Downs 1967, chs. 2 and 13). Extensions of Shepherd's model could employ it.

The regulatory life cycle inherent in Shepherd's approach is summarized in figure 2.3. It, too, could use further development.

3.3 THE LIFE CYCLE OF AGENCIES

Processes and patterns of change in organizations over time are not well understood in the literature. Though work in those areas is grow-

---

[16] In chapter 9, we shall discuss the process of deregulation. We shall argue there and in chapter 3 that the agency may preserve itself through being relatively better able to control its environment. This argument is somewhat consistent with Shepherd.

[17] See footnotes 14 and 15 above.

ing, there is especially little about *processes* of creation, and of decline or reduction, and termination. These generalizations apply to regulatory agencies, as well as to utilities and any other organizations involved in the regulatory process. The widely cited and summarized life cycle theory of regulatory agencies presented over twenty years ago by Marver Bernstein (1955, ch. 3), or any extension or elaboration of it, has still not been subject to extensive empirical test (but see Meier and Plumlee 1977, 1978). Similarly, Anthony Downs's (1967, chs. 2, 13) explanation for the life cycle of bureaus does not seem to have been accorded much empirical study. These works therefore remain major, if largely unsupported statements, and warrant some consideration here.

3.3.1 Bernstein's Life Cycle of Regulatory Commissions

Marver H. Bernstein (1955) has argued that although there are "unique elements" in the experience of each agency, "the history of commissions reveals a general pattern of evolution more or less characteristic of all," with "roughly similar periods of growth, maturity, and decline." The length of periods may vary across commissions, and periods may sometimes be skipped, but there is yet a "rhythm of regulation" that suggests a "natural life style" (Bernstein 1955:74); see also Jaffe's (1954) "arteriosclerosis theory"; Cary's (1967:67) "hardening of the arteries"; and Redford (1952:226–27, 381–86). Of note is Bernstein's argument that the cycle can repeat in the same agency. Four periods are identified: gestation, youth, maturity, and old age (see figure 2.4).

Gestation may require twenty or more years, in which a rising distress leads to the formation or activation of groups who demand legislative remedy to protect their interests. After a struggle, a statute containing "vague language" and reflecting "unsettled national economic policy" is passed. It is a compromise, which largely succeeds in passage only because of crisis or near-crisis conditions. Groups desiring the regulation want immediate relief from abuses of business, and do not consider longer-range goals or policy in the area. The statute will often be out-of-date because of the length of the struggle (Bernstein 1955:74–79).

During the second phase, *Youth,* the agency is crusading and aggressive, and operates in a conflictual environment. Lacking administrative experience, possessing vague objectives and untested legal powers, the commission faces well-organized and experienced opposition from the regulated groups. The agency quickly gets into liti-

Figure 2.4.   Bernstein's (1955) Life Cycle of Regulatory Commissions

Gestation:
  – twenty years or more
  – sparked by crisis
  – marked by group struggle
  – regulation is compromise
  – regulatory statute out of date when enacted
  – regulation emphasizes short-term over long-term considerations

Youth:
  – crusading, aggressive in conflictual environment
  – agency lacks experience
  – agency has vague objectives
  – untested legal powers are tested, but legal process is incomprehensible to public
  – experienced, well-organized opposition from industry
  – loss of public support and political leadership as groups who pushed for regulation retire; regulated industry successful in rewarding regulators and affecting attitudes

Maturity:
  – passivity/apathy; adjusts to conflict it faces
  – agency lacks Congressional and public support
  – acts as manager rather than policeman
  – relies on precedent and routine
  – maintains good relations with industry
  – most of time spent in litigation
  – parochial professionalism
  – backlog of cases develops
  – Congress and Budget Office refuse appropriation increases
  – "becomes a captive of the regulated groups"

Old Age:
  – debility
  – procedures sanctified
  – "working agreement" with industry to maintain status quo
  – "recognized protector of agency"
  – Congress and Budget Office refuse funds
  – staff declines in quality; poor management
  – agency fails to keep up with societal change

But   scandal/emergency/crisis can trigger new drive for regulation: cycle repeats

gation in order to determine the scope of its powers, but the legal proceedings are "highly specialized, technical, and frequently obscure" to the public. The regulated industry tries to determine appointments to the commission and tries to reward and punish regulators who are, respectively, for and against them. Loss of public support and political leadership for the regulation occurs as the groups that backed the regulation tire and retire from the field, believing "they have earned a rest from political turmoil;" as those who supported the legislation assume that administration of the statute will take care of itself; as defenses in the courts are technical and remain incomprehensible to the public; as the regulated industry begins to have success in changing public attitudes and in affecting the commissioners' attitudes as well by ways such as holding out the implicit promise of a future lucrative position in the regulated industry; as legislative champions find no advantage in continued advocacy and intraparty differences are smoothed over; and as the "inchoate, relatively unorganized (and frequently disorganized) public" is no match for cohesive industry groups; leaving the commission in "splendid isolation." The zeal of the commission in its youth itself arises to a large degree from "the general political setting," including the prevailing ideology of the proper role of government. This of course may be different for agencies created at different times. (Bernstein 1955:79–86)

In *Maturity*, the third phase, the agency undergoes a "process of devitalization." Lacking external Congressional and public support, the commission adjusts itself to the conflict it faces. It becomes more like a manager than a policeman, and more like the business managements it supposedly regulates, in viewpoint. It relies increasingly on precedent and routine; "precedent, rather than prospect, guides the commission." Without external pressure, conflicts are avoided; the agency seeks to maintain good relations with the industry and to escape unpleasant interpersonal relations. In order to avoid trouble from charges of unfairness that may be substantiated during judicial review, the agency allows private parties easy challenge to its actions and spends most of its time in adjudication. Professionalism grows in the staff, but is parochial, and tends to encourage the emphasis on precedent. As a result of these factors, the agency develops a large backlog of cases. Congress and the Budget Office will not approve larger appropriations to hire staff to reduce the backlog because they believe the agency is not well-managed. Thus "the commission finally becomes a captive of the regulated groups." (Bernstein 1955:86–91)

Finally, in phase four, *Old Age*, the passivity and apathy of phase three "deepens into debility." The agency's procedures undergo sanctification. It develops a fixed "working agreement" with the regulated parties that leads to maintenance of the status quo and establishment of the agency as "recognized protector of the industry." Congress and the Budget Office notice the debility of the commission and refuse additional aid, fearing that increased adherence to old procedures and policies rather than efficiency would result. The staff declines in quality, and the agency becomes more than ever dependent on the regulated industry for staff. The agency is poorly managed and exhibits doubt about the objectives of regulation. The commissioners as a group develop "certain understandings among them which act as powerful deterrents to efforts to improve their managerial quality." The agency fails to keep up with changes in technology and economic organization, and is insensitive to its "wider political and social setting." Scandal or emergency, i.e., a crisis, can, however, by dramatically highlighting the failures of the regulation, trigger a new drive for regulation. The cycle repeats. (Bernstein 1955:91–95; cf. J. E. Moore 1972)

Unlike Glaeser, Farris and Sampson, and Shepherd, Bernstein focuses his life cycle arguments mostly on changes in the regulatory agency rather than on the regulated party, other parts of the regulatory environment, or some combination of these. Although Bernstein's model is probably the classic statement of the regulatory life cycle in the literature, it can be subject to a number of criticisms (see, e.g., Sabatier 1975, for a discussion of some of these). Bernstein mixes description and explanation, sometimes requiring the reader to interpret reasons for the importance or relevance of a given factor or to reconstruct them from considerations of the rest of his argument and the examples.[18] He is literary at the expense of logical (this is also true of Glaeser to some extent), and tends to use metaphors and dramaturgical language that brighten the reading but add imprecision to the analysis. To some degree, this is a reflection of an older style of writing, but it does seem to interfere with specification of the model.

For example, Bernstein, after referring to the "trial by legal combat" that occurs during initial litigation of the regulatory statute, writes: "The arena in which the legitimacy of regulation is attacked and defended is highly specialized, technical, and frequently obscure. Few nonlawyers are able to follow the legal proceedings, which ap-

---

[18] This may contribute to variations in the way Bernstein's model is described in the literature; see, e.g., Meier and Plumlee's (1977) reconstruction of the model, which differs from Bernstein's strict statement of it.

pear incredulous or mysterious to the uninitiated'' (Bernstein 1955:81–82).

One can infer that the significance of the obscurity of the legal process is that the general public is unable to follow the course of the litigation and offer support in the agency's fight against skilled utility lawyers. But Bernstein does not actually say this. Moreover, he does not state who the ''uninitiated'' are who are important to his model, nor does he specify what courts and/or what parts of the legal process are the subject of his comments. In addition, one can ask if Bernstein means that it is the legal process alone that is technical and obscure, or whether it is the subject of the litigation and the legal issues debated that are of this character? Or is it both? The difference is important to building one aspect of an explanation for the evolution of the agency.

Sometimes the difference between stages is unclear. In both phases three and four, for example, Congress and the Budget Office refuse additional appropriations, in Maturity because they believe the agency is not well-managed, and in Old Age because they fear increased adherence to old procedures and policies rather than efficiency will result (Bernstein 1955:90–93). It is not immediately apparent that Bernstein has made any real distinction here.

Interestingly, Bernstein's ''working agreement'' seems somewhat like Shepherd's ''social contract.'' But Bernstein ignores the possibility that the regulation was sought by the regulated party from the outset, for its own protection, an assumption that is central to Shepherd's model. Perhaps what appears with respect to consumer or ''public interest'' goals as debilitation is really only evidence of effective service and protection. As a number of writers on regulation have observed, regulation is often *explicitly* supposed to promote and protect the industry (e.g., Sabatier 1975:303).

In the end, any life cycle model requires empirical support. Bernstein offers anecdotal support using the federal agencies, but the generality of his model requires systematic support from the experience of agencies at other levels, as well as more careful and complete analysis of the careers of the federal agencies (for one attempt, see Meier and Plumlee 1977, 1978). Because Bernstein does not specify the length of any period subsequent to Gestation, however, it is hard to do this (Sabatier 1975:304). Would we really want to argue that an agency that, say, was apparently ''vigorous'' and ''youthful,'' in Bernstein's language, for fifty years and then passed through Maturity and Old Age in five years, to be reborn in crisis as a youthful agency, followed Bernstein's life cycle? Maybe it would be more accurate to describe such an agency as *normally* "youthful," and look for reasons other than an inherent life cycle for its occasional periods of debility. Similarly, an agency that seems perpetually in Maturity or Old Age may not be in a cycle. It may have essentially started out that way.

But Bernstein's life cycle model is intuitively appealing. The occurrence of initial activism, which soon fades, is a sufficiently remarked-upon phenomenon throughout regulation to suggest the existence of underlying pattern and explanation. Bernstein colors such a portrait well, if occasionally vague about the logic or the details.

3.3.2 Downs's Life Cycle of Bureaus

The life cycle of regulatory agencies can be viewed as a special case of the life cycle of bureaus. Life cycle theories such as Bernstein's that seek to explain the ultimate rigidification and "capture" of regulatory agencies are, in fact, frequently generalized beyond the independent-commission context in which Bernstein first developed it. There are important differences, of course, between the so-called independent regulatory commission and the regulatory office, division, or department. The commission is a bureau that has a group rather than single executive (though the chairman may be given major administrative supervisory responsibility) and the relation of the regulatory unit to the legislature and to executive departments and elected officials may differ. Such differences, as well as others, may have consequences for the performance of the unit, but regulatory agencies may at least have bureaucracy in common.

One can argue, however, that it is not structural differences of this kind per se but, rather, differences in the extant incentive system facing regulators, that best explain any performance differences (or similarities). Structural differences, of course, may affect the incentive system. In addition, the preferences of the regulators for various rewards may vary, though the variation may be no different from what it is for bureaucrats in general. Anthony Downs and some other recent writers, mostly economists (see, e.g., Tullock 1965), have applied an approach of this type to study bureaucracies, including regulatory agencies.

Thus, both commissions and offices/divisions/departments are to some extent hierarchical, bureaucratic units and, further, regulators in both types face somewhat similar incentive systems that derive from the nature of the regulatory relationship. This permits a generalized discussion of regulatory agency behavior. We shall discuss the mechanism of regulatory "capture" again in chapter 3.

Anthony Downs (1967, chs. 2, 13) has developed a model of the life cycle of the bureau that, with appropriate adjustment, may be applied to both departmental and commission forms. Among Downs's basic assumptions are that bureaucrats can be viewed as rational, in the sense of acting with consistency with respect to given goals, and that an important component of their goal set (which he also specifies) includes basic self-interest. In the rational choice approach, behavior is explained as the result of individuals rationally pursuing their goals in an environment characterized by differentially distributed goal satisfactions, i.e., in effect, differentially distributed incentives. Downs goes on to distinguish several types of bureaucrats based on differences in purely self-interested, and in mixed, motives. These types are used to explain occurrences in the bureaucratic and, by implication, the regulatory life cycle.

There are several defenses in the literature of the use of the rational-choice and self-interest assumptions, as well as the employment of rational choice models in general (see, e.g., Downs 1957; Buchanan and Tullock 1962; Riker and Ordeshook 1973); we shall not review them here. One important argument is that the rational choice approach may permit explanation and prediction of behavior in different or changing settings, given stability in the subject's goal set.

3.3.2.1 Downsian Bureaucrats

In Downs's typology (see figure 2.5), *climbers* seek only their own self-interest goals of power, income, and prestige; *conservers* seek only their own self-interest goals of convenience and security, seeking to retain what power, income, and prestige they have; *zealots* are mixed motive in that they possess similar self-interest goals, but also strongly desire to achieve or implement a relatively narrow policy, program, or concept; *advocates* are mixed motive and value, in addition to self-interest goals, the broader goals of the organization (or a broader set of "functions"); and *statesmen* are mixed motive and desire in addition to self-interest to achieve goals relating to the benefit of society as a whole (Downs 1967:88–89). Note that the "mixed" goal types possess "mixed" goals that represent levels of a hierarchy: organization, society, ideation (policy, concept).

In figure 2.5, the Downs typology is generated in a systematic

Figure 2.5: A Typology of Actors

I. Extended Form of Typology: Actors by Goal, and by Existence and Level of Goal Holder

(1) Self or Other Goals Only

	Self-Other Dimension	
Existence and Level of Holder Dimension	Actor Has Self-Goal Only	Actor Has Other-Goal Only
No holder exists (ideational)	null	null
Holder exists: individual level	climber[a] conserver[a]	(altruists, e.g., Good Samaritan)
organizational level	(e.g., classical firm)	(e.g., ideally philanthropic foundation)
societal/systemic level	(e.g., stereotypical colonial country?)	(e.g., heaven?)

(2) Self and Other Goals (Mixed Goals)

Self-Goal	Other-Goal			
	No holder exists	Holder exists: individual level	organizational level	societal/systemic level
No holder exists	null ———————————————————————→			
Holder exists: individual level	zealot[a]	loyalist	advocate[a]	statesman[a]
organizational level	(e.g., religious missionary organization)	(e.g., emperor's palace guard)	(e.g., consulting firm)	(e.g., army)
societal/systemic level	(e.g., religious missionary movement)	?	?	?

II. Reduced Form of Typology: Individual-Level Actors by Goal, and by Level of Goal Holder

		Self-Other Goal Dimension	
	Level of Goal Holder	Actor Has Self-Goals Only	Actor Has Self- and Other-Goals
Actor Has Self-Goals Only	Level of Holder of Self-Goal:		
	individual	climber[a]	—
		conserver[a]	—
Actor Has Self- and Other-Goals	Level of Holder of Other-Goal:		
	individual	—	loyalist
	organizational	—	advocate[a]
	societal	—	statesman[a]
	ideational	—	zealot[a]

NOTE: Actors are presumed to have self- and/or other-goals that are sought by "holders" of the levels specified. Actors that are statesmen, for example, have an individual-level holder of their self-goals (e.g., the bureaucrat) and a societal/systemic-level holder of their other-goals. In other words, statesmen may act for themselves, and for society's goals.

[a]Type identified by Anthony Downs in Inside Bureaucracy.

fashion. Although the typology appears complex, it is really constructed simply. Dimensions of self- vs. other-goal (including both), and existence and level of "holders" of the goal(s), are crossed with one another. Here "other-goal" is the "mixed" motive, or goal of the "principal" or "other" party for which the bureaucrat can be viewed as "agent." In the holder existence and level dimension, a "holder" may or may not exist for the goal. If one does exist, the levels of the holder may include individual, group or organizational, and societal or systemic. If no holder exists, we may understand the goal as relating, for example, to a concept, ideation, or policy.

Thus the level of a "holder" of an other-goal is equivalent to the level of the principal in an agency (i.e., agent-principal) relationship. If no holder of an other-goal exists, then the other-goal in question is not associated with a principal of any level. An example would be an actor behaving as an agent for "truth" or for a religious concept.

The typology of figure 2.5 is a general typology of purposive actors; bureaucrats may be understood as only one type of individual-level actor that can be characterized by the typology. Furthermore, the general typology includes actors of levels besides the individual level, i.e., organizations and societies or systems. Since our concern is only with individual bureaucrats, we shall focus only on cases involving individual-level holders of either self-goals or both self- and other-goals. These common cases are indicated in the "reduced form" of the typology. The general typology is similar in construction to one we shall develop in chapter 4 to classify conceptions of the public interest.

In the boxes in figure 2.5's typology are some types or examples of actors that fall in the specified categories. Actors that are *advocates,* for example, have an individual-level holder of their self-goals (e.g., the bureaucrat himself) and an organizational-level holder of their other-goals. In other words, advocates may act for themselves, and for an organization's goals. Actors that are climbers, on the other hand, may act only for self-goals, i.e., for themselves.

Looking at figure 2.5, we see that the Downs list of types can be understood as a subset of a larger typology of actors. There are potentially purely "altruistic" types where the bureaucrat-agent possesses only other-goals; purely self-interested types; and mixed types. In the chart in which we allow the actor to have both self- and other-goals, we see that a category that Downs has omitted is generated:

the case where the bureaucrat is acting for another individual. For the mixed goal situation, we have named this type, the "loyalist."

Identification of a loyalist type should have utility beyond pointing out how the Downs typology is perhaps incomplete when more systematically generated. Loyalists may play major roles in situations where, for example, a charismatic figure heads an agency over a relatively long period of time (e.g., J. Edgar Hoover), or an elected official seeks to gain control of a bureaucracy by appointing lower-level officials who are loyal primarily to him.

Because of the possible scarcity of true altruists, we shall not carry these types through subsequent discussions. This leaves us with Downs's basic five types plus the loyalist.

Note that the charts may be used to generate types when the agents of interest are of levels higher than the individual, e.g., in an organizational-level model in which organizations like whole firms, public bureaucracies, and so on, are the units of analysis. We have included some examples, mostly at the organizational level, in parentheses, though for our immediate purposes, i.e., for the individual-level model, these categories are null.

3.3.2.2 Downsian Bureaucrats and the Life Cycle

Downs (1967:5) argues that bureaus originate in one of the following ways: They are begun either by followers to perpetuate the ideas of a charismatic leader, by groups who see a need to perform a given function, as a division split off from an existing unit, or through the entrepreneurship of a group promoting a policy that gains support. It would appear that all except the first type may often apply to the founding of regulatory agencies, though the first type is conceivable where, for example, a social movement is headed by such a leader.

Once started, the bureau is dominated initially by advocates or zealots, must seek external support to survive, and begins to grow rapidly. Those who pushed for the establishment of the bureau, whether followers of a charismatic leader, groups seeking to have a function performed, or entrepreneurs for a policy, are likely to be represented in the personnel of the agency whose activities they care so much about. In addition, zealots who pushed for separation of a bureau from the larger unit may also be found in the new bureau. Note that the followers of the charismatic leader may be labeled "loyalists" in our extension of Downs's model. Members of the larger unit from which the bureau is split off may install loyalists in the new agency to retain control. Where groups external to the government have sought the new agency, it is likely that members of these groups will be placed in it in leading positions. At any rate, recruiting for the new agency will probably be most successful, of course, among those who favor the agency.

This description is somewhat consistent with Bernstein's discussion of the phase of Youth, in its depiction of the likely crusading spirit or zealotry of the early agency. But it is also consistent with a view of regulatory establishment that emphasizes protection of the regulated party, e.g., Shepherd. The regulators could conceivably be active advocates of promotion of the industry.[19] This is an aspect that, as with the rest of life cycle analysis, requires empirical study.

The agency must convince groups with influence over needed resources, e.g., key elected officials and the legislature, that the agency's services are desirable. Zealots and advocates will seek support both to allow continuation of their program and organization, and simply to satisfy their own self-interest in survival of the agency. Similarly, loyalists will seek support both to serve the interests of their principal and to help themselves. Recall that Bernstein implies that the loss of public support in the early career of the agency is an important factor in the "capture" of the agency.

A bureau is said to reach its "initial survival threshold" when it has reached a size sufficient for it to offer "useful services," and an age sufficient for routinized relationships to have developed with its major clients (Downs 1967:9). It is especially vulnerable before this point. This threshold is generally attained after a period of rapid growth. Bureaus that split off have often already reached the threshold. Bureaus born new try to build up to it rapidly before being blocked by other bureaus or by groups which oppose its function, or before they run out of resources. Newly established bureaus whose zealots have active counterparts in their environment may be relatively more successful. We can add that loyalists may count on their powerful principals to supply or mobilize sufficient support to guarantee the bureau's attainment of such a threshold.

The major effects on the growth and decline of bureaus have their sources in factors in the environment of the bureau, though relatively small changes in the composition of the personnel in the bureau may

---

[19] The regulators could also, of course, think they are vigorously performing regulation in the consumer or public interest, while actually serving the regulated industry's interest best.

have substantial impact. Downs argues that if officials in key posts are preponderantly of one type (conservers, zealots, etc.), "the bureau and its behavior will be *dominated* by the traits typical of that type" (Downs 1967:11). He explains the dynamics of growth and decline largely in terms of changes in bureau composition due to changes in the environment. Acceleration in growth may begin when the bureau's social function gains in importance and the bureau's sovereign directs it to expand. The expanding bureau attracts climbers, who see opportunities for advancement, and scares away conservers. The climbers rise, so that the bureau is increasingly directed by them. The climbers innovate and seek expansion in order to better themselves. The bureau requires innovators to serve its expanded function. So growth accelerates. Brakes on acceleration include competition from other bureaus, the increasing difficulty of getting impressive results as the organization grows larger and more complex and encounters problems in drawing more talent to an already talent-rich agency, and the internal check of conflicts among ambitious climbers.

Deceleration mirrors acceleration up to a point. Forced by a decline in the importance of its social function to decrease its size, the bureau finds that climbers jump out of the bureau or lose hope of substantial promotion and become conservers. The bureau is then less willing and able to take advantage of innovation and expansion opportunities. The deceleration is not perfectly symmetrical with the acceleration because the climbers who remain will still rise more quickly than the nonclimbers; because the number of high positions sought and filled by climbers will rise faster during acceleration than it falls during deceleration; and because of the argument that since all officials, including both climbers and conservers, resist a drop in their resources, the resistance to reduction will be greater than the enthusiasm of growth.

In general, Downs argues that bureaus will seek to expand because an organization that is rapidly expanding can attract better personnel and more easily keep the best personnel; can provide personnel in leadership positions with increased power, income, and prestige if expansion is successful; can reduce internal conflicts over scarce resources and rewards; and can improve the quality of its performance and its likelihood of survival (which may satisfy both loyalty and self-interest). In addition, public bureaus may seek to expand because officials are not subject to the market constraint of measuring marginal gains against marginal costs; they receive greater rewards for increasing than for reducing expenditures. Note also that expansion of agencies in which loyalists play a major role may also satisfy the desire of the loyalists' principal for more power, as well as satisfy the loyalists' own self-interest.

Downs (1967:18) introduces a life cycle simile by noting that "bureaus, like men, change in predictable ways as they grow older." In particular: 1) They learn to perform better. 2) They develop formalized rule systems that cover more situations and in effect record the bureau's experience. This improves performance in previously encountered situations, tends to divert officials from social function performance to rule conformity, and increases the structural complexity of the bureau and its consequent inertia from sunk costs. 3) They shift their goals in practice from performing certain social functions to survival as the growing rule structure increases the importance of conservers. 4) They modify the formal bureau goals in order to guarantee the survival of the bureau's administrative mechanism. This stems from the career commitments of officials who wish to avoid the costs of losing status and seniority, looking for a new job, and so on. 5) Their administrative component increases because lower-level workers are discharged first in shrinkages; because the greater number of functions performed by the older bureau requires more coordination; and because, unless modern business-machine technology happens to be applicable to administration, the production or lower-level jobs may be more subject to mechanization, which is more likely to be introduced with age.

The effects of age lead Downs to cite his "Law of Increasing Conservatism: All organizations tend to become more conservative as they get older, unless they experience periods of very rapid growth or internal turnover." Thus "the older a bureau is, the less likely it is to die" and "the best time to 'kill' a bureau is as soon as possible after it comes into existence" (Downs 1967:20). In addition, older bureaus usually serve a broader scope of social functions. This is because bureaus acquire additional functions to protect themselves as their original social functions decline in importance. But they still perform the older functions: "as time passes, bureaus, like private firms, tend to diversify to protect themselves from fluctuations in demand" (Downs 1967:20).

Recall that Glaeser observed a tendency for regulatory agencies in his last evolutionary "epoch" to combine regulation and policy-making in several previously separately treated, but related, areas. Thus the ICC brought in competing transportation means and was to develop a National Transportation Policy. Farris and Sampson noted regional expansion and increased cooperation among utilities in their later stages. Shepherd noted a tendency for later regulation to bring under control competing new forms, though on terms favorable to the already regulated industry. All of these observations may be to some extent consistent with Downs's comment regarding diversification of functions served by the bureau. Shepherd and others may argue that diversification of regulation is evidence of industry protection at work, but we can offer a perhaps equally convincing hypothesis: diversification is evidence of a regulatory agency protecting itself, i.e., bureau protection at work. In chapter 3, we shall offer a bureaucratic theory of regulatory origin, and shall argue that the capacity of the regulatory agency to control its environment may facilitate such protective strategies as diversification in coverage.

Downs argues that bureaus die when their social functions are not important enough to draw sufficient resources. This may occur because the basic functions decline in importance, the bureau performs them inefficiently, or some other bureau performs them better. But established bureaus are unlikely to die: 1) bureaus will alter their functions to survive; 2) clients, who often do not pay the costs of bureau services, pressure for their continuance past the point at which the services are justifiable; 3) some clients of the bureau obtain such large and irreplaceable net benefits even when others do not that they continue to press for the service; 4) the absence of the quid pro quo exchange of the market hides situations in which maintenance of the service is unjustifiable and permits the self-interest of bureau members to operate to keep it alive; 5) bureaus are more reluctant to engage in conflict with other bureaus than firms are with other firms because the competition would not be impersonal (the opponent would be more obvious) and such competition is not needed for survival, and because bureaus in conflict would attract the investigatory attention of the central allocation agencies (e.g., legislature and budget office) and public criticism by the bureau's opponents; 6) the large size of bureaus enables them to survive fluctuations in resources; and 7) even if a bureau cannot attract enough external support to go it alone, it might survive by getting another, expanding bureau to absorb it (Downs 1967:22–23). We shall consider regulatory "death," i.e., deregulation, in chapter 9.

3.3.2.3 Downsian Bureaucrats and the Rigidity Cycle

Downs (1967, ch. 13) also describes what he terms the "rigidity cycle," which is consistent with his discussion of the general life cycle. He is not very precise, however, in defining "rigidity." It seems to involve the development of complex and restrictive regulations, and relative inflexibility in the operations of the bureau, so that it takes more time to make decisions, with much effort devoted to filling out forms, following superfluous procedures, and writing elaborate justifications for actions; there is much effort channeled into monitoring activities like making numerous inspections; and there is great difficulty in generating innovations and getting them approved (Downs 1967:160). Thus rigidity seems to consist of three interrelated elements: 1) lack of speed in decision; 2) lack of innovation; 3) lack of flexibility in decisions, including task choice and resource allocation, in that given procedures and rules, together with elaborate monitoring and enforcement of these procedures and rules, must be adhered to or performed.

Downs specifies that the rigidity cycle has eight phases but he neglects to label all of them in the text. The cycle begins, at any rate, with a great and rapid expansion of the new bureau. Officials experience "leakage" of their authority and try to counter it. But these attempts lead to increasing rigidity.

Rigidity results from the following: 1) Bureau leaders employ a separate monitoring agency to counter the authority leakage. The monitor imposes complex regulations, requires use of resources in responding to the regulations, and finds that resources are used to evade it. Less resources are thus available to pursue bureau goal achievement. 2) Growth of the bureau leads to specialization and thus coordination problems, loss of perspective on the overall task, and demands by the monitor to have approval rights in order to coordinate spillovers. Thus it takes longer to make decisions and get things done. 3) Key decisions tend to be made higher up in the organization, but the greater distance leads to difficulties and delays in decision-making. This escalation of decision-making results from the increasing specialization, which requires coordination at a high level; from the search for, and imposition of, organization forms successful in one part of the bureau on the other parts, which do not work well and lead to rigidity; and the promotion of zealots who favor certain management techniques which they then impose on the whole organization.

Thus the increasing size leads to delayed decisions, with multiple approvals and excessive reporting requirements, and difficulty in innovation because it may not fit existing control processes.

An urgent situation may, however, lead to creation of a separate bureau as part of the larger bureau, but with better staff and resources, fewer regulations, and so on. But even this special organization will tend to degenerate as it finds that success requires it to interact with other bureaus and yield some decision-making power; some ties with the ossified bureau remain and create bottlenecks; events in the uncontrollable environment prevent the isolation from continuing; and officials in the host bureau lose interest or attention to competing urgent matters.

The control structures created under expansion persist even though the functions which they govern shrink. This is because of economies of scale in the operation of the control unit, so that it may need to retain some minimum core; because top officials keep it at the same size to increase control; and because the proximity of the control unit to the top officials allows them to keep their power, income, and prestige. Note that, as Downs argued earlier, the increased regulations lead to conserver domination in the bureau.

Downs (1967:163–64), in discussing implications of the analysis, cautions that, even given these arguments, "bureaus rarely become completely ossified." The bureau's sovereign would hear protests from groups and organizations, including other agencies, with which it deals. Bureaus are less likely to ossify where there is more of such feedback. Sabatier (1975), in fact, argues that capture of regulatory agencies is retarded where there is an active group interest that provides feedback of this type. Another implication is that, in bureau-dominated societies, leaders must establish special organizations to accomplish urgent tasks. This is in spite of the fact that the huge bureaucracy results in such authority leakage that some low-level bureaus have considerable autonomy. The fact that many regulatory agencies are created in response to a crisis is consistent with this.

A final implication is that large bureaucracies often undergo a "reorganization cycle" as top-level officials seek to control them (cf. J. E. Moore 1972). This cycle involves: 1) rearrangement of higher and intermediate but not lower level relationships; 2) short-run effectiveness; 3) gradual disappearance of these performance gains; and 4) return of the lack of control, which stimulates another cycle. This pattern of reorganization is apparent in the history of regulatory reform, especially since the 1930s. Each cycle is marked by the appearance of one or more critical studies, some of whose recommendations are usually adopted. Problems persist, though small gains are sometimes noted. Eventually, a new cycle is triggered. Examples of such studies include the 1937 President's Committee on Administrative Management ("Brownlow Committee"), First Hoover Commission (1949), Second Hoover Commission (1955), James Landis's "Report on Regulatory Agencies to the President-elect" (1960), the 1971 Report of the President's Advisory Council on Executive Organization ("Ash Report"), and a series of studies of regulatory agencies done for Congressional committees and private organizations, beginning about 1975.

Downs (1967:165–66) argues that the short-run gains in effectiveness are due to a breakup of some rigid lines of authority and communication that "may release energies and ideas that have previously been held back by ossification" and that "may also force free enterprising bureaucrats to follow their superiors' orders more closely, until they can determine exactly how much autonomy they now enjoy." Working from Downs's own "Law of Increasing Conservatism," however, we can see why there may be some short-run gains. Downs specifies that growth and turnover may interfere with the conservatism trend. Regulatory reform often involves bringing in a new Mr. Clean to head or chair the agency. Examples include Joseph Swidler and the New York Public Service Commission, and Miles Kirkpatrick and the Federal Trade Commission. As part of the "honeymoon" usually granted new agency heads, some extra funds are made available (Noll 1971a:88). This may produce some small growth in the agency. The new man brings in some of his own loyalists or zealots, and does some rearranging within the agency (Welborn 1977:60–63). This causes the careers of some within the agency to be blocked, and others, aided. Conservers near retirement age who see some of their rewards threatened may quit; climbers whose paths are blocked and loyalists to the old agency head may "jump" out of the agency. Thus the new man produces some turnover, not necessarily intentionally. Together with the growth, it may lead to increases in agency effectiveness, insofar as effectiveness is linked to increases in decision speed, innovativeness, and flexibility. But once these changes are made, the old rigidity pattern reasserts itself, as Downs describes.

3.3.2.4 Rigidity and Regulatory vs. Nonregulatory Agencies

Downs's discussion of the life cycle implies that regulatory agencies are not alone in their evolutionary passage to rigidity. One might think from a reading of Bernstein, for example, that regulatory commissions are distinct in their susceptibility to this process. What differences might we infer about the life cycle behavior of bureaus in general and regulatory agencies in particular? And what differences might there be between what we shall refer to as the department form of regulatory agency—i.e., the hierarchical, single-headed office, division, or department—and the commission form?

Consider first the differences between the regulatory and nonregulatory agency. Looking back over Downs's discussion, we can isolate several interrelated factors that interfere with progression of the cycle (see figure 2.6). By considering which factors are relatively more active in which type of agency, we can speculate on possible differences.

In figure 2.6, a simplified adaptation of Downs's model, the increased importance of the agency's social function leads to the formation of a concerned and active public constituency, and to the agency sovereign's requesting or permitting growth of the agency. The "public constituency" may be understood as an interest group or set of groups concerned with performance of the agency's formal regulatory "public interest" goals. The growth is characterized by increased size (more personnel) and accompanying increases in other agency resources (i.e., higher budget). This growth produces turnover through promotion and creation of new positions. The active constituency lobbies for greater allocations to the agency, leading also to increased resources. Turnover in the agency draws climbers to the agency and scares away conservers. In addition, new positions and positions opened up through promotion and departure are filled by advancing climbers. The result is an increased proportion of climbers to conservers. For reasons discussed earlier, climbers seek growth (if only to permit more climbing), so that there is an element of positive feedback in the model (an aspect of Downs's "accelerator" effect). Climbers are also more innovation-prone and may seek to expedite the work of the agency and make it more flexible in order to facilitate growth and help their careers. Note that innovation-prone

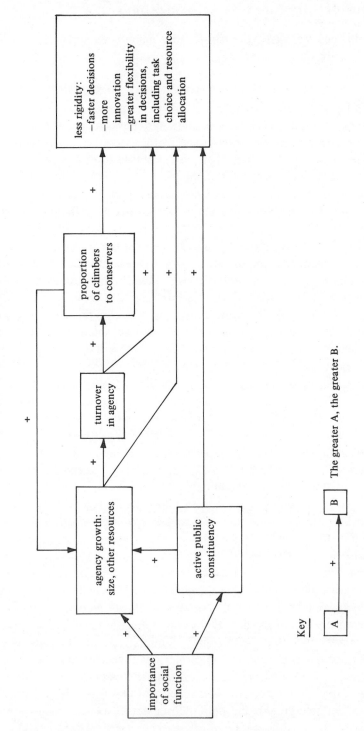

Figure 2.6. A Simplified Adaptation of Down's Rigidity Model
to Explain Prevention of the Rigidity Cycle

zealots may also be attracted to the agency. Thus the growth of rigidity is retarded. Turnover may break up rigidifying lines of communication and authority, permitting quicker and more flexible decisions, and so also reducing rigidity (see, e.g., Price 1977:104–10). Increased resources allow faster decisions, more (and more risky) innovations, and greater flexibility, with the result less rigidity. And the active public constituency keeps an eye on it all, ready to participate and pressure if the agency does not behave according to its conception of the "public interest" reflected in the agency's formal regulatory goals.

We shall organize the discussion of agency differences under four of the variables employed in the model: importance of a bureau's social function, growth, the existence of an active public constituency, and turnover in the agency:

1. The *increasing importance of a bureau's social function* leads to bureau growth and may guarantee a growing and active "constituency" for the bureau. Although regulatory agencies, after the crisis period of their founding, have historically displayed a long-term pattern of growth (see, e.g., Stigler 1975:152–58), their growth has not been steady (see also Noll 1978a:81–88) nor has it apparently been related directly to growth in the regulated industry. If the social function served by regulatory agencies has not been of steadily increasing importance (or maintained at a level of importance sufficient to produce growth tied to that in the industry), the regulatory agencies may be more subject to the rigidity/life cycle effects noted by Downs than other kinds of public agencies. The recent increasing importance of regulation in the "social"[20] (as contrasted with the economic) area (see Lilley and Miller 1977) has in fact corresponded with the advocacy of active constituencies in the form of public interest groups (see Berry 1977).

2. *Continued growth* in the agency leads to higher turnover in the agency, so that more innovation-prone climbers and perhaps zealots are attracted. As noted above, regulatory agencies usually do not have records of steady or continued growth; they have shown inconsistent growth with periods of growth alternating with stability and even occasional decline. We may expect, then, relatively more rigid-

---

[20] The sense in which "social" is used here is different from that in "bureau's social function." Lilley and Miller (1977) mean to refer to recent regulation of individual behavior, interindividual behavior, and external impacts on individuals (e.g., OSHA, CPSC, EEOC).

ity in the regulatory agencies than in those government bureaus that have experienced steady growth over this period.

3. An *active public constituency* may supply the feedback pressure that will inhibit development of rigidity and overidentification with the interests of the regulated party (see also Sabatier 1975; Jaffe 1973; on bureaucratic clienteles, see, e.g., Rourke 1976). Regulatory agencies have in the past been relatively "backwater" in that they have dealt with relatively esoteric matters in an esoteric fashion, from the public's perspective. The details of securities regulations, for example, or the procedures which govern hearings conducted by administrative law judges in regulatory agencies, have this status. Recent events, such as interest in environmental regulation and food and drug regulation, may be changing this in some areas. But such obscurity may inhibit the development of a "constituency" in the public which has the interest and expertise to participate effectively. Frequently the only "constituency" that possesses these attributes is the regulated party. The agency may come to serve this active "constituency" well. Thus rigidity and "capture" by the regulated party tend to accompany one another. Government bureaus, in general, that suffer from such obscurity may also be more likely to become rigid, but frontline government departments that provide important and easily perceptible services may be relatively less likely to follow the pattern. Note also that the relatively high specialization in regulatory agencies (recall Bernstein's comments on professionalism) may promote rigidity.

4. *High turnover* disrupts ossifying authority and communications patterns and provides opportunities for (and so draws and promotes) relatively more innovation-prone climbers and zealots (see, e.g., Price 1977:104–10). Inconsistent growth in regulatory agencies compared to other bureaus could mean relatively less turnover, and so facilitation of rigid authority and communication patterns and a relatively lower proportion of climbers and zealots. Plateaus in the pattern of uneven growth could permit the entrenchment of conservers who could then interfere with the achievement of the normal effects of growth in subsequent expansion periods.

3.3.2.5 *Rigidity and Regulatory Commissions vs. Departments*

Consider now the differences between the department and commission form of regulatory agency. Important structural differences, again, include the multiple head of the commission and the commission's frequent status as an "independent" agency. In addition, commissioners may be appointed, while many bureau heads and high-level personnel may be Civil Service or career bureaucrats. The discussion will be organized under the factors used to compare regulatory and nonregulatory agencies:

1. There would not seem to be important differences related to the *increasing importance of a bureau's social function*. In principle (though not necessarily in practice), it might be harder for the effects of changing social function to be transmitted to an "independent" commission than to a line bureau. We shall consider the effects of "independence" below in our discussion of the "active public constituency."

2. Under certain conditions, *growth* in the regulatory commission will be less favored than growth in the department form. But mechanisms to permit growth in the commission can be developed and lead to consequences different from those in Downs's model.

Commissioners, whose salaries may be set by the legislature, may find it relatively more difficult to increase them, and because of their fixed term of appointment, uncertainty over their being reappointed, and the implicit lucrative job opportunities that they may perceive in the regulated industry, they may value such increases relatively less (see, e.g., Eckert's arguments, 1973). If work load increases, commissioners may not be able to easily secure from the legislature increases in the number of commissioners to handle it; the commissioners, after all, if not always primary decision makers in the regulatory agency, are usually at least a kind of appeals court through which agency decisions must flow. Thus, unable to increase their salary, receiving prestige only from the regulated industry as they officiate in a "backwater" agency, and subject to personal increases in work load if they try to expand the agency's regulatory coverage or seek to make the regulations more complex, the commissioners may even oppose growth. They may design regulations that are simple to administer and define the scope of their regulatory mandate narrowly (see, e.g., Eckert 1973). These effects are additionally encouraged by the need to avoid reversals of agency decisions by the courts (i.e., the regulators make the decisions on simple, narrow, largely procedural grounds) which could reflect unfavorably on the regulators.

Note that these arguments are often also consistent with the making of regulations consistent with the wishes of the regulated party. Thus, setting of a uniform price throughout the market and permitting monopoly of service may also serve the interests of a regulated industry. The occurrence of such regulation then *need not* be evidence of "capture," i.e., of an industry successful in securing protective regulation for itself. It is the *commission* which is obtaining its own protection.

Growth in the department may permit the regulators increased salary, increased status and prestige from having more subordinate personnel, and less of a work load through having subordinates perform it (see, e.g., Eckert 1973; on commissions vs. bureaus, see also DeAlessi 1974). If commissioners could obtain these results from growth they would seek it, too. In fact, it is possible to interpret the increased use of the "institutional decision" (see, e.g., Davis 1972:226–44) in regulatory agencies as a mechanism for securing the personal benefits of growth.

In an "institutional decision," the agency's ruling is the product not of the deliberations and writing of the small group of formally accredited decision makers, i.e., the commissioners, but the resultant of the activities of personnel throughout the agency and is often merely "signed off" by the commissioners. Thus agency staff may do an analysis of a pending case, with contributions possibly including recommendations from both legal and technical staff. An administrative law judge may make an "initial decision;" he may have staff help in writing it or putting it together. Commissioners, similarly, in supposedly reviewing the judge's decision, may actually read only a summary and recommendation prepared by staff.

It can be argued that institutional decisions are a way of coping with high regulatory caseloads, of increasing the expertise that goes into the decision through specialization of consideration of its aspects, and of expediting the decision. It is also a method of diffusing responsibility for the final decision among agency members, this argument also being consistent with the model we are using. But our major point here is that institutional decisions may permit growth and its rewards to the top regulators. More specialists with higher professionalization are hired, which increases the status of the people on top. Fragmentation of the decision also fragments the work load on the commissioners.

Growth of this type, however, may not, as in Downs's model, lead to less rigidity, but to more. As Downs argues, specialization leads to coordination problems and the growth of internal rules and procedures. The need to preserve this complex administrative structure enhances the role of conservers. The number of considerations and sign-offs required by fragmentation of the decision together with the requirement to follow complex administrative procedures can lead not to expedition, but to increasing delay. A major complaint, in fact, that has been directed at many of the federal commissions that have developed this decision method is the too-frequently extreme time it takes to generate the final decision (see U.S. Senate, Committee on Governmental Affairs, vol. 4, 1977). Rigidity, in the end, is enhanced, not reduced.

Thus the institutional decision could be seen as a response to the desire of commission heads for the personal benefits of agency growth, while confounding the "normal" effects of growth in reducing rigidity. Of course, this is speculation based on the consideration of a modification of Downs's model in the context of the commission structure, but it is suggestive of the potential payoffs from taking a bureaucratic/organizational perspective.

3. Insofar as the actions of an independent commission are more visible than a department, where the regulatory function may be buried in a subsidiary office, the maintenance of an *active public "constituency"* may be encouraged. But we see no a priori reasons why the department form may not also be "visible," given a similar regulatory function. In fact, arguments have been offered to suggest that the "independence" of the independent regulatory commission may lead to isolation from active, corrective public constituencies and, in fact, can promote "capture" by the regulated industry.[21]

Bernstein (1955:130) offers three definitions of "independence": "location outside an executive department; some measure of independence from supervision by the president or by a Cabinet secretary; immunity from the president's discretionary power to remove members of independent commissions from office." Fesler, in a study of state regulatory agencies, finds that "independence" has been used to mean "independence of control by the governor and legislature, independence of control by utility companies, and independence in the sense of integrity and impartiality" (Fesler 1942:22; on independence see also, e.g., Fesler 1946; Redford 1952:275–83; U.S. Senate Committee on Governmental Affairs, vol. 5, 1977; Eastman 1928). The degree of such "independence" in any or all of these senses has been a major issue in the design of regulatory agencies. Discussions have not usually gone beyond structural

---

[21] For a discussion of the "independence" question, see, e.g., Bernstein (1955, ch. 5).

conditions and what they are supposed to do to influence commission behavior, to considerations of the effect of "independence" on the incentive system faced by the regulators and consequences for behavior.

Isolation from executive directives or supervision can mean that public protests to elected officials cannot be channeled effectively back to the regulatory agency; indirect "heat" from the public may not warm—and inform—the commission's behavior (see figure 2.2). It may, of course, still affect commissioner chances for reappointment. But the commissioner who looks forward to more lucrative employment in the regulated industry may not be overly concerned about this; in fact, the average tenure of the federal commissioners has not been very long (see, e.g., Graham and Kramer 1976: 406–7; U.S. Senate, Committee on Governmental Affairs, vol. I, 1977). Isolation from executive directives may also mean that commissioners can afford to be relatively less responsive to active public constituencies that approach the commission directly. Even if the commission permits intervenors from such groups to enter its proceedings, leading to appeals of its decisions, the commission can protect itself from court reversal by making narrowly based procedural decisions. As Bernstein notes, the life of groups that actively pushed for regulation in some "public" interest is short, and subsequent active constituencies can also expect to have problems in maintaining advocacy (on such problems see, e.g., Berry 1977). And though the cycle of interest-group interest may be relatively short, the regulated industry's intense interest will always be there. Independence from executive policy directives and from public constituencies does not also mean independence from a constituency from which the agency will not be isolated—the regulated industry (McConnell 1966:289–90).

Commissions that are formally independent can sometimes be used by elected officials as targets or scapegoats for rhetoric aimed at political gain. Independence can also be a method of isolating the elected official from any public blame heaped on the regulatory agency (Baldwin 1975:9). Should commissioners care about their prospects for reappointment, the status they enjoy as commissioners, or their professional reputation and its contribution to their opportunities for a satisfactory future position outside the agency, attacks by elected officials can effectively reduce any formal independence that exists. Fesler quotes one apparently not unbiased observer:

> The heat generated by gubernatorial campaigns for election . . . has seemed to produce in a governor a berserk rage against the light and power industry. Hence the first official act of many of them is to go out and rattle sticks along the bars where the utilities are caged, and to make snoots at their keepers, the regulatory commissions. (Fesler 1942:22)

Isolation from executive policy directives can also mean isolation from changes in administrative, economic, and social life to which other agencies respond. Active public constituencies may contribute to awareness of such changes. Thus, once the commission is administratively rigidified and its procedures (and precedents) judicialized, it may be insulated from new management techniques and new ways of viewing emergent economic and social problems.

Regulatory agencies that are not commissions but which are given "independent" status may be subject to some of the same problems, of course, but the commission form itself is usually granted an "independent" status.

Finally, even if active public constituencies do concern themselves with the work of the commission, they may be stymied by the lack of individual responsibility that results from the commission's collective leadership (as well as the effects of decisions made institutionally). Individual commissioners may escape blame for commission decisions and pressure to change them, and may continue to enjoy the subtle rewards bestowed by the regulated industry.

"Independent" commissions are, however, hardly isolated; Krasnow and Longley (1978), among others, describe many potential paths of influence. But it seems structural independence is likely to have some effects, as described, on the incentive system faced by the commissioners.

4. *High turnover* at the uppermost level of the commission is not unusual; historically, commissioners do not on the average have long tenure (e.g., Graham and Kramer 1976:406–7) and frequently depart for relatively lucrative jobs that deal with or are in the regulated industry (e.g., Graham and Kramer 1976:413–18). We shall review the empirical literature in this area in chapter 3. Yet the regulatory commissions have often been held up as the prototypes of agencies with a life cycle culminating in rigidity.

Regulatory commissioners are, however, not normally advanced to their positions from within the agency; as many observers have noted, commission appointments have most often involved political pressures or been patronage rewards (see, e.g., Graham and Kramer

1976, ch. 23). Thus the path of promotion within the agency terminates below the commissioner level and turnover at the top level alone provides no incentive for climbers to join and stay with the agency. Superficial change at the top level may also not have much effect in an agency in which decision is "institutional" anyway. The judicialization of procedure in the agency is formalized and would often be hard to change even if a new commissioner wanted to change it. For the case of the regulatory commission, therefore, turnover at the top level may not retard the growth of rigidity that Downs explains in his theory. This is in contrast to the department case in which high-level turnover can permit promotion and/or entry of climbers.

3.3.2.6 Downs and the Life Cycle: Concluding Comments

Compared to the life cycle/evolution models described earlier, Downs's is better developed and, with the possible exception of Shepherd, more explicitly explanatory in approach. But though his explanations are superficially deductive and logically developed, they are not very well organized. For example, his discussion of the rigidity cycle is clearly related to and overlaps, but is offered separately from his discussion of the life cycle. He does not identify or label stages in the cycles (there may be none—there is no reason to suppose that life cycles are linear progressions), but even when he asserts there are a certain number of stages, he does not bother to specify them. His presentation is more a logical linking of intriguing insights, than a model with a clearly defined overall structure. One can extract some structure, or use the basic arguments to develop a model, as in the simplified model represented in figure 2.6, but it is easy to develop special cases and exceptions, as we have done in our discussion of the rigidity cycle. Downs's model requires a more careful specification of the conditions under which it will be operative, including the impact of organizational structures on the incentive system, as in the case of the commission form. Though Downs tries to be deductive, he clearly assumes certain features of the agency and its environment that are not made explicit. As a result, generalization of the theory is perilous.

Still, one must admire the sheer density of the analysis, including the number of insights, reasons, and small explanations distinguished, as well as the promise of an approach similar to the one he takes if developed more carefully.

3.4 LIFE CYCLES AND EVOLUTION: CONCLUSION

3.4.1 Assessment of the Models

In figure 2.7 we summarize some criticisms that apply to all of the life cycle models.

Perhaps the most important caution that can be made about the foregoing discussion of evolutionary patterns and "life cycles" in regulatory bodies and those they regulate is that it is based largely on anecdotal evidence, casual observations, and apparent patterns in a

Figure 2.7. General Criticisms of Existing Life Cycle Models

- Lack of rigorous empirical support.
- Poor specification in models in general.
- Relatively unitary treatment of organizations.
- Questions regarding correctness of life cycle metaphor, regularity of stage emergence, existence of stages, cyclical nature vs. evolutionary nature of flow.
- Lack of careful consideration of intrastage evolution.
- Vague specification of stage boundaries.
- Lack of careful specification of explanatory developmental processes; frequent emphasis on description over explanation.
- Failure to perceive components of regulatory system as open, adaptive subsystems in an interdependent *system*.
- Failure to explicate processes of external access or influence in system, as well as developmental patterns for other components of the system, such as interest groups.
- Failure to comprehend vast variation and complexity in units of analysis and system.

few agencies or industries. And the regulated industry models, after all, apply only to utilities. Shepherd probably goes farther than any of the others in trying to attach his analysis to events in a broad range of the subjects studied (see his chart relating utilities to approximate dates of passage through his stages; Wilcox and Shepherd 1975: 349). But far more in the way of empirical verification is needed (for one attempt, see Meier and Plumlee 1977, 1978). Life cycle or evolutionary stages analysis may turn out to have more heuristic than explanatory or predictive value.

Most models are, in addition, poorly or vaguely stated and organized, and are imprecise or ambiguous about stage and developmental characteristics.

Many aspects of the life cycle that would aid explanation of agency and utility behavior have yet to be addressed. Some of the authors, of course, such as Glaeser, put far more emphasis on description of the phases than on explanation of why they occur in the form they do, and how they originate and evolve into later stages. There is a general need to incorporate organizational variables, and variation, in a more complete and systematic way. The question of whether organizational development in utilities and in agencies is evolutionary or truly cyclical and repeating, and the consequences of the answer, need closer attention.

Models tend to treat all organizations as either unitary bodies—black boxes that behave as single persons might—or as bodies in which one or a very few rational types of individuals determine the organization's course. But organizational action may be a resultant of the behavior of individuals in a collectivity, none of whom has complete control over organizational outputs (or goal-setting) (cf. Banfield 1961:324–41). The problematic nature of organizational goals has long been recognized (see, e.g., Georgiou 1973). In the political science literature, the utility of recognizing alternative "levels of analysis" in organizational settings has also received recognition (Allison 1971).

The life cycle metaphor itself may be misleading. Organizational careers may not be like lives that begin at birth and pass through discernible stages. Organizations may start (and stay mostly) at one "stage," whether it is "old age" or "youth." Organizations may not "cycle"; they may evolve one-way. And there is no reason to suppose that the evolutionary process can be conceptually decomposed into a series of stages; a seamless evolution may be a more appropriate depiction. If organizations do evolve into new statuses that may be considered "stages," they must also evolve within "stages." The nature of the changes within "stages," and the boundaries that separate "stages" are not made clear. In general, life cycle models, though purporting to describe organizational dynamics, are remarkably static. They provide pictures of subsequent stages, describe some processes or behavior or interdependencies that seem to lead to changes, but rarely provide clear statements of carefully explicated and linked developmental processes that explain the evolution or life cycle.

Except for Shepherd's analysis (and even in his discussion the detailed changes in the regulatory body are not explicated), the evolution/life cycle theories do not treat the units of study as comprising a system. Looking again at figure 2. 1, it is easy to see that the stages through which regulators pass are probably intimately related to the stages of the regulated party. In addition, if the other elements in the regulatory environment (e.g., interest groups) pass through characteristic stages (or are encouraged or induced to pass through some series of stages due to the interaction of the central units of interest), it would in general be necessary for full understanding to include them. Similarly, patterns or processes of external access or influence that characterize this interactive system are not well described. Any unit in the overall regulatory system may be treated as an open, adaptive system (cf. Fiorino and Metlay 1977).

Implicit in some of the stages analysis we have discussed, for example, is a possible life cycle pattern for public interest groups. Thus, Bernstein notes the initial activism of such groups in response to the crisis conditions that lead to founding of the commission. This activism fades after the agency's formation, but is revived as the agency in Old Age fails to respond to a renewed crisis. An analysis of the dynamics of the growth and decline of interest groups could have important consequences for the explanation of regulatory life cycles, especially if, as Sabatier (1975) argues, "constituency" activism may help prevent agency "capture".[22]

Finally, both industries (and other regulatory subjects) and agencies exhibit vast variation in all of the aspects sought to be described, explained, or included in life cycle models. Organizational and systemic structures, personnel, regulatory controls, environmental political, social, and economic conditions, and so on, present a vast array of contingencies that are subject to condensation and simplification (or, simply, lack of consideration) in existing life cycle formulations. Such complexity has led at least one writer to dismiss the feasibility of developing a theory of regulation as "almost a logical impossibility" (G. W. Wilson 1976:702).

Variation and complexity are problems in the study of almost any social setting. Given the foregoing criticisms, however, the utility of life cycle analysis beyond heuristic value remains to be demonstrated.

[22] For models that may be adapted to this purpose see, e.g., M. Schwartz (1976:193–98) on the "life of protest organizations" and Mitnick (1974:398–402) on the evolution of advocacy in interest groups.

3.4.2   Future Theory Development

Life cycle theories are somehow intuitively appealing ways to represent observed change in the careers of regulatory organizations. Their present status as satisfactory descriptive or explanatory mechanisms, however, is questionable. There is clearly a need to specify the models more carefully, include or deal with internal and external (and time dependent) complexity, subject new as well as developed models to empirical test, and so on.

Of key importance to the development of a better understanding of change processes and patterns in the regulatory system is further work on what we shall call the bureaucratic or bureaucratic protection theory of regulation. Public organizations are not passive and/or defensive responders to client-manipulated incentives or disincentives. And they are not merely collections of individuals with different goal sets who respond rationally to the available distribution of goal satisfactions. Regulatory organizations possess, almost by definition, unusual powers to regulate and control their environments. They are characterized by different structures (e.g., commission vs. bureau form) and different technologies of regulating (e.g., routine vs. complex). They are adaptive in that they can both affect and be affected by environmental change. Different structures, technologies, and environments can, of course, be understood as contingencies affecting extant incentive systems. But the temptation to reduce *all* explanations of regulatory behavior to simple rational choice calculations involving individuals should be resisted.

The institutional decision, for example, is marked by specialization and structural differentiation in the agency. The effects of such a decision method on organizational performance therefore represent the resultant of individual actions in this structure. If the institutional decision permits regulatory officials some of the personal benefits of growth (while reducing some of the costs that would result in the commission form), we can perhaps understand adoption or extension of this method as an individually rational act. Institutional decisions may not even be sought directly; they could grow out of individual desires to practice professional skills and increase subordinate staff. But the regulatory behavior itself (e.g., agency actions to set rates, issue licenses, restrict trade practices, and so on) is a resultant of individual actions in the organization and not necessarily the intended act of an individual or of a given set of individuals. The apparent paradoxes that occur in similar social situations are eloquently discussed by Schelling (1971, 1974, 1978).

A related problem arises in any collective decision-making in which the aggregated choice of many individuals must be ascribed to a single, rationalized point of view, or in which an explanation is sought by deducing single or consistent reasons or motives from collective actions. Examples include multimember courts (where the problem is solved by permitting reporting of differing concurring opinions) and university promotion and tenure review committees (where reporting of reasons to the candidate may simply be discouraged).

Having made the argument for sensitivity to organizational complexity, we do note that simplified but satisfactory explanations for general purposes *can* sometimes be constructed. At a fairly abstract level of explanation it would not be inaccurate, for example, to speak of a "bureaucratic behavior theory" of regulation in contrast to "industry protection" or "consumer protection" theories among possible alternative theories. Explanations falling under the bureaucratic theory would derive importantly from the goals of bureaucrats and indicated rational behaviors given extant structures, technologies, and environmental contingencies. Resultant collective behaviors would still be included even if intended by no individual. Industry protection and consumer protection theories, in contrast, would explain regulatory behavior largely in terms of actions by industries or consumer groups following their goals in the given regulatory area. Any complex resultant collective behaviors could also be included. We shall consider theories of regulatory origin in chapter 3.

At any rate, adequate models or explanations of general regulatory behavior as well as evolution or life cycles probably await study of the components of the regulatory system as the organizations that they are.

4.0 Conclusion

In this chapter, we have focused on dynamic elements in the administrative/regulatory system, including the creation of administrative units, trends in the history and evolution of regulation in the United States, and the evolutionary/life cycle patterns of two major elements in the regulatory system—the regulatory agency and the regulated industry. In the next chapter, we shall examine the origins of regulation more carefully, reviewing some theories of regulatory origin, specifying some elements of a theory or theories of regulatory origin, illustrating these theories with a review of the history of the Interstate Commerce Commission, and presenting a partial theory of regulatory "capture." This will lead us to basic questions regarding the goals and rationale of regulation, which are treated in chapters 4 and 5.

III

Theories of Regulatory Origin

THE CREATION OF regulatory organizations, and the creation, implementation, and administration of regulation, may be understood as special cases of the general policy-making process. To some extent, this is consistent with our emphasis on regulation itself as process. Though they are special cases of the general process, it is still possible, of course, to distinguish theories that seek to explain regulatory origin from theories of the ongoing regulatory process. In fact, existing approaches have been directed at a variety of dependent variables, not all of which have been linked explicitly to stages in the policy process. Thus, theories have been offered regarding regulatory origin, the effects of regulation, the process of regulation in operation, and general aspects of bureaucratic behavior, of which behavior in regulatory agencies is only a subset.

Unfortunately, some scholars have discussed general theories of regulation without clear distinction of regulatory origin (whether of new organizations or of new regulations within existing organizations) from ongoing regulatory practice, e.g., choice of particular outcomes under existing regulation. And most approaches, as we shall see, have been limited to only parts of the overall policy-making process, and cannot serve as adequate explanations of regulatory origin or of regulatory practice.

After describing the policy-making process in simplified form, we shall review some of the leading theories of regulation. Because theories of regulatory origin are usually closely related to (or not distinguished from) theories of regulation in general, we shall look broadly at such theories. Our focus, then, will be on those that are, or could be, linked to regulatory origin. One objective of the analysis will be to demonstrate that these theories are really partial theories and that an integrated approach is needed.

Following this review, we shall outline four simple "interest" theories of regulatory origin, and argue for, and develop, the bureau-cratic/organizational approach. A major feature of this is a general in-centive systems approach to organizations. We shall then offer a dis-cussion of aspects of regulatory entry, in which some components of the general policy-making process are developed for the case of regu-latory origin. Following this, the four simple interest theories are applied, illustratively, to discuss the growth of transportation regula-tion by the Interstate Commerce Commission. Finally, the incentive systems approach is applied to develop a partial theory of regulatory "capture," i.e., a theory of how regulators may acquire predisposi-tions to add new regulation that serves the regulated interest, or to produce ongoing regulatory activities that serve the regulated interest rather than public interest ends.

1.0 The Policy-Making Process

The process by which public policies are proposed, reach a formal public decision forum, are chosen, are implemented, are administered in the routinization that follows implementation, have impacts, feed back on earlier stages in the process, and are (rarely) terminated is a complex one (see, e.g., Jones 1977; Cobb and Elder 1972; Cobb, Ross and Ross 1976; on regulation cf. Sabatier 1977). Theoretical study of the area is in its infancy; there are now no powerful theoreti-cal tools to apply to the whole process like those available to and employed by economists, as we shall see, to study parts of the pro-cess. This policy-making process can be conceptually divided into the following stages (see the works cited above for more detail and other views): access (issue creation, issue expansion, agenda entrance), decision, implementation, administration, impacts (and their evalua-tion), and termination. Since termination can itself be viewed as a policy process (i.e., the intention to terminate must be proposed, get on the agenda, and so on), it will be omitted in the subsequent dis-cussion.

A full theory of regulation must therefore explain how regulation is proposed, formally considered and approved, put into effect, ad-ministered, has impact, is evaluated, and is altered. The regulation may be a new agency with a new regulatory mandate, a new adminis-trative rule or standard in an existing agency, or any of the other forms of external choice restriction we include under "regulation."

A full theory of regulatory *origin* must at minimum extend from the access stage into the administration stage; much of what is effective and meaningful in any piece of regulation is frequently created as a broad or vague regulatory restriction emerges from formal adoption in the decision stage and is given concrete identity and detailed specification for action during implementation. In chapter 6 we shall analyze the relation between legislative decision and administrative implementation—delegation. Analysis of regulatory origin, however, can include any or all stages in the policy process; some theories work backward to an explanation of origin from effects or generalize from the form and content of formalized regulatory policies. Furthermore, sometimes the intentions of groups involved in regulatory origin can only be understood by examining intended—or actual—effects. For these reasons, we shall include all stages through impacts/effects in our discussion.

The stages in the policy-making process in the context of regulation are presented below in outline form together with major and/or illustrative variables, or variable categories, for each stage (cf. Cobb and Elder 1972; Cobb, Ross and Ross 1976; Anderson 1975; Jones 1977; Sabatier 1977). Some of the concepts in the access stage will be discussed and applied to regulatory entry later in this chapter. There is no general agreement in the literature on conceptual divisions, i.e., stages, in the policy process; the outline below is an attempt at integrating and extending some of the existing approaches. Some scholars distinguish only three stages, for example: *policy formulation* (or policy intention formation), which includes our access and decision stages; *policy implementation,* which includes our implementation—here meaning the establishment and putting-in-effect of the program or administrative apparatus—as well as our administration—operating an established program—stages; and *policy evaluation,* which includes impacts/effects, their evaluation and feedback, and any changes, such as termination.

I. Access
1. Issue creation (initiation and specification of the policy intention)
    1.1 Nature of parties proposing regulation
    1.2 Nature and form of regulatory issue—issue specification (dimensions, symbol usage)
    1.3 Dynamics of creation (e.g., crisis vs. gradual)
    1.4 Contextual/situational conditions affecting creation (e.g., com-

peting groups, status in political system, social, economic, and
cultural conditions, physical environment, historical factors)
2. Issue expansion (building coalition of additional parties)
   2.1 Nature of parties targeted for inclusion in coalition
   2.2 Nature of issue-entrepreneurs managing expansion of issue
   2.3 Strategies of individuals/groups advocating/opposing regulatory
      issue
   2.4 Dynamics of expansion (e.g., speed of conversion to emotional
      issue)
   2.5 Contextual/situational conditions
3. Agenda entrance (issue reaches consideration on the public or societal agenda, and on the formal, institutional agenda)
   3.1 Nature of individuals/groups managing entrance
   3.2 Nature of agenda "gatekeepers" governing entrance
   3.3 Locus of agenda entry (e.g., executive, legislative, existing in-
      dependent agency)
   3.4 Strategies of entrance managers; patterns of entry
   3.5 Dynamics of entry
   3.6 Contextual/situational conditions

II. Decision

1. Nature of key decision makers (including motives or objectives)
2. Nature of policy advocates/opponents (including motives, resources
such as legitimacy, funds, strategic position, size, external esteem,
and so on)
3. Nature of the decision-making process (e.g., legislative vote, vote
by commissioners in agency; institutional decision in agency)
4. Locus of decision (e.g., legislature, executive, "independent"
agency)
5. Strategies of policy advocates/opponents during decision process
6. Processes of coalition and support-building for, or legitimation of,
proposed policies
7. Dynamics of decision
8. Nature of policy approved (policy outputs)
9. Contextual/situational factors in decisions

III. Implementation

1. Relation between decision locus and implementation locus (including delegation factors)
2. Nature of implementers (including motives or objectives, level of
information-expertise, and so on)
3. Nature of advocates/opponents of regulation outside implementing
unit
4. Resources of implementing unit
5. Nature of implementing process (e.g., number of clearances,
number of parties that must be involved, and so on)
6. Strategies of implementers and of advocates/opponents outside and
inside implementing unit

7. Dynamics of implementation (time and change factors)
8. Contextual/situational factors in implementation

IV. Administration

1. Nature of administrators (e.g., motives including risk preference, cognitive capabilities—bounded rationality, expertise, and so on)
2. Nature of parties supporting/opposing regulation
3. Standard operating procedures of administration
4. Organization and structure of administrating unit
5. Resources of administrating unit
6. Strategies of parties participating in (supporting/opposing) regulation
7. Dynamics of administration
8. Contextual/situational factors in administration

V. Impacts/Effects

1. Nature of administrative outputs
2. Nature of effects of administrative outputs
3. Nature of parties affected
4. Distribution of impacts
5. Relation of impacts to affected parties' preferences
6. Intensity of preferences of affected parties regarding the effects
7. Attempts to evaluate and feed back evaluation results to the earlier stages in the policy process

Existing theories of regulation typically link parts of this process but fail to include, and to explain, other parts. Simple "economic" theories of regulation, for example, sometimes link a few aspects of issue creation with a few aspects of decision and with some aspects of impact. This would be no failure if the theories were explicitly limited in scope, but few are. The process abstracted above is an enormously complex one; the categories listed are not complete and fully descriptive. Thus a theory that dealt adequately with all, or even most, aspects of this process would be a powerful one indeed.

It can be argued that the value of parsimony and the goal of adequate prediction could lead one to feel happy with a theory that derived adequate prediction from a simple relation of a few factors. But the prediction may relate only to a limited set of dependent variables, such as impacts or effects. Theories of regulation, however, should seek to explain more than this. Prediction is valuable, but, we feel, understanding through explanation may be more so. Standards of adequate explanation, and understanding, can vary. "Understanding" can exist for some people at different levels of abstraction, using variables that are more or less inclusive, or "natural" or descriptive or operational, and for some people who require a greater or lesser capability for prescriptive use or manipulability. We would certainly not claim that any adequate theory of regulation would employ in key roles all of the variables listed in, or implied by, the list above, as well as others. But any adequate theory of regulation ought to be able to account for and to explain the behaviors observed through the process.

2.0 Theories of Regulatory Origin

To a large extent, theories of regulation have always been theories of "interest." For example, references have ranged from the older term "parties-in-interest" to later discussion of the "preferences" of members of groups or the "utility-maximization" of bureaucrats or other actors. These assumptions have not at all been identical or even very similar; "interest" itself is a concept with a variety of usages.[1] But whatever the terms used, such theories have usually had some core assumption regarding the seeking of interest satisfaction or attainment. Usually, public regulation, directly or indirectly, is the instrument through which that interest satisfaction is achieved.

The distinction is not always made, however, between the interests of those seeking regulation and the interests of those served by regulation. Sometimes it is assumed that the regulation sought and achieved by some party then operates as the interest of that party would prefer; i.e., there are no intervening events or conditions to deflect satisfaction. Perhaps parties seeking regulation of a certain sort with certain effects never actually achieved those effects, right from the start, though the regulatory form itself was obtained. As we saw in chapter 2, regulation can also be viewed as evolving or changing over time, so that the interests served do not remain those served initially. In the latter case, the *effects* of regulation which may formally have the same structure or organization as previously may have changed. Existing theories of regulation do not always make these distinctions, though at least one writer, as we shall see below, argues for the utility of his approach based on its attempt to combine explanations of origin and evolution (Weingast 1978).

A further distinction of relevance is whether the regulation is new or is an addition to or modification of existing regulation. Theories

[1] The literature on "interest" is quite extensive; we shall not review it here. See, e.g., Held (1970) and chapter 4.

which concentrate on the role of external interest groups, e.g., the Grangers or the railroads in the founding of the Interstate Commerce Commission, may ignore the role of the regulatory administrators and other parties who can play a major part in later additions to the regulation, e.g., any role played by the Commission and by the group of lawyers specializing in ICC cases, i.e., the ICC bar, in, say, the Transportation Act of 1920, or the Motor Carrier Act of 1935 (adding trucking).

In order to organize the discussion of theories of regulation, we return to our definition of regulation as intentional restriction of choice by a party not directly involved in, or performing, the regulated activity. The extremes of intentional action may be classified into those that reflect private, egoistic, selfish or "self" interests or goals, i.e., self-regarding preferences, and those that reflect "other" interests or goals, i.e., other-regarding preferences.[2] Let us contrast, in particular, that case where the other-goal referent is the public at large, or society, with those cases with goals that have private or particularistic referents. This distinction is similar to that made between "public-regardingness" and "private-regardingness" (Wilson and Banfield 1964, 1971; Barry 1965: 12-13). It also potentially carries the same problems, of course, of determining to which category a given case belongs. At any rate, we may identify theories of regulatory origin according to whose genuinely held goal or interest, public or private, would be primarily realized by establishment of the regulation (cf. Posner 1974). Thus, the theories are to be categorized by whose *intention,* public or private, is realized by the form of the new regulatory interference. There is no presumption that the regulation would actually have this *effect* either at the start or over time.[3]

The only scholar to present an extended discussion of regulation organized around the stages of the policy process is James Q. Wilson (1974). His consideration of the "politics of regulation," however, takes this approach only implicitly; he writes that he seeks to explain "the circumstances under which regulation becomes politically possible, the pattern of regulation that is likely to emerge from a given political context, and the forces that will influence how a regulatory

---

[2] On "self-goals" and "other-goals" see Mitnick (1974).

[3] On public vs. private theories of regulation, see, e.g., Posner (1974); Stigler (1971); Abrams and Settle (1978). The distinction is usually made between "public interest" theories and "economic" theories of regulation, in which an economic model is made of the supply of regulation in response to the demand of private parties. An "agency" based distinction (see below) has not been employed.

agency does its job" (J. Q. Wilson 1974:137). Because of his approach, consideration of Wilson's arguments provides an appropriate
introduction to the more specialized models that are reviewed below.

Like many of the other models, Wilson's can also be considered a
theory of "interest." Rejecting reliance on perspectives that assume
regulation is instituted to serve either public interests or private,
regulated-industry interests, Wilson argues for allowing "a variety of
political causes" and asserts "that it is necessary, in order to understand why regulation occurs, to specify the circumstances under
which one or another cause will be operative" (J. Q. Wilson 1974:
138–39). We shall put forth a related view in the discussion of four
simple interest theories and the ICC case later in this chapter. Wilson
introduces the "interest" concept by considering how the perceived
costs and benefits of the regulation are distributed in society by a
proposed regulatory policy. Two assumptions are made about the
ways these costs and benefits impact: Individuals and groups are
more sensitive to decreases rather than increases in their net benefits,
and political action is more likely when costs or benefits are concentrated on a relatively small, homogeneous group rather than spread
diffusely over a large, diverse one.

Three main patterns of the distribution of costs and benefits are
identified. Under a proposed regulatory policy involving *concentrated
benefits, diffused costs,* the benefited groups (e.g., licensed occupations, taxi companies) are likely to successfully introduce and maintain the policy. The regulation itself is likely to involve lessening or
removing price competition in the industry; entry barriers; a strong
influence of the benefited group on the regulatory agency; the seeking
of low visibility by the industry and the agency to prevent opposition
from forming; and, in any controversy, a defense of the regulation
through claims that the regulation removes the evil effects of price
competition, promotes safety, and so on.

Under a proposed regulatory policy involving *concentrated benefits, concentrated costs,* a struggle between two organized groups
leads to a formalized imposition of costs and recognition of benefits
(e.g., labor–management struggles). The regulation that results will
contain a "charter" defining the rights and obligations of each side;
neither side will dominate the regulation's administration indefinitely;
each side will continually seek to improve its position under the
"charter"; and continual conflict, attempts to enlist allies, and court
appeals will keep visibility of the regulatory issues high. Wilson's

regulatory "charter" seems reminiscent of Shepherd's regulatory "social contract," discussed in chapter 2, in which the relation between regulator and regulatee is institutionalized.

Finally, under a proposed regulatory policy involving *diffused benefits, concentrated costs,* a small group is unable to escape imposition of costs by a large, diffusely-benefited group (e.g., consumer, safety, environmental regulation). Scandal or crisis may encourage this, but is not necessary. Many of these proposals originate in Congress, rather than the executive branch, and may be championed by Congressmen during committee hearings that give their champions substantial publicity. The regulation will tend to focus on some "evil" in order to get attention; the regulatory legislation will be strong and moralistic in order to mobilize support (since compromise is at this stage not yet required); many procedural—not substantive—bargains will be made to accommodate existing or potential state programs in the federal system; and the political process represented by the legislative fight for passage of the regulatory bill will condition the actual legislation as much as any a priori consideration of the problem by itself.

In discussing the role of Congressional champions of groups receiving diffusely-spread benefits, Wilson is effectively considering the role of *agents* in solving collective action dilemmas for diffusely-affected constituencies. It would seem that at the core of any discussion of how groups lacking existing leadership and organization participate in regulatory creation, and any discussion in which even organized groups are represented by and give instructions to particular parties that seek benefits for them through the political process (e.g., lobbyists), lies some treatment of what are, in effect, the problems and processes of agent–principal interactions (for interest groups, cf. Curry and Wade 1968; Frohlich, Oppenheimer, and Young 1971). Where "public interest" ends are sought, so that agents *must* exist to seek the "public" ends, agency concerns are perhaps particularly central. We shall return to this below when we consider "public interest" theories.

In this article, Wilson ignores a fourth category of distribution of costs and benefits—the case of *diffused benefits and diffused costs.* This effectively completes a two-by-two typology generated by dimensions of concentrated/diffused benefit and concentrated/diffused cost. This fourth category does not, however, appear to be a null or empty one. A great deal of regulation in such areas as general business or trade practices, retirement pension regulation, and safety regulation could fall in this category. Perhaps general industrial safety regulation, such as OSHA, is better classified here since it cuts across all industries and workers. Although impacts on particular industries may be high, impacts are widely distributed across diverse industries that, apart from general business groups like the Chamber of Commerce, have no particular central organization representing all of them in this area. If Wilson means to limit his concept of "concentration" to both high impacts and small groups, one wonders if there is a place in the typology for a regulation like OSHA in which group size is exceedingly large (all businesses over a certain size), and individual impacts can vary from nominal to very large.

Perhaps the "concentrated/diffused" concept should be disaggregated into level of impact on individual parties, and number or scope of parties affected. One could also distinguish a measure of basic diversity or difference in kind among affected parties. Parties may have differences regarding their preferences for outcomes from the general policies being sought for the group. Depending on their situations, parties may reduce the likelihood of unfavorable group action by not participating, or influence a particularly favorable group action through participation (cf. Stigler 1974). The costs of organizing diverse parties could be relatively high.

Wilson's prediction regarding group advocacy success rests on the incentives individual parties have to participate, given the costs they face (e.g., organizing and advocacy) and the likelihood of sharing in benefits brought by the group even if they do not participate in or contribute to the group's struggle (see discussion in our chapter 5 regarding "collective" or "public goods"; Olson 1965). Groups are therefore less likely to form and seek to control regulation when the effects on them are both individually small and distributed over a large number of different parties (i.e., costs of organizing high). Of course, net benefits/costs and risk/uncertainty factors, as well as the collective properties of the benefits supplied to the group, must be considered. The collective action problem is actually considerably more complicated than this brief account suggests. Thus Wilson's "concentrated" must mean more than "high per capita," as he perhaps inconsistently indicates at one point (J. Q. Wilson 1974:158). At any rate, it appears that classification of many regulatory policies in the typology as presented by Wilson could be problematic.

As in the case with the other "diffused" categories, the role of agents in producing—or not producing—the regulation can be particularly important in the diffused/diffused category. Agents can help solve the collective action dilemmas of "diffused" groups by providing expertise and a locus for group organizational actions.

Following this consideration of what we have termed the access and decision stages, Wilson proceeds to consider the nature of the regulation that is produced (i.e., more on the decision stages), discusses "regulatory administration" (our implementation and administration stages, together with some consideration of impacts/effects), and considers, finally, "some preconditions of effective regulation" (including, of course, many aspects of impacts/effects and their linkages to earlier stages). By looking at stages subsequent to access and decision, Wilson looks, in effect, at how intentions in regulatory creation do or do not lead to or correspond to actions under regulation.

Wilson observes that the "domain of regulation" will be enlarged under regulatory administration—i.e., new regulation or greater specificity added to existing regulation—1) where standards or criteria are imprecise and are then given content on a case-by-case basis that tends to create a patchwork quilt of standards such that almost anything can be rationalized; 2) where regulation is added to correct the unanticipated loopholes and consequences of the original regulation (McKie's "tar-baby effect"); 3) where the regulatory agency is used as a vehicle for meeting complaints about, and solving problems from, the impacts of industry performance; and 4) where the agency promulgates regulatory controls in order to increase its power over the regulated industry to meet its regulatory objectives, "to increase its nuisance value and thus what its members can charge the industry in graft or favors," and to simply "hold the initiative," i.e., retain power by making the agency less predictable (J. Q. Wilson 1974:156).

Regulatory "capture" is seen as only one of the outcomes possible under regulatory administration. Wilson argues that "capture" will be most likely in the concentrated benefits–diffused costs situation, but cautions that some regulation was created with industry support and given a formal mandate to protect the industry. Such promotional regulation cannot really be considered "capture." The concentrated benefits–concentrated costs situation is said to be unlikely to produce "capture"; any control of the regulation that develops will tend to shift back and forth between the contending parties. Under Wilson's third category, concentrated costs–diffused benefits, industry may seek to block or emasculate regulatory legislation, or affect its administration. Such factors as active public or consumer interest groups can reduce the likelihood of industry success.

Wilson goes on to discuss a number of factors affecting agency performance in regulatory administration. Of particular importance in understanding the politics of regulation (and politics in general) are "the creation, reaffirmation, and institutionalization of symbols" (J. Q. Wilson 1974:166). Even regulation that is largely symbolic in impact can be important for the symbolic legitimation it provides for government action in the area. Furthermore, as Cobb and Elder (1972; see discussion later in this chapter) have also argued, "the decisive stage in the ebb and flow of social conflict is control over the public agenda: what government may or may not do is chiefly determined by what people have come to believe is properly a 'private' or a 'public' matter" (J. Q. Wilson 1974:166). We shall give special attention to the importance of the agenda-building, or access stage in regulatory origin, later in this chapter.

Although Wilson covers all stages of the policy process, his insightful article is far from a theory of regulation, or of regulatory origin. He presents us with a framework for organizing the explanation of behavior in the access and decision stages, i.e., the concentrated/diffused benefit/cost typology. Explanations are constructed in this framework from considerations of what actions would be rationally pursued by parties potentially subject to some distribution of costs and benefits and facing constraints such as the costs of organizing. Although intuitively appealing, the typology may not be easy to apply, its dimensions may need development (the "concentrated/diffused" concept), and it can be systematically extended at least to a fourth category.

Wilson also presents, in effect, a list of factors relevant to, and some arguments regarding the role of these factors in, subsequent stages. Parts of the analysis can perhaps be extracted and presented as partial theories; he discusses, for example, a number of factors relevant to compliance with regulatory directives (see Marcus 1978). There is a rich stratum of observations and arguments that may be mined to build more complete and systematic theories. The benefit/cost typology can perhaps also be extended by allowing the locus of impact to vary; Wilson assumes, for example, that in the concentrated benefit–diffused cost situation the benefit goes to industry and the cost goes to the public-at-large or to consumers. The situation could be the reverse—particular groups of consumers may receive benefits, with industry (and maybe the public-at-large) diffusely subject to the costs. An example of this may be the use of general tax funds to support administrative procedures that protect consumers, or a consumer advocacy agency, or a consumer counsel in a general trade regulation agency.

Thus, although Wilson touches on all stages in the policy process, we must look further in searching for a theory of regulatory origin. We begin by reviewing the literature on "public interest" theories of regulation.

2.1 "PUBLIC INTEREST" THEORIES OF REGULATION

2.1.1 Agents and Interest Theories

"Public interest" theories of regulation assume that regulation is established largely in response to public-interest-related objectives. Unless one assumes that the state or public mystically acts for itself in seeking the regulation, public interest theories require, in effect, that parties seeking regulation be *agents* for the public interest. These agents may satisfy their self-interest instrumentally through pursuit of public interest objectives (e.g., politician championing consumer regulation to aid reelection), but the theory requires that at least some preferences for the public interest be genuine and terminal.

It is easy to dismiss the potential of public interest approaches on the grounds that there exists no single public interest conception (see chapter 4). Public interest theories can be viewed as vague and indeterminate because views of the public interest are often vague and can be conflicting. This is not necessarily so and does not necessarily affect a theory which recognizes and includes this, or is merely based on a specific, well-defined public interest conception. The potential of public interest theories can also be dismissed because of the absence of a mechanism through which public interest conceptions can be advocated, defended, and managed through the formal decision process of regulatory creation. But this ignores the role of agents like entrepreneurial politicians and public interest groups (cf. Posner 1974:340–341), a role which has received increasing attention in the literature (see, e.g., Berry 1977; Curry and Wade 1968). As long as agents exist to believe in and act for the public interest, construction of public interest theories should be feasible.

In actuality, *all* parties in controversies over regulatory creation are usually agents. This includes private groups, who are usually represented through agents. Henry Ford II may testify to Congressional committees on proposed automobile emission controls, but most of the Ford Company's advocacy will be through agents such as lobbyists and legal counsel. Even the legislative representatives deciding, and the regulators who must implement and administer, are usually all agents. As agents, all these parties are subject to the standard information problems of agents in determining their principal's preferences and in acting for them (see, e.g., Mitnick 1974).

It has been argued that agents acting with discretion under formal contractual arrangements are commonly subject to special expectations, i.e., the *fiduciary norm*. Such agents are instructed by the norm to act solely in the principal's interest, without regard for their self-interest. Of course, before entering the contractual agreement, the agent may have calculated the probable costs to him of action for the principal. The risks that those costs will be high may of course be reflected in a risk premium added by the agent to his fee. But should the agent's actions for the principal lead to costs to the agent exceeding his predictions, the agent is still bound by the norm to act to the best of his ability with fidelity to the principal's interest (see Mitnick 1974, 1975a, 1975b, and chapter 4). The fiduciary norm is frequently held genuinely, and agents are trained (in law school, in training for the Foreign Service) to prefer the behavior specified in the norm.

Agents for the public interest may possess the fiduciary norm genuinely, as part of their sense of mission, and could be expected to behave as fiduciaries at least as much as agents for private interests. The genuinely held, terminal preferences of public interest agents for the conception of the public interest for which they act may even reinforce their fiduciary preferences.

Thus, given these arguments, there may be no reason to suppose that public interest theories could not be created complete with adequate mechanisms to insure (and explain) translation of the interest into some regulatory form.

2.1.2   Public Interest Forms Used in Theories

The forms taken by the "public interest" in public interest theories can, as one would suspect from the nature of the concept, vary greatly. For example, the "public interest" in such theories can refer to:

   1. A *balancing* concept in which the public interest results from

the simultaneous satisfaction of selected aspects of several different particularistic interests. The balancing result gives satisfaction to interests that may to some extent be contending or competing.

2. A *compromising* concept in which particularistic interests are made to concede part of what they desire so that the overall result is in the "public interest."

3. A *trade-off* concept in which particularistic interests affected by regulation are made to provide some costly service or other benefit judged to be in the public interest in exchange for certain private benefits to them. For example, utilities may be permitted to charge rates in excess of marginal costs for some services, which then subsidize below-cost services required under regulation.

4. An overriding *national* or *social goals* concept in which certain social, societal, or national objectives are held to be in the public interest and to supersede private interests. For example, public interest goals relating to national defense or sectoral or regional development may be held to be overriding.

5. A *particularistic, paternalistic,* or *personal dictated* concept, unitary in character (see chapter 4), in which the public interest is equated with the preferences of a particular person, group or organization, or system. These preferences, which may, for example, be those of a charismatic leader or dictator or a political party, can be any of the previously listed types, e.g., a national or social goal. The distinctive feature of this concept, however, is its attachment to, or equation with, the preferences of a particular entity, whatever its level (person to system).

The general concept of the public interest will be explored more systematically in chapter 4.

2.1.3   Deviation from Public Interest Effects in Public Interest Theories

There are, as we have seen in chapter 2, various descriptions and theories of how regulation changes over time. Regulation which is sought in a "public interest" that may fall in one of the categories listed above may not continue to (or ever) serve that interest. Theories that seek to explain such change are not, strictly speaking, theories of regulatory origin. Because of changes in regulatory functioning and effects, however, it is possible to stretch the point and argue that change can "create" new regulation, i.e., new interferences, where none had existed before, or eliminate previously existing regulation. Thus, a brief look at some explanations for the change is in order here.

In general, three views may be distinguished; we shall focus initially on the regulators rather than on organizational or contextual factors. Regulation may then cease to serve the "public interest" because: 1) the regulators are or become venal or evil; 2) the regulators are or become incompetent; 3) the regulation becomes "captured" by the private regulated interests.

1. The *venality* view holds that regulators are corrupted by opportunities for personal profit, so that the regulation they administer is warped to serve their personal interests. Actions taken by such regulators to benefit themselves can even be illegal. Regulators may then accept bribes, alter regulation so that industries or businesses in which they have a personal stake benefit, embezzle or divert public funds to their personal gain, and so on.

Needless to say, this is an older view of public service, perhaps more descriptive of the era of robber barons than of now. Many state commissions in the late nineteenth century have been described as being (and/or were thought at the time to be) in the pocket of the railroads (see, e.g., C. F. Adams 1887:133–34; Cushman 1941:52). Instances of corruption still occur today, and recent adoption of ethics policies and legislation by legislatures at all levels reflects attempts at eliminating the appearances, if not the actualities, of conflict of interest. The tradition of muckraking journalism is congenial with aspects of this view, and some of the investigative work inspired by the renaissance of concern for public values represented by the Ralph Nader organizations is inspired by it. This view is frequently consistent with the third view, "capture," since usually only the regulated industry would be willing and able to offer the kinds of favors that such a regulator might seek.

2. The *incompetence* view holds that regulators are like other people as far as ethics are concerned, but are simply either less able than other officials to perform their jobs, or just not up to the particular demands of the regulatory office at that time. Incompetence in the agencies may have several sources. The ordinary rewards, e.g., salary, status, working conditions, provided to regulators may be claimed to be insufficient to draw competent people. Remedies involve raises in salary, changes in position title, changes in status of the regulatory organization within the government, and so on. The nature of the times may be such that the best people have better job

opportunities elsewhere. Thus, during the Depression, many of the most able law school graduates entered the public service, which was viewed as more challenging and glamorous (Landis 1960:11–13; Jaffe 1964). Use of administrative agencies as repositories for political patronage, opportunities for reward of political cronyism, and sites for extension of partisan influence can lower the quality of appointees (U.S. Senate, Committee on Governmental Affairs, vol. 1, 1977).

Thus, the appointments process can play a major role in determining the quality of appointees. Consultation and "clearances" with the regulated industry can result in appointment of regulators who are both not anti-industry and less able (cf. Noll 1971a:42–43). The lack of knowledge of how to regulate effectively in changing sectors or declining industries or the persistent application of regulation misdesigned in ignorance years before can make regulators appear incompetent. And an emphasis on the wrong kinds of knowledge, such as legal over economic expertise, can have similar effects (cf. Friendly 1962). But above all the failures are due to a lack of "good men": "The prime key to the improvement of the administrative process is the selection of qualified personnel. Good men can make poor laws workable; poor men can wreak havoc with good laws" (Landis 1960:66).

3. The *capture* view holds that the regulatory mechanism is basically workable and desirable but is somehow "captured" by the regulated parties so that it serves their interests rather than the public interest (on sources of "capture," see, e.g., Redford 1952:251–52). The term "capture" is actually used in several ways related to this view. "Capture" is said to occur if the regulated interest *controls* the regulation and the regulatory agency; or if the regulated parties succeed in *coordinating* the regulatory body's activities with their activities so that their private interest is satisfied; or if the regulated party somehow manages to neutralize or insure *nonperformance* (or mediocre performance) by the regulating body; or if in a subtle process of interaction with the regulators the regulated party succeeds (perhaps not even deliberately) in *coopting* the regulators into seeing things from their own perspective and thus giving them the regulation they want; or if, quite independently of the formal or conscious desires of either the regulators or the regulated parties the basic structure of the *reward system* leads neither venal nor incompetent regulators inevitably to a community of interests with the regulated party

(see, e.g., Noll 1971a:39–46). We shall return to the reward system theories, which we employed, in effect, in part of the discussion in chapter 2, again below. Note that "capture" can sometimes be consistent with, or promoted by, factors that encourage incompetence in, or mediocre performance by, the regulators. Later in this chapter we shall present a theory of regulatory "capture."

Excluded from the above discussion is a view that says the reason that public interest effects do not obtain has nothing whatsoever to do with the regulators; public controls cannot bring about the desired public interest effects. This may be due to a kind of technological or societal determinism that denies the efficacy of public action. Even the most able, honest, disinterested, and aware regulators would be unable to reach the specified public interest ends. This view is usually absent from public interest theories, which sometimes emphasize the perfectibility of governmental regulatory endeavors (see Blachly and Oatman 1940). A related view is that regulation can never succeed in reaching public interest ends because the reward system of regulators inevitably produces perverse results and cannot be altered to encourage more desirable ends (see, e.g., Noll 1971a). We note also that it is possible for all three conditions—venality, incompetence, and capture—(or any combination) to exist in the same agency at the same time.

J. Q. Wilson (1974) has argued that deviation from public interest ends can simply be a casualty of the operation of the political process: "When government regulation fails to compel businesses to serve socially desirable objectives, it is not usually because of the incompetence or venality of the regulators but because of the constraints placed on them by the need to operate within the political system" (J. Q. Wilson 1974:147). Thus, in regulatory controversy, needs will be dramatized and failures emphasized; advocacy and the need to build support can mean that the provisions of regulation will reflect what has been effective in the political controversy, rather than what is likely to work in regulation. Subsequent performance that deviates from public interest ends would then be unremarkable.

Finally, there are a host of procedural, organizational, and systemic factors that can interfere. In chapter 2, we discussed, for example, the potentially rigidifying effects of reliance on the institutional decision.

2.1.4 Structural/Legal/Rights Protection Public Interest Approaches

In the older literature it is only rarely that something like an explicit "public interest theory" of regulation is put forth. This is largely a construct imposed by later work. The "public interest" perspectives in this earlier literature are largely implicit. To illustrate, we shall review a few of these works below.

Many of the works in the older literature on regulation, particularly those in the public administration or legal traditions, employed what could be called structural/legal/rights protection public interest approaches. These works emphasized formal structure, organization, and operations of the agencies; classified the agencies' duties and powers; examined the legal and constitutional bases for administrative action; reviewed the historical additions to agency mandates; and spent a great deal of time and effort concerned with the implications of regulatory structure and action for the protection of personal rights and freedoms. In some cases, administrative regulation was even viewed as a method of equitably settling conflicts. (For related, more recent views, see Wilson 1974:164; Schultze 1977; Owen and Braeutigam 1978.)

This literature does not necessarily present a rigid, mechanistic view of government. On the contrary, it contains many works by scholars advocating the need for discretion in administration and stressing the value of flexibility and informal processes in the administrative process. On these points there was, however, some disagreement. Elements of the structural/legal/rights protection approach can be found throughout all works of this period (mostly the 1930s and 1940s), including those we have chosen to identify below as "group" approaches to the public interest.

Robert E. Cushman (1941) wrote what is perhaps the standard work on the origins of the major federal regulatory agencies, *The Independent Regulatory Commissions*. The book is an enormously scholarly, well-organized, and highly descriptive account of the legislative histories, subsequent mandate changes, legal and constitutional status, and major organizational problems of these agencies. Cushman sees the independent commissions as created to solve major economic problems. The problems usually stem from recurrent abuses in the regulated industry or arise because some goals in the national interest are not being achieved in the private sector.

Congress responds to these problems with regulation, which is viewed as an experiment to be corrected through trial and error. Even where segments of the business community favor some public controls (and, contrary to the implication of some recent writers, many earlier works like Cushman *do* recognize that business in many cases sought protection through regulation), the Congress imposes those controls largely with the public interest at heart. Thus Cushman writes regarding the founding of the Interstate Commerce Commission that "it was clearly recognized that the important problem of federal railroad regulation would have to be solved by trial and error. A major purpose in creating a commission was to provide machinery to secure the accurate and expert information necessary to the solution of that problem. Congress felt it wise to move slowly" (Cushman 1941:64).

Regarding the ICC and the Federal Reserve Board, Cushman writes, "The two bodies bore only a very superficial resemblance to each other, but one thing they had in common—they were both independent of the executive branch. Each was created in order that government control of a great economic problem could be made effective" (Cushman 1941:146). Regarding the beginning of the Federal Trade Commission, Cushman says, "Underlying the whole trade commission movement lay a steadily growing antagonism to trusts and monopolies, and a growing belief that they were increasing in number and power" (Cushman 1941:178). And "businessmen themselves tended to agree that a trade commission ought to be created" (Cushman 1941:179). Regarding maritime regulation, the creation of the Shipping Board was not so much protectionist of the industry as it "was an attempt to halt the long and steady decline of the American merchant marine" (Cushman 1941:228), a goal in the public interest. Even in the development of communications regulation, where the "industry was clamoring to be regulated for its own protection" (Cushman 1941:297), the creation of the Federal Radio Commission by the Radio Act of 1927 is viewed as an "interesting experiment" (Cushman 1941:302) which was later improved as the public interest and the lessons of trial and error seemed to indicate.

Another "public interest" view, resembling in some aspects that of Cushman, is that advanced implicitly by Blachly and Oatman:

> In establishing administrative agencies for particular purposes, Congress has acted, on the whole, both wisely and consistently. Hence the administrative structure is not a haphazard assemblage of miscellaneous parts. It is a system, and an organic system, in which specialized organs perform differen-

tiated functions. Further evolution, however, can improve the system. . . .
In the course of the past fifty years the federal government has been confronted with important new problems, particularly in the field of economic
control. That it might meet these problems, the government has been compelled to assume numerous functions which it had not previously carried on,
and to allocate these functions to authorities.

Because the regulatory process might interfere with personal or property
rights by commanding or compelling something to be done or by refusing to
permit something to be done, special forms of action were developed which
(1) enable the government to function in its sublegislative and subjudicial capacity, and (2) at the same time guarantee that as it does so, individual rights
shall be protected. (Blachly and Oatman 1940:5–6)

Furthermore, "The organization and operations of the administrative agencies, particularly those agencies which perform functions affecting individual rights, are carefully devised to *combine the protection of guaranteed rights with the promotion of administrative
efficiency*" (Blachly and Oatman 1940:140; emphasis added).

Thus regulation is a deliberate, carefully organized, and perfecti-
ble response to economic problems. It is designed not only for administrative efficiency; the rights of parties subject to regulation are
to be given special attention and protection. It is noteworthy that administrative efficiency, and formal organizational and due-process-
related matters (in the context of the administrative agency not judicial model), are paramount. Apparently, considerations of economic
efficiency in the *effects* of regulation are, if relevant at all, somewhat
less important (cf. Owen and Braeutigam 1978).

2.1.5 "Group" Public Interest Approaches

A number of the earlier writers on regulation employed variations
on the group approach to politics developed by Bentley (1908; see
below). Unlike Bentley, however, they usually either harbor implicitly, or eventually explicitly introduce, a role for the state in introducing or guiding regulation in the public interest. Many of these
works are enormously rich in their descriptions of group activity and
of the interactions of groups with government. Many are suggestive
of work in political science and economics that appeared many years
later and whose authors unfortunately either ignored, or were un-
aware of, this earlier literature. With perhaps a very few exceptions,
these works are not explicitly theoretical as later traditions would
prefer. Theories are not clearly specified; hypotheses not specifically
offered and then tested. Despite their defects, these works deserve a

more prominent place in the progression toward adequate theories of regulation.

We have already considered Bernstein's (1955) life cycle theory in chapter 2, and will not review it in detail here. It is, in essentials, a group public interest approach. Regulatory bodies originate during a "gestation" stage in which groups seeking redress of abuses by business gain a public-interest-spirited regulation. The regulation is, however, likely to be a compromise; the commissions "carry out the terms of the treaties that the legislators have negotiated and ratified. They are like armies of occupation left in the field to police the rule won by the victorious coalition." (Bernstein 1955:76, quoting a work by Earl Latham). Though the groups appear to be largely consumer in character, Bernstein's discussion of the regulation seems to imply that it is established "to act in the public interest" (Bernstein 1955:81). This the commission tries to do during its "crusading" "youth" stage, only to succumb to "devitalization," "debility and decline" in "maturity" and "old age."

Fainsod and Gordon (1941), in one of the best of the numerous business-and-government texts that were written just before, during, and for a few years after World War II, use the group approach and echo the "regulation solves problems created by business abuses" argument. In this work and in an article (Fainsod 1940) written about the same time, however, Fainsod tried to develop the parties-in-interest perspective on regulatory creation more comprehensively, explicitly, and perhaps in a way closer to more recent theoretical approaches than others of his era. An understanding of the nature and methods of the major parties-in-interest and the environment in which they operate, as well as the political instruments of regulation, is held critical to an understanding of regulation. Regulation is seen as a public-interest-inspired attempt, supported perhaps by aggrieved groups, and perhaps ultimately of a balancing or compromise nature, to control "abuses" and thus solve "problems":

> The more one ponders the history of the growth of regulation in the United States, the clearer it becomes also that this growth has not been the product of any farsighted plan or design or the result of any thoroughly worked out rationale or theory. Step by step, whether in state or nation, it has represented a series of empirical adjustments to felt abuses. It has been initiated by particular groups to deal with specific evils as they arose, rather than inspired by any general philosophy of governmental control. (Fainsod and Gordon 1941:226)

The "empirical adjustments" sound a lot like Cushman's "experiments" and "trial and error." Furthermore,

> The regulatory machinery . . . does not operate in a vacuum. Important parties-in-interest have a vital stake in the formulation, execution, and—on occasion—frustration of public policy. They seek to make their influence felt. A realistic examination of the regulatory process must take them into account, consider their claims, their demands, and the intensity of the pressure which they are able to bring to bear on the contest to determine policy. (Fainsod and Gordon 1941:238)

Fainsod goes on to identify and discuss seven major parties-in-interest in railroad regulation.

The best statement of Fainsod's approach is in his classic article on the regulatory process (Fainsod 1940). Regulation, he asserts, is best understood as a process, much as Bentley and the group theorists claim (see below). But there is to be more than just a focus on group activities; in this Fainsod goes beyond many of his contemporaries. One must consider: "(1) the conditioning factors which make up the institutional context of regulation, (2) the parties in interest who are concerned with the character of regulation, and (3) the actual political instruments which provide the pattern of operative controls" (Fainsod 1940:299). After establishing this, Fainsod examines each of these three factors in turn.

1. Conditioning factors include "technology, economic organization, ideology, law, and other institutional factors" which "establish the context within which the parties in interest as well as the regulatory instruments are compelled to function. These factors may be labeled institutional because they contribute elements of continuity, stability, and even rigidity to the regulatory process" (Fainsod 1940:299).

2. The parties in interest typically include investors, (financial) "control groups which determine policy," management, labor, consumers, and suppliers to the industry. Though all groups "are vitally dependent upon the welfare of the industry with which they are identified," "the problem of allocating the income stream of the industry among the various parties in interest" leads to conflict. Conflict tends to be resolved according to "the relative bargaining power which the parties in interest are capable of mobilizing in the economic realm." Some groups, particularly the "control groups," have an advantage here. Weaker parties can then "begin to demand public controls and seek to use political power to make their demands effective." This

"constitutes a form of bargaining" to try "to secure a more satisfactory adjustment of relationships within the industry." At any rate, there will be "groups with vital interests in regulation which are ignored" and "other parties in interest who perhaps exercise more power in shaping policy than ought properly to be exercised by them." These points anticipate the later literature on agenda-building in the policy process (see, e.g., Cobb and Elder 1972), which we shall be employing again below. Fainsod thus perceives a tension between each party in interest's concern with the collective welfare of parties in the industry, i.e., between the welfare of the industry as a whole, and the party's own special interest. (Fainsod 1940:301–2)

Fainsod proceeds to discuss the role of each party in interest in regulatory creation. When the industry is expanding, "control groups," which are doing well—along with the management and investors who respond to them—will oppose regulation. If labor is successful in collective bargaining in the now profitable industry, it may not have reason to press for regulation. Thus it was that "the dissatisfactions which produced the beginnings of regulation in expanding industries in the United States have been chiefly consumer in origin;" the consumers, "as in the case of farmers and small business men in the railroad field, have provided most of the initial driving impetus behind the regulatory movement." (Fainsod 1940:303)

In a declining industry, all parties want to avoid loss and so "each seeks to shift the burden of readjustments to other interests." In partial response to threats of this type from other parties, each party may then seek help from government through protective regulation and promotional efforts. (Fainsod:303–4)

Fainsod then discusses the factors affecting the likely success of each group in influencing the regulatory process. We will not review these arguments in detail, but will note some of the factors Fainsod identifies as important. These include: 1) resources, e.g., the financial resources of the "control groups," and their consequent ability to buy lobbyists, provide campaign contributions to legislators, pay lawyers, and use the media; 2) "strategic position" in the industry and in the social strata of business and society; 3) opportunities for building coalitions or acquiring effective political entrepreneurs within the existing "broader movement of social and political forces" ("The influence which the parties in interest in a particular industry exert at any given time is largely measured by their ability to find effective political champions or allies capable of fusing their demands into a general program of wider appeal.''); and 4) ability to organize "for independent political action." Small investors and consumers are said to have particularly difficult organizational problems compared to the other, larger, parties in interest. Small investors are "dispersed, scattered" and "in regulated industries where the stake of the individual consumer is relatively slight the incentive to active collaboration is absent." The problem of assuring consumer advocacy requires some permanent mechanism, Fainsod argues, like "Consumers' Counsels"; "the regulatory agencies themselves find it difficult to serve as vigorous protagonists of consumer interests in the absence of an active and continuous manifestation of consumer support." (Fainsod 1940:302–9)

These arguments again find Fainsod remarkably prescient as far as the academic literature twenty-five to thirty-five years later is concerned. He effectively identifies many of the variables later used in models of agenda-building (e.g., Cobb and Elder 1972), perceives key problems in motivating group action (e.g., Olson 1965), and recognizes some factors later judged important in maintaining social interests like the consumer interest in the active decision calculus of regulatory agencies (e.g., Sabatier 1975).

3. The "pattern of operative controls" includes "competitive party politics, legislative activity, the exercise of administrative discretion, and judicial determination." The regulatory agency may to various degrees "respond to or resist the pressures" from the parties in interest. (Fainsod 1940:309–10) But "the regulatory agency itself is capable of generating a certain amount of independent power to change its environment" (Fainsod 1940:299).

Fainsod now specifies more clearly the "public interest" theory nature of his approach. He discusses various ways to increase administrative efficiency in "supervising industry" and asserts that both the ICC and the FTC "were established to develop new social values in the public interest." The discretion that administrative agencies possess is extremely important in facilitating the adjustment processes among interests as well as the deliberate manipulative attempts by the regulators that occur in the regulatory process. The regulatory agencies play a "creative role": "In theory at least, and frequently in practice, they are capable of recognizing some interests as more 'public' or more 'general' than other interests and of adapting, fusing, and directing group pressures toward such a recognition." (Fainsod 1940:309–23)

Avery Leiserson (1942) and Pendleton Herring (1936a) both wrote important works employing the group approach in what is essentially a public interest theory framework.

Leiserson's (1942) work explored the forms and ways in which interest groups could be represented before regulatory agencies or participate in the formulation of administrative policy. The degree of group participation can vary from simple advocacy through consultation and shared decision-making. He argues that "a satisfactory criterion of the public interest is the preponderant acceptance of administrative action by politically influential groups" (Leiserson 1942:16). Thus administrative structures must be designed to promote this acceptance. The administrator is not, however, merely a conduit or forum. He is limited by his statutory powers and duties and existing public policy. Though in conflicts between the agency and private groups the agency legally must prevail, conflict would represent a breakdown in the necessary cooperation between group and agency. Thus there is a "balance between the two sources of authority" that "is continually contingent and precarious" (Leiserson 1942:279). The regulatory agencies themselves are said to be created to serve groups or classes, e.g., "shippers against carriers" (ICC), "businessmen against competitors using unfair methods" or restraining competition (FTC), "investors against certain practices of promoters, dealers, and brokers of securities" (SEC), and so on (Leiserson 1942:6–7). But the public interest is served in this process as groups accept the regulation.

Leiserson cites approvingly (1942:11–12 n. 23) the public interest view expressed by Herring (1936:23–24):

> Although it is clear that the official must balance the interests of the conflicting groups before him, by what standards is he to weigh their demands? To hold out the *public interest* as a criterion is to offer an imponderable. Its value is psychological and does not extend beyond the significance that each responsible civil servant must find in the phrase for himself. Acting in accordance with this subjective conception and bounded by his statutory competence, the bureaucrat selects from the special interests before him a combination to which he gives official sanction. Thus inescapably in practice the concept of the public interest is given substance by its identification with the interests of certain groups.

Regarding interest groups, Herring (1936a:viii) argues:

> In theory our government should strike a balance among these conflicting forces so as to promote the welfare of all. In fact some groups are placed

more advantageously than others within our governmental structure and under our industrial system.

In response, government must experiment:

> Weaknesses, abuses, and failures are frequently found. But experimentation continues. No logical a priori theory can embrace the flux of actual government. New laws, new administrative forms appear. There is a persistent search for some workable means of adjusting the forms of governance to the uneasy needs of men. The story of the federal bureaucracy today is kept in a looseleaf ledger. (Herring 1936a:viii)

Like Leiserson's, Herring's work is devoted largely to a study of how bureaucrats can develop a noncorrupting, working relationship with the groups facing the agency. Administrators acting with discretion within a constrained mandate seek to realize the public interest in a changing environment by balancing the interests of the relevant groups.

We have tried to point out some of the contributions of the public interest approaches so far described. Their limitations require attention as well. These approaches usually do not distinguish origin explanations from operation explanations, as we observed earlier, and usually do not really provide us with adequate and systematic theories. In some cases (e.g., Herring 1936a), the author seems to imply that aspects of the regulatory process defy "logical a priori" theories.

Working from the policy process outline offered earlier, we can see that these approaches tend to link aspects of the access stage to the decision and administration stages, but leave numerous areas untouched. They generally ignore effects, or assume that effects follow automatically and are justified, implicitly, by the "need" for the regulation rather than some rational calculation of both benefits and costs. The literature generally ignores the behavioral factors affecting delegation from legislature to agency, though matters of administrative discretion, usually in a legal context or in the context of a recitation of advantages or disadvantages of flexibility and informality, are treated. The process of legislative influence and agency oversight requires elaborated attention. Problems of implementation are largely ignored in favor of a focus on decision and administration.

Although the group theorists provide valuable descriptive materials on the kinds, characteristics of, and positions taken by groups, and explore the variety of ways in which groups can be integrated in government, many basic questions remain. Some conditions leading to the formation of groups, e.g., economic need, are reviewed, but are not carefully treated. What factors affect group success in formation and in advocacy, for example? Why do groups hold together if members are dispersed and the net gain to the individual member is relatively small? Fainsod goes further than the others in actually developing a model, but even his work falls short of a systematically explicated theory.

The group approaches seem to assume that groups are all-pervasive and, for the most part, will spring up to represent any interest (we have noted some exceptions for some writers, but they are never developed). But groups are usually relatively small in numbers, and there is a need to explain how smaller and/or poorer groups sometimes "defeat" larger and/or richer ones (see Schattschneider 1960; Cobb and Elder 1972). The role of groups in conflicts settled entirely within the government is unclear. If groups are so pervasive and important, why are some issues never raised at all, or languish in obscurity for years, or suddenly become important at one time—but not before (Cobb and Elder 1972)? What explains the dynamics of regulatory controversy?

2.1.6   Functional Public Interest Theories of Regulation

Some recent theories of regulation have focused on some governmental functions apparently served by regulation and have attempted to explain the regulation on this basis. These may be considered in a broad sense "public interest theories."

Richard Posner has suggested that "an important purpose in fact of public utility and common carrier regulation is to compel, by the device of the internal subsidy, the provision of certain services in quantities and at prices that a free market would not offer, much as the conventional taxing-spending power is used to the same end" (Posner 1971:41).

Thus regulation serves the public-finance function of taxation. Regulation frequently permits, in effect, internal subsidies by requiring firms to provide some services below cost while allowing collection of higher than warranted fees for other services. Purchasers of those other services are effectively taxed through these higher prices to provide (and internally subsidize) the below-cost service. Examples include unprofitable airline service to localities, public-affairs programming by broadcasters, and commuter rail service. Posner discusses how this approach casts light on various aspects of regulation and analyzes some possible advantages and disadvantages of the approach. We shall not review his arguments here; the reader is referred to his paper.

However intriguing Posner's suggestion that regulation is taxation by other means, it represents a public interest theory that essentially links only the decision and/or administration stages of the policy process to the impact stage. Posner considers the device's effects in the areas of equity and efficiency, and examines administration, enforcement, and oversight problems and advantages. He does consider the desirability of delegating the taxing function to regulatory agencies and observes that delegation would economize on the legislature's time. This bears on the implementation stage. The article's discussion centers on the appropriateness of taxation by regulation as a means to attain certain effects.

Thus, although the taxation function is designed to produce public interest ends, it is not clear that we truly have an alternative public interest theory. It is more like recognition of wide use of a regulatory tool which apparently is aimed at producing public-interest-related ends. Of course, use of the tool implies something about the purposes of regulation. It may not tell us very much, however, about the public policy process access stage, including the creation, expansion, and entrance to the agenda of regulatory issues, and it does not explain much about where these public interest purposes come from.

William S. Comanor and Bridger M. Mitchell (1972:178) argue that the "statutory positions" of regulators "afford them the power to leave their impact on the structure of the industry in ways which they perceive as in the public interest." Thus regulation becomes a method or tool of *planning*. [4] Because the regulators have no funds to pay for the ends they seek, they procure these funds indirectly through protection of firms and regulation producing internal subsidization. The model is therefore closely related to Posner's taxation by regulation. It is, however, more of a public interest theory of regulation because it tells us a little bit about the origin of the particular regulation, i.e., it serves the interests of economic planners in implementing the legislative act. Internal subsidization remains, of course, the tool, and Comanor and Mitchell inform us why it is selected by the planners (i.e., it is a ready source of otherwise unavailable funds

---

[4] On planning in the regulatory context, cf. Kahn (1971); Slesinger and Isaacs (1968:12–14).

and thus permits planning in the relevant industry). The authors illustrate their theory with an examination of how the public interest objectives of "diversity" in programming and "localism" in ownership and management were sought by the Federal Communications Commission. Internal subsidization provided a tool for these planning objectives.

Comanor and Mitchell's study focuses mostly on the relation between the administration of a regulatory policy and its effects, though it bears also on the decision, and perhaps on the implementation, stages in the policy process. But it does not really tell us how a given policy intention is in general created and arrives on the agenda of the economic planners, who seemingly prefer it (beyond that its objectives are implied in the legislative act or have been standing policy for many years). Thus *planning by regulation* tells us more about choice, use, and effects of a tool in an area already regulated than about basic origins of regulation.

Before closing this section on public interest theories of regulation, we note that some works contrasting alternative theories of regulation often create "straw men" public interest theories or "public interest" theories of a highly specialized character. Russell and Shelton (1974:49), for example, distinguish in their coalition theory (see below) regulators "who may expect to act for the regulated, those who may expect to act for consumers, and those who may expect to act for the public interest." In a footnote, the authors define "public interest" in the following comment, "Since the rise of the New Welfare Economics, the public interest has come to mean optimal resource allocation, given the existing income distribution" (Russell and Shelton 1974:49). This is perhaps the *economist's* public interest, i.e., efficiency, not *the* public interest or even a conception that could be claimed as being most widely shared in this society. There is nothing wrong with Russell and Shelton's use of it as the public interest except that the reader should be aware that the authors are using a specialized model. Their conclusions regarding the public interest case cannot be compared with those of any studies using different public interest conceptions. A similar situation arises where theorists use the "consumer interest" as synonymous with, part of, or an indicator for the "public interest."

2.2 "PRIVATE INTEREST" THEORIES OF REGULATION

The development of private interest theories of regulation may be seen as a progression in increasing logical organization and a filling in of areas about which early theories are blank. This is perhaps as it should be, but there seems to be a way yet to go before entirely adequate theories are developed.

Work on theories of this kind has progressed from the older group-balancing approaches, through the "economic theory of regulation," which formalized the relation of groups and government and provided an explanation for the occurrence of regulation of a given sort, and through individualistic theories of the regulatory process that attempted in various ways to fill in the blanks between supply and demand left by the "economic" theory. We shall examine, in turn, a few of the major theories in this progression. Recall that, due to the nature of the public interest, to some extent many public interest theories can be viewed as special cases of private interest theories.

2.2.1 "Group" Private Interest Theories of Regulation

Fainsod (1940:297–98) offers an elegant summary of the group argument represented by Arthur F. Bentley's classic work, *The Process of Government* (1908):

> Government in this view can do little more than register the shifting balance of forces in the community; regulatory agencies become prizes in the struggle for power. That interest or group of interests which captures control of them impresses its policy upon them. . . . The idea of public interest becomes a fiction used to describe an amalgam which is shaped and reshaped in the furnace of their conflicts.

For Bentley the group, not the individual or society as a whole, is determinant: "When the groups are adequately stated, everything is stated. When I say everything I mean everything. . . . We shall have to get hold of political institutions, legislatures, courts, executive officers, and get them stated as groups, and in terms of other groups" (Bentley 1908:208–10). The term "interest" is taken as "the equivalent of a group," and "group" itself is taken not as a static mass or collectivity but as a "mass activity," as "so many men, acting, or tending toward action—that is, in various stages of action" (Bentley 1908:211). Bentley's emphasis is therefore on *process* (see Peter H. Odegard in Bentley 1908, 1967:xxxvii). The interpretation of group activity cannot be done in isolation, without consideration of the activities of other groups:

> Nor will it suffice to take a single interest group and base our interpretation upon it, not even for a special time and a special place. No interest group has meaning except with reference to other interest groups; and those other inter-

est groups are pressures; they count in the government process. (Bentley
1908:271)

Bentley's group model is supposed not only to be descriptive; it is
said to produce desirable results:

> The greater portion of the detail of governmental work, as embodied espe-
> cially in the law that is being daily sustained, is composed of habitual reac-
> tions which are adjustments forced by large, united weak interests upon less
> numerous, but relatively to the number of adherents, more intense interests.
> If there is anything that could probably be meant by the phrase 'control by
> the people' just as it stands, it is this. (Bentley 1908:454)

If these interests representing numerous people are threatened, a
corrective mechanism stands ready:

> Now when government, as the representative of the 'absent' or quiescent
> group interests, is distorted from this function to any noticeable extent by the
> concentrated pressures of smaller group interests . . . , we see the formation
> of a group interest directly aroused in opposition to the interests which have
> gained objectionable power. (Bentley 1908:454–55)

Fainsod criticizes Bentley for ignoring both the conditioning factors and "underlying context of institutional arrangements out of
which the interest groups themselves take shape," and the role of the
"political instruments," e.g., the regulatory agencies, themselves,
which have important effects (Fainsod 1940:298–99). Mancur Olson,
Jr., observes that Bentley does not say much about why group needs
get translated into effective group pressures, what leads to effective
group organization and action, and why certain groups become sa-
lient in certain societies and at certain times, and not others (Olson
1965:122). Schattschneider (1960) observes that the number of people actually represented by groups is relatively small, and that the
large groups do not always win. In addition, Bentley's corrective
mechanism does not always function effectively or at all (see, e.g.,
Cobb and Elder 1972:32–33).

In terms of the policy process, Bentley deals largely with only certain aspects of access, decision, and impact; and fails to adequately
consider many other aspects of access, including issue creation, expansion, agenda entrance, as well as implementation and the other
stages.

Later work by some of the group theorists attempted to fill some of
these gaps. David B. Truman (1951) allows influences from the wider
institutional setting and argues that groups will arise as a result of in-

creasing societal specialization and complexity and in response to societal needs stemming from economic "disturbances" and "dislocations." These groups will exert corrective political pressure. But the actual means and processes of formation and the reasons why groups maintain themselves are less clear. Olson (1965:126) notes that the group theorists

> generally take for granted that such groups will act to defend or advance their group interests, and take it for granted that the individuals in these groups must also be concerned about their individual economic interests. But if the individuals in any large group are interested in their own welfare, they will *not* voluntarily make any sacrifices to help their group attain its political (public or collective) objectives.

After all, self-interested individuals in a large group, knowing they will receive the collective benefit from group success whether or not they contribute, can simply choose to be "free riders" on the group.

Thus Bentley and the other group theorists do not offer a comprehensive theory adequate to explain regulatory origin and the regulatory process. But there are many promising elements here, e.g., the emphasis on the importance of process; the perception of government control and use of its powers as the variable prize of group conflict; the observation that the supply of regulation, including its form and effects, can be responsive to group demands. A view of regulation as part of an economic process of supply and demand goes beyond the group formulations, but we can perhaps see its logical roots here.

2.2.2 "Economic" Theories of Regulation: The "Black Box" Is
        Constructed

In a stinging appraisal written about the same time as Fainsod's classic paper, Horace M. Gray declared that the then existing formal rationale for public utility regulation had become, in effect, the emperor's clothes:

> the public utility status was to be the haven of refuge for all aspiring monopolists who found it too difficult, too costly, or too precarious to secure and maintain monopoly by private action. Their future prosperity would be assured if only they could induce government to grant them monopoly power and to protect them against interlopers, provided always, of course, that government did not exact too high a price for its favors in the form of restrictive regulation. (Gray 1940, in American Economic Association 1949:283)

Regulation therefore tends to be sought by industry for its own protection and subsequently serves this purpose (see also, e.g., Keyes

1958; Plott 1965). This conclusion is the usual outcome (though not, as some exponents hasten to add, the only outcome) of the "economic theory of regulation" developed by Thomas G. Moore (1961), George J. Stigler (1971), William A. Jordan (1972), Richard A. Posner (1974), and others. Perhaps the most influential work has been that by Stigler (1971); we shall review his arguments.

Stigler asserts that "two main alternative views of the regulation of industry are widely held": 1) "regulation is instituted primarily for the protection and benefit of the public at large or some large subclass of the public," and "regulations which injure the public . . . are costs of some social goal . . . or, occasionally, perversions of the regulatory philosophy;" and 2) "the political process defies rational explanation: 'politics' is an imponderable, a constantly and unpredictably shifting mixture of forces of the most diverse nature" ranging from acts of "virtue" to those of "venality" (Stigler 1971:3).

Though probably held by many at the time, these views are largely "straw men;" certainly the academic community was not unanimous. The literature in political science, though mostly "public interest" oriented as far as origin beliefs are concerned, included many scholarly works critical of regulatory performance and a huge critical literature of policy studies and commission reports. The leading work on regulation was probably that by Bernstein (1955), who was strongly critical of contemporary regulation and developed the classic formulation of the life cycle hypothesis. Thus "occasionally" simply does not describe the received wisdom among the essentially "public interest" theorists at the time. Most writers acknowledged that regulation did not work well and, in fact, often protected the regulated industries. Furthermore, as we have seen, group theorists had developed a model which did not require (and in many forms rejected) an overriding "public interest" view. In economics, Gray (1940), Moore (1961), and others had argued the protectionist origin view, and economic historians had begun to support this position (e.g., Kolko 1965; MacAvoy 1965; Hilton 1966).

The "defies rationality" view might have been held by some political scientists, perhaps those who viewed the group process as unpredictable, but was surely not one of the "two main alternative views." Thus Stigler strangely chooses to contrast his innovative approach with what are essentially more examples of the special-case public interest theories we mentioned above.

Stigler's basic theme is the following:

> We assume that political systems are rationally devised and rationally em-
> ployed, which is to say that they are appropriate instruments for the fulfill-
> ment of desires of members of the society. This is not to say that the state
> will serve any person's concept of the public interest; indeed the problem of
> regulation is the problem of discovering when and why an industry (or other
> group of like-minded people) is able to use the state for its purposes, or is
> singled out by the state to be used for alien purposes. (Stigler 1971:4)

This statement has much in common with earlier work, as we have
seen, but unlike much of these earlier materials, Stigler is attempting
to develop an explicit, predictive theory of regulation.

Having made the general statement, which applies to all groups,
Stigler implicitly limits his theoretical analysis to the perspective of
industry as the group seeking regulation. He observes, as many have
(see, e.g., Rainey, Backoff and Levine 1976), that the powers of the
state are sought because they are backed by coercion. The benefits
that the state can provide are then considered, with four "policies"
identified: 1) direct subsidy, 2) control over entry, 3) powers affecting
substitutes and complements, and 4) price-fixing. The political process puts limits on what the industries can get. Limitations, which are
viewed as predictable, include: 1) the possibility that "the distribution of control of the industry among the firms in the industry" will
be changed, e.g., from the political decision's consideration of the
political, not market strength, of each firm; 2) the costs imposed by
the procedural safeguards of the administrative process; and 3) the
admission of "powerful outsiders to the industry's councils," e.g.,
groups affected by the industry's operations. (Stigler 1971:4–7)

The acquisition of the benefits is not without cost, and so Stigler
considers some costs of obtaining regulatory legislation, as well as
why the industry is able to exploit the democratic system for its own
ends. Stigler derives what is essentially a rationale for the necessary
employment of agents—full-time representatives and political parties—in a democracy from consideration of the otherwise simultaneous, frequent voting by all citizens—a physical impossibility—and
from the observation that the voting does not exclude uninterested
voters and "does not allow participation in proportion to interest and
knowledge." The costs of information to the voter, especially where
he is uninterested and thus uninformed, are high. Hence representatives and parties seek to discover and fulfill these interests and are
rewarded through reelection and the perquisites of office holding.
(Stigler 1971:10–12)

Thus the industry seeking governmental controls goes "to the appropriate seller, the political party," and pays with votes and resources, e.g., campaign contributions. Given that the "political 'market' " is fixed in size, larger industries may have relatively more success than very small ones in getting protection. If one political party either errs badly or becomes extortionate, another may be elected to take its place. The elected officials may receive compensation from the benefited industries, often in an indirect fashion, e.g., through a lawyer-legislator's law firm or a bank patronized by both industry and official. Stigler observes that free-rider questions are raised in determining how industries organize for political advocacy and that there is no "satisfactory theory of group behavior." He draws the analogy to oligopoly, and conjectures that "the more concentrated the industry, the more resources it can invest in the campaign for legislation." (Stigler 1971:12–13)

Stigler performs two empirical studies, one of regulation of motor carriers and the other of occupational licensing. In the first, he successfully links state regulation of weight limits on trucks to three variables derived from consideration of interests likely to push for or oppose higher weight limits (agricultural interests needing heavy trucks, the degree of possible competitiveness with railroads, and the public-at-large's interest in preventing damage to the highways by heavy trucks). Thus aspects of affected interests are tied to particular regulation. In the second study, the occurrence of occupational licensing is related to characteristics which might be expected to ease the occupation's task of securing favorable legislation, i.e., size of its labor force and concentration in cities. Stigler also compares licensed, partially licensed, and unlicensed occupations to see whether his economic approach to regulatory supply is supported, i.e., relating the level of incomes, stability of membership, employment by business enterprises, who may "have incentives to oppose licensing," and presence in national markets to licensure. The results were mixed, but some support is provided. (Stigler 1971:7–9, 13–17)

Aside from briefly considering some of the roles of, and rewards sought by, politicians and political parties, Stigler (at least until the article's conclusion) ignores what one would think should be the centerpiece of the analysis—the parties who often actually choose and administer the regulation (assuming regulation is not solely by direct legislation, a possibility). Administators often have considerable discretion. Furthermore, they are often not elected and not even subject to political appointment; they may be Civil Service employees. There is therefore a "black box" in Stigler's theory of regulatory supply and demand (at least as it appears in this article)—the regulatory agency itself. Now, it may be that the unit makes no difference. This is interesting of itself and worthy of comment. There is, after all, a large literature on regulatory reform attesting to the "failures" of continual tinkering with regulatory organizations.

But regulators apparently *can* make a difference. Purchasers of airline tickets before and after Alfred Kahn became chairman of the Civil Aeronautics Board can attest to the difference in their wallets. The change was brought about initially by no new legislation. Dramatic occurrences of this sort have been uncommon in the history of national regulation; the situation in state and local regulation often goes unreported. Perhaps there are systematic mechanisms inside the regulating body, or affecting the regulators, which are conditioned by the more "distant" external factors considered by Stigler. The effects of these internally mediated mechanisms might be only imperfectly predictable by studying those external factors. At any rate, as we saw in chapter 2, the regulatory unit may be seen as part of a complex system of which interest groups are only a part.

In his conclusion (and certainly in some later work; see Stigler 1975),[5] Stigler seems to recognize the potential importance of regulators and the need to link analysis of external factors to the nature and situation of the regulator. He comments, regarding reform of the ICC, that "the only way to get a different commission would be to change the political support for the Commission, and reward commissioners on a basis unrelated to their services to the carriers" (Stigler 1971:17–18). To this point, Stigler has been offering a theory of origin which implicitly is also a theory of regulation in practice; the conditions of origin presumedly remain. If reform is possible, then a theory of regulatory change is needed. Stigler's economic theory of origin might be able to provide an explanation of how factors characterizing groups different from industries can lead to different regulation; but there is no accounting for the transaction costs of change; the effects of possession of "entrenched" or strategic positions by the industry; and the effects of different processes of, or methods of

---

[5] In other work, Stigler has indeed contributed to models of regulators as utility maximizers; see, e.g., Stigler (1975:167–77). In our review, however, we wish to illustrate the variety and development of theories of regulation, and have thus treated Stigler (1971) apart from later work.

carrying out, the change. Why does change occur at one point in time and not another, and involve one interest group and not another? Perhaps Stigler's economic theory can be extended to cover these factors.

Stigler's analysis concerns itself with some aspects of the access stage (e.g., nature of parties, contextual conditions) and relates these to aspects of the decision stage (e.g., nature of some of the key decision makers, locus of decision in legislature, nature of policy approved). He ignores many features of the agenda-building process (e.g., dynamics of creation, expansion, entry; issue specification), the decision process, the implementation process including delegation to regulators, and the administration stage. He does not deal here much with impacts; perhaps effects are assumed to follow directly from the regulatory policy formally adopted. In this article, Stigler seems to assume, much as an older school of public administrationists and public interest theorists of regulation did, that implementation and administration take care of themselves.

Actually, Stigler has elsewhere been quite sensitive to the effects of regulation; with Friedland (1962), he wrote a leading article that questioned whether utility regulation had had any effect, and provoked a whole subfield of research on the effects of regulation. Stigler and Friedland found it apparently had not had significant impact. At the start of his article on the theory of economic regulation, Stigler asserts the "central tasks" of such a theory are to explain regulation's benefits or burdens, forms, and effects on the allocation of resources (Stigler 1971:3). His theory then tries to explain how regulation of a certain kind, i.e., producer protection, comes about. As Pressman and Wildavsky (1973) and others have described, however, it is one thing to have a formalized policy intention, and another to see it work as intended. That linkage is a nontrivial problem for theories of public behavior.

Stigler's arguments regarding the capture of government and the succession of control are really quite similar in some ways to those of the group theorists. In fact, although the economic theory is explicitly ultimately based on assumptions regarding individuals, most of the analysis proceeds as if we could substitute "group" or "firm" for individual. Thus firms may be said to have free-rider problems in joining for political action, i.e., firms (groups) are treated as rational self-interested single actors. Stigler's empirical study of licensing, of course, occurs in the individualistic context.

The other literature employing the simple supply-demand economic theory of regulation exhibits most of the same biases, e.g., largely ignoring the regulator and the regulatory process, as well as strengths. Other work using an economic theory approach, it should be noted, has indeed sought to develop a model of the regulator and thus fill in the "black box;" we shall review some of this work later.

Before leaving Stigler's model, it is well to recall some of the significant contributions it makes. It is explicit and better specified; it permits some prediction and empirical testing. Parenthetically, we note that Bentley placed a high value on empiricism and formal analysis (see Peter Odegard's introduction in Bentley 1908, 1967). The theory promises perhaps a more careful and systematic analysis of some aspects than was offered by previous theories of regulation, though the theory itself appears incomplete.

In an extensive review, Posner (1974) analyzes and extends the economic theory of regulation. He builds on Stigler's observations regarding the application of a supply and demand framework to the occurrence of regulation. Supply and demand can be explained by using the economic theory of cartels modified to include the political process. Like cartelization, regulation can protect industries by bringing about shared rules for behavior—rules which insure higher than competitive rates, protection from potential competitors, and so on.

The determinants (though not necessarily, it appears, the routes) of political influence, however, must be mapped into the cartel formulation. We shall summarize briefly only part of Posner's arguments. Though small numbers of actors facilitate cartelization, large numbers can be effective in securing protective regulation. Large numbers can use their votes, for example, to influence the decision process. Small numbers might succeed in cartelizing by themselves, while large numbers face free-rider problems in maintaining agreements. In general, industries whose costs of securing influence in the political process are less may exhibit more, and more favorable, regulation.

Posner and Stigler do not really develop a fixed and coherent theory of regulation; what they do, rather, is introduce a promising approach that suggests what some of the key variables ought to be that predict to regulation. Although he makes a case for the economic theory as the best available approach, Posner recognizes this: "The economic theory is still so spongy that virtually any observations can be reconciled with it. . . . At best it is a list of criteria relevant to predicting whether an industry will obtain favorable legislation. It is not a coherent theory yielding unambiguous and therefore testable hypotheses'' (Posner 1974: 348, 349).

William Jordan (1972), like Stigler, argues that regulation tends to serve the purpose of producer protection. He offers three "hypotheses" regarding regulatory *effects*. These hypotheses essentially define three theories of regulation.

1. The *consumer protection* hypothesis says that regulation will simulate the effects of a competitive market and protect consumers "by reducing prices until they equal marginal costs, by preventing discriminatory pricing, by improving service quality (at existing prices), by encouraging the entry of firms that are more efficient or that offer more preferred price/product combinations, and by reducing industry profits to the market rate of return" (Jordan 1972:152). Since regulatory agencies don't appear to act this way, Jordan (1972:152) says some "propose the supplementary perversion hypothesis," i.e., that the regulated industries somehow pervert the regulators into industry protectors.

2. The *no-effect* hypothesis says just that—regulation simply has no effect, except the cost of the regulatory process itself. Of course, the perversion hypothesis could also produce this effect.

3. The *producer protection* hypothesis argues that "the actual effect of regulation is to increase or sustain the economic power of an industry" (Jordan 1972:153). Regulation can convert a competitive situation to a cartel, help an existing cartel, or protect a cartel from potential competitors. Evidence for the hypothesis would see regulation "increasing prices, promoting price discrimination, reducing or preventing the entry of rival firms, and increasing industry profits" (Jordan 1972:153).

Jordan argues that, once the prior market structure is taken into account, the evidence supports the third over the first two hypotheses. He then reviews the existing evidence, finding support for his view that the effects of regulation have been largely producer protection. In particular, he finds the "supplementary perversion hypothesis" to be "a forced and tortuous way to accommodate the consumer-protection hypothesis with the existing evidence" (Jordan 1972:175), though he does not offer a more detailed critique of the hypothesis itself.

In essence, Jordan appears to commit the fallacy of linking effects with origin, though he does not directly argue this; he seeks to determine the "purpose" of regulation and notes (pp. 175–76) that installation of regulation was often supported by the respective industries. Thus, "where there is little or no monopoly power in the prior market structure, regulation should have an important impact by helping formerly independent producers form a cartel for their benefit and protection" (Jordan 1972:176).

Jordan's work is valuable as that of one of the early proponents of a revisionist producer protection theory, derived in the context of what is, effectively, an economic theory of regulation. But, in terms of the policy process, Jordan's arguments are rather limited, essentially linking only origin and regulatory policy (vaguely), and regulatory policy with effects.

Stigler, Posner, and Jordan are only a few of a growing group of scholars, mostly economists, who have been developing the economic theory of regulation and its stepchildren. Abrams and Settle (1978) have recently applied the economic theory of regulation to the case of regulation of political campaign financing. They argue that legislators will try to design the regulation to serve their self-interest rather than in some "public interest." Thus incumbents would seek "regulations designed to 'control entry' of potential opponents." And the majority political party will seek to remain so by acquiring protective regulation that is adverse to the minority party (Abrams and Settle 1978:247–48). The authors find significant support for their hypotheses.

It is really not surprising to find Congressmen and political parties acting in their self-interest. Though the results are suggestive, we really need more to support an economic theory of regulation (as against a simple rational choice model of the behavior of politicians). One can perhaps distinguish an *economic theory of regulation,* with the supply-demand framework and the assumptions about individual actors, from an *economic approach to modeling regulation,* which relies mainly on the assumptions and techniques of economics but not necessarily on the structure of, parallelism with, or appropriation of, existing models in economics. The structure of the economic theory of regulation, at any rate, needs fuller explication to build it above the basic supply-demand, rational choice framework.

The Abrams and Settle study can be viewed as a bridge to that work which develops explicit economic models of regulation centered on the politician as regulator, which we shall consider below. In that literature, the black box between supply and demand is filled with utility-maximizing politicians. The economic theory becomes more of an economic approach to developing theory in regulation.

2.2.3 Utility-Maximizing Theories: Efforts to Fill in the Black Box

Regulation can be seen as the outcome of rational choices by public officials maximizing their utility, i.e., the satisfaction of their preferences, under varying constraints and with varying reward opportunities. Models typically assume that there is a single type of rational key decision maker whose decisions will be determinant and effective.

In this approach, regulatory organizations cease to be complex structures in which individuals with varying abilities and preferences practice varying professions; perform varying tasks with varying technologies; interact in varying formal and informal channels; receive varying stimuli from external organizations; and so on. Regulation is said to be the result usually of a decision or a bargain, not a resultant of collective behavior. This is a major criticism, we believe, but one whose importance can perhaps ultimately be determined only by empirical test. Perhaps in many situations, and under many conditions, the individualistic model could still work well. In small regulatory organizations, especially, such as taxi licensing boards, this may be true.

The utility-maximizing key decision-maker approach has exhibited two major variants. One route has been to focus on a particular type of key decision maker and build the model around him. The other route has been to look at the characteristic behaviors and relationships that exist in regulation, i.e., to focus on the activities that the key decision maker participates in. We shall term the first variant the "focal decision-maker" approach and the second, the "behavioral" approach.

2.2.3.1   The Focal Decision-Maker Approach

The focal decision-maker approach selects a key decision maker, assumes he has some particular (or typical) set of preferences, usually characterized by self-interest (e.g., reelection, salary, status, future security), and specifies the constraints and reward opportunities, i.e., opportunities for preference satisfaction, that he finds in his regulatory setting. Regulatory decisions are said to follow then from the decision maker's rational decisions in this setting.

Frequently, the decision maker is assumed to be no different in respect to his preferences and abilities than any other of his type in settings other than regulatory. Politicians are politicians and bureaucrats are bureaucrats, whether or not they are assumed to be regulators. Reward opportunities, however, tend to administer rewards selectively, so that bureaucrats who in one setting would pursue salary increases might in another seek convenience on the job and future job security.

Although the "no difference" claim is often made, in practice some differences are assumed. The bureaucrat/politician rarely acts as agent for some policy goal in these models, and certain preferences are implicitly assumed more important than others. It seems questionable, moreover, to assume that certain preferences are important and determinant merely because they can be satisfied in a given setting. Few of the existing models in this area have employed distinctions like those made by Downs (1967) regarding types of bureaucrats determined according to kinds of rewards sought (see chapter 2).

The focal decision-maker models have tended to cluster around two decision-maker types: the regulator as politician, and the regulator as bureaucrat. We shall consider some representative models for each type.

1. *The Regulator as Politician.* The regulator has been modeled as a politician who seeks survival, i.e., reelection, by choosing regulating policies to serve groups who may offer him their support. Variations on this approach include assuming the regulator is a vaguely defined elected politician who determines regulatory policy so as to maximize votes received; a legislator who acts instrumentally within the legislative committee system, whether through oversight or service provision, to please his constituency and thus obtain reelection; or an elected politician who must build and manage a "coalition" in order to stay in office.

Sam Peltzman (1976) has developed what is essentially a model of wealth redistribution by elected politicians seeking to maximize votes. His model is really more general than one of the regulator alone; one of the major criticisms that can be offered, in fact, is that his is not really a model of regulation. It is a model of legislation-making, with analysis of why legislation with a typically regulatory character, e.g., specifying certain cross-subsidies, occurs.

In Peltzman's formal model, which he views as an extension of Stigler's model but which goes somewhat beyond Stigler, the "regulator'' seeks to maximize his expected vote majority. In the simplest version of the model (closest to Stigler's model), the probability of the politician receiving support from a beneficiary is taken to be a function of the average net gain to the supporter, i.e., dollar gain (transferred to the beneficiary) minus the ''dollars spent by beneficiaries in campaign funds, lobbying, and so on, to mitigate opposition'' minus the ''cost of organizing both direct support of beneficiaries and efforts to mitigate opposition,'' all divided by the ''number of potential voters in the beneficiary group'' (Peltzman 1976:214–15). The regulator chooses the size of the group to be benefited, the amount of dollar gain to the beneficiary group, and the amount spent by that group to mitigate opposition in his behalf. The wealth going to the beneficiary group is viewed as a tax at a certain rate on the wealth of all outside the beneficiary group. Opposition comes from those paying the tax and is ''assumed generated by the tax rate and mitigated by voter education expenditures per capita'' (Peltzman 1976:216). Through manipulating this formal model, Peltzman derives the following results:

> 1. With a few ambiguities, the thrust of imperfect information about both the gains and losses of regulatory decisions and of costs of organizing for political favors is to restrict the size of the winning group.
> 2. But this winning group will not obtain even a gross gain through political action as great as is within the power of the political process to grant it.
> 3. Moreover, even if groups organize according to an economic interest (producers v. consumers), political entrepreneurship will produce a coalition which admits members of the losing group into the charmed circle. (Peltzman 1976:221–22)

Peltzman's version of Stigler's model really goes beyond Stigler in more than its formalization. Stigler's view seems to be one of groups using the political process, including legislative representatives and parties acting as agents or entrepreneurs for these groups. The resulting regulation is funneled through these agents' self-interest in reelection, but they seem to play a less central role in the supply side than that of the groups whose needs and characteristics determine the demand side for regulation. In Peltzman's model, the supply side—the politicians—are clearly central; the model is organized around the decision-making politician. This is why we have included Peltzman's model in this group, rather than among the general economic theories of regulation, though it is clearly a development from them.

Peltzman's version of Stigler's model can be subject to a number of criticisms (cf. those by Hirshleifer and by Becker appended to Peltzman 1976). Chief among these is that regulators are *not* normally legislators or other elected officials. Usually only the top regulatory officials, e.g., commissioners and a few key staff, are even appointed. The rest are there and stay there courtesy of Civil Service. Thus Peltzman (and Stigler) have really developed models of legislative decision on regulation. This is surely relevant to considerations of regulatory origin, but it is scarcely sufficient for a theory of regulation. As we have observed before, administrators invariably have some discretion. Models like Stigler's or Peltzman's raise the question of how and in what form the administrators receive the legislation; why some things (and not others) are delegated and so left to administrative discretion; how administrators implement, oversee, and enforce the regulation; and so on. Does the role of the legislator stop once regulatory legislation is approved? What about legislative oversight of regulation? Are there informal ways in which the "politician" regulators—the legislators—convey their changing preferences to the "bureaucrat" regulators? Maybe these questions would turn out to be irrelevant ones, but they need attention.

The Stigler-Peltzman models further assume, implicitly, that all the relevant parties, such as consumers and producers, also believe the buck stops with the legislators. Otherwise, the model would be incomplete since it ignores the costs incurred by consumers and producers in participating in the administrative process. Maybe these costs are covered under the costs-to-mitigate-opposition that are included in the model. If the agencies are irrelevant and regulation is put into effect as intended, why do we have the apparent going through the motions of decision in the agencies at all? Perhaps the model assumes implicitly that if the regulation is not implemented and administered as intended, both the affected groups and the legislators, who each have a stake in the regulation being effective, will police the administrators perfectly (and costlessly?). What of findings like those of Stigler and Friedland (1962) regarding the apparent ineffectiveness of regulation (Peltzman does note this as a potential problem)?

Another aspect of Peltzman's model that is questionable is his assumption that the funds spent by beneficiaries in support of the politician both directly and, partially, in organization costs, go to "mitigate opposition." The beneficiary is supposed to spend funds on the politician's campaign, on lobbying, and on educating the *opposition*.

In fact, the empirical evidence has largely been that private interest groups *stay away from their opponents*. Overwhelmingly, they lobby their friends, e.g., getting out the vote, insuring that lukewarm supporters do not leave the fold, and so on (see, e.g., Bauer, Pool, and Dexter 1963; Dexter 1969; but cf. Hayes 1978). Jeffrey Berry's recent (1977) study of *public* interest groups had one finding that was interesting because of this: apparently public interest groups sometimes *do* lobby their enemies, though most often they lobby their friends as private interest groups do (Berry 1977:216–23). Thus Peltzman's model appears inaccurate on this score; perhaps a change in the assumed use of funds and an altered rationale can repair it.

Peltzman does not stop with formalization of the Stigler model; he generalizes it by assuming the politician's objective function, i.e., utility, is a function of the wealth of consumers and of producers. The politician will receive more support and more votes by keeping consumer prices low (consumer wealth) and producer wealth high. Later he generalizes the model to allow the politician to have two prices (i.e., the wealth of two consumer groups) as well as the wealth of the producers in his objective function. Peltzman uses these models to investigate price-entry regulation and the regulated price structure and derives a number of interesting results. The most significant is that the regulator will tend not to favor any single group; since he wants to maximize votes, he would prefer to build the broadest possible coalition of supporters. Jack Hirshleifer summarizes the point well:

> For example, in some circumstances a technological advance might lead to a new market solution lowering cost but not lowering price—so that all the benefit would otherwise go to the producers and none to the consumers. In these circumstances the regulators would impose a price reduction, assuring that some portion of the social gain goes to consumers as well. . . . Similarly, the regulators tend to assure that burdens are spread among all parties, if a social loss has been incurred. And where some would gain and others lose from the unconstrained market process, the regulators 'lean against the wind' so as to moderate the final outcome. (Peltzman 1976:243)

Thus Peltzman is able to derive a rationale for the pervasive occurrence of internal subsidization in regulation.

Peltzman's approach suffers from some of the same problems as Stigler's in terms of its comprehensiveness as a theory of regulation. It ignores several important parts of the policy process, e.g., implementation and administration. One supposes effects follow directly from the regulatory legislation and/or are costlessly policed by the legislators and the interested groups. The relation between the politicians, presumably legislators (or, possibly, the chief executive, since as "politicians" those subject to the analysis must be elected), and the regulation administrators is not considered. The mechanisms by which groups approach and reward politicians is really only sketched in the broadest way. It is not clear exactly how regulatory issues arise, gather supportive coalitions, and get on the agenda. Thus the access stage remains largely a mystery.

Barry Weingast (1978) has offered what he terms a "political cycles" model of regulation that also focuses on the regulator as politician-legislator. In Weingast's model, it is clear now that the "politician" is a legislative representative who performs the duties (e.g., serving on policy-making committees) and has the ordinary goal (reelection) of legislators (cf. Fiorina 1977). The key to Weingast's model, however, is its attention to the role played by legislative committees in originating legislation and performing oversight on the regulation in operation.

The policy-making process is said to proceed in two stages: The legislature: 1) considers alternatives, and 2) "implements and manages ongoing policies and programs" enacted previously (Weingast 1978:11). But, contrary to this description, legislators do not implement and manage. Administrators do, for some of the reasons discovered by the Continental Congress and discussed in chapter 2 (and in chapter 6). Oversight is not of the same order as implementation and management.

Legislative candidates "wishing to maximize the probability of election will choose the stand which they perceive corresponds to the median voter in their district" (Weingast 1978:10). As issues vary, candidates will switch their positions to maximize their election chances. Unlike Stigler and Peltzman, Weingast argues that votes, not wealth used in a way tantamount to bribery, is the key factor. He sets up a formal model centering on the institutional rules governing the committee system, i.e., legislation must come from the proper committee; legislation is subject to majority rule; oversight is delegated to the appropriate committee; and representatives are assigned, if possible, to the committee they desire.

Weingast then discusses factors inhibiting issue formation and contributing to waning of support for a policy once it is passed and into the oversight stage. These factors include the information cost to a citizen of remaining informed on an issue/policy's status, and a collective action dilemma existing among legislative districts: Why pay the costs of raising an issue and converting one's representative if he is only one among many needed? Let the other districts do it; we may be a free rider on their efforts. The most interested districts will tend to see that their legislators get themselves appointed to the relevant oversight committees.

But as support fades, representatives from less-interested districts will "jump" out of the committee, leaving open the possibility that a majority of representatives will remain who are hostile to the, say, public interest aims of the original legislation. A "policy reversal" can occur. A regulatory agency now exists so that gains and losses among parts of the population can change; the original movement may therefore not re-form to counter the reversal. But it can, creating the possibility of a "political cycle."

Weingast goes on to elaborate his model by distinguishing "producer," "consumer," and "mixed districts," and discussing how factors such as their existing organization, lack of free rider problems, and continual need to interact with the regulatory agency lead producers to dominate oversight. Changes on the oversight committee in composition, preferences, and intensity of preferences (permitting vote-trading) result as legislators follow the type and level of concern in their districts.

Weingast argues that this "political cycles" model is particularly valuable because it can include both the cartel-by-design origin theory (original producer protection) and the life cycle theory (perversion/capture over time). The agency's origin can be marked by either consumer protection or producer protection biases, depending on who dominates the movement establishing the agency. Subsequently, control can shift either way.[6] In view of the distinctions we made earlier, it is hardly surprising that an origin theory and a life cycle theory are argued as complements, not substitutes, in a broader model. What is of interest (and question) is the degree of robustness of the "political cycles" formulation as a general model.

[6] Weingast, like a number of others, employs a specialized interpretation of the "public interest theory" of regulation. Referring to regulation, he writes, "Since the agencies often benefit an industry at the expense of consumers, this form of market intervention poses a dilemma for the public interest theory as an explanatory model of the policymaking process" (Weingast 1978:1–2). Thus Weingast apparently takes the consumer interest as indicative of the public interest, if not synonymous with it, and one supposes his analysis should be understood in this light.

It has no mechanism of agenda-building; Weingast admits he does not know how issues form, given the inhibiting factors he identifies, and recognizes this requires more study (Weingast 1978:15). Does the model really describe a "cycle"? Why not a path of evolution; after all, Weingast allows the process to start and stop at various points. The model still largely ignores implementation and administration *by* the regulatory agency. The oversight committees meddles, but it must be doing this because the agency is acting with discretion counter to its intentions. Administrators do have some discretion, as we have already pointed out several times in connection with other models. In chapter 6, we shall consider why the legislature delegates and creates this discretion. If the legislators are so important, why do industries bother with the regulators, offering them attention, jobs after they leave, and free lunches?

Furthermore, regulatory oversight has historically been usually of a perfunctory nature, save in times of crisis in issues in the relevant area (though recently this is changing; see Aberbach 1977; Ogul 1976; U.S. Senate, Committee on Governmental Affairs 1977, vol. 2). This can be consistent with agreement between oversight committee and agency (e.g., on producer protection), but it could also mean other things. Perhaps regulation is too trivial to bother with (or used to be this way); nearly all legislators may prefer to spend their vote-getting time elsewhere. There are empirical questions: Do legislators jump on and off oversight committees in the way described? Can districts be homogeneously characterized as producer or consumer (who represents the truckers? the railroads? the securities brokers?)? As we saw in chapter 2, life cycle theories (e.g., Bernstein, Downs), though flawed, are perhaps more substantial than Weingast presents them. A closer comparison of evolutionary mechanisms is in order.

In spite of these criticisms, Weingast's work clearly begins to fill a gap—the gap between the external factors that affect groups and lead them to seek regulation, and the operation of the regulation. The sides of the box were erected by Stigler and Posner. Peltzman put a "politician" in it. Weingast has made the politician a legislator and has attempted to give him an institution to operate within. One can sense the puzzle pieces fitting together.

William Niskanen (1975) has amended his previous work on bureaucracy (1971) to develop models of the utility-maximizing bureaucrat and the vote-maximizing legislator. His more recent work is relevant here because his analysis of legislators has some features in common with the models we have just considered, and because he juxtaposes a bureaucrat model with a legislator model, recognizing the logic of considering both. We shall consider his legislator model briefly.

Like Weingast, and overlapping with him, Niskanen (1975, p. 623) offers several descriptive assumptions about the legislature: "majority rule decision making, committee review, vote maximizing behavior by legislators, and legislator discretion in the use of his own time and available staff resources." Also like Weingast, Niskanen (1975:624–25) assumes that "most committees are dominated by legislators who have higher demands for the services reviewed than the median demand in the whole legislature and the committee decisions are very seldom amended or reversed by the whole legislature." He notes (p. 625) recent studies that "confirmed the casual observations that most legislators receive the committee assignments they request and that the requests are correlated with services that are most important to their regional constituencies."

Legislators are said to have high discretion in their use of their time and staff. These may go to services to constituents (cf. Fiorina 1977) or campaign contributors (who may thus aid reelection) and to "monitoring," i.e., oversight tasks on committees. But "the monitoring function . . . is a public good within the legislature; the benefits of monitoring accrue to the whole population as a function of their tax costs" (Niskanen 1975:626). This leads to a potential free-rider problem.

Niskanen's model (1975:627) then specifies votes for the legislator as "a linear function of the specific services he performs for his constituents and contributors, the level of output of some aggregate government service, and the taxes paid by his constituents." Taxes are equated to cost of the number of units of government services that would be paid for by taxes from the district. The legislator's time is said to be divided between constituency-related and "monitoring" activities. Using the legislator's time as a constraint, Niskanen maximizes an expression for votes derived from the above. He notes that from this "the most important observation is that a legislator from a district that pays a small share of the total taxes will spend most of his time on activities specific to his district" (Niskanen 1975:628). At the same time, investment of time in monitoring may be low.

Thus, though some of his assumptions are similar, Niskanen's

model reaches a conclusion possibly hostile to Weingast's formulation. Committee assignments may be sought after because they facilitate services; oversight, which is at the core of Weingast's model,
can run a poor second. Emphasis upon the legislator as key to an understanding of regulation may be misplaced, though inclusion of the
legislative decision, service, and oversight processes are probably essential.

Regulators as "politicians" must not always turn out to be legislators. Several writers have identified regulators as officials in regulatory agencies who attempt to build "coalitions" in order to assure
their "survival." Thus, although the setting bears relation to that of
the regulator-as-bureaucrat models discussed below, the basic character of the analysis is that of externally colored political, not bureaucratic, survival.

Russell and Shelton (1974) assume regulatory agencies are distributors and redistributors of wealth, regarding which allocation their
top officials have considerable discretion. Effects of decisions are not
easily predictable; decisions are basically judgmental and there are no
objective standards on which to base them; the judicial review process is limited to due process rather than considerations of fact or
substance; and legislatures have provided no specific regulatory standards, i.e., usually nothing more than "just and reasonable" and
similar exhortations to public interest behavior. Thus, within some
"zone of reasonableness," regulators can redistribute wealth at their
discretion.

Regulators are assumed to maximize their utility. They will seek:
1) to assure their post-commission futures, and will thus not wish to
alienate future benefactors; 2) to attain "survival," e.g., protection
against those who are harmed by their decisions, through forming and
maintaining a "political coalition"; 3) to retain their integrity by not
voting against their individual notions of the public interest (a weak
constraint since rarely is anything clearly against all views of the
public interest); and 4) to retain their reputations among their associ-
ates and peers.[7]

Regulators may then behave so as to insure their future well being,
and can elect one of three patterns of behavior: 1) for the regulated
firms; 2) for the consumers; and 3) for the public interest. The public

---

[7] For another model employing the survival goal, cf. Baldwin (1975).

interest is identified by Russell and Shelton (1974:49) as "optimal resource allocation, given the existing income distribution." As we have seen, this is a special-case definition.

The distribution of regulators by these three types is expected to depend on the expected gains from each pattern of behavior. Organization and decision costs are greater for consumers than for the small group of regulated firms (usually on a given issue there is only one firm), and consumers may face free-rider problems. Industry expenditure on regulation will be greater and can be taken as "a proxy for the positions in regulation available to ex-commissioners" (Russell and Shelton 1974:50). Since the benefits obtained by type (3), public interest regulation, are public goods and spread throughout, and organization costs are even greater than for consumers, little support for it will appear; commissioners "should expect to find in such service its own reward" (Russell and Shelton 1974:50). Thus type (1), behavior for the regulated firms, would probably be encouraged.

In order to maintain their coalitions, regulators wish to avoid appearing biased, since an appearance of bias will limit their influence. Thus the regulator will seek to draw support from outside his "core constituency." If the regulator adopts type (1), pro-firm, behavior, he will probably seek at least some supporters from the other groups anyway. One way of doing this is through some internal subsidization, i.e., providing some below-cost services to some consumers. There is of course a limit to the amount of such cross-subsidization that can be "safely" imposed. But only the public interest regulator will oppose it, on efficiency grounds. Cross-subsidies must be balanced by permitting extra profit in other services, which could draw in new competitors in these services. To protect the internal-subsidization system, regulators will therefore institute entry controls.

Russell and Shelton develop a formal model from this basis and derive a number of other results. They also argue that agencies will not behave differently even if shown that their behavior is not consistent with some social goals or if the agencies are populated by "better" commissioners: "The behavior of regulators is a function of the *situation,* not of the men" (Russell and Shelton 1974:60).

It is not clear, however, that level of regulatory expenditure by parties approaching the agency is a reliable surrogate for future job opportunities. One must at any rate consider the number and variety of future positions available in all areas against the relatively small number of commissioners. Some regulators (e.g., the Alfred Kahns) may not depend at all on the parties affected by regulation for future jobs, or may not care. It seems strange to assume this goal may play such a primary role, though as one goal it seems possible. The observation that regulators upon leaving the agency overwhelmingly go to work in a position related to the industry is really quite different from the assumption that regulators will make decisions on the basis of this future possibility. They may get jobs related to the industry *no matter what they do* because they are held to be expert regarding the regulatory process and friendly with the remaining incumbents.

The idea of a "coalition" is interesting but may have limited applicability. Russell and Shelton define their discussion and model in terms of utility regulation by commission. What "coalition" would the head of a taxi licensing bureau form? If it were a municipal taxi commission, would the arguments be different? "Coalition" as a useful concept here could require scale and multiple-headed agency direction. The traditional isolation and esoteric nature of regulatory units may cast some doubt on the need for or appropriateness of "coalitions." What of regulation where internal subsidization is lacking? Who exactly is in the "coalition" and what means do they use to interact with and support the regulators?

Russell and Shelton's model is basically one of ongoing regulatory decision rather than origin; it focuses on the administration stage of the policy process. It may be possible to generalize the arguments to include the decision stage, where the new regulation is an addition to existing regulation. We remain curious about regulatory access, implementation, and impacts.

Thus, models of the regulator-as-politician have looked at both sides, legislature and agency. But many things are still lacking, especially on the agency side. Russell and Shelton's model, though it discusses "coalitions," ignores organizations. The regulatory process really provides only the boundaries of a "zone of reasonableness" in their model. Are regulators affected by their status as organizational creatures? Agencies can vary greatly in size, but though the larger ones are often small compared with the firms they regulate and other units of government, they still rank as complex organizations. Can we really treat regulators as the sole determiners of organizational action, almost as if the organization were itself an individual? Can the organizational goals which some organization theorists even reject as useful conceptual tools be treated simply as the goals of a group of top officials?

2. *The Regulator as Bureaucrat*. There are several existing models of the regulator as bureaucrat; unfortunately, none of them addresses all of the questions we have posed above. Typically, the regulator is assumed to be the top official in a regulatory organization, who in his basic preferences is similar to other bureaucrats. His behavior is then structured by the constraints of the organizational setting and his reward opportunities, which he pursues rationally. Most of these models predict to "capture" of the agency by the regulated industry, or at least regulatory outputs that consistently favor the industry.

The regulator-as-bureaucrat models may be seen as special cases of more general models of bureaucratic behavior. Downs (1967) and Tullock (1965) have applied the rational choice framework to bureaucrats, as has Niskanen (1975, 1971), some of whose work we discussed earlier. Managerial discretion models of organizations assume that organizational members have some discretion over allocation of organizational resources. Usually this choice is between return to personal goals and return to organizational goals. The organization member is assumed to choose among the possible allocations rationally, given the constraints of the organizational setting (see, e.g., Williamson 1964; Migue and Belanger 1974; Mitnick 1974; and Borcherding 1977). Russell and Shelton (1974) explicitly cast their discussion of regulation in terms of managerial discretion, as does Mitnick (1975b).

Variations on the regulator-bureaucrat model have been presented by Noll (1971a, b, c); Hilton (1972a); Eckert (1973); Noll, Peck, and McGowan (1973:120–26); Mitnick and Weiss (1974); Mitnick (1973b, 1974, 1975b); DeAlessi (1974, 1975); and others. We have already discussed a variant of this model in chapter 2. As an illustration, we shall present below a version of this approach taken largely from parts of the arguments in Mitnick and Weiss (1974) and Mitnick (1973b, 1974); it involves a combination and extension of work by Noll and Eckert. Mitnick's full model as it appears in these papers is better categorized in the general framework of agent-principal relations, however, and as such will be described later under the heading of behavioral models.

The model of regulatory behavior employed in these regulator-as-bureaucrat approaches assumes that the actors are rational, in the broad sense of taking actions consistent with given goals, and that they are the recipients of incentives in scarce and differentially distributed supply. They are also self-interested; three groups of goals are identified:

Organizational goals of the commissions are in practice (Noll 1971a): 1) nonreversal of its actions by the legislature through oversight review or new legislative act or by the courts through judicial review; 2) preservation of the regulated interest, where that interest is typically that of some industry or spectrum of industries. If many decisions or actions of the commission are reversed or modified by legislative or judicial action, then the commission is clearly not doing its "job" of properly disposing of the matters entrusted to it. Although some commissions have been formally charged with promoting the regulated interest (which may often patently conflict with other explicit regulatory aims), preservation has a more basic origin. The very existence of the regulatory agencies gives official recognition and legitimacy to the special interests they regulate. Having legitimated those interests, an agency that regulated them out of existence would be perceived as acting against its mandate. Furthermore, the agency's task of regulation involves policing with respect to some standard, which implies that the regulated party should not be allowed to fall below this standard. Thus commissions must both avoid reversal and preserve the regulated interest.

Personal goals of the commissioners generally include: 1) status; 2) ease of working conditions, including work load, pleasant and reinforcing interpersonal relationships, and absence of debilitating client pressures; and 3) expectation of future rewards for current service, such as remunerative positions of high status in the regulated industry or in organizations such as law firms that practice in that area. These goals may also apply to some key commission staff, such as examiners. Other goals common among the bureaucrats in other administrative agencies are not directly operative because of the incentive system faced by the regulators. Thus, because their salaries are set by law and difficult to alter, and because of their fixed term of appointment and uncertainty regarding reappointment, regulators cannot satisfy salary goals through current service; for this reward, they depend on future remunerative positions (Eckert 1973). Expansion in agency coverage with increased work load would likely bring increased status and perhaps salary to a bureaucrat, since he would be managing a larger staff and have a higher rank in the hierarchy of his department. In a regulatory commission, however, the increased work load in the form of cases would have to funnel eventually through a set of commissioners fixed in number by law and thus difficult to expand, since it would require legislative approval. Even if more staff were added, the status of the commissioners, already heads of an independent agency, would not be much affected, since with respect to other agencies the regulatory commission by nature will almost always be smaller and less significant, at least over time, than a major operating department of government. And it would remain basically constrained in expansion by its regulatory mandate. Regulators may receive rewards of status, however, from the members of the regulated industry, to whom the decisions of the agency are of intense interest.

Client goals are, generally: 1) those of the regulated industry, i.e., favorable regulation; 2) those of "public interest," consumer, or other activist groups, i.e., regulation consonant with their interpretation of the public interest. Clients are also expected to act in their self-interest in other ways, e.g., seek efficiency in the use of their resources.

Regulatory actions are likely to have a diffuse impact on the large number of scattered consumers, but a direct and concentrated impact on the regulated industry. Consumers are likely to face higher organization and decision costs than the industry, as well as free-rider problems. Consumers will pay higher information costs on regulatory matters, since their individual contacts with the regulated product or service, and with the regulatory agency, are only occasional. The industry, of course, has constant involvement with the product or service and, because it is regulated, must have regular contact with the agency. For these reasons, action by the industry during regulatory proceedings is likely to be better organized, funded, and informed. The regulated industry may be better able to make a case that will receive favorable decision from the agency and survive any challenge on appeal to the courts.

Because of the structure of the existing incentive system, the commissioners can become, in effect, the *agents* of the regulated industry rather than, say, of some conception of the public interest (Mitnick 1973b, 1974, 1975b; Mitnick and Weiss 1974). The regulated industry may offer commissioners and key staff the incentive of lucrative jobs after retirement from government service. They may also be a source of helpful advice in necessary day-to-day contacts. In addition, the industry accords the commissioners, whose actions are so important to it, the respect and prestige they receive from nowhere else. Public interest groups who contest regulatory cases may lower the status of the commissioners and their staff by publicly claiming that the commission is not acting in (their) "public" interest, may greatly increase the work load of the commissioners and the personal pressures on them, and can in general offer either no, or small, prospects of future rewards in the way of jobs.

Failure to satisfy organizational goals will also threaten the personal goals of the commissioners. The commissions are expected by their review mechanisms to maintain the regulated interest without its collapse and to avoid reversal. To avoid the loss of status and of the prospect of lucrative future employment that could accompany poor performance with respect to these goals, the commissioners are motivated to discourage public interest group objections and to decide cases on as narrowly procedural grounds as possible to preclude subsequent reversal in the courts. Since the courts check to see only if the agency's decision was procedurally correct, the commissioners offer reasons for their actions that they had offered before and found acceptable. Since objections to these reasons are likely to come from the public interest group clients, and not from the industry clients, such a decision method is likely to safeguard rewards the commissioners receive from the industry. It also involves less work for the commissioners than comprehensive substantive consideration. In order to avoid objections from public interest groups, the commissioners may try to co-opt those groups symbolically, that is, without really increasing commission work load by genuinely considering problems brought up by the groups, and without threatening current or future rewards from the industry. It is easy to see how an incentive system of this sort could lead to the "capture" of the regulatory body by the regulated industry.

Because they are unable to increase their salary, receive prestige only from the regulated industry as they officiate in a "backwater" agency, and are subject to personal increases in work load if they try to expand the agency's regulatory coverage or seek to make the regulations more complex, regulators in a commission may oppose growth in the agency. They may design regulations that are simple to administer and define the scope of their regulatory mandate narrowly (see, e.g., Eckert 1973). These effects are additionally encouraged by the goal of avoiding reversals of agency decisions by the courts, which like the agency (as far as possible) will make decisions on simple, narrow, largely procedural grounds. The situation in a regulatory bureau, as we discussed in chapter 2, is different, since regulators can gain by increasing the size and budget of the unit.

Simplification of regulation—e.g., setting a uniform price in the market and allowing monopoly or near-monopoly of service—and narrow definition of mandate can be consistent with the interests of the regulated parties. Thus the occurrence of such regulation need not be evidence of "capture," i.e., of an industry successful in securing protective regulation for itself. We would get the same result if the *commission,* not the industry, is obtaining its own protection. Of course, the two may coincide, which may account for the prevalence and persistence of these effects.

In discussing agency protection, we are moving beyond the arguments normally given by the modelers of the regulator-as-bureaucrat, though writers such as Eckert (1973) and DeAlessi (1974, 1975) have explicitly considered the effects of alternate organizational forms (e.g., bureaus vs. commissions, public vs. regulated private organizations) on observed behavior. In addition, we have spoken of "incentives" to indicate the potential relevance of an approach centering on existing incentive systems.

There are many problems with the rational-choice-bureaucrat model, as with the other kinds of models we have considered. The regulator-as-bureaucrat models are usually cast in the context of predicting regulatory outputs from ongoing regulation, i.e., focus on the administration stage of the policy process. The model is also sometimes linked to the effects stage (see, e.g., DeAlessi 1974). It is usually not employed to develop explanations for the access, decision, and implementation stages, and thus for regulatory creation. But this may not necessarily be a fault of the approach. The incentive system facing bureaucrats may be expected to play a major role where additions or modifications are made to an existing regulatory mandate. The behavior of bureaucrats of the agency affected by the new regulation may be central to an understanding of regulatory creation under these circumstances.

The regulator-as-bureaucrat models invariably focus on the top officials. There may be important differences between appointed agency heads and the Civil Service bureaucrats on the staff. It is not clear that such bureaucrats have the same future job possibilities as the top officials or even covet them at all. Bureaucrats may prefer to work for public rather than private organizations because their preferences for job security are relatively higher ranked than their preferences for salary gain (on such differences, see, e.g., Rainey, Backoff and Levine 1976).

There may be differences, moreover, between officials who head the agency, and "line" regulators—e.g., reclamation inspectors— who may have the most common and direct contacts with the regulated party and do the major work of regulating.

All regulators-as-bureaucrats may not, of course, have the same goals; in chapter 2 we considered some types of bureaucrats based on differences in goal sets.

A regulator-as-bureaucrat model of the type described does include legislative oversight, as the politician models generally do. But the nature of the oversight function is not developed well. There may be an opportunity here for integrating the two approaches. Furthermore, the bureaucrat model includes consideration of the effects of judicial review, i.e., provides a linkage to the judicial system that appears lacking in the politician models.

The bureaucrat model is, however, most often a small group or individualistic model; the complexity of organizational behavior is usually absent. The work of Eckert (1973) and DeAlessi (1974), and the arguments we developed in chapter 2 (e.g., the institutional decision as a means of permitting agency growth), do begin to introduce such elements. We feel this is essential to an adequate model of regulation.

Before leaving the focal decision-maker models, we note one study in which the agency and its behavior are viewed as somewhat more complex than in some of the bureaucrat models. Porter and Sagansky (1976) model the agency as having a multi-argument objective function subject to multiple constraints. They contrast this formulation with that of a simple "capture" theory in which the agency acts only for the regulated party. They propose four non-mutually-exclusive explanations for regulatory behavior derived from their approach:

> First, the regulatory agency's instrumental goal designed to maximize its chances for survival may be economic efficiency, and it may possess the data required to reach the efficient solution; the decision and the efficiency of the outcome are determined by the expertise available to it. Second, the agency's goal may be again economic efficiency, but its decision is constrained by the practical and administrative problems of gathering and analyzing the data it needs. Third, the agency may prefer economic efficiency, but its decision is determined by the control and influence exercised by the entities it regulates over the key pieces of information it needs to make its choice. Finally, the agency's goal may not involve economic welfare at all; its decisions reflect its desire to survive in a political environment and thus

result from the balancing of the political forces acting on it. (Porter and Sagansky 1976:265–66)

Porter and Sagansky (1976:266) found in a case study of airfreight regulatory decisions by the Civil Aeronautics Board "that each explanation and the interactions among them contribute to explaining the . . . decisions." Apart from possible problems in distinguishing individual from organizational goals, Porter and Sagansky are effectively suggesting the very real complexity of explaining decisions in a regulatory organizational setting. Single factor, simple theories of bureaucrat behavior may be inadequate.

2.2.3.2   The Behavioral Approach

The second major category of utility-maximizing theories may be called the behavioral approach. Like the focal decision-maker models, the behavioral approach assumes that regulators will be rational, utility maximizers. It is complementary to those models, however, in that it focuses on relational, procedural, or organizational factors or behaviors that tend to be brushed over or ignored in the other approaches.

The leading proponent (and the developer) of the behavioral approach in the context of regulation (on the firm, see, e.g., Cyert and March 1963) is Paul Joskow. He has applied it to model, among other things, the setting of the allowed rate of return by a regulatory commission (1972), the decision by regulated firms to apply to the regulatory commission for price changes (1973), and the dynamic interaction of regulatory agencies and regulated firms (1974).

Operating under a considerable degree of flexibility or discretion, "agencies seek to minimize conflict and criticism appearing as 'signals' from the economic and social environment in which they operate, subject to binding legal and procedural constraints imposed by the legislature and the courts. The agencies' organizational structure, regulatory instruments, and operating procedures are chosen so as to achieve this goal" (Joskow 1974:297). The "signals" come from actors like consumers, public interest groups, and politicians pursuing their interests. The agency in minimizing conflict achieves an equilibrium "which *satisfactorily* balances the conflicting pressures from the external environment"; it then exhibits "a well established organizational structure and regulatory procedures and instruments that are well defined and used repetitively and predictably" (Joskow 1974:297).

Parties in the environment can disturb this equilibrium, e.g., consumers and public interest groups may become active with rising prices, deteriorating service, or damage to the environment, and regulated firms may seek price rises or a lowering of service quality as their costs rise. In trying "to satisfy these conflicting interests in a way that minimizes formal legal proceedings that are time consuming, expensive and bring the regulators into public view" (Joskow 1974:323), the agency can enter an "innovation mode." Recent inflation and environmental activism have led agencies, for example, to develop new routines to handle them.

Agencies are normally said to play a fundamentally *passive* role; firms, not the agency, will usually initiate a rate of return review. The agency does not, as folklore might have it, continually monitor and enforce some set rate of return.

In Joskow's " 'organizational' view of regulatory agencies" (1974:297), the explanation seems to proceed almost on the organizational rather than the individual level, in that it is the "agency," not the individual commissioners, which seeks to minimize the conflict encountered from other organizations (consumer and public interest groups, regulated firms) and, occasionally, individuals in organizational roles (e.g., politicians). We have included Joskow's behavioral approach under the general heading of utility-maximizing decision-maker approaches because the parties involved are assumed to act rationally, selecting various behavioral rules of thumb or targets that are reasonable given the uncertainty and the costs of information. Behind the largely organizational-level discussion, one suspects that there lurk utility-maximizing individuals. But it is in essentials an organizational-level analysis.

George W. Hilton (1972a:48) has argued from an individualistic rational choice model that "a regulatory commission of members who serve for finite periods must be expected to engage in a great deal of 'minimal squawk' behavior." The commissioners must always be concerned with their subsequent employment and do not wish to antagonize future employers, i.e., the regulated industry. Thus Joskow's arguments could be linked to the individual level through this or a similar argument.

Joskow (1974) develops and tests a number of propositions regarding the agency-firm interaction, e.g., that "during periods of falling average cost we expect to observe virtually no regulatory rate of return reviews." Firms will not initiate them. Joskow generally finds support for his hypotheses from data on U.S. utility regulation. His

other studies, e.g., Joskow (1972, 1973), are also generally successful in empirically linking various behavioral rules of thumb or indicators to the firm's decision to apply for price changes (1973) and the
setting of the rate of return by the regulatory commission (1972).

Although Joskow says he takes an "organizational view," in reality his approach is more of a procedural/decisional view. Organizational variables, e.g., structure, communications flow, technology,
professionalization, individual and role attributes, which do not deal
directly with the nature of the decision, are ignored. But these may
be crucial to an understanding of why various rules of thumb are
adopted, why the agency seeks to minimize conflict, and many other
aspects of Joskow's models that are posited or assumed.

Thus, from a broader perspective, Joskow's models are largely
descriptive and predictive rather than truly explanatory. They explain
and predict behavior on the narrow basis of decisional attributes. Explanation, of course, may lie in the eye of the beholder, and Joskow
himself (1973) argues against a purely predictive model. His models
present major contributions in countering conventional wisdom (and
earlier and still-current models by others) regarding exactly how commissions and firms make decisions. But what explains the major contextual, determinative characteristics of the Joskow regulatory commission? What explains avoidance of conflict and commission
attitudes toward active versus passive regulation? Why does the
agency rely on industry information and how does this situation
arise? What explains the persistence of limited expertise in the
agency? We do not mean to commit the common critical excess of
carping about things that an author does not do where he did not intend to do them anyway; we mean only to point out that an adequate
theory of regulation probably requires much more.

Joskow's assumption that commissions will play a purely "passive" role can be questioned. Perhaps "reactive" would be a better
characterization, because in responding to actions by groups in the
agency's environment, the commission (within Joskow's model) can
be active indeed in devising new routines or procedures that will permit it to return to its "satisfactory" equilibrium. Furthermore, as we
shall argue in chapter 9, agencies have played very active roles in
their defense in deregulation controversies. Similarly, agencies, we
shall argue later in this chapter, can play active roles in regulatory
creation. Regulation explicitly provides an agency with environmental control capabilities, which can be exploited by the regulated

parties and others, and which can be used by the agency to protect itself. The models discussed earlier in which agencies or regulators
sought "survival" are consistent with this.

Thus, we propose that agencies, though most often reactive if they
are commissions not bureaus, should be viewed and understood as
central *actors,* not passive deciders. Recall that the regulator-as-
bureaucrat models, as discussed earlier in this chapter and in chapter
2, developed growth and antigrowth or maintenance rationales (as
well as a mechanism to permit growth in the commission without
reducing rigidity and without necessarily aggressive external expansion of mandate). Regulatory agencies, if bureaus, can be just like
other bureaus (as regulators can be like other bureaucrats) in seeking
expansion of their "territory" (see, e.g., Downs 1967) and acting on
their environment. They can seek diversification in mandate coverage, as investors diversify portfolios, to protect themselves against
environmental turbulence and consequent risk.

Joskow's models can possibly be made consistent with a number of
organizational models that link individual action with organizational
outcomes. We noted the potential complementarity with Hilton
(1972) above. But, because Joskow does not concern himself with
the individual-organizational action linkage, his model can probably
be made consistent with models of organizational action as the resultant of purposeful individual behaviors, where the organization action
itself may not be desired by anyone under ordinary circumstances.

"Institutional" decisions, because they could result in an apparently nondirected or inconsistent series of actions in which there is
no one guiding hand to lead the organization in action on its environment, can make the commission appear "passive" or at any rate
"reactive." Externally generated demands force the commission to
action, which requires it to both act and to present a rationale for its
action. Rules of thumb may be adopted as described by Joskow as the
agency's institutional decision is generated.

We might hypothesize that the greater the external pressure, the
more consistent and better rationalized (and the less randomly institutional) the commission's decision will be. After all, it may be subject
to challenge in the courts. The regulator-as-bureaucrat models tell us
that top officials may then be careful to devise defensible decisions.
There are, of course, extra costs involved in the preparation of extra-
careful decisions and in the potential imposition of particular positions on the institutionally fragmented agency decision and operating

procedures. Normally, the perfunctory, procedurally based rationales generated through the institutional decision should be sufficient to protect the agency and its members.

As far as the policy process is concerned, Joskow's models essentially describe the administration stage, link administration actions to effects, and illuminate the interaction between administration decisions and effects. Joskow's work fits neatly into the gaps left by other models we have described. Although his model is one of regulatory practice, not creation, and ignores access and policy decision on, and implementation of, basic regulation, he does attempt to describe how changes in regulatory practice are introduced as the result of agencies seeking to devise procedures to minimize conflict. Many other models assume in effect that administration takes care of itself; Joskow tells us how it does this, and how external, environmental effects and conditions provoke interaction with the agency.

Joskow's analysis of the regulatory process as a series of largely firm-initiated interactions between the agency and the regulated firms in effect raises the question of whether there is some overall conceptual structure that can be applied to understand the agency-firm relationship over time. Other environmental parties also enjoy a long-term relation with the agency.

John R. Baldwin (1975) comes close to specifying such a relation in his behavioral model of the regulatory agency: "A regulatory institution should be regarded as one type of agent adopted by the government to effect particular bargains" (Baldwin 1975:6). Logrolling—mutual concessions or trades to favor the particular objectives of each party in order to build overall support for an issue—is a bargaining process much described in legislatures. Because of the costs of information and participation, voters select agents to do such bargaining for them. Governments, too, may employ agents to act for them, and the self-interest of the agent—the regulatory agency—will lead it to insure its own survival by trying to insure the government's reelection by satisfying government supporters. Then two general circumstances contribute to the creation of such regulatory agents:

1) The government acts as arbitrator in disputes between parties with strongly opposing interests, such as consumers vs. business (or two forms in one industry, such as trucking vs. railroads). Because of high transactions costs and uncertainty, the groups cannot bargain by themselves to an optimal solution. But, more importantly, the welfare of the opposing parties depends on their legal rights. They

thus seek advantageous rights from the government, at least one party being unwilling to accept the solution that would be the result of bargaining by themselves. To avoid alienating the groups, government then establishes the regulatory body. That body then performs what is in effect logrolling with respect to the interests of the parties before it.

2) The government acts as arbitrator in costly conflicts among firms, such as that conflict represented by cutthroat competition. Backed by the coercion of the state, the government can reach a solution that insures that all firms benefit. In effect, the government applies a coercive solution to a collective action dilemma. This case is quite similar to the first one, and logrolling may be employed to resolve the problem. If consumers do not realize that the regulation has in effect created a cartel, the regulatory body will engage mainly in bestowing privileges like franchises or monopoly rights. If consumers are aware of the cartel, the regulatory body will have to give benefits to consumers as well.

Participants accept the regulation not only for the net benefits they gain, but also because both sides can substitute a unanimity rule— gain for both—for majority rule or a payoff to just one side. And to permit payoffs to both, the legislation establishing the regulation will be vaguely worded.

The role of independence in the position of the regulatory agency is then explained not in terms of its contribution to efficient administrative decision-making, but because it serves the self-interest of the government. Those parties actually paying the costs of the benefits going to the participants in the regulatory process will be less likely to discover this; the regulation will have the image of a series of technical decisions made in the public interest. If the incidence of the costs is discovered, independence will permit the government to disassociate itself from the policy. In addition, independence can mean that parties that are dissatisfied with the regulation will not retaliate by seeking defeat of the government in order to reverse the regulatory policy.

Baldwin goes on to discuss the behavior of the regulatory agency. He reasons that the agency will seek survival, with policies determined largely by the costs to interested groups of information on particular policies, and the costs to the agency of employing alternate forms of side-payments (e.g., subsidies, entry barriers) to the contending parties before it in order to reach a result acceptable to all.

The approach is then applied to the case of the Canadian air transport industry.

Like Joskow, Baldwin treats the regulatory situation essentially on the organizational rather than individual level. It is not immediately apparent how individual preferences are transformed, for example, into an agency self-interest goal of survival. Baldwin does, however, consider regulatory origin explicitly, as well as regulatory behavior. He clearly begins to suggest some elements of an overall conceptual structure that can characterize agency–environmental relationships; his explicit use of agent–principal references is suggestive of other work in this area (e.g., Mitnick 1974; Goldberg 1976). He, in effect, identifies aspects of the central role of regulation in resolving collective action dilemmas, i.e., in resolving problems of groups in insuring individual behaviors that will achieve group outcomes beneficial to the members. His approach allows satisfaction of more than one narrow interest; it is, for example, no simple industry protection theory. Moreover, Baldwin's model covers the access, decision, administration, and effects stages, though not all aspects of these stages are considered. The methods by which the regulatory agency and its programs are implemented, however, remain unclear.

Goldberg (1976; see also 1973, 1974) presents a model of regulation in which the regulator is explicitly conceptualized as an agent administering a long-term contract in the interests of the community at large. He contrasts this long-term contract model with the usual discrete transactions approach used in economics. Formation of the contract itself must consider such factors as the producer's right to serve and the consumer's right to be served, and the contract should permit the agent flexibility over time in administering the contract, e.g., through a flexible pricing mechanism under the control of the agent. The agent must in administering the contract choose some mix of actions that will serve the public; this mix can involve trade-offs among different objectives. Typically, the agent in administering and policing a regulatory contract will experience the ordinary problems encountered by agents, e.g., determining and acting upon principals' preferences. In Goldberg's approach, the justification for regulation lies not in such conditions as a natural monopoly (see chapter 5), but in the need to administer a long-term contractual relationship in the collective interests of societal groups.

Thus, broadly speaking, we can include Goldberg's approach among the "behavioral" models, since it focuses on the relations and activities of regulators, e.g., the "contractual" relation with parties in the public and the activities required in administering the contract, while assuming the parties themselves are rational utility-maximizers. In terms of the policy process, Goldberg's model has something to tell us about access, decision, implementation, administration, and effects, though in its present level of development only a few aspects of each stage are addressed. The model discusses, in effect, some reasons for regulatory creation, decision on the regulatory contract, the agent's problem in implementing and administering the contract under uncertainty, and the relation of the agent's behavior to impacts.

Like Baldwin and Goldberg, Mitnick (1973b, 1974, 1975b, 1976) has applied agency concepts—i.e., concepts relating to relationships between agents and principals—to the study of regulation. Mitnick's efforts, however, have developed out of work on a theory of agency as an approach to a wide class of social relationships, rather than as a convenient and productive framework to apply to regulation alone.[8]

Mitnick (1974) distinguishes two broad classes of agency relationships, based on formalization of the agency role: "formal occupational" and "consistent structural agency." Many of the helping professions, such as medicine or social work, have formalized agency roles, often reflected in canons of ethics specifying appropriate and inappropriate agency behaviors. In consistent structural agency, unlike formal occupational agency, the agent's social role does not formally involve agency. Analytically, however, he or she acts relatively consistently as agent for a given party. This typically occurs because of the stability of the extant incentive system; acting for the party in question may increase return to agent self-goals.

---

[8] A theory of agency as an approach to a broad variety of social relationships was first proposed, independently, by Stephen Ross (1973, 1974) and by Mitnick (1973b, 1974). Use of agency concepts has not, however, been foreign to the social science literature; agency has, of course, existed for many years as a distinct area in the law. In social science, for example, agency concepts have been used in social psychological studies of authority (e.g., Milgram 1974), political economic studies of democracy (Downs 1957), political philosophical studies of obligation and representation (e.g., Tussman 1960; Pitkin 1967), and political behavioral studies of interest groups (e.g., Curry and Wade 1968), corruption in government (e.g., Banfield 1975), and rational behavior in coalitions (Riker 1962). Studies in economics and finance have applied agency concepts in such areas as welfare economics (e.g., Arrow 1970), internal firm organization (Mirrlees 1976; Stiglitz 1975), theory of the firm (Jensen and Meckling 1976), and contractual relationships (e.g., Harris and Raviv 1978). Agency concepts are also being applied in accounting, where the nature of auditing and accountant-client relationships make it particularly appropriate (e.g., Evans 1978; Magee 1978; Ronen 1979). Some of this work has overlapped in content; cf., for example, Jensen and Meckling (1976); Ronen (1979) with Mitnick (1973b, 1974, 1975b). This is only a short list of examples; work using agency concepts has been expanding rapidly.

Formal systemic, organizational, and other social divisions may bear no resemblance to the pattern of structural agency. Because of this, an observer focusing on formal structural divisions may see what appears to be paradoxical behavior. Regulatory commissions, for example, which are supposed to regulate certain industries in the public interest, are observed to regulate against the public interest. In order to understand such behavior, one must examine how the incentive systems producing these agency relationships arise and operate.

Mitnick's general agency framework (1973b, 1974, 1975a, 1975b, 1976) includes a typology of agency relationships generated from such dimensions as the level of consent between agent and principal regarding the agent's acts (e.g., whether or not a contract exists, a contract which may be formal or informal), the source of specification of the agent's acts (agent or principal), and the level of discretion possessed by the agent. Various norms, such as the fiduciary norm, can influence the agent's behavior. The relationships of agency observed under regulation are taken as frequently contractual in character, although the contracts themselves may be informal or implicit.

In order to organize the analysis of the incentive systems producing the agency relationships under regulation, the organization and its environment is divided into three groups, each with its set of goals. These groups represent three very general roles: that of client, that of manager, and that of "guardian" with respect to the central organization (in this case, the regulatory agency). The client is the consumer or beneficiary of the formal organization task, product, or output. The manager directs the organizational production of its task, product or output. The guardian meters and/or polices the organization's behavior with respect to the formal organization goals (which can therefore generally be viewed as the goals of the guardian).[9] For example, in a firm these roles correspond to the consumers and suppliers, managers, and stockholders; in a regulatory commission they correspond to the regulated industry and general public and "public interest" groups, the commissioners, and the review mechanisms of legislature and courts.

Considerations of agency relations between client, manager and guardian can generate a theory and therefore an explanation of orga-

[9] The "principal's problem" (see Ross 1973) may in this context often be the problem of how to make the manager's self-goal consonant with the guardian's, where the principal is the guardian. See, e.g., Barrett (1970); Manne (1965). Cf. Henry Daniell as Lord Wolfingham to Claude Rains as Don Alvarez in *The Sea Hawk*, "Don Alvarez, we serve others best when at the same time we serve ourselves."

nizational behavior.[10] A simplified model of this type at the organization level may not be able to explain many behaviors of interest. It is only useful, of course, where we could in fact identify three groups with these roles. Their goals and the structure of their interactions must of course be tractable to the agency approach. These conditions are not, however, uncommonly met; the producer-manager, receiver/supplier, policeman-regulator trilogy is perhaps a logical and "natural" one where there is a task performed by one party, with an output received by another, and where some quality of performance in that task is of concern to a third party.[11]

The client, manager, guardian model can be thought of as adjoining or extending the Barnard "economy of incentives" approach to intraorganizational behavior (Barnard 1938; see also March and Simon 1958; Clark and Wilson 1961). In the Barnard model, a single executive manipulates his fixed supply of incentive resources toward some organizational end, perhaps, as Clark and Wilson (1961) maintain, organizational survival. The incentive-receivers in this case are the organization's employees. The client, manager, guardian model takes a step back in focus. The manager may still be the executive feeding incentives to his now invisible employees, but the organization and its incentive system are now seen as embedded in a larger environment. The manager-executive is himself the recipient of incentives of various kinds from two sources in particular, clients and guardians.

This interorganizational incentive system may then affect both intra- and interorganizational behavior, as it organizes agency relations of various types. The acts of the manager if he is an agent may include, for example, manipulating the internal incentive system to meet certain goals of his principal, who may be, say, guardian stockholders desirous of profitable return on their investment. The manager may under other conditions be the principal in an agency relation with either the clients or guardians. Stockholders may be "used," for example, to ratify management's actions. Clients may be induced by the manager as principal to purchase more of the organization's product, permitting expansion in organization size and increased status and salary to the manager.

---

[10] Evan's organization-set model can be re-cast in this form, possibly with some gains. See Evan (1966, 1972). Litwak's discussion of interorganizational relations is applicable to the client, manager, guardian model in the context of agency theory (Litwak with Rothman 1970).

[11] Cf. "policing" or "metering" models of the firm. See, e.g., Alchian and Demsetz (1972).

The use of the client, manager, guardian model is subject to criticisms similar to those of the Barnard approach when considered as an adjunct to that approach (see Georgiou 1973; Mitnick 1974). Many important employee incentives do not flow through the manager-executive, for example; incentives coming from organizational clients and guardians may bypass the manager, as when the manager's salesman develops relations of friendship and trust with a customer. Incentives to employees may even come from sources outside the client, manager, guardian system, e.g., from professions or other organizations to which the employee belongs or from fellow employees. A more general organization theory employing goals, norms, incentive dimensions and types, and relations may offer better explanation of a wider range of organizational phenomena (Mitnick 1974; Mitnick, Backoff, and Rainey 1977; Backoff and Mitnick 1978).

The three-fold categorization may also be used within organizations. Thus a segment of a hierarchy may be broken down into managers of the task at that level, clients of its output, and guardians of its performance (who may be other managers). The point again is that the client, manager, guardian model is an analytical tool that does not respect formal boundaries and, given its limitations, may be used with agency theory in a variety of situations, and at a variety of levels.

Note that the guardian role can include regulatory interference. Thus the model could be adapted to sort behaviors in ordinary social and economic regulation of the firm. The guardian regulatory agency may regulate managerial compliance to organizational goals set by that guardian agency (e.g., safety, affirmative action). The manager may face dual guardians with conflicting goals—e.g., the stockholders and the regulators—and be also constrained, of course, to deal with (and/or manipulate) the demands of clients (e.g., customers, suppliers).

In the context of the independent regulatory commission, the client, manager, guardian model may be applied to identify three groups of goals: 1) Organizational goals of the commissions, including a) nonreversal of its actions by the legislature and b) preservation of the regulated interest (see Noll 1971a). These are goals of the commission guardians, the legislature and the courts. 2) Goals of the commissioners, including a) status, b) ease of working conditions, and c) expectations of future rewards such as jobs after leaving the commission. These (admittedly self-interest goals) are the manager goals. 3) Goals of clients, including *a*) those of the regulated industry, i.e., favorable regulation, and *b*) those of public interest, consumer, or other groups.

In the section on the regulator-as-bureaucrat, we have already presented the logic of regulatory behavior that follows under these assumptions and under given institutional constraints, and we shall not repeat it here. The client, manager, guardian division provides a way to organize the discussion of the regulator incentive system. As we saw earlier, the rational choice arguments tend to predict the creation of a relation of agency between the commission as agent and the regulated industry as principal. This relation is governed by the implicit and explicit provisions of a regulatory "contract."

Mitnick (1974, 1975b) has also applied agency concepts to discuss the problem of insuring regulator compliance to some specified public interest criteria.[12] His approach links agency concepts with the "managerial discretion" model of the firm (Williamson 1964).[13] Under conditions of "organizational slack" (Cyert and March 1963), the managers of an organization may be viewed as possessing some fixed quantity of discretionary resources to dispose of. In the firm, for example, revenue that is discretionary may be devoted to increments of profit to the "guardian" stockholders or to increased emoluments or staff that benefit the managers.

Similarly, the discretionary resources of the regulatory agency may be assumed to go either toward extra satisfaction of some "public interest" criteria[14] through their indicators, e.g., careful examination of rate applications, or toward increasing the commissioner's status, easing his workload, and insuring the likelihood for him of lucrative future employment. These commissioner rewards may be offered largely by the regulated industry, and may be attained by commission activities that favor the industry. The commissioner's preferences reflect a trade-off between such public interest, and self-interest, goals. The commissioner's choices of allocations of his discretionary

---

[12] Portions of the following discussion are drawn from Mitnick (1974, 1975b).

[13] Cf. the similarities of the discussion below to the model later advanced by Jensen and Meckling (1976).

[14] These may be viewed as a set of criteria, aggregated by some calculus into a single dimension. This is obviously difficult to do, if only because of problems of measurement and of operationalization, not to speak of the need for basic value or welfare trade-offs. Since decisions are nevertheless made all the time according to such criteria, we shall assume that, at least in principle, such a public interest dimension can be constructed.

resources to his own ends, and to public interest ends, are restricted by the technology of regulating and the constraints of the institutional environment. Since under these conditions the commissioner will not then ordinarily act purely for public interest criteria, questions of degree of deviation, and of policing compliance, arise. The regulators are thus seen as agents to be policed to adherence to the "public interest" goals of some principal "public."

The fixed supply of discretionary resources may include such factors as the commissioner's supply of incentive rewards to distribute within his agency to produce behavior toward one of these ends, and the commissioner's disposition of that portion of his own time not already appropriated by certain commission activities. Public interest activist groups (among other possible sources of demands on the agency), seeking to police the agency to behavior reflecting the group's conception of "public interest" ends, may successfully divert part of the discretionary overhead into extensive litigation.

But such policing is not costless; like other agency relationships in which the agent at least partially prefers divergent behavior (or lacks the knowledge or skills to act perfectly for the principal), there are costs in insuring agent behavior that satisfies the principal's preferences. Principals must pay *specification costs* to identify acts of the agent that would satisfy the principal's preferences, and *policing costs* in monitoring and enforcing compliance.[15] Agents, too, may pay specification costs in ascertaining and acting for the principal's preferences. Herein can lie the attractiveness to principals of norms like the fiduciary norm and the rationale for the frequent existence of agent training mechanisms that inculcate such norms (e.g., foreign service schools; law schools): such norms permit principals to economize on both specification and policing costs.

Public interest groups as prospective principals face both specification and policing costs: in gaining access to the regulatory process; identifying regulatory actions that would satisfy their preferences; and conveying this information to the regulatory agents (specification costs); and in detecting and policing agency behavior that they believe is deviant (policing costs). Litigation and other activities by public interest groups may have the effect of diverting, removing, or using up some of the regulatory agency resources (e.g., regulator

---

[15] For extended discussions of specification and policing costs and behaviors, see Mitnick (1974). Cf. Jensen and Meckling's (1976) reference to "agency costs."

time) that might otherwise go into the regulator's discretionary over-head.

Thus it is possible that, due to the institutional constraints on how the regulator may distribute his or her net discretionary resources, withdrawal of resources to be devoted to specification and policing activities may by itself lead to *less* return to public interest ends. This occurs because the removal of discretionary resources takes away not only the portion that would go to regulator self-interest ends, but also the portion that the regulator would devote to public interest ends. Remember, we assumed that the regulator has preferences both for self- and for public-interest ends.

With a policing mechanism in operation, it is possible (but not at all assured) that the public interest may realize a net gain. Over time, the regulator may come to prefer public interest ends more highly or may discover, for example, that greater adherence to public ends can be instrumental to future jobs. A new incentive system encouraging more public interest-related behavior could even attract to the regulatory agency more regulators who strongly prefer such behavior.[16]

Because degradation in the actual, net return to the public interest can occur as a result of group activities, a question is in order about the rationality of public interest groups that challenge the commissions. The rational principal attempts policing only if he expects a net return, discounted for the intervening adjustment time when his return is below the original level. We suggest that because of bounded rationality and information costs, not to speak of fundamental problems in valuation, the return to the given public interest criteria may be more difficult to measure and predict than certain obvious indicators wrongly assumed to be correlated with return to that interest (cf. Niskanen's comments, Migue and Belanger 1974:43; Alchian and Demsetz 1972). And these indicators are then relied on in actions that public interest groups consider very rational indeed.

A major indicator is the degree of apparent commissioner fidelity, i.e., how much of the discretionary agency resources he diverts to his self-goals, perhaps through the instrumental means of appearing in his conduct to favor the regulated industry. Note that the real measure of agent fidelity is the difference between what he actually appropriates for his self-goals and the level of discretionary return to agent

---

[16] For a model of the policing process describing these stages, and a discussion, see Mitnick (1974, 1975b).

self-goals at which discretionary return to the principal is maximized. Since the latter may be unknown, the focus inevitably shifts to simply reducing discretionary return to the agent. If by some chance the organization is already operated to give maximum discretionary return to the principal, then reduction in agent return will probably result in a reduction in principal return as well. Public interest groups that object to this "necessary" level of discretionary agent return, e.g., comfortable offices, will thus be acting rather directly against their interest. If, given the information that this is so, such groups persist in such behavior, we would assume either that they are irrational, which is not likely, though possible, or that what they really prefer is the appearance of agent fidelity and not the maximization of return to the public interest.

In addition, the legal and other weapons that such groups may use can frequently be directed only against evidence of agency manager infidelity, rather than to insure some given return to the public interest. For example, a group may use litigation to force an agency to prepare an environmental impact statement, or to force an agency that prepared only a *pro forma* statement to put some content into it. But the group generally cannot litigate to determine that content, i.e., to insure the level of return to the interest they represent that they prefer! Thus even if a group focuses on return to the public interest rather than on fidelity it may only be able to act on commissioner infidelity, hoping the outcome will not be perverse.

At the heart of the argument is the observation that agent fidelity in the sense used here does not necessarily correlate with level of principal return. By focusing on apparently improper behavior by the commissioners, such as reliance on the industry for helpful advice, "ex parte" contacts with industry that may involve exchange of inside information, field visits and spending time with industry representatives rather than with commission staff or "impartial" experts, allocating discretionary resources within the agency to engineering sections with close ties to the industry rather than, say, environmental evaluation sections, and so on, the public interest groups may succeed only in securing an honest agency that doesn't regulate, and, ultimately, a righteous government that cannot govern.

Although Mitnick's other work on the theory of agency permits coverage of all stages in the policy process (as does Goldberg's), the arguments summarized above relate mostly to the administration and effects stages. The nature of the incentive relation in agent-principal relations is not conceptualized clearly here (but see chapter 6), and, although contracts play a major role in the agency formulation (see Mitnick 1974), the implications of the regulatory contract are not developed as they are in Goldberg's and Williamson's work. The models perhaps contain insufficient organizational detail and variation, and tend to rely on relatively simple rational choice arguments like those advanced by Noll and others. The power of an approach based on the theory of agency (and related incentive system concerns) appears, however, to be considerable. We shall develop it further later in this chapter and in chapter 6.

Before concluding this review of theories of regulation, we wish to note the comprehensive conceptual and descriptive model of regulation offered by Warren Samuels (1973). He presents the regulatory system as one of "power" relationships, in contrast to "legal" and "economic" "paradigms." In an integrating collection of propositions and observations about regulatory behavior, Samuels discusses the system as a total institution comprising commissions; utilities; executive, legislative and judicial governmental components; interest groups; and so on. Parties exercise power through available choice, and the institution structures this power and is the object of control by parties who seek their own ends. Thus regulation is an instrument sought by parties to serve their own interests. Usually regulation ends up in the control of the regulatees.

Samuels employs a number of features of several of the models discussed earlier, including those of the regulator as bureaucrat, but casts his model in a much broader setting and adds many distinctions of his own. We shall not recapitulate Samuels's complex analysis, but wish to suggest that adequate future models of regulation will probably have to be integrating in character. Whether or not they focus on relations of power, as Samuels's model does, future formulations will need to be comprehensive and deal with the regulatory system or "institution." Models that do not must be clearly indicated as of a specialized character, limited in scope, and perhaps for specialized application.

2.3 CONCLUSION

In this review we have indeed seen how "theories of regulation" have usually been limited in scope though their authors present them as general in character. In figure 3.1 we have indicated, roughly, those parts of the policy process emphasized by some of the major

Figure 3.1. Theories of Regulation and the Policy-Making Process

Stages in Process Covered by Theory

Theorist	Access	Decision	Implementation	Administration	Effects
2.1 Public interest theories					
Structural/legal/rights protection and group					
Cushman (1941); Blachly and Oatman (1940); Bernstein (1955); Fainsod (1940); Fainsod and Gordon (1941); Leiserson (1942); Herring (1936a)	X	X		X	
Functional					
Posner (1971)		X	(X)	X	X
Comanor and Mitchell (1972)		(X)	(X)	X	X
2.2 Private interest theories					
2.2.1 Group					
Bentley (1908); Truman (1951)	X	X			X
2.2.2 Economic					
Stigler (1971); Posner (1974)	X	X			
Jordan (1972)	(X)	X			X
2.2.3 Utility-maximizing					
Focal decision maker					
(1) Regulator as politician					
Peltzman (1976)	(X)	X			
Weingast (1978)	(X)	X		X	
Niskanen (1975)		X		X	
Russell and Shelton (1974)				X	
(2) Regulator as bureaucrat					
Noll (1971); Eckert (1973); Mitnick and Weiss (1974); DeAlessi (1974, 1975)				X	X
Behavioral					
Joskow (1972, 1973, 1974)				X	X
Baldwin (1975)	X	X		X	X
Goldberg (1976)	X	X	X	X	X
Mitnick (1973b, 1974, 1975b, 1976)				X	X

Columns marked summarize treatment of works described in that category; each work in a category may not cover all marked columns. Parentheses indicate lesser treatment of stage. Major theory categories are keyed to the section numbers that appear in the text.

regulatory theorists. Our discussion has sought in some places to indicate some obvious areas of complementarity among the approaches. Note that, of the various parts of the policy process, theorists have apparently largely ignored implementation. And, although various scholars consider aspects of access, recall that their analyses are usually static and do not consider the strategies and processes of agenda-building during access.

In the next sections of this chapter, we shall suggest an integrating approach to a theory of regulation and develop further a specialized model that we feel has been neglected in earlier theories of regulatory origin—the bureaucratic theory of regulation. Our review has been structured to suggest the integrating framework from its identification of deficiencies in existing models: A theory of regulation may be constructed around the various stages in the policy process. Explanations within that framework may be generated through application of an incentive systems (and agency relationship) approach. Though all stages of the policy process are considered, the model centers on the regulatory organization and the incentive system faced by organizational members. We shall not, however, actually present an integrated theory of regulation applicable throughout the policy process.

3.0   Four Interest "Theories" of Regulatory Origin; the Bureaucratic/Organizational Approach

3.1   THE POLICY-MAKING PROCESS AND THE INCENTIVE SYSTEMS APPROACH

An adequate theory of regulation should encompass all stages in the policy process: access, decision, implementation, administration, and effects. An adequate theory of regulatory origin should probably carry us into the administration stage. Ideally, we should be able to explain any behaviors of interest throughout the process. For many purposes, however, specialized theories which seek to explain only certain behaviors in certain stages may be sufficient.

However admirable the goal of a comprehensive theory of regulation, we shall not develop one here. Such a theory, in full development, would undoubtedly be complex. We do suggest that the policy-making process can act as a framework to order development of the components of such a theory. As we saw earlier in this chapter, many existing approaches appear complementary or possibly can be made so. Rational choice or "economic" models of legislators and of bureaucrats, for example, seem in some areas to adjoin one another.

Neither shall we develop what could be considered a fully adequate theory of regulatory origin; we shall not attempt to address all of the issues raised in our review of the literature. We shall, however, suggest a modeling approach that is consistent with at least some of the partial theories we have examined. This approach has the potential, we believe, of developing an adequate origin theory. And we shall argue that an especially useful approach to understanding regulatory behavior, including origin, would focus on the regulatory unit itself, as organization.

We propose that explanations for behavior in the policy-making process in regulation may be developed from, and integrated through use of, an incentive systems approach.[17] In figure 3.2 we depict a simple incentive relation at the individual level. Incentives are assumed (see chapter 6) to define a relationship between an incentive sender and an incentive receiver in which transfer of an incentive reward (or punishment, i.e., negative reward) is made contingent on some behavior of the incentive receiver. The sender may attempt to establish an *agency* relationship with the receiver. Of course, we may have multiple senders, receivers, and transferred rewards (not depicted). We assume that senders and receivers have given but alterable preferences and act rationally given extant conditions of risk and uncertainty. Use of an incentive systems model can be viewed as a natural or logical consequence of modeling regulatory relations as instances of the general agent-principal relationship. Here the principal is the incentive sender and the agent, the incentive receiver.

In figure 3.2 (see Mitnick, Backoff, and Rainey 1977 for an elaborated approach and explanation), the sender may transmit an "incentive message" regarding specified behaviors and contingent rewards to the receiver within the structure of the sender-receiver relation. That relation may or may not be formalized; it may be characterized by a contract as in an employment relation. The receiver will process the message and act rationally upon it. The sender will then receive information on the receiver's action and release the reward to him. The incentive transaction may not always occur in this basic way, of

[17] On the incentive systems approach, see, e.g., Barnard (1938); March and Simon (1958); Clark and Wilson (1961); J. Q. Wilson (1973); Mitnick (1974); Mitnick, Backoff and Rainey (1977); and Backoff and Mitnick (1978). On bureaucrats' incentives, see, e.g., Downs (1967); Loevinger (1968); Kaufman (1971, 1977); Eckert (1973).

Figure 3.2. A Simple Incentive Relation at the Individual Level

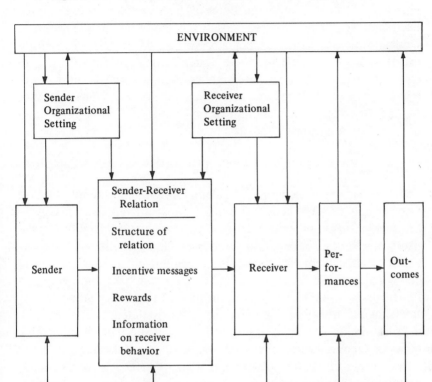

course; the transfers may be simultaneous, for example, and the transaction may not always be completed. The transaction will be affected by organizational variables in the sender's and in the receiver's organizational setting (e.g., organization structure, technology and climate, communications patterns, roles, norms, and so on) and by factors in the wider environment (e.g., aspects of cultural, political, economic, and social conditions).

Rational choice models like those employed in the regulator-as-bureaucrat models can be cast in this form. The objective would be to analyze systematically the incentive systems of parties whose behavior is of interest at the relevant stage of the policy process. Thus we would seek to systematically model the incentive relationships between legislators and constituents, regulated parties, other interest groups, and the regulatory body. The explanation would be constructed through consideration of the preferences of the involved parties, the rewards transferred and contingent behaviors, intervening and conditional institutional or organizational variables, and so on.

In figure 3.3, for illustration, we depict a simplified and greatly abbreviated model of the regulator's incentive relation with the regulated industry. This is based loosely on the regulator-as-bureaucrat models discussed earlier. A better model would include other parties active in the regulator's incentive system, e.g., other regulators, interest groups, legislators on oversight committees, and so on. Later in this chapter we shall present an explicit incentive systems theory of the industry–regulator relation; a theory explaining, in part, the phenomenon of regulatory "capture."

3.2 FOUR SIMPLE INTEREST THEORIES OF REGULATORY ORIGIN

In the context of economic regulatory origin, four simple interest theories may be identified. These may represent the objectives of parties seeking the regulation, and are derived from considerations of the likely possibilities of origin, given our previous discussion. We identify the four "theories" to provide a framework for our arguments below regarding the centrality of the bureaucratic behavior theory and for illustrative application later to the case of regulatory origin for the Interstate Commerce Commission. As discussed, adequate full theories might be constructed from consideration of the incentive relations among these four parties and other relevant actors.

Any given case of regulation might be explained by one of these core interest theories alone or by a mixture or superposition of multiple theories. There may be a coincidence of interests among groups seeking regulation. The resultant regulation may only occur because of such coincidence. But conditions of such cases must be carefully specified to avoid undermining the explanatory potential of the core theories.

In general, we may classify theories of regulatory origin according to whether private or "public" interests are served:

1. *Private interest theories*
   a. *Consumer protection theory:* The goal relates to protection of the consumers of the product or activity. Consumers and their agents constitute the parties seeking regulation.
   b. *Industry protection theory:* The goal relates to protection of the producer of the product or activity. The industry and agents for it constitute the parties seeking regulation.
   c. *Bureaucratic behavior theory:* The goals are those of bureaucrats who perform (and seek) the regulation. We may divide this theory into: (1) *Maintenance theory.* Bureaucrats' goals are best served through de-

Figure 3.3. A Simplified, Abbreviated Model of the Regulator's Incentive Relation with the Regulated Industry

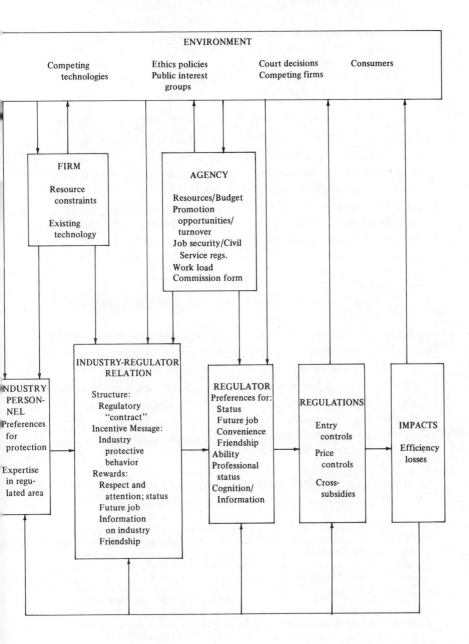

fensive maintenance or status quo survival of the bureaucracy. (2) *Expansion theory.* Bureaucrats' goals are best served through aggressive expansion of the bureaucracy and its mandate.

2. *Public interest theories: social goals theory:* The goals formally relate to concerns affecting or balancing the interests of the community or public at large. The goals can include, for example, national social goals like development of certain regions or aid to certain social groups. The conception of the "public interest" here may vary as described earlier in this chapter (see also chapter 4).

In figure 3.4, we list some typical evidence for each of the origin "theories." These are discussed in works dealing with these approaches (see, e.g., Jordan 1972; see also J. Q. Wilson 1974) or are hypothesized by the author. They are individually not determinant, and some overlap with another theory. Furthermore, these factors generally constitute either aspects of the achieved regulation or aspects of the observed regulatory procedure and are therefore highly suspect. Regulation, as we observed, may not be directly sought; it may be a resultant of individually (not collectively) rational behaviors.

3.3 THE CENTRAL ROLE OF THE REGULATORY AGENCY AS ORGANIZATION

It will be our contention that, although adequate theory must attend to all relevant parties and stages in the policy-making process for origin, the regulatory unit can play a central role in the analysis. As organizations, regulatory agencies interact with their environments and can, as regulatory bodies, have major influence on those environments. This can provide a rationale for the importance of the agency.

3.3.1 Public versus Private Organizations and Environmental Control

Public organizations in general may often be relatively better able to control their environment than private organizations.[18] Such con-

---

[18] Private organizations with some of the characteristics of many public organizations, e.g., large size, may also possess this ability. For a review of public/private differences, see Rainey, Backoff, and Levine (1976). On public-private differences in termination, see Behn (1978). Jeffrey Pfeffer has noted that regulation can be a means to manage the environment; it is "an outcome of the competition between organizations or interest groups to use the power of the state for their own economic advantage," i.e., to manage the environment in their interest. See Jeffrey Pfeffer (1974:475; see also Pfeffer and Salancik 1978; Krasnow and Longley 1978; Rickson 1977; Williamson 1971; Kaufman 1971). We shall modify and extend this argument, discussing the use of regulation to resolve collective action dilemmas, and specifying a more active role for the governmental unit. On organizational environments in general, see, e.g., Aldrich and Pfeffer (1976); Litwak with Rothman (1970); Starbuck (1976).

Figure 3.4. Typical Evidence for Origin Theories

Consumer Protection

- product or service quality controls
    - e.g., basic performance
- maximum price restriction
- marginal cost pricing
- nondiscriminatory pricing
- entry by efficient firms favored
- low industry profits
- broad service requirements
- guarantee/accountability requirements

Industry Protection

- entry restrictions
- price control/minimum rates
- price discrimination encouraged
- high industry profits
- exclusive service restrictions
    - product
    - geographical area
- product quality controls
    - e.g., high reliability, frills
- fixed technology/production process protection
- extreme judicialization/proceduralism
- case backlog

Bureaucratic Behavior

- increasing bureau size associated with increased mandate
- increasing diversification in agency mandate
- increasing funding
- decreased complexity of regulations in fixed size agencies or top official corps
    - e.g., exclusive service
        single price
- increased complexity of regulations in variable size agencies or top official corps
- acquisition of functions of other agencies
- increased professionalization, specialization
- greater use of "institutional decision"
- extreme judicialization/proceduralism

Public Interest/Social Goals

- geographic/social group trade-off in benefits as part of national policy
    - e.g., cross-subsidization
        value of service pricing
- apparently uneconomical service to certain groups or areas
- departures from marginal cost pricing that balance incomes from given products or services
- collective action coercion for collective benefits, where no single group is clear beneficiary

trol means that the organization may be able to determine behavior among entities in its environment that promotes achievement of individual member or organizational goals, including survival of the organization. The most widely noted aspect of this is probably the potential of coercion that backs governmental actions. The coercion itself need be applied only rarely; belief in the ability to mobilize such coercion is sufficient. In addition, the consumption of goods and/or services supplied through government is consequently frequently structured to be relatively unavoidable. The nature of the goods and/or services often supplied, i.e., "public goods," sometimes contributes intrinsically to this jointness of consumption. Thus, governmental actions may not only be deliberately coercive in individual cases, but widely and generally unavoidable. The availability of coercion may even in many (and possibly most) cases be secondary; persons are taught from an early age that governmental rules and institutions and actions flowing from them are to be to some extent heeded as "right" or "proper," i.e., legitimate. Merely symbolic actions by governmental organizations may then lead to more substantive activity in their environments. The sheer size of many governmental organizations may stabilize their environments by creating relations of power-dependency with smaller organizations that associate with them. These and the other arguments in this area are fairly standard ones, though the focus is usually on public-private differences rather than on aspects that permit one type of organization a relatively greater ability to control its environment.

Empirical support for these arguments is not usually offered in the literature, as is evident from the recent review by Rainey et al. (1976). Counterarguments can thus be made, which chiefly focus on the organization's ability to implement programs, i.e., to achieve formal programmatic or organizational goals. Legislative prescriptions may inhibit response by governmental organizations to environmental contingencies; support through allocation rather than the sale of goods or services may require the need to cultivate "constituencies" and build external interest group coalitions, leading to actions responsive to those constituencies (cf. Holden 1966; Rourke 1976:42–80); the "publicness" of actions and mechanisms for facilitating public participation can permit, and even promote, effective opposition to proposed actions from adversely affected groups.

For these reasons, it may be argued that many governmental organizations (including regulatory ones) may manage their environments most effectively in the areas of insuring survival and persistence of the organization, and realization of the goals of organizational members through it, rather than in achieving given programmatic or formal organizational goals (cf. Baldwin 1975). We shall see in chapter 9 how the instrumentality of organizational survival to achievement of individual goals may play a role in the strategies adopted by agency personnel during decline or in periods of threat of decline.

3.3.2   Regulatory Organizations and Environmental Control

Consider now regulatory organizations. Regulation explicitly carries the grant of the ability to restrict choice in the regulatory organization's environment. Like other public organizations, the regulatory agency over time adapts, is forced to adapt, or forces others to adapt to it. Each of these occurs, but regulatory organizations, more so than many other organizations, and many other government agencies, can control their environments. For example, in the area of economic regulation:

1. Regulatory agencies often have the ability to structure their environment, including the number and relationships of the units subject to regulation. Thus entry restrictions, merger controls, marketing restrictions, and service requirements may structure a regulated market.

2. Regulatory agencies possess considerable reward power, i.e., can supply various tangible and intangible, and positive and negative, rewards or incentives. The agency, for example, may be a source of legitimation for actions of the industry, permitting or encouraging its operation through legitimation of its societal role; a source of expertise or a depository of information as well as a supplier of other services such that the agency may become a service bureau on which the industry is dependent; a source of psychic reward to industry members that affirms to industry members that what the industry is doing is good and proper; and, of course, a source of regulations that may have immense impact on the financial health of the industry.

3. Regulatory agencies may guarantee the stability and maintenance of exchange relationships, thereby absorbing uncertainty in the environments of regulated organizations (as well as, probably, in that of the agency itself). Insofar as regulated industries value such stability, it can be viewed as a component of the regulatory agency's reward power, and thus be among the incentives an agency can offer.

3.3.3   Regulation and the Collective Action Dilemma

One reason that has been offered for the origin of regulation has been, in effect, that firms failed in controlling their environments. This explanation posits the presence of a "collective action dilemma" (see, e.g., Olson 1965; Olson and Zeckhauser 1966; Coleman 1966; Hardin 1975). In such a dilemma, individual actions which, in the given means, are necessary for all members of the group to benefit do not occur. Ways to guarantee such action must be devised, or other means developed, to supply the benefits. Typically, individual self-interest may lead some members of the collectivity to avoid contributing to, or participating in, the collective action. This may, for example, allow them to be "free riders" on the group benefits obtained by others, or permit them to exploit in other ways any collective action agreement applying to behavior in the group.

Thus, firms in a market that is not perfectly competitive may gain short-run competitive advantage from, say, price cuts. This forces competitors to do the same, leaving all worse off than previously. Collective agreements reached to forestall such price wars may be unstable because of the short-run advantage to be gained from breaching them, and may in many cases be illegal. The industry may then secure governmental regulation, in effect a governmental agent, in order to create and enforce the needed collective agreement. For example, it has been argued that the railroads obtained federal regulation in the form of the Interstate Commerce Commission in 1887 as a means of bringing stability to an industry characterized by frequent rate wars that interrupted collusive "pooling" agreements (see Hilton 1966; cf. Posner 1974).

The collective action dilemma rationale may be applied to other kinds of regulation. Consumers faced with the problem of acquiring information on risk from a food additive may elect to be "free riders" and let others bear the cost of supplying the information. But an insufficient number (possibly, none) of the consumers may then be willing to pay the costs. And no single consumer or small group of consumers may be willing or able to absorb the costs of provision so that all may benefit. Thus no information could result. Consumers may reduce the uncertainty in their environment in such situations by creating a governmental agent to supply the information and collectively coerce themselves through taxation to pay for it. Or they may arrange to have the agent coerce a third party into supplying it. For example, regulation may require firms to pay the costs of research to prove the safety of their product.

In effect, the (to be) regulated parties or other clients of the regulation (e.g., consumers) seek the creation of regulatory bodies as agents administering collective agreements that resolve their collective action dilemmas and thereby manage their environments (cf. Goldberg 1973, 1976; Baldwin 1975:7–8; Mitnick 1974). It follows that if the regulatory agency has been established to mediate the environments of the regulated parties, it may, through the same powers, control its own environment to some extent.

3.3.4   Illustrations

These arguments will be illustrated with a couple of brief cases. We shall look ahead to the discussion of the development of the Interstate Commerce Commission that appears later in this chapter. The railroad industry in this country in the 1870s and 1880s was characterized by alternating rate wars and attempts at collusive "pooling" agreements. Most of these agreements continually broke down as firms in an overbuilt industry sought to gain relative advantage in transport between given locations. Although other explanations exist (and can be used in conjunction with the following one), it has been argued that railroad interests obtained federal regulation in the form of the Interstate Commerce Commission in 1887 as a means of bringing stability to the industry and thereby protecting their investments and assuring their incomes (see, e.g., Hilton 1966). In the 1920s the trucking industry was similarly characterized by cutthroat competition and consequent instability. Although the Motor Carrier Act of 1935 that brought truckers and other highway carriers into the ICC was at least partly written by the Association of Railroad Executives, it was supported by much of the trucking industry as a way of reducing this instability (Fainsod et al. 1959:290). Note that the rise of the new transport mode, trucking, posed a potential threat both to the railroad industry and to the agency that regulated it, the ICC. Bringing the truckers and other motor carriers in thereby stabilized the environments of all three parties: railroads, truckers, and the ICC.

The ability of regulatory agencies to manage their environment, often in the interest of the regulators themselves, is also illustrated by Eckert's (1973) study of the taxi industry. He hypothesized from a model of regulators as utility maximizers that cities with a commission form of taxi regulation would be more likely to have a monopolistic or nearly monopolistic taxi industry, adopt simplifying market division restrictions like exclusive taxi stands, and require uniform rates, than cities with a bureau form. In other words, regulatory commissions would have less complex regulatory environments than regulatory bureaus. Regulators in commissions would find it relatively more difficult to increase their salaries because of the need for legislative action, and would value salary increases less, due to their shorter tenure, than bureaucratic regulators. Thus increasing regulation and/or making it more complex would not lead to salary increases, but *would* increase the commissioners' work load. Bureau regulators rewarded in salary by scope of duties and length of service, however, would be more likely to seek increases in regulation and its complexity. Eckert found some support for the above hypotheses: regulatory agencies apparently successfully managed their environment in a way consistent with the likely self-interest of agency officials.

3.3.5 The Incentive System, Regulator-Bureaucrats, and Environmental Control

Regulator-bureaucrats may be expected to exploit the environmental control capabilities of the regulatory unit to further their interests. They will do this, of course, within the bounds of the extant incentive system. Thus Eckert's commissioners simplified their regulation at least partly to reduce their work load; their available rewards, existing preferences, and environmental "tools" apparently conspired to this outcome.

Using the bureaucrat types derived in chapter 3, we can thus discuss the propensities of regulator-bureaucrats in the context of regulatory origin.

Climbers may be expected to seek expansion in regulatory agency size and mandate, and to push for ever-more-complex regulations. More regulation will provide an excuse for more workers, and so more status for the regulatory official. In a commission, however, more regulation will have costs in increased work load if the climber is a commissioner. Since the climber seeks self-interest goals, he may not be resistant to an industry orientation if he foresees the possibility of "jumping" to a lucrative position in the industry. Thus the potential exists for the climber to both expand regulation and employ or interpret the new regulation in the industry's interest, i.e., use the agency's environmental control capabilities to serve the industry. Growth in the regulatory agency may lead to less rigidity, as discussed in chapter 2, but not to less of an industry orientation.

Conservers, who seek to retain their existing rewards, would generally oppose expansion of the agency and its mandate because of the threat thereby posed to the existing incentive system. New internal agency organizational arrangements, additional (unpredictable) staff, and new industry constituencies could alter the reward structure. Conservers may then use the environmental control capabilities of the agency to repress change in the industry, since this could alter the stable reward system existing between industry and conserver-regulators. Thus regulation that "locks in" obsolescent technologies and protects against new competitors may not just be evidence of industry protection; it may be the agency maintaining stability in its environment in its own interest.

Conservers may, however, favor mandate extension and even growth if their rewards are clearly going to be maintained or increased. This would be so if mandate extension brought in the new industry or regulated area "on the terms" of the old. Thus, as we shall see in our discussion of the ICC later in this chapter, the trucks were brought in on the railroad model, i.e., the trucking regulation was keyed to existing railroad controls. In a commission, however, any increases in mandate will increase work load and pose a threat to commissioner rewards. Conserver-commissioners will thus oppose it unless it can be finessed through an institutional decision.

Advocates seek to protect the agency's goals or functions. If through expansion a threat to survival of the agency's programs is co-opted or removed, they will back it. Thus they may act on the environment, perhaps internalizing part of it within the agency, in order to protect the agency. Note that it is possible for climbers, conservers, and advocates all to back expansion, but for different reasons. Advocates face the same problems as the others in the commission form, though as advocates it is not clear that they would be prepared to deal with it through fragmenting decision and potentially interfering with achievement of organizational or program goals. They might do this if they believed increased specialization or professionalization might aid the agency in some way.

Loyalists will be agents for some individual and may act as he wishes, assuming their self-interest permits. Thus we would want to determine whether the individual in question is a climber, conserver, advocate, zealot, or statesman. Without this knowledge, we cannot speculate on his likely behavior.

Zealots may characterize a new agency; they will push for achievement of their narrowly conceived programs. Unless the zealot's program involves industry protection (a possibility), he will generally oppose industry influences that threaten his project. He will favor maintenance or expansion as necessary to defend his project; organization form could again involve a trade-off, but if he is sufficiently intense about his project, it may not make a difference. If the industry truly gets the regulation it wants, as the producer protection models claim, we should see zealots for the industry among the founding bureaucrats. This does not seem descriptive of agencies allegedly established this way, such as the ICC, and leads us to question either the industry-protection or the bureaucratic-protection approach. Of course, mixed cases are possible as well.

Statesmen will do what they think is best for society, within the constraints of their mixed motives. No predictions regarding maintenance or expansion seem indicated.

Having discussed the likely behavior of bureaucratic types during regulatory creation, we turn to consideration of the *access* stage, i.e., the process by which new regulation reaches a formal agenda for decision.

4.0 Aspects of Regulatory Entry

We consider now some descriptive aspects of the *access* mechanisms by which parties seek regulation. We will briefly look at some features of these means that are likely to be similar for all theories of regulation. Regulatory entry is a special case of what has been called agenda-building, the process by which issues are brought to a formal institutional agenda and transformed into policy intentions. Cobb and Elder (1972; see also Cobb, Ross, and Ross 1976) identify three stages in the agenda-building process: issue creation, issue expansion, and agenda entrance (see figure 3.5). These stages are summarized below in the context of the simple interest theories of regulation identified earlier.[19]

1. *Issue creation:* A "triggering device," which in the case of regulation is often a crisis in the subject activity, precipitates a controversy or conflict with some aspect of the activity as the issue, or subject matter, of the conflict. The crisis involves satisfaction of the goals of one or more of the following parties: consumers of the activity, producers of the activity, potential or existing overseers of regulation of the activity, or the general "public." At this or any later stage of the policy intention formation process, a proposal to deal with the crisis, in the form of institution of regulation of a certain form, may be made by those of the above parties who may genuinely benefit from resolution of the crisis in the proposed fashion or by their agents. The issue and/or regulatory proposal may be defined at the outset by an "initiator" and then guided towards agenda entrance by a chaperon or champion who may be the same party as the initiator.

2. *Issue expansion:* If the issue or proposal is not directly placed on a formal institutional agenda,[20] as it might be by an agent for the "public" who may be a legislator in the social goals theory, or a bureaucrat in the bureaucratic behavior theory, adherents must mobilize support for their position on the issue. This support is to be used to gain access to decision makers who control the formal agenda. Decision makers who participate directly in formal agenda formation, and who wish to place a regulatory issue on that agenda, may need to mobilize support among fellow decision makers.

Adherents of regulation must stimulate and coordinate contribu-

[19] To simplify discussion we have omitted much detail of the Cobb and Elder model, including issue dimensions, symbol utilization, dynamics of issue expansion, and conflict containment strategies, among other things (see figure 3.5). The purpose of our discussion here is to suggest some factors involved in the creation of a regulatory issue and its transformation into a policy intention. This linkage has not often been examined in previous work on regulation. Our presentation is not sufficient, however, for an adequate understanding of the process; the reader is referred to the Cobb and Elder work. We have added to the Cobb and Elder model brief considerations from the "economic theory of regulation." Bernstein (1955:74–75) includes a few arguments in his "gestation" stage that are similar to some in Cobb and Elder's agenda-building model.

[20] Cobb and Elder distinguish two types of agendas: "The systemic agenda consists of all issues that are commonly perceived by members of the political community as meriting public attention and as involving matters within the legitimate jurisdiction of existing governmental authority." The formal institutional agenda is "that set of items explicitly up for active and serious consideration of authoritative decision-makers." In policy intention formation, issues may proceed from the systemic to the formal agenda. (Cobb and Elder 1972:85–86)

FIGURE 3.5: COBB AND ELDER'S AGENDA–BUILDING MODEL

ISSUE CREATION   ISSUE EXPANSION   AGENDA ENTRANCE

Initiator:
(Existence of)
Readjuster
Exploiter
Reactor
Do-Gooder

Trigger Device:
(Existence of)
Internal events
External events

Issue Existence

Issue Dimensions:
Lack of specificity
Social significance
Temporal relevance
Lack of complexity
Lack of categorical precedence

Symbol Utilization
Historical precedence
Credibility
Lack of saturation
Reinforcement
Urgency portent

Mass media attention

Speed of development of issues

Speed of conversion into emotional issue

General public
Attentive public
Attention group
Identification group

Entrance Patterns
Automatic
Brokerage channel
Threats of imminent sanctions
Disruption

Systemic agenda entrance

Formal agenda entrance

Systemic (cultural) constraints on appropriate government action

Appearance on political party agenda

Attention by media opinion leaders

Support of key decision makers

Lack of group legitimacy

Organizational scale

Resources
Strategic position
Esteem in which group is held

Identification of decision makers with group

Interest Group Variables

Symbolic Group Strategies
Arousal of latent community support
Provocation of another group
Dissuasion of opponents
Demonstration of strength of commitment
Affirmation (internal support)

Conflict Containment Strategies

Group-Oriented:
Discrediting the group
Discrediting the group leaders   } Direct
Appeal over the leaders to members
Co-opt leaders   } Indirect

Issue-Oriented:
Symbolic rewards
Tokenism
Creating new organizational units
Anticipation   } Direct
Symbolic cooptation
Feigned constraint
Postponement   } Indirect

Compiled from Cobb and Elder (1972), chs. 5–10.

tions to their cause, i.e., manipulate the incentive system of target parties. These contributions may be in the form of resources, including positions of influence that promote access, and joint advocacy. In addition to the collective good [21] of the achievement of a given policy intention on regulation, adherents may try to offer selective benefits, i.e., incentives, for participation that may not be directly related to the proposed policy intention in substance (Olson 1965). Public interest groups, for example, may offer the intrinsically rewarding incentive of a feeling of "doing good" for participating. Also, variations in the proposed regulation may affect possible contributors differently, leading some to participate to insure regulation of a particular form (see Posner 1974:346; Stigler 1974).

The larger the number of contributors, the larger the total contribution, and the more likely that access will be attained. If the contributors are voters, for example, larger numbers present a greater threat to an official's reelection. Therefore adherents often try to expand the conflict to include more participants. This may involve redefining the issue to attract more supporters. But larger numbers also entail larger costs in coordinating their collective activity and in policing their adherence to the group goal and to group advocacy procedures. Where there are large numbers, a given contributor may withhold his contribution in the expectation that he will receive the benefits of the collective good anyway (see Olson 1965; Chamberlin 1974; Hardin 1975). Selective and asymmetrically distributed benefits may, as noted above, overcome this. The latter case may lead to an approximation of the small numbers condition, where contribution is encouraged by the greater impact of a given contribution (Stigler 1974).

Groups can use a number of symbolic strategies to try to expand the conflict and obtain more supporters. Many of these strategies involve manipulating symbols and issues and exploiting the mass media. Groups can use the media to try to arouse latent community support; can try to provoke opposing groups to action and thereby gain sympathetic attention for their own cause; can attempt to use attractive or distasteful symbols to dissuade opponents; can through dramatic action attempt to demonstrate strength of commitment; and can try to show affirmation of the group identity through the use of symbols to reinforce group solidarity (Cobb and Elder 1972:141–50).

---

[21] A pure collective good is a good such that when it is supplied to any party it cannot be withheld from supply to any other party, and/or such that supply to one party does not diminish supply to any other party (see ch. 5).

Opponents can elect a number of group- and issue-oriented strategies to try to contain the conflict; these are listed in figure 3.5.

3. *Agenda entrance:* We assume that there exists some set of decision makers who determine entrance to the formal institutional agenda from which the policy intentions of regulation may be authorized. Groups seeking regulation must induce these "gatekeepers" to put the issue or proposal on the formal agenda and then to authorize its implementation. In some cases, of course, adherents of regulation may already be key decision makers. For the case of regulation these gatekeepers are generally the members of a legislature and key bureaucrats in any relevant regulatory bureaucracy. Regulation may result, of course, from acts of the legislature or from actions of the regulatory agency such as rule-making in accord with its original broad mandate. Access to decision makers may depend on the endowed positions of adherents of regulation. These may include, for example, resources such as numbers of members and perceived legitimacy of groups seeking regulation, and position of the regulatory adherents in the structure of the political system—is it easy or difficult for them to exert influence on the decision makers? Also in the category of endowed, at least at the start of the process, may be the opinions of decision makers regarding the issue or proposed regulation, and the opinions of the groups espousing it.

In order to gain agenda entrance, and, later, in order to influence key participants in the *decision* stage, adherents of regulation may seek to coerce, convince, or reward decision makers, i.e., to offer negative incentives, to change the preferences of the decision makers, or to offer positive incentives. Coercion may be legal or extralegal. In the latter case groups may use tactics of embarrassment, confrontation, or disruption.[22] In the former case, groups may exploit the coercive power of government, as when they go to the legislature to pass legislation to force a recalcitrant regulatory body to act in a certain way, or when they adopt a strategy of legal advocacy to widen a regulatory mandate through reinterpretation by the courts. Or they may exploit the legal coercive power of other tactics, such as that of the pressure group that threatens to withhold votes. Groups may try to convince decision makers, perhaps through personal lobbying. They may supply information, relying on the force of their argument. They may act as brokers or obtain agents to act for them to persuade

[22] On strategies of interest group advocacy, see Berry (1977). We have combined some of Berry's work with Cobb and Elder's and reorganized the result.

decision makers, reaching compromise positions that reflect changes in initial preferences. And groups may seek to reward decision makers, whether through the promise of votes or campaign contributions, through assurance of remunerative jobs in the regulated industry when the bureaucrat or legislator leaves office, or through more subtle rewards like advice that eases daily work load, or prestige or status incentives that the official can get nowhere else. Note that many of the tactics employed during the *access* stage may also be used in the *decision* stage.

Thus regulatory entry, like regulation, is itself a process. Opponents of regulation may interfere with the process at any stage, seeking to prevent the creation of the issue, the expansion of support for the regulatory position, and consideration of regulation by decision makers.[23] Of course, key decision makers who oppose regulation may simply refuse to act. Because of the difficulty of organizing, especially for the case of shorter-term or idiosyncratic goals, or in situations where the adverse impact of the regulation is widely and diffusely spread, opposing regulation is often difficult. Organized groups like the regulated industry may face greater problems, however, in sustaining their own advocacy than in contesting access with unformed interests like the general public (see, e.g., Bauer, Pool, and Dexter 1963, part 4: "The Pressure Group").

5.0   An Illustration: The Interstate Commerce Commission

To illustrate the simple interest theories of regulatory origin listed above, we shall take a brief look at the origin and growth of the Interstate Commerce Commission.[24] Evidence for each of the theories is presented; the ICC may be a case of partial coincidence of goals. It is possible to argue that in any case in which parties representing each of the theories become actively involved, the resultant will be a pluralistic common denominator; the system will operate to give satisfaction as far as possible to all who seek it (cf. Fainsod 1940). At times, however, some parties may benefit more than others. The new regulation may also be internally contradictory, or be interpreted or

---

[23] For more on conflict containment strategies, see Cobb and Elder (1972:124–29).

[24] We shall not, however, apply the Cobb and Elder model; information to give full content to that model is often lacking and would at any rate expand the presentation more than is appropriate to this work.

administered inconsistently over time, as regulation is added to it. This is unsatisfactory as an explanation of regulatory origin unless we can, as we required above, disentangle the conditions leading to common-denominator coincidence, and/or inconsistent content, interpretation, or administration. We shall not attempt to do so here, and merely offer the ICC case illustratively.

5.1 PRIVATE INTEREST THEORIES AND THE ORIGIN OF THE INTERSTATE COMMERCE ACT OF 1887

5.1.1 Consumer Protection Origin Theories

An ideological aversion to private monopoly, concentrated political power, and industrialism, together with belief in agrarianism and laissez faire, or nonintervention in economic activity, meant that the first attempts at regulation in the nineteenth century were generally directed at circumscribed areas with marked abuses and at local and then state levels before national regulation (Fainsod et al. 1959:242–43; see also our chapter 2). So it was for the beginning of railroad regulation.

At first, for the farmer and shipper in the mid-nineteenth century, "railroads were blessings" (Fainsod et al. 1959:246). But there was an agricultural depression in the late sixties and early seventies, accompanied by complaints that rates had become extortionate, discrimination was practiced against individuals and localities, collective practices set unfair rates and eliminated competition, state officials were corrupted, and capital stock was watered and manipulated into worthlessness (Fainsod et al. 1959:246).

Friedlaender (1969) notes that railroads practiced extensive price discrimination with respect to shippers, localities, and commodities (on bases for discrimination, cf. H. C. Adams 1898:435). Big shippers were given secret rebates. Localities were discriminated against through long-haul/short-haul differentials. For example, a railroad competing in the long haul against water transport between, say, river ports on the Mississippi and Ohio rivers, would lower its rates to compete successfully. But on shorter interior runs on the same line, say between a river port and inland city, rates were kept high, so that rates for short hauls were often higher than those for long hauls. It was more expensive to ship grain via the Pennsylvania Railroad between Chicago and Pittsburgh than between Chicago and New York

(Hoogenboom and Hoogenboom 1976:5; on long-haul/short-haul discrimination and the ICC, see Crumbaker 1940).

The third form of discrimination was in type of commodity, between so-called "high-valued" manufactured goods, and "low-valued" bulk agricultural or natural resource commodities. Because consuming areas had multiple sources of supply, bulk commodities could often come by water. Since, in addition, transportation costs were a relatively large fraction of their final price, shipment of such goods was especially sensitive to changes in rail rates; elasticity of demand for rail services was high. Manufactured goods, on the other hand, often had few transportation alternatives, and transport costs constituted a relatively small fraction of their price. So demand for rail transport was relatively insensitive to changes in rail rates, or inelastic. Railroads could then charge high rates for the "high-valued" manufactured goods, and low rates for "low-valued" bulk commodities; this was called "value-of-service" pricing (Friedlaender 1969:10–11; on discrimination, see also Kirkland 1961; Locklin 1966; Hillman 1968).

There are a number of vivid contemporary descriptions of these discriminatory practices (see, e.g., C. F. Adams 1887:118–26; Stickney 1891; Larrabee 1893; H. C. Adams 1898; Meyer 1903; Ripley 1912; Buck 1913). Ripley (1912), for example, concludes:

> In brief, the contemporary evidence all goes to show that,—quite aside from evil intent,—the railroad business of the United States in the middle of the eighties, was in a highly disorganized state. . . . Competition had run mad. And out of this unsettled condition of affairs there had sprung the usual mushroom crop of speculation, fraud and corruption which is bound to flourish at such times. . . . finally, in seeking to understand the economic situation in 1887, the intolerable arrogance of great railway managers must be kept in mind. . . . It is certain that there was no well-defined sense of responsibility to the public. (Ripley 1912:449–50)

Indeed, the self-interest goal of profit was to be vigorously pursued and, where possible, protected. As Charles Elliott Perkins, President of the Chicago, Burlington and Quincy Railroad, wrote to William Larrabee in 1887, "It is a recognized principle of political economy, or rule of human conduct, that men will not invest their savings in hazardous enterprises and assume the risk of loss if they are not permitted to have a corresponding chance of profit" (Cochran 1953:446).

Critics claimed that the railroad system "was founded on a theoretical error . . . that in all matters of trade, competition, if allowed perfectly free play, could be relied upon to protect the community from abuses" (C. F. Adams 1887:117). Government intervention—regulation—could repair these market defects. I. L. Sharfman, author of perhaps the most extensive study of a regulatory commission—the ICC—ever written, observed that "Sharp resentment at the manifest injustice and baleful consequences of the rebating evil and at the subversive industrial tendencies inherent in rate maladjustments was the most potent factor leading to federal legislation" (Sharfman 1931, 1:18).

This is the traditional view of regulatory origin, i.e., that regulation is begun at the behest of adversely affected groups to correct abuses. These groups are frequently consumers of the regulated product or service; hence, we deal here with the *consumer protection* theory of origin. But which groups, out of those apparently adversely affected, will take action that results in regulation? Which of the groups that push for regulation are key to the enactment of that regulation? How do they gain access to the political decision-making system? Is the regulation that is achieved actually that which is desired, and does it produce the desired effects?

We shall not address all of these questions for the case of the ICC; the literature is marked with sharp disagreement on many of these points. We shall, however, identify a few of the groups said to have played major roles in seeking abuse correction through federal regulation of the railroads (for analysis of groups seeking railroad regulation, see, e.g., Purcell 1967; Garraty 1968; McCraw 1975; Hoogenboom and Hoogenboom 1976). There is no single, simple consumer explanation for the origin of federal railroad regulation; disagreement exists as to which consumer groups were prominent in this process.

The Granger movement, which was strongest in the midwest, sought at first, among other things, to protect farmers from these abuses through state-level regulation of the railroads (see, e.g., Larrabee 1893; Meyer 1903; Buck 1913; Stover 1961; G. H. Miller 1971). The Grangers likened the railroad owners to robber barons:

> The history of the present railway monopoly is a history of repeated injuries and oppressions, all having in direct object the establishment of an absolute tyranny over the people of these States unequalled in any monarchy of the Old World, and having its only parallel in the history of the medieval ages, when the strong hand was the only law, and the highways of commerce were

> taxed by the feudal barons, who, from their strongholds, surrounded by their armies of vassals, could lay such tribute upon the traveller as their own wills alone should dictate. (From a Granger declaration of grievances, 1873; C. F. Adams 1887:129.)

In the early 1870s, "Granger legislation" establishing state regulatory commissions was enacted in a number of states. It was strongly opposed by the railroads, who were successful in eventually modifying or amending laws in many states to make them more acceptable to railroad interests (on railroad lobbying, see, e.g., Cochran 1953; Kirkland 1961:113–14). Railroads were also able to influence favorable appointments to the commissions and to control some commissions through outright corruption (see, e.g., Adams 1887; Larrabee 1898; Cushman 1941; Stover 1961:129–30).

Granger legislation led to the so-called "Granger cases" in the courts, the most notable being *Munn* v. *Illinois,* 94 U.S. 113 (1877). This case, which we shall discuss further in chapter 4, upheld the constitutionality of railroad and grain elevator regulation by the states. A distinction was made between a business "clothed" with a public interest (that could be regulated), and one which is essentially private (and cannot be) (see, e.g., Fainsod et al. 1959:246–47).

It has been argued that the "fundamental principles" of railroad regulation in this country developed in the Granger movement, and were later reflected in federal railroad regulation (Buck 1913:205; see also, e.g., Meyer 1903:189–94; Sharfman 1931, I:15). The Granger movement was a "forerunner" that "paved the way for the more extensive agitation" that resulted in federal regulation (Buck 1913:231). Some have gone further to argue that the occurrence of federal regulation in 1887 can be ascribed directly to the Grangers, though most (see, e.g., Hoogenboom and Hoogenboom 1976:8; Buck 1913:230) have stopped short of this (for citations to those in the older literature who give credit for the Interstate Commerce Act of 1887 (ICA) to the Grange, see Buck 1913:230; on the Grange as explanation, see also C. F. Adams 1887:126; Meyer 1903:189–94; Huntington 1952:470–71; Warner et al. 1967:640). The Granger movement was already fading by the time the federal Act was passed.

Farmers are not the only consumers of railway services to whom the origin of railroad regulation is credited. George H. Miller (1971) ascribes the Granger laws chiefly to merchants and to shippers in the river towns of the Midwest, rather than to farmers alone. Lee Benson (1955) argues that the push to the Interstate Commerce Act was led not by midwestern farmers and shippers, but by New York merchants, though many groups wanted some regulation. Nash (1957) identifies independent oilmen in Pennsylvania fighting Standard Oil, which received large rebates from the railroads, as a key group in the drive toward federal regulation. The oilmen's bill contained language and provisions similar to that which emerged in the Interstate Commerce Act, and that Act can be traced to it. But Nash, too, hastens to caution that he would not offer his oilmen as the sole group of importance in explaining the ICA: "Such was the diversity of the groups desiring regulation that no one-sided approach, whether sectional, urban, or agrarian, will suffice as an explanation" (Nash 1957:189; see also Buck 1913:230).

Purcell (1967) maintains that many economic groups, including businessmen in general, favored some federal regulation of the railroads:

> It was neither "the people" nor "the farmers"—nor even "the businessmen"—who were responsible for the government regulation of railroads. Rather, it was many diverse economic groups in combination throughout the nation which felt threatened by the new national economy and sought to protect their interests through the federal government. (Purcell 1967:578)

Some groups, believing that regulation would protect the railroads or that laissez faire and free enterprise should be protected, did oppose regulation. Some of these groups included those who were enjoying high benefits from the status quo, such as big shippers who received large rebates (Purcell 1967:571–73).

5.1.2 Industry Protection Origin Theories

Included among the businessmen said to favor regulation in the views of Purcell and others were many of the railroadmen themselves. In fact, in contrast to the traditional view of regulation as instituted to correct abuses, there is a revisionist view that federal regulation of the railroads was actively sought by the railroads and can be best explained as the result of railroad efforts to use the coercive powers of the government to their own benefit (see especially Kolko 1965; Hilton 1966; see also, for a contemporary view, Stickney 1891:219–23). This is in essence an *industry protection* theory of regulatory origin.

George W. Hilton describes the railroad industry in the 1880s as being in a "mature state of cartelization" (Hilton 1966:87). Because few railroads served each city, there were considerable incentives to collusion. Since, in the short run, demand for transportation was inelastic, or would not change much with change in price, and alternatives to railroads were poor, there was a fixed pie to divide up if railroads cooperated and did not compete away potential profits. Thus, after 1870, the railroads engaged in "pooling," involving pooled or jointly decided allocations of traffic or revenue to lines serving major terminals in common. In 1879, there were eight major pools. Monopoly gains overattracted resources to the industry; overbuilding of railroads (with respect to demand) occurred, with many parallel lines and consequent excess capacity.

But the existing structure was unstable, because a railroad could try to capture more business and raise its revenues, or drive out competitors, by cutting rates. So rate wars alternated with collusive pooling. Whereas in the 1870s and earlier, rates had been relatively high (and shippers—including Grange members—had suffered accordingly), during the 1880s rates were falling as the railroads built up and periodically competed. Instability in the industry caused losses to railroads, which, according to Hilton, then saw regulation as a reluctantly acquired means of mediating this instability (Hilton 1966:87–94; see also Kolko 1965; MacAvoy 1965). But only a minimum of regulation was desirable—enough to eliminate instability, but not interfere with the collusive practices that guaranteed overbuilt, unnecessary railroads their incomes. Because of overbuilding, some economies of scale (decreasing costs), and the level of demand, efficiency criteria dictate that the industry should have been allowed to "shake down" into fewer, more efficient firms, allowed to compete among themselves and with other transportation modes.

Spann and Erickson (1970) argue that the railroads were not a decreasing cost industry in which "the cost of operation grows less rapidly than the volume of business done" (Ripley 1912:71). According to such a rationale, which was an argument applied to the railroads at that time to support regulation, promotion of competition can be wasteful in resources; it is more efficient—cheaper—to combine firms (or allow consolidation) and operate at a larger scale (on "natural monopoly," see our chapter 5). Then, "since the markets for railway service are monopolistic or oligopolistic some type of control over the pricing of railway services is essential to the protection of the public interest" (Harbeson 1967:232).

Railroads in the late nineteenth century appeared to have declining

costs because of technological improvements, however, and not because of anything inherent in the cost structure. In fact, Spann and
Erickson argue, the railroads had essentially constant costs with increasing scale. With decreasing costs one would expect to see
mergers and rapid growth of the larger firms; on the contrary, growth
of the larger firms was not faster than that of the industry at large,
and cartels, not mergers, were the predominant railroad strategy in
the period before regulation. Thus, consistent with the Hilton conclusion, Spann and Erickson (1970:236) assert that regulation stabilized
an "unstable cartel situation."

Contemporary support for the thesis that at least some railroads (in
particular, railroad executives) acquired and supported regulation is
extensive. Stickney (1891) claimed that

> For a quarter of a century [railroad owners] have been attempting, by agree-
> ments between themselves, to make and maintain uniform and stable rates.
> But as such contracts are not recognized as binding by the law, they have
> rested entirely on the good faith of each company, and to a great extent upon
> the capacity as well as good faith of each of the traffic officials and em-
> ployees. In the past they have not been efficacious. . . . Their alternative
> protection is the strong arm of the law. Let the law name the rates, and let
> the law maintain and protect their integrity. (Stickney 1891:222–23)

Stickney's observations seem consistent with our own arguments
earlier regarding the function of regulation to resolve collective action
dilemmas.

A few typical examples should suffice to indicate railroad executive support for regulation. William H. Vanderbilt, son of the Com-
modore and an executive in several railroads, when asked during the
Hepburn Committee investigation of New York railroads in 1879
whether he might prefer a rate war or federal regulation, replied, "I
am not opposed to general legislation by the general government on
this question; I rather favor it, and have for years past" (Martin
1974:361).

After the Interstate Commerce Act was passed, railroad executives
were quick to note ways in which it could be exploited in their own
interest. Perkins, writing to his General Manager, Henry B. Stone, in
1889, advised, "Let us ask the Commissioners to enforce the law
when its violation by others hurts us" (Cochran 1953:198). Again,
we see elements of the collective action dilemma resolution rationale.

Perhaps one of the most widely cited bits of evidence that railroads
were aware of and supported the exploitation of federal regulation in

their own interest is Richard Olney's letter to Perkins in 1892. Olney had just been appointed Attorney General by Grover Cleveland, and advised Perkins not to push for repeal of the Interstate Commerce Act:

> My impression would be that looking at the matter from a railroad point of view exclusively it would not be a wise thing to undertake. . . . The attempt would not be likely to succeed; if it did not succeed, and were made on the ground of the inefficiency and uselessness of the Commission, the result would very probably be giving it the power it now lacks. The Commission, as its functions have now been limited by the courts, is, or can be made, of great use to the railroads. It satisfies the popular clamor for a government supervision of railroads, at the same time that that supervision is almost entirely nominal. Further, the older such a commission gets to be, the more inclined it will be found to take the business and railroad view of things. It thus becomes a sort of barrier between the railroad corporations, and the people and a sort of protection against hasty and crude legislation hostile to railroad interests. . . . The part of wisdom is not to destroy the Commission, but to utilize it. (Josephson 1964:526)

A number of recent writers have accorded railroads a role among groups desiring federal regulation, but have taken an approach less extreme than that of Gabriel Kolko (1965) and George W. Hilton (1966), who view the Interstate Commerce Act mainly as regulation sought by the railroads to further their own interests (for critiques of Kolko 1965 and Hilton 1966, see Harbeson 1967, 1972; Purcell 1967; Martin 1974; McCraw 1975; Hoogenboom and Hoogenboom 1976). In this broader view, regulation was a compromise among, or resultant from, conflicting interests, each of whom wanted some regulation, but not necessarily all of the regulation as it appeared in the ICA. Railroads, as well as other groups, turned to federal control to solve their problems, but were clearly opposed to certain provisions of the final Act (see, e.g., Benson 1955; Purcell 1967; Harbeson 1972:633; Hoogenboom and Hoogenboom 1976:8–17).

Of course, creation of regulation, and the effects of its operations, are two different things, as we discussed earlier. Conceivably, too, an explanation that ascribes the major role in regulatory origin to a particular group need not also require that the regulation which is actually enacted be exactly what the key group wanted. To make a baseball metaphor, particular teams (or points of view) may be greatly helped in reaching the World Series by the presence of "most valuable players" on their squads; such teams may also end up losing the Series itself. There may have been no ICA without railroad support, or the support of other groups, for some regulation. But this is no guarantee in general that the decision that emerges from the institutional decision structure, i.e., Congress in this case, will reflect only the interest of the group or groups most responsible for getting the issue there. Recalling our discussion of agenda-building, we observe that those groups most successful in expanding an issue in order to reach an institutional agenda during the access stage still face the problem of getting their desired policy intentions approved during the decision stage.

5.1.3 Bureaucratic Behavior Origin Theories

Besides consumer and industry protection theories, we have distinguished a *bureaucratic behavior* theory of regulatory origin. Although no federal railroad regulation existed before the Interstate Commerce Act of 1887, we can perhaps see in the literature some precursors of it in the railroad context. Charles Francis Adams, Jr., chairman of the Massachusetts railroad commission, observed, in criticizing the Granger state commissions, that

> . . . the inclination of the American mind is not bureaucratic. Recourse is had in this country to commissions, as our bureaus are called, with great reluctance. Experience, it must also be admitted, fully justifies this feeling of distrust; as a rule they do not work well. Not only do they develop in too many cases a singular aptitude for all jobbery, but, even when honestly composed, they rarely accomplish much. Once created, also, they can never be gotten rid of. They ever after remain part of the machinery of government, drawing salaries and apparently making work for themselves to do. (C. F. Adams 1887:132)

Adams attributed the failures of the Granger commissions to a lack of expertise among the appointees, rapid turnover (with officials quickly moving into positions in the railroad industry), and a prosecutorial orientation that eschewed investigation and judicial contemplation in favor of advocacy and hostility to the railroads. Governors in appointing commissioners viewed "any antecedent familiarity with the railroad system as a total disqualification. So afraid were they of a bias, that they sought out men whose minds were a blank" (C. F. Adams 1887:133; see 131–35).

Of course, the reluctance to resort to commissions that Adams observed has long since passed, but his discussion of reasons for poor performance is still relevant. We have already considered some of these factors in chapter 2, and will incorporate some of them in the theory of regulatory capture we shall present later. The dilemmas of how to find experts to regulate without relying on industry sources, for example, and of how to keep them in office and reward them independently of the regulated industry, are as much quandries in our time as in Adams's.

Samuel P. Huntington (1952) has argued in his study of the development and performance of the ICC that

> Successful adaptation to changing environmental circumstances is the secret of health and longevity for administrative as well as biological organisms. . . . to remain viable over a period of time, an agency must adjust its sources of support so as to correspond with changes in the strength of their political pressures. If the agency fails to make this adjustment, its political support decreases relative to its political opposition, and it may be said to suffer from administrative marasmus. (Huntington 1952:470)

Huntington maintains that, until World War I, the ICC relied for support on the farmers and commercial shippers, which were "the groups responsibile for its creation" (Huntington 1952:471). After the War, the ICC shifted its dependence to the railroad industry, where it remained. As the railroad industry declined due to changes in the transportation industry as a whole, so did the ICC.

Huntington's environmental support dependence arguments are clearly related to aspects of our previous discussion of the central role of the regulatory agency as organization acting in and on its environment. In effect, Huntington is arguing that the history of the ICC from its creation can be best understood as that of an organization acting so as to defend and maintain its key sources of external support.

5.2 PUBLIC INTEREST THEORIES AND THE ORIGIN OF
THE INTERSTATE COMMERCE ACT OF 1887

In contrast to private-interest-theory explanations for railroad regulatory origin that rely on one or more groups, such as various consumer or industry entities, are public interest approaches. Perhaps typical of an older view of the origins and functioning of federal agencies is the following description of the ICC taken from a school civics text:

> By the Interstate Commerce Act passed in 1887, the national government prevents railroads that are doing business in more than one state from managing their affairs simply for their own benefit and without regard for the public good. It compels these railroad companies to charge reasonable rates;

to treat all persons, corporations or localities alike; and it prevents the companies from charging more to haul freight a short distance than for a long distance under similar conditions.

Under this act an Interstate Commerce Commission was created, whose duty it is to see that the provisions of the law are carried out. . . . In this way the rights of all citizens may be properly protected. (Finch 1934: 154–55)

The "public good" is contrasted with "private benefit" and there is an implicit assumption that creation and operation are as intended.

Stickney (1891), in discussing the rationale for federal regulation, offered a theory of the railroads as agents of the state, using it to support the institution of rate regulation. He wrote:

If . . railway companies are performing functions which belong exclusively to the sovereignty of the State, under its license, or as its trustees or agents, and are collecting revenues by exercising the sovereign prerogative of collecting taxes, . . . it is not only the right but the duty of the State to fix the rates of taxation, as well as to regulate the methods of collection. (Stickney 1891:171)

It follows that new regulation would originate and operate from State attempts to control its agents, the railroads. It is less clear, however, how the state obtains its authority and determines what actions of its agents are desirable.

Another essentially public interest view is that the Interstate Commerce Act of 1887 "was intended to strip the railroads of the enormous economic power which they had attained. . . ." According to Albro Martin, the railroads needed regulation that would permit them to cartelize, but these practical desires were subordinated to "the deep-seated mistrust, hatred, and fear of large, insulated aggregations of power" (Martin 1974:343, 370). The eventual result of this misguided conception of where the public interest lay (i.e., against economic power) is said to be the decline of the railroads. We shall return to Martin's argument later.

Finally, and perhaps easiest to understand as a consistent "public interest" perspective on the ICC's creation and history, is an explanation developed by Ann F. Friedlaender (1969) based on the ICC's protection of value-of-service pricing. Preservation of such pricing practices by the railroads is said to contribute to national development goals, as described below, and is thus a case of a "national social goals" theory of regulation.

As the Grange had protested, farm incomes in the West were low.

This threatened development of Western frontier regions. The federal government was subsidizing such development through vast grants of land to the railroads (see, e.g., Sanborn 1899; Goodrich 1960; Kirkland 1961; Stover 1961; Locklin 1966). Value-of-service pricing caused transfers between different income and different commodity groups—and between different regions. Agricultural producers in the West with low incomes were, in effect, receiving hidden subsidies from consumers of manufactured goods in the East with relatively high incomes. Because the West received some (i.e., bought some) manufactured goods in exchange for agricultural commodities, one might think these effects would cancel. But consumption and production in the West did not necessarily coincide, and most consumption of manufactured goods was in the North and East. So the rate structure had definite redistributive effects. Regulation that removed discrimination by shipper and locality, and preserved that by commodity, would then serve the public interest, broadly construed (Friedlaender 1969: 12–16; see also Harbeson 1972:636–37). Note that removal of shipper and locality discrimination coincides with what would be expected under the consumer protection theory.

We shall pick up the threads of these theories, and add more elements of the bureaucratic behavior one, below. We consider now the founding of the ICC.

5.3 CREATION OF THE INTERSTATE COMMERCE COMMISSION

The creation of the ICC was precipitated by the U.S. Supreme Court decision in *Wabash, St. Louis and Pacific Ry. Co. v. Illinois,* 118 U.S. 557 (1886). It said that states could not regulate portions of interstate journeys that were within their boundaries. This threw out much of the power of the state commissions (see, e.g., Fainsod et al. 1959:250–51). Thus any national regulation would be instituted in response to a *crisis,* to plug the gap made by the Court.

Hilton (1966:94–103) argues that there were four possible courses of policy open:

1. *Enforcement of competition.* Few argued it. Arguments for: It would drive out excess resources in the industry and reduce the cost of transportation. It would reduce, eventually, the instability disliked by the industry. Arguments against: Real competition was not possible because the number of railroads could never be great enough, and so collusion and cartels were inevitable. Competition would bankrupt

some railroads. Hilton notes this is the standard way in economic
theory to reduce excess (it is happening today in the railroad industry). But railroad losses, as against capital flows out of an industry,
would be irrecoverable, a large dead loss.

2. *Nationalization, or public ownership.* Supporters included the
Knights of Labor, the populists, and John P. Altgeld, elected reform
governor of Illinois in 1892. Arguments for: It would end instability
in the railroads and their discriminatory policies; end the corruption
of legislators by the railroads; bring more equality in the wages of
railroad workers; avoid further monopoly gains; end excess railroad
construction. Arguments against: The United States had an inadequate bureaucratic tradition for an enterprise as large as a state railway. Unlike European states like Belgium, it lacked administrative
skill. Furthermore, the U.S. bureaucracy was corrupt already; the
railroad would just be opportunity for more corruption.

3. *Public-utility-type regulation.* Such regulation simulates competition by setting a rate structure that yields a fair rate of return on investment. Arguments for: These are similar to those above involving
removal of abuses and of instability in the industry. Arguments
against: It was not required by the courts of the time; fair return was
not called for until *Smyth* v. *Ames*, 169 U.S. 466 (1898). In 1887,
maximum rates of a business clothed with the public interest could be
regulated by *Munn* v. *Illinois* (1877). But stability, not excessive
rates, was the problem; rates were already falling. State maximum-
rate regulation was not thought to have worked out well. It was
thought that railroad costs varied too much for statutory maximum
rates to be set.

4. *Facilitation of collusion.* For this, there was "abundant precedent" (Hilton 1966:101); it would be an essentially incremental decision, an extension to the national level of certain state-level practices.
There were two types of state commissions, and each, by the late
1880s, facilitated collusion. One model was the Massachusetts state
commission, which could not set rates, but could investigate and
publicize rates and try to persuade railroads to adopt safety devices
and discontinue undesirable practices. It was little more than a board
of arbitration but it helped settle rate disputes, preventing rate wars,
and facilitated collusion. It was considered by the railroads to be
quite successful. "Granger commissions" could set maximum rates
and prohibit certain discriminatory practices. But, as we have seen,
these commissions were gradually reduced in power by railroad-spon-

sored legislation, and through outright corruption (on the state commissions, see, e.g., C. F. Adams 1887; Stickney 1891; Larrabee 1893; Meyer 1903; Buck 1913; S. L. Miller 1924:698–732, Cushman 1941; Kirkland 1961; Stover 1961; G. H. Miller 1971; Hoogenboom and Hoogenboom 1976). The Georgia state commission worked closely (and legally) with the Southern Railway and Steamship Association, the most successful of the cartel pools. The experience in Great Britain also served as a model for collusion. Hilton argues, of course, that his last alternative, facilitation of collusion, was the one adopted in effect, and that enforcement of competition might have led to "better" long-term results for the country (Hilton 1966:113).

Though these may have been the policy options possible, we do have a record of the actual Congressional debate on whether to establish a commission to handle the matter, which led to the Act of 1887. Cushman (1941:45–54) summarizes the legislative history:

Arguments for:
  1. The commission would be flexible and expert; railroad problems were "both vague and complex," "better handled by a body of experts," and the alternative of "inflexible law" enforced in the courts would be inadequate.
  2. The commission, being expert, could plan, advising Congress on railroad policy and, since continuing in nature, could accumulate experience that would be reflected in legislation.
  3. The commission would protect the public and shippers from the railroads. It would defend those with few resources.
  4. The commission could mediate disputes among the railroads, thereby preventing cutthroat competition.
  5. The commission would help the courts by providing expertise, though it would not "exercise any final regulatory power."
  6. The experience of the states and England was offered in support of a commission.

Arguments against:
  1. The discretion of the commission would "soften the force of statutory legislation." The Grange representatives had testified that they did "not want our justice strained through a commission. . . ."
  2. Railroads would influence appointments to the commission, and would dominate the commission, as they dominated legislatures and executives in the past.
  3. The commission would be tainted with politics because of the President's potential abuse of the appointments process to exercise undue authority, and the requirement that it be bipartisan; it would be "the foot-ball of politics," according to Representative Campbell of Ohio.

4. Railroad regulation was too big a job for "a single administrative body to perform."
5. Formation of the commission would lead to delays in regulation; one Congressman argued that "in my judgment a more troublesome and intricate . . . piece of legal machinery was never suggested."
6. State regulation by commission had not worked.

Note that these arguments contain elements of three of the simple interest "theories" of origin: consumers of the activity (shippers), the railroad industry, and the country as a whole might be served by regulation by commission.

The act that was finally passed, in 1887, to fill the gap made by *Wabash* v. *Illinois,* also contained elements of all three positions:

It eliminated abuses by requiring that rates be "reasonable and just," by declaring that preferential treatment of individuals through special rates, rebates, and so on was "unjust discrimination" and unlawful, by prohibiting undue or unreasonable preference or advantage to any person, company, firm, or type of traffic, and by prohibiting the practice of charging more for short hauls than long hauls (see, e.g., Hilton's brief summary, Hilton 1966:107). So in these respects the Act served the consumer interest.

But the Act did not prohibit value-of-service pricing, which, as we saw before, was a method of cross-subsidization or taxation that met national social goals by supporting Western development. So, by protecting Western enterprises against abuses, and in effect subsidizing their operations through value-of-service pricing, the Act was consistent with the social goals theory.

But elimination of abuses also stabilized the railroad industry by preventing ruinous competition through secret rebates and other discriminatory practices. And although the Act did prohibit pooling of traffic or earnings, it had nothing in it to prohibit other forms of collusion; for example, rate-fixing agreements. Thus the Act promised to bring the railroad industry the stability it wanted; by putting reins on some abuses of cutthroat competition it also protected the overbuilt, excess-capacity railroad industry from reducing itself more rapidly to efficient dimensions. And so there is evidence also for the industry theory.

Friedlaender cites evidence for the social goals theory in the way the original ICC conceived of its mandate. In its *First Annual Report* (1887), the Commission wrote:

> The public interest is best served when the rates are so apportioned as to encourage the largest practicable exchange of products between different sections of our country and with foreign countries; and this can only be done by making value an important consideration, and by placing upon the higher classes of freight some share of the burden that on a relatively equal apportionment, if service alone were considered, would fall upon those of less value. With this method of arranging tariffs little fault is found, and perhaps none at all by persons who consider the subject from the standpoint of public interest. (Friedlaender 1969:12)

But the influence of the consumer point of view is also apparent during this period: The ICC was originally put in the Department of Interior. But Brownlow argued (Bernstein 1955) that the ICC was made an independent commission in 1889 because " '. . . Mr. Reagan of Texas, the author of the interstate commerce bill, said that since a railroad lawyer named Ben Harrison had been elected President, he did not trust the President any more with this matter, so he invented the . . . independent commission' " (Bernstein 1955:23). Reagan, who had been Postmaster General of the Confederacy (Nash 1957), had argued the case for the shippers in the controversies leading to the Act of 1887 (Hilton 1966:104–5).

The innovative flexibility of the procedures of an administrative agency had been held to be one of its advantages. But the new ICC was set up like a court: Its first chairman, a distinguished judge and law professor, Thomas M. Cooley, made its procedures like a court of law—case by case consideration (see, e.g., C. A. Miller 1946: 15–19). Judicialized procedures have persisted to the present day in such agencies. There were, however, some reasons to support procedures of this form (Bernstein 1955:29): 1) Courts, which had the power of review of agency activities, would back ICC decisions if the agency behaved more like a court than a novel form, the administrative agency. 2) Commission members, exemplified by Cooley, preferred the known advantages of the judicial form to the unknown ones of the administrative process. 3) Because of legal actions by railroads, much of the agency's business involved the courts; consequently, and because the agency wanted to win, it tailored its procedures to the judicial model. 4) As a new form, the ICC was on shaky ground and faced threats to its existence. It faced opposition to both its substantive duties and novel form. So it was prudent, in order to preserve the agency, to take a conservative approach; hence, the judicial model.

In the above can be seen aspects of a bureaucratic behavior model of regulatory behavior; we return to it below.

Although many railroad officials "expressed vigorous disapproval of the Act" (Cochran 1953:198; see also Hoogenboom and Hoogenboom 1976:17; Benson 1955; Purcell 1967; Harbeson 1972:633), and some tried to abolish the Act (Hoogenboom and Hoogenboom 1976:32–33), they also disliked the continuation of many of the discriminatory practices that had brought instability to the industry. Kolko (1965:45) asserts that the law was "welcomed" by the railroads. There is some disagreement in the literature regarding the relative effectiveness of the early ICC in controlling these practices, and about railroad attitudes toward the regulation as it developed. In the advice of Olney and even Perkins, we have already seen recognition by the railroads of the new law's potential utility to them. But there may have been, at least initially, some lack of adherence to the Act's provisions in at least some parts of the country (but see Mac-Avoy 1965:126). Perkins wrote to John Murray Forbes at the beginning of 1888, after the Interstate Commerce Act had been in effect over nine months, that

> I am inclined to think there is more cheating going on to-day than ever before, in the way of secret rebates of one kind or another. . . . Such a system of doing business is very demoralizing to all concerned, and especially to the railroad agent. . . . The struggle for existence and the survival of the fittest is a pretty theory;—but it is also a law of nature that even the fittest must live as they go along and will always leave at least a fair share of the struggle to posterity. (Cochran 1953:447)

The staff of the early ICC was too small to be very effective. In addition, it had difficulty getting evidence on violations and, because of its reliance on the industry, information in general (Fainsod and Gordon 1941:247; Hoogenboom and Hoogenboom 1976:25). In this regard, the ICC was experiencing a problem that most regulatory agencies that were created in its wake in the decades following have also encountered.

In spite of these problems, the ICC, at least until the economic depression of 1893, may have had a measurable effect on the railroads (see, e.g., Hoogenboom and Hoogenboom 1976:35; MacAvoy 1965:125–53; S. L. Miller 1924:741), whether that effect was to protect shippers or enforce an industry cartel (or both). Cooley himself has been praised highly by most writers for his efforts in implementing the Act (see, e.g., Hoogenboom and Hoogenboom 1976), though some have seen Cooley as little more than a tool of the railroads (e.g., Kolko 1965). At any rate, whatever powers the ICC had established for itself out of the Interstate Commerce Act were soon limited by the courts.

5.4 THE EXPANSION OF THE ICC'S MANDATE

A series of Supreme Court cases in the 1890s severely limited the powers of the ICC. In the *Maximum Freight Rate* case (167 U.S. 479 [1897]), the ICC was denied the power to set new rates to correct existing rates it judged unreasonable. In the *Trans-Missouri Freight Association* (166 U.S. 290 [1897]) and *Joint Traffic Association* (171 U.S. 505 [1898]) cases, the Supreme Court, acting under the Sherman Antitrust Act, forbid the railroads from making agreements through traffic associations to set rates. The ICC had accepted these private arrangements as part of its regulatory policy. In the *Alabama Midland* decision (168 U.S. 144 [1897]), the Court made it impossible for the ICC to enforce section 4 of the Interstate Commerce Act, which forbade long-haul/short-haul differentials. This was done by interpreting the section to permit railroads to easily establish exceptions to the regulation (on these cases, see, e.g., Sharfman 1931, vol. 1; Ripley 1912; Fainsod and Gordon 1941:248–50; Cushman 1941; Hillman 1968; Hoogenboom and Hoogenboom 1976:35–37). In that case, Justice John Marshall Harlan wrote in dissent:

> . . . the present decision . . . goes far to make that Commission a useless body, for all practical purposes. . . . The Commission was established to protect the public against the improper practices of transportation companies engaged in commerce among the several states. It has been left, it is true, with power to make reports and to issue protests. But it has been shorn, by judicial interpretation, of authority to do anything of an effective character. (Sharfman 1931, 1:32)

The ICC did not respond *passively* to these decisions and prudently accept and consolidate its newly limited role in order to insure its survival in an increasingly hostile environment. We might possibly expect such a passive, conflict-containing pattern, given such behavioral models of regulation as that of Joskow (see discussion earlier in this chapter). Instead, the Commission *reacted* with what seems to have been considerable outrage, actually provoking external attacks, and sought legislation restoring its powers. In its annual report for 1897, the Commission wrote:

> The Interstate Commerce Commission can conduct investigations and make reports. It can perhaps correct in a halting fashion some forms of discrimination. It collects and publishes statistical information which would be of value, if under the law it could be obtained and published within a reasonable time. But by virtue of judicial decisions, it has ceased to be a body for the regulation of interstate carriers. . . . The people should no longer look to this commission for a protection which it is powerless to extend. (Fainsod and Gordon 1941:249)

It is interesting to note how *The Commercial and Financial Chronicle,* a publication reflecting a segment of business views that was both pro-railroad and opposed to ICC regulation, criticized the ICC's posture in that report. It commented, "In other words, according to their own statements, the Commission still has a great many functions left" ("Wanting More Power" 1897:1149). The *Chronicle* also observed that, in its opinion,

> the discussion is not conducted in a calm and dignified way. The language is in some instances quite intemperate. The spirit displayed by the Commission is occasion for deep regret. There is altogether too much censuring and scolding of the U.S. Supreme Court in the document to make it of any value as a contribution to the study of the important questions at issue. ("Wanting More Power" 1897:1148)

Furthermore, the Commission was said to

> argue strenuously for more power than the courts have decided they possess . . . The position of the Commission regarding pooling is curious, and serves well to illustrate how grudgingly and with what bad grace the members yield anything asked for by the carrying interest. . . . The existing situation may be unsatisfactory to railroad and shipper alike, but we imagine it will be a long time before any considerable portion of our people will be willing to grant a public body any such extraordinary powers as the Inter-State Commerce Commission is seeking. ("Wanting More Power" 1897:1149)

In April 1898, the *Chronicle* reported the reaction of a committee of the New York Chamber of Commerce to a bill restoring some of the ICC's powers: "In its report this committee, after pointing out that the tendency of all government bureaus is to seek greater power, announces its adherence to the old maxim that that government 'governs best that governs least' " ("The Financial Situation" 1898:683).

The ICC of this period contained at least three commissioners (Knapp, Prouty, and Clements) who have been described as "relatively effective" and variously praised for their expertise and "strength of character and force of will," and for being "ardent" and "formidable" (Hoogenboom and Hoogenboom 1976:42–43). They were joined in 1906 by perhaps one of the most able persons ever to sit on a federal regulatory commission, Franklin K. Lane. It was confidently and ingenuously asserted at the time of his death in 1921 that, had he not been born in Canada, Lane would have been President (C. A. Miller 1946:53). It is possible that, given the considerable body of literature critical of the historical pattern of regulatory appointments (see discussion later in this chapter; see also Hoogenboom and Hoogenboom 1976), including those to the ICC, a Commission this able was never again constituted. It was this Commission (with several apparently distinguished additions in the first decade or so of the century) that pushed so strongly and successfully for an increase in the powers and mandate of the ICC. As we shall see, beginning in 1903 the ICC was the beneficiary of a stream of enabling legislation that culminated in the Transportation Act of 1920.

It is plausible that advocacy of increased powers by the ICC and its supporters during this period reflected *active* attempts at bureaucratic survival—and, ultimately, expansion. A survival policy had been set in the Commission's early days as evidenced by the judicial cast of its procedures. The limiting Supreme Court decisions threatened the Commission's survival by leaving it little to do. In addition, the decisions and the lack of powers they brought lowered the prestige of Commission officials. Thus it could be argued that the Commission wanted new powers not only for their substantive content but for their contribution to the status of Commission members and the insurance they brought that the subsequent value to them of their positions would not be devalued further through dissolution of the Commission. Such powers provided environmental control. An additional argument here stems from commissioner identification with his role. Perhaps officials appointed to the Commission wanted to regulate; they gained intrinsic satisfaction from doing a job, and doing it well. They would thus be expected to push for powers that renewed their ability to regulate, no matter what the substantive nature of the regulation.[25] Finally, of course, commissioners (especially those on the ICC of this period) may have had a genuine belief in the public need

---

[25] For a statement of the regulation-for-its-own-sake argument, see J. Q. Wilson (1971). See also Jaffe (1954) and McCraw (1975:182) for "regulation-mindedness"—a presumption by regulators that perceived problems can always be cured through additional regulation (cf. McKie's (1970) "tar-baby effect").

for and efficacy of the new regulatory programs that were proposed.

We may therefore have a case in support of the bureaucratic behavior theory. Organization protection through environmental control attempts is explained, speculatively, through reference to individuals seeking to protect and/or enlarge return to their personal goals. Organization protection could also occur, of course, through organization-level mechanisms that may not be tied directly and rationally to individual preferences, i.e., established by individuals as instrumental to their goals. Institutional decisions, for example, which could grow out of staff desires to practice professional skills (and key staff and commissioner desires to expand the size of the agency, increasing their own status through hiring more professionals) can produce detailed, technical defenses that will stand up to court review and protect the agency (and the commissioners and staff) from reversal.

This period also marks the beginning of the ICC's growth as a complex, professionalized organization. Henry Carter Adams, the first Ph.D. graduate from Johns Hopkins University and an economist who was among the founders of the American Economic Association, served the Cooley commission as director of its statistics unit, and "emerged as the commission's key man" as the Court stripped away the ICC's regulatory powers (Hoogenboom and Hoogenboom 1976:37–38). The whole staff of the ICC to which Adams belonged numbered between 104 and 133 during the 1890s (Sharfman 1937, 4:68; Hoogenboom and Hoogenboom 1976:37). It expanded enormously in the first two decades of the century as the expansion in ICC powers required the addition of numerous specialists.

The ICC's activism at this time, and the quality of the commission and key staff, suggest a basic question about the relation of individual regulators to regulatory performance. We have touched on this point earlier, and will do so again, later in this chapter. Do "good men" make a difference? If they do, as Landis and others have claimed, then models of regulatory origin, or of performance, must assume that a certain large-number uniformity or average character to the workforce in the agencies studied will nevertheless persist. Though "good men" come and go (and, as the literature suggests, this has been mostly "go"—see the discussion later in this chapter), the incentive system they face may remain the same and produce consistent behaviors from the typical bureaucrats who also remain. If occasional "good men" do have important effects, we need to incorporate into more complex models factors that identify such individuals, and explain their entry into and behavior in the agency.

The other theories of origin also find supportive evidence in this period. We shall review the nature of the reform movement in the early 1900s and the railroad regulation that was enacted, and comment on some of this evidence and on further evidence for the bureaucratic theory.

The early 1900s saw the growth of the Progressive reform movement. This included a "belief in the efficacy of changes in the machinery of government," "faith in the expert," "distrust of the politician," and a tendency to view the "government as separate from the rest of society" (Bernstein 1955:45–46; see also J. Anderson 1962). Government would be an impartial, expert, "clean" vehicle of social reform. Bernstein (1955:36) notes three techniques the Progressives offered to bring this about: 1) Reform the electoral process by changing the machinery of voting, e.g., the secret ballot, direct primary, initiative-referendum-recall, and so on. 2) Use sound management and business methods to make government efficient. 3) Escape politics by giving governmental functions to independent regulatory commissions free to make expert, impartial decisions. As in earlier years, an ideology supported the form of new administrative bodies. The Progressive movement thus led to the founding of numerous commissions at the state level, and the Federal Trade Commission, in 1914, at the national level (on the origin of the FTC, see Stone 1977). A series of acts through the early 1900s gave the ICC greater powers, especially in rate-making.

The Sherman Act prohibited the railroads from engaging in rate-fixing and other collusive practices. With pooling outlawed through the Act of 1887, the railroads could avoid destructive competition, such as rate wars, through consolidation—and consolidate they did. The financial problems many railroads faced during the 1893 depression also contributed to this process. Alexander J. Cassatt, president of the Pennsylvania Railroad in 1899, developed the idea of "community of interest" in order to control rate cutting. By purchasing stock in competing railroads, a firm could acquire an interest in their operations and thus be less willing to engage in rebating and other discriminatory practices that could harm them (Hoogenboom and Hoogenboom 1976:39–42; on the size of "communities of interest," see Chalmers 1976:47). The plan worked; rebating decreased.

In 1903, Congress passed the Elkins Antirebating Act, almost unanimously. The Act, which was written at least partly by James A. Logan of the Pennsylvania Railroad, has been termed "a truce of the principals to abolish piracy" (Ripley 1912:494; also cited by Sharfman 1931, 1:38 and Hoogenboom and Hoogenboom 1976:45). It outlawed rates other than one filed with the ICC, thus preventing rebates and other rate cutting. In beginning to repair the damage of the Supreme Court decisions, and reinforcing the effects of Cassatt's communities of interest, the Act seems, as the quote suggests, another example of the collective action dilemma rationale discussed earlier.

In the *Northern Securities* case (193 U.S. 197 [1904]), the Supreme Court used the Sherman Antitrust Act to dissolve the Northern Securities Company, a railroad holding company which went somewhat beyond a mere "community of interest." The strategy of consolidation appeared limited (Hoogenboom and Hoogenboom 1976:46–7). An industry protection theory might suggest that the railroads would turn to government to maintain their cartel.

Pushed strongly by Theodore Roosevelt and the ICC, the Hepburn Act of 1906 gave the Commission the power to set maximum rates, extended its jurisdiction to express and sleeping car companies, oil pipe lines, and other areas, and allowed it to specify accounting and reporting procedures. It also increased the size of the Commission to seven members (from five), their terms of office to seven years (from six), and their salaries (by one-third). Both the work load of the Commission and the size of its staff jumped. In one year, formal complaints filed with the Commission went from 82 in 1906 to 415 in 1907 (Sharfman 1931, 1:40–44). The staff went from 178 in 1905 to 474 in 1908, and expenditures of the Commission went from $337,000 in 1905 to $740,000 in 1908 (Sharfman 1937, 4:66, 88). Whether one agrees with a bureaucratic behavior theory explanation or not, the bureaucratic rewards of expansion were considerable.

Franklin K. Lane, an unsuccessful "antirailroad" candidate for governor of California in 1902, joined the Commission in 1906 (Hoogenboom and Hoogenboom 1976:48, 54; C. A. Miller 1946: 53–55). Lane apparently saw his role on the Commission both as impartial arbiter and as agent of the shippers. Writing to E. B. Beard in 1908, he asserted that "it is not my business to fight the railroads, but to hear impartially what both sides may have to say and be as entirely fair with the railroads as with the shippers. . . . My aggressiveness on behalf of the shipping public has brought upon my head much criticism. . . .'' (Lane and Wall 1922:68). However Lane perceived his role, he has been judged "a friend to shippers" (Hoogenboom and Hoogenboom 1976:54).

In implementing the Hepburn Act, the ICC retained the case-by-case approach developed under Cooley and, with its new rate powers, retained and, in effect, sanctioned value-of-service pricing.

In the Mann-Elkins Act of 1910, the ICC was given the power to suspend any changes made in rates and put the burden for showing the reasonableness of rates on the railroads. It also strengthened the long-haul/short-haul restriction, established a Commerce Court to review ICC decisions, and gave the Commission new authority over telegraph, telephone and cable lines (Sharfman 1931, 1:52–62; Hoogenboom and Hoogenboom 1976:61). Commission staff went from 527 in 1909 to 702 in 1912, and expenditures from $994,000 in 1909 to $1,471,000 in 1912 (Sharfman 1937, 4:66, 68). The Commerce Court, which reversed a number of the ICC's decisions, was terminated by Congress in 1913.

In the period before the United States entered World War I, the ICC heard several extensive and complex rate cases and either turned down railroad requests for rate increases or granted increases smaller than desired. In this, the Commission appeared responsive to the views of shippers, who were represented by, among others, Louis D. Brandeis. Value-of-service pricing continued to be protected (Hoogenboom and Hoogenboom 1976:62–73).

Formally recognizing the need expressed by many to be able to regulate railroad rates and investment more accurately, the Valuation Act of 1913 set up a bureau in the ICC to value railroad properties. Commissioner Prouty resigned to head the bureau, which by itself became larger than the rest of the ICC (Hoogenboom and Hoogenboom 1976:68; see also C. A. Miller 1946:43–44). The staff of the ICC went from 731 in 1913 to 2,254 in 1917, and expenditures rose from $1,561,000 in 1913 to $5,229,000 in 1917 (Sharfman 1937, 4:66, 68).

To handle the work load, the ICC asked Congress repeatedly for an increase in the number of commissioners. The increase to nine was granted in 1917. The ICC was split into divisions, each headed by three commissioners, and examiners (first authorized in 1906) were permitted to prepare "proposed reports" subject to division or full Commission review (Sharfman 1937, 4:49–58, 70–86; Hoogenboom and Hoogenboom 1976:81–82). The institutional decision was developing.

Albro Martin (1971, 1974) maintains that the decisions of the ICC during the Progressive era starved the railroads of needed capital and led to their decline. In a way, the commissioners ignored the economics of the situation and responded to public criticism or to their personal conceptions of the "public interest." Martin has been criticized for his own use of economics (see Hilton 1972b; McCraw 1975), but his arguments could be used in support of the consumer interest (and possibly a "public interest") theory. One of the persistent criticisms of regulatory agencies, in fact, has been their ignorance of economics (e.g., Friendly 1962; Stigler 1975) in the midst of the agencies' sometime recognition of its importance. Franklin Lane wrote in 1909 that "The trouble with the Courts is that they know nothing about the question. Fundamentally it is not . . . law but economics that we deal with" (Lane and Wall 1922:71).

In this capsule description of the pre-World War I ICC, we see the interwoven strands of the four simple interest theories. The trend of bureaucratic expansion and differentiation (e.g., the institutional decision) is well-documented. Of course, mere expansion could simply be an indicator that consumers, the industry, or the public-at-large is getting the extensive and effective regulation that they desire.

From the point of view of the industry protection theory, the granting of rate-making powers to the ICC was a method of getting around the constraints imposed by the Sherman Act. If the industry was prohibited from colluding on rates to get stability in the industry (consolidation could only be taken so far in the face of antitrust statutes), the government could do the industry's collusion for it (see Hilton 1966; Kolko 1965).

From the point of view of the consumer theory, the granting of rate-making and other powers were added controls on the industry to insure operation that protected the consumer.

From the point of view of the social goals theory, value-of-service pricing would be insured if the Commission were granted more powers over setting rates. In addition, there appears to be some evidence that at least some commissioners thought they were acting as agents for the public interest.

In World War I, the railroads were placed under federal direction, with a new Railroad Administration, rather than the ICC, in control. Early in the War, the railroads had performed poorly and it was thought that strong central direction was necessary. Substantial rate increases were granted under the Railroad Administration, as well as a number of labor reforms (Sharfman 1931, 1:138–76; Cushman 1941: 105–15; Hoogenboom and Hoogenboom 1976:82–89). It appeared as if, by taking rate and other controls from the ICC, a tight lid was raised from the railroads and their operations—support, perhaps, for a consumer interest theory.

5.5 THE TRANSPORTATION ACT OF 1920 AND BEYOND

The trend to increased ICC powers culminated in the Transportation Act of 1920. A bill on which the final Act was mostly based was probably written by Commissioner Clark of the ICC (Hoogenboom and Hoogenboom 1976:94). The Act specified a total fair rate of return on investment of 6 percent; the ICC was given an affirmative duty to insure railroad revenue. The ICC could set minimum rates, specify services, control entry and exit to and from the industry, as well as aspects of capital formation, consolidation, and pooling (see Locklin 1928; Sharfman 1931, 1:177–244; Cushman 1941:16–29; Hilton 1966:111; Fainsod et al. 1959:269–70; Phillips 1965:454–55; Hoogenboom and Hoogenboom 1976:90–97). Hilton (1966) argues that these steps only made the industry, through the management of the ICC, into the cartel it had long sought to become, insuring stability. While earlier regulation was overly concerned with abuses, with "no-saying," the Act of 1920 introduced protection explicitly by specifying a fair rate of return. The switch from no-saying to yes- and no-saying involving protection was an important event in the development of regulatory commissions and was reflected in many subsequent commissions. Thus the industry theory can be supported.

The consumer theory receives some support because the ICC was given wide-ranging powers to specify conditions of service.

The social goals theory is supported because the ICC could now "order a carrier to acquire facilities or build an extension where the public interest, convenience, or necessity justified such action" (Fainsod et al. 1959:270). Subsequently, in the 1920s, during another agricultural depression, the commission frequently acted with its new powers to keep agricultural rates relatively low, preserving value-of-service pricing (Friedlaender 1969:17–19).

The bureaucratic behavior theory is also supported because the Act of 1920 involved a great increase in the complexity of what the ICC did. This conceivably served bureaucrats' goals by insuring survival of the Commission by creating work for it to do. In addition, the added powers increased the status of Commission officials. Status would also be increased if the increased tasks of the agency made it necessary for officials to hire more subordinates. Although the budget and number of employees dropped in the early 1920s in response to a "national economy program," Sharfman (1937, 4:67–68) observes that "the important legislative enactments of 1906, 1910, 1913, 1920, 1933, and 1935 have been largely responsible for the growth of, and for the changes in, the number of the Commission's employees."

Furthermore, the ICC had argued that, in the new legislation, railroads should be allowed to consolidate under the ICC's supervision. Thus "by eliminating many competing railroads, consolidation would reduce and simplify rate cases" (Hoogenboom and Hoogenboom 1976:94). Recall that simplification of the burden falling on the fixed set of commissioners can be evidence of bureaucratic protection (cf. Eckert 1973, on taxi commissions). Before the War, the ICC had had several difficult and extensive rate cases involving many railroads. They had asked for and received two more commissioners and had delegated work to examiners; by the Act of 1920 they received two additional members, raising the Commission to eleven.

The work load did not diminish, however, and neither did the ICC's reliance on its staff. Commissioner Woodlock, after leaving the Commission in 1930, described the staff's role:

> All these cases finally come to the commissioner in the form of a report prepared for adoption by the commission or a division as the case may be. These reports summarize the pleadings, the testimony and the contentions of the parties and contain the findings proposed by the writer or the reviewing authority as the case may be. The commissioner's business is to apply the law to the facts in the case. He has, first, to be sure that he has all the pertinent facts before him and, second, to be sure that when he decides upon his vote he is correctly applying the law to the facts. For this surety he must rely largely upon his staff, and the staff of the commission. It is their business to see that the report accurately reflects the testimony, that the testimony is accurately analyzed and weighed, that the precedents upon which reliance is placed are properly applicable and sufficiently support the proposed finding, and, if there is defect in any of these requirements, to point it out to the commissioner. The aim of the staff is so to sift down the whole case as to place before the commissioner, stripped of all non-essential details, the fundamental issues on which he must pass judgment. (Sharfman 1937, 4:295)

The process of bureaucratic expansion, differentiation, delegation of decision and—as critics maintain—rigidification was developed in its familiar form.

It is interesting to note that Woodlock's appointment to the Commission, in 1925, was marked by controversy over his alleged bias toward business, especially railroad interests. Robert M. LaFollette predicted "that for four years big business would govern the nation" (Hoogenboom and Hoogenboom 1976:111–12). We have observed earlier that structural aspects of bureaucratic protection (e.g., simplification of regulation) can coincide with industry protection; appointments of commissioners who may be predisposed to favor industry interests and who interpret their own role as narrowly as Woodlock apparently did, would only exacerbate this coincidence.

Legislation conferring regulatory powers on the ICC, such as the Act of 1920, as well as actions taken by the Commission, assumed implicitly that the monopoly of the railroads over transportation of goods would continue; the growth of competing means, such as trucking, was not anticipated. This is a common fault of regulation—it often tends to freeze and protect the existing industry against innovative competing forms.

Trucks and buses were first subject to regulation, which covered such aspects as safety, physical characteristics of vehicles, driver licensing, number of operating hours for drivers and, later, rates and services, in the 1920s (see, e.g., S. L. Miller 1933; Healy 1940). But as it was earlier with the railroads, state regulation could not apply to interstate service. Railroads strongly supported trucking regulation as a means of controlling threatening competition—advocating control of entry, rates, and other factors (see, e.g., Healy 1940:427; Huntington 1952:478; cf. Morgan 1953 and Huntington, Williams, and Morgan 1953). The Association of Railroad Executives even helped to write the trucking legislation. Many truckers (especially the larger firms), like the railroads before them, supported regulation to stabilize conditions in their industry, i.e., to control rate wars and other aspects of cutthroat competition (see, e.g., Healy 1940:428; Fainsod et al. 1959:289–90; Locklin 1966:670–1; T. G. Moore 1972:25–26). Thus, extension of regulation to motor carriers by the ICC, in the Motor Carrier Act of 1935, can be seen in the light of the industry protection theory. Some shippers also supported this legislation because regulation would end unstable rates and could have supported it to repair unsatisfactory service resulting from cutthroat competition (the situation was more complex than this—see Healy 1940: 428–29; but see Huntington 1952:478). Thus the consumer theory may get some support. But many shippers, including farmers, who benefited from rate cuts, were opposed to regulation. The Act gained support when amendments removed agricultural goods from coverage under it (Hoogenboom and Hoogenboom 1976:131; on the Act generally, see Healy 1940:424–33).

Friedlaender argues that the old bulk-commodity-subsidization rationale was relevant. During the Depression the railroads had excess capacity and losses in revenue. They could not raise already high rates on manufactured goods because trucking was now an effective competitor in these goods; similarly, they could not lower rates to try to capture more traffic because truckers could also lower rates. So the railroads sought to raise the relatively low rates on bulk and agricultural commodities, for whose transportation they had an advantage. The ICC would not let them. After trucking was brought under regulation by the Act of 1935, the ICC based truck rates on the existing level of rail rates, and raised truck rates whenever they threatened the railroads (Friedlaender 1969:20–21). This constituted protection of the railroads, of course, but it can be seen in the light of permitting continued subsidization of bulk and agricultural commodities (see also, e.g., Hoogenboom and Hoogenboom 1976:132–33). Friedlaender claims that ICC "rate and regulatory policies are understandable if one accepts the following basic premises: 1) rates on agricultural and bulk commodities must be kept down; and 2) competitive rate-making would undermine the financial strength of the railroads and cause them to increase rates on their noncompetitive bulk traffic" (Friedlaender 1969:26).

Because the new transportation form, trucking, threatened the survival and status of an agency centered on the railroads, the extension of regulation to the new industry can be seen as evidence for the bureaucratic behavior theory. Both the ICC and state regulatory commissions strongly supported the new regulation (see, e.g., Healy 1940:427–28). After delays due to a filibuster on appropriations by Senator Huey Long, and a personnel hiring problem with the Civil Service Commission, the ICC staff expanded from 1,631 in 1935 to 2,173 by the end of 1936, and the expenditures of the Commission went from $5,577,000 in 1935 to $7,247,000 for the fiscal year ending June 30, 1937 (Sharfman 1937, 4:67).

Note that extension of regulation came during the Depression, a time of crisis for the regulated industries, and was subject to the ideological preference for economic intervention characteristic of the New Deal.

The Transportation Act of 1940 brought some water carriers under ICC regulation. Like earlier regulation, the Act proscribed certain abuses, required reasonable rates, and gave the ICC power to set maximum and minimum rates, and so on, and would prevent instability. But the Act was opposed by some shippers and water carriers who feared that the railroads would control regulation under the ICC. The railroads had actively sought this added protection against competition. As a result of the opposition, most water carriers were excluded from regulation, and the Act contained a national transportation policy to alleviate the fears of those who remained. According to this, the ICC was "to recognize and preserve the inherent advantages of each of the transportation forms" (Friedlaender 1969:22–23; Fainsod et al. 1959:297–98). The Act can thus be seen as an industry protection measure since it served the interests to some extent of all of the regulated industries. Value-of-service pricing was preserved, as required by the social goals theory (Friedlaender 1969:22–23). Consumer shippers received protection. And the bureaucracy of the ICC extended its control, even capturing some functions that had been performed by the then U.S. Maritime Commission.

Having illustrated the place of the four "theories" of regulatory origin in the founding of the ICC and the extension of its regulation to competing modes of transportation, we shall stop here (for more on the history of the ICC until recent years, see, e.g., the series by W. H. Jones 1975; Hoogenboom and Hoogenboom 1976; T. G. Moore 1972; Hilton 1969; Fellmeth 1970; Vaden 1976; R. E. Cohen 1977; R. J. Samuelson 1979). There does appear to be at least some support for each of the theories at many places in the ICC's history.

Whether regulation was added to serve consumer, industry, public or bureaucratic interests (or all of them), the ICC appeared most often to play a reactive role: "Rather than act upon the nation's transportation problem, the ICC reacted to it" (Hoogenboom and Hoogenboom 1976:118). The character of that reaction may have differed, possibly reflecting such factors as commissioner and staff quality, differentiation and delegation in the regulatory process, and the nature of external stimuli or demands. Reaction may have ranged from active attempts to recapture, reformulate, and expand regulatory powers (in the early years of the century), to more passive attempts to define all new regulation in terms of the existing railroad model (with trucks and barges) and thereby defend it (and/or, possibly, the organization).

Perhaps, acting as an organization in which value attaches to the retention of the existing social (incentive) system, "having achieved the increased power it had agitated for, the commission used that power to preserve existing relationships" (Hoogenboom and Hoogenboom 1976:188). Perhaps each interest was, in so far as possible, protected, so that the Commission acted as arbiter of a balance of interests, rather than the advocate or defender of any one interest. A vice chairman of the ICC has written that "This regulatory mission, in my judgment, is to safeguard the public interest within a free, competitive, and privately-owned transportation system, through the striking of balances between diverse and often conflicting interests" (Brewer 1974:356).

The "public interest" which, as we shall see in chapter 4, is so often used in ways lacking in real or consistent content, becomes equivalent to something which may be very different from other notions of the public interest potentially applicable to this case—i.e., becomes equivalent to a "balance of interests." If the agency functions in practice as arbiter among or balancer of interests, it seems clear that one must seek understanding of its central role as *organizational* processor of interests. This, of course, is independent of whether the set of interests processed includes the bureaucratic one in addition to a selection from (or all of) the other simple interests we have identified.

As we have cautioned earlier, we have not tried to offer full explanations for the historical behavior of the ICC and its expansion. Rather, we have indicated how it is possible to construct alternative explanations. The case of the ICC, at any rate, may require a synthesizing explanation.

6.0 Some Observations on Regulatory Origin

We offer some generalizations about regulation based in part on the foregoing.

1. Regulation has often been an incremental, piecemeal response to specific, perceived abuses and current crises. The target of regula-

tion is generally quite narrow and specific and, in fact, apparently viewed in isolation. Regulation is often tried first at local, then state, and finally national levels, after it has failed at the lower level for some reason, e.g., the problem crosses state boundaries, the influence of the regulated party could not be overcome at the lower level, and so on.

2. The mandate received by the administrator of the regulation where regulation is delegated is often poorly defined. After all, if the legislature could define it perfectly, it could—except for completely routine cases such as registration—leave administration of the regulation to the courts and the judicial process. Delegation is held necessary, among other reasons, because of a presumed need for flexibility, and therefore discretion (see chapter 6). So almost by definition, regulatory mandates cannot be completely specified. But assertion of expertise in the agency delegated to is also often an excuse to disguise the unwillingness or inability of the legislature to decide the terms of the mandate. For example, although regulation may be desired by consumers, by the industry, by the regulatory agency, and in support of national social goals all at the same time, the exact content of the desired regulation may differ in each case. A legislature may find it easier to simply pass a broad delegation of powers—since everybody wants regulation of some kind—and leave it to the agency to decide whose goals it will satisfy. Because regulation of the same area may be sought by different groups for different reasons, the regulatory agency may appear inconsistent at the same time, and over time, as it tries to regulate with respect to conflicting goals.

3. The range of possible alternative means or forms of regulation are generally not considered when regulation is imposed. Traditional or previously used forms, or forms supported by ideology as "proper," or accidental forms are adopted. As Redford has observed regarding the origin of the Civil Aeronautics Act of 1938, "we have here an outstanding example of how institutional history fixes an idea which in turn becomes determinative of future policy" (Redford 1969:28). The CAA was modeled after the ICA. Thus, both ideological and institutional histories often determine the choice of regulatory mechanisms.

4. Regulation is regularly imposed but it is rarely removed. Because regulation frequently is sought and/or enjoyed by parties to regulation (including the bureaucracy that administers it), who would oppose its removal, it is probably easier to impose than to remove.

Elaborations and additions to the regulatory coverage rarely involve reevaluation of the basic rationale for regulation. Thus the regulatory mandate becomes a reflection of a history of perceived abuses and crises (or of environmental problems solved for the central parties) rather than an integrated set of instructions to meet a well-defined problem or need.

5. Whether regulation serves national social goals and/or consumer interests, or neither, the regulated industry has often supported the imposition of regulation (though not always all features of the specific regulation proposed or approved). And if the regulated industry originally opposes regulation, it almost invariably comes to be one of the regulation's strongest supporters, with time.

6. Change in the regulated industry, such as technological advances that alter the basic characteristics of the industry or permit the appearance of competing modes, is generally not foreseen, and its possibility ignored. By assuming in effect that the essential characteristics of the industry will remain the same forever with perhaps only incremental change, regulation tends to freeze the industry into the forms current when regulation took effect. Regulation has thus often acted to "protect" industries against innovative basic changes. Note that such a freeze also protects the procedures of the regulatory agency and would be consistent with the bureaucratic behavior theory.

7.0 The Incentive Systems Model of Organizations and Regulatory "Capture"

We began this chapter by reviewing the structure of the policy-making process and the literature on theories of regulatory origin. These theories were analyzed partly with reference to the stages of the policy process that they covered. We then presented the general incentive systems approach; described four simple interest theories of regulatory origin; argued the central role of the regulatory agency as organization; and considered some aspects of regulatory entry. The four simple interest theories were then applied to the case of the Interstate Commerce Commission. Our discussion to this point has emphasized the earlier stages in the policy process and the origin of new regulatory programs or organizations; an adequate theory of regulatory origin should, as we observed earlier, take us through the administration stage of that process. An adequate theory of origin should also include the origin of new regulation in existing programs and organizations.

In this section, we shall present a partial theory explaining the development of a predisposition by regulators to make decisions and take actions consistent with the preferences of the regulated industry. This can include the origin of new regulations in an existing program or organization, or just actions in such areas as regulatory interpretation, management, and enforcement, that favor the regulated industry. Actions that aid the industry can simply include mediocre rather than consummate performance of regulatory tasks.

We thus go beyond strict consideration of regulatory origin alone; the theory applies not only to the industry protection situation of regulatory origin, but also to the explanation of certain aspects of ongoing regulatory practice—and performance. In section 2.1 we discussed some views of how regulation may deviate from serving public interest ends; these included "venality," "incompetence," and "capture." Thus we shall in this section present a partial theory of regulatory "capture." By developing a predisposition to make decisions and take actions consistent with the preferences of the regulated industry, regulators become, in effect, the agents of the industry (Mitnick 1974). This is the sense in which we shall treat "capture."

The theory is a logical adjunct to our earlier discussions of regulatory origin. The approach taken is related to the rational choice models of regulators as bureaucrats and the models of regulation as agency that were discussed earlier in this chapter (e.g., Noll 1971a, b, c; Hilton 1972a; Eckert 1973; Noll, Peck and McGowan 1973:120–26; Mitnick and Weiss 1974; Mitnick 1973b, 1974, 1975b; DeAlessi 1974, 1975; Goldberg 1973, 1974, 1976; Baldwin 1975). But the present approach utilizes an explicit incentive systems model of organizations (Mitnick, Backoff, and Rainey 1977), extends and makes significant additions to the earlier approaches, and depicts the posited relationships explicitly and systematically. Use of an incentive systems approach follows directly from modeling regulatory relations as instances of the general agent-principal relationship.

The theory offered here is, however, only a partial theory. It is an individual-level model limited largely to the relationship between the industry and the regulator and how aspects of this relation can promote "capture." Recall that in figure 3.1 we displayed a model of a simple incentive relation at the individual level, and in figure 3.2 we

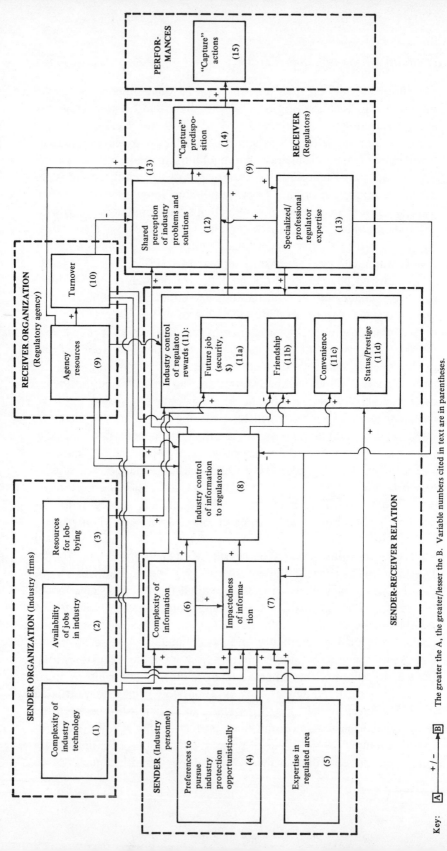

Figure 3.6 A Partial Incentive Systems Theory of Regulatory "Capture"

SENDER ORGANIZATION (Industry firms)

Complexity of industry technology (1)

Availability of jobs in industry (2)

Resources for lobbying (3)

SENDER (Industry personnel)

Preferences to pursue industry protection opportunistically (4)

Expertise in regulated area (5)

RECEIVER ORGANIZATION (Regulatory agency)

Agency resources (9)

Turnover (10)

Shared perception of industry problems and solutions (12)

"Capture" predisposition (14)

Specialized/professional regulator expertise (13)

RECEIVER (Regulators)

Complexity of information (6)

Impactedness of information (7)

Industry control of information to regulators (8)

Industry control of regulator rewards (11):

Future job (security, $) (11a)

Friendship (11b)

Convenience (11c)

Status/Prestige (11d)

SENDER-RECEIVER RELATION

PERFOR-MANCES

"Capture" actions (15)

Key: [A] → [B]   +/−

The greater the A, the greater/lesser the B. Variable numbers cited in text are in parentheses.

listed some common variables in each of the incentive model's categories for the case of the regulator's incentive relation with the regulated industry. In figure 3.6, we have further simplified the presentation to an explicitly depicted partial theory of "capture," omitting the environmental and some of the other variables. Many potentially important factors are thus not included. But we do mean the theory to reflect what is the most common or prototypical situation.

Thus, for example, as we discussed in the sections on the regulator as bureaucrat and on aspects of regulatory entry, an active public constituency supporting "public interest" ends is frequently absent and difficult to mobilize. And, also as we have discussed earlier, agency structure (such as a bureau rather than a commission form) can, as Eckert (1973) describes, affect the reward system faced by regulators and, ultimately, their actions for or against the regulated industry's interests. We do not consider variations in personnel practices among agencies.

Furthermore, since the theory deals only with the direct relation between regulators and the industry, it omits situations such as that sometimes referred to in the context of federal regulation as the "unholy" or "iron triangle" (e.g., Weaver 1978). Besides the agency and the industry, this "triangle" includes the legislative committee of oversight (e.g., Seidman 1975a:38–68; Krasnow and Longley 1978:69–93; Cary 1967; Bibby 1966). Influences relevant to "capture" considerations can be exerted through such committees (cf. the discussion of Weingast 1978 earlier in this chapter). The discussions of these situations that we presented earlier should therefore be seen as appendages and extensions of the present theory. The theory itself may be seen as a "slice" of a more general theory and as a prototypical or core set of arguments applicable at all levels of government, i.e., at levels other than the federal "unholy triangle" and at levels perhaps lacking such a "triangle."

7.1 A PARTIAL THEORY OF REGULATORY "CAPTURE"

Information plays a central role in the theory. In figure 3.6, the complexity of the industry's technology (1) means that the information needed to make regulatory decisions will also be complex (6). The industry's opportunistically pursued preferences to secure protection for itself (4), and the expertise it possesses in the complex technology it employs (5), lead to a condition of "information impactedness" between the industry and the regulatory agency (7). The complexity of the information itself (6) (with associated uncertainty, with the bounded rationality of the parties in dealing with such information, and with the potential relative expertise of the industry in the area) can also contribute to the "information impactedness" (7) (cf. Porter and Sagansky 1976).

Williamson (1975; Williamson, Wachter and Harris 1975) uses this term to refer to a condition in which "true underlying circumstances relevant to the transaction, or related set of transactions, are known to one or more parties but cannot be costlessly discerned by or displayed for others" (Williamson 1975:31). The condition can occur whether or not each of the parties to the transaction have identical information, and may result from opportunism (strategic behavior in pursuit of self-interest; see Williamson 1975:26–27), a small-numbers bargaining situation, uncertainty, and bounded rationality. Where information is identical, incompleteness in the information and/or deception from opportunism can lead to information impactedness. Where information is asymmetrically possessed, there may be "high costs to obtaining information parity" (Williamson 1975:31). As noted, this situation frequently characterizes the relationship between the regulatory agency and the regulated industry.

Opportunism (4) by the industry can also lead to control by the industry over such regulator rewards as satisfaction of status/prestige, convenience, friendship, and future job goals (11). The industry must, of course, as indicated in figure 3.6, possess sufficient resources to be devoted to lobbying and/or other rewarding personal contacts with the regulators (3), and, in the case of future job rewards, possess attractive jobs for regulators after they leave the agency (2).

Specialized or professional expertise held by regulators in the regulated area (13) can work against the information impactedness condition (7), and against industry control of the information needed for regulation (8). This is because it can to some extent counter industry interpretative expertise (5) and the problems raised by the complexity of the information on the industry necessary for regulation (6). But the industry is likely to retain advantages in the "expertise" area of supply of current operating information on the industry (5). And industry opportunism (4) with possible exploitation of the small-numbers agency-industry bargaining relation, bounded rationality, and remaining uncertainty, can still promote information impactedness (7). Information impactedness (7) and information complexity (6), of course, can lead to industry control of the information needed for regulation (8).

Industry control of information needed in regulation (8) can permit the industry a measure of control over regulator rewards in such areas as friendship and convenience (11b, 11c). By doing the regulators "favors" and satisfying everyday job performance needs through supplying information, the industry can ease regulators' work loads (i.e., increase their level of "convenience") (11c) and create friendships between industry members and agency personnel (11b). Industry control over the information needed by regulators (8) can lead to shared regulator–industry perceptions of industry problems and appropriate solutions (12). Information can, of course, be supplied selectively to the regulators or distorted with an industry bias. Through control of information, the industry can succeed in co-opting the regulators (see, e.g., Selznick 1949), i.e., in making the regulators perceive the regulatory task through an informational framework and orientation provided by the industry.

The occurrence of specialized/professional expertise (as against generalist, e.g., legal, regulator expertise) in the regulatory agency (13) can provide fertile opportunities for the industry to control regulator rewards (11). Specialized concern for the industry and/or related professional matters can mean that the regulator will value expressions of respect (or status or prestige) from other experts, including experts working in the industry (11d). Although the specialized expert may not be as dependent on the industry for information as the nonspecialist, he may still find much of his information controlled by the industry. Supply of information by the industry can, as we have noted, reduce the work load of all regulators, specialist or nonspecialist, and thus increase their level of what we have termed "convenience" (11c). This contributes to the industry's control over regulator rewards. The specialist may simply have narrower or better defined information needs, and he, too, may find the industry helpful in increasing his level of on-the-job "convenience" (11c).

Long-time interest in the field, membership in professional associations in the area, attendance at professional meetings, and job-related industry contacts by regulatory agency specialists can all lead to the development of friendships with specialists and others working in the regulated industry (11b). Actions by regulators counter to industry interests could then produce negative impacts on personal friends of the specialist–regulator. Thus the industry may in effect control this source of specialist–regulator rewards. Finally, quite apart from any potentially opportunistic behavior by the industry (4), the specialist–regulator will find that most of his future job possibilities inevitably lie in, or dealing with, the regulated industry that relies on such expertise (11a). Furthermore, jobs in the industry are likely to mean increased salary and, for non-Civil-Service regulators, increased security. Opportunistic behavior by the regulated industry in recruiting regulators through offering them unusually attractive positions will only exacerbate the problem.

Because of their long-time interest in and ties to the regulated industry, it is likely that specialist–regulators (13) may come to share the industry's perceptions of its problems and the best solutions to them (12). This may not occur necessarily; specialists like some academicians, for example, who may study an industry at arm's length, avoiding personal ties and possessing job security in a tenured university position (as well as the supposedly disinterested norms of scholarly inquiry), might avoid this sharing of perceptions. Even academicians, however, may depend on the industry for information and for other rewards, such as consulting arrangements, and can thereby acquire an industry orientation.

We note the paradoxical nature of the need for specialist–regulators: Though they may reduce the industry's information (especially, expertise) advantage in regulation, they may also be more subject to rewards mediated (and possibly manipulated) by the regulated industry.

The greater the regulatory agency's resources (e.g., budget, permitting a larger number of personnel, greater investment in research in the agency's problems, more monitoring stations and inspectors, and so on) (9), the less the information impactedness (7) and the less the industry's control over information needed by the regulators (8). In addition, more resources (9) will permit the hiring of more specialist–regulators (13), thus also reducing information impactedness (7) and industry control over information (8) (but increasing regulatory agency susceptibility to specialist–regulator rewards mediated by the industry (11)). Greater resources (9) can in general reduce industry control of regulator rewards (11) since the regulatory agency may then be able to provide higher salaries (and thereby reduce the attraction of future jobs in the industry) (11a), create better, more "convenient" working conditions (11c), offer more of the physical trappings of status and prestige (e.g., fancier offices, close-in parking spaces, more trips to conventions, private secretaries) (11d), and promote friendships through being more supportive of the regulatory agency social system (e.g., more banquets, comfortable lounges, more personnel with which to interact) (11b).

Increases in regulatory agency resources permitting growth in the agency (9) will lead to increased turnover (10) (on the general effects of turnover, see Price 1977). Turnover can include both changes in jobs within a regulatory agency and agency exits and entrances. This can occur as new positions open up due to expansion and the need for additional supervisory personnel. Higher turnover (shorter regulator job tenure) (10) can mean increased information impactedness (7) and increased industry control over information needed for regulation (8). Regulators will thus have less job experience and possess less of the particular information on the industry that is needed to perform their jobs (Price 1977:106–7). They will have less of an opportunity to learn the idiosyncratic tasks and information bases associated with their positions (cf. Williamson, Wachter, and Harris 1975:260–61). The industry can therefore increase their relative information advantage. Note that increase in agency resources (9) can tend both to decrease and to increase industry control over information (8). The former occurs as more resources permit hiring more experts, performing more monitoring, and so on. The latter effect proceeds, of course, through turnover's (10) effect on information control (8). That is, more resources produce higher turnover, but higher turnover increases information impactedness and industry control of information.

Turnover (10) can, on the other hand, inhibit the development of regulator–industry friendships (11b) and thus reduce the possible ability of the industry to mediate regulator rewards in this area. Turnover (10) can also interfere with the development of shared regulator–industry perceptions regarding the industry's problems and appropriate solutions to those problems (12).

Industry control over regulator rewards (11), and shared regulator–industry perceptions of industry problems (and solutions) (12), are associated with regulator predispositions to make decisions and take actions consistent with industry preferences (14). And these predispositions are associated with actions that favor the industry, i.e., "capture" (15).

As we noted earlier, the theory depicted in figure 3.6 is really only a partial one. We have really treated only the industry–agency relation, and have not considered such factors as the relationship of the regulatory agency to the legislature and to the courts (e.g., the agency will act to avoid reversal of its decisions), the effects of alternate regulatory agency structures (e.g., commission vs. bureau forms), and the relations between the regulatory agency and consumer and public interest groups.

In closing this section in which we presented an incentive systems theory of regulatory "capture," we would like to note a basic (and contestable) assumption made in this approach. This is that the regulator rewards important in understanding this phenomenon are all self-interested in character. Regulators are assumed to be officials basically like most other officials; and they are assumed to be without some crusading, altruistic interest in forwarding some regulatory policy or program (cf. Eckert 1973). Regulators of this sort do, of course, occur, and in general we may presume that regulators may be at least mixed-motive in seeking both self-interest and the other-interests of programs, policy, or various publics (see chapter 2). The theory in figure 3.6 would still apply, of course, to the self-interest component of mixed-motive regulators, and in its information control–shared perception and other linkages would still apply to all. At any rate, we could simply add a variable relating to the occurrence of regulator preferences for policy, program or "public interest" ends. This can obviously oppose "capture." In this way we can perhaps introduce the effects of (the possibly only occasional) "good men."

7.2 FEDERAL AND STATE REGULATORS: EVIDENCE FOR SOME VARIABLES IN THE THEORY

In this section, we shall take a quick tour of some of the available evidence for a few of the variables in the theory. Empirical evidence is not available for each level—federal and state—for each of the variables in the theory discussed in the previous section. In fact, the study of regulators has been overwhelmingly directed at the federal level. Furthermore, most works that have studied regulators focused on the top officials, usually commissioners (and sometimes also key or high-level staff members). Top state regulatory officials, and federal and state staff, are less studied. Where data on states exist, it is almost entirely for state public utility commissions. State and local regulation, of course, is far more extensive than this.

We shall in essentials focus on questions of career mobility (on career mobility of federal bureaucrats, see McGregor 1974): (1) What kinds of backgrounds or pre-job expertise do regulators have (relevant to variable 13 in figure 3.6)? (2) Where do regulators go after they leave the agency, and why do they leave (variable 11a)? (3) How adequate are agency resources perceived to be, especially as they relate to regulator salaries (variables 9, 11)? (4) What is the turnover rate in regulatory agencies (variable 10) and would it appear to promote or inhibit industry control of information (variable 8) and of regulator rewards (variable 11)? We shall limit consideration of turnover to how long regulators remain in the same agency rather than extend it as well to intra-agency job changes. It should be cautioned that we have no direct data on "capture" itself; the theory is *not* being directly tested.

We shall consider the federal agencies first.

7.2.1   Federal Regulators: Backgrounds

Besides arguing that "good men" are the "prime key to the improvement of the administrative process" (see quote cited earlier in this chapter; Landis 1960:66), Landis asserted that "good men are primarily attracted by the challenge inherent in a job" and that salary is only "secondary" as long as it is sufficient "to meet reasonable standards of living comparable to [the regulators'] positions in the society" (Landis 1960:66–67). And longer tenure of office is desirable to compensate for the severing of "past connections," to allow long-term planning, to eliminate anxiety over reappointment, to reduce turnover and permit expertise to develop, to encourage "the spirit of independence," and generally to promote "the concept of devotion to a career rather than that of a stepping stone to further political or professional advancement" (Landis 1960:68).

Landis's observations were not new, and neither were the problems he had observed. Thirty years before, Robert Cushman wrote regarding the state commissions that "with really able and honest men in control even very mediocre administrative machinery seems to run with relative smoothness. Without such men, no amount of modern streamlining gives sound and efficient administration" (Cushman 1941:498). Thus, commissioner backgrounds as well as basic administrative talent have long been considered key factors in regulatory performance. We review some of the literature on backgrounds below (see also Lichty 1961–62, 1962; Williams 1976; Scher 1961; Nagel 1969; Welborn 1966; Canon 1969).

Pendleton Herring noted in his 1936 study of the federal commissioners (covering the beginning of the agencies until January 1, 1935) that they exhibited a very diverse set of educational backgrounds. He commented favorably as far as occupation is concerned:

> In general no uniform background can be found. This is in itself significant. No clear ties of an economic or social variety point to the development of a bureaucratic class. Very broadly viewed our commissioners are for the most part professional men. Their training has been legal and academic rather than technical. Much more likely than not they have participated in politics and held minor public office. They have seldom been chiefly concerned in running for major elective offices. They have taken some interest in their political parties, but this has often been an activity of a rather incidental sort. The party hack is very rare; the lawyer, educator, journalist, and banker is more usual. (Herring 1936b:33)

And,

> The characteristic of our system is this: that our public servants are lawyers or businessmen or professors. They are not administrators primarily. They have given their loyalties elsewhere before they enter the government. (Herring 1936b:43)

Herring observed that it was difficult to get able businessmen to hold appointments as commissioners for very long, and "even if this were possible, our regulatory commissions obviously should not be dominated by the industrialist. . . . the record to date suggests that we are more likely to get from college faculties than from great corporations competent men who are willing to serve for a long period" (Herring 1936b:60). There was a pattern of appointment of some retired, defeated, or unsuccessful politicians in elective office, but "the aged politician usually has little to offer and only a brief time to serve" (Herring 1936b:60). Appointments, at any rate, had frequently been made for political reasons.

Finally, as far as background is concerned, Herring noted that "an avenue has opened from state to federal regulatory commissions for quite a few men." This could be significant and improve regulation at both levels, he argued, since "most of the state commissions have long been handicapped and discouraged. The practice of federal appointments as rewards to the able would 'tone up' the personnel greatly" (Herring 1936b:49).

From Herring's data on background, it is clear that by far the most popular employments at time of appointment, and primary occupations, were law and public service. Law constituted 25 and 27 percent, and public service 45 and 34 percent, respectively, of the time-of-appointment-employment and primary occupation responses. It has often been observed (particularly for legislators) that it can be relatively easy for lawyers to take jobs in the public sector, since they have a profession to which they can easily return (see, e.g., Eulau and Sprague 1964). Note that Herring both saw public service as a steppingstone to (more rewarding) service on a regulatory agency, and the agency as a reward for significant past public service. This theme will return below.

Stanley, Mann, and Doig's 1967 study overlaps with Herring's (from the first administration of Franklin Roosevelt) and effectively updates his work to April 30, 1965. The percentage of commissioners with law degrees had risen to 59 percent. Educational backgrounds were still diverse. A smaller percentage of commissioners attended elite or prestige private pre-college schools than other high-ranking political executives in the federal government (Stanley, Mann, and Doig 1967:120–21, 124–25). Fewer commissioners had had business occupations, many more had had public service backgrounds, more are likely to have worked at other levels of government, and more (except for cabinet officers) had held elective office than the other political executives studied by Stanley, Mann, and Doig (1967:34). The data seem to recall the observation regarding commission service as reward for service elsewhere.

Stanley, Mann, and Doig compared their results directly with Herring's. Far more of the commissioners in the later group had public service backgrounds, with corresponding drops in all other areas except law. Herring's observations regarding steppingstones to the agency from lower levels of government and the agency as resting place for ex-politicians receive increased support. But eleven percent of the commissioners had at one time served in the U.S. Congress compared with 13 percent in Herring's study (Stanley, Mann, and Doig:44), i.e., the frequency of appointment of ex-Congressmen was about the same.

Significant numbers of commissioners were found to have been employed in, or retained by, the regulated industries, but the pattern was not consistent across agencies. Relatively small percentages of career or noncareer agency employees ever became commissioners in their agencies, though again the pattern was inconsistent. Commissioners tended to be appointed more often without prior federal service, and tended to stay a bit longer, than executive personnel in other agencies. Almost half the commissioners, in fact, had been local officials or part-time state and local officials. (Stanley, Mann, and Doig 1967:136, 140–41, 143, 144.) Herring had found a higher percentage with nonfederal experience in the public sector (76 percent versus 43 percent) and more local officials and state legislators (Stanley, Mann, and Doig 1967:47). But the same percentage, 13 percent, was found in both studies to have held positions in corresponding state-level regulatory agencies (Stanley, Mann, and Doig 1967:48). Commissioners were more likely to have served previously in government in general, and for greater lengths of time, than other federal political executives (Stanley, Mann, and Doig 1967:48–49). As for position held immediately before appointment, Stanley, Mann, and Doig (1967:146) found that law had dropped from Herring's 25 percent to 12 percent, and public service had risen from Herring's 45 percent to 78 percent.

Thus, Herring's observation that the commissioners were "not administrators primarily" was no longer true. But while Herring argued for the development of career regulators within the same agency, Stanley, Mann and Doig could show the development of a class of public servants who simply made a career (or frequent stopover) of government. This career then included service in regulatory agencies.

Graham and Kramer's (1976) study of twenty-five years (approximately, 1949–1974) of appointments to the Federal Communications Commission and Federal Trade Commission provides by far the best documentation of the details of the appointments process (cf. Fellmeth 1970:1–5 for additional details for the case of the ICC). They observe that

> Partisan political considerations dominate the selection of regulators to an alarming extent. Alarming, in that other factors—such as competence, experience, and even, on occasion, regulatory philosophy—are only secondary considerations. Most commission appointments are the result of well-stoked campaigns conducted at the right time with the right sponsors, and many selections can be explained in terms of powerful political connections and little else: Commission seats are good consolation prizes for defeated Congressmen; useful runner-up awards for persons who ricochet into the appointment as a result of a strong yet unsuccessful campaign for another position; appropriate resting berths for those who have labored long and hard in the party vineyards; and a convenient dumping ground for people who have performed unsatisfactorily in other, more important Government posts. (Graham and Kramer 1976:391)

Appointments of commissioners who had served on the agency's staff were not as uncommon in the two agencies as the earlier studies indicate; about 20 percent had seen such service. But, as Graham and Kramer's (1976:396–97) analysis makes clear, this hardly constituted a recognized ladder for promotion and reward for achievement. Staff were "promoted" both because they had powerful political sponsorship and because they lacked partisan identification but had a "nominal party affiliation" and the support of the chairman of the agency.

Graham and Kramer's data on the FCC and FTC commissioners whose appointments they studied is reproduced in table 3.1. Out of a total of 58 appointments, one-half were serving in a position in the federal government at the time of their appointment, another 9 percent were serving in state government, and 29 percent were working in a private law practice. This is consistent with our earlier observations. While the principal occupation of 9 percent appeared to have been elective office, 64 percent were practicing lawyers (and 67 percent had law degrees). Graham has observed that the quality of many appointments to the federal commissions by the Carter administration has, on the basis of apparent job knowledge and professional skills, been relatively high.[26]

A study by the staff of the Subcommittee on Oversight and Investigations of the Committee on Interstate and Foreign Commerce, U.S. House of Representatives (1976; see also 1975), covering 1961 to 1975, has partially updated the earlier results described above. Table 3.2a and b lists the numbers of commissioners or top officials in a selection of federal regulatory agencies that, through evidence of some participation "in any activity or organization promoting a consumer, environmental, or conservationist cause," seemed to have demonstrated "consumer sensitivity" prior to their appointments (U.S. House of Representatives, Subcommittee on Oversight and Investigations 1976:450–51). The numbers are small. The Subcommittee (1976) also found that about 35 percent of the appointees "had prior direct or indirect employment in the regulated industry," and that this percentage had been increasing (pp. 451–52); see table 3.3a. Finally, the Subcommittee (1976) observed that nearly half of the appointees (34 percent federal, 14 percent state) have had prior

---

[26] James M. Graham, personal communication (April 1979). Graham and Kramer (1976:383–84) note that the quality of appointments tends to be higher in the early years of an Administration.

TABLE 3.1. THIRTY-ONE MEMBERS OF THE FEDERAL COMMUNICATIONS
COMMISSION AND TWENTY-SEVEN MEMBERS OF THE
FEDERAL TRADE COMMISSION WHO SERVED
BETWEEN 1952 AND 1975

	FCC	FTC	Combined
I. Position immediately preceding appointment:			
Academic	2	—	2
Broadcaster	2	—	2
Engineer, private	2	—	2
Federal Government (total)	17	12	29
(a) Staff, same agency	5	2	7
(b) Congressional staff	2	2	4
(c) Congressional Member	1	2	3
(d) Executive branch	6	7	13
(e) Other Federal regulatory agencies	2	—	2
Law, private	5	12	17
State government	3	2	5
Other	—	1	1
II. Regulatory background: [a]			
In staff of same agency	8	6	14
In regulated industry, same agency	8	3	11
In other Federal regulation	6	6	12
In State regulation	5	—	5
No background in regulation	11	12	23
III. Principal occupation prior to appointment:			
Academic	2	—	2
Broadcaster	2	—	2
Engineer	5	—	5
Lawyer	15	22	37
Elected officeholder	1	4	5
Other	6	1	7
IV. Employment subsequent to agency service:			
Academic	2	2	4
Federal public office	2	2	4
State public office	—	1	1
Private employment in agency-related work	14	10	24
Public interest employment agency-related work	1	—	1
Retired	3	5	8
Other	2	4	6
Still in office	7	3	10
V. Party affiliation:			
Democratic	16	11	27
Republican	14	13	27
Independent	1	3	4

	FCC	FTC	Combined
VI. Race:			
Caucasian	30	26	56
Black	1	1	2
VII. Sex:			
Male	29	25	54
Female	2	2	4
VIII. Education (highest level):			
Advanced degree in law (LL. M.)	3	1	4
Law degree	15	24	39
Bachelor's degree	10	—	10
Some college	3	—	3
No college	—	2	2
IX. Age: [b]			
Median age at appointment	47.5	49.5	48.5
Median age at departure	55.0	53.5	54.5
X. Tenure:			
Appointed to an unexpired term (less than 7 yrs)	13	14	27
Resigned before expiration of term	10	12	22
Served 7 yrs or more	9	8	17
Still serving	7	3	10
Average length of service as commissioner [b]	6.7	4.6	5.6
Average length of service as chairman [b]	2.8	3.2	3.0
XI. Reappointment:			
Number reappointed	7	6	13
By same administration	4	4	8
By 1 or more subsequent administrations	4 [c]	2	6

SOURCE: Graham and Kramer (1976:422).

[a] Totals for the 1st 4 categories exceed the number of commissioners, since some regulators had backgrounds in several relevant areas.
[b] Years.
[c] Robert E. Lee was reappointed by the same and by subsequent administrations.

employment in a public sector job (see table 3.3b). The regulatory agencies have thus continued to be a place for employment for former public servants.

Meier and Plumlee (1978) in their attempt to find support for Bernstein's life cycle theory reported some data on regulatory backgrounds. Unfortunately, their data is impossible to evaluate and compare to other studies because they are not specific as to which "agency elites" (commissioners? key staff?) they include. The percentage of "agency elites" from the regulated industry, and that of "agency elites" with prior expertise at time of appointment vary a

TABLE 3.2. COMMISSIONERS OR TOP OFFICIALS IN SELECTED FEDERAL
REGULATORY AGENCIES DEMONSTRATING "CONSUMER
SENSITIVITY" PRIOR TO APPOINTMENT

*3.2a. Commissioners or Administrators with Demonstrated Consumer Sensitivity,
FY 1961–75*

Agency	Number	Total regulators appointed
CPSC	1	5
FCC	1	19
FPC	0	16
FTC	2	15
ICC	0	21
SEC	0	19
EPA	2	2
FDA	1	6
NHTSA	3	5
Total	10	108

*3.2b. Chairmen or Administrators with Demonstrated Consumer Sensitivity, FY
1961–75*

Agency	Number	Total regulators appointed
CPSC	0	1
FCC	0	4
FPC	0	3
FTC	0	4
ICC	0	6
SEC	0	4
EPA	2	2
FDA	1	6
NHTSA	3	5
Total	6	35

SOURCE: U.S. House Subcommittee on Oversight and Investigations (1976: 451). Biographical
data provided to the subcommittee by the agencies.

great deal over time and across agencies; no strong patterns emerge.
Consistent with what we have already seen, Meier and Plumlee did
observe some general recruitment from the industry. Most of the
elites were credited with prior expertise, which is not consistent with
some of the other studies. Finally, very high percentages of the elites
had had legal training. (Meier and Plumlee 1978:89, 92, 93)

TABLE 3.3. PRIOR EMPLOYMENT OF COMMISSIONERS OR TOP
OFFICIALS IN SELECTED FEDERAL REGULATORY AGENCIES

*3.3a. Commissioners and Administrators Appointed with Prior Direct or Indirect
Employment in Regulated Industry, FY 1961–75* [a]

Agency	Employment in Regulated Industry		Total regulators appointed
	In last 5 yrs	In last 15 yrs	
CPSC	2	2	5
FCC	5	10	19
FPC	1	2	16
FTC	5	8	15
ICC	3	4	21
SEC	5	10	19
EPA	0	0	2
FDA	1	2	6
NHTSA	0	0	5
Total	22	38	108

[a]Information received from agencies in September 1976 shows that 2 of 7 Commissioners appointed in fiscal year 1976 had such prior employment in regulated industry.

*3.3b. Prior Employment of Individuals Appointed Commissioners or Administrators of
Regulatory Agencies, FY 1961–75*

Agency	Private Sector (total 56)						Public Sector (total 52)				
	Regulated industry	Industry	Law practicing before Commissions	Other private practice of law	Certified public accountant	Educator	Career federal service	Professional staff of the Congress	Member of Congress	State government	Total
CPSC	2	—	—	—	—	1	2	—	—	—	5
FCC	6	—	4	3	—	—	2	2	1	1	19
FPC	1	1	1	2	—	1	2	2	1	5	16
FTC	—	—	8	2	—	—	4	—	—	1	15
ICC	—	2	4	3	—	—	2	5	1	4	21
SEC	—	—	9	—	1	—	5	1	3	—	19
EPA	—	—	—	—	—	—	1	—	—	1	2
FDA	2	—	—	—	—	1	3	—	—	—	6
NHTSA	—	1	—	—	—	1	—	—	—	3	5
Total	11	4	26	10	1	4	21	10	6	15	108

SOURCE: U.S. House Subcommittee on Oversight and Investigations (1976:452,455). Replies to the subcommittee questionnaire of June 1975. Biographical data provided to the subcommittee by the agencies.

There is much less information available regarding staff in the federal agencies. Herring (1938) studied 500 upper-level federal regulatory officials. Forty percent had law degrees (but except for the SEC, there were no law review men); many had no college or professional degrees. Although few had had direct political experience, about half had held positions in other, usually federal agencies, including other regulatory agencies. A significant component of the staff in some agencies   had   worked   in   the   regulated   industry.   Herring (1936b:99–100; also 1938) reported a typical pattern for 165 cases in the ICC: few of these senior staff members had college degrees on entry; they later completed their educations in night school and worked their way up over 10–20 years.

Information on federal regulatory staff, especially lower-level staff, is still scarce. Information in each of the areas we are reviewing (background, future job, resources, turnover) has been gathered by several studies for federal employees and/or agencies in general; some regulatory staff are undoubtedly included, but it is not generally possible to separate their responses (see, e.g., Bendix 1949; Warner et al. 1963; Kilpatrick, Cummings, and Jennings 1964; Stanley 1964; Corson and Paul 1966).

The study by the House Subcommittee on Oversight and Investigations (1976) did report data on prior employment of upper level (GS–15 and above) Civil Service personnel in the regulated industry (see table 3.4). It found that 14 percent had come from the regulated industry.

7.2.2   Federal Regulators: Departures

We turn now to consideration of where federal regulators go when they leave the agency, and why they leave.

Herring observed that

> In general, the men engaging in business after service were simply returning to their former occupation. . . .The common activity for the ex-commissioner is the practise of law in a field closely allied to his administrative experience. . . . A lawyer after service on an important regulatory commission has no difficulty in getting wealthy clients. . . . It would not only be unfair but untrue as well to say that the members of our federal regulatory commissions withdraw from public life in order to exploit the experience and knowledge that they have gained in government service for the benefit of private interests. To account for the short careers of our commissioners a confused variety of causes must be examined. (Herring 1936b:67, 68, 70)

TABLE 3.4. PRIOR EMPLOYMENT OF UPPER LEVEL CIVIL SERVICE (GS-15 AND ABOVE) PERSONNEL IN REGULATED INDUSTRY

Agency	Having prior employment in regulated industry	Total upper level personnel	Percent total from regulated industry
CPSC	0	77	0
FCC	24	179	13
FPC	29	140	21
FTC	64	178	36
ICC	15	266	6
SEC	42	116	36
EPA	51	524	10
FDA	15	272	6
NHTSA	22	165	13
Total	262	1,917	14

SOURCE: U.S. House Subcommittee on Oversight and Investigations (1976: 452). Replies to the subcommittee questionnaire of June 1975.

Herring found that a significant number of the federal commissioners served again in government following their commission appointment (Herring 1936b:133; the data are not clearly consistent with that on p. 135). Many returned to law practice; Herring writes that, for the commissioners from three of the agencies, "it can be definitely said that their contact with the federal government brought them clients and encouraged them to set up their offices in the capital" (Herring 1936b:135).

Stanley, Mann, and Doig (1967:73) noted that commissioners were more likely than most other federal executives "to go into new organizations in their old professions. In many cases this meant moving to a different law firm." Only 6 percent went into business related to their agency work. But, obviously, those who were lawyers and those whose work was in an area related to the regulation but not in business could also be benefiting directly from their service.

The House Subcommittee on Oversight and Investigations (1976) found that one-third of the commissioners or administrators became directly or indirectly employed in the regulated industry within five years of their leaving office (see table 3.5). Fellmeth (1970: 19–22) describes a strong pattern of post-ICC job-taking in the transportation industry. In the hearings that preceded the House study (U.S.

TABLE 3.5. SUBSEQUENT EMPLOYMENT OF COMMISSIONERS OR
ADMINISTRATORS DIRECTLY OR INDIRECTLY IN
REGULATED INDUSTRY, FY 1961–75 [a]

| | Employment in Regulated Industry | | | Total leaving |
Agency	Direct	Indirect	Total	agency
CPSC	0	0	0	0
FCC	3	1	4	16
FPC	0	2	2	16
FTC	0	6	6	15
ICC	2	0	2	17
SEC	2	10	12	19
EPA	0	1	1	1
FDA	2	1	3	5
NHTSA	1	0	1	4
Total	10	21	31	93

SOURCE: U.S. House Subcommittee on Oversight and Investigations (1976: 453). Replies to the subcommittee questionnaire of June 1975.

[a]Information received from the agencies in September 1976 shows that 6 of 12 Commissioners who left agencies in fiscal year 1976 became employed in the regulated industry.

House of Representatives, Subcommittee on Oversight and Investigations 1975), former FPC Chairman Lee White remarked,

> Being very perceptive, I noticed that as people were coming to the end of their term and they didn't know whether the President was going to appoint them or not, there was a subliminal process at work. Some of them, believe it or not, began dickering as to how they ought to be voting on some issues. So it occurred to me that that last period is especially tender and sensitive, and that the worst thing in the world is to be looking for a job when you know that your term is going to end, say, on June 30, and you are making decisions all through January and June of that year. . . . If you haven't married a wealthy woman and acquired money, or a wealthy husband, all of a sudden the payroll stops, those salary checks stop. (U.S. House of Representatives, Subcommittee on Oversight and Investigations 1975:72)

Meier and Plumlee (1978) report the percentages of "agency elites" who retired to the regulated industry for each of all four-year periods from the founding of the agencies studied until 1975. Again, we note that "agency elites" is not defined in the article. The authors comment that "members retiring to work in the regulated industry is hardly universal, but occurs with sufficient frequency to cause concern" (Meier and Plumlee 1978:90). This would appear to be a reasonable assessment of the available evidence on agency commissioner departures. A note of caution is necessary, however, regarding too-simplistic generalizations from such observations of post-agency ties to the industry. The report on the regulatory appointments process prepared by James M. Graham for the U.S. Senate Committee on Governmental Affairs "Study on Federal Regulation" (1977) describes a number of cases in which blanket condemnation of the practice could be questioned.

We shall consider reasons for leaving again when we discuss turnover below. We do note that once failure of reappointment, death in office, and compulsory and voluntary retirement are considered, the sample size to examine for "reasons" is considerably reduced (see Stanley, Mann, and Doig 1967:157).

The available data on departures of staff in the federal regulatory agencies is sparse. The House Subcommittee on Oversight and Investigations (1976) did report reasons for leaving for upper-level staff members in nine regulatory agencies between fiscal years 1971 and 1975 (see table 3.6). Twenty-seven percent of the staff members cited "job frustration," 12.5 percent cited "lack of money and promotion opportunity," and 38 percent cited "accepted better job" as their reason for leaving. The Subcommittee report argued that, "if the number who left for a better job (38%) were attracted by some-

TABLE 3.6. REASONS FOR LEAVING CITED BY FORMER EMPLOYEES OF 9 REGULATORY AGENCIES [a]

Agency	Job frustration	Lack of money and promotion opportunity	Accepted better job	Others	Totals
CPSC	3	0	5	0	8
FCC	11	4	13	6	34
FPC	6	1	13	13	33
FTC	11	13	32	24	80
ICC	12	8	16	7	43
SEC [b]	0	1	4	3	8
EPA	10	4	13	15	42
FDA [b]	4	2	7	3	16
NHSTA	2	1	1	4	8
Total	59	34	104	75	272

SOURCE: U.S. House Subcommittee on Oversight and Investigations (1976:459) Survey, April 5, 1976.

[a] Based on responses of those attorneys, GS-11-14, and executives, GS-15's and above, that left the agencies between fiscal years 1971–75.

[b] Does not include attorneys.

thing other than an increase in money, a reasonable assumption, considering that so few complained of a lack of money or advancement—it could be inferred that more than half left because they were dissatisfied with the agency's performance. In any event, the salary levels clearly were not unsatisfactory to the majority of those who left" (U.S. House of Representatives, Subcommittee on Oversight and Investigations 1976:459). From the data reported, however, it is still possible that salary was often a contributing factor.

7.2.3 Federal Regulators: Resources, Especially Salary

We consider now the adequacy of agency resources, especially the level of regulator salaries. Relatively high regulator salaries could lessen the industry's control over regulator rewards through reducing the attractiveness of future jobs in or related to the industry.

Overall, agency resources as represented both by budget and by number of personnel have not exhibited steady growth, and periods of growth have not shown a steady growth rate. In general we do see long-term growth (see Noll 1971; Stigler 1975; Meier and Plumlee 1978:87).

As for salary, Herring summarized the situation in his sample pointedly: "For men who feel the need of very high financial rewards the federal government cannot compete" (Herring 1936b:69). Calls for increased regulator salaries and fringe benefits have been frequent over the years. The first Hoover Commission noted that "with the present scale of salaries for the commissions, it has become harder and harder to attract men of caliber and capacity for the arduous work required or to retain them on the commission for substantial periods once they have been appointed" (Commission on Organization of the Executive Branch of the Government January 1949:24). Landis (1960) recommended maintenance of adequate salaries and increased fringe benefits as a supplement to his call for "good men." Although federal salaries have been substantially increased, it is still true, as Graham writes, that "public service for many of those persons sometimes means considerable financial sacrifice for the term in government" (U.S. Senate Committee on Governmental Affairs 1977, 1:64).

With respect to staff salaries, the First Hoover Commission observed that "inflation has made it increasingly difficult to attract and retain qualified men for top positions. Since salaries for such jobs have not been adjusted to offset rising prices, they are far less attractive than in the past and can scarcely compete with comparable private positions'' (Commission on Organization of the Executive Branch of the Government January 1949:23). Although the House Subcommittee on Oversight and Investigations (1976:459) commented that "so few complained of a lack of money or advancement" and "the salary levels clearly were not unsatisfactory to the majority of those who left," this "few" who cited pay or promotion still amounted to 12.5 percent (see table 3.6). And it is not at all certain that responses citing "accepted a better job" didn't include better salary as a component of "better job." Federal staff salaries are perceived as significantly better, however, than those in the states (Mitnick 1979).

7.2.4 Federal Regulators: Turnover

The final question posed at the start of this section dealt with the turnover variable (on federal bureaucrats in general, see McGregor 1974). Herring (1936b:98) identified "the average brevity of service" as one of "two major faults in our present system." The other was "the lack of intimate knowledge of administrative duties on the part of most appointees," who tended to leave the agency too quickly. He observed that "service on a federal commission is no more than an interruption in their normal careers. It is often a strange interlude, and one they are anxious to conclude" (Herring 1936b:44).

The two factors of tenure and expertise are related in our theory, and by Herring (1936b:98): commissioners "have not remained in office long enough to develop the necessary expertness or to give the government the full advantage of what competence they possess." The quality of regulators was subject to a panel study as part of the Senate Governmental Affairs investigation. That study concluded that the observed lack of quality was "not a matter of venality or corruption or even stupidity; rather, it is a problem of mediocrity" (U.S. Senate Committee on Governmental Affairs 1977, 1:10). "Mediocrity"—relatively low quality due to background, job skills, and basic ability—is an aspect of the incompetence rationale for deviation from public interest ends that we discussed earlier in this chapter. If longer tenure in fact increases expertise, then an original mediocrity will surely have no opportunity to improve.

The First Hoover Commission observed a "rapid turn-over" (Commission on Organization of the Executive Branch of the Government January 1949:24). Although Stanley, Mann, and Doig

(1967:69) found that commissioners tended to serve longer than other political executives in a given position, for most agencies the median tenure was less than a full term. In spite of this brevity, it was longer than that observed by Herring for the agencies covered by both studies (Stanley, Mann, and Doig 1967:70). The brief median tenure observed was partially a result of low rates of reappointment (Stanley, Mann, and Doig 1967:154). The median lengths of service over the lives of the agencies or since 1930 are compared to terms of appointment in table 3.7 (U.S. House of Representatives, Subcommittee on Oversight and Investigations 1976:452); in each case tenure is less

TABLE 3.7. SHORT TERMS SERVED BY COMMISSIONERS OF REGULATORY COMMISSIONS

| | Median term service | | Term of appointment |
Agency	Years	Months	(years)
SEC	2	8	5
FTC	3	6	5
FCC	4	5	7
FPC	3	2	5
ICC	6	7	7

SOURCE: U.S. House Subcommittee on Oversight and Investigations (1976:452).

than term (for the recent FTC and FCC see also table 3.1). Meier and Plumlee (1978:91) found that turnover was independent of the age of the agency, though again we remain unsure of which "elites" they were describing.

We do not have any readily available data on turnover for federal staff comparable to that for the commissioners. Herring (1938:91) did report that he had observed the appearance of "a career corps of permanent officials" in the older agencies; the ICC lawyers had an average tenure of 25 years. In 1970, Fellmeth and the Nader group found that fourteen top policy-making staff members in the ICC had an average tenure of 29 years (Fellmeth 1970:14, 350). There was an apparent "age lump" (Downs 1967): nine of the fourteen had been at the agency since before or shortly after trucks were added to the ICC's mandate by the Motor Carrier Act of 1935. Thus it is reasonable to suppose that these men participated in the original implementation of regulation in this area (and in the barge area as well). Fellmeth (1970:13–15) argues that such long-time employees tend to perpetuate a viewpoint of regulation appropriate to the earlier, rather than the present era, and tend to socialize younger staff members in this potentially outdated view, a view which becomes commission policy (cf. Kaufman 1960). Hoogenboom and Hoogenboom (1976:189) maintain that poor performance by the ICC can be attributed at least partly to weak appointments at the commissioner level facing an "entrenched" staff that protected "a comfortable status quo" and that was influenced subtly over time by the persistent pressures of the regulated industry. In the 1969 FTC, before its reorganization by new chairman Caspar Weinberger, twenty-two out of thirty-one top-level staff had been in the agency over twenty years; the average age of the thirty-one was 55.82 years (U.S. Senate Committee on Governmental Affairs 1977, 1:208–9). Thus it is possible that although commissioner turnover has been rapid, in at least some agencies key staff may be part of Herring's "career corps" (cf. McGregor 1974). Unfortunately, the accusation is that very long service has led not to the enlightened expertise that Herring and others revere but to conserverism, and rigidification (see the discussion of rigidification in chapter 2, e.g., figure 2.6; see also the "capture" theory of figure 3.6; cf. Jaffe 1954:1132–133).

The sources of turnover among commissioners, and staff, are many. Commissioners may not be reappointed due to change of President, policy differences with the President, pressure from the regulated industry, or other factors. Turnover can result from death; departure for better jobs or more money; a view of commission service that it is a short-term job with one's main life work elsewhere; being eased out due to incompetence; policy differences with other commissioners such that the commissioner in question feels he or she cannot accomplish what he or she desires; and many other reasons (see Graham and Kramer 1976; U.S. Senate Committee on Governmental Affairs 1977, vol. 1).

Thus, for the federal commissioners, the pattern seems to be one of mediocre politically-colored appointments of people with diverse backgrounds who are not in general well-prepared in the specifics of the regulated area. A very large percentage have come from, or previously held, other jobs in government. Some appear upwardly mobile, e.g., from lower-level regulatory agencies or staff positions; others seem to receive the post as reward for notable past service, usually political in character. Commissioners leave for a variety of reasons, with substantial numbers becoming directly or indirectly employed in the regulated industry at some time after they leave. Many were lawyers and return to law practice, perhaps after intervening additional public service. Lawyers, of course, are in a good position to benefit from service on a regulatory agency. Agency resources have not shown steady growth. Commissioner salaries were in the past not competitive with salaries in the private sector and usually still represent some financial sacrifice. Turnover is unquestionably rapid; commissioners tend to stay less than their appointed terms. The data on staff is sketchy, but there may have been a tendency in some agencies toward development of an "entrenched" (conserver) senior staff of long tenure.

Thus, in general, there would appear to be some support for "capture" performances, if the relationships in our theory are correct. A panel study for the Committee on Governmental Affairs did inquire about the panelists' perceptions of commissioner responsiveness to the regulated industry and to consumers. The results varied across commissions but did not in general indicate perceptions of excessive responsiveness to either group (U.S. Senate Committee on Governmental Affairs 1977, 1:290–91).

7.2.5   State Regulators: Backgrounds

We turn now to state regulation. All of the readily available data on the questions posed earlier deal with state public utility regulation, and so the following discussion will be limited to those agencies.

It is unfortunately probably true that in some states at some times the composition of the commissions has matched *The New York Times'* editorial description of the Public Service Commission of New York in the early 1960s:

> No agency of state government has been more conspicuously in need of basic overhaul than the Public Service Commission. A well-upholstered dumping ground for defunct Republican party stalwarts, it has had a noisome record of nonperformance in areas of utmost importance (*New York Times,* December 23, 1969:30).

At the time, the PSC consisted entirely of Republicans who were former office-holders or party officials appointed by a Republican governor.

Fesler (1942:8) noted that "statutory prescription of minimal qualifications for commissioners is rare" (see also Cushman 1941:492). A study by the Ohio Legislative Service Commission in 1977 found the situation not much changed: "Only ten of the reporting states list some job-related qualifications'' (Ohio Legislative Service Commission 1977:9). A 1967 survey of state utility commissions for the Subcommittee on Intergovernmental Relations of the Senate Committee on Government Operations (1967:5) found that over one-third of the commissioners then serving had a legal background, frequently accompanied by other public service. Substantial numbers had worked in business or in state and local government. In 1978, 40 percent of the commissioners were attorneys (Smith 1978:14). In 1967, there were no Ph.D.'s among the commissioners (there were two other doctorates) and only three-fourths of the commissioners had a bachelor's degree. Very few had had previous experience on a regulatory commission (U.S. Senate, Subcommittee on Intergovernmental Relations 1967:5–6). By 1978, more appointments from other regulatory agencies were being observed (Smith 1978). Commissioners usually do not come directly from the regulated industry (Ohio LSC 1977:15–6). (On the possible effects of better educated commissioners, see Pelsoci 1978.)

Besides law, politics is the most frequent former occupation of commissioners (Ohio LSC 1977:11; Smith 1978). This is not surprising when it is remembered that commissioners are elected in some states. But political considerations in appointments continue to be important. In 1978, 5.8 percent of the commissioners had advanced from the staff (Smith 1978:14). There has been a recent surge in appointments from among those with more specialized expertise, e.g., economists (Smith 1978; for more on specialization among commissioners see Smith 1952, 1955, 1957a, 1957b, 1958, 1959).

With respect to staff backgrounds, Fesler (1942:11) noted that "although competent staff members have been obtained and retained by state commissions, the utility companies have yet better men to pit against the public's experts." But appointments, though not outstanding, were not usually political: "Politics . . . characteristically takes a holiday with respect to the technical positions on commission staffs" (Fesler 1942:12). In 1967, 58 percent of the responding commissions had up to 10 employees who formerly worked for the regulated utility (U.S. Senate Subcommittee on Intergovernmental Relations 1967:15). In 1977, few state commissions seemed to employ retired utility personnel (Ohio LSC 1977:13–14). There has been observed in state governments in general an increase in the quality and professionalization of officials (see, e.g., Wright 1978:310; Elazar 1974; on the effects of more and better staff, see Pelsoci 1978).

7.2.6 State Regulators: Departures

Regarding where commissioners go after they leave the agency, Herring (1936b:70 n. 9) cites a study by Mosher and Crawford indicating that in 1929 only a relatively small percentage of the commissioners left for employment in the regulated utility. But work in areas dealing with the industry must also, of course, be considered. Instances of abuse are regularly reported (see, e.g., Adams 1976). In the Ohio Legislative Service Commission survey (1977:15–16), although only two of the commissioners in the survey had "come directly from working with or representing a regulated utility," at least 14 had "on leaving the commission, taken direct or indirect employment with such an organization." Commissioners frequently tend to return to law practice, but it is clear from the data that many also go on to other public service (Ohio LSC:11–12). Smith (1978:13) notes several recent cases of state commissioners moving to federal agencies.

Fesler (1942:11–12; see also Cushman 1941:497) notes that "during the last few years the state commission staffs have been 'training schools' not for the utilities, but for federal and state commissions in the utility field." He cites the case of the Wisconsin Public Service Commission, in which 27 out of 30 technical employees went to state, federal, or other public service. This route is still much travelled, at least in some state regulatory agencies (see Mitnick 1979). A partial explanation for the lack of employment in the utilities in Fesler's day was the occurrence in a few states of "a gentlemen's agreement" by the utilities "not to 'raid' the commission, as they have in the past incurred criticism and ill will by such tactics." In the 1967 Senate survey, 54 percent of the states reporting specific figures indicated up to 10 former employees were then working in the regulated utilities. The Ohio LSC study (1977:15–16) found small percentages of former staff working in the regulated industry. Thus mobility into the industry, though not dominant, is a regular part of the present pattern.

7.2.7 State Regulators: Resources, Especially Salary

Cushman (1941) noted the small size and resources of the state utility commissions. Specialization by function was difficult: "The discussion of this problem in many states will remain purely academic for a long time to come because of the meager staffs with which many of the state commissions are provided. A body may be too small to be divisible, and this is true of some state commissions" (Cushman 1941:489). He cited two reasons: "Small staffs result in many cases from legislative desire to keep down the cost of state government; in some cases they are due to influences which do not desire too aggressive enforcement of state regulatory policy" (Cushman 1941:497). Salaries at that time, and probably now as well, followed "the salary level of the state government as a whole, and usually no special attention is paid to the value or demands of a particular job" (Cushman 1941:496; on relatively low budgets and salaries in the states at this time, see also Barnes 1942:181–82). Salaries still vary a great deal from state to state (Ohio LSC:9–10). Fesler (1942:12) noted that staff salaries were below those of the regulated utilities.

The 1967 Senate survey asked whether the state commissions considered their budget sufficient; 37 percent said it was not. For nineteen responding agencies, the median percent of increase reported as needed was between 20 and 25 percent, a substantial amount (U.S. Senate Subcommittee on Intergovernmental Relations 1967:21). Of course, traditional budget gamesmanship could be at play here. Salaries of commissioners were perceived as inadequate by 76 percent of the reporting commissions. The staff size was perceived as inadequate by 55 percent of the reporting commissions, and the median increase in staff size reported as needed was in the range of 10 to 20 percent. Staff salary was perceived as inadequate "to attract and retain competent and qualified persons" in 68 percent of the reporting commissions. The median commissioner and key staff salary increase reported as needed was in the range of 20 to 30 percent (ibid.:16). Support for state agencies in general has risen since then; general state salaries are also not perceived as low as previously (Wright 1978:310). But this long history of state agency malnourishment has scarcely been completely reversed.

7.2.8   State Regulators: Turnover

Like the federal commissioners, the turnover of state officials has been rapid. Fesler (1942) reported that tenure is his sample averaged 5.75 years, and he cited a study by Ruggles of a larger group that had a 5.44 year average (see also the discussion of the Ruggles study by Barnes 1942:180–81). The six year term of office was, and continues to be, most prevalent; thus, even at this earlier time state commissioners were not serving out even one full term. The 1967 Senate study calculated a median tenure of 5 years for the 160 commissioners it covered. At that time, 35 out of 55 responding commissions had 6 year terms, and 11 others had 4 year terms. Smith (1978) cites an average tenure of only 4 years. The tenure of state commissioners has therefore been decreasing and is usually well below the length of the term of appointment.

According to Fesler (1942:11), the tenure of state staff members was long during the Depression years, possibly due to "its relative security, comparatively good salary scale, and increasing prestige." The data of the 1967 Senate survey permit us to estimate median tenures for some state agency professional staff members. For attorneys, this was about five years for responding commissions; for engineers, about ten years; for rate analysts, about nine years; for inspectors or investigators, about six years; and accountants, about eight years. There was, however, great variance among the states. Perhaps the relatively brief tenure of the attorneys reflects the relative fungibility of their skills. At any rate, although some staff may linger not much longer than the commissioners, overall their turnover seems a bit less.

Reviewing the results for the state commissioners, we see again the pattern of dominance by lawyers, the lack of specialist backgrounds, and, perhaps even more so, the tie between participation in politics and appointment. On leaving, state commissioners go back to law, move to another government post, or take positions dealing with the regulated industry (including law practice). The staff is often a training school for service elsewhere. The state agencies have historically not been well-funded, with salaries at all levels perceived inadequate and/or below those in comparable jobs in the regulated utilities; the situation has apparently been more extreme in this regard than that in the federal agencies. Turnover at the top level has been rapid; so has turnover among some staff positions.

Overall, the evidence in the four variable areas for the federal regulatory commissions and state public utility commissions suggests that, if the theory is correct, there may have been a tendency toward "capture." Regulators have rarely been specialists in the regulated area, resources have not always been plentiful, and turnover has been relatively rapid at the highest level. This could contribute to industry control over information. And industry control of information, according to the theory, leads to shared agency–industry perceptions of industry problems and thence to "capture" (although turnover could interfere). Relatively low agency resources and salaries, together with industry control of information, leads according to the theory to industry control of regulator rewards and so to "capture." Another exception to this prediction in the theory, it is true, is turnover's effect on control over the friendship reward. But friendships may develop quickly, escaping the constraint of relatively rapid turnover, if industry control of information requires frequent industry–agency contacts. Thus, the observed conditions in the federal agencies and state public utility commissions are somewhat consistent with the levels of the theoretical variables requisite to encourage "capture" behaviors. Of course, as we cautioned earlier, this is not a test of the theory, since we have analyzed no independent indicators of "capture."

7.2.9   The Case of the State Reclamation Inspectors

It is important to remember that the known patterns in the federal regulatory commissions and state public utility commissions need not be representative of regulation in general. In fact, there are likely to be significant differences in the conditions obtaining in regulation at different governmental levels, in different functional areas, and at different organizational levels, even within the same agency. We did see some intra-organizational differences in the review above. In illustration of some of the conditions that can occur in agencies other than those considered in the review, and to point out some areas of difference, we shall briefly review some results of a study by Mitnick (1979) of a state reclamation agency.

Inspectors in this agency, in a large midwestern state government, were engaged in enforcing the coal strip mining provisions of the Surface Mining Control and Reclamation Act of 1977. The study involved a questionnaire sent to all inspectors in the agency (the results for twenty-nine, or 85 percent, are discussed here) as well as interviews with some agency officials. Part of the questionnaire was adapted from Rainey (1977); most of it was developed for this study. Since only one agency was investigated, the results should of course be taken as only suggestive. The agency was not chosen because of any suspicions regarding "capture;" if anything, it would appear that the regulatory performance of the agency as viewed by the federal Office of Surface Mining—which oversees the Act—has been good.

The agency's implementation plan for the Act was among several chosen as models, and the federal Office has tried to hire some top agency officials.

The inspectors tended to be young, right out of school, and educated in local public colleges of average quality with majors relevant to—but not necessarily specializing in—their work. Thus, unlike the top levels of the federal and other state agencies we reviewed, the state inspectors had no prior major work experience elsewhere whether public or private, did not of course have law degrees, did not have political connections (they became Civil Service employees), and often sought their positions based on some previous educational training in a relevant area. Unlike the ideal administrators of Herring and other scholars, the inspectors are not necessarily prospective career agency employees; many state as the primary reason for coming to the agency an expectation of future work elsewhere. Inspectors perceived that large percentages of their colleagues came to the agency thinking they could get a good future job in the mining industry or in the federal government as a result of their experience in the state agency.

When they leave, inspectors mostly go either to a job with (or related to) a regulated coal company, or get "promoted" to a federal job with the Office of Surface Mining. The perceptions of the inspectors regarding departures are consistent with this. Clearly, the reclamation agency is a training ground for the regulated industry and for the federal service. Both Herring's ladder to the federal level, and the notorious "revolving door" to the industry—in this case perhaps merely opening rather than revolving—are apparent.

Due to federal support under the Act, resources in the state reclamation agency have been growing. But salaries are set by the state and have continued to be substantially lower than those in the federal service and in the mining industry. The inspectors are well aware of this, and all cited pay as a perceived primary reason why inspectors left the agency. Like the federal and state commissions described earlier, pay has been a problem. But much more than the federal and state commissions, the state reclamation agency is most definitely a way station for the upwardly mobile; future, not past rewards, are uniformly relevant.

Turnover, accompanying rapid growth in the size of the agency to meet the demands of the federal Act (and an earlier state statute), has been rapid; the rate has been estimated at 15 to 20 percent per year.

The median tenure among a sample of a dozen recently departing inspectors was about three years. Thus, like the other federal and state officials, the inspectors do not tarry long with the agency.

The situation of the inspectors, with their dual destinations of regulated industry and federal service, suggests an interesting possibility about the likelihood of "capture." Inspectors seeking to be "promoted" to the federal Office of Surface Mining may also seek to enforce the federal regulations as the federal agency would prefer they do. Depending on the circumstances (including expressed preferences) of the federal agency, this could significantly interfere with the chances for "capture" by the regulated coal mining companies. The control over future job rewards held by the federal agency would partially counter the industry's exploitation of persisting low agency salaries. Of course, the mining companies would continue to attract many inspectors, but the effect of control over rewards would be diluted. Exploitation of the future job ladder in regulatory design may then be one way of breaking out of the flow towards "capture" dictated by the theory in figure 3.6. And it may also be a way of influencing regulatory behavior at lower governmental levels so that it is conducted closer to the preferences of federal regulators in the subject area.

Interestingly enough, partial delegation of regulation in the federal system can therefore, up to a point, be seen as a mechanism to improve the performance of regulation. In being attracted to state-level agencies, regulators may be induced to trade lower salaries for future job prospects (lowering the overall cost of regulation from what it would be if performed entirely at the federal level), and to perform better while doing so. Maintenance of a federal systemic scheme of regulation (and promotion ladder—with salary and perhaps status differentials for workers at different levels), rather than total or extensive decentralization or fragmentation of regulatory control to states or localities, would be necessary to sustain the incentive relationship (cf. Ostrom 1973; McConnell 1966:91–118).[27]

Once state (or local) staff are promoted to the federal level, however, they may conceivably, through long tenure, enter the rigidification process; as Downs (1967) observes, over time there is a trend toward conserverism. There is no where else for regulator-climbers to go—except to the regulated industry. Thus regulatory design

---

[27] I would like to thank Bert Rockman for pointing out the implicit consequences of this argument for democratic theory and the design of the federal system.

should perhaps pay attention to what we may call *incentive safety valves*—future job opportunities, perhaps outside the agency, that act as regulators of current performance.

There are, in conclusion, some significant differences between the data available for the federal commissions and state public utility commissions and that for the single state reclamation agency. We cannot proclaim, from a single example, any generalizations here. But it is probable that other state or local regulators facing similar incentive systems could produce similar differences. This suggests the potential utility of the incentive systems approach we have taken.

Perhaps "good men," as Landis and Cushman argued, can always make any administrative machinery work well. But in their relative absence—a condition history says we must frequently expect—perhaps an incentive systems perspective in regulatory design could help produce the kind of regulatory agents and behavior we desire.

8.0   Design and the Public Interest

This concludes the section of this book on "creating regulatory forms." We now turn to "designing." Chapters 4 and 5 will examine the basic (chapter 4; public interest) and more instrumental or intermediate (chapter 5) rationales used to support regulation. These are formal rationales; we have seen that regulation may be sought and may operate to serve interests unrelated to the formal, public rationales. Why, then, are they worth examining?

First, agents for the public interest exist and will act for that interest, whatever their private self-interest in that advocacy. As long as there are public interest advocates, there is a chance regulation may indeed be "public interest" in character.

Second, there appears to be much support for regulation actually serving some variant of the public interest, if we give credence to arguments like those of Friedlaender (1969). Much regulation in the noneconomic areas, e.g., "social" regulation, appears to have genuine public interest rationales in founding (if not always public interest effects). There are, however, many variations on the "public interest." If some are sometimes realized, we should seek to understand the concept.

Third, even if the public interest is a facade, its content and forms may be of interest. Why this rather than another rationale? What are the purposes of this rhetoric?

Finally, we need to examine the public-interest-related rationales because of our basic design perspective. Even if regulation is pervasively undesirable in effects, perhaps it need not be. If these effects are correctable, not inevitable, then a design capability is essential. Design must be guided by appropriate criteria and rationales. There is really little current systematic knowledge of design of major forms of regulatory instruments. We may only become sure that nothing will work after we understand the mechanism of working.

IV

The Concept of the Public Interest

IN ORDER TO choose regulatory mechanisms, we need to evaluate them with respect to the intention, goal, or "rule" of the interference involved in the regulation. Why is the given regulatory interference desirable? What goals does it, or should it, seek to achieve?

There is a potentially vast array of such goals that could be used to evaluate an also vast array of potential regulatory means. Logic and common usage dictate, however, that some of the goals are relatively more instrumental and specific than others in particular regulatory contexts. This is not to say that a given hierarchy or ordering of goals (from basic or "terminal" to specific or instrumental) exists and is generally accepted for any or for all regulatory areas. Such goal hierarchies do not, in general, exist. And this is not to say that goals relevant to regulatory situations do not conflict; the general case is that goals *do* conflict.

At the base of most regulatory instruments, however, is some formal rationalization that the regulation is to proceed in the "public interest." Later in this chapter we shall consider why public interest rhetoric (if that is what it is) is so commonly employed. And in chapter 5 we shall discuss more instrumental/specific goals of regulation. Note that here we are speaking of formalized rationalizations for regulation, which, as discussed in chapter 3, may not be the same as the reasons for, or sources of, regulatory origin. Regulation which is formally supposed to serve the "public convenience and necessity" may be really sought and instituted, for example, to protect an industry. This it may do by managing the competitive environment of subject firms in a way which provides stability and other benefits to firms in the industry.

Some critics of the usage of the phrase "the public interest" have noted that the breadth and diversity with which the concept is used is such that it reduces in effect to "whatever the government does."

For example, some agency general standards include: "just and reasonable rates, undue preference or prejudice, public convenience and necessity, discrimination discouraging membership in a labor organization, bargaining in good faith, unfair methods of competition . . ." (Friendly 1962:8). Such relatively vague, often almost contentless phrases can be used to support a variety of sometimes conflicting governmental actions, as well as to justify any expedient action (see, e.g., Loevinger 1966:131; Bonbright 1961:27–28).

As many writers have noted, however, "public interest" language has been employed so as to subsume a number of different, but identifiable, meanings. The same phrase, in different contexts or at different times, has been used to mean different things. The range and circumstances of such usage have been subject, in effect, to considerable dispute in the literature. But whether or not the public interest concept employed is operative at face value or used merely symbolically, we must seek to understand these usages in order to understand the rationalization for regulation.

The main object of this chapter is therefore to present a typology of conceptions of the public interest. Before discussing and presenting the typology, we shall very briefly review the origins of the concept in the context of public utility regulation and summarize the constitutional and legal underpinnings of the concept as used in regulation in the United States. One of the points to be made is that this constitutional/legal history and setting provide few guidelines to the "public interest" as well as to the choice of when public regulation is desirable.

1.0 The Public Interest Concept in Utility Regulation: The Public Utility Concept

The concept of the "public interest"—or something like it—has a long history in the context of the regulation of business.[1] Glaeser (1957) and Phillips (1965) discuss several forerunners of this concept (see figure 4.1).

The medieval notion of the "just price" was developed by the early Church in opposition to the Roman law notion of "natural price" that had come from Stoic philosophy. The "natural price"

[1] There are many discussions of the public utility concept in the literature. See, for example, Barnes (1942); Glaeser (1957); Phillips (1965); Liebhafsky (1971).

Figure 4.1. Precursors of the Public Interest Concept in the Regulation of Business

Medieval notion of "just price" (as against "natural price")

Obligations of the guilds in medieval towns

State or social goals underlying royal charters or franchises in the sixteenth century

Rights and duties or obligations of "common callings" developing under the common law

Obligations:
- serve all who request service
- give safe and adequate service
- serve all on an equal basis
- require only a "just and reasonable" price

Rights:
- right of protection of private property
- right to receive a reasonable price and not be compelled to take a loss
- right to offer services and to terminate services, and to make limited restrictions on services, such as some business practices
- right of eminent domain

Source: see Glaeser 1957; Phillips 1965.

doctrine justified any willing exchange; "just price" recognized the implicit coercion of exchange that could arise under difficult economic circumstances, e.g., famine. Unjust enrichment was forbidden under "just price," which was to be determined by what was customary. Glaeser (1957:196) notes that political and economic instability contributed to the adoption of the "just price" doctrine by the later Roman Empire. Seeking to discourage revolution, Emperor Diocletian set maximum prices for about eight hundred articles. In spite of Diocletian's motives in installing it, the "just price" doctrine implied the existence of a justification for interference by the state in private economic activities. This doctrine continued in the scholasticism of medieval philosophers like St. Thomas Aquinas, who identified the "just price" as that which will reimburse production costs, viewed broadly.

A second forerunner of the public interest concept in the context of business regulation appears in the guild system in medieval towns. The guilds were strictly regulated and had to serve, at reasonable prices, whoever requested service. In return, they received a monopoly of their trade. We can see in this apparent exchange of regulation for monopoly the bare form of the public utility regulation of recent times; William G. Shepherd's "basic social contract" (e.g., Wilcox and Shepherd 1975:348–52; see chapter 2) comes to mind.

A third early form was implicit in the royal charters or franchises that conferred monopolies during the age of mercantilism. Developing in France in the sixteenth century, the franchises to some extent shifted the locus of control from the local, town level to the national level. Although the state did not want to perform those activities subject to charter itself, they were judged governmental in nature, involving state or social goals. And so here again we have the germ of an idea of interference with respect to a "public interest."

A fourth precursor lay in the common law specification of certain occupations, "common callings," as subject to special rights and duties, explained by the nature of the business. Such occupations, involving patronage of the public, were said to be "affected with a public interest." They included "surgeons, smiths, bakers, tailors, millers, innkeepers, ferrymen, wharfingers, and carriers" (Phillips 1965:53). These "callings" had to serve whoever requested service and to charge them reasonable prices. Chief Justice Waite, in *Munn v. Illinois* (94 U.S. 113 (1877), at 127) cited a now widely quoted passage from Lord Chief Justice Hale's seventeenth-century treatise, *De Portibus Maris:* [2]

> A man, for his own private advantage, may, in a port or town, set up a wharf or crane, and may take what rates he and his customers can agree for cranage, wharfage, housellage, pesage; for he doth no more than is lawful for any man to do, viz., makes the most of his own. . . . If the king or subject have a public wharf, unto which all persons that come to that port must come and unlade or lade their goods as for the purpose, because they are the wharfs only licensed by the king, . . . or because there is no other wharf in that port, as it may fall out where a port is newly erected; in that case there cannot be taken arbitrary and excessive duties for cranage, wharfage, pesage, etc., neither can they be enhanced to an immoderate rate, but the duties must be reasonable and moderate, though settled by the king's license or charter. For now the wharf and crane and other conveniences are affected with a public interest, and they cease to be *juris privati* only; as if a man set out a street in new building on his own land, it is now no longer bare private interest, but is affected by a public interest.

Thus, like the "just price" doctrine, "common callings" required the imposition of some societally instrumented values to achieve outcomes in opposition to what otherwise might result from the opera-

---

[2] Cf. Phillips (1965:53); note the small differences in the text.

tion of the uncontrolled market place. In particular, such a situation is said to be one "affected with a public interest."

Under the common law, the body of court-made "law" that has evolved through successive court decisions, there grew a group of rights and duties that attached to businesses regulated as "common callings." These have come to be applied to many regulated businesses, particularly public utilities. The rights and duties gave specific content to the required behavior and to the limits attached to such required behavior, under the implicit or explicit regulations applied to "common callings." These rights and duties were developed and elaborated over time, were later included in regulatory statutes, and remain at the core of regulation "in the public interest" (cf. the development of the business corporation from earlier corporations with special benevolent or public service purposes; Seavoy 1978). They do not, however, tell us when a business is to be regulated, nor what the "public interest" is in a general way.

Phillips (1965:80–83) lists the obligations and rights of regulated industries developed under the common law: Obligations were to serve all who request service; to give safe and adequate service; to serve all on an equal basis, forbidding unjust discrimination; and to require only a "just and reasonable" price for services. Rights included the basic general right of protection accorded to private property; the right to receive a reasonable price for services, where regulatory authorities may not compel a business to operate at an overall loss, though reasonable return is also not (always) guaranteed; the right to offer services and to make limited restrictions on the services, i.e., to offer services constrained by reasonable rules and regulations, e.g., office hours and business practices, and the right to terminate service under stipulated conditions, with due notice given to customers; and the right of eminent domain, i.e., the right to condemn and take private property for "public use," subject to the payment of a "just compensation."

Medieval regulation gave way in the eighteenth century to a renewed emphasis on, and belief in, the "natural laws" of the market in many areas of economic life. Crystalized in Adam Smith's *The Wealth of Nations,* the new doctrine of "laissez faire" meant, in practice, deregulation on a massive scale. Smith argued that the individual economic actor, "generally, indeed, neither intends to promote the public interest, nor knows how much he is promoting it. By preferring the support of domestic to that of foreign industry, . . .

intends only his own security; and by directing that industry in such a manner as its produce may be of the greatest value, he intends only his own gain, and he is in this, as in many other cases, led by an invisible hand to promote an end which was no part of his intention'' (Smith 1909:335).

Thus, in its assumption that the general welfare in some form will be achieved through a reliance on individual economic self-seeking, laissez faire was not merely a return to a reliance on the natural laws of Stoicism. A concept of the "public interest" is not abandoned to one of private interest but, rather, said to be realized as the resultant of private action.

It is but a short step from the argument that private competitive action will lead to a realization of optimal collective benefits to an ideology which supports the general desirability of competition as the form for organizing economic activity.

Under the new doctrine, many economic controls were deregulated. By the early part of the nineteenth century, relatively few industries and occupations were subject to the kinds of obligations (and rights) described above. Recall the kinds of early nineteenth century regulation described in the utility evolution models discussed in chapter 2. Regulation during this time was largely promotional, was limited to the common law, a few statutes, and franchises and charters, and was applied to a limited extent in such areas as transportation (e.g., turnpikes, canals).

Abuses and poor performance during the promotional period, and the subsequent "competitive" era, could not seem to be remedied by the limited regulatory controls employed. Were there some conditions for which Smith's invisible hand would not work?

The reassertion of regulation in the later nineteenth century, which has traditionally been identified with a need to control the excesses of industry (e.g., Glaeser 1957; Farris and Sampson 1973), was accompanied by the appearance of a more sophisticated notion of the public utility concept, as well as a set of regulatory mechanisms intended to compensate for the failures of Smith's perfect market. The obligations and rights of regulated industries listed earlier were developed further and formalized. If the rise of the regulatory commission in this period is explained not from such public interest grounds, but as the result of industries seeking to use the coercive authority of government to protect themselves (e.g., Gray 1940), the rationalization for the new controls, i.e., the public utility concept, could be understood perhaps in a symbolic role that merely promoted public acceptance of the regulation. At any rate, it is probably possible to posit or extract a dominant version of the public interest concept for each of the stages or periods of regulatory evolution identified by Glaeser, Farris and Sampson, and other writers in this area.

There is some dispute as to what the necessary conditions are for which Smith's invisible hand should be replaced by "public utility regulation." That is, while the conditions which must obtain for free competition to produce, unequivocally, the collective benefits claimed for it are reasonably well understood, the conditions for which public utility regulation is the desired alternative are less clear. In chapter 5 we shall consider both the characteristics of perfect competition, and the alleged defects of "natural monopoly" as a rationalization for regulatory intervention of this kind.

Furthermore, the public utility concept, and the notions of public protection or the "public interest" that lay formally behind it, continued to evolve following the renascence of regulation in the late nineteenth century. In the next section of this chapter we provide a very brief overview of the evolution of the legal basis for regulation, i.e., how the public interest rationale was formally extended to new potential regulatory objects. First, however, we close this discussion of the origins of the public interest notions inherent in the public utility concept with a summary of a mature version of that concept.

Bonbright (1961) identifies four defining elements of the public utility as private organization subject to regulation: 1) The regulation involves "direct control of its rates of charge for services" (ibid.:4); 2) "the primary purpose of the regulation must be, ostensibly at least, the protection of the public in the role of consumers rather than in the role either of producers or of taxpayers" (ibid.:4); 3) the regulation is applied only "as a matter of long-run policy rather than as a temporary expedient in wartime or in some other emergency" (ibid.:6); and 4) the enterprise is "a 'business' even though subject to regulation and even when directly owned and operated by the government," i.e., "public utility services are designed to be sold at cost, or at cost plus a fair profit" (ibid.:22–23).

Public utility status is, furthermore, generally conferred for two reasons, which can be seen as elaborations of the public protection element of the definition: 1) The services regulated are viewed as necessary or essential, and the regulation itself is essential in assuring adequate provision of these services; and 2) utility plants possess "technical characteristics leading almost inevitably to monopoly or at least to ineffective forms of competition'' (ibid.:8), i.e., leading to "natural monopoly,'' so that regulation is necessary to protect the public from exploitation while permitting the public to enjoy the efficiency of the monopoly form under these conditions.

Thus the public interest notion surrounding this view of the public utility concept involves protection of a public of consumers from both exploitation and loss of efficiency in service, through the means of regulation of a particular kind to be instituted in special circumstances. Bonbright's definition does not explicitly include the "common callings'' rights and duties, though some of these could perhaps be seen as following from the public protection or service aspects of the definition.

In contrast, Barnes (1942) offers a definition different from Bonbright, explicitly reflecting some of the "common callings'' requirements: "Those industries are public utilities which are required to render service at reasonable and nondiscriminatory prices to all who apply for it'' (Barnes 1942:1). In fact, of course, there are a great many such definitions in the literature. They reflect both a group of public interest related concepts and a group of mechanisms held implicitly as means to implement or protect that interest (e.g., "reasonable and nondiscriminatory prices''). And our consideration of the public utility concept has limited us to the context of economic regulation; the varieties of public interest conceptions and implementing mechanisms are greater still when we consider "social'' regulation (e.g., Lilley and Miller 1977) as well as "economic'' regulation. What is needed is a systematic presentation of the possibilities inherent in the public interest concept, i.e., a typology of conceptions of the public interest, and a systematic treatment of the mechanisms of regulation. Preferred public interest conceptions can then be chosen and used to evaluate alternate mechanisms.

We shall make a first step toward such a goal later in this chapter, with presentation of a basic typology of conceptions of the public interest. Before doing so, however, we turn to a brief review of the development of the legal basis for regulation in this country.

2.0 The Constitutional/Legal Basis of Regulation in the United States

In the previous section, we took a brief look at the development and content of the public utility concept. We now turn to a consideration of the development of the formalized rationale for regulation, i.e., the constitutional/legal basis for regulation in the United States. Rooted in the older common law concepts discussed earlier, the formal rationale for government regulatory interferences finds expression in basic constitutional provisions and in statutes, together with their evolving court interpretations. We shall focus on only a few of the major developments, with the aim of making a basic point: To a very large extent today, there are no fixed, definitive legal expressions of what can (and cannot) be regulated, and why. And if the legal guidelines are empty or ambiguous, the importance of the development of systematic representations of public interest conceptions and of the regulatory rationale becomes that much greater.

Controversies over the appropriateness of government regulation in the United States have tended historically to center around: 1) the appropriate level or locus of regulation, state vs. federal, and 2) the appropriate objects of regulation, in particular those objects which, due to their being "affected with a public interest," may be regulated by government.

Controversies over level or locus of the regulator usually are linked to interpretations of Constitutional provisions of powers explicitly given to the federal government, left to the states, or interpreted as implicitly resting with the federal government or the states. In the context of economic regulation, federal regulation is based on the "interstate commerce clause" in Article I, Section 8 of the U.S. Constitution, which gives Congress the power "To regulate Commerce with foreign Nations, and among the several States, and with the Indian Tribes." Other powers given to Congress in Section 8 are also relevant to regulation, such as those relating to the "Power To lay and collect Taxes, Duties, Imports and Excises, to pay the Debts and provide for the common Defence and general Welfare of the United States"; the power "To borrow Money on the credit of the United States"; the power to make uniform laws on bankruptcies; the power "To coin Money, regulate the Value thereof, and of foreign Coin, and fix the Standard of Weights and Measures"; the power "To Establish Post Offices and Post Roads"; and the power to make copyright and patent laws.

The "implied powers clause," also in Article I, Section 8, effectively extends these and other powers: Congress shall have the power "To make all Laws which shall be necessary and proper for carrying into Execution the foregoing Powers, and all other Powers vested by this Constitution in the Government of the United States, or in any Department or Officer thereof."

State regulation is based largely on the police power, i.e., the power to regulate the health, safety, morals, and general welfare of the public. Although not cited in the Constitution, this power has been recognized by the courts under the Tenth Amendment, which requires that "The powers not delegated to the United States by the Constitution, nor prohibited by it to the States, are reserved to the States respectively, or to the people."

According to Article VI, where federal and state regulation conflict, federal shall supersede state: "This Constitution, and the Laws of the United States which shall be made in Pursuance thereof; and all Treaties made, or which shall be made, under the Authority of the United States, shall be the supreme Law of the Land; and the Judges in every State shall be bound thereby, any Thing in the Constitution or Laws of any State to the Contrary notwithstanding." Individual rights are protected against regulation by Constitutional safeguards of due process, equal protection, and so on, and by guarantees of judicial review.

These are hardly clear-cut distinctions, and it is not surprising that an enormous and sometimes inconsistent case history grew around them. What, for example, is to be included under "commerce"? What, indeed, does "among the several States mean"? Conant (1974) reviews the evolution of meanings applied to these words by the courts. Some scholars have argued that "Commerce . . . among the several States," given the common meanings applied to these terms in the eighteenth century, meant not a federal power to regulate only commerce "between the States" but, rather, "a general or plenary power to regulate all commerce of the United States" (Conant 1974:84). Consequently, the extent of things "affected with a public interest," and therefore presumably subject to regulation, is similarly broadened. But this is a particular scholarly view, not one shared initially by the courts.

At any rate, the case history has generally been one of expanding the domain of federal controls over state ones. The interstate commerce clause was interpreted ever more broadly. And given the new possibilities of business regulation, as well as the ambiguity of "commerce" and the other Constitutional language, there grew a need to distinguish among businesses that can or cannot be regulated, i.e., that were or were not to be seen as being "affected with a public

interest." Thus controversies over the appropriate objects of regulation tended to center around various tests of what "affected with a
public interest" meant in business practice, as well as around interpretations of the coverage implied by the relevant Constitutional
clause(s).

The preeminence of federal over state regulation under the interstate commerce clause was first affirmed in *Gibbons* v. *Ogden,* 22
U.S. 1 (1824), in which Chief Justice Marshall broadly defined the
scope of the commerce clause and asserted the ascendancy of federal
over state controls. The case dealt with the question of whether New
York State could assign the exclusive rights to operate steamboats in
traffic between New York and New Jersey to a private party. Marshall found that this commerce was covered by the Constitutional
clause, could not be regulated by New York, and went on to offer a
definition of "commerce among the several States" that both asserted
federal control *among the states* and reserved commerce *inside states*
(that did not have effects outside) to state control (see, e.g., Conant
1974:86).

In *Cooley* v. *The Board of Wardens of the Port of Philadelphia,* 53
U.S. 298 (1851), an operator of ships between Philadelphia and New
York claimed that he did not have to use approved pilots or pay a
substitute fee in leaving the port of Philadelphia because his interstate
commerce could be subject only to federal, not Pennsylvania state
regulation. The Supreme Court disagreed, arguing that the states may
perform "local," not "national" regulation in the absence of federal
controls in the area. This "separation theory" thus distinguished between "general" problems to be subject to a uniform system of regulation at the federal level, and "local" problems, which could be left
to the states in the absence of Congressional action (Farris and Sampson 1973:48–49).

The powers of states over interstate commerce in the absence of
federal regulation were temporarily extended in the Granger cases in
the 1870s. States were permitted to exercise control over interstate
railroads through their new regulatory commissions. Chaos resulted,
and in *Wabash, St. Louis and Pacific Railway Co.* v. *Illinois,* 118
U.S. 557 (1886), the Supreme Court responded by effectively ter-
minating existing state regulation of interstate rail commerce. This it
did through invalidating an Illinois regulation restricting long-
haul/short-haul abuses (see chapter 3).

State powers over interstate commerce remain restricted; state controls must not be found to be an "undue burden" on such commerce (Conant 1974:106). Chief Justice Stone discussed the permissible conditions for state control in *Southern Pacific* v. *Arizona,* 325 U.S. 761 (1945), in which the Court struck down an Arizona statute regulating the length of trains:

> There has thus been left to the states wide scope for the regulation of matters of local state concern, even though it in some measure affects the commerce, provided it does not materially restrict the free flow of commerce across state lines, or interfere with it in matters with respect to which uniformity of regulation is of predominant national concern. (See, e.g., Conant 1974:107.)

Such language is hardly very informative as a potential guide in individual cases, though the national "uniformity of regulation" rationale could perhaps offer some help. The case law following such broad declarations can often be suggestive of particular conditions and exceptions (see, e.g., Conant 1974:108–12; Farris and Sampson 1973:50–51).

In situations in which there are relevant federal actions or controls preempting local or state initiatives, the federal of course take precedence (see, e.g., *City of Burbank* v. *Lockheed Air Terminal, Inc.,* 411 U.S. 624 [1973]). In a few cases, states may be recognized as possessing some powers on the basis that other parts of the Constitution conflict with the provision in question, i.e., the commerce clause, and must be accorded supremacy over it (see, e.g., *National League of Cities* v. *Usery,* 426 U.S. 833 [1976]). But one can assert that, with a few such conditions and exceptions, states usually cannot regulate general characteristics of interstate commerce, even without any federal controls in the area.

On the other hand, Federal regulation has been extended even to some apparently *intra*state commerce. Under the "Shreveport Doctrine," first enunciated by the Supreme Court in *Houston, East and West Texas Railway Co.* v. *United States,* 234 U.S. 342 (1914), federal regulation can be applied to intrastate commerce to correct a situation which adversely affects or is "discriminatory" in its effect on interstate commerce. In the 1914 case, railroad rates from Shreveport, Louisiana, to eastern Texas (i.e., interstate), regulated by the Interstate Commerce Commission, were much higher than non-federally-regulated intrastate Texas rates from Houston and Dallas to the same area. This in effect discriminated against the interstate rates, giving the Houston and Dallas originated traffic an unjust advantage.

Where there was such an interdependency between federal and state regulation, the federal government was permitted to exercise its supreme authority to protect interstate commerce (and, in effect, its interstate regulation). The Court wrote that "Whenever the interstate and intrastate transactions of carriers are so related that the government of the one involves the control of the other, it is Congress, and not the State, that is entitled to prescribe the final and dominant rule, for otherwise Congress would be denied the exercise of its Constitutional authority and the State, and not the Nation, would be supreme in the national field. . . ." (at 354–55; see, e.g., Farris and Sampson 1973:52–53; Barnes 1942:158–59).

Though the scope of federal regulation generally widened at the expense of state control, the range of activities held to be allowable subjects of regulation under the interstate commerce clause did not. For a period beginning in the latter part of the nineteenth century and extending well into the Depression years, the Supreme Court applied restrictive interpretations to the meaning of the interstate commerce clause. The broad interpretation of Marshall's opinion in *Gibbons* v. *Ogden* was narrowed to limit it to transportation between states and to activities judged to directly affect such transportation (Conant 1974:90). And the possibilities for control in transportation were themselves limited. For example, in *Hammer* v. *Dagenhart*, 247 U.S. 251 (1918), the Court restricted federal control under the interstate commerce clause to articles that were harmful or deleterious, e.g., lottery tickets or impure food and drugs. Manufacturing was distinguished from commerce and held outside the scope of the clause (see e.g., Conant 1974:93; Fainsod and Gordon 1941:138; Liebhafsky 1971:108).

The return of a broad interpretation of federal regulatory powers under the interstate commerce clause came in a narrow decision in *N.L.R.B.* v. *Jones and Laughlin Steel Corp.*, 301 U.S. 1 (1937). The Court wrote, "When industries organize themselves on a national scale, making their relation to interstate commerce the dominant factor in their activities, how can it be maintained that their industrial relations constitute a forbidden field into which Congress may not enter . . . ?" (Conant 1974:97). The ruling of *Hammer* v. *Dagenhart* was reversed in *United States* v. *Darby*, 312 U.S. 100 (1941), which not only broadened the scope of activities covered by the interstate commerce clause, but also asserted more strongly the ability of the federal government to regulate intrastate behavior that affected interstate commerce. The case concerned a sawmill operator in Georgia who paid less than the minimum wage and, because his lumber was shipped out of state, thereby violated the Fair Labor Standards Act of 1938. Justice Stone wrote,

> Whatever their motive and purpose, regulations of commerce which do not infringe some Constitutional prohibition are within the plenary power conferred on Congress by the Commerce clause. . . . The power of Congress over interstate commerce is not confined to the regulation of commerce among the states. It extends to those activities intrastate which so affect interstate commerce or the exercise of the power of Congress over it as to make regulation of them appropriate means to the attainment of a legitimate end, the exercise of the granted power of Congress to regulate interstate commerce." (See, e.g., Farris and Sampson 1973:53–54; Conant 1974:98–101.)

The extent of the return to Marshall's broad definition of the commerce clause in *Gibbons* v. *Ogden* is well illustrated by Justice Jackson's opinion in *Wickard* v. *Filburn,* 317 U.S. 111 (1942). The case concerned a farmer who had planted more than his allotment for wheat under the Agricultural Adjustment Act of 1938. Filburn was subject to a fine under the Act and argued that, since the wheat was entirely local production for local consumption, he should not be subject to the regulation; the relevant provisions of the act were unconstitutional under the commerce clause. Justice Jackson wrote:

> Whether the subject of the regulation in question was "production," "consumption," or "marketing" is, therefore, not material for purposes of deciding the question of federal power before us. . . . even if appellee's activity be local and though it may not be regarded as commerce, it may still, whatever its nature, be reached by Congress if it exerts a substantial economic effect in interstate commerce, and this irrespective of whether such effect is what might at some earlier time have been defined as "direct" or "indirect." (See, e.g., Liebhafsky 1971:110.)

Even where alternative Constitutional supports seem available, the Court has sometimes been willing to rely on this broad interpretation of the commerce clause. In *Heart of Atlanta Motel, Inc.,* v. *United States,* 379 U.S. 241 (1964), a motel with an interstate clientele sought to escape the anti-discrimination provisions of Title II of the Civil Rights Act of 1964. Quoting John Marshall's opinion in *Gibbons* v. *Ogden,* Justice Tom Clark eschewed reliance on the Fourteenth Amendment in favor of the interstate commerce clause:

> In short, the determinative test of the exercise of power by the Congress under the Commerce Clause is simply whether the activity sought to be regulated is "commerce which concerns more States than one" and has a

real and substantial relation to the national interest. (See, e.g., Liebhafsky
1971:110; cf. Justice Clark's opinion in *Katzenbach* v. *McClung,* 379 U.S.
294 [1964].)

Thus, particular kinds or areas of interest have broadened to a "national interest," a phrase close to simply asserting control in an uninformative and general "public interest."

Federal controls remain very extensive in potential (and, of course, in practice), and the interstate commerce clause has largely retained its broad interpretation. But considerations of the locus and extent of control do not usually tell us much about the "public interest" for which control may be exercised. Of course, restrictions such as those specified in *Hammer* v. *Dagenhart* do indicate articles or activities which are held undesirable, and thus may be seen to be not in the "public interest." But we end up with little knowledge about the supposedly guiding "public interest" concept itself.

There has, in fact, been a line of cases that considered what determines whether a business is sufficiently "affected with a public interest" to permit regulation. These could also be taken as more or less indirect indicators of the "public interest."

Munn v. *Illinois,* 94 U.S. 113 (1877) concerned the case of operators of a grain elevator in Chicago who refused to abide by an Illinois statute licensing such operators and regulating their rates (see, e.g., Barnes 1942:2–4; Phillips 1965:56–60; on state cases leading to *Munn,* see Scheiber 1971). The number of such elevators in Chicago was relatively small, the sites on which they could be constructed were limited, and all the elevators were controlled by nine companies, who set grain storage rates by joint agreement. The Supreme Court supported the regulation. Chief Justice Waite wrote that

> Property does become clothed with a public interest when used in a manner to make it of public consequence, and affect the community at large. When, therefore, one devotes his property to a use in which the public has an interest, he, in effect, grants to the public an interest in that use, and must submit to be controlled by the public for the common good, to the extent of the interest he has thus created. He may withdraw his grant by discontinuing the use; but, so long as he maintains the use, he must submit to the control" (at 125–126; see Phillips 1965:58–59).

The monopoly aspects of the grain storage business in Chicago were important in establishing that "public consequence," and thus became a basic rationale for regulation. Justice Field noted in dissent, however, that "there is hardly an enterprise or business engaging the attention and labor of any considerable portion of the community, in which the public has not an interest in the sense in which that term is used by the court in its opinion. . . .'' (at 140–141; see Phillips 1965:60).

Impact on "the community at large" makes property of "public consequence" and thereby "clothes" it with a "public interest." Though monopoly in a widely used service or business affects "the community at large" and could thereby be seen as a defense for regulation, Justice Field made a prescient point regarding the extent of activities which can be shown to affect such a "community." Where does that effect have to begin, and to stop? How many must be affected, and with what severity? We can easily multiply such questions, which bear on basic problems in the identification of a "public interest."

As it turned out, Justice Field's warning was well-taken, for after years of trying to add content to "affected with a public interest" by specifying necessary conditions or industries that were so affected, the Supreme Court essentially abandoned the effort, and relaxed such controls on regulation rationalized in this way.[3]

In *Budd* v. *New York,* 143 U.S. 517 (1892), the Court determined that the monopoly conditions attaching to elevating, weighing, and discharging grain from ships meant that that business was "affected with a public interest." Justice Brewer, in a dissent, tried to distinguish property devoted to a public use, and a public interest in the use of property. Only the former constituted grounds for regulation, since "there is scarcely any property in whose use the public has no interest" (at 549–50; see Phillips 1965:61). In *Brass* v. *North Dakota* ex rel. *Stoeser,* 153 U.S. 391 (1894), the regulation of rates for grain storage by North Dakota was upheld without reliance on monopoly characteristics. The Court noted the size of the elevators, the volume of business, and the intention of the legislature. In *German Alliance Insurance Co.* v. *Kansas,* 233 U.S. 389 (1914), the Court again supported regulation by finding a public interest in the regulation of insurance by Kansas. But now the public interest could cover "more than the mere rendering of service by means of tangible,

---

[3] For a review of this effort to specify industries "affected with a public interest," see Phillips (1965:60–80). Barnes (1942:19–22) summarizes industries that were, or were not, held to be "affected with a public interest." He also presents several "theories" developed to specify the basis of the "public interest" in regulation; Barnes (1942:13–19). On such theories, see also Swenson (1924:133–43).

physical property'' (Phillips 1965:64; see also, e.g., Barnes 1942:4–5). There was no monopoly governing distribution of some indispensable commodity, though purchase of insurance was referred to as "practically a necessity to business activity and enterprise" (at 414–15; see Phillips 1965:64–65).

In *Wolff Packing Co.* v. *Court of Industrial Relations,* 262 U.S. 522 (1923), a Kansas price and wage control statute was struck down as unconstitutional. Chief Justice Taft attempted at length to develop criteria for finding businesses "affected with a public interest." He identified three classes of such businesses: 1) Those receiving grants of special privilege, e.g., franchises or rights of eminent domain; 2) those involving historically regulated occupations; and 3) those industries already subject to regulation (see, e.g., Barnes 1942:5–7; Phillips 1965:65–67). These distinctions are scarcely informative; it does not tell us much to say that that which has been regulated may also now be regulated.

Dissents in some subsequent cases foresaw the eventual Court position. Justice Holmes, in a dissent to *Tyson and Brother* v. *Banton,* 273 U.S. 418 (1927), a decision declaring a New York law controlling ticket scalping unconstitutional, declared that

> I think the proper course is to recognize that a state legislature can do whatever it sees fit to do unless it is restrained by some express prohibition in the Constitution of the United States or of the State, and that Courts should be careful not to extend such prohibitions beyond their obvious meaning by reading into them conceptions of public policy that the particular Court may happen to entertain. . . . [I] think . . . that the notion that a business is clothed with a public interest and has been devoted to the public use is little more than a fiction intended to beautify what is disagreeable to the sufferers. The truth seems to me to be that, subject to compensation when compensation is due, the legislature may forbid or restrict any business when it has a sufficient force of public opinion behind it. . . . (at 446–47; see Phillips 1965:68)

And Justice Brandeis, in his dissent to *New State Ice Co.* v. *Liebmann,* 285 U.S. 262 (1932), a case in which the Court overturned Oklahoma regulation of entry into the ice-manufacturing business, wrote that "The notion of a distinct category of businesses 'affected with a public interest,' employing property 'devoted to a public use,' rests upon historical error. . . . In my opinion, the true principle is that the State's power extends to every regulation of any business reasonably required and appropriate for the public protection" (see Phillips 1965:75).

This string of cases struggling with the definition of "affected with a public interest" ended, effectively, with *Nebbia* v. *New York,* 291 U.S. 502 (1934), in which a New York statute regulating milk prices and trade practices in the industry was upheld. Justice Roberts, who switched from the majority in *New State Ice Co.* v. *Liebmann,* concluded that "the phrase 'affected with a public interest' can, in the nature of things, mean no more than that an industry, for adequate reason, is subject to control for the public good. . . . there can be no doubt that upon proper occasion and by appropriate measures the state may regulate a business in any of its aspects, including the prices to be charged for the products or commodities it sells" (see Phillips 1965:77; Conant 1974:137–38).

Thus the effort to give a meaning to "affected with a public interest" sufficient to determine, unambiguously, what may or may not be regulated, failed. The legislature was left to regulate within the controls of Constitutional constraint, existing statute, and public desirability expressed through the representative process. Although conceptions of the public interest relating to the "community at large" or general or significant effect on the public were distinguished, usually in a fairly vague way, no specific conception or systematic range of conceptions emerged. There is therefore from this legal history little in the form of basic criteria that can be taken to determine the desirability of regulation and to permit choice among alternative regulatory means. Consequently, we turn to the political philosophy literature on the concept of the public interest and then to development of a systematic typology of public interest conceptions.

3.0   A Typology of Conceptions of the Public Interest

The meaning of the phrase "public interest" has been the subject of a voluminous literature in political theory, and there remains no accepted definition of the phrase, much less an accepted operational definition offering indicators that we may use to determine empirically whether something is in the public interest. A typology of conceptions of the "public interest" may then have utility here. Besides serving the aim of clear and unambiguous discourse, providing for the present purpose a clearer understanding of the range of basic criteria for regulation, and potentially contributing to an improved rationale for regulation and to choice among regulatory means, such a typology could be employed to relate various public interest notions to behavior. It may be that a useful theory in which behaviors may be explained and predicted using observed or posited conceptions of the public interest could then be constructed. Our aim, then, is a logically constructed typology that can serve these purposes. Later in this section we shall consider reasons for the employment of public interest rhetoric, a notable aspect of regulatory decision-making and controversy.

3.1 SOME EXISTING TYPOLOGIES

Existing typologies of the public interest have not been designed with the theory-building objective in mind. Present typologies in the political philosophy literature are most commonly constructed by aggregating schools or theories of the public interest into convenient lists, without regard for the overall structuring of categories in a logical or systematic manner. Many typologies are created as sets of straw men so that the author's preferred conception of the public interest is highlighted.

Classifying rules need to be established that locate categories in a parsimonious way, on a few dimensions. These rules should permit an inclusive or exhaustive mapping of possible conceptions. This mapping should include both conceptions offered in the past, and related but unused or little-used conceptions that may be employed in comprehensive theory-building or used in the future. The typology should therefore cover the full range of meanings of the public interest offered previously. Because of differences in classification method, and thus perhaps definition, categories of earlier typologies may not coincide with categories of the new typology. We shall not then "force" conceptions from previous categories or the old categories themselves into new categories. Some support for our choice of classifying dimensions may, however, come from observation of frequent previous use of the dimensions, whether implied or explicit. This would increase the likelihood that we are in fact covering the full range of meanings. The classifying dimensions should also be relevant to, or descriptive of, the natural phenomena under study, i.e., be important in applications of the public interest concept. They should have theoretical utility in the explanation and prediction of social events, if we seek in the long range a theory relating conceptions to behavior. And the dimensions should for these reasons be empirical variables. Categories created by the classifying dimensions should be explicit and unambiguous. We seek a typology that is systematic and logical, in that each category would be determined by different sets of values of the same few classifying variables, varying in a systematic fashion. (On typologies, see, e.g., Altman 1968; Bailey 1973 and 1975; Deutsch 1966; Sokal 1974.)

Consider, for example, some relatively recent typologies in the political philosophy literature (see figure 4.2). Sorauf (1957) identifies five definitions of the public interest: as commonly held value; as the wise or superior interest; as moral imperative; as balance of interests; and as a vague, essentially undefined value. Quite aside from the question of whether this list is inclusive and mutually exclusive is the fact that it is basically an unstructured list, i.e., lacking classifying dimensions, and is unsuitable for use in theory construction in the way we have described.

Similarly, the typologies of Schubert and Cochran are essentially lists long enough to include within a few categories all previous writers on the subject considered sufficiently important. Schubert (1960) identifies three categories: According to the "rationalist" category, the public interest is determined by the government acting in accord with the actual values held by a majority, or all, the people. In the "idealist" category, the moral dictates of the conscience of the decision maker in determining the public good replace the actual values of the people as a guide to the public interest. In the "realist" category, the government mediates conflicting interests, with the public interest, so far as it may be said to exist, as the resultant. Cochran (1974) lists four categories: According to the "normative" theory, "the public interest becomes an ethical standard for evaluating specific public policies" with the common good of the community as a whole as referent. The "abolitionist" category includes theorists who would do away with the concept. "Process" theorists "define the concept by reference to the political processes through which policy is made." Subcategories include: "(1) an aggregative conception which views the public interest as a sum of interests; (2) one which views it as the result of a clash of interests; and (3) one which views it as the democratic process of interest reconciliation or as fair procedure." "Consensualist" theorists "view the public interest as a vague, but valuable, term which refers policy debate to a public value consensus" (Cochran 1974:330–31).

The typology of Leys and Perry (1959) does make a logical contrast between its two major categories, but contains unstructured or

Figure 4.2.   Some Existing Typologies of the Public Interest

Unstructured Lists:

Sorauf (1957)
   As commonly held value
   As the wise or superior interest
   As moral imperative
   As balance of interests
   As a vague, essentially undefined value

Schubert (1960)
   Rationalist
   Idealist
   Realist

Cochran (1974)
   Normative
   Abolitionist
   Process
   Consensualist

Structured Lists:

Leys and Perry (1959)
   Formal meanings:
      Simple: e.g., intention of king or parliament
      Pluralistic: sanctioned by any legal or political process
   Substantive meanings:
      Utilitarian or aggregationist
      Decision resulting from proper procedures
      Normative conception of public order

Held (1970)
   Preponderance theories
   Common interest theories
   Unitary theories

Banfield (1955)
   Unitary:
      Organismic
      Communalist
   Individualistic:
      Utilitarian
      Quasi-utilitarian
      Qualified individualistic

weakly structured lists within each category. They distinguish between "formal" meanings of the public interest, which involve
"whatever is the object of duly authorized, governmental action,"
and "substantive" meanings, which describe "the object that *should*
be sought in governmental action (or in nongovernmental action that is
a delegation of governmental power or accepted in lieu of govern-

mental action).'' Formal meanings include "simple" conceptions ("the intention of king or parliament") and "pluralistic" conceptions, with objectives "sanctioned by any legal or political process, it being assumed that, as a matter of fact, decisions are made in various ways and in various places." Substantive meanings include: 1) the utilitarian or aggregationist conception ("the maximization of particular interests"); 2) "the decision which results when proper *procedures* are used," including simple conceptions such as due process and pluralistic conceptions involving the rules of the decision-making legal or political process; and 3) "a normative conception of public order" (Leys and Perry 1959:44).

Held's (1970) categories are constructed from considerations of relations between statements regarding the public interest and individual interests: "x is (is not) in the public interest," "x is (is not) in the interest of individuals $I_1 \ldots I_{n-1}$," and "x is (is not) in the interest of individual I_n" (Held 1970, p. 42). But Held does not consider all possible relations of validity and equivalence among these statements, though she may consider the most probable ones; she writes that "considering theories of the public interest in this light, one can discern, I think, three fundamental outlines" (Held 1970:42). Thus the scheme of her typology is perhaps secondary to the aim of gathering major theories into a few categories; one is left to wonder about the status of the categories that can be determined by the scheme but are not considered. It seems, at any rate, a cumbersome way (for the purposes we envisage) to identify three simple categories: "preponderance" theories, where the public interest coincides with the claim of those "with a preponderance of individual interests," which may involve, for example, power, votes, or calculations of utility; "common interest" theories, where the public interest is equated to "those interests which *all* members of a polity have *in common,*" including, for example, interest in the system of government, in a decision method for settling differences, or "their common interest in maintaining some arrangement that benefits every single individual or group"; and "unitary" theories "according to which it is justifiable to assume or appeal to a single ordered and consistent scheme of values" (Held 1970:43–45). Although it may be possible to develop empirically based indicators for Held's categories, the broadness of the categories may require an elaboration of the schema, and of the indicators necessary.

The existing typology closest to what we propose below is that of

Banfield (1955). He divides conceptions of the public interest into a "unitary" category, where "the whole may be conceived as a single set of ends which pertain equally to all members of the public," and an "individualistic" category, where "the ends of the plurality 'as a whole' are simply the aggregate of ends entertained by individuals." Unitary conceptions include "organismic," in which the plurality is an entity with ends that may differ from the component individuals', and "communalist," in which the ends are universally or almost universally shared by all individuals. Individualistic conceptions include "utilitarian," in which individual utilities, treated alike, are aggregated to see if a net gain indicating the presence of the public interest results; "quasi-utilitarian," in which more weight is given to the utility of some than others in the aggregation process; and "qualified individualistic," in which certain ends are excluded from the ends of individuals aggregated to discover the public interest (Banfield 1955:323–26). Note the logical contrast between the unitary and individualistic categories, and the evident, though not explicit, relations between the subcategories in each category. The subcategories in each category are not, however, developed in a parallel fashion across categories; there is still no overall systematic mapping of the kind we are looking for.

3.2 A TYPOLOGY OF PUBLIC INTEREST CONCEPTIONS

Consider briefly what we would like to know about the concept of the "public interest" in order to build and employ a typological set of useful definitions: 1) How *is* the phrase the "public interest" actually used? This is an empirical question. We look at all contexts in which it is used and observe and compile its apparent meanings—or at least define the variety of contexts. (See Held 1970:2–3, citing Flathman 1966 and Barry 1965.) This information may suggest the dimensions used to construct the typology. The task of identifying meanings of the public interest has been performed in effect by the diverse literature on the subject, though material on empirical meanings is less common than conceptual argument. We leave open the possibility that study of usages will warrant change in the typology we propose. 2) What "public interest" usage *should* be employed in each context? Given the information acquired in response to question 1, we decide whether "public interest" is used "correctly" in each of the classes of empirical contexts. This involves deciding what meaning we wish to infer in each of the empirical classes of contexts.

It means excluding vague, conflicting, or "wrong" meanings. Note we may simply adopt names other than the "public interest" for these other or associated meanings; we need not restrict our vocabulary of meanings. This task involves using the logically constructed typology to map the empirical world. 3) What is the "public interest" in this particular case? We use the results to question 2, identifying the class of which the case is a member, and employ the meaning of the "public interest" indicated. This identification may involve the development of indicators for each class. Note that in defining the "public interest" we could decide that it is to have the same meaning in all contexts, or we may allow variation in meanings across contexts, as long as we can consistently identify contexts with indicated meanings in order to avoid ambiguity.

Assume now that there is a proposed act or case for which a determination must be made whether or not it is in the "public interest." Assume that a single determination of the public interest is to be made; we exclude, a priori, nondeterminative definitions of the public interest, e.g., where several conflicting views are each determined simultaneously as the "public interest." What typology may we construct to classify it?

There are, of course, many possible typologies of the type we seek that can be constructed. It is thus necessary to support our choice of classifying dimensions. Central to the concept of "interest" is the notion of "preference." "Interest" itself has been widely used in previous typologies, though it has, in general, been subject to many meanings in the literature (see, e.g., Connolly 1972; Held 1970). Thus, there may be a reduction in ambiguity by focusing on one aspect of "interest," the more neutral concept of "preference." A set of preferences or preference schedule are terms taken to mean, in effect, a set of instructions specifying what would constitute successful pursuit or realization of the desired objective or goal. Thus the preference schedule is a set of predispositions that maps out the particulars of how a goal is preferred, i.e., how the (potential) actor's desires (would) vary with respect to the levels at which his objective may be received (see McClintock 1972:443; Nagel 1975).

Definitions of the public interest typically vary in the extent to which they admit of variations in preferences, reflecting judgments based on variations in fundamental "values" regarding the proposed act. Thus, some definitions specify only a single set of preferences, while others permit multiple sets. If multiple, the sets may be alike or may differ. The *number of* basic guiding values, or ends, or interests, or *sets of preferences* has been a common variable in previous typologies. Specification of single or multiple interests figure in all of the typologies we reviewed above. It is a "natural" variable, relating directly to the nature of holding a conception of the public interest; as "interest," it is, after all, part of the common description of the concept itself. It has potential theoretical utility because the concept of preference is basic to the literature on collective or social choice, and we may expect that it may figure prominently in public choice theories developing in this area.

A set of preferences may exist, abstractly, apart from specification of any actor, though action in accord with such preferences would obviously require an actor. We may then specify for our typology *whether a holder of preferences is required,* and, if it is, the *level of the actor holding the set of preferences:* no holder required—ideational (the preferences may exist apart from any actor); holder required—individual, group or organizational, and systemic. For convenience we shall exclude from discussion mixed-level cases, e.g., where actors include both individuals and groups. Such cases may be added through simple extension of the arguments. We have also combined the individual and group/organizational levels for discussion, where we could easily separate them for empirical classification.

Definitions may also be characterized as to the *degree and character of participation,* i.e., the existence of a set of acts or procedures, required of members of the polity in order to determine the "public interest"; some definitions, on the other hand, may be characterized as "passive" or "investigatory," in that any inquirer into the public interest can determine that interest without specified participatory acts of units or members of the polity up to the polity as a whole. Participation is a "natural" variable because activities undertaken to discover the public interest in a case frequently do require specified behaviors, such as voting or procedures associated with due process. Previous typologies often include categories with behavioral aspects, or at least frequently include conceptions inherently requiring some specified behavior. Cochran, for example, identifies a category of "process" theorists, and Leys and Perry have "pluralistic" and procedural subcategories involving behavior. In addition, a participatory/passive dimension may be seen to be theoretically important because of our future aim of relating public interest conceptions to behavior.

A final dimension relates to *whether or not determination of the public interest is rule-determined,* i.e., there are, or are not, formal or informal rules that parties involved in the determination of the public interest must follow, whether these parties are members of the polity whose preferences are being aggregated (if there are multiple sets of preferences), or are parties who are analytically essentially outside the subject polity who are assessing the public interest. By "rule" we mean a guide for action or choice that is independent of any specific instance, applicable at different points in time, and consistent in pattern. Rules may be more or less specific or constraining; we may consider those instances when there are weak rules like "refer to party A's intuition" as essentially non-rule-governed.

Addition of the rule dimension enables us to better characterize the participatory/passive nature of the public interest determination. Participation may be orderly and guided by a rule, or, as in the work of the group theorists, marked by non-rule-governed conflict. Insofar as participation is a "natural" variable, characterization of that participation or lack of it by rules is also a "natural" variable. In addition, conceptions of the public interest may supply rules for organizing society and deciding on appropriate public policy. Rules inherent in the given public interest concept—or their absence—may thus be crucial to an understanding of such organization and decision. Many conceptions of the public interest in the literature are governed implicitly by rules. For example, the moral dictates of the conscience of the decision maker in Schubert's "idealist" category constitute a set of rules for decision on the public interest, and the requirement of certain procedures in Cochran's process category, and in the categories of Leys and Perry, imply rules. The utilitarian position cited, for example, by Cochran and by Banfield involves a rule of aggregation of individual utilities. A rules dimension may have theoretical utility because it enables us to link the rulelike aspects of public interest concepts with more specific decision rules in the public sector. This enables us to identify the full chain of rationalization that leads to public action, and may permit us to better describe aspects of behavior in the public sector.

Thus, classifying dimensions for the typology will be: 1) number of sets of preferences regarding the proposed act that are considered when determining the public interest, and the occurrence of agreement or disagreement among them; 2) the existence and level of the actor holding the preferences (ideational, or individual, group or organizational, systemic); 3) whether determination of the public interest requires participation of units of the polity in certain acts, or is

Figure 4.3. Typology of Conceptions of the Public Interest

Level	Participatory/ Passive	Rule/ Nonrule	Number of Sets of Preferences — Unitary one	Combinatorial multiple same	Combinatorial multiple different
ideational (No holder required)	participatory	rule	Null	Null	Null
	participatory	nonrule			
	passive	rule	NORMA- TIVE		
	passive	nonrule			
individual/group- organizational	participatory	rule	DICTA- TORIAL	CONSENSUAL: unanimity Paretian consensual majoritarian	PLURALISTIC AGGREGATION: e.g., due process, election
	participatory	nonrule			e.g., outcome of group con- flict
	passive	rule			e.g., Benthamite, conflictual majoritarian, weighting
	passive	nonrule			e.g., random
systemic (Holder required)	participatory	rule	COM- MUNAL	Null (for single system)	Null (for single system)
	participatory	nonrule			
	passive	rule			
	passive	nonrule			

merely passive or investigatory in nature; and 4) whether determination of the public interest is, or is not, essentially rule-determined.

We shall present the categories as if satisfaction of the indicated set of preferences does occur, or is required, in order that the situation of satisfaction be characterized as in the "public interest." A variation here is to allow satisfaction of preferences to be possible but not necessarily certain for each member (see Benditt 1973).

We shall try to indicate which categories appear to be null or empty, whether for empirical or logical reasons (see figure 4.3). Citations to the numerous conceptions in the literature (see, e.g., Held 1970) will be made only occasionally for illustrative purposes.

I. *Unitary*

There exists a single, particular set of preferences, not selected or combined from a collection of such sets for the proposed act or case, that determines the "public interest." According to existence of holder and level we have:

A. *Normative*

The set of preferences are unattached to any particular or type of holder (the ideational level); they reflect persisting and ultimate values. Thus, although no one may hold the set of preferences regarding the public interest for a case (all may hold different preferences, and thus be wrong), only this one set is the correct one reflecting *the* public interest. This category is fundamentally passive or investigatory and is rule- or non-rule-determined; determination rests on correct examination of values, and not on any procedures required of members of the polity. If rules are not required, knowledge of the public interest may be arrived at, for example, through insight or reference to conscience. Use of "insight" could of course be considered the relevant rule. The participatory categories seem to be null.

B. *Dictatorial or Impositional*

The set of preferences indicating the public interest is that of a single unit or member of the polity. (We combine the individual and group/organizational levels.) They reflect the public interest because they are held by that one unit or member, regardless of their being shared by other units or members. This category may be participatory, or passive/investigatory, and rule- or non-rule-determined. Thus determination of the public interest may, or may not, require certain procedures or ritual, e.g., sacrifices before the oracle. In addition, the dictator's preferences may or may not be coercively imposed on the polity, which in the former case may obviate the need for rules other than "refer to the dictator's preferences." The possible arbitrariness of a dictator makes this situation possibly non-rule-governed.

C. *Communal*

The set of preferences are those of the polity as an organic, communal whole (the systemic level). The public interest is the "common good" of that organic whole; it is *not* determined by reference to interests of parts or

members of that whole (cf. Cochran 1974). This category may be participatory, or passive/investigatory. Thus determination of the public interest
may require governmental legitimation, i.e., the public interest is what the
government does, acting as agent for the polity as a whole. Or, in another
participatory sense, individual determination of the communal notion of the
public interest may require procedures such as putting oneself in the position
of fiduciary (see below), a completely disinterested party acting in this instance to benefit the whole (e.g., judge, ombudsman). Individuals holding
private interests therefore could not determine the common good. Rules may
or may not be required; in the latter case a person may be expected to naturally sense or intuitively know the locus of the common good, with perhaps
the only rule, "refer to intuition."

II. *Combinatorial*
There exist multiple sets of preferences for the proposed act or case; determination of the public interest involves combination or selection from
these sets. Systemic-level categories would appear to be null because we are
dealing with one system and require multiple preferences. If we have multiple systems, e.g., the international system, this level would not, of course,
be null. Multiple normative conceptions at the ideational level, i.e., no
holder required, are possible. In the instance of similarity between conceptions, of course, the "multiple" distinction becomes unnecessary. Where
there are multiple different normative conceptions, it would be possible, in
principle, to develop both participatory and passive means of reaching decision on the public interest, as well as both rule- and non-rule-determined
means. But such means do not appear to be generally distinguished in the
literature. We shall thus limit our discussion to the individual and
group/organizational levels, and shall consider them together.
A. *Consensual*
Similarity of the sets of preferences held by all, or nearly all, units or
members of the polity (or indifference to the act or case proposed) is the determining factor; the set so held determines the public interest. We distinguish three situations in order of weakening consensuality:
  1. *Unanimity:* Each set of preferences is identical to every other; all hold
the same set.
  2. *Paretian:* Each member either holds the same set of preferences, or is
indifferent to the act or case proposed. A Pareto optimum may be said to
exist when no change is possible that satisfies some people's preferences
without dissatisfying other people's preferences. Any change that helps
some people without hurting any is then Pareto efficient.
  3. *Consensual Majoritarian:* The same set of preferences must be held by
most, or nearly all, members of the polity; the preferences of the minority
are treated as irrelevant, no matter their "intensity," i.e., the extent to
which they would exchange valued goods for satisfaction of their preferences.
Note that the sharing of preferences in this category may vary in exten-

siveness (number of areas of preference shared) and intensiveness (similarity in intensity).

The subcategories may be participatory, or passive/investigatory. Thus, given perfect information on preferences, the nature of the public interest is determined in the passive/investigatory case; in a less perfect world the participatory requirement of willingness to pay may serve as an affirmative expression of the presence of consensuality, and thus determine the public interest (see Steiner 1970:37). The subcategories may also conceivably be ruled- or (essentially) non-rule-determined.

B. *Pluralistic Aggregation*

There exist multiple, different sets of preferences for the proposed act or case, reflecting in general different sets of values. We may distinguish participatory and passive/investigatory subcategories, and then further divide these subcategories as to whether determination of the public interest is, or is not, rule-determined.

1. *Participatory*

a) Rule-determined: Members or parties follow or engage in set acts or procedures; the outcome is labeled in the public interest. We identify two common approaches: 1) The public interest determination is effectively independent of the substantive nature of the sets of preferences held by the participants (though we require of course that these preferences exist, and be multiple and different); determination depends largely on the following of the specified procedures. 2) The determination of the public interest involves the processing of the sets of differing preferences through specified procedures; determination of the nature of the public interest depends on the given sets of preferences as well as on procedure. An example of the first type is a "due process" notion of the public interest—an outcome is in the public interest if certain procedures have been followed. An example of the second type is an election—determination of the public interest involves participatory expression of preferences according to a combinatorial rule.

b) Non-rule-determined: Determination of the public interest involves participation, but not according to some rule. Thus it may involve a group conflict marked perhaps by force or deception, and perhaps characterized by struggle over control of access to policy-determining resources or positions. The outcome of the group conflict may be called the public interest (see Held 1970:78–82, on Bentley and other group theorists; see also our chapter 3). Included here also are incrementalist conceptions.[4]

2. *Passive or Investigatory*

a) Rule-determined: Sets of preferences are assessed or aggregated according to some rule; the outcome is the public interest. Examples include: 1) Benthamite simple summation of utilities,[5] 2) *conflictual majori-*

---

[4] That is, decisions that are the product of incremental decision-making, i.e., marginal, remedial, serial, fragmented, and so on, are in the public interest. On incrementalism, see Braybrooke and Lindblom (1963).

[5] The net satisfaction of the group of individuals (or units) is determined by summing measures of their individual satisfaction.

tarian—a decision rule of majority or greater is applied to determine the public interest; unlike *consensual majoritarian,* the existence of a disagreeing minority is implicitly recognized; 3) a weighting scheme is applied to distinguish sets of preferences either according to (*a*) the particular members who hold preferences (e.g., extra weight for being poor)—some members may even be excluded, or (*b*) the content of the preferences—certain sets of preferences are excluded a priori, or given positive or negative weights like racehorses (see Banfield 1955; Steiner 1970:42–44).

   b) *Non-rule-determined:* Selection is made by chance or random selection, for example, or according to the whims of the determiner.

Note that we have tried to categorize the various public interest conceptions so that empirical cases may be classified. One looks for the degree of sharing of preferences, the level of the actor holding the set of preferences (and whether such an actor is required), the occurrence of participation, and the existence of governing rules. A step beyond what we have attempted here would be to relate public interest conceptions as classified by this typology to forms of behavior. It may be that the structure of this typology would not prove conducive to such theory-building; it would, at any rate, provide a start.

In addition to its possible theoretical uses, the typology may be employed descriptively. For example, a recent notable trend in administrative regulation has been the drift from investigative/passive conceptions of the public interest to participatory ones, and from non-rule-determined to rule-determined ones. Rather than passively aggregate preferences according to rule, sitting back in a trusteeship relation, or rely on a group conflict to sort out the public interest, administrative agencies increasingly require or, more often, are required to follow certain procedures. The administrators and/or the parties subject to administration must actively involve themselves in the decision-making process. Administrators must investigate affirmatively, following procedures determined for and by them; hearings must be held; affected parties must be given, or allowed, representation in administrative proceedings that affect them. See, e.g., Mitnick and Weiss 1974; *Natural Resources Defense Council* v. *NRC,* 547 F. 2d 633 (1976); but see *Vermont Yankee Nuclear Power Corp.* v. *Natural Resources Defense Council; Consumers Power Co.* v. *Nelson Aeschliman,* 435 U.S. 519 (1978); 46 LW 4301 (1978). Some writers have argued for, or observed, trends away from trusteeship decision-making by allegedly impartial and expert administrators toward legislative or representative forms (see, e.g., Haefele 1973a,

1973b). The value of the typology here is that we can plot these and other such changes or comparisons.

Consider now where some of the public-interest-related conceptions discussed earlier in this chapter in the context of the evolution of the public utility concept, and of the legal basis for regulation, belong in the typology. Many of the early concepts were unitary in character; we can tentatively identify a general trend from unitary to combinatorial. Thus notions of "just price," the obligations of guilds, and the state or social goals underlying royal charters or franchises were largely unitary. They reflected essentially passive, rule-governed determinations of a single group of preferences made by an organization or individual, e.g. the Church, the guild or aristocratic protector of the town, the sovereign or his government. The rights and duties of common callings under the common law came to be similarly "dictatorial" in nature, since they represented a rule-governed, passively held, single set of preferences administered by the judges of the court system.

The "public interest" that resulted from laissez faire, on the other hand, represented the resultant of individual economic actors with multiple, often different, preferences seeking satisfaction through participation in a largely non-rule-governed trading system. The category is therefore participatory, non-rule-governed "pluralistic aggregation."

A further historical trend for development of the concept in essentially democratic societies has been one of movement from non-rule-governed to rule-governed forms of pluralistic aggregation, though other, competing conceptions continued to exist. Thus although the (essentially "dictatorial") rights and duties of the common callings were formalized in the public utility concept in the late nineteenth century, the trend in interpreting what was "affected with a public interest" seemed largely to be toward whatever the legislature deemed was in that interest. This implies a reliance on participation in the rule-governed representative system to pluralistically aggregate multiple preferences into a "public interest" for any case.

At the same time, some of the earlier judicial gropings for a "public interest" concept referred to the "community at large," and language of this type seems to remain in statutes and other repositories of formal rationales or guides for regulation. These expressions may represent a competing "communal" notion of the public interest, where decision on regulation is supposed to somehow benefit the community as organic whole. Perhaps the failure of these notions as guides for judicial action, however, led to the abandonment to the legislature characterizing *Nebbia* and the later cases.

"Communal" notions can perhaps then be seen as symbolic justifiers of a legislative collective choice process. One cannot usually offer a clear rationale for a group decision in which hundreds of people, each possibly representing and aggregating thousands or millions of potentially different sets of preferences, take part. But such a justification is often needed, if only to pacify (or deceive) losers in the decision (see the discussion of public interest rhetoric below). And implementation under the new regulation occurs in a risky and uncertain environment, requiring guides for action and means of defending the action against those who are adversely affected and take legal steps to oppose it. In chapter 6 we present a model of delegation by a legislature that suggests how such ambiguities (and therefore a need for further specification and justification) arise.

The typology we develop is still some distance from a systematic set of goals that can be used to rationalize and choose among alternate regulatory means. We believe that it does take an important step in that direction by providing a systematic organization for the most basic kinds of public interest conceptions that have been, and may be, used to support regulation.

The typology has some other obvious potential difficulties. It may not be easy to determine the extent of sharing of preferences, and decisions on the presence of rules, especially when they are weak or relatively nonspecific in content, may be difficult. Participation may blend into passiveness, with no clear demarcation. Certain uncommonly complex notions of the public interest might not be able to be fitted comfortably into one of the given categories alone; mixed situations involving some participation, some passive/investigatory, some rule-determined and some non-rule-determined behavior, all in the same public interest determination, may occur and be hard to classify. The dimensions chosen for classification may not prove to be important ones for organizing empirical conceptions of the public interest and relating them to forms of behavior. Use of the typology could demonstrate these and other problems, or perhaps show them to be of little concern.

3.3 PUBLIC INTEREST RHETORIC

In this section we shall attempt an explanation for the occurrence of public interest rhetoric, i.e., rhetoric invoking variants of the "public interest." Such rhetoric is used in governmental settings even where a variant of the public interest is not actually formally operative (Posner 1974:355). As we saw above, public interest rhetoric invariably accompanies legislative and judicial decision-making in the regulatory area. Why is public interest rhetoric, and not some other rhetoric, employed?

Assume the political system is pluralistic, and democratic in that it is structured to be responsive to constituent demands under certain constraints. This may usually imply a combinatorial, pluralistic aggregational notion of the public interest.

Because the state cannot act for itself, no one possesses the public interest as a genuine self-goal, i.e., as the subject of genuine self-regarding, or private, egoistic, selfish preferences. Therefore all who act for the public interest are *agents*.

All government actors must appear to act for the public interest. This is:

1) In order not to appear to be granting special favors to certain groups. Other groups may protest. Due to the possibility of successful access in a pluralistic democratic system, such protest may interfere with the receipt of those favors. Thus public interest rhetoric may be adopted to cloak actions involving favors for certain groups.[6] Edelman (1967) argues that rhetoric of this type may be used symbolically to produce quiescence among those who might protest. The use of public interest rhetoric may be a rational strategy to cloak the lack of unified justification that can result from the legislative collective decision process, as we observed earlier, and thus be a defense against group protest. The pressures toward legislative delegation, evident from the model in chapter 6, would contribute to the lack of such a unified justification. Going beyond the protest argument, we could also argue that public interest rhetoric could satisfy any basic need for legitimacy or justification possessed by members of the polity—a need whose lack of satisfaction is exacerbated by the nature of the legislative decision process.

And 2) because systemic normative constraints in the form of a widely shared value consensus will inhibit deviating language and actions (cf. Downs 1962). This consensus is on the form of government, the nature of "democratic" procedures, certain core values

[6] Posner (1974) argues that public interest rhetoric is used to increase the information cost of those seeking to determine the true beneficiary of government action, i.e., that public interest rhetoric is a study in the information costs produced by fraud. If this is so, one can still ask why public interest rhetoric is used to raise information costs—why not other language? We offer reasons for this.

frequently not operational like "equality," and so on. The variety of meanings appearing under the concept "legitimacy" include as one conception the existence of a shared consensus on, or support for, a government. Should the consensus be reflected in a uniformity of preferences regarding the public interest, we would of course have a "combinatorial consensual" conception of that interest. Language regarding governmental actions that bear on or reflect the general consensus will therefore tend to take the form of public interest rhetoric, reflecting that consensus. And the particular public interest conception and language employed, and any governmental action, must of course be reasonably consistent with this agreement on values. Governmental actors who ignore this value consensus in their rhetoric and actions may expect opposition, whether they speak or act for themselves or others. They may fear such opposition, again, because of the possibility of successful access in a pluralistic democratic system. If these agents for the public interest genuinely share in this value consensus (or believe genuinely in some particular public interest conception reflecting some individually held value set), of course, they may employ public interest rhetoric anyway.

In addition to the existence of a shared value consensus, we posit that the agency role itself involves a widely shared norm of service. Members of the polity expect this norm in agents for the public interest much as they expect the fiduciary norm in many agency relations in ordinary social behavior. Recall (chapter 3) that an agent who holds the fiduciary norm must act solely for the goals of his principal, or beneficiary, without regard for any other goals that may be relevant to the situation, including any self-goals of the agent. (On the fiduciary, see Mitnick 1974, 1975a, 1975b.) The norm is prescribed in situations of contractual agency—i.e., where there is a mutual agreement establishing the condition of agency; and is more strongly prescribed the greater the discretion of the agent—i.e., where the agent may choose acts that affect return to the goal of his principal. The norm of service to the public interest may then reinforce the value consensus surrounding acts for that interest. Note that the degree of ambiguity frequently surrounding the conception of the public interest that is operative reinforces the norm.

We may then divide governmental actors into *pure fiduciaries,* i.e., those who act solely according to some conception of the public interest; *lexicographic, or "lexical," fiduciaries,* who from all possible acts choose, first, that set equivalently optimal according to the public interest, and, second, from that optimal set, that act which also benefits them the most; and *false fiduciaries,* who may merely appear to act according to the public interest, but are acting primarily for their own benefit. Some false fiduciaries may act for the public interest only instrumentally, though of course they may genuinely prefer suboptimal acts for that interest, i.e., acts that offer some return to public interest goals.[7]

Because lexical and false fiduciaries consistently choose acts that benefit them, with the false fiduciary unconstrained by what is best with respect to the public interest, they may do relatively better for themselves than the pure fiduciary. Under uncertainty, if return to the public interest is relatively low, the lexical and false fiduciaries may be suspected of dishonesty, and the pure fiduciary, of incompetence. In order to avoid this appearance in the (possible uncertain) event return to the public interest is relatively low, lexical and false fiduciaries may attempt to disguise the fact they are doing well for themselves. The lexical fiduciary may undertake such deception only if it does not adversely affect return to his principal's goal. The pure fiduciary remains of course indifferent to the use of such deception, and will, along with the lexical fiduciary, use public interest rhetoric as rationalization because he means it, though he may not emphasize it. Lexical and false fiduciaries may adopt the rhetoric of the public interest, and emphasize in addition other factors, such as the accouterments and appearances of service, in order to continue receiving the benefits of their positions as agents. Such agents may be policed, for example, by other governmental agents specialized for this purpose, or by parties outside the government who may gain access according to our assumption of a pluralistic democratic system. Formal policing attempts, or outside protest, may in some cases result from perceptions of any violations of the basic value consensus noted above, which may (or may not) be codified in the legal system. Thus

---

[7] We could, of course, subdivide this category into "mixed" and "purely false" fiduciaries depending on whether or not there is a genuine preference for suboptimal acts for the public interest. Elsewhere (Mitnick 1974, 1975a, 1975b), we have distinguished "lexical self-interest agents" and "pure self-interest agents," both of whom may be false fiduciaries. Lexical self-interest agents who are governmental actors choose, first, that set of acts equivalently optimal with respect to their self-interest, and, second, from that optimal set, that act which also benefits the public interest the most. Pure self-interest agents choose what is best for them without regard for the public interest. Note that in policing the agent (see Mitnick 1975b) there is a logical progression from pure self-interest agent to lexical self-interest agent to lexical fiduciary to pure fiduciary. Note also that it is possible for the structure of benefits to be such that all types of agent choose the same act, though this would perhaps be uncommon.

whether or not we have pure, lexical, or false fiduciaries—true or false agents—public interest rhetoric will be used. Only in the case of the pure fiduciary, ironically, is public interest rhetoric not emphasized. And since we can assume that most governmental actors are probably not pure fiduciaries and allow self-interest to figure in, we expect to see public interest rhetoric.

The fiduciary origin of such rhetoric is in addition to, and reinforces, the other reasons discussed above—value consensus and the avoidance of protest of special favors. Note that the special favors case becomes a special form of the fiduciary argument if we substitute acts for special interests for acts for self-interest in the calculus of the lexical and false fiduciaries. That is, public interest rhetoric may be used to disguise the fact that return to the special interests favored by the lexical and false fiduciaries is high relative to return to the public interest. Such acts for special interests may of course be instrumental to self-interests, as when the regulatory commissioner who favors the regulated industry is in effect rewarded with a job in that industry after his retirement from the commission.

Note that different conceptions of the public interest may be subject to choice by fiduciaries who have considerable discretion in their choice. The conception chosen may then reflect the goal set of the pure, lexical, or false fiduciary.

3.4 CONCLUSION

After reviewing some forerunners of the public interest concept in the context of regulation of business, i.e., the public utility concept, and examining briefly the constitutional/legal basis of regulation, including judicial attempts to give meaning to the phrase "affected with a public interest," we presented a typology of conceptions of the public interest. We found that there was little in this history to inform choice among alternative regulatory means and that the range of public interest conceptions potentially to be dealt with, or actually dealt with, was nowhere systematically displayed. We thus set out to provide such a typology.

Conceptions in the typology range from unitary to combinatorial interest versions, involving various levels, and participatory/passive and rule- and non-rule-determined forms. We do not argue for adoption of a single definition, preferring instead to categorize ways in which the phrase may be used. Different circumstances—for example, different kinds of agents for the public interest in different situations—may employ different usages; the "public interest" is often used as rationalization for administrative action. A useful theory to explain choice of specific rationalization for each case remains to be formulated. We have suggested some reasons for the use of public interest rhetoric in general, involving the avoidance of protest, the constraints of general value consensus, and the behavior of fiduciaries. Development of a general theory relating public interest conceptions to behavior may be aided by construction of typologies like the present one.

Having examined the basic formal rationalization for regulation, the "public interest," we turn to consideration of the more specific or instrumental goals that support regulation, and a closer look at some of the conditions for which regulatory interference has often been judged appropriate in the "public interest," e.g., natural monopoly.

V

Intermediate Goals and the Rationale for Regulation

THE TYPOLOGY of conceptions of the public interest we have developed in chapter 4 may not permit us to directly evaluate and choose among alternate means of regulatory interference; the conceptions are defined at an extremely abstract and general level. And we still need something of a guide as to when such interference is warranted, given some more specific "intermediate" goal set. Remember, we are moving towards building a capability for regulatory design.

Thus, in this chapter we shall consider the public interest––intermediate goal (and lower-goal) hierarchy, and present an approach to the rationale for regulation based on these considerations, the arguments we have made regarding regulatory interferences, and the existing literature.

1.0 Decision on the "Public Interest"

Rationalization of public decisions, including ones involving regulatory matters, usually refers to or invokes some notion of the "public interest." In chapter 4 we developed a typology of conceptions of the public interest and discussed reasons for the employment of public interest rhetoric. There is, of course, no accepted single meaning of the concept. Thus, if one were to use the "public interest" as rationale for public action, an implicit first decision involves which concept meaning to employ.

Usually, there is little or no real decision made regarding such concept usage; traditional or contextual factors often select the meaning. Neither absolute kings nor legislatures usually deliberate, in effect, whether to employ a unitary or a combinatorial usage; previous decisions regarding the form of government—absolute monarchy or democratic representation—will predispose choice of usage.

A basic problem noted in chapter 4, however, is that of rationalizing a collectively made decision resulting from aggregating multiple different sets of preferences into a single "explanatory" preference set. Legislatures, like many other groups, usually need to offer a single coherent reason for the collective decision, as if a single individual were deciding. This will tend to reduce uncertainty for organizations in the legislature's environment, e.g., administrative agencies (including regulatory agencies) implementing legislation and courts interpreting it. (On the legislature as organization, see Cooper 1975, 1977.) Because of demands from groups in the environment of these organizations, e.g., interest groups and regulated industries, who prefer unambiguous decisions for their own reasons, agencies and courts (members of the legislature's "organization-set" [Evan 1976]) will prefer legislative rationalizations that are nonconflicting, i.e., that express a single set of ends. But the legislative decision does involve aggregation of different preferences, and agencies and courts may prefer criteria that permit them to satisfy, perhaps inconsistently over time, their most insistent (and threatening) clients as well as the changing preferences of their own members. For these and other reasons (see the model of delegation in chapter 6), vague legislative rationalizations tend to be offered.

Therefore, the need to construct a sufficiently vague or broad rationale could often lead legislatures to some debate over the formal public interest language to employ.

Recall again that we do not claim that regulation is always instituted to, and operates to, realize some conception of the public interest; we just note that this is the common formal rationalization given. In fact, of course, regulation has apparently been frequently sought and used by private parties to serve their own interests.

2.0 Decision on Intermediate Goals

Because of the multitude of things that can be desired, basic public interest conceptions usually specify whose interests are to be determinant, certain nonsubstantive aspects of the interests, such as rules or procedures to be followed, and/or certain processes or activities that are required in order to determine or express the given interest (e.g., examine entrails at Delphi). The typology developed in chapter 4 is consistent with this. The problem therefore remains of linking basic public interest conceptions to specific, substantive goals: How do we move from a public interest conception to a substantive, contextual goal? Exactly what preferences are to be sought, once we have settled whose preferences they are to be, how they are to be selected and manipulated, and what general characteristics they must have?

This is perhaps a far more difficult conceptual problem than choosing among basic public interest conceptions. There is also no systematic typology of substantive goals that may be elected in the "public interest," and no logic now available which relates such goals to different basic public interest conceptions.

Because the process appears to be one of moving from very general and encompassing to more specific and special-circumstance criteria, we may perhaps conceive of the goals as arrayed in a fairly complex hierarchy. The hierarchy would reflect *both* increasing specificity of goals and increasing instrumentality of goals. This is because lower-level, i.e., more specific goals, are rationalized by higher-level goals, and ultimately by the most general goal, the "public interest." For example, flammability standards in pajamas are supported by more general safety goals, which are in turn supported by a public interest conception involving legislative decision.

We can identify types of "intermediate" goals, i.e., goals that give substantive content to the broad public interest conception but are fairly general in that they are largely independent of specific cases. Regulatory "intermediate" goals will tend to result in restrictions on choice regarding various activities of the regulated party. Our problem in constructing a typology of intermediate goals then resolves into one of categorizing aspects of activities potentially subject to such regulatory interferences.

We can divide intermediate goals into those which deal with aspects of the regulated activity by itself—i.e., in isolation from its effects on other parties, including people performing it—and those which deal with external impacts of performance of the activity. Within these two groupings, we can distinguish static and dynamic factors (see figure 5.1). For ease in exposition, we have combined the typology's cells into four categories, described below: [1]

[1] This typology was generalized partly from McKie's (1974) list of goals. For identification of a number of evaluative goals, see Backoff (1974).

Figure 5.1. Typology of Intermediate Goals

			Activity by Itself	Activity with Environment
Static:	Acting/ Performing		Aspects of quality of activity performance e.g., efficiency	Aspects of activity performance impacts e.g., safety, equity
Dynamic:	Changing:	No Change	Aspects of activity existence, maintenance, support e.g., stability, reliability	Aspects of activity support impacts
		Change	Aspects of activity evolution and development e.g., innovation, growth	Aspects of activity evolution impacts

Activity by Itself
Static
   1. Aspects of the quality of activity production or performance. For example, efficiency.
Dynamic
   2. Aspects of activity existence, maintenance and persistence, or activity support. For example, stability, continuity, reliability.
   3. Aspects of activity evolution and development. This may involve change in (*a*) the nature of the activity—for example, innovation, progress through changes in kind; or (*b*) the extent or scope of the activity—for example, growth, promotion of activity, progress through expansion. In short, this involves aspects of change in the activity over time.
Activity with Environment
Static and Dynamic
   4. Aspects of activity impact evaluation. This may involve characteristics of impact on activity performers or suppliers, consumers, or third parties. This includes both aspects of the impact of isolated characteristics of activities (e.g., safety), and the impact of relative characteristics (e.g., equity) on the parties in question. This category will be taken to include, for convenience, both static and dynamic impact factors. Thus, for example, we include both goals relating to the effects of efficient production on clients of a firm, and goals relating to effects of

activity reliability and of activity innovation on others, including members of the firm. Safety and equity goals would fall under the static dimension, i.e., aspects of the impact of performance.

Note that we have placed both maintenance/support and evolution/development aspects under "dynamic." Although support/maintenance seems at first glance to be a "static" factor, it relates principally to correction/steady-state/equilibrium/defense-against-change kinds of considerations, and is, we think, usefully contrasted with the evolution/growth change factors.

Application of these intermediate goals requires identification of a still "lower" class of goals, subject-specific rules or standards (see, e.g., Dubnick and Walker 1979). A frequent criticism, exemplified by Friendly (1962), is that such standards have been insufficiently developed and inconsistently applied. Against this view are the advocates of the wisdom of administrative discretion and rationalization, who argue that very specific standards limit the flexibility of the administrative process (Landis 1938).

The intermediate goals are not necessarily consistent with each other, of course. Safety requirements may reduce productive efficiency, for example. Resolving the trade-offs that inevitably must be made is a major problem of regulation in the abstract ideal, as well as in practice. It is therefore evident that certain aspects of one form or mechanism of regulation that appear to be "advantages" may become "disadvantages" or may lose all relevance when evaluated by a different and conflicting intermediate goal.

Consider again the general problem of moving through the goal hierarchy—from public interest to intermediate goal to subject-specific rule or standard. It would be helpful if we could develop a logical structure or linkage that could guide us up and down through this hierarchy. Sometimes the passage through the hierachy is partially easy and direct, e.g., the pajama safety case mentioned earlier. The complexity of the regulatory situation, however, seems at this point of our understanding to forbid all-encompassing, determinant guides or ties. Instead, we must rely largely on careful identification of the given regulatory situation and of the goals and standards and attempt to trace the logical dependencies through the goal set.

Some of the linkages through the goal hierarchy may turn out to be frequently occurring or important ones. For example, there may be a relatively more frequent or "stronger" tie between activity performance goals, such as efficiency, and unitary conceptions of the public interest. Because of acceptance and/or enforcement of a single set of preferences, intermediate goals may focus more on successful performance of, or implementation questions regarding, that set of preferences, rather than on relationships among competing preference sets. On the other hand, there may be more frequent or "stronger" ties between activity impact evaluation goals, particularly those relating to relative impacts, e.g., equity goals, and combinatorial (especially pluralistic aggregational) conceptions of the public interest. Thus, where preferences differ and must be somehow included or aggregated in the final goal determination, attention may focus on intermediate goals (like equity) that explicitly reflect such aggregation (or, in this case, balancing).

These are really only potential tendencies. Clearly, efficiency can allow "more" to go around, thus perhaps permitting more (and possibly different) preference sets to be satisfied. This would link activity performance goals (e.g., efficiency) to a combinatorial public interest conception. We shall return to this contrast in chapter 6.

It is possible, in fact, for all intermediate goals to be related to all public interest conceptions (see figure 5.2). In any given case, of course, ambiguity would not necessarily remain; the circumstances of the case would hopefully indicate the ties between public interest conceptions and intermediate goals. Recall that all relationships of conflict, as well as consistency, can exist *among* the intermediate goals, complicating the analysis greatly.

Figure 5.2.   Relationships between Public Interest Conceptions and
Intermediate Goals

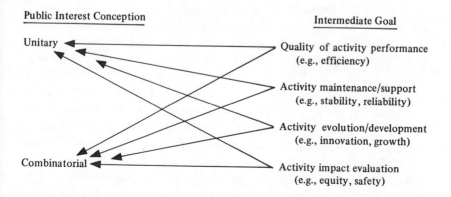

Activities of the sort subject to regulation do not occur in a vacuum; they are performed within the social framework of the larger society. Given an assumption of rationality, the intermediate goals we have outlined above ought to be reflected in this framework. In chapter 4 in our discussion of public interest rhetoric, we noted the existence of a limited value-consensus on some broad aspects of the public interest. Thus we can postulate, analytically, a set of rules, reflecting or implementing a set of consensual general intermediate goals, ultimately rationalizable in the consensual "public interest," that describes, implicitly, fundamental societal organization. These intermediate goals are essentially "general" in their removal from specific cases and their consequently broad application, and "consensual" in that they are very widely, if not universally held. Note that there can still be conflict where such a consensual goal is applied to a specific case, perhaps conflicting with particularistic goals, e.g., a generally desired "equity" implemented through affirmative-action requirements. And intermediate goals can conflict with other intermediate goals; consensuality on goals does not mean that they are always consistent with one another.

The fundamental societal rules are exemplified by notions of law and order, property rights, freedoms of transaction, and so on. They establish, implicitly, the boundaries and general forms of social and economic organization, and can be "constitutional" in character (cf. Buchanan and Tullock 1962). Within this framework, our activity subject to regulation occurs. This activity has its own set of rules that guide and define its performance. Organizational task performance, for example, may be structured by norms of rationality (Thompson 1967), producing patterned or rule-governed activities. These activity rules reflect or implement: 1) some particularistic goals that overlap with some intermediate goals which *are* consensual general ones; 2) some particularistic goals that overlap with some intermediate goals which are *not* consensual ones; and/or 3) some particularistic goals (e.g., private self-interest, profit), which are not intermediate goals at all (see figure 5.3).

Recall now that regulation formally involves interference by a party analytically an outsider to—i.e., not directly involved in or part of—the activity performed. Consider the case of implementation or defense of some societally consensual intermediate goal set. Clearly no such interference, i.e., no regulation, would be necessary if the activity rules prove consistent with the societal rules by producing be-

Figure 5.3. Consensual Societal Goals and Regulatory Interference

(1) Regulation aimed directly at protecting or maintaining some fundamental societal rules, so that outcomes consistent with some societally consensual general intermediate goals result.

(2) Regulation aimed at modifying the rules of the activity, so that outcomes consistent with some societally consensual general intermediate goals result.

(3) Regulation aimed at modifying the rules of the activity, so that outcomes consistent with some intermediate public goals result. Note: The intermediate public goals here need not be consensual general intermediate goals.

(4) Regulation aimed at modifying the rules of the activity, so that outcomes consistent with some particularistic activity goals result. The particularistic activity goals (a) may be consensual general intermediate goals, (b) may be intermediate but *not* be consensual general intermediate goals, and/or (c) may *not* be intermediate public goals at all.

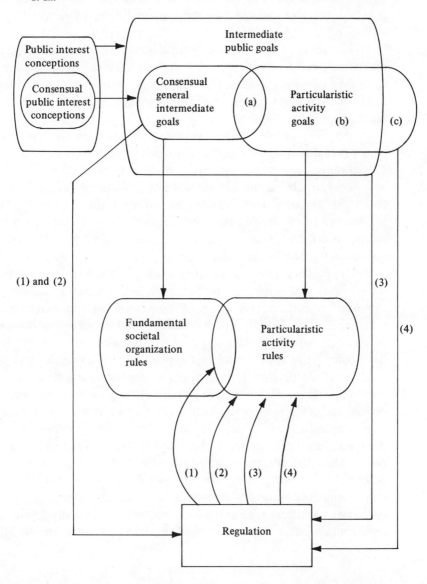

havior consistent with those rules, and thus with our particular societally consensual intermediate goal set established in the public interest. If regulation is judged necessary because inconsistency exists (and, of course, regulation is judged effective and desirable), then it may be aimed at two levels:

1. Regulation aimed directly at protecting, or maintaining, some fundamental societal rules, so that outcomes consistent with some societally consensual general intermediate goals result. This may involve the elaboration or enforcement of societal rules. For example, it may involve enforcement of the property rights of people hurt by pollution.

2. Regulation aimed at modifying the rules of the activity, so that outcomes consistent with some societally consensual general intermediate goals result. For example, fossil fuels with a certain maximum sulfur content may be prescribed for an electric utility to maintain the public health.

In practice, of course, the analytical distinctions we have made here often dissolve. Protection of property rights occurs instrumentally through requiring certain types of fuels to be employed; it could also occur, of course, by providing a law prohibiting damage to property rights through pollution, and an advocacy office empowered to sue the utility for each instance of damage. Thus the regulation may occur, in effect, a step or two away from the activity rules and the consensual general intermediate goals.

But regulatory interferences need not always be related only to some consensual general goals. In fact, regulation may be elected and imposed in the clear absence of consensus on the given goals, whether through dictation (perhaps unitary public interest conception) or through some less-than-consensual group-decision process (perhaps combinatorial public interest conception). Thus regulatory interferences could potentially reflect any of the intermediate goals, and even any of an infinite set of particularistic activity goals such as private self-interest or profit. In the latter case, as we saw in chapter 3, parties such as industries may mediate regulatory interferences in their own activities to serve their own particularistic goals. These possibilities are illustrated schematically in figure 5.3, and listed below:

3. Regulation aimed at modifying the rules of the activity, so that outcomes consistent with some intermediate public goals result. The intermediate public goals here need not be consensual general inter-

mediate goals. For example, regulation seeking equity in income distribution may be implemented over the objections of wealthier citizens.

4. Regulation aimed at modifying the rules of the activity, so that outcomes consistent with some particularistic activity goals result. The particularistic activity goals (*a*) may be consensual general intermediate goals, (*b*) may be intermediate but *not* be consensual general intermediate goals, and/or (*c*) may *not* be intermediate public goals at all. For example, regulation may serve to maintain the domestic merchant marine, protecting it against foreign competition through controls requiring shipments in American "bottoms." Note that in this case the particularistic goal (maintenance of the domestic merchant marine through protection) may be consistent with the intermediate activity maintenance/support goal of keeping a viable merchant marine available for use in war.

Note that the intermediate goals we have mentioned may easily, and frequently, conflict. The societal rules themselves are, in fact, often inconsistent. A major problem in many existing areas of regulation is that, having been established as the result of crisis or in response to specific abuses, piecemeal regulation often does not make the necessary trade-offs with full consideration of what these are. But trade-offs between goals are implicit in the empirical consequences of several uncoordinated lines of regulation.

We shall now discuss the rationale for regulation with respect to intermediate goals and the public interest. Recall again our discussion of "interferences." Interferences may be intentional or unintentional; regulation, of course, is intentional. The *objects* of regulation may also be either intentional or unintentional activity. Thus regulation may aim:

1. *To correct or restrain intentional activity* that (*a*) is judged desirable in its ideal form but which malfunctions in practice, or (*b*) is judged undesirable according to our set of intermediate goals rationalized in the "public interest." Examples include many defects of the economic system, including competition or "natural monopoly" that has some undesirable features (we shall discuss these in a moment), and breakdowns in maintenance of the fundamental societal system, e.g., questions of law and order, property rights.

2. *To control unintentional activities and their effects which are by-products of basic activities.* Examples include externalities, to be discussed below.

Figure 5.4. Outline of Rationale for Regulation

I. To correct or restrain intentional activity that

        (a) is judged desirable in ideal but malfunctions in practice

or

        (b) is judged undesirable with respect to the public interest (including instrumental goals)

II. To control unintentional by-products of activities

Under I:

    Market (perfect competition) ⟶ Intermediate goals ⟶ Pareto optimum, Other public interest conceptions

Therefore, regulate where:

    (a) competition can't survive

    (b) competition exists but, because of imperfections, does not get competitive results

    (c) competition exists, but other policy opposes reliance on it

        Under (b), some defects in competition that may call for regulation:

           Defects in market actors:
               (1) Buyer ignorance

           Defects in market exchange:
               (1) Excessive risk ⟶ no market develops
               (2) Competition is discriminatory or selective – violates many buyer/seller ignorance requirement
               (3) Competition is hurtful to service

Under II:

    Externalities: situations of unintentional activity are distinguished according to:

    (a) actor/bystander
        e.g., production/consumption (economies/diseconomies)

    (b) effects
        e.g., positive vs. negative; marginal vs. nonmarginal

    (c) responses
        e.g., relevant/nonrelevant; Pareto-relevant/Pareto-irrelevant

In practice, of course, our distinction between intentional and unintentional activities may blur; many activities may have both intentional and unintentional aspects. The arguments we present here constitute an outline for ordering what is an extensive literature on the regulatory rationale (see figure 5.4); it is not meant as a complete discussion (for a brief discussion of the rationale, see Green and Nader

1973). We divide our presentation into the rationale for regulating intentional and for regulating unintentional activities. The focus will be on regulation of economic activity.

3.0 The Rationale for Regulating Intentional Activities

First, consider some intentional activities subject to regulation. Because of its importance, we shall use economic activity as an example. Competition is the basic or, at least, ideal form of economic activity in ours and other "capitalist" economies. Why would anybody advocate this as a good way to organize economic activity? There are many reasons; a major one for our purposes is the remarkable theoretical result that "perfect competition"—a theoretical construct rarely realized in practice—produces a Pareto-optimal allocation of economic resources. We shall not discuss the reasons for this equivalence; they are set forth in most texts on microeconomics.[2] We shall be concerned with some consequences of this result. Remember that the Pareto optimum was one of the definitions of the public interest discussed above, falling in one of the combinatorial categories. An act is desirable according to the Pareto criterion if at least one person is helped by (while the rest are indifferent to) the act, and undesirable if any person is hurt by the act. It is, of course, a rather weak condition for the public interest, since it has nothing to say about all acts that help some and hurt some, even where nearly all are helped or hurt.

Perfect competition exists when the following conditions are met (see, e.g., Henderson and Quandt 1971:104-5):

1. The goods produced by firms in the market are homogeneous, i.e., an item with the same characteristics is produced by all, and the consumers of these goods are also identical as far as the firms are concerned. Thus firms and consumers, respectively, cannot be distinguished from one another.

2. There are many firms and many consumers, with each transaction small compared to the total purchases/sales in the market. Thus the actions of any buyer or seller cannot measurably affect price.

3. Perfect information about price and about the product is held by firms and consumers, who then use this information to their own best

---

[2] For an elementary explanation of the relation of perfect competition to Pareto Optimality, see Sharp (1973:1–33); Mansfield (1970, ch. 15).

benefit. Because the goods are homogeneous, because the number of actors in the market is large so that the action of any buyer or seller cannot affect price, and because all have perfect information on these factors, the price will be the same throughout the market.

4. There are no long-run barriers to entry into and exit from the market for all firms and consumers. The flow of resources, including labor, into areas or applications in which they may be most advantageously used is unimpeded; the resources themselves are infinitely divisible and completely mobile. Thus resources are free to be devoted to their use of greatest demand with greatest efficiency.

Note carefully, however, some of the assumptions underlying the model of perfect competition (see figure 5.5). It assumes a "greed," or "more is always better," rationality toward economic resources. Irrationality is excluded. Thus efficiency is valued (note it qualifies as one of our intermediate goals) because in increase it permits greater production from the same inputs, and thus permits some to be made better off while none are hurt—i.e., by allowing "more to go around" it is consistent with the Pareto principle. Efficiency may exist with respect to production, i.e., with respect to the efficient employment of inputs to produce various desired production units; and with respect to distribution, i.e., with respect to distribution of economic goods to best satisfy consumers' preferences so that it should not be possible to make consumers better off through trade in these goods—any trade in a distributively efficient condition would make someone worse off. Although concepts of preference are sufficiently flexible to include within such a model those who always prefer the same or less of a resource (and are perfectly rational in doing so), the model generally assumes that more return to economic goals is preferred and, in fact, that the preference structures of the participants either totally reflect, or can be translated into, desire for economic goods. Clearly, it would be difficult to declare that a Pareto-efficient change in the distribution of economic goods was in the public interest if the public interest related entirely to noneconomic concerns that could not be evaluated in economic terms.

The model assumes that aggregate behavior can be explained by combining the behavior of individuals; groups are combinations of individuals and do not have emergent properties based on the group itself. Individuals are assumed to be the best judges of what they want and to know what they want; the consumer, not some expert dictator, for example, has sovereignty over his desires. Individuals do not err,

Figure 5.5. Some Assumptions (and Criticisms) of the Model of Perfect Competition

– "Greed" form for preferences, i.e., "more" is always better, is assumed; individuals are rational with respect to such preferences. Model in simple form omits those who prefer the same level, or less, or who are irrational.

– Preferences either totally reflect, or can be translated into, desire for economic goods. Model in simple form does not treat preferences for noneconomic goods that cannot be so translated.

– Groups are combinations of individuals and do not have emergent properties; emergent properties are therefore excluded from the model in simple form.

– Individuals are assumed to be the best judges of what they want and have "sovereignty" over their desires. Thus error or lack of expertise or ability to judge or presence of overriding social or group goals is not permitted in the model in simple form.

– Individual endowments are taken as given, so that gains by a rich and by a poor man are equivalently optimal. There is therefore a bias in the simple form of the model toward efficiency goals over impact evaluation goals like equity.

– The market is not structured in an inefficient way, given the technology of production. For example, it is assumed that a market with only one firm will not permit more efficient production than the model's market of many. But such markets do exist, and are thus not covered by the model in simple form.

– The market is assumed to exist and to include the relevant good. In simple form the model includes only one good, but this can be extended in a more complicated model. Some goods, however, are never produced in a competitive market, and some goods which are produced are rarely included in the market (e.g., noise, soot).

– Goods are assumed homogeneous, and firms and consumers, respectively, indistinguishable. This is rarely the case.

– Firms and consumers are assumed to be many, with individual transactions small compared to the scale of the market. Many markets exist, however, without these characteristics.

– Firms and consumers are assumed to have perfect information about the good and its price, and the price is consequently the same throughout the market. Such information rarely exists and price typically varies.

– There are no barriers to entry into and exit from the market, and resources are such as to be fully mobile within it. But such barriers often exist, and resources devoted to particular uses, e.g., railroad track, are often not fully mobile.

have the expertise to judge what is good for them, and do not consider, prefer, or are subject to overriding community, group, or other social goals.

The model assumes all incomes or endowments as given; changes that give more to a rich man, and to a poor man, are equivalently Pareto-efficient. Thus it is clear that intermediate goals of activity im-

pact evaluation, such as equity, may conflict with the goal of efficiency, which is at the core of the model.

The model assumes that the structure of the market is not inefficient, given the technology of production—i.e., that it is not more
efficient to have one firm produce all the goods than the perfect competition situation of many producers. This implies no increasing returns to scale. If it is more efficient to have one firm rather than
many, we may have a market that is a "natural monopoly," and the
perfect competition model does not apply; we return to this below. In
fact, markets in which the "many firm" assumption leads to inefficiency are not uncommon.

The model in simple form assumes that the market exists and that
the relevant good is included within it. The simple model can be extended to include multiple goods in multiple markets. Thus it is assumed that all goods can be traded; all exchanges are reflected in the
market. But this is often not the case: 1) Some goods tend not to be
produced by the competitive market. "Public" or "collective"
goods, for example, are said to be "goods that can be consumed by
one person without diminishing the consumption of the same good by
another and where exclusion of potential consumers is not feasible"
(Bish 1971:25). In other words, collective goods, once supplied to
one party, cannot be withheld from any other. National defense, for
example, is a public good. We may also identify public "bads," like
some kinds of pollution. Who would pay for a public good if he
knew that he could share in the benefits of purchase of the good by
just one other consumer? We assume, of course, that our consumer is
self-interested and not altruistic, and that he feels certain that the fact
of his *not* purchasing the good will not affect its supply—i.e., he
feels that the situation where all must contribute if any may benefit
does not hold. 2) Some goods tend not to be included in the market.
Thus unintentional by-products of economic activity, such as noise or
soot, have in the past rarely been priced and traded.

Beyond these points, of course, we can make the obvious criticisms about the limitations of the model in the simple form presented
here: 1) Goods are never perfectly homogeneous and few markets
exist in which firms and consumers cannot, respectively, be distinguished; in fact, firms usually attempt vigorously to distinguish themselves and "discriminate" their product through advertising, reflecting the possibility of such distinction in the given market, and
external factors like geography often conspire to distinguish firms and
consumers. 2) Many markets do not contain a very large number of

buyers and sellers; geography and transaction or communication costs over distances (besides demand and technology) often limit, for example, the effective number of firms in a local market. Monopoly/oligopoly (one firm—few firms) and monopsony/oligopsony (one buyer—few buyers) are not uncommon. Individual sales or purchases can indeed sometimes affect price, as with purchases of steel by General Motors. 3) Firms and consumers rarely have perfect information about the product or its price, and the price itself is usually not the same throughout the market. 4) There are often considerable barriers to entry and exit. These can even be geographical in character, e.g., need to use river water as coolant or to build on an already occupied site. Resources are usually not completely divisible and transferable; there are few alternate uses for a railroad right-of-way a hundred miles long and, say, thirty feet wide, and for the steel track and wooden ties that lay along it.

Thus it is perilous to use the model of perfect competition as ideal if it is merely an almost purely heuristic model, and is rarely realized in practice. Absent the special conditions, there is no guarantee that the public interest criterion of Pareto optimality will be achieved. Even close approximations to the conditions may not be particularly desirable if they do not actually produce Pareto optimality.[3]

Of course, if our criterion is not Pareto optimality but "consensual majoritarian" (i.e., most or nearly all agree, with the minority treated as irrelevant), perhaps some set of similar but weakened conditions will suffice. This could be similarly possible for a criterion implied in chapter 4 but not specified; we could call it "Pareto consensual majoritarian." Here we allow either similarity of preferences regarding the act, or indifference toward it, among most or nearly all parties, with the (now clearly opposed—or nonparticipating) minority again treated as irrelevant. We suggest that because of the infrequency with which the formal conditions of the model of perfect competition are realized in practice, adherence to that model as a desirable guide to organizing economic activity usually implies no "more" than one of the consensual majoritarian criteria. That is, some minority may be affected negatively but are implicitly ignored. Thus something "less" than Pareto optimality is in effect employed, and consequently the use of the model of perfect competition as ideal becomes questionable.

Let us assume, nevertheless, that perfect competition should be

---

[3] See the "theory of second best;" e.g., in Henderson and Quandt (1971:286–88).

sought and held as ideal because it satisfies the Pareto principle and thus brings about results in the public interest. This is the traditional view; some markets may very nearly be perfectly competitive. It may also be that the implied consensual majoritarian criteria that could turn out to be implicit in near achievement of perfect competition conditions are held desirable. Furthermore, it is possible that actual situations approaching perfect competition may just be more likely to produce Pareto optimal results. This is at least partially an empirical question.

Goals beside efficiency can be supportive of perfect competition as a means of organizing economic activity. The value of free choice, for example, may be held to be more nearly realized under the decentralized choice conditions of perfect competition in which consumers have sovereignty. "Free choice" can be viewed as an activity-impact-evaluation goal. Thus the rationale for perfect competition would flow through the public interest–free choice, rather than public interest–efficiency, connection. More such ties are possible, of course. Regulation which more closely preserves free choice (e.g., incentive rather than directive means; see chapter 6) could similarly be held relatively more desirable.

Thus, assuming that there are benefits to the public interest from maintaining perfect competition, regulation may be imposed when: [4]

1. "Competition . . . cannot exist or survive for long," so competitive results are not achieved by the unregulated market.

2. Competition exists, but because of imperfections, competitive results do not occur.

3. "Competition exists, or could exist," and could produce competitive results, but because of other policy considerations—i.e., our set of intermediate goals—"competitive results are unsatisfactory" in some respects.

3.1 WHERE COMPETITION CANNOT EXIST

Consider first the first category—where competition does not exist or survive. In particular, we shall consider the case of "natural monopoly."

A natural monopoly has been defined to exist "if the entire demand within a relevant market can be satisfied at lowest cost by one firm rather than by two or more, . . . whatever the actual number of

[4] The conditions below are from Kaysen and Turner (1965:189–90) and, generally, pp. 189–213.

firms in it" (Posner 1969:548). Such markets tend to approach monopoly as firms merge or fail, i.e., competition tends not to survive. Such "decreasing-cost" conditions of natural monopoly often occur when some large initial investment is necessary, for example, a railroad (but see Spann and Erickson 1970). This essentially traditional definition has been attacked. Bonbright (1961), for example, argues that

> What favors a monopoly status for a public utility is not the mere fact that, up to a certain point of size, it operates under conditions of decreasing unit cost—an attribute of every business, including a farm or a hand laundry. . . . It is due, rather, to the severely localized and hence restricted markets for utility services—markets limited because of the necessarily close connection between the utility plant on the one hand and the consumers' premises on the other. (Bonbright 1961:12–13)

Thus the technology itself, reflected usually in necessary ties to the local market, rather than the cost conditions produced by the technology, is the determining factor for existence of a natural monopoly. Natural monopoly public utilities therefore are usually "transportation or transmission agencies" (Bonbright 1961:13).

In fact, a natural monopoly can and often does exist under increasing cost conditions. For example, this may be so when a power utility exhausts its potential of cheaper energy-production methods—e.g., water power—and must use more and more of some more expensive means—e.g., nuclear power (see Bonbright 1961). Actually the cost curve may be U-shaped, since decreasing costs may exist at the outset after the utility's expensive physical plant is built and begins exploiting the cheaper power-production method. Later, as more expensive power production is added, the curve may turn upward. At any rate, competition may not be efficient as a means of organizing such industries.

But even this presumed abandonment of competition may not be quite so reliable an assertion in a world of technological innovation. Although the industry may be monopolistic, substitutes may arise in other industries that could compete in function. For example, power utilities based on different fuels (e.g., gas vs. oil vs. electric heating) or transportation competitors (e.g., buses vs. trains vs. planes) or communication competitors (e.g., telephone vs. telegraph vs. radio) can develop. Regulation may act to minimize disruption in functional areas where such substitutes arise (see chapter 2). In transportation, for example, the truckers were brought into the Interstate Commerce

Commission largely on the terms of the existing regulated industry, the railroads. But such competition is rarely pure competition; frequently only a few substitutes, and sometimes only a few firms in the substitute industries, develop.

Thus a look at the undesirable characteristics that could manifest themselves in the situation where competition fails to survive seems appropriate. Such undesirable features are supposed to be controlled or corrected through regulation. We shall therefore review some of such criticisms applied to natural monopoly, a case where pure competition does not exist. Posner (1969) provides both a critique of natural monopoly, and a thorough critique of the conventional critical wisdom, and we shall summarize some of his arguments here.[5] Criticisms of natural monopoly include:

1. Monopoly permits the monopolist to extract supracompetitive profits through charging higher prices. This enables him to obtain value that would otherwise be kept by the consumer. Monopoly prices are considered socially undesirable because of effects on: (a) Income distribution—it involves the transfer of wealth from the relatively poor consumer to the relatively rich monopolist. (b) Overall economic stability—demand is lowered, contributing to any possible recession, because monopolist investors save a larger proportion of their income; when demand is decreasing, monopolists may be slower to lower prices, thus contributing to recession; higher prices contribute to any inflation; since the monopolist tends to employ less of the factors of production, he may contribute to unemployment. (c) Allocation of economic resources—the higher monopoly price may exclude consumers who would otherwise purchase the product, leading them to substitute more costly or less useful ones. Thus society's resources are not used optimally. (d) Proper business incentives— easy profits may dull the incentive to efficient operation.

But against the actual occurrence of such monopoly practices is the revisionist theory of the firm; managers may not, for example, seek profit, but, rather, status, pleasant working conditions, and other rewards. But managers are constrained by investors and other forces to work for profits. And even if managers have such objectives, they may still charge monopoly prices whether to finance more such rewards or because their slack management allows firm costs to rise.

---

[5] Posner's article is far more densely written than is indicated here; the reader is referred to it for extensions and elaborations. For criticisms of Posner see issues of the *Stanford Law Review* subsequent to his article.

Posner qualifies the result that high monopoly prices should occur: (a) Because competing entrepreneurs might be tempted to enter, and legislatures tempted to threaten him if his prices are consistently excessive, the monopolist's long-run price may be lower than his short-run. (b) Because of the prevalence of oligopoly, it is not proper to compare a monopoly with competition; it should be compared with oligopoly. Prices and profits may not be that much higher.

Posner offers several criticisms of the above arguments regarding the occurrence of monopoly profits. Monopoly profits serve, in general, as an incentive to efficiency, although this may be hard to distinguish from mulcting the customer. The income-distribution point is not convincing, for example, if the stockholders are ordinary citizens, and if equality of opportunity rather than of rewards is the goal. The economic-stability arguments are not viable because the natural monopoly sectors comprise too small a proportion of the economy to have much of an effect, and monopolist investors will not necessarily accumulate large savings from the profits because the stock of the excessively profitable monopolist would be bid up, making it more expensive, and less profitable, to new investors. Regarding the allocation of resources, it is argued that reduction of excessive prices in one sector, the monopolist one, may not increase overall efficiency in a complex, interconnected economy, and that the monopolist may discriminate in his pricing in order to maximize profit, charging more to those who will pay more, so that he may as a result be more efficient. The business-incentives criticism may not be valid because the situation is similar to a competitive firm in that increase in profits remains the motive. And excessive profits would not come so easily to subsequent investors as the firm's stock is bid up.

2. Another criticism of natural monopoly is that it leads to internal inefficiency, or departures from cost minimization in the firm. Without the ability to make comparisons to other firms in the industry, and without competitive pressures, it may be difficult for a natural monopolist to discover cost-minimizing methods. Also, managers of the firm may have goals other than profit maximization; as noted above, they may seek various self-rewards. They may seek political support for long-term interests like security for themselves and protection for the firm. Cost minimization, however, is generally consistent with such goals, since it would allow more profit to be devoted to them. Posner argues that internal inefficiency would be more serious than monopoly profits, since the former would involve waste of

resources, while the latter would involve only a transfer. We note, however, that this assumes efficiency goals should be dominant in evaluating the situation. Other social goals might support any such "waste" of resources.

3. Another alleged failing of natural monopoly is an inability to make optimal use of technological change. Posner argues, however, that we cannot distinguish theoretically between competition and monopoly in this regard. Both the competitive firm and the monopolist gain from innovation. Both either have, or could obtain, the necessary resources. Concern for survival may favor short-term innovation in the competitive firm; long-term goals regarding political viability favor innovation by the monopolist. While diversity in the competitive market favors innovation, since several approaches are likely to be supported, diversity also may be encountered either in the regional organizations of the natural monopolist or in associated industries. Note that technological change is one of the intermediate goals we noted earlier.

4. Monopolists have been accused of arbitrary refusals to serve, the offering of inferior goods and service, and a lack of responsiveness to what consumers desire. Posner argues that the monopolist will simply lose profit if he refuses to serve. And lowering the quality of goods to save costs, and thus earn greater monopoly profit, depends on what consumers will pay for. We note, however, that the consumer may within a wide range be constrained to purchase some quantity of the monopolist's good, whatever its quality, e.g., electric service. Lowering quality may then be a viable means of extorting more profit. Relevant here are goals in our category of activity impact evaluation.

5. Markets that are natural monopolies may be subject to ruinous or wasteful competition if more than one firm remains in them. Posner argues that the nature of natural monopoly inevitably means shakedown to one firm, by exit or merger. At any rate, price wars may not be as destructive or prolonged as has been thought; participants will soon see the value of mergers if they are permitted to merge. Thus natural monopoly should be allowed as a defense for merger under the antitrust laws.

6. Monopolists are said to engage in unfair competition, such as predatory pricing to drive out rivals or firms in another market that the monopolist is entering. Posner argues that predatory pricing is

rarely a rational strategy, partly because losses will have to be re-couped by higher subsequent prices; this could draw in new competi-tion if entry is not too difficult. Merger would be a better strategy.

7. The monopolist's economic power has been thought to threaten democratic processes. Posner notes, however, that the objection is really to large firms, rather than monopolists.

8. Finally, it is argued that, lacking market correctives, manager-ial incompetence may persist in the monopolist. Posner agrees that this could occur, since it may be difficult to distinguish managerial failings from other factors without market evidence.

Thus, Posner argues that natural monopoly does not necessarily ex-hibit those features for which it has been subject to regulation. This raises doubts about the wisdom of a general policy of regulating mar-kets that are natural monopolies. Given the enormous literature in the area, and the long history of regulation of natural monopoly, the po-tential validity of even only some of Posner's observations seems distressing. But Posner's arguments are not at all determinant; it still appears possible that natural monopolies can display, at least some of the time, at least some of the features that have seemingly provoked regulation.

Demsetz (1968) has proposed a substitute for regulation of natural monopolies, a substitute that he claims may prevent or curb the un-desirable features of unregulated monopoly while performing in a manner superior to ordinary regulation. He would let firms participate in an auction to determine who would be permitted to supply the mo-nopoly services in question for a given period of time. Firm bids for this franchise would specify the per-unit price they would charge for the service, and the lowest such bid would be the winner. The trans-action would occur in the absence of risk and uncertainty, in a "fric-tionless" world with zero transactions cost. Assuming that resources to supply the service are readily available, and that the cost of collu-sion is high, the presence of many rivals in bidding will keep the price close to what it would be under perfect competition (cf. the dis-cussion of "pollution rights" auctions in chapter 7).

Demsetz's proposal has received a great deal of discussion in the literature, with important analyses by Trebing (1976), Williamson (1976), Goldberg (1976), and others. We shall review some of the major criticisms; a recurrent theme among them is that the real-world "frictions" inherent in the contract bidding process would tend to prevent it from working as described. Corrections to these "frictions" typically involve regulation-like mechanisms. Consequently, regulation, at least in some cases, may remain preferable.

Trebing (1976:114–18) offers several counter-arguments to the bidding alternative. He asserts that price discrimination by the firm may still be possible, even if the firm's profits are what it would receive under competition. Controls and monitoring/enforcement could be necessary to avoid such discrimination, but this is tantamount to regulation.

The franchise bidding system would increase uncertainty. This would raise capital costs, raise problems of arbitrating re-opened long-term contracts, raise problems of high transaction costs and risks in the case of short-term contracts, and raise the need to monitor quality of service. The government bargaining agents may be incompetent and/or lack sufficient information to manage the auction system. We have already seen this disadvantage, and some of the others, in chapter 2's discussion of nineteenth century regulation by franchise.

Societally desirable levels of service may not be equivalent with that determined through the bidding process. Under the bidding process, franchise holders may lack the incentive to innovate since there may be no recourse if costly failure results, and since cost-saving innovation could lead to a push by the government for renegotiation of the franchise contract. Firms might simply abandon service if the costs on succeeding contracts go up.

Finally, bidding may just constitute an opportunity for the largest and/or strongest firm to take over the market, limiting entry by competitors. Low bids submitted in order to do this may be subsidized by earnings in other markets. Overall, then, the bidding process may simply not work sufficiently well in practice to be a replacement for regulation, though it could be a supplement or adjunct to it.

Williamson (1976) focuses on the contractual difficulties likely to inhere in the bidding process. He examines three possible forms of contracts that could be chosen under a franchise bidding arrangement. "Once-for-all contracts" include complete contingent claims contracts and incomplete contracts. The former must be enormously complex in order to deal with all contingencies under uncertainty, and the latter run the risk of being subject to opportunism and share the problems of incomplete long-term contracts, noted below.

A second type of contract is the "incomplete long-term contract,"

in which unforeseen contingencies are managed by allowing renegotiation of terms, subject to penalties (Williamson 1976:79). Under
such a contract, low bids may not be able to take sufficient account of
the uncertain future; those submitting them must be risk-takers. The
auction authority must have measures of the quality of service desired
and the ability of alternative service providers to perform. But it may
be hard to select specific, reliable criteria to evaluate and choose
among candidates. Simple reliance on lowest bid under these conditions may be a poor choice.

Incomplete long-term contracts may face execution problems as
well. The franchisee is likely to hold the franchise over the whole
period of the contract; the long-term contract seeks to give the franchisee an incentive to invest in substantial, lasting facilities. Attempts
at displacing the franchisee may be characterized by litigation and
transition costs, and the franchise authority will be reluctant to admit
its judgment in the choice of franchisee was in error. Thus one can
examine likely execution problems for the franchisee over the length
of the contract.

Under uncertainty, bids for the franchise that specify fixed prices
may not be workable; costs will change. Problems similar to those
encountered under defense contracts in deciding the incidence of
these additional costs could occur. These could include difficulties in
auditing and lack of incentive to keep costs down (e.g., the cost plus
defense contract).

If the contract is incomplete, as assumed, franchisees can adhere to
the letter rather than the spirit of the contract. Since consumers, who
lack information and expertise, are unlikely to be able to police this,
consummate performance may only be assured through regulation-
like monitoring and enforcement. In addition, accounting ambiguities
are likely to be permitted by the franchise authority, since failure of
the franchise would reflect on its judgment. Thus regulation-like accounting controls may be needed.

The circumstances of renegotiation are likely to emphasize the
presence of political skills in franchisees, since they may contribute
more to bidding success than performance skills. Finally, incumbent
franchisees, for reasons discussed below, are likely to have an advantage at contract renewal time.

The third type of contract is the "recurrent short-term contract."
Such contracts could, of course, permit needed adjustments under uncertainty, compensating for the problems faced under incomplete

long-term contracts. The sequential decision-making characterizing such a contractual arrangement serves the bounded rationality of the participants, and curbs the potential opportunism of franchisees who know they must soon compete again to win the franchise from the authority.

The major problem with such contracts attaches to the advantages enjoyed by incumbents. Transfer of capital equipment from one franchisee to the next may be beset with the valuation problems so prominent in rate-of-return regulation. Transfer may not be necessary, of course, if the equipment is relatively unspecialized, or if it is simply used up in service. But this will not generally be the case.

Significant difficulties also attend to the disposition of human capital. Experienced workers in the incumbent franchisee have invested in job performance skills idiosyncratic to the particular task of the franchisee. These include idiosyncracies related to use of particular equipment, production methods, informal team relationships, and communication means. It may be inefficient to replace these workers with a new franchisee. The incumbent workers are also more likely to be able to provide (and, presumably, to support the offering of bids specifying) the least-cost service.

Moreover, workers are likely to prefer to remain with the present owner of the franchise due to informal understandings about their personal job situation (e.g., promotion, job security) that are more costly to reach with outside owners, and that would be more risky with new owners than the original relationship. Thus incumbents are likely to have advantages stemming from aspects of information acquisition and the nature of the informal social system in their organization. And so franchise bidding would not be able to operate as the efficient substitute for regulation that Demsetz claims it is.

Williamson goes on, in fact, to describe regulation from the perspective of its contractual advantages (cf. Shepherd's "social contract;" see chapter 2):

> At the risk of oversimplification, regulation may be described contractually as a highly incomplete form of long-term contracting in which (1) the regulatee is assured an overall fair rate of return, in exchange for which (2) adaptations to changing circumstances are successively introduced without the costly haggling that attends such changes when parties to the contract enjoy greater autonomy (Williamson 1976:91).

Williamson's analysis is consistent in part with other models we have reviewed of regulators as bureaucrats and regulation as a long-term behavioral relation that structures outcomes. Perhaps more extensive analysis of the likely behavior of the bureaucrats administering the contract would enhance his argument; references to saving face are probably by themselves not completely convincing. Since Williamson is restoring some of the real-world complexities assumed away by Demsetz and other economists working from classical market models, it would seem useful to go further, if possible, and consider more of the likely behaviors and institutional constraints which administrators of regulatory contracts are likely to engage in or face. Williamson's very major contribution is in breaking down and analyzing the conceptual structure of the regulatory contract, i.e., informational and informal relations aspects and idiosyncracies.

Given the admitted complexities of the situation, rigorous as well as descriptive models can be difficult to construct (cf. Goldberg's remarks in Goldberg 1976). They can involve greater conceptual development, as against manipulation of existing formalism, than is common in economics. They tend to build bridges to other areas of social science, e.g., small group analysis and organizational behavior, though as approaches they can remain distinct. There is a shift, as we saw in chapter 3, from models in economics to a blending of economic approaches with "alien" concepts from the other social sciences and, particularly, from law. But, as witnessed by Williamson's work (and by Goldberg's and others'), the payoffs can be significant.

Williamson's work should be seen as complementary to models of regulation that introduce similar *relational* elements (e.g., Goldberg 1973, 1974, 1976; Mitnick 1973b, 1974, 1975b; Baldwin 1975). In particular, these models portray regulation as consisting of some pattern of agent-principal relationships governed by a "contract." Victor Goldberg (1976; see also 1973, 1974) has applied this perspective to examine the natural monopoly rationale for regulation. Like Williamson, he emphasizes the critical role played by complex contractual relationships in economic exchange; he observes the bias of economists in assuming such exchange occurs in the form of discrete transactions. He suggests that such a focus can provide a potential rationale for natural monopoly regulation (or, at least, a framework for examining that rationale) if, as Demsetz demonstrates with his market-like solution, the traditional decreasing costs explanation is insufficient.

Goldberg argues that, at the stage at which contracts are formed, the agent (regulator) must establish in the contract some measure of protection both for the producer's right to serve and the consumer's right to be served. The producer may prefer some long-term protection of his status as sole provider of the service since this will permit him to invest in the long-lived capital equipment necessary for success. Consumers would also prefer some protection if they wish to assure service reliability for equipment complementary to that of the service provider. Consumers might also, however, wish to be able to terminate the relationship should superior (or less costly) technologies become available. Thus the agent-regulator must make a trade-off between producer and consumer interests.

The regulator acting as the consumer's agent could seek protection from competing technologies through entry control (as he obviously would as agent for producers); such protection is a frequent criticism of regulation. Consumers might want it to permit the producer to invest in innovation. The amount of protection provided may be more or less than what would be optimal, but it is not clear that private contract would do any better. Under private contract, consumers may still wish to retard competing technologies for the same reason, and private agents may still have to use restrictive mechanisms like those in regulation. If they do not, they will use substitutes like patents, trade secrets, and so on, that do the same thing. At any rate, the private market does not always supply the goods and services that are desired.

Under long-term contracts, flexible pricing for the natural monopoly service may be adopted since it permits adjustment to changing circumstances. This may be some cost-based pricing system, such as that in rate-of-return regulation. So again we see a similarity to regulation.

Consumers will be interested in assuring their right to be served under the long-term contract. After the service has begun, the producer could "hold up" the consumer, threatening to terminate service; the consumer may have few or no alternatives. Consumers may also wish to avoid arbitrary and capricious treatment at the hands of the producer. Producers can also demand compensation for "honest mistakes" made when the contract was formed. For these reasons, the agent (regulator) may seek contractual protection for the consumer in these areas; we often see such protection, of course, in regulation. Such protection can be costly—consumers may be asked to pay a premium price to cover the supplier's risks.

The agent-regulator must administer this long-term contract. Disagreeing with Posner, Goldberg argues that the problems apparently endemic to regulatory oversight stem not from the regulation but from the nature of the service. Private contracts face similar problems; Goldberg discusses as example the problems of overseeing university food service contracts. Such private contracts, like public regulatory contracts, produce problems in determining and allowing costs and what a "reasonable profit" should be, overseeing service quality in detail, responding to consumer complaints, and so on. Undesirable effects, such as Averch-Johnson-like overexpenditures on capital (e.g., Kahn 1971, vol. 2:49–59, 106–8), can result if the restrictions in private contracts are similar to those in public regulatory ones. Goldberg (1976:444) concludes that "many of the problems that arise in regulated industries would arise even if the industries were not under the jurisdiction of a regulatory agency (although the magnitude of the problems need not be the same)."

Thus the rationale for regulation where competition does not exist stems not from natural monopoly per se, but from the need to manage long-term relationships, i.e., contracts, among the parties in question. Like Bonbright to some extent, for Goldberg natural monopoly and its regulation rest on the need to manage service provision for particular technologies over time.

Goldberg's agent-regulator, as he himself explicitly cautions, is taken to be "a faithful representative of his principals' interests" (Goldberg 1976:430). This can be equivalent to what we have elsewhere termed a "pure fiduciary" (see chapter 4). Such an assumption, as Goldberg notes, assumes away consideration of regulatory politics and possible "capture" by the producer. He suggests that private contract may also be subject to similar kinds of influence. But it is not at all clear that the conditions of public and private contract would still be similar if we allowed such considerations. There is a large, uneven, and underdeveloped literature on public and private comparisons that suggests that there can be significant differences (see Rainey, Backoff, and Levine 1976; on regulation, see, e.g., DeAlessi 1974, 1975). Given goals that may be more vague, different forms of oversight, possibly different kinds of personnel with differing motives, different funding or allocation systems, and so on, the mythical public contract could operate in a substantially different environment than the private contract. What Goldberg does show, however, are how certain core relational considerations of oversight produce strikingly similar problems in both private and public contract.

If the agent is assumed "faithful" to some degree, we would be interested in learning, for example, the sources of his initial faithfulness (e.g., fiduciary norms, special training, external policing?) and what policing mechanisms operate to maintain some measure of this orientation. We have suggested elsewhere (Mitnick 1975b) that the costs of policing regulatory agents may be such that there can be a net gain to public interest criteria through some tolerance of deviation. In a real contractual world like that which Williamson and Goldberg endeavor to describe, considerations of policing of agent fidelity to contractual provisions can play a very significant role. Given public-private differences, public agents could be more difficult to police than private ones (cf. Wilson and Rachal 1977). This could lead to divergences in performance under public and private contracts.

The agents' self-interest must at some point be recognized and its effects considered. Like Williamson's managerial discretion model of the firm (1964), regulators may be viewed as making a trade-off between self- and organizational-goals under institutional and environmental constraints, i.e., in administering the "regulatory contract" (Mitnick 1974, 1975b). The relationship between the agent and his constituency-principals must be analyzed: how is the relationship formed; how does it operate; how is it terminated?

The agent, moreover, is not an individual, or even a perfectly coordinated organization, or "team." As we discussed in chapter 2, collective organizational action can deviate from individual action, and individual intentions. This may not be due only to self-interested organizational members; it can result even where all members seemingly have the "best" of intentions (cf. Schelling 1971, 1974, 1978). In chapter 2, for example, we discussed how division of labor under the "institutional decision" can produce perverse, rigidifying outcomes. It is thus risky to extrapolate from rational individual to rational organizational behavior. And it is thus risky to look for a rationale for regulation in this way.

In summary, Bonbright has argued that the traditional natural monopoly definition has a questionable basis, and Posner has shown that the traditional natural monopoly rationale is leaky. Demsetz has shown that in a perfect world a market-like alternative—franchise bidding—can substitute for regulation. Trebing, Williamson, and

Goldberg have taken issue with the perfect-world characteristics and likely performance of Demsetz's substitute. Williamson and Goldberg have provided a new potential rationale for—or at least a framework to develop alternatives to—the institution of regulation where competition does not exist or cannot survive. They have done this by introducing the complexity of real world exchange, challenging the traditional simplifying assumptions of microeconomics.

Clearly, many theoretical and empirical questions remain to be answered. Perhaps a future theory will indicate when regulation is indicated, and when it is not, when competition fails to survive.

3.2 WHERE COMPETITION EXISTS, BUT IS IMPERFECT

Consider now category two—where competition exists, but is imperfect. What are the kinds of defects that would make us want to regulate? (See, e.g., Kahn 1970, vol. 2.) We can sort them into 1) a category dealing with defects in the market actors themselves or what they possess, and 2) a category dealing with defects in the market exchange that occurs in competition, including aspects of the content and the structure of the exchange. We list a few of such defects:

Defects in Market Actors

1. *Buyer ignorance:* imperfect information about the nature and quality of the product, or of market characteristics like price, held by the buyer. This includes information about safety, or the risk associated with the product (see, e.g., Kelman 1974). Note this involves activity-impact-evaluation goals. Such risk information is often not obtainable easily through experience with the product or reliably from other consumers. Governments promulgate safety regulations, for example, to overcome such information problems.

A number of other "defects" in market actors can stem from or reflect real-world limitations on human information processing, i.e., "bounded rationality" (e.g., March and Simon 1958).

Defects in Market Exchange

1. *Extreme risk.* An extreme case of imperfect information occurs when a market fails to develop extensively because of the risk involved in producing the commodity. To induce private investment in such extremely risky fields, a government may grant a franchise monopoly to one producer, protecting him against competitors and so guaranteeing him all profits in the field. An example is the trading

companies established in the sixteenth and seventeenth centuries to develop the newly discovered lands. The social goals here are promotional, i.e., developmental/growth, in nature.

2. *Competition is discriminatory or selective,* violating the many seller–many buyer ignorance condition of perfect competition. Examples here include the long haul/short haul abuses of railroads and the rebates and special favors given selected shippers. Relevant here is an equity goal, an aspect of activity impact evaluation.

3. *Competition is destructive in that it is hurtful to service* in the area: (*a*) Hurtful to basic services. Because the industry is inherently subject to this hurt, regulation must be instituted. An example is the argument given in favor of regulation of trucking, an industry that is not a natural monopoly—that regulation was necessary to prevent rate wars.[6] (*b*) Hurtful to part of services that are deemed desirable of continuation. An example is "cream-skimming" in the transport industry, where, with free entry, competitors enter only the very lucrative markets of a service area, e.g., the Boston-Washington eastern corridor. Established firms suffer, and service worsens in noncreamy markets no longer subsidized by the no-longer-available extra revenue from the creamy markets. (*c*) Hurtful as a by-product of excessive nonprice rivalry. An example is airline competition on meals and service. This causes inflation of service costs; it is inefficient because consumers would prefer simpler service at lower cost. Several intermediate goals are relevant here under "hurtful to service," e.g., efficiency, promotion, or regional development.

There are many other defects of competition for which regulation may be adduced as a cure; this list is not complete. A major point is that defects in competition can be related to the intermediate goal set and thus be sufficient reasons for considering regulation.

3.3 WHERE COMPETITION COULD EXIST, BUT IS NOT DESIRED

The third category was where competition could exist, but for policy considerations—i.e., one or more of our intermediate goals—it is

[6] Examples of the terms used in public controversy to characterize below-cost competition marked by rate wars, i.e., "cutthroat competition," are given by Redford (1969:28). These include "condemnations of 'unbridled,' 'cut-throat,' 'disastrous,' 'destructive,' 'wasteful,' 'unregulated,' competition and of 'chaotic conditions,' 'unsound ventures,' 'haphazard growth,' 'blind economic chaos,' and industry sowing of 'wild oats.' What was favored was 'orderly and sound growth,' 'orderly planning,' 'a measure of stability,' and 'financial stability.' " Of course, regulation instituted to prevent alleged hurt to basic services through control of cutthroat competition (a public interest rationale) may in reality be sought by industry for its own economic protection. The destructive competition rationale can be only a facade.

considered undesirable. For example, most nations no longer hire mercenaries, preferring to provide their own national defense. But they could. Nations may adopt redistributive social goals, transfering wealth from their richer to their poorer citizens. Perfect competition, as noted above, takes initial endowments for granted, and may not therefore be desirable in the context of such an intermediate goal.

We have now considered regulatory interference to correct or restrain intentional activity that malfunctions or is judged undesirable. We now consider the rationale for regulating unintentional, by-product activities and their effects.

4.0 The Rationale for Regulating Unintentional Activities

Unintentional activities may be subject to regulation, in the ideal case, when they impact adversely on intermediate goals and, ultimately, the public interest. The intermediate goals may consist, of course, of goals like efficiency, equity, and the value of free choice (including consequent or related basic preferences for the unregulated market system). In general, the class of effects that are by-products of unintentional activities (recall the discussion in chapter 1) is referred to as "externalities," "neighborhood effects," or "spillovers."[7]

We can distinguish situations of unintentional activity according to: 1) the kind or nature of the *actor* and the original activity generating the unintentional activity and its effect; 2) the kind or nature of the *bystander* subject to the unintentional activity and its effect, and the basic activity in which the bystander is engaged; 3) the kind or extent of the *effect* of the unintentional activity on those subject to it, i.e., bystanders; and 4) the *response* of the bystander to the unintentional activity and its effects. We shall consider a few characteristics in

---

[7] Definitions of these terms, and of dimensions relevant to them, such as some of those discussed below, tend to vary in the literature. For discussions of externalities, the related concept of "public goods," and some of these dimensions, see, e.g., Arrow (1970); Baumol (1965); Baumol and Oates (1975); Buchanan (1968); Chamberlin (1974); Cowhey and Hart (1973); Davis and Hulett (1977); Davis and Kamien (1970); Frohlich, Oppenheimer, and Young (1971); Hardin (1975); Head (1962); Lin (1976); MacRae and Wilde (1979); Macaulay and Yandle (1977); Meade (1973); Mishan (1971); Musgrave and Musgrave (1973); Olson (1965); Olson and Zeckhauser (1966); Plott and Meyer (1975); Riker and Ordeshook (1973:240–71); Samuelson (1954, 1955); Schelling (1978:211–43); Staaf and Tannian (1972). Baumol and Oates (1975:17) define an *externality* as "present whenever some individual's (say A's) *utility* or *production* relationships include real (that is, nonmonetary) variables, whose values are chosen by others (persons, corporations, governments) without particular attention to the effects on A's welfare."

Figure 5.6.   Some Dimensions of Externalities

Actor/Bystander

    Level: individual, group or organizational, system

    Nature of the basic economic activity –production or consumption:
        Complementary
        Separate
        (Economies/Diseconomies)

Effects

    Direction of effect: positive vs. negative

    Dynamics of effect: existent vs. acting vs. changing
        Marginal vs. nonmarginal

    Dispersal/uniformity

    Collective good vs. particular good character
        Nonexcludability
        Jointness of supply (nondepletability)

    Intensity of effect

    Directness of effect
        Indirect (e.g., pecuniary) vs. direct (e.g., technological)

Responses

    Awareness: information condition regarding externality

    Action
        Relevant vs. nonrelevant externality
        Direct vs. indirect action

    Resolution
        Pareto-relevant vs. Pareto-irrelevant
        Regulation

each of these four categories, i.e., actor, bystander, effects, and responses (see figure 5.6). The discussion will proceed largely in the context of economic regulation, as above.

4.1   ACTOR/BYSTANDER

Both actors and bystanders can be characterized as to *level,* i.e., individual, group or organizational, systemic, and as to the *nature of the basic economic activity* performed by the actor or bystander, i.e., *production* or *consumption.* Thus individuals, groups or organizations, or systems can engage in production or consumption activities which can produce unintentional activities and consequent effects among bystander individuals, groups or organizations, or systems engaged basically in production or consumption activities.

Note that both production and consumption basic activities can produce unintentional activities/effects, where these activities/effects may impact on production or consumption activities that can be either *complementary* to the basic acting economic mode, or entirely *separate* and potentially unrelated to it. That is, the interfering actor's production (consumption) may be consumed by (produced by) the bystander (i.e., complementary), or may be entirely separate, perhaps in a separate industry, from that of the bystander. These possibilities are depicted in figure 5.7. The empirical distribution of these possibilities is unclear; the unintentional effects of consumption on a by-

Figure 5.7. Relations Between Interfering Actor and Bystander Basic Activities

Interfering Actor's Basic Activity Generating Unintentional Activities/Effects	Bystander's Basic Activity Affected by Interfering Actor			
	Production		Consumption	
	Complementary	Separate	Complementary	Separate
Production	Null			
Consumption			Null	

stander engaged in separate production may not be obvious. A further distinction is whether effects of production on bystander production, and consumption on bystander consumption, involve the same production or consumption activities, or the same produced or consumed items. This would permit expansion of the discussion into consideration of factors like effects on competition and jealousy effects.

Depending on their positive or negative effect on bystanders (see below), we can have production or consumption external *economies* or *diseconomies* (see, e.g., Mansfield 1970:427–29; see figure 5.8). Here changes in scale of production or consumption produce "external" effects, i.e., effects on parties not directly involved (bystanders). An example of an external economy in production where the consumer bystander is "complementary" occurs when large-scale purchases of passenger aircraft by major domestic airlines permit the development of safety devices and their inclusion as regular equipment. Smaller foreign or domestic airlines, with smaller orders, then benefit since they also receive planes equipped with these devices. An example of an external diseconomy of production where the pro-

Figure 5.8. Economies/Diseconomies As Effects of Unintentional Activities That Are By-Products of Production and Consumption

Interfering Actor's Basic Activity Generating Unintentional Activities/Effect	Effects on Bystanders	
	Positive Effect on Bystanders	Negative Effect on Bystanders
Production	Production Economy	Production Diseconomy
Consumption	Consumption Economy	Consumption Diseconomy

ducer bystander is "separate" occurs when increases in production due to new business at a nearby factory produce truck traffic and production wastes that damage growth at a heretofore unaffected tree nursery. A consumption diseconomy on similar but "separate" consumers is crowding at the beach for those who dislike crowding; a consumption economy is crowding at the beach for those who enjoy crowding, perhaps because it helps them meet people.

4.2 EFFECTS

We have already discussed some effects of unintentional activities, i.e., external economies and diseconomies, in the context of considering interfering actors and bystanders subject to the interference. There are many potential ways to characterize external effects, i.e., externalities; we shall distinguish several dimensions below.

I. *Direction of effect: positive* vs. *negative.* Externalities (as we saw with external economies/diseconomies earlier) can be positive or negative, depending on whether their effects are perceived as beneficial or harmful (recall our discussion in chapter I).

2. *Dynamics of effect: existent* (being) vs. *acting* (behaving) vs. *changing* (becoming). Externalities can be produced merely through existence of the interfering actor, which generates the by-product activity and effect, e.g., a particular actor in a particular location produces a "neighborhood effect;" through action by the interfering actor, which generates the by-product activity and effect, e.g., a "spillover;" and through change in the scale or nature of the interfering actor's activity, which generates the by-product activity and effect, e.g., an "external economy" or "diseconomy." Change may be characterized by *marginality.* Externalities in which "a small

change in the level of activity generating the externality alters the magnitude of its effects'' are called "marginal," whereas externalities in which "an all-or-none situation exists over some range of changes in the level of the externality" are called "nonmarginal" (Bish 1971:20).

3. *Dispersal/uniformity:* Externalities can vary as to *dispersal* or *extensiveness* of their effects, i.e., number of bystander parties affected, and *uniformity* of effect, i.e., similarity in effect among affected bystanders.

4. *Collective or public good* vs. *particular or private good character.* Externalities that are collective or "public" goods may be characterized by any of the numerous dimensions that have been distinguished in studies of such goods.[8] The two which have been accorded the most prominence (definitions of "collective good" usually include at least one of these dimensions) are *nonexcludability,* and *jointness of supply* (or *nondepletability*):

a. *Nonexcludability:* The externality may be such that supply of it to any bystander means that it cannot be withheld from any other; any bystander cannot be excluded from receiving it. For example, air pollution from a factory (or radiation from a malfunctioning nuclear power plant), once emitted and affecting anyone in the community, cannot be withheld from others in the community. In these cases, it is conceivable that exclusion could be achieved through use of, say, individual air filters in the one instance, and lead houses, in the other. Thus exclusion may be difficult or costly, rather than impossible.

b. *Jointness of supply (or nondepletability):* The externality may be such that provision of it to any individual does not affect its availability to others. Usually, this means that consumption by one person of the good in question does not reduce the good's availability for consumption by others, i.e., the good is nondepletable (see, e.g., Head 1962; Baumol and Oates 1975). Examples include bridges (up to the level of congestion), air pollution, and sunny days.

This sense of "jointness" is regarded as the "pure" or extreme case; public goods can also "be understood in the less extreme sense

---

[8] Other terms that have been used in definitions to categorize public goods include nonrivalness (i.e., nondepletability), indivisibility, non-rejectability, forced availability, no selectivity in supply, impossibility of appropriation, and others. See the works cited in footnote 7. The complete and exact set of phenomena and/or conditions to be definitionally associated with the term "public good" still seem to be in dispute in the literature. Cf., for example, Head (1962), Olson (1965), Baumol and Oates (1975), Cowhey and Hart (1973), and Plott and Meyer (1975).

that a given unit of the good, once produced, can be made at least partially available, though possibly in varying degrees, to more than one individual'' (Head 1962:202). Thus the good may not be *equally* available; some people may find more or less of the good available or supplied to them than others. Bridges do become congested, and even sunny days may not be equally available on a beach crowded with umbrellas.

The dimension of dispersal/uniformity, identified above, is consequently clearly of relevance in considering public goods aspects of externalities. How widely is the externality provided or experienced, given that some (or none) can be excluded, or given that it is available in partial or full degree to some (or none)? What are the boundaries of the group to which the good is supplied? Once supplied, how even or uniform is that supply? Dispersal/uniformity can therefore characterize both private good, and public good, externalities.

5. *Intensity of effect:* Externalities can vary in the intensity or severity of their effects on bystanders, whether those effects are positive or negative. Intensity of effect can be measured through determination of what the affected party would give up to remove (negative externality) or to acquire (positive externality) the externality.

6. *Directness of effect: Indirect* (e.g., effects through price system) vs. *Direct* (e.g., effects on valued activities or rewards). Another distinction often used to characterize the effects of externalities is that between *pecuniary* and *technological* externalities. In pecuniary externalities, the externality effect, which is reflected in, and operates through, a change in price, occurs as a result of changes in levels of ordinary market activities. For example, increased demand for an industry's product can be reflected, as an externality, in price changes in the raw materials used to make it, and consequent effects on purchasers of the materials. Baumol and Oates (1975:29) cite the hypothetical case of a rise in leather prices as a result of higher demand for shoes. Technological externalities, on the other hand, involve direct (if unintended) effects; one party has control over or affects directly a valued activity or source of reward (positive or negative) for the other party. The classic example of factory soot dirtying clothes hung out to dry is an externality of this type. This distinction can be of particular interest where efficiency goals are relevant; under perfect competition, pecuniary externalities may not produce resource misallocations (see, e.g., Baumol and Oates 1975:28–30).

The pecuniary/technological externality contrast may be generalized to one of *directness of effect;* pecuniary externalities operate indirectly, through changes in the price system, while technological externalities operate directly on valued activities or rewards of the affected bystander. Of course, there are undoubtedly other mechanisms of indirect effect besides pecuniary externalities; a distinction based on a contrast between effects transmitted indirectly through the price system, and effects occurring directly on quantities of valued activities or rewards, is obviously of direct concern to economists constructing particular market models of exchange and resource allocation. Under a more general framework employing a generalized conception of externality as unintended by-product, the pecuniary/technological distinction can be seen as only one contrast possible under a "directness of effect" dimension.

Looking ahead to the means of regulation to be distinguished in chapter 6, we can perhaps generalize the pecuniary/technological contrast to one between incentive-like and directive-like modes of effect. The first operates through affecting the attractiveness of alternative choices of activities by the subject party (in this case, the bystander); the second operates through direct circumscription or specification of choice by the subject party. Since regulatory effects were logically contrasted with externality effects in the construction of chapter 1's figure 1.1, there would be a certain satisfying symmetry in identifying incentive/directive dimensions under both regulatory effects and externalities. We could also take the other dimensions identified under externalities and reciprocate, specifying direction, dynamics, dispersal/uniformity, collective vs. particular good character, and intensity of effects of regulation. This suggests, of course, a typology of effects of intended (i.e., regulatory) vs. unintended (i.e., externality) actions, i.e., interferences.

The dimensions identified above are of course only a few of the distinctions of effect dimensions possible here.

4.3 RESPONSES

Insofar as the externalities by themselves are concerned, we may, of course, expect affected parties to desire the removal of negative externalities and the conservation or promotion of positive externalities. Goals affected by removal, conservation, or promotion could be any of the types distinguished earlier.

In considering responses to externalities, three basic problems present themselves—*awareness, action,* and *resolution:*

1. *Awareness:* There is potentially a basic information problem regarding the effects of externalities. Because these effects are not intended, they are often not anticipated and, if anticipated, not formally recognized. Parties generating negative externalities may wish to avoid potential (costly) protests from adversely impacted bystanders. Factories, for example, do not advertise their air pollution. Even if perceived to exist, there may be measurement problems attendant on discovering the exact extent and severity of impacts. This can be because existing monitoring devices are designed to measure the basic activity, not its by-product activity and effects; because the lack of intentionality in the by-product activity can distribute its impacts in initially unpredictable ways; and because lack of functional intentionality may disperse effects in an unconnected, diffuse, and extended fashion that could subsequently be difficult and costly to measure. The actual impacts, especially long-run, as with carcinogens, may be poorly understood or unknown, even if aspects of the by-product activity, e.g., supply of air pollutants, are well-known.

Affected parties can face a collective action dilemma merely in regard to information, much less corrective action to remove a negative externality. That is, individual affected parties, with no knowledge of the potential benefits from gaining information on the extent of, say, air pollution and its effects on them, but suspecting that the benefit from such knowledge would be less than the cost to them of supplying it by themselves or with a few others, may simply opt to be free riders on whatever information is supplied by their neighbors. As a consequence, little of such information may be produced. Regulation can be imposed just to supply this information through using coercively (and legitimacy) backed tax contributions to support the information generation. For example, the Consumer Product Safety Commission and the Food and Drug Administration have major formal responsibilities, in effect, in the supply of information on risk (see, e.g., Kelman 1974).

2. *Action:* Even if complete information exists on the externality, there may be no necessary action on the part of the subject bystanders to remove, conserve, or promote it. The larger trade-offs among benefits and costs in acting figure here of course. Buchanan and Stubblebine (1962; see also Bish 1971:18–20) distinguish *relevant* vs. *nonrelevant* externalities. Externalities that make a sufficient difference to stimulate action to remove or increase them are "relevant;" those that do not are "nonrelevant." This of course leaves

open the mode of response, and the nature, if any, of the resolution achieved as a result of the action. Regulation may be sought to resolve collective-action dilemmas stemming from externalities that cannot be removed (or promoted) without such collective action. Choice of regulatory means as well as means of access to the formal policy-intention agenda (recall the discussion of agenda-building in chapter 3) must be made.

In general, strategies of action can be either *direct* or *indirect*. Direct strategies involve attempts by affected bystanders to change the interfering actor's behavior through direct influence attempts or other approaches to that actor. An example of a direct strategy would be a payment or bribe to the interfering actor to reduce a negative externality. Indirect strategies may involve appeals to, and participation by, some third party, e.g., a regulatory agency.

3. *Resolution:* Resolution of problematic externalities can occur, of course, in a great many ways, from bribery to coercive intervention by third parties like governments. Buchanan and Stubblebine (1962) distinguish *Pareto-relevant* from *Pareto-irrelevant* externalities. Externalities in which the parties affected are willing to pay what the originator of the externality is willing to accept to change his or her action are termed "Pareto-relevant." If such an exchange is not possible, the externality is "Pareto-irrelevant."

Assuming we have a negative externality, Pareto-relevance means the externality may be removed through a simple exchange—a bribe, if you like—between the generator of the externality and those affected. Both parties are better off after this exchange. But in some cases our set of intermediate societal goals may rule out such exchange. Equity may dictate that the polluter, for example, should pay to clean up his own mess rather than be bribed to do so by those subject to pollution. In other cases, exchange to undo a Pareto-relevant externality may be impractical or unfeasible due to structural costs—costs of organizing to pay the bribe may reduce the externality below Pareto-relevance, for example. And some externalities, of course, although "relevant," may not be Pareto-relevant—they may be in the category of life's little annoyances that incite sporadic, but ineffective efforts at correction (e.g., yelling "shut up" at the neighbors' howling cat), even though their "correction" may be consistent with societal goals. Thus *regulation* of some sort may be necessary to deal with these situations in order that resolution occur. It is assumed, of course, that the evaluation of such an externality resolution (including the cost of regulation) according to societal goals warrants this action.

The dimensions we have specified under "actor/bystander," "effects," and "responses" can be greatly extended; they are perhaps the core of a typology of externalities that can be constructed from them and other dimensions. Though we shall stop our analysis here, a systematic understanding of the variation in externality characteristics could be employed to develop a theory of externality promulgation and control. Clearly such a theory would assist in the development of a fuller rationale for regulation.

5.0 Conclusion

In this chapter, we sought to present the outline of the rationale for regulation in the ideal case. We noted some aspects of choice of the basic public interest rationale, presented a typology of—and discussed the role of—a set of "intermediate" goals that can rationalize regulation, and considered the rationale for regulation as an attempt to correct or restrain intentional activity (e.g., natural monopoly) and as an attempt to control unintentional, by-product effects of activities (i.e., externalities).

Having considered the basic criteria and the rationale for regulation in chapters 4 and 5, we are ready to move to an analysis of alternative regulatory means, in chapter 6. Recall a basic theme of this work: regulation should be a dynamic creative, not a static, standard form. Understanding of creation, design, and removal of regulation requires understanding of alternative criteria for regulatory establishment and for choice among potential regulatory institutions.

VI

Organizing Regulation: Considerations in Regulation by Incentive and by Directive

HAVING DISCUSSED the concept, origin, basic formal goal, and rationale for regulation, we turn to consideration of regulatory design. A major point we wish to make is that there are a wide variety of potential regulatory means, most of which are usually not considered in any given situation of regulatory creation or reform, and that systematic evaluation of potential means is desirable for design.

The design of regulatory organizations has historically *not* been the subject of systematic analysis. The history of regulatory reform is littered with prescriptions for organizational changes, often contradictory, that are aimed at removing perceived abuses (see, e.g., Bernstein 1972). The basic regulatory methods used by such organizations, as well as the overall structural means of regulation, have only relatively recently begun being subjected to systematic comparative analysis (see, e.g., Baumol and Oates 1975; Buchanan and Tullock 1975; Samuels and Schmid 1976; Vladeck 1975).

In this chapter, we intend to contribute to such systematic analysis of choice of general means for regulation. Recall that in chapter 3 we discussed the incentive system facing regulators. Now, in chapter 6, we shall contrast the major tools used in regulation: incentives and directives. Thus we move from a discussion of the regulator as incentive receiver, to one of regulator as incentive (and directive) sender. We shall introduce the analysis by reviewing the rationalization of regulatory forms and acts, and by modeling governmental action as agency, and legislative delegation to administrative agents. We shall then identify and compare two means of control in basically hierarchical settings—regulation by incentive and by directive. The results may be applied generically to problems of control in all organizations, though our focus is on regulation.

1.0   Sources of Rationalization of Regulatory Institutional Forms and Acts

We may distinguish decisions on the rules by which regulatory acts are selected; and decisions on the acts themselves. The basic set of rules constitutes an organizational framework within which acts are determined. Thus, for example, a set of "constitutional" rules, embodied in a regulatory agency's enabling statute and regulations, outlines the functioning of the agency, with decisions on regulatory acts made by regulators in this framework. (For arguments on constitutional rules, see Buchanan and Tullock 1962.)

Consider now decisions on the basic rules. We can conceive of an infinite regression of such decisions, of course. Decisions on acts require decisions on the rules which determine the acting framework; decisions on rules require decisions on a rule-making system; and so on. We have, for example, the constitutional convention (decisions on rule-making system) which establishes a legislative assembly (decisions on rules) which delegates to a regulatory agency both rule-making and acting powers (decisions on rules and decisions on acts). But on what basis can we make decisions on rules? Whose values should determine the form of the acting (and/or rule-making) organization? This is equivalent to asking, by whose warrant should the decision be made—quo warranto? (Haefele emphasizes this; see, e.g., Haefele 1973a, 1973b.)

Rationalization of public decisions usually refers to or invokes some notion of the "public interest." As we observed in chapter 4, there is, of course, no accepted meaning for this concept. We do not claim that regulation is always instituted to, and operates to, realize some conception of that interest; we just note that this is the common formal rationalization given. And though the public interest remains as the ultimate justification, we can, as we did in chapter 5, also identify several broad areas of "intermediate" goals frequently offered as "in" the public interest. Given an activity to be evaluated, the first three areas of goals relate to the activity by itself, and the fourth area of goals relates to the activity with its environment (i.e., relating to its impacts):

1. Aspects of the quality of activity production or performance. For example, efficiency.

2. Aspects of activity existence, maintenance and persistence, or activity support. For example, stability, continuity, reliability.

3. Aspects of activity evolution and development. For example, innovation, growth, promotion of activity.

4. Aspects of activity impact evaluation. For example, equity, redistribution, safety, removing discrimination. Criteria in this category can relate to impact evaluation for any of the other three categories, e.g., impacts of performance on bystanders.

Below these intermediate goals we can identify a third level of goals: subject-specific rules or standards.

These intermediate goals can conflict with one another, of course. Equity frequently conflicts with efficiency, for example. A major problem of regulation is to resolve such trade-offs. It is therefore evident that certain aspects of one form of regulation that appear to be "advantages" may become "disadvantages," or may lose all relevance, when evaluated by a different and conflicting intermediate goal. We shall choose no determinant goal set and no instructions for resolving conflicts through trade-offs; different goals and different trade-offs may be chosen in different regulatory settings by different actors. Advantages and disadvantages that arise from any or all such goals will be cited in our compilation below. In effect, a checklist will be created from which advantages and disadvantages may be selected in a given situation by given goals.

Even then, choice will not be easy. The present state of knowledge regarding effects of major types of regulatory means is rudimentary; determinant, global choices of means are not always possible. But we can begin to lay the grounds for such a capability.

Furthermore, the intermediate goals may be applied at *two* levels: that of the activity subject to regulation, and that of the regulation itself as activity. This distinction is rarely, if ever, made in the literature, but can be crucial in evaluating forms of public action; reliance on traditional regulatory means often conceals implicit decisions on goals. Thus regulatory means may be evaluated both for their effects and for themselves. We may, for example, seek a regulatory means that both assures efficiency in the regula*ted* activity, and is itself efficient in regula*ting*. This can complicate the analysis considerably. As is the case with goals applied to the regula*ted* activity, it is often difficult to evaluate the degree of intermediate-goal attainment from election of a given regula*ting* activity.

Goals relevant to the regula*ting* activity can assume major importance. We saw in chapter 2 that ideological preferences for the form of administrative organization can strongly influence resulting institu-

Figure 6.1. Typology of Intermediate Goals Applied to Regulating and Regulated Activities

ASPECTS OF ACTIVITY	REGULATING ACTIVITY		REGULATED ACTIVITY	
	ACTIVITY BY ITSELF	ACTIVITY WITH ENVIRONMENT (IMPACTS)	ACTIVITY BY ITSELF	ACTIVITY WITH ENVIRONMENT (IMPACTS)
Quality of Activity Performance	e.g., efficiency in regulating procedures	e.g., equity in dealing with public	e.g., efficiency in regulated industry	e.g., safety, equity in regulated industry
Activity Existence, Maintenance, Support	e.g., reliability in regulatory procedures	e.g., impacts of regulatory stability on regulated industry	e.g., stability, reliability in regulated industry	e.g., impacts of activity reliability on suppliers of industry
Activity Evolution and Development	e.g., innovation in regulatory procedures	e.g., impacts of regulatory innovation on other agencies	e.g., innovation, growth in regulated industry	e.g., impacts of activity innovation or growth on community

tional structures; administration by committee during the American Revolution, for example, was supported by an aversion to the executive government imposed on the pre-Revolutionary colonies. The device of a Public Counsel may help assure equitable due process in the regula*ting* as well as in the regula*ted* activities of industry. Goals in regulatory procedure, such as greater public access and participation, and widened investigative responsibilities (see, e.g., Mitnick and Weiss 1974), have been central factors in some recent agency decision-making.

Contrast, for the moment, a framework in which an "expert" makes the decision on regulatory acts, with a framework in which representatives of the people for whom the decision is being made, make the decision. The comparison is expert trusteeship vs. representative decision-making. The trustee is technically expert on regulatory matters and assumes that whatever preferences guide his decision can be easily known. The representatives are not technically expert but assume that the people they represent know what's to their own good. A unitary notion of the public interest would select the trusteeship framework; a combinatorial notion could be consistent with either framework (see chapter 4).

Note, however, that an intermediate goal concerning aspects of activity performance, such as efficiency, might make us lean toward the expert regulatory framework both because a single expert may be more efficient in regulating than a group of nonexperts, and because an expert on the regulated activity might be better able to achieve efficiency in the activity through the regulation he enacts. And a goal of activity impact evaluation, such as democratic responsiveness, may implicate the representative framework for its own sake. We might suppose that the ultimate rationalization should be in terms of the effects on the regulated activity, but this is not necessarily so where the regulatory framework itself has intrinsic value.

The other intermediate goals could also be applied to evaluate both such a regulatory framework—i.e., the regula*ting* activity—and the effects of regulation on the regula*ted* activity: Is the framework reliable, providing continuity in regulation? Would the framework be consistent with promotion of reliability and continuity in the activity being regulated? Is the framework responsive to (desirable) change? Would the framework promote or be tolerant of (desirable) change in the activity subject to regulation? In figure 6.1, the typology of intermediate goals is applied to both the regula*ting* and the regula*ted* activities. Examples of goals or valued impacts are given for each category produced.

2.0 Governmental Action in Choosing Forms and Acts as Agency

In the example in the previous section, both the trusteeship and representative framework face the following problems:

Problem of determining preferences

Problem of choosing acts to meet those preferences

Problem of finding out how to perform those acts

Problem of determining who should perform the acts.

Thus what we have is a problem in *agency*—in *acting for* others. If one cared to do it, it could be argued that the science of politics is in the broadest sense the study of agency relations. Design problems in governmental action then often include, given a preference set for the principal: Who shall the agent be? Which acts should he perform? In the context of regulation, this may mean comparing the forms and process of the agent-regulator in the light of their impact on the regulated activity, as well as in the light of criteria that may be applied to the regulating activities themselves. The intermediate goals identified above may be used to evaluate the forms and process of the agent-regulator in terms of both their effects on the regula*ted* activity and aspects of the regula*ting* activity itself.[1]

The values of a democratic system generally select a representative system as the decision-making system on basic rules. In particular, these values constitute a participatory combinatorial notion of the public interest (see chapter 4). The problems of agency of such a decision-making system then become those of:

Choosing representatives

The representatives determining the preferences of their constituents, given a distribution and intensity spread of those preferences; the constituents face the problem of holding their agent-representatives accountable to their preferences

[1] On the theory of agency as an approach to understanding a broad class of social relationships, see Mitnick (1973b, 1974, 1976); Ross (1973). On governmental action as agency, cf. Banfield (1961:307–23; 1975); Curry and Wade (1968); Goldberg (1976).

The representatives choosing a method of aggregating their views in order to reach a decision

The representatives choosing rules (i.e., making decisions on the form of the acting system) and perhaps also acts to meet those preferences for the specific case

Someone, perhaps determined by the representatives, or being the representatives themselves, finding out how to perform the acts or construct and operate a framework according to the rules

Someone, perhaps the representatives, performing the acts or operating the framework—the problem of determining who should do this.

The "someone" selected is then also an agent. As agent for the representatives, he is, in a telescoping relation, agent for the principal public. In the context of regulation, this agent is often the regulator (though regulation may also, for example, be performed directly by the representatives acting together). In chapter 2 we saw how solution of these agency problems led to the federal executive departments. Under some of the theories of regulatory origin discussed in chapter 3, e.g., the industry protection theory, private groups in effect acquire governmental agents to resolve collective action dilemmas. Such groups may gain these agents by manipulating the representative decision-making process, or by influencing existing agent-regulators to become agents for the groups.

3.0 Delegation as the Creation of Agents

We can consider the representatives' problem in choosing the agent-regulator an example of the general problem of delegation, i.e., the creation of substituting agents. In particular, we are speaking of delegation by a legislature. The substituting agents may specify aspects of the criteria guiding public action and/or the mechanisms of implementing and administering such criteria (cf. Sorg 1978 and Mitnick 1974, on the concept of "discretion"; see also, e.g., Jaffe 1973). We considered some problems of decision by legislature in our discussion of older regulatory means in chapter 2.

Assume that a legislature is an elected body of many agents of diverse backgrounds, with many, generally conflicting views; who meet in one place under some conditions of uncertainty to reach many decisions on policy intentions for the collectivity. Assume also

that several common and generally consensual intermediate goals and
conditions held instrumental to them—e.g., efficiency, equity, responsiveness to change, continuity goals, and expertise, expedition,
conflict-management conditions—can be applied to evaluate and design the decision process. And assume the legislator agents are rational and can act both in their self-interest and in the interests of their
constituents. Action for constituents may be either instrumentally or
genuinely motivated. The legislator-agents face the ordinary, natural
limits on information-processing and collective decision-making—
e.g., time, ability to consider alternatives comprehensively, and so
on. Similarly, parties in the legislative environment are assumed rational, mixed motive, and facing information-processing constraints.
In general, all parties desire to reduce or manage the uncertainty they
face because of resulting gains to their mixed goal sets. Then the following constraints may be loosely deduced and lead to delegation: [2]

1. *Inexpertness in decision:* Legislatures are in general inexpert:
substantively inexpert in technical matters, and structurally inexpert
in that they lack firsthand knowledge or information (on this distinction, see Mitnick 1974). This follows from the fact of legislators with
diverse backgrounds meeting in one place. As agents, the legislators
may be supposed expert on the preferences of their constituent-principals, or at least able to determine a set of preferences to act on in
lieu of, or instead of, knowledge of their actual preferences. The
remedy for the substantive and structural lack of expertise is to acquire substantive experts and field agents, i.e., to delegate to administrative bodies.

2. *Slowness in decision and limited case-handling capability:* Because of necessary consultation and deliberation among many with
differing views, the decision process is slow. Nonexpert legislators
must devote time to educating themselves in the areas of cases. The
need to make many decisions conflicts with the natural limits on the
legislator-agents, so that case handling is slow and limited in volume.

---

[2] Cf. the discussion by Hurst (1950:409–10). On the legal/constitutional issues in delegation,
see, e.g., Barber (1975); Davis (1958, 1:75–158; 1970:40–78); Jaffe (1965:28–86);
B. Schwartz (1976:31–86). On delegation in organizations, see, e.g., Kochen and Deutsch
(1977); March and Simon (1958:40–44). See also Dahl and Lindblom (1953:90–91); Downs
(1957:230–34). The legal/constitutional literature on delegation deals largely with normative
prescriptive questions, e.g., when is delegation allowed or permitted under a constitution or
statute? But we are interested in delegation from an organizational theoretical perspective, e.g.,
when does it tend to occur, or how can it be explained? The latter has not received extensive attention, at least in a systematic fashion, though it is critical to an understanding of the design of
a representative governmental system.

Decisions may then be speeded and increased in volume if given to a body better designed for rapid and large-scale decision-making, i.e., an administrative body (cf. Ehrlich and Posner 1974).

3. *Lack of continuity in decision:* Because legislators are elected, continuity in the composition of the legislature is not guaranteed. Constituent-principals may always recall—deny reelection to—their agent-legislators. Continuity and coherence in policy-intention formation can therefore be lacking. Continuity in policy intention may, however, be provided by delegation to a body with this characteristic, e.g., an administrative body.

4. *Lack of full-time oversight:* Legislator-agents must make many decisions and, given the natural limits on their time and information-processing capability, will be unable to provide full-time oversight—including implementation and administration—of activities selected by their decisions. Furthermore, unless the given activities were selected consensually, some members of the legislature may be against performance of the selected activities. If given responsibility for oversight, or allowed to share oversight with other members, these negative legislators could subvert, damage, or divert the activities in question. The pro-activity legislators will be unable to provide oversight both of the selected activity and of their fellow, anti-activity members. Thus it will be in the interest of those members who do wish the activities performed to delegate this task to a body outside the legislature. At any rate, the possible lack of expertise due to diversity of backgrounds can mean a lack of capability to effectively oversee the selected activity.

5. *Subjection to political-partisan influences:* Because legislator-agents may act for their self-interest, they may—while participating in the collective decision process in the legislature—act in ways likely to promote their reelection. Of course, it is possible that such reelection is also in the interest of their constituents. Legislators can also be responsive to the interests of groups likely to aid them in reelection, e.g., parties, interest groups. Fidelity to self- (and possible constituent) interests can mean lack of fidelity to, or inconsistent action with respect to, previously enunciated views on prospective legislative acts. Behavior of this sort, i.e., adherence to individual, group, or constituency interests apart from decision-relevant "issue" or "programmatic" interests, is usually termed "political" or "partisan" in this context.

We have not assumed a particular form for the legislative process.

Particular structural opportunities may exist to further individual, group, or constituency interests, e.g., vote trading to exchange votes on less intensely preferred outcomes to acquire votes on more intensely preferred ones. We would expect the legislator-agent to take these opportunities, depending on his preferences.

Delegation to an outside body, such as an administrative agency, presumably could escape these political or partisan effects. Of course, delegation would then only be desirable if the values applied rejected political or partisan behavior or their effects. As Haefele (1973a, 1973b) and others have argued, however, such behavior can be highly desirable in permitting optimal satisfaction of constituent preferences, e.g., allowing most intensely desired outcomes to be achieved.

6. *Broad or vague decision from conflict resolution:* Legislatures are mechanisms to resolve conflict. Legislatures integrate, resolve, and express varied views to form policy intentions; they are vehicles for compromising decision where values conflict. Where conflicting views are balanced, the policy intention chosen will tend to be broad; detailed matters over which there is conflict will be pruned out in order to reach agreement, or at least build a coalition large enough to formally adopt the policy intention. Or agreement will not occur. Because of the expectations of at least some of the constituent-principals that their agents will act for them in some way, and the reelection threat that may be exercised by them, the agents will want to act or appear to act, i.e., reach some agreement. Generalized opposition or inactivity is not likely to be rewarded; constituents will want their representatives as agents to get at least some things for them. The reaching of consensus has inherent advantages (see, e.g., Buchanan and Tullock 1962), if only because it avoids the imposition of costs on the losers, a position any legislator can at some time expect to be in. There are also costs to the winners in building coalitions large enough to win. Thus a general policy of seeking a (bland or vague) consensus can be advantageous. Then:

A. Delegation is a method of restoring detailed content to broad directives; in effect it reflects a division of labor in which broad policy intention formation is left to the legislature and detailed policy intention formation is delegated, perhaps to an administrative body.

B. Delegation may be necessary because the policy intention chosen by the legislature, reflecting resolution by least common denominator—i.e., the broad principle or platitude—is completely or largely uninformative as a guide to action. Then another body, perhaps courts (early in historical development) or administrative bodies (later, historically) must be relied on to make the real decision. Unlike case A, the broad policy intention is too broad to provide any substantial guide.

C. Given conflicting views, a broad policy intention may be agreed on with delegation for detailed policy intention formation in order to displace the wrath of principal-constituents who may be adversely affected by specific acts (cf. Baldwin 1975:9; Cutler and Johnson 1975:1401–2). Here determination of specific acts, and general knowledge of the distribution of adverse impacts, become known only after detailed specification under delegation. This strategy may be adopted manipulatively either with respect to expected impacts on given groups, or merely as a strategy, given uncertainty, to displace possible criticism from any adversely affected groups (cf. the discussion in chapter 4 on use of public interest rhetoric).

D. Given conflicting intra-constituent-principal views on appropriate legislative action, agent-legislators may feel constrained to advocate least-common-denominator views, or views common to groups that constitute at least a majority of the constituency. Should such views be adopted by the legislature, they are likely to be broad and require more detailed supplementary policy intention formation. Thus delegation is made necessary.

E. Delegation may be employed as a device to transfer policy intention formation to a place where it may be more subject to the influence of particular parties (cf. Posner 1974:350–51). Due to conflicting views in the legislative body, a group or "interest" with a particular set of preferences regarding legislative action may find it impossible to realize their detailed aims. Those agent-legislators who are also, in effect, agents for the group may then seek agreement at the broad least-common-denominator level, with the expectation that subsequent detailed policy intention formation will be strongly favorable to the preferences of their group-principal.

7. *Need to offer single, broad or vague rationale:* Whether or not the decision is consensual, legislatures are constrained to offer a single rationale for it. As with some other forms of decision-making groups—e.g., multi-judge courts—the reasons why the members of the winning coalition voted the way they did can differ widely. Legislators may choose a given piece of legislation because they have traded their vote on another issue; because they have an incorrect idea

of the legislation's contents or impacts; because the legislation achieves goals for them that differ from the goals sought by their also favorable colleagues; and so on.

Organizations and other parties that are affected by the legislature's decisions, such as administrative agencies, require a single rationale both to reduce uncertainty for themselves in planning their future relationships with the legislature, and in planning their future internal operations; and because client groups demand such a single rationale. Groups receiving services or regulation from administrative agencies will similarly wish to reduce uncertainty in their relationships with the agency, and in their future consumption of services and regulation. Courts settling disputes involving legislative decisions need a single guideline, and contesting parties will prefer some explanation for the court's own decision.

Furthermore, the intermediate consensual goal of equity can require that a single, consistent rationale be produced to validate action. This goal can be, and often is, formalized. Courts, for example, may invoke any existing formal rules that administrative action not be arbitrary or capricious in character.

Parties in the environment of legislatures may not, however, desire high specificity in the rationale they require. Their own environment is turbulent, with clients presenting changing, conflicting demands. Thus these parties—e.g., courts and agencies—may prefer rationales that allow them to satisfy, perhaps inconsistently over time, their most insistent (and threatening) clients, as well as to accommodate the changing preferences of their own members regarding the actions at issue. Therefore vague or ambiguous, but single, rationalizations tend to be demanded, and supplied. Note that a trade-off may have to be made in the specificity of the single rationale in order to accommodate both the planning and environmental adaptation needs.

Since the rationales supplied are vague, there is consequently a need for delegation to fill in the specifics. As noted below, such broad delegations can be in the self-interest of the delegatees for other reasons.

As we observed in chapter 4, public interest rhetoric, which is usually vague, may be used to cloak any absence of the requisite single justification for the legislature's decision. In fact, the very availability and acceptability of such rhetoric can permit and expedite delegation.

8. *Desire of the delegatees for expansion:* Broad or vague deci-

sions can require more criteria refinement, implementation, and administration than decisions that are highly specified by the legislature. This may require delegatee-agencies to hire more personnel to perform these tasks. Growth in the administrative agency can be in the interest of existing agency officials, in particular, officials that are climbers, advocates, and, possibly, zealots (see chapter 2). Thus the interests of bureaucrats in such agencies may lead them to prefer broader, more ambiguous decisions from the legislature and so act as a spur to delegation.

9. *Need to make new rationales for legislative decision formally consistent with past rationales:* Legislators find that they need not only to offer a single rationale, but also a rationale that is consistent with existing rationales for past action in the area—rationales to which the new one is an adjunct or modifier. As in the earlier case, an intermediate equity goal may be operative, in this instance requiring consistency with still-existing but older rationales. It can be difficult to provide a specific rationale to cover potentially diverse activity areas, as well as mesh consistently with existing rationales for these areas. Decision criteria, as well as rationales for public action, therefore tend to become more vague as the scope of coverage widens (cf. Lowi 1969, ch. 5; see our chapter 2). Formal rationales for regulating railroads under the ICC widened, for example, from controlling abuses in railroads (and other factors) to providing a national transportation policy by the time trucks and barges were added. Increasing broadness and vagueness in criteria and rationales can mean greater reliance on delegation.

10. *Need to resolve collective action dilemmas for constituents and client groups:* As we argued in chapter 3, regulation can be sought by prospective regulatees because it solves collective action problems for them, reducing uncertainty and achieving collective ends. Regulation, for example, can reduce uncertainty for firms by providing stability of competition, and can provide information on risk to consumers who as individuals would never supply this information to themselves. The need to provide such regulating tasks translates into a need for delegation, given the constraints noted earlier regarding direct legislative action.

11. *Lack of capability to deal with change/uncertainty:* Under uncertainty, legislatures may not be able to be very specific about the proposed regulation; they cannot predict all future contingencies in the environment. They may be unable to respond quickly and

Figure 6.2. Occurrence of Delegation under Varying Conditions of Desire and Ability

Desire of Principal That Task Be Performed	Ability of Principal to Perform Task Himself	Desire of Party Delegated to, i.e., Agent, to Perform Task			
		Desire of agent—yes		Desire of agent—no	
		Ability of agent to perform—yes	Ability of agent to perform—no	Ability of agent to perform—yes	Ability of agent to perform—no
Desire of principal—yes	Ability of principal—yes	Possible delegation	Delegation possible after training	Delegation possible with sanctions	Delegation possible with training and sanctions
	Ability of principal—no	Delegation	Delegation after training	Delegation with sanctions	Delegation with training and sanctions
Desire of principal—no	Ability of principal—yes	No delegation	Possible delegation	Possible delegation	Likely delegation
	Ability of principal—no	No delegation	Possible delegation	Possible delegation	Likely delegation

frequently enough to changes in the environment with appropriate new legislation, or to write legislation sufficiently flexible to anticipate changing economic and technological conditions. This follows from our previous observations: decision will tend to be slow; continuity in decision-making may be absent, so the base detail work done for earlier related decisions will be lost; expertise in the subject area may be lacking and acquired only at a cost including time; and opposition from adversely affected parties, including those with a vested interest in previous decisions, will delay action. In addition, legislatures may be unable to predict changes in constituent-principal preferences regarding governmental action. Rather than administer the policy intention themselves (subject to lack of speed, lack of expertise, and so on), they may therefore delegate. Thus uncertainty leads to "flexibility" or discretion in the administrative body.[3]

As is by now evident, the reasons for delegation are extensive and complex. Besides the reasons deduced above, which mostly involve achieving some (possibly biased or altered) program performance, there can be other informal, symbolic, or covert ones; these can involve insurance of nonperformance. For example, legislators may not desire to act or perform a given task themselves and may not want the task performed at all. They may have made a collective decision to authorize the task because of pressures from constituents and wish to appear in favor of the action. To resolve this dilemma, legislators can deliberately delegate the activity to an agency that will not act or, if it does act, will do a minimal or poor job.

In figure 6.2, we display the delegation possibilities, considering only the positive or negative desires of the principal delegating a task, and of the agent to whom the task is delegated; and the ability of the principal, and of the agent, to perform the task themselves. This is in effect a typology applicable to all agency relationships involving delegation.

Assume the principal is rational and able, at a cost, to supply his agent with positive sanctions (rewards) and/or negative sanctions (e.g., coercion, loss of rewards), and/or able, at a cost, to raise the ability of the agent and/or himself through training in task perfor-

---

[3] The need for "flexibility" or discretion is illustrated, obliquely, by the so-called Henry VIII clauses put in some English legislation in the sixteenth century. These gave "the administrative power to modify the provisions of legislation insofar as it may appear to be necessary to bring the scheme of regulation into effective operation." Of course, in practice at the time, they just legitimized the king's power to do as he liked. But some have proposed such clauses, with a time limit, to help make U.S. regulation more effective. See Landis (1938:52).

mance. The alternative actually chosen depends on the relative costs of the available options. The principal may elect a costly sanctioning or training alternative because the cost of finding and engaging a suitable new agent exceeds the costs of sanctioning and/or training.

Legislators are unlikely to have the ability to perform the task themselves, nor to pay the costs of training themselves to perform the tasks, since they lack the time to do them anyway. Smaller legislatures at lower governmental levels, e.g., town councils, that do not meet the "many decision" assumption made earlier, should of course be distinguished here. Rational principals who wish to minimize costs and desire that the task be performed probably will not elect (in a choice among agents) the agent who either does not desire to perform the task or lacks the ability to perform it. Should the principal find that his existing agent is of this type, he may search for another agent.

The categories in which the principal does not desire that the task be performed include two in which the principal is unlikely to elect delegation, because the agent is likely to perform the task. The categories in which the agent neither desires to perform the task nor has the ability to do it are likely ones for delegation (assuming delegation itself is not costly), where the principal's desires involve purely symbolic efforts.

In general, of course, the more costly the training and sanctioning of the agent, where the principal has the desire and ability himself to perform the task, the less likely is delegation.

The analysis of delegation in this section is largely static, i.e., the resort to, occurrence of, or single instances of delegation are explained. But delegation can be seen as an ongoing, dynamic process involving feedback and continual adjustments. As Hurst (1950:410–11) points out, delegation is itself a process rather than a summary act. The legislators may refine the mandate they give the administrative body, based on that body's elaborations of the mandate. The legislators may act formally to revise the mandate, or they may in a process of consultation, formal or informal, make clear to the body their present interpretation of the mandate. The legislators may influence the administrative body indirectly, for example, through the attention they give to complaints about the body's administration of the mandate; or they may seek certain assurances when administrators come to the legislature for funds. (On delegation, cf. Friendly 1962; Jaffe 1973.)

As we observed at the beginning of this chapter, the history of regulation has been one of continual tinkering, with numerous proposals (and numerous attempts) at regulatory reform. Perhaps a better understanding of delegation, as well as of the alternate means of regulation that can be created through delegation, can improve the success of such efforts.

4.0 Interferences and Comparing Institutions

4.1 LOCI OF INTERFERENCE

Having reviewed the process of rationalizing governmental acts, and having presented models of governmental action as agency and legislative delegation to administrative agents, we can begin to consider the choice of such agents from among the alternate forms they can take.

Given delegation, choice must be exercised as to the *form* of the administrative agent to be delegated to, as well as to the *acts* to be performed by that agent. In addition, a goal of aspects of activity evolution and development may imply *changes* in the mechanism that chooses acts. Preferences of constituent-principals may change, for example, so that new decision-making procedures are called for to correspond to the new preferences and perhaps to new problems. So both because of basic design questions and because of the possibility of change, a focus on comparative institutions seems indicated (cf. Ostrom 1973; Levine et al. 1975; Schultze 1977; Majone 1975; Goldberg 1974). We should be able to design an organization "appropriate" with respect to our goals from our knowledge of comparative characteristics, advantages and disadvantages, of the different possible forms. We should be prepared to change forms as our goals dictate.

Reform or change in an administrative system by definition involves an interference with an existing system; at least, a change in what otherwise would have occurred (on administrative reform, see Backoff 1974a). The extent or quality of the change or interference may vary. The existing system may be maintained with changes merely in the mechanism of the system, or a new *framework*—essentially a new system—substituted. We thus have interferences with regulatory frameworks that: 1) alter the basic framework, or 2) alter aspects of the regula*ting* activity within that framework. For example, the basic framework may be changed from the commission to the bureau form, and the regulating activity changed from rate regulation to regulation of service quality. Distinction of changes in framework from changes in mechanism within a framework will be left as basically a matter of analytical definition. The *interference* with the regula*ted* activity is, of course, just the regulation itself. Thus we can interfere with: 1) the basic framework, 2) the regula*ting* activity, and 3) the regula*ted* activity.

We have to make, therefore, *decisions* on interferences with the basic form of the organizational framework, and with the forms of the regulating activity within that framework (decisions on changes in the rules), and decisions on interferences with the subject activity in the course of regulation (decisions on regulatory acts). Change in, or interference with, the regulatory acts chosen may result from change in, or interference with, the rules. Decisions on interferences that are decisions on changes in the rules can reflect, and in effect choose, societal goals that then guide subsequent decisions on acts made under the new rules. The decisions on rules can even specify both a completely new basic framework, or rule system for deciding on acts (a "social choice" process), and the goals for acting selected for that process. Regressing backward, the decision maker on interferences with the framework can itself be one of several possible types of such "social choice" processes. And it may in some cases delegate choice of general, or, more commonly, specific, societal goals to the basic framework—itself a social choice process—that it chooses.

4.2 INTERFERENCE WITH BASIC FRAMEWORKS: SOCIAL CHOICE PROCESSES

Four basic social choice processes are commonly identified, though not always in the same way (see, e.g., Dahl and Lindblom 1953; Bish 1971): market, hierarchy, voting, bargaining. The general comparative advantages and disadvantages, and consequent uses of these processes, are discussed in places in the literature (e.g., Dahl and Lindblom 1953; Elkin 1974; Davis and Kamien 1970), and more narrowly defined forms are occasionally compared and critiqued in a more formal way (e.g., Rose-Ackerman 1973). Within some of the general types there is considerable work on varieties of the given general type (e.g., Black 1963; Fishburn 1973). But there is no systematic derivation of the set of basic social choice processes, at least in general use. This is surprising, given the importance of an understanding of basic social choice processes to both theory and prescriptive policy intention formation. What is needed is a typology that enables location of each social choice process on a parsimonious set of theoretically interesting dimensions that defines a set of inclusive and mutually exclusive categories.

Perhaps no generally accepted, systematic typology of social choice processes exists because of the apparent dimensional complexity of the processes. A few of these dimensions are listed below:

Exchange vs. one-way choice

Contingency vs. noncontingency of behavior on exchange

Variable vs. fixed terms of exhange

Centralization vs. decentralization of choice

"Upward" vs. "downward" choice

Few vs. many participants in choice

Low vs. high price or cost for participation in choice

Deliberate vs. emergent choice

Little vs. much freedom of choice or discretion by participants in choice

Specificity vs. generality of choices expressed

Contingency vs. noncontingency of choice by one participant on choice by other participant(s).

In figure 6.3 we present a simple and admittedly inadequate classification of social choice processes. The two dimensions are exchange vs. one-way expression of choice, and centralized vs. decentralized expression of choice. Hierarchy falls in the centralized,

Figure 6.3. Simple Typology of Social Choice Processes

| | | Centralization of Choice | |
		Centralized choice expression	Decentralized choice expression
Reciprocity of Choice	Exchange in choice expression	Centralized exchange	Market Bargaining
	One-way choice expression	Hierarchy	Voting

one-way category; voting falls in the decentralized, one-way category, and both the market and bargaining fall in the decentralized, exchange category.

There is also one category in which none of the traditional social choice processes fall, which we have labeled, for want of a better term, "centralized exchange." Typologies can demonstrate their utility, of course, if they permit identification of heretofore unrecognized possibilities. An example of centralized exchange would be a trading system like a latter-day colonial empire, in which centralized choices or allocations are made in response to peripheral-unit expressions of need from the center; peripheral colonies may exchange raw materials for an allocation of manufactured goods made at the center. Other examples may exist in loose federations or franchise systems.

A better typology would, however, clearly distinguish between the market and bargaining. Bargaining, like the market, can be seen as a trading system. But exchanges in bargaining are contingent ones, and due to the need to exchange bargaining messages, usually involve only a few actors (or agents).

We shall not then develop the systematic typology that is necessary. Perhaps the possibly large number of requisite classifying dimensions generate a number of either null or sparsely populated categories, so that the four commonly identified social choice processes remain the major, or core, processes identified. But we believe that, even if this proved to be the case, such a systematic typology could add greatly to understanding by elucidating the major underlying structural factors or dimensions.

The four commonly cited social choice processes are defined below:

1. *Market:* "Perfect" markets are trading systems usually defined by such factors as homogeneity of traded commodity and purchasers, many buyers and sellers, yielding a uniform price, perfect information regarding price and purchase opportunities, and lack of barriers to entry and flow of resources. In addition there are assumptions about participants, e.g., rationality and self-interest. Less "perfect" markets involve relaxation of some or all of these requirements.

2. *Hierarchy:* A hierarchy is an organization whose members are arranged in a series of superior and subordinate levels (cf. Dahl and Lindblom 1953). Superior levels in some way control the behavior of subordinate levels. Thus relationships between subordinate and superior levels are in general ones of agency, with subordinates acting for

the goals of superiors. The organization, which may be defined abstractly for purposes of analysis rather than constitute a formally recognized (though still fundamentally abstract) entity, may have any number of levels, and is in effect a network of agency relationships in which lower-level participants act directly or indirectly for upper-level ones.

3. *Voting:* Voting is a system of collective choice in which individual choices are aggregated according to some rule of overall decision. Choice may be made directly by voting individuals or indirectly through their representatives.

4. *Bargaining:* Bargaining is interaction involving contingent exchanges of valued resources.[4]

Mixtures of two or more of these types are, of course, the general case. It is possible to identify further varieties of frameworks within each of the four basic types, though we shall not do this here.

In general, in the context of regulation we are concerned largely with *hierarchical frameworks,* in that regulation by definition involves restriction of choice of behavior by a governmental entity not directly party to the activity, so that regulatory superiors may be seen as controlling choice in regulated subordinate performers of the activity. It is important to note that production of desired behaviors or realization of desired outcomes need not occur, however, within frameworks traditionally used to secure them. Thus Haefele (1973a, 1973b) suggests that voting systems may sometimes produce more desired outcomes, e.g., in satisfaction of preference intensities, than traditional hierarchical forms. And Friedman (1962) has proposed that marketlike voucher systems replace hierarchical ones in supply of education.

For the purposes of analysis of alternate regulatory means, we shall artificially constrain our comparisons to types of hierarchical means. A fuller and more adequate analysis would consider as well substitutes for hierarchical regulatory means—such as types of markets (see, e.g., Rose-Ackerman 1977), voting systems, or bargaining arrangements. Consideration of the multitude of possibilities here would greatly expand the scope of an already extensive discussion. In the subsequent consideration of hierarchical regulatory means, we do

---

[4] Cf. the definitions of bargaining given by Schelling and by Bish: Bargaining involves "situations in which the ability of one participant to gain his ends is dependent to an important degree on the choices or decisions that the other participant will make" (Schelling 1960:5). And, "Bargaining is interaction among individuals who have opportunities for increasing their welfare by exchanging resources over which they have discretion" (Bish 1971:11).

touch on some aspects of such means that have a mixed character, e.g., that introduce marketlike elements into a basically hierarchical setting. Many of the advantages of incentive means in hierarchical regulation, for example, are similar to those offered in support of the similarly decentralized choice-system of markets.

4.3 INTERFERENCE WITH REGULATING AND REGULATED ACTIVITIES: FORMS IN THE CONTEXT OF AGENCY

Having identified basic framework forms, we turn to consideration of interferences with the regulat*ed* activity and with the regulat*ing* activity.

The extremes of interference in the regulat*ed* activity (as distinguished from interference with the regulatory form or framework) are, clearly, actual government performance of the activity to be regulated (strictly speaking, this is definitionally not regulation at all, since, in regulation, the regulator is not directly party to the activity), and laissez faire, i.e., no interference at all. In between we have different kinds, and degrees, of interference. We could, as Dahl and Lindblom (1953) do, identify a number of dimensions relevant to this interference, i.e.:

Voluntary–compulsory

Direct control–indirect control

Autonomy–prescription

Compulsion–information

Public–private ownership.

We prefer to identify, however, two very general kinds of interference that are applicable to analysis of interferences with both the regulat*ed* and the regulat*ing* activity. These are the concepts of "incentive" and "directive" mechanisms. Applicable to considerations of design of control in all hierarchies, they are therefore useful in the context of regulation because of its generally hierarchical setting. (Recall that the present analysis is limited to the hierarchical social choice process.) Thus we may distinguish interferences that occur by:

1. Circumscribing or directing choice in some area—i.e., making rules for behavior that may be transmitted as instructions (e.g., in directives or regulations). We may call this interference, regulation by directive.

2. Changing the perception of the nature of the alternatives for ac-

tion subject to choice; i.e., changing the relative attractiveness of alternatives. Thus, rather than being circumscribed or directed externally, choice is left to the performer, with certain alternatives for choice made more attractive. We may call this interference, regulation by incentive. Included in this category are interferences that increase the relative attractiveness of alternatives by either: (a) changing the alternatives or features associated with them; or (b) changing the performer of the activity so that he evaluates or perceives the alternatives differently. The net effect of an incentive is to reward an actor for performing a given act (and perhaps not other acts). We may distinguish positive incentives from negative incentives. Positive incentives increase, and negative incentives decrease (or threaten to decrease) the relative reward to an actor for performing a given act. In general, the incentive mechanisms to be considered involve positive incentives.[5]

The term "incentive" has not received consistent definition in the literature (see Rainey 1977). Mitnick, Backoff, and Rainey (1977) proposed that the term "incentive" actually refers to a relationship, to be called an "incentive relation," rather than to an isolated entity, transferred object, or particular property. A basic incentive relation possesses five defining properties: 1) stimuli are mutually sent and received; 2) the stimuli sent by the sender involve or promise reward to the receiver, i.e., increased return to the receiver's goals; 3) the stimuli are linked to, or made contingent on, given receiver behavior; 4) the receiver behaves in response to the stimuli; and 5) the receiver's responding behavior is rational, i.e., the receiver will behave so as to acquire or avoid the positively or negatively valued stimuli.

The standard incentive transaction (Mitnick, Backoff, Rainey 1977) consists of: 1) the transmission of messages concerning the rewards to be provided contingent upon performing certain behaviors (the "incentive message"); 2) information to the sender or provider of the rewards that the behavior in question is (or is not) performed; and 3) the actual transfer or provision of rewards to the behavior performer. Variations on this basic flow are possible and frequent, e.g., simultaneous steps, incomplete flows, and so on.

[5] On incentives, see, e.g., Clark and Wilson (1961); Schultze (1970); Mitnick, Backoff, and Rainey (1977); Backoff and Mitnick (1978). For an application to regulatory design, see Mitnick and Weiss (1974). W. P. Welch has argued (personal communication 1979) that the key difference between incentive-like and directive-like things is the autonomous character of choice in the incentive situation. This emphasizes the many similarities between market social choice processes, and incentive alternatives under a hierarchy social choice process.

Thus, when we refer to "incentives," as we have in previous paragraphs, we shall be implying the existence of a relation of the type defined. For convenience, we shall usually refer just to "incentives," though more careful discourse might substitute "incentive relation" or just "rewards."

The term "directive" can actually be understood as a variety of incentive relation involving negative incentives. In a directive, the incentive message specifies desired behavior as an instruction, standard, or rule. Noncompliance with the instruction is usually associated, formally or informally, directly or indirectly, with negative rewards; e.g., fines, penalties, demotion, termination of existing positive rewards, expulsion from the association or organization, various forms of coercion. Thus the "directive message" usually includes the threat of application of negative rewards (cf. Redford 1952:164–75, on sanctions).

Directives can also have normative backing. For example, because given directives are accorded "legitimacy" by the directive receiver, i.e., valued as rightful and proper perhaps due to their source in a legitimate authority or directive sender, noncompliance may have the character of a negative reward for the receiver.

In order to contrast regulatory means, we shall assume that "incentive" regulatory means involve either positive rewards or reductions in some initially imposed negative rewards, so that the net effect is that of a positive reward. Directive means will then involve instructions backed (perhaps distantly, but still backed) by negative rewards. The basic incentive-relation concept includes both, of course.

Note that regulation by incentive implicitly assumes for its effectiveness that the interference "makes a difference" or is "relevant" (see chapter 5; Buchanan and Stubblebine 1962) to the subject being regulated; regulation by directive assumes it "makes a difference" only indirectly—in provision for enforcement. A subject may of course be indifferent to a prohibition under regulation by directive, which may be adopted only because non-adoption carries penalties.

Return now to the context of incentives and directives as alternate regulatory means.

Consider first the case of the regula*ting* activity. Constituent-principals may wish to control the activity of their agent-legislators, who in turn seek to control the activity of agent-administrators or regulators. And within the regulatory entity, superiors seek to control subordinate agent-regulators. Regulators may then be controlled by directive means (e.g., conflict of interest laws) and by incentive means (e.g., hypothetically, pay bonuses to effective and/or equitable regulators).

Consider now the case of the regulated activity. The regulatory entity seeks (at least formally) to restrict choice in the regulated activity so that it is performed according to the wishes of legislative constituent-principals, i.e., seeks to create agents in the regulated activity in some more-or-less narrow area. These may not, of course, be willing agents. The mechanisms of interference to restrict choice may, as in the case of the regulating activity, be incentive or directive. Thus polluters can be given subsidies (incentive) to construct treatment facilities, or be instructed by administrative rule or standard (directive) to reduce pollution below a certain level.

In general, incentive and directive mechanisms are means that may be adopted by *principals* to control *agents*. The relevance of comparing incentive and directive means in organizing regulation then follows from the modeling of governmental action as *agency*. Thus the regulatory body, itself an agent of the legislature (and, ultimately, the public) employs incentive and/or directive means to create agents (of that body and therefore of the legislature and, ultimately, the public) in the regulated entity.

The incentive vs. directive conceptual distinction is not foreign to the literature, though we believe the conceptual analysis presented here is more careful and intends a considerably more systematic and precise comparison of regulatory means than is available. Contrasts of "regulation" with incentives, often in particular contexts such as pollution control—or using particular regulatory means such as standards versus effluent charges—have appeared increasingly often in recent years. Similar comparisons, however, have a long history in the literature (see, e.g., Kneese and Schultze 1975; Buchanan and Tullock 1975; J. Q. Wilson 1974:148; Schultze 1970; Dahl and Lindblom 1953).

4.4 CHARACTERIZATION OF REGULATORY MEANS BY INTERFERENCE TYPE

Regulatory means can be characterized according to whether regulation by incentive or by directive predominates. In figure 6.4 we list some common regulatory means that fall in each category.

Regulation by directive includes, for example, public enterprise, in which the activity may be performed directly by the government (it is not strictly regulation, being an extreme case since the government is directly party to the activity); common law, a body of case-by-case court-made law; and administrative rules and standards, which may be prescribed by a regulatory commission. Regulation by incentive includes tax incentives, which are tax credits or rebates for performing, or not performing, certain acts; user and effluent charges, which effectively price certain resources, such as water or air, that may not normally be priced or certain services that often deal with such resources; subsidies, which are grants to support performance or nonperformance of an activity; a promotion campaign, i.e., changing the performer rather than the alternatives he faces; and laissez faire (again an extreme case), in which the activity that would be regulated is left alone.

Figure 6.4.   Regulatory Means

Regulation by directive: Public enterprise (extreme case)
                                Common law
                                Administrative rules or standards

Regulation by incentive: Tax incentives
                                Effluent/user charges
                                Subsidies
                                Promotion campaign
                                Laissez faire (extreme case)

Note that permit or rights auctions, in which scarce pollution rights are established and auctioned off to the highest bidder, are a kind of mixed social choice process. The formalization and structuring of the market process involved, i.e., its boundaries and enforcement provisions, are regulatory, and hierarchical in character, but the means of controlling pollution is fundamentally a market. Thus we have not listed permit or rights auctions among the hierarchical incentive and directive alternatives in figure 6.4. We shall, however, briefly consider the advantages and disadvantages of this means and compare it to the other means later, in chapter 7.

4.5 COMPARING REGULATORY MEANS

On what grounds, or by what criteria, can we evaluate the regulatory means in each category: incentive and directive? The advantages and disadvantages of each regulatory means may be supported by one or more intermediate goals in the classes that we have identified, and may be more or less directly related to them, i.e., follow directly or in a more tenuous instrumental fashion. Ideally, we could evaluate each regulatory means according to each intermediate goal in turn, thereby generating a full (and possibly contradictory) set of reasons for and against each means. We shall not, however, attempt here to make such necessarily complex evaluative arguments, even for only the two broad categories of incentive and directive means; recall that the intermediate goals may be applied both to the level of the regulated activity and to the level of the regulating activity. We shall cite the relevant intermediate goals explicitly in a few cases where they are directly relevant, and offer some important advantages and disadvantages for each category; there are undoubtedly other reasons that we shall be omitting.

The critique will, however, be organized in order to promote comparison. Regulatory means must be established; administered; change, respond to change, and effect change over time; and manage enforcement of, and secure compliance with, regulatory objectives. These may be considered among the basic functional "problems" of regulatory systems (see chapter 1). The intermediate goal categories of aspects of performance, maintenance, and of impact evaluation in these areas, fall largely but not entirely in the administration and enforcement areas. The intermediate goal categories of aspects of activity evolution and development, and of impact evaluation in this area, suggest inclusion of regulatory process or change areas. That process must have a start, and must cause and respond to change over time; thus we have two more areas: establishment and change.

Identified in figure 6.5 in outline form are the areas in which we shall compare incentive and directive means. These are, in many cases, areas of relatively prominent difference that are sometimes discussed in the literature in the context of specific types of incentive or directive means; as we remarked above, there are probably others. The advantages and disadvantages are loosely deduced, given the definitions of incentive and directive mechanisms and certain common (and largely implicit) assumptions regarding the nature of the regulators, the regulated party, and the environment in which the regulation is operative. In spite of these caveats, including the lack of evaluation by the full set of intermediate goals, the discussion below marks a beginning toward systematic analysis of basic alternative regulatory means.

Figure 6.5. Incentive vs. Directive Mechanisms

Directive Advantages	Incentive Advantages	Functional Categories
		I. Establishment factors
X		... A. Existence of given preferences of the regulated party
X		... B. Information cost to establish regulation (especially on preferences)
	X	... C. Coincidence of regulation with preferences of the regulated party
		II. Change factors
		A. Change in the regulated party that affects or is affected by regulation
		1. Change in regulated parties that affects regulation
X		..... a. Change in the preferences of regulated parties
	X	..... b. Acquisition of norm-like status by the regulation, with consequent legitimacy and collective support
	X	.... 2. Change in the regulated party is affected by regulation (e.g., innovation)
		B. Change in the regulation that affects or adjusts to the regulated party or the environment
		1. Flexibility in application of the regulation
	X	..... a. Distributional factors (e.g., decentralization, individual adjustment to change considerations)
	X	..... b. Level of regulation factors (e.g., "tuning")
		c. Rate of impact factors
	X	...... 1) Rate of accommodation in regulated party permitted
X		...... 2) Effectiveness in crisis
	X	.... 2. Cost of change in regulation

5.0 Advantages of Incentive, and of Directive, Mechanisms

We compare incentive with directive mechanisms in this section. In figure 6.5, we indicate areas of comparison and whether the area of difference described is an advantage of incentive or of directive

		III.	Administration factors
			A. Process of regulation
			1. Cost of process
X		. . . . .	a. Intrinsic cost of mechanism (e.g., value of incentives)
	X	. . . . .	b. Cost of operating the mechanism
			2. Coordination and planning factors
X		. . . . .	a. Cost and feasibility of coordination
X		. . . . .	b. Predictability of impacts
			3. Flexibility in design of regulation
X		. . . . .	a. Availability/scarcity factors relating to employment of the mechanism
X		. . . . .	b. Malleability/divisibility aspects
			B. Impact of regulation
X		. . . .	1. Redundancy factors (e.g., same behavior without regulation; inefficiency; effects of overreward)
	X	. . . .	2. Choice factors (value of free choice)
	X	. . . .	3. Centralization/decentralization considerations
		IV.	Enforcement factors
			A. Methods and difficulties in policing
	X	. . . .	1. Enforcement costs
	X	. . . .	2. Cost of extension of policing
			B. Factors affecting likelihood of compliance
X		. . . .	1. History of supply of regulation/"saturation" of receiver
X		. . . .	2. Use of coercion
	X	. . . .	3. Credibility of supply of sanction (positive or negative) associated with the regulation
			4. Likelihood of compliance if enforcement apparatus is absent or faulty
	X	. . . . .	a. Coincidence of interests
X		. . . . .	b. Effects of norm-like status—e.g., legitimacy, collective support
	X	. . . .	5. Likelihood of compliance under changing conditions

mechanisms. Incentive advantages are taken as directive disadvantages, and vice versa. The advantages discussed below for each means are keyed to figure 6.5 by the outline's letters and numbers, which are in parentheses.

5.1 ADVANTAGES OF INCENTIVES

1. *Establishment Factors*

—A system involving positive rewards (or one involving both positive and negative rewards) may be easier to establish—meet less resistance—than a system involving only negative incentives (including coercion)—e.g., directives (though directives could also conceivably be held intrinsically desirable) (cf. Riker's arguments, Riker and Ordeshook 1973, ch. 10). (I.C.)

2. *Change Factors*

—Incentives may not acquire the norm-like status that sometimes attaches to (directive) rules, and may thus be easier to change. Directives as norms may be supported by collective prescription and held legitimate, and be therefore relatively harder to change. Of course, an incentive schedule, level of incentive, or characteristics of incentive-offering may have rulelike aspects and acquire the same impediment to change. (II.A.1.b)

—Incentives may permit and/or encourage innovation more than directives. Incentives may be made contingent on innovation. Some of the incentive resource may absorb some of the cost of innovation. And efficiency in the regulated party's performance of the activity (which activity is tied to the incentive), perhaps through innovation, may permit the party to obtain and/or keep more of the valued incentive or divert it to other rewarding uses. Such a surplus may itself permit innovation.

Of course, if the directive system is designed to impose coercion or other penalties for failure to innovate, or for failure to reach some goal or engage in some behavior that can only be met or performed through innovation, the directive system may extract innovation. (II.A.2)

—The decentralized decisions of subjects under an incentive system permit individualized adjustments to changing environmental conditions. This may lead to more efficient and equitable (two intermediate goals) distributions of resources and impacts. A directive system that involves centrally administered uniform directives could not accommodate local change. (II.B.1.a)

—Once established, (the effects of) many incentive means can be continuously "tuned" through relatively small changes in the incentive schedule. This could require, of course, an information cost in obtaining feedback on the effects of existing schedules, as well as a sensitivity to such changes on the part of the incentive receiver. Directive means are not generally described as being as capable of such fine-adjustment effects. Reasons for the latter may involve the cost of expertise to adjust the directive's content, as well as difficulties in overcoming the legitimacy and supportive prescription that may attach to the directive as norm. Where the action tied to the incentive is large or indivisible, however, the tuning ability of the incentive (or, obviously, the directive) may not be valuable or relevant. (II.B.1.b)

—Incentives may permit gradual change, since individuals may be able to control the impact on themselves. Of course, rapid change desired by the individual may also be permitted. Directive systems may produce rapid, destabilizing—and even violent—change, because of deadlines for compliance associated with them. Of course, deadlines can in some circumstances be staggered, and stretched, if such change is produced. But efficiency, equity, stability, and reliability goals would seem to favor the incentive means. (II.B.1.c.[1])

—Cost of change in regulation under an incentive system may be less than under a directive system if the major costs of expertise and information were expended at the time of establishment of the incentive system. The level of the incentive need only be altered until the desired behavior is observed (see the "tuning" advantage, above). Directive systems subject to continual creation or modification, however, may require expenditures on information and expertise, for example, with each directive creation. Of course, some directives (depending perhaps on their purpose and target) may be as easily altered as incentives. (II.B.2)

3. *Administration Factors*

—After start-up costs, many incentive means are relatively inexpensive to operate, requiring little administrative attention unless they are being tuned. Since controlling choices occur at the location of each participating unit, rather than centrally, central administration costs may be less. Centralization of control in a directive system, on the other hand, generally entails a higher administrative cost than a decentralized incentive system. The regulatory apparatus usually formed to set and administer rules and standards may require expenditure on a continuing body of technical experts and establish a set of costly procedures. These procedures guarantee activity impact evaluation goals like equity and due process that may be especially threatened where the regulation is to some extent (at least formally) imposed and not voluntary. If continual promulgation of directives is required, there may be a relatively high central administration cost in processing feedback from previous directives and designing and issuing new ones. (III.A.1.b)

—The choice of behavior that is often permitted subjects of incentives may be held desirable in itself as an activity impact evaluation goal. Directive systems, on the other hand, may severely restrict the choice of parties subject to them. On this criterion, mixed incentive/directive systems might also be held preferable to pure directive systems. (III.B.2)

—The decentralization of action decisions under an incentive system allows a variety of behaviors and permits adaptation to local conditions where multiple parties in different situations or environments are subject to it. This would not be possible where a centrally administered, uniform directive is in effect. Such decentralized adaptation may serve activity performance goals like efficiency and activity impact evaluation goals like equity. (III.B.3)

4. *Enforcement Factors*

—Enforcement costs may be less under an incentive mechanism because the incentive distributed by the principal is desired by the agent, so that the agent may be more likely to behave in the way required for incentive supply. On the other hand, enforcement costs, including monitoring and sanction application costs, may be relatively high in a directive system, especially if it involves coercion or other negative incentives that parties may seek to escape (as well as escape the undesired directive). Of course, the very severity of penalties could increase compliance and reduce costs if subjects come to fear them. A relatively inexpensive policing system could involve the imposition of extremely high penalties on relatively rare occasions, with extensive subject knowledge of, or observation of, penalty application. (IV.A.1)

—Since the enforcement cost is less, per capita enforcement cost is less, and control may be extended to more parties than under a directive system, given a comparable expenditure level. (IV.A.2)

—Since incentives are generally supplied more often than the negative incentives or coercive punishments that may accompany directives in the form of threats, the subject may have greater knowledge of and, based on the history of supply, greater belief in the likelihood of supply of the incentive. He may therefore be more likely to respond to the mechanism. Incentives are frequently supplied or calibrated in marginal units (e.g., hourly wage), while the negative sanctions that may be associated with noncompliance with directives are usually less divisible and their supply less frequent and more disrupting. With poorer information on penalties, the subject may find them less credible. Thus the principal may have to interrupt his agent's performance of a desired task to administer a penalty (e.g., suspension without pay), and thereby forfeit the gains from even substandard performance during that time. And repeated penalties may lead an agent to acquire an aversion to the task he is performing (and his relation to the principal), with consequent decrements in performance. Although we argue that the tendency in common situations is as above, we admit the possibility that certain directive systems (e.g., by the public display of severe if rare penalties) may convince subjects of the likelihood of supply and be as credible (and effective in enforcement in this regard) as incentive systems. (IV.B.3)

—Since positive incentives are coincident with the interest of the regulated party, rather than being a coercive mechanism as is often the case with directives, the incentive may produce desired behaviors to some extent even if enforcement is: (a) nonexisting, (b) inadequate, or (c) partially faulty. Parties subject to directives may seek to escape, and may succeed under such conditions. It is possible, of course, that deception may occur relative to the actual occurrence of agency in response to an incentive means. Undesired or irrelevant behaviors or merely preference satisfaction without ties to behavior could be produced. (IV.B.4.a)

—Some incentive systems may maintain compliance under some changing situational or environmental conditions, since they allow the subject to adjust his consumption of the incentive (and of course his contingent behavior) to the change. For example, an effluent charge system permits changes in total payment of charges depending on amount of effluent emitted (which may be altered, say, by production-process changes).

Typically, a lag between directives causes faulty compliance as conditions change faster than the directives. The regulatory agency must become aware of the changes through monitoring, and then design, promulgate, and enforce new directives. This takes time. The regulated party is not likely to inform the regulatory body of changes that are favorable to the party but that would be controlled or compensated for under the regulation. On the other hand, if change adversely affects the regulated party, he may complain to the regulatory body to have the regulation adjusted in his favor. Thus "regulatory lag" may lead to gains for the regulated party and at any rate may fail to closely achieve the aims of the regulation. The decentralized, individual adjustments that may be possible under some incentive systems, however, may therefore insure more immediate responses to change and better compliance. (IV.B.5)

5.2 ADVANTAGES OF DIRECTIVES

1. *Establishment Factors*
—The goals to which the incentives are directed must exist, be relevant, and be major or important, given the desired action. This serves as an obvious constraint on incentive system design, particularly when goals are nonpecuniary, or idiosyncratic. Remember that the incentive-directive distinction applies to all agency relationships, not just pollution control. Hermits, for example, may be insensitive to sociability rewards. In contrast, the preferences at which the negative incentives or coercion in directive systems is aimed are usually (nearly) universals and are probably better known to system designers. (I.A.)
—The information cost involved in determining the subject's goals and preferences, gathering information on the regulated activity and its environment, and using expertise to *initially* set the mechanism in the proper form and at the proper level to secure desired behavior is frequently less for a directive than an incentive means. Directives can initially require certain outcomes specifically; incentives must be set so that individual responses produce those outcomes. This requires more information. Some directives, however, especially if aimed at intermediate processes (e.g., control technologies rather than ambient or effluent levels in environmental regulation) can also have high initial information costs. As noted earlier, however, in directive systems the preferences to which negative incentives including coercion are directed are usually universally shared. In general, preferences are particularly hard to measure, and often must be implied ("revealed") from action. But if the program of control is new there may be relatively little information on preferences; there may have been little opportunity for revealing activities. This might suggest that where this is a particular problem, control might begin with a directive system and then switch to an incentive one once sufficient information exists. At any rate, as far as relative costs of this sort are concerned, directive means may have a relative advantage in establishment, and incentive means, in administration. (I.B)

2. *Change Factors*

—Directives offer predictability of performance if the preferences of the subjects are changing; they will not require compensating change. This generally occurs because some preferences, to which such negative incentives as coercion are addressed, tend to remain the same. The incentive means, on the other hand, is subject to any changes in preferences (to which the incentive is directed) that could destroy the mechanism's effectiveness. This would of course require changes in the regulatory form. Thus incentive means can be particularly vulnerable to such preference change and require compensating alterations. The body establishing the mechanism (e.g., a legislature) may be slow or cumbersome in acting, so that responding modifications in the incentive mechanism are slow in coming. Perhaps the establishing body has chosen the incentive means with its relatively low administration requirements and costs because that body expects its (slow and cumbersome) participation will be largely limited to establishment. (II.A.1.a)

—Directives may have more direct and rapid effects than incentive means because they do not have their indirect and possibly time-consuming mechanisms of adjustment. They may thus be more effective in crises. (II.B.1.c.[2])

3. *Administration Factors*

—Directives may have relatively small intrinsic cost since, unlike many incentives, they do not involve distribution of a scarce valued resource (or foregone rewards, e.g., tax credits). Application of negative incentives associated with directives could be costly, but such incentives are often invoked only rarely. (III.A.1.a)

—Centralization of control in a directive system provides an opportunity for coordination and comprehensive planning in policy intention implementation. Thus coordination and planning may be more feasible and less costly than in an incentive system where choices of activity are made by possibly dispersed individual subjects. (III.A.2.a)

—Centralized choice through directive may permit relatively more predictability (by regulatory agencies or others) of collective or combinatorial impacts (i.e., uncertainty is reduced in this area) than under an incentive mechanism's decentralized, individual choice. (III.A.2.b)

—Unlike incentives, there may be no intrinsic scarcity in directives, i.e., no intrinsic limit on directive promulgation. Limits due to the costs of directive creation and promulgation (e.g., notification costs) are still relevant, of course. The incentive resource, on the other hand, may be scarce. Such scarcity insures the value of the incentive but also constrains the extent to which it can be distributed to produce desired behaviors. The extent of the incentive possible may be also structurally limited; for example, unless "negative" tax is allowed, the amount of a tax incentive may be limited by the amount of the tax. In contrast, there may be no intrinsic limit on directive promulgation. (III.A.3.a)

—Unlike incentives, there may be no intrinsic limit on directive malleability or specificity. In practice, of course, limits related to the directive target (e.g., feasibility of regulating angels on pins), and directive creation and promulgation costs, may affect these areas. In contrast, the incentive means often requires divisibility in the resource that is distributed as incentive (e.g., status distinctions and gradations in value attached to the distinctions). Where the available incentive resource is all or nothing in character or occurs in large steps, usage as an incentive may be restricted. (III.A.3.b)

—Although some costs are likely to be present (e.g., notification, monitoring, policing), redundancy—performance of the desired act occurring anyway—may be relatively less important in directive than in incentive systems. Because incentives themselves are frequently scarce and valued, redundancy (say, with respect to a given party's action) may be more important (and costly) than in a directive system. In systems where there is a number of subjects with varying preferences, redundancy under both incentive and directive systems might be unavoidable. There may be an information cost to ascertain that the incentive or directive would *not* in fact be redundant. And where preferences are uncertain or changing, the risk of redundancy might be considered well taken.

Incentives that exceed the agent's minimum cost in acting may be inefficient as far as the principal is concerned. In addition to the added, perhaps to some extent unnecessary expenditure, the agent may feel less "pressure" to reduce costs in acting. This has been an argument in some discussions of subsidy systems. Here it is of course assumed that the agent distinguishes the incentive from his own valued resources. In contrast, under a directive system in which he is compelled to expend his own resources in acting, the agent would seek to be efficient. It is hard to see, however, why the agent would not also seek to be efficient in the use of the incentive if he were allowed to keep, or direct to other satisfactions, the excess amount of the incentive supplied. Of course, if he were not allowed to keep the excess, the agent might reduce his costs in acting by not paying the information, auditing, and other costs of assuring efficiency.

Over-reward in incentive systems may also produce more of the behavior the incentive may be designed to control or reduce. More producers of the behavior may be drawn in. Although each is then over-rewarded for reducing the amount of the undesirable behavior (e.g., air pollution), there may be an increased overall production of the undesirable behavior due to the increase in producers (cf. Baumol and Oates 1975). (III.B.1)

4. *Enforcement Factors*

—Directives backed by coercion or other penalty may be less likely to lose effectiveness with repeated or recent supply. This is because the preferences to which the coercion or other penalty (in the extreme, for example, imprisonment; loss of job) that may back directives is aimed are frequently basic ones that are always subject to dissatisfaction. Of course, for example, repeated pain may be deadening; that may not mean, however, that threat of additional pain may not be effective. And some directives may be ignored if repeated sufficiently often, particularly if they are unenforced. In contrast, the receiver of the incentive resource may be saturated, or satiated with it. Recent or extensive receipt of the incentive resource may inhibit response to it. (IV.B.1)

—Because coercion is generally directed at intensely—and nearly universally—held stable preferences, directives backed by it may be relatively more effective. Incentive systems that permit some choice limit the application of coercion and may not then insure that exactly the desired behavior results.

The incentive means sometimes requires, or is associated with, some ultimate coercion, though the degree of coercion and the specificity of the enforcement mechanism may vary. There may be special enforcement mechanisms associated with some incentive means, such as tax incentives, while regular civil and criminal remedies suffice for others. Governments may coercively require, for example, that industry pay *some* effluent charge if it pollutes. Thus, at the boundaries, some incentives may have the same enforcement problems as directives, and so have some enforcement costs as well. Note that such *mixed* incentive systems may not also have all the enforcement advantages of such directives since some choice may remain. (IV.B.2)

—Directives that as rules acquire the status of norms may be accorded collective support and legitimacy. This may reduce the need for coercive backing, reduce enforcement costs, and increase the likelihood of compliance even when the enforcement apparatus is lacking or faulty. Of course, any rules governing incentive dispersal may attain norm status so that incentives could be similarly supported. (IV.B.4.b)

6.0   Assessment of Comparative Advantages: A Hypothetical Environmental Case

Looking at Figure 6.5, which depicts the advantages listing above, no pattern favoring incentives or directives appears. Except for effectiveness in crisis, and change in the regulated party's preferences, incentive means do appear to have a comparative advantage in the change categories. But regulation is often introduced in response to a crisis (see chapters 2,3).

In the other categories, there is no clear pattern. Establishment of incentives may be easier, but more costly and require that certain preferences exist. Directives appear to have general comparative advantages in the administration categories of coordination/planning and flexibility of design, and are less of a problem as far as intrinsic cost and redundancy are concerned. But they can have high operating costs and do not offer the advantages of free and decentralized choice. Incentive means have a high intrinsic cost but low operating cost and do provide the advantages of free and decentralized choice.

In enforcement, incentives have comparative advantages in costs of policing, in credibility, and, except for the possible advantage of having norm-like status, in likelihood of compliance if enforcement is imperfect or conditions are changing. Directives depend less on the history of supply or "saturation" of the receiver, enjoy the backing of coercion, and can have a norm-like status.

In order to illustrate the potential utility of the incentives-directives regulatory means analysis, we shall present and discuss a hypothetical case of environmental regulation.

IRON TOWN

Iron Town sits at the confluence of two rivers which join at a point and merge to form a larger river which serves as a major avenue of commerce. The economy of Iron Town is dependent largely on a few heavy industries whose numerous plants are scattered along the consequently polluted basins of the two smaller rivers. Many of these plants are old, with antiquated technologies. Due to high costs, a sluggish regional economy, and the competition of foreign imports, these industries are not prospering, and their plants are currently operating below capacity. Economic forecasts for the Iron Counties area are good, however; the availability of skilled labor and Iron Town's status as a transportation and commercial center are expected to facilitate future growth.

Iron Town politics have been historically dominated by these industries. As a result, pollution control legislation has been rarely enacted and, when enacted, ineffectually enforced. Recently, however, unusually low water flow conditions in the river system coincided with a large discharge of highly toxic chemicals by a mill along one of the rivers. There was a large fish kill many miles down the major river, at a point where the pollution was normally greatly diminished. There was a severe impact on sports and commercial fishing and recreational uses. More seriously, the toxic chemicals found their way into the public water systems of numerous towns along the major river. In the resulting crisis, a regional pollution control authority for the Iron Counties area was created. Limited expertise, inability to provide full-time oversight, and other factors may have led local legislatures to delegate pollution control to the authority. The authority's resources are likely to be limited, at least in the short run, as historical political patterns reassert themselves. Change in the region's economy and the modernization of its industrial base could affect this and permit greater support in the future. The authority is expected to be able to establish and implement some form of pollution control mechanism. (Cf. Roos and Roos 1972; Wenner 1972; Jones 1975.)

What type of regulatory mechanism should be chosen?

The pollution authority will have to select, either explicitly or implicitly, goals for control. Assume the authority desires to attain and encourage economic efficiency both in regulating and in the regulated industries, to seek or seek to permit growth and innovation, and to realize equity in the regulatory process and in regulatory impacts. Given the political role of large industry in the area, the authority may feel that an emphasis on individual choice in pollution control as an impact goal could be expedient and accord with the business ideology of the region.

We shall assume that the authority selects an essentially hierarchical alternative, permitting us to contrast incentive and directive alternatives in the context of this case. We do this because of the focus of this chapter, which has the limited objective of developing the incentive/directive regulatory distinction. But there *are* alternatives besides the hierarchical one; we included a brief discussion of social choice processes to point this out. It is entirely possible that Iron Town's problems might be better served by another control regime, e.g., a market of pollution permits (see, e.g., Rose-Ackerman 1977; see also chapter 7).

Consider the characteristics of the Iron Town problem. The numerous plants produce numerous pollution sources, control of which could be administratively costly if a centralized directive system (e.g., standards) were selected. Planning and coordination could, however, be easier with such a system. Existence of the older plants with antiquated technologies and their effects suggest that choice of a regulatory means that would encourage or speed innovation would be desirable. Innovation could also increase efficiency and reduce costs in the industries and contribute to improvement in the region's economy. An incentive means would seem appropriate. As plants build production up to capacity as the region recovers, more pollution would be produced. Thus the regulatory means chosen must be able to accommodate to this growth. The "tuning" capability of some incentive regulatory means would seem useful here.

Growth in the region could mean both more pollution and more sources to control, leading potentially to higher administrative costs. New technologies could mean a need for expertise to design new directives, e.g., new directives to govern use of new fuels or new processes with differently polluting characteristics. Continual promulgation of central directives could be costly. Recall, that, at least in the short run, available resources, including presumably expertise, will be in short supply to the pollution authority.

Enforcement can be a problem in this region because of its historical character as well as because of the technical problems and the costs of control in a large and growing area. Growth and resource constraints could therefore imply the need for a strategy with low per capita enforcement costs. An incentive strategy with a low incentive resource cost might serve well.

Due to the region's history and the possibility that future political influences could, at least in the short run, reduce either the diligence of oversight or the degree of constraint in newly issued directives, a strategy that relies only on directives backed by negative incentives could be in trouble. There is no reason for firms to refrain from evasion of controls, a policy consistent with previous behavior. An incentive strategy where the firm's interest coincides to some extent with that of the pollution authority would aid compliance even if enforcement is imperfect (perhaps because of resource problems). A mixed system which requires compliance but encourages it through some incentive provision would seem desirable.

A directive system sensitive to the individual needs of numerous plants could be costly to operate, requiring considerable expertise guiding the promulgation of numerous specialized directives. As far as the equity goal is concerned, there may be no best solution. There is an inevitable trade-off between the fairness involved in sensitivity to special local circumstances and that which requires that all parties be treated in some sense equally. The individualized adaptation to controls permissible in incentive systems can resolve some but not all problems of this sort since individuals are given some choice in responding. But local advantages, e.g., position on the river or technology used, could make it easier for some to clean up and so raise equity questions. Consider two plants, one upstream and the other downstream. The upstream facility has an advantage which comes at a cost to the downstream facility, i.e., is an externality, if the overall system of control is one that seeks uniform river quality. The capacity of the downstream part of the river to absorb pollution may be reduced due to the upstream dumping. No problem may result, however, if the regulation involves standards on effluent quality and accepts some variation in river quality.

An essentially incentive system such as an effluent charge system may not only have a low incentive resource cost; in fact, instituted from scratch, the system will generate revenue. The effluent charge puts a tax on units of effluent. The polluting firm must pay the tax, so at the boundary, so to speak, the system is directive. But the firm may pay less tax if it pollutes less. Since there is a potential net gain to the regulated party, we are dealing with an incentive strategy. (On effluent charges, see, e.g., Freeman and Haveman 1972; Kneese and Bower 1968; Kneese and Schultze 1975; Rose-Ackerman 1973; see also chapter 7.)

There are many possible problems with effluent charge systems (see, e.g., Rose-Ackerman 1973 and 1977; Wenner 1978; Majone 1976; chapter 7); the analysis of the advantages and disadvantages of such a system in the situation we have described is considerably more complex than as presented. We do wish to show how the basic comparison of incentive and directive means can lead to choice of one for a particular case. The particular form, whether effluent charges, another incentive means, or some mixed system, must still be selected or designed.

A major problem for the pollution authority, however, will be establishing the regulation. An incentive system such as an effluent charge system requires coercively backed payment of a tax, i.e., the effluent charge. Since a tax would be imposed, the system would be opposed. But those subject to it may realize that, if some regulation is inevitable, it may be more advantageous than a directive system that forces them to, say, construct treatment facilities. At least they may pay less tax as they gradually reduce pollution through the most efficient (and potentially innovative) way they can find (e.g., process changes, input changes, etc., which may have costs different from treatment). Because of their stake in the region, industries are likely to support regulation that encourages or permits efficiency and growth in the area. In addition, the pollution authority is faced with the high initial costs of the incentive system. It may find ways to pay these costs (e.g., borrowing or transfers from other governments, borrowing from the public, stretch out of planning and system creation), realizing that it will be able to sustain the relatively lower operating costs of the system.

After an initial "tuning" period, the charge will require little supervision unless change and growth in the region is not as predicted and individual adjustments under the existing charge schedule are inadequate. In that case, further "tuning" may be necessary. But the administrative costs could still be less than under a directive system.

Iron Town's pollution crisis led to creation of the pollution authority, but is now past. If Iron Town were faced with an immediate pollution crisis in the absence of regulation, a directive form would clearly be indicated. With time for implementation, the presence of an incentive means in operation could forestall any new crisis.

We have conveniently assumed that the pollution authority, riding the wave of the crisis, will be able to institute some form of regulation. We have ignored the agenda-building phase—getting the pollution issue on the formal agenda of local or state government (see Cobb and Elder 1972). In the decision stage, on the agenda, the form of regulation is likely to be subject to bargaining among the special interests concerned, such as public interest and industry groups. The choice of means may not be quite so centrally rational as our discussion seems to imply (Majone 1976). But we have argued that in this case an incentive means may be in the best interest of the regulated parties, the industries who have controlled Iron Town politics and are in turn dependent on the region's economic well-being.

Understanding of nearly all regulatory means, not only effluent charge systems, is insufficiently developed. Experience with effluent charge systems is still short, but systematic analysis of even means employed for many years has only begun relatively recently. In view of the complexity involved, some have called for experiments so that alternative means may be compared based on controlled practice.[6] Taking a prescriptive public interest view of regulation, however, one could argue that problems won't wait.

7.0 Conclusions

In this chapter, we have compared two means of organizing regulation: incentive and directive mechanisms. We reviewed a set of categories of intermediate goals that may be used to rationalize governmental forms and action; presented a model of government as agency;

---

[6] See, e.g., Wenner (1978). Many older works on regulation also viewed development of regulation as an experimental process of trial and error (see chapter 3).

discussed delegation by legislative agents to administrative agents; discussed the nature of regulatory interferences, identifying the four commonly described social choice processes as basic frameworks for organizing activity; and developed the incentive-directive distinction from considerations of the concept of "incentive" and of control processes in agency. We then systematically compared incentive and directive mechanisms according to a set of functional dimensions (i.e., establishment, change, administration, and enforcement factors). Advantages were determined largely according to success in performing the functions identified, with frequent reference to goals from the set of intermediate-goal categories. The advantages were loosely deduced from the definitions of incentives and directives and mostly implicit, but common, assumptions about the nature of the regulators, the regulated party, and the environment in which the regulation is operative. To illustrate the analysis, a hypothetical environmental case was presented and discussed.

A major weakness in the analysis concerns the method used to compare incentive and directive means. The functional categories are not closely derived from the basic intermediate-goal set, and the goals are not systematically factored through the means to yield advantages.

Assumptions regarding regulators, regulated parties, the environment, and, in some cases, common forms of the incentive and directive means, are for the most part left implicit. The deduction of advantages and disadvantages can consequently be termed "loose." Arguments in support are sometimes somewhat speculative and refer to "common" cases; exceptions can probably be identified in some instances.

The aspects of the functional categories actually compared are ones selected for the incentive/directive differences they would display. They are frequently interesting and important aspects, but a more complete treatment would derive them as part of a systematically constructed typology that also identifies aspects in which incentive and directive means do *not* differ. Since these aspects of difference are not systematically derived, there are undoubtedly others we do not consider.

Thus, the present effort should be considered a first or early step in understanding the systematic design of regulatory organization. In spite of the limitations cited above, the analysis should prove to be a valuable start in integrating, extending, and applying our fragmented knowledge of the effectiveness of alternate regulatory means. Systematic knowledge of the type we seek could finally interrupt the cycle of regulatory reform noted at the start of this chapter.

As we indicated at the outset, the analysis is applicable to hierarchical frameworks in general, being to some extent a consequence of general considerations in the relation of principal and agent. We do think that a better understanding of the science of politics may be gathered from the study of what may be its characteristic feature, the relation of agency.

In chapters 7 and 8 we shall move to comparisons of particular forms of the general means discussed in chapter 6: tax incentives, subsidies, and effluent charges as incentive means, and various types of administrative rules and standards, and public enterprise as an extreme case, as directive means.

VII

Regulation by Incentive: Tax Incentives, Effluent Charges, and Subsidies

THERE ARE, of course, many different forms of regulation by incentive. In this chapter we shall consider some advantages and disadvantages for three such forms: tax incentives or credits, effluent charges, and subsidies. A fourth and related means, auctions of property rights (e.g., pollution rights), will be reviewed briefly later in the chapter. All of these methods have been widely discussed in the literature in the context of environmental problems, frequently as alternatives.[1] The first three constitute, however, major types of means of regulation by incentive (with effluent charges seen as a type of user charge). Although the discussion will proceed in the context of environmental regulation, many, if not most, considerations are easily generalizable to problems of regulation in general. In many places we have presented the arguments in an abstract manner in order to encourage perception of applications outside the environmental context.

---

[1] Most of the advantages and disadvantages listed in this chapter were compiled, derived, or extended from discussions in the following works: Aaron (1971); Ackerman et al. (1974); Baumol and Oates (1975); Bird and Waverman (1972); Brenner (1973); Brumm and Dick (1976); Buchanan and Tullock (1975); Carbone and Sweigart (1974); Comptroller General of the United States (1977); Dales (1968); Davis and Kamien (1970); Dewees, Everson, and Sims (1975); Ferrar and Horst (1974); Freeman and Haveman (1971 and 1972); Freeman, Haveman, and Kneese (1973); Gerhardt (1972); Gorr et al. (1975); Hall (1949:413–26); Hines (1973); Kneese (1977, 1972, 1971); Kneese and Bower (1968); Kneese and Schultze (1975); Lee (1973); Macaulay and Yandle (1977); Madden and Morris (1971); Majone (1975, 1976); Mäler (1974); Mills (1966); Mushkin and Vehorn (1977); Nagel (1974); Olson (1965); Orr (1976); Posner (1971); Roberts (1971, 1970); Roberts and Stewart (1976); Rohlfing et al. (1941:430–50); Rose-Ackerman (1977, 1973); Rosenthal (1972); Rothenberg (1974); Ruff (1970); Schultze (1977); Seneca and Taussig (1974); Smead (1969:31–43); Surrey (1957, 1970); *Tax Incentives* (1971); Thompson (1973); Wenner (1978); L. J. White (1976); R. White (1976); and Wilcox and Shepherd (1975:633–61). The materials in Anderson et al. (1977) were not completely reviewed for this chapter because the work was received by the author after the chapter was largely complete.

1.0 Tax Incentives, Effluent Charges, and Subsidies

In the United States, under the tenth amendment to the Constitution, the police power, which involves regulating health, safety, morals, and the general welfare (therefore responding to goals of aspects of activity impact evaluation), was left to the states. But a federal power was in effect created through use of the Congressional power to regulate interstate commerce. In addition, a police power was sometimes executed through manipulation of federal tax provisions. The ability to do this has sometimes been restricted by the courts. It has been thought by some observers that the taxing power can only be used to raise revenue, or must augment or supplement another delegated power, like regulating commerce. Others have maintained that the taxing power may be used freely to obtain the general welfare, and need not be specifically limited to association with delegated powers, or raising revenue. In general, regulatory taxes that have satisfied the first position have been historically more likely to be judicially approved. But the recent trend has been to allow the taxing power to be used as a regulatory means in this country at the federal level (see Lee 1973; Conant 1974:167–75). Thus controversy over use of the tax system as a means of applying negative incentives has often revolved around essentially normative questions, i,e., permissibility under constitution and/or statute, rather than around feasibility, design, or efficacy in comparison with other regulatory means.

The remission of taxes in some form, such as deferrals, deductions, credits, exclusions, or preferred rates (Thompson 1973:168), contingent on some act (or the omission of some act), is a tax incentive. Note that it involves taxes forgone, taxes that would normally have been collected. It has not usually been used to refer to taxes instituted to proscribe certain behavior, a form of regulatory taxation we shall not discuss here in its general form.[2] Effluent charges constitute tax incentives in the broad sense, but they generally involve imposition of a new tax schedule on discharges that is designed to induce some behavior, rather than selective reductions in an essentially existing schedule that might have been designed for other use. Many tax incentives, for example, are built into income tax systems. Tax incentives, or "tax expenditures" (provisions for remission) that in-

---

[2] On taxes used as negative incentives, see, e.g., Lee (1973); Smead (1969:31–43); Hall (1949:413–26); and Rohlfing et al. (1941:430–50).

duce certain action, have in recent years amounted to a considerable sum. Most tax expenditures are tax incentives; in 1977, the total of such federal expenditures was about $111.6 billion.[3]

An effluent charge puts a price on free resources, such as "common property" resources like air and water, that are used in the production process and then returned to the environment in altered, "polluted," state. Theoretically, society could place a value on reduction in such pollution; a value could be attached to each additional reduction of a unit of such undesirable discharge, representing the social damage caused by that unit. This value would thus represent the marginal social cost of each additional unit of pollution or, alternatively, the marginal social benefit from eliminating that unit of pollution. In general, the marginal social benefit from additional reductions in pollution will be decreasing; reductions of the first units will be judged more valuable than reductions in the nearly pure state.

How, then, could we choose a level of waste treatment? Reduction in wastes has costs, whether from treatment mechanisms, internal-production-process changes, or other means. The polluter (and, let us say, society) theoretically knows the costs to him of reducing each additional unit of pollution. These marginal costs will in general be increasing, since it is often more expensive to reduce pollution further in the nearly pure state. Assume that society wishes to obtain some optimum level of pollution control at minimum cost to the polluter and/or anybody else. Then we should keep reducing wastes, paying the costs, as long as the marginal social benefit of reduction of a unit of pollution exceeds the costs of actually reducing it. At some point, of course, the costs of pollution reduction will begin to exceed the marginal social benefits. Given our assumptions about the ways the marginal social benefits and reduction (e.g., treatment) costs change with the number of units of waste dealt with, it should be clear that the minimum cost of pollution control consistent with so-

---

[3] U.S. Bureau of the Census (1978):265–66; but see cautions in headnote, at 265, regarding a rough summation like that made here. Also see Aaron (1971) for a listing of federal tax incentives, restrictively defined. Posner (1971) has suggested, in effect, that additional tax expenditures are hidden in the internal subsidization established and protected by much regulation (see chapter 3). For example, airline regulation insures maintenance of below-cost service to small communities. In effect, all customers of regulated firms are taxed through excess service fees to pay, indirectly, for the below-cost services. The tax does not go through government. We could view this taxation method as efficient in a limited sense (apart from inefficiency due to misallocation of resources) as far as the regulating mechanism is concerned, since it economizes on use of the administrative taxing apparatus. Of course, the regulatory apparatus is substituted, which, although it might exist for other purposes, could conceivably be marginally even more costly.

cietal benefits would be where the marginal social benefit of reduction equals the marginal cost of reduction. With more waste reduced, the marginal cost will exceed the marginal benefit; with less waste reduced, the marginal benefit will exceed the marginal cost, and more benefit can be obtained through more waste reduction.

Society could then charge the polluter the marginal social cost (which is the same as the social benefit of reduction) per unit of pollution at the level of waste reduction at which the polluter's reduction costs are minimized for optimal societal benefit. Thus the marginal social cost would in effect be attached to each unit of pollution or waste, and the polluter would be subject to the fee on all units of waste that he discharged. The free resource would no longer be free. The polluter, if he had a choice, would minimize his waste-reduction cost by choosing the level of waste reduction at which this "effluent charge" (equal to the marginal social benefit of reduction or the marginal social cost of damages per unit of pollution) equals his marginal cost of reduction per unit of pollution. If he chooses a level of waste reduction below, where the charge exceeds the marginal reduction costs, he will have to pay the extra costs of the effluent charge on that portion of his wastes that is untreated (if treatment, for example, is the method of reduction). But he can gain by treating more waste because the charge he must pay on it anyway is greater than his marginal treatment cost. If he chooses a level above, his marginal reduction cost will exceed the charge and he will prefer to pay the charge; it is cheaper. Under the charge scheme, the polluter's solution is thus to reduce wastes on all units of effluent up to the socially optimal level, and pay the charge on wastes emitted above it.

Because the polluter is in effect being charged for using the environment, the effluent charge can be viewed as a kind of user charge.[4] User charges can be assessed, for example, to pay for sewage treatment. While the legal rights to use of a sewage treatment facility are clear, the rights to use of the common property resources of the environment have been disputed (Freeman and Haveman 1972:325–26). But the recent judicial and legislative tendency is to vest those rights in the public, so that establishment of an effluent charge system amounts to asserting the polluter's responsibility to the public for the damages he creates.

Because effluent charges constitute an extension of the price sys-

---

[4] On other types of user charges see, e.g., Mushkin and Vehorn (1977); and Walters (1968).

tem, they represent a marketlike solution to pollution control. Note this occurs within a hierarchical, regulatory context; someone must administer the charges. Recall (chapter 5) that a perfectly competitive market can produce results that realize one conception of the public interest; in particular, it can produce efficient allocations of resources. Similarly, effluent charges, through obtaining a cost-minimizing outcome, are said to produce an efficient use of resources in pollution control. There are other marketlike approaches to pollution control, notably schemes involving the sale or auction of transferable "pollution rights." It has been argued that such a scheme could in many respects be superior to an effluent charge system; we shall consider some relative advantages and disadvantages of rights markets later in this chapter (see Dales 1968; Ackerman et al. 1974; Rose-Ackerman 1977).

Subsidies, like the other regulatory means, can take many forms. They may be in the form of direct rewards for performing (or not performing) some activity, as with subsidies tied to pollution reduction, or more indirect support that will lead to changes in the activity, as with subsidies for waste treatment facilities. Subsidies are therefore positive incentives, involving the transfer of valued resources contingent directly or indirectly on certain acts, and do not feature the remission of resources otherwise requisitioned, as with tax incentives. Subsidies may be tendered in incremental steps—as when the recipient must perform a series of actions to receive the total sum, or when each act required is independently valued—or they can be offered in an all-or-nothing fashion. And subsidies may be partial or full when offered in indirect support of certain actions, as when they pay some percentage of the cost, or the total cost, of a waste treatment facility.

We shall now consider in turn the advantages and disadvantages of tax incentives, effluent charges, and subsidies.

2.0 Tax Incentives

2.1 ADVANTAGES OF TAX INCENTIVES

1. *Establishment Factors*
   —Because a tax incentive is a "hidden" subsidy, it may be approved more easily; "hidden," perhaps deliberately, among technical tax provisions, it is harder for the lay public to notice, and to protest. This is

perhaps the outstanding and most frequently cited advantage of tax incentives (see, e.g., Surrey 1957, 1970).

—It may be easier to enact because its cost, in terms of revenue forgone, falls diffusely on the tax-paying public, with no one group hurt by the loss in revenue; meanwhile the intensely concerned benefited group may lobby for it.

—The participation of the private sector in social programs that results from a tax incentive system may lead to further, voluntary involvement, as well as being considered intrinsically desirable according to societal goals. There is at least a partial coincidence of interest between the taxing authority and the subject firm. The tax incentive, it can be argued, may, in conjunction with the firm's officers' shared feelings of corporate social responsibility, be enough to trigger firm participation. The firm may also consider it a prudent environmental defense to participate in such programs, especially where subsidized to some extent. Publicity for these endeavors could help forestall future societal demands on the firm's resources.

—The preferences to which the tax remission is directed, i.e., financial, obviously already exist, and the reward is of course already valued. This can facilitate establishment.

—The information cost necessary to determine the subject party's preferences is therefore less, though it is not necessarily known whether the tax credit will be sufficient, in conjunction with existing preferences of the subject party, for the desired action itself. Thus some information cost in establishment remains.

2. *Change Factors*

—Tax incentives may be a more permanent and stable means, because they would be defended by an intensely concerned interest against a diffuse one. This may be more so with tax incentives than with subsidies, because the diffusely distributed cost of the tax incentive is only revenue forgone, rather than perceived as a real, continuing cost, and tends to be valued less as a result.

—They may be more permanent and provide stability, because they generally require legislative, rather than administrative, acts to change them.

—The preferences at which tax incentives are directed are unlikely to change and destroy the existing utility of the device. Tax incentives deal with pecuniary gain and loss and are thus translatable, or convertible, to other forms of reward. The institutional setting, i.e., individuals or organizations and the tax system to which they are subject, tends to be relatively stable in major aspects. Of course, the value placed on a given level of reward through tax credit can vary as actors and environmental conditions vary.

—Tax incentives can allow some measure of gradual accommodation among the class of subject parties. All may not have to accept the tax incentive at the same time; individual parties may accept it at a time when it will be most efficient for them to do so. Tax incentives can be set up on a percentage, matching, or scale basis, also permitting gradual accommodation.

—In principle, tax incentives can be "tuned" until desired action is produced. Existing individual preferences for the desired action, as well as for the reward comprising the tax credit, can vary; initial information regarding them may be poor and costly to obtain. Thus the "proper" level of the tax incentive could be set through experimental "tuning." If the level of the tax incentive is legislatively set, as seems likely, it may, however, be difficult to alter.

3. *Administration Factors*

—Tax incentives are claimed to be relatively simply structured and do not require as much bureaucratic involvement. Thus administrative operating cost could be relatively less. But tax incentives need not be simple; they may require complicated eligibility certification (Surrey 1970:716–18).

—Tax incentives make it easy (less costly) for recipients to deal with the government, cutting "red tape," since they are obtained at the same time as taxes are paid. But a subsidy could also be obtained as simply as filling out an IRS form, it is argued, if the program were designed properly (Surrey 1970:716–18).

—It is claimed that tax incentives promote private decision-making on activities to be performed, which is held a good thing that helps solve social problems. Private decision-making can be held intrinsically desirable because of the value placed on free choice. But a subsidy program could also be "volunteeristic." For example, the system of charitable deductions could be rearranged with the government matching private gifts with grants on a no-questions-asked basis (Surrey 1970:718–19).

—Tax incentives may provide funds to firms or other organizations that do not have easy access to capital markets. This may promote societal goals served by such organizations—organizations which otherwise would be unable to perform the desired acts.

—The distributional cost effect may be held desirable according to societal goals because one class is not made to pay for it, as with effluent charges; the impact is diffuse.

—Action decisions under a tax incentive will be decentralized, permitting a variety of implementing behaviors with adaptation to local conditions; subject, of course, to the provisions of the tax incentive.

4. *Enforcement Factors*

—Tax incentives can exploit the experience and existing apparatus of the tax collection system. The tax collection agency, such as the IRS, already has an audit staff, for example, that could be used with any new tax incentive. It might be necessary to create such a staff in an operating department. But departments already do run audits in many areas.[5]

—The enforcement apparatus already exists for ordinary taxes and could be relied on for tax incentives, reducing costs.

[5] See discussion by Robert T. Cole and reply by Surrey in *Tax Incentives* (1971:74–76).

—Because the relevant treasury department would, through its collection of taxes, oversee the provisions of the tax incentive, a supervisory check is, in effect, placed on the activities of the relevant operating departments: the treasury department would have to consult with the operating departments regarding the regulated areas. But it is argued that such supervision belongs in the bureau of the budget, and such duplication would be undesirable.[6]

—Because they constitute a positive incentive, tax incentives may not require excessive enforcement, and enforcement costs. The remission of funds represented by a tax credit coincides with the interest of the subject party, potentially easing enforcement. But if the behavior contingent on the incentive is more costly than the credit involved, as is often the case, the effect of coincidence can disappear. Resultant action may rely on preexisting preferences for action of this kind.

—Because enforcement costs could be relatively less, control could be extended to more parties with the savings; i.e., per capita costs of extension of control could be less.

—If the tax incentive permits adjustments in level of consumption of the incentive reward and variations in contingent behavior, compliance might be maintained under changing environmental conditions.

2.2 DISADVANTAGES OF TAX INCENTIVES

1. *Establishment Factors*

—Funding by tax incentive is often considered in legislatures by finance committees, notably the House Ways and Means and Senate Finance Committees in the U.S. Congress. But these committees are substantively inexpert, unlike the departments or the committees in the subject areas, and could as a result write bad legislation.

—Establishment of a tax incentive, it has been asserted, involves an implicit ownership claim against the citizen income remitted. This has been criticized on the grounds of societal goals involving the "economic independence of citizens" and the maintenance of pluralistic power centers, both of which contribute to a "free society" (Madden and Morris 1971). Establishment can be opposed on these grounds.

—An information cost to determine the likely efficacy of given levels of credit remains.

2. *Change Factors*

—Because they work indirectly, tax incentives (as well as, for example, subsidies) have a lagged effect and consequently may not be effective in crises.

—Because they are probably supported by an intensely concerned recipient group that faces a diffusely concerned public, tax incentives may be difficult to adjust rapidly in crisis.

—In a crisis, the legislative acts necessary to alter a tax incentive may be

[6] *Ibid.*

more difficult to obtain quickly than, for example, administrative adjustments.

—In general, change in the tax incentive may be difficult to obtain where legislative action is required.

—Because a tax incentive rewards special interests, it may be difficult to alter or reduce it because of those interests' opposition.

—Tax incentives do not usually cover the full costs of contingent action. As a result, they may not pay the direct costs of innovation as well as cover the risk premium involved. Thus innovation may not be encouraged as much as with incentive means that do cover costs more fully.

3. *Administration Factors*

—A tax incentive is clearly useless where there is no power to tax.

—The size of the tax incentive is often modest or insufficient, and may not cover the full cost of the activity it is supposed to induce. As a result, it may be ineffective, or induce activity at suboptimal levels.

—The tax incentive may be redundant; the activity it is supposed to induce may have occurred anyway. Thus there may be an unnecessary significant cost due to the intrinsic costs of revenue forgone. But this criticism also applies to subsidies (as well as other incentive means).

—Tax incentives can produce counterproductive or inefficient behavior. For example, they may be specified to encourage construction of end-of-line treatment plants when, in some cases, internal process changes may be more efficient. In general, tax credits are easily structured to support capital expenditures or equipment purchases, and as a result may induce such activity even when it is inefficient.

—Tax incentives are of more utility to high rather than low-income taxpayers, and cannot benefit those who, because their income is low, or because they are tax-exempt for some reason, do not pay taxes. Small businesses, for example, may be relatively hurt by it; and it may tend to help richer firms while letting poorer ones die off. Thus tax incentive systems may often be inequitable, though they sometimes may be recast to improve their equity characteristics.

—Tax incentives reduce revenues, thus increasing tax rates for taxpayers at large; they have intrinsic cost due to the revenue forgone. They may, in particular, put a heavy burden on the federal budget (U.S. Bureau of the Census 1978:265–66; Aaron 1971). Of course, subsidies also place a burden on the budget (Surrey 1970).

—Tax incentives generally pose problems of overall control of government expenditures. They are uncontrollable expenditures, having been authorized by the legislature and subject to the demand level of their recipients. They are generally uncoordinated with other existing administrative programs in substantive content and with direct expenditures in the same and related areas. Of course, they could be coordinated, but, as described elsewhere, are politically "hidden."

—Tax incentives require a cost in administration in processing applications for the tax exemptions, which competes in funds with monitoring and enforcement activities.

—Tax incentives are likely to be administered by the substantively inexpert tax-collection agency, such as the IRS, rather than the departments.

—Tax incentives complicate the tax code, raising the difficulties, and therefore the costs, of tax collection. Because of their frequent inequities, they may damage the integrity of the tax system.

—In the context of environmental problems, tax incentives are unlikely to minimize pollution with efficiency because of their uniform applicability within the locality establishing the tax. Typically, the assimilative capacity of the environment may vary from place to place, and inducing the construction of identical treatment facilities in such different areas may lead to overinvestment or a distortion of desirable efficient investment in treatment. We would expect that, in other contexts structured in the same way, tax incentives could be inefficient.

4. *Enforcement Factors*

—When one includes the costs of the necessary enforcement apparatus to collect taxes and detect cheating, the advantage of incentives that they do not require heavy enforcement, with its associated costs, may be lost. But the incremental cost of yet another tax incentive may still be small. Tax incentives are directive at the "boundary" and could share the directive's disadvantage in this regard. Usually, however, enforcement costs are presented as an advantage.

—An audit of the tax incentive program by the tax collection agency that administers it is more likely to be antagonistic to it than one administered by a substantive department.[7] Thus, tax collection rather than programmatic goals may characterize the enforcement effort and determine the success of the program.

3.0 Effluent Charges

3.1 ADVANTAGES OF EFFLUENT CHARGES

1. *Establishment Factors*

—A charge system may appeal to the public at large because it appears to them that the polluter is paying for the pollution control; under a subsidy arrangement, for example, it appears that the taxpayer is paying. Thus a charge system has the potential of winning wide public support where pollution affects nearly everyone and is caused by only a few. But where the hurt to each member of the public is relatively small, and the impact of the charges on the polluter is relatively great, the public of course experiences difficulty in organizing to contest the strong opposition of the polluters.

[7] See discussion by Robert T. Cole in *Tax Incentives* (1971).

—The indirect mechanism of the charge permits a transition period as the polluter gradually switches to a more efficient pollution control method or methods. This may be contrasted with the potential disruption of a specific standard or even a flat prohibition. Because of the relative impact, polluters facing regulation may sometimes prefer establishment of the charge system. Besides, the possibility of future gains through using the most efficient control method are possible.

—It has been argued that the implementation of effluent charges is harder to delay than that of directives, and so effluent charges are likely to be opposed by polluters for this reason. Under technology standards, firms can claim that the requisite technology is unavailable, operates unreliably, or is simply uneconomical. Thus automobile manufacturers successfully delayed implementation of more restrictive emission standards (L. J. White 1976). But under a charge system, firms have a simple alternative—pay the charge. Furthermore, firms then have a marginal, as against an all-or-nothing alternative. Annual costs to the firm of paying the charge may be substantially less than the capital costs of pollution control equipment, making it harder for firms to appeal symbolically and dramatically to the public or the legislature for assistance. Finally, under standards, the ultimate enforcement tool available to government is threat of closing the facility. But because of the impacts of such closing, the threat is often not a credible one and has, in fact, been exploited by industry in dramatizing the potentially adverse impacts of the regulation. Thus directive regulation linked to pollution control technology or even to pollution levels can provide polluters with more advocacy opportunities—and produce more delay in implementation—than a charge system. Regulation may be postponed indefinitely and, effectively, defeated. (On these points, see L. J. White 1976.)

—An effluent charge system asserts by implication the government's or public's property rights in the environment. This may be held to be intrinsically desirable. A system that implicitly recognized polluter's rights, such as a subsidy, could establish what some would consider an undesirable precedent perhaps difficult to alter. Establishment of a charge system may be supported on this basis.

—Although charges can have high establishment information costs in general, in comparison to the particular directive strategy that seeks to match required control technology with production technology charges may come out ahead. This is because that directive strategy requires extensive information on the firm's and industry's production technology, potential control/abatement methods, and so on. The directive must be able to specify the control technology that will produce the desired effects in the environment (hopefully, at minimum cost). In effect, the directive strategy requires information to make a choice that under a charge system would be left to the regulated party (cf. Anderson et al. 1977). Directive strategies that simply specify preferred environmental end-states (e.g., ambient standards) or effluent qualities (e.g., effluent standards) may have lower information requirements, though at the risk of imposing severe costs on the firm and possibly promoting societal inefficiencies.

2. *Change Factors*

—Effluent charges provide an incentive for research and development for new, cheaper, and more efficient pollution control methods. The polluter who seeks to minimize his costs will seek more efficient ways of controlling pollution, since the charge structure permits him to gain by doing so. It is not clear, however, that incentives will in fact be sufficient to produce meaningful research (see Rose-Ackerman 1977:399–401).

—Rather than being subject to administrative discretion, as with rules or standards, where bargaining, political influence, and decay of agency enthusiasm through its life cycle (see chapter 2) adversely affect regulatory actions, a charge system may be a relatively fixed, stable or continuing incentive.

—A polluter has no incentive to lower pollution more than a standard prescribes (since to lower it further would be costly), but the total charge on effluent under a charge system would be reduced with each reduction in pollution. This provides a continuing effective incentive for reduction. Such a continuing incentive would obtain under a standard only if the polluter wants to discharge more than the standard, and then the incentive would exist only down to the level of the standard. Thus, although charges have been called a "license to pollute," they are far less of a license than a standard.[8]

—In a world of imperfect information, government may overinvest, or invest inaccurately, in treatment facilities or other means of pollution abatement; effluent charges, however, may be adjusted experimentally to reduce pollution discharge, thus being superior under conditions of uncertainty. The charge is merely adjusted until the desired level of pollution reduction occurs. Note that information about the costs to the polluter of increments of reduction, and about the incremental damages to the environment from each unit of pollution, need not be extensive. The charge may be set approximately, and then adjusted, with only the actual, more easily measured, level of pollution observed. This represents an advantage because it may be difficult, costly, and perhaps impossible for the government agency to obtain full information on pollution damages and reduction costs. Also, if the situation changes (e.g., new technology is employed in industrial processes), effluent charges can be adjusted accordingly, but area-wide treatment facilities, for example, would be a sunk cost and hard to change.

But effluent charges are not always superior under the foregoing reasoning: effluent charges serve as an incentive for industry, say, to treat its own waste or change its production process. Changes in charges may need to be followed, however, by potentially expensive changes in treatment facilities at each plant (where treatment would only be selected if

---

[8] Descriptions of the "license to pollute" argument and its counter appear in many places; see, e.g., Thompson (1973:184).

the cost of treatment changes would be below the increment in the cost of charges from not treating or changing).

—An effluent fee schedule is very flexible in response to change; its targets and structure can be varied in many ways, and respond to increases in knowledge.

—It has been claimed that effluent charges can be adjusted relatively quickly; changes are said to require less information and analysis (and so less cost) than other methods (Thompson 1973:183).

—A charge system permits gradual accommodation by those subject to it. This can minimize adverse impacts and insure that the accommodation that does occur is the most efficient.

3. *Administration Factors*

—It is claimed that effluent charges generally entail a lower total cost than alternative strategies. They lead to both an efficient allocation of resources devoted to pollution control, and a least-cost solution for pollution control, where each polluter minimizes his costs (see Baumol and Oates 1975, ch. 10; Ferrar and Horst 1974). Each polluter can adjust his response individually (and most efficiently), taking advantage of the differing cost conditions faced by each. The polluter may, for example: store wastes, change his production process, change the input mix or nature of raw materials, treat the wastes, cut back production, change the mix or nature of his output, or pay the effluent charge (see, e.g., Kneese 1972:136). In the case of uniform effluent charges, more pollution control would tend to occur where marginal costs are less. This situation may be compared to a rule requiring uniform percentage reduction in pollutants, which would be more costly because it ignores variations in control costs (Kneese and Schultze 1975:81).

—Depending on whether the polluter can pass on some of his pollution control costs in the form of higher prices for his goods (the market may not be competitive), a charge system may cause consumption to shift to substitute goods producing less environmental damage. This result, which "prices" the environment, is held desirable because pollution would be reduced overall.

—An effluent charge system yields revenue (rather than depleting the treasury as with subsidies and tax incentives) that could be devoted to environmental projects. The revenue could be used to provide central treatment facilities to improve environmental quality still further.

—The charge system does not bias pollution control toward one means, e.g., end-of-line treatment, as with some types of subsidy. Thus there may not be a large sunk cost all in the same control means (which could later be shown not to be optimal).

—The agency administering the effluent charge program need not estimate the internal reduction costs of firms; it can set the charge experimentally. This saves on information costs during administration of the charge. The experimental method of setting charges is valuable for regulatory purposes because it makes possible the acquisition of information on the costs of pollution control for different levels of pollution reduction (Freeman and Haveman 1972:324).

—Charges are administratively as simple as the income tax system; they would involve self-reporting, subject to systematic audits. Thus administrative cost could be relatively less. A charge system could avoid the delays and dilutions of restriction that can result from negotiation of rules or standards through the administrative process.

—A charge schedule may be constructed in many ways, with many targets, and is therefore flexible in this regard, in addition to being flexible in response to change.

—Redundancy will not be a problem as it would be with some incentive systems where the system has an intrinsic cost. Firms that have already reduced pollution simply ignore the charge.

—Charges respect the value held by some regarding voluntary, noncoercive controls; the fact that choice of pollution control means is left in private hands is felt to have intrinsic value.

—A charge system permits decentralized, individual adaptation; particular and/or local conditions can be respected. This can serve both efficiency and activity-impact-evaluation goals like equity.

—Charges can be viewed as equitable because they place the costs of control on those who cause the pollution, who may ultimately be the consumers of the goods produced.

—Charges may be viewed as equitable by polluters where a uniform charge affects them all at the same time; a permit system subject to negotiation, delays, and nonuniform application may not be so viewed.

4. *Enforcement Factors*

—A charge system permits graduated enforcement, which is an advantage over a rule that when relaxed, perhaps as the result of political influence or negotiation, has no effect.

—A charge system does not rely on the enthusiasm of the enforcers; it is not subject to decay with the "life cycle" of an agency (see chapter 2).

—Effluent charges are self-enforcing to some extent, because of their incentive nature; reduction in pollution corresponds with reduction in charge-costs to the polluter. Thus, they may not require a very costly enforcement apparatus.

—The enforcement experience and expertise with other taxes is useful with effluent charges.

—The structure of effluent charges as a tax leaves less room for bargaining in enforcement, and thus defends against active special interests who may have political influence.

—Charges will be effective even if polluting firms do not maximize profits, as long as they minimize costs. Thus enforcement may occur even where firms seek goals other than profit (e.g., rewarding the firm's managers), so long as they are consistent with cost minimization.

3.2 DISADVANTAGES OF EFFLUENT CHARGES

1. *Establishment Factors*

—An effluent charge system may require substantial information costs to implement, even if an experimental charge-setting approach is adopted.

If the original level of the charge is not approximately correct, there will be potential misallocations of resources on pollution control; investment may be wasted in control techniques inappropriate to the governmentally intended level of pollution reduction. It may be difficult and costly to ascertain or measure internal pollution reduction costs and environmental damage costs. Like some standards, charges require the measurement of effluent; there are similar information requirements on the rate of discharge. Many firms themselves do not know what they discharge. It also may not be possible to separate out the effects of individual polluters; they may combine in a complicated, nonlinear fashion.

—The subject polluters will strongly oppose a charge system since they must pay the cost (or pass it on, making their products less competitive with substitutes). Under a subsidy or tax incentive scheme, of course, the cost is spread diffusely over the taxpayers.

—Some environmentalists effectively put an infinite value on the environment, and oppose a charge scheme because it permits some waste discharge.

—Unlike a rules or legal-orders approach, which symbolically implies eventual complete elimination of pollution through a series of increasingly severe restrictions, a charge system does not, and has been opposed by some environmentalists on these grounds. It has been called, as we noted above, a "license to pollute."

—Some (e.g., the polluters subject to it) may object to the appropriation by the government of property rights over common property resources implied by a charge system and oppose it. Note that the opposition could be either on purely symbolic or ideological grounds, i.e., that the government has no particular rights to these resources, or on economic grounds, i.e, that appropriation means the taking of valuable resources from those with rights to use them.

—In some cases, the costs of pollution are infinite, irreversible, or much greater than the benefits, as with dangerous substances, and so an effluent fee may not be a desirable method, or if set very high may be equivalent to prohibition anyway. Its establishment may be opposed on these grounds. Note that an effluent charge system generally requires divisibility in damages, unlike some other methods, e.g., standards.

—Under an effluent charge scheme in operation, a polluter must pay both for pollution reduction, which may involve waste treatment, and the tax on what it still discharges. The cost imposed by the need to pay the tax, which may be justified as compensation to the public for the damage done, may put marginally surviving industrial firms out of business. This would occur in spite of the fact that the damage done did not warrant this. Rules which under perfect information set pollution reduction levels optimally would not have this added cost feature, and would permit the firms to survive (Rose-Ackerman 1973:310). Firms which would suffer under this reasoning would, of course, oppose establishment of a charge system.

—During its implementation stage, an effluent charge can be especially costly to the subject firm since the firm must both invest in pollution control (whether, for example, in waste treatment or process changes) and pay the charge before the control mechanism goes into effect. This double payment can be a severe blow to marginal firms who must still face, of course, the costs of the system in operation. A "grace" period or lowered charge during implementation has been suggested,[9] but this would probably delay implementation of the charge system or be exploited by marginal subject firms to delay costly pollution control investment. (Cf. Dewees, Everson, and Sims 1975:135–37.)

—Where major polluters are other governments, e.g., municipal waste treatment, it may be difficult to set the charge effectively; subject governments may oppose establishment of the control system. Bargaining between governments can affect the type of system adopted and its effects. The municipality may receive its charge payment back in the form of a subsidy or other intergovernmental transfer. A workable charge system could require establishment of a river-basin-wide authority to administer it. But cooperation and agreement among numerous local (and possibly state) governments could be difficult to obtain. Thus we may expect problems in intergovernmental relations associated with establishment of a charge system.

2. *Change Factors*

—The information necessary to adjust a charge system may be difficult to obtain and therefore costly. There are problems of measurement, quantification, and basic knowledge about impacts and production processes.

—Effluent charges may require seasonal variations to account for changing environmental conditions (e.g., high stream flow with good waste assimilation in the spring) and seasonal changes in industrial production and processes perhaps due to changes in demand. But a permit system, for example, would also be subject to such changes.

—Exercise of the flexibility potential in a charge system could produce an unstable, uncertain environment for the activity of the polluter. In addition to hampering management of the firm's operations, it may prevent the development of a consistent and comprehensive pollution control system by the organization. And frequent changes may provide more opportunity for the intervention of undesirable political influence in the charge-setting process.

—Adjustments in charges under experimental charge-setting, or for other purposes, may be disruptive and costly, since there is generally some sunk cost in specific means of pollution control.

—An effluent charge schedule may require change as individual firms grow and more of them pollute at the level set by the charge, the number of firms in the region grows, and their total effluent grows. Inflation can also dilute its effect. But increases in the charge will be opposed by sub-

[9] These points were called to my attention by Debbie Gross-Sidlow, graduate seminar paper (Autumn 1977).

ject firms and changes will at any rate be difficult due to the mechanism of the political process that would have to be followed, whether legislative, administrative, or both. Of course, other means, such as standards, would also require change and could face similar problems. Over time, new and more efficient pollution control technologies could develop. Under an effluent charge, a firm has a "continuing incentive" to find such new, efficient ways to reduce emissions. This could possibly deal with some of the added pollution from firm and regional growth.

—Because they work indirectly, effluent charges may not be an effective means of control in a crisis. There may be great uncertainty about the effects of a new fee schedule and about the time necessary for it to produce results. In addition, the charges may be difficult to adjust rapidly through the political process.

—If the effect of an effluent charge falls short of societal goals of pollution reduction, it may be politically difficult to raise it. It could require renegotiation of the political compromises or consensus that permitted the establishment of the charge system, and give new opportunities to the charge's opponents to defeat it. Furthermore, the failure to reach goals reflects unfavorably on the administrators of the charge. Because of information difficulties, high uncertainty and consequent "failures" are likely. For this reason, administrators are said to favor more direct controls, such as rules (Baumol and Oates 1975:155).

—Because pollution reduction, including treatment, is likely to become more expensive in the future as pollutants become more complex, an effluent charge will require upward adjustments. But for the reasons given above, these adjustments are likely to be opposed and could prove difficult. Similarly, inflation may make (difficult) increases in the charge necessary.

3. *Administration Factors*

—Where there is perfect information, a standard will work as well as an effluent charge in obtaining some level of pollution reduction at minimum cost. This is because the standard can simply be set at the optimal level of reduction otherwise selected by the charge. Thus the argument for effluent charges generally depends on there being imperfect information. But charges still present problems under uncertainty, as we have noted elsewhere. The point here is that some of the stated advantages for charges disappear under those conditions when information is more complete.

—The cost of making a mistake in setting an effluent charge may be, formally, greater or less than a standard (see Rose-Ackerman 1973). But correction of the error may be more difficult in the case of the charge because the effect of the charge is indirect, with feedback on it delayed. Thus more damage could conceivably be done in the interim, before the undesirable effects of the charge can be known. Of course, feedback with other means of control could also be delayed. Furthermore, it has been argued that the cost of making a mistake under a charge scheme may be large if the benefits from reducing pollution do not vary smoothly, or are discontinuous, with respect to reductions in pollution (Rose-Ackerman 1973).

—An effluent charge increases a polluter's costs, leading to increased prices for his product (assuming he can pass some or all of the cost on to consumers). Societal goals may require, however, that the polluter pay for his own pollution. Or societal goals may seek to protect a certain class of consumers or prevent them from being made relatively worse off.

—Effluent charges may not be effective where the polluting firm is in a noncompetitive market, e.g., a public utility. The firm may be able to pass on the entire cost to the consumer, especially if it is in the position of a monopoly. An inelastic demand for the monopoly's good would facilitate this. In this case the firm may simply elect to pay the charge without reducing pollution at all. Or it may choose an inefficient means of reducing pollution that responds to other goals of the firm. Standards, however, would be effective in the noncompetitive situation.[10] But the passing-on of costs is a process that takes time; in the short run there may be some pressure to comply with the intent of the charge.

—In general, in any market structure, if the demand for the good produced by the polluting firm is relatively inelastic, i.e., relatively independent of the price of the good, it would be easier to pass the cost on to the consumers. Again, the polluting behavior of the firm could then be unaffected by a charge scheme.

—Revenue will be decreasing as firms respond to the effluent tax; thus its advantage as a revenue source is overstated.

—The administrative body or board setting the effluent charge could become revenue oriented and set the tax with revenue rather than societally optimal pollution control in mind.

—Effluent charges would have to be varied to take into account geographical differences. Thus low- and high-pollution-area polluters would under a uniform charge and identical internal-cost conditions reduce by the same amount. But society may judge that the low area was reducing pollution by an unnecessarily large degree. And the assimilative capacity of the air or water sink into which waste is discharged may vary, again indicating possibly excessive pollution control in some areas. This variation in charges could result in an impossibly complicated system, with extremely high information (and possibly administration) costs, as charges could have to be set for each individual firm. Of course, the existence of a variety of types of discharges could add to the difficulty of setting charge schedules for a wide geographical area. It is possible that, under such conditions of complexity, a simple standard, such as the requirement of reduction of a uniform percentage, could prove more efficient. At any rate, rules may more easily differentiate among regulatory targets and situations, allowing for localized variations.

—There is the administrative problem of setting boundaries to the geo-

---

[10] These points were called to my attention by Wilpen Gorr.

graphical region to be subject to charges. This could lead to equity controversies over the inclusion or exclusion of various polluters.

—A charge system generally will not induce a group of polluters to build a joint treatment plant in the optimal place (Rose-Ackerman 1973).

—Because effluent charges are a decentralized approach involving independent decision-making on pollution control means and levels, they do not provide the basis for comprehensive planning. Centrally administered rules or standards would, however, permit such planning.

—There is an administration cost of running an agency to determine such information as environmental damages and costs, pollution reduction costs, and to monitor and inspect the self-reporting charge system, and enforce it.

—An effluent charge system can result in an increase in charges to other polluters, and so an increased overall cost, if one polluter prefers to pay the fees (through error, likely under the uncertainty we have described, or because his industry is noncompetitive) rather than reduce wastes. The increase in charges would be necessary to reduce pollution further among the compliant parties to compensate for the one who refuses.

—It is hard to tell whether an effluent charge system did in fact achieve efficiency, since one would have to measure the internal processes of firms, know their alternatives to paying the charge, and the effects of choosing them.

—Threshold effects may throw off the analysis of the optimal pollution control point. Thus the relationship expressing marginal benefits of pollution reduction as a function of pollution reduction may have several peaks, for example, where a river is good for swimming, fishing, boating, or nothing at all. Near the boundaries of these regions relatively small changes in pollution control costs may have large effects, determining which region is selected by the charge. Thus setting of the charge must be done carefully, and may of course be difficult under the uncertainty we have described (Rose-Ackerman 1973).

—There are also discontinuities in the marginal cost of treatment that may complicate the analysis. Treatment plants, for example, may only come in certain sizes (Rose-Ackerman 1973). Efficiency in treatment could vary greatly by size of treatment plant; it could be very inefficient for each firm to abate or treat its own wastes.

—Effluent charges reflect, after all, an implicit standard or level of pollution control, selected by society. As a standard, it is subject to some of the same criticisms.

4. *Enforcement Factors*

—Monitoring effluent may be difficult and costly. In some cases, technology to monitor, or monitor at low cost, given pollutants does not exist. In this regard, standards specifying treatment methods could be superior.

—A charge system involves, ultimately, coercion, since either charges must be paid or pollution reduced. So its advantage as a voluntary means, respecting goals of self-determination, is overstated. And because enforcement must occur, there are inevitably enforcement costs; some will try to escape paying the charge or reducing pollution, and these must be caught and punished.

—Charges depend on an enforcement system to collect. In some situations, however, workable enforcement systems cannot be established, e.g., when international boundaries must be crossed. It has been suggested that a system of bribes could then substitute (Mäler 1974:10).

—If collusion is prevented but the number of polluters is small, polluters may try to induce other polluters to perform more than their share of pollution reduction (while performing, themselves, less than their share). They could do this by overstating their costs of pollution control, inducing other polluters who rely on this information to overinvest in control. If polluters suspect that cost information is inflated, they may go slow in developing their own facilities for control. This may lead, overall, to delayed or less-than-optimal pollution control (Rose-Ackerman 1973).

—Polluters can collude. They may agree to treat wastes to a level above the optimal, knowing that administrators of the charge will then lower it. The savings from the lowered charge can more than offset their increased pollution reduction costs. A polluter could then cheat on his fellow polluters by lowering his treatment of wastes (i.e., raising polluting discharges). The administrators, of course, are handicapped by lack of accurate information about what level of treatment is in fact optimal (Rose-Ackerman 1973).

4.0 Subsidies

4.1 ADVANTAGES OF SUBSIDIES

1. *Establishment Factors*
   —A subsidy may be relatively easier to establish because of the diffuse impact of its costs; the burden is on all taxpayers rather than one group. Due to the relatively small individual impact, and the well-known difficulty of organizing a large number for collective action (see, e.g., Olson 1965), opposition to the subsidy is likely to be weak.
   —If the subsidy enables the firm to convert the waste into a revenue-producing resource, then the subsidy need not cover the total cost of pollution reduction, e.g., a treatment facility, in order to be effective. This should make establishment of the subsidy easier, since those who will benefit from it under these conditions, will lobby for it.
   —In general, the group benefited by the subsidy will be relatively small and therefore perhaps better able to organize itself to lobby for the subsidy; organization costs as well as "free rider" problems may be less.
2. *Change Factors*
   —Subsidies that are tied directly to pollution reduction rather than structured, indirectly, to support treatment facilities or other capital expenditures, may constitute a continuing incentive to reduce pollution to socie-

tally optimal levels. They are similar to effluent charges in this respect. But in order to be set properly, they require considerable information, as do charges. And a firm could exaggerate the amount of pollutants discharged in order to receive a larger subsidy. It could actually encourage entrance of additional firms into the polluting industry (Thompson 1973:166).

—A subsidy could encourage research and development on more efficient means of pollution control, since the firm could keep the additional profits it gained from the subsidy by using the more efficient means. That is, the amount of the subsidy may then exceed the cost of control.

—The regular review of a subsidy scheme during the appropriations process in a legislature may indicate and generate support for change, should changes be necessary.

—Subsidies that are not tied to specific behaviors, e.g., specific environmental treatment modalities, can allow individualized adaptations and varying accommodation schedules.

—Subsidies may be a more permanent and stable means because they would be defended by an intensely concerned interest against a diffuse one.

—They may also be more permanent and stable because they generally require legislative, rather than administrative, acts to change them.

3. *Administration Factors*

—Subsidies can be directed to specific targets or to a class of targets; they are flexible in this respect.

—Unlike tax incentives, subsidies are easy to include in budget setting, in planning, and in setting priorities for resource allocation.

—Subsidies are not subject to the distortions of tax incentives. They are not regressive; they can benefit people outside the tax system, or who have tax losses, or who are otherwise exempt from taxation. They do not complicate an existing tax code or provide loopholes subject to equity questions. They permit aid to go to firms too small to benefit from tax incentives.

—Subsidies may help organizations that do not have easy access to capital markets.

—Subsidies can respect the value of free choice; if they are not attached to coercively backed regulations, individual parties may freely elect them.

—The distributional effects of a subsidy may be different from an effluent charge, and according to societal goals may be a reason for choosing it. An effluent charge increases a polluter's costs, leading potentially to increased prices and lower demand for the product. At least part of the cost may then be borne by the class of consumers that purchase the product. A subsidy, on the other hand, is paid for by increased taxes or lower governmental expenditure in other areas. Thus costs may be spread more diffusely.

—Responses to subsidies may be decentralized and respect particular and/or local conditions, in the absence of specifications to the contrary attached to them.

—Subsidies may be designed to cushion the effects of other regulatory means; as such cushions, they may be judged desirable according to societal goals regarding amelioration of certain regulatory side effects.

4. *Enforcement Factors*

—The fact that the acts induced by the subsidy may be relatively costless may mean that enforcement costs are less; a subsidy enjoys the advantage of being a positive incentive.

4.2   DISADVANTAGES OF SUBSIDIES

1. *Establishment Factors*

—Even if a subsidy covers the full cost of the desired action (and, as noted below, it usually does not), a firm would be indifferent about electing the specified behavior. Thus establishment requires either additional costs such as more-than-sufficient subsidies or directive enforcement with consequent enforcement costs, or some coincidental preferences held by the firm, e.g., some side benefits for the firm.

—A subsidy, in effect, rewards those firms that have resisted the most; it thus serves as an incentive *not* to comply voluntarily. Subsidies would therefore be sought by such firms.

—A subsidy may encourage a firm to pollute more at the outset than it normally would in order to receive a larger subsidy on which it could make a profit.

—Subsidies are subject to pork-barrel treatment in legislatures. They may as a result tend to serve local/special interests rather than higher level, or more general, interests. They are subject to acquisition by wealthier interests who can afford to lobby effectively for them, and may be considered inequitable for this reason.

—Subsidies must be paid for by new taxes or by transfers from existing expenditures. In the first case, it may be difficult to get a legislature to enact new revenue-producing legislation, especially if it is an election year. In the second case, transfers of funds will be opposed by those administrators and their clients who now receive them.

—The cost of information to select desired behaviors to be made contingent on the subsidy can be high. In the environmental area, much uncertainty can exist as to the most efficient (and, sometimes, the most politically feasible) means of control to support. Information on the initial pollution level may be needed to set the subsidy accurately, and this information could be costly.

2. *Change Factors*

—Because subsidies work indirectly, having a lagged effect, they may not be effective in a crisis. And because their authorization may require a legislative act, they may be politically difficult to adjust rapidly.

—A subsidy could lead to less research and development on pollution-reducing methods, since implementation of such innovative methods could result in elimination of the subsidy. If the subsidy were eliminated, the innovation would no longer be profitable. So if the firm expects surveillance and removal of the subsidy if it is not "required," then it will not make major cost-saving innovations.

—Because a subsidy rewards special interests, it may be difficult to alter or reduce the subsidy because of those interests' opposition.

—The subsidy program will be subject to regular review during the appropriations process in the legislature. This may lead to the putting of substantive curbs or fiscal limits on the program.

—The cost of change in a subsidy-based scheme of regulation could be great, since, in the context of environmental controls, it could involve alterations in physical-treatment facilities built at great cost.

3. *Administration Factors*

—The subsidy often does not cover the full cost of the activity it is supposed to induce. As a result, it may be ineffective, or induce activity at suboptimal levels.

—Subsidies generally do not encourage reduction in waste generation, just increase in treatment. This is because in their most common form they are linked to a particular method—waste treatment. Process or fuel changes, or curtailment of operations, or other means of pollution reduction, may be more efficient but are generally not encouraged by subsidies.

—The treatment plants built from subsidies are often operated poorly. This is because only construction, not efficient operation, is encouraged by the subsidy program. Subsidies must be comprehensive in covering desired behaviors, or the subsidy distributors must feel that uncovered behavior will occur anyway. Efficiency is rarely a criterion in subsidy decisions, though there is no reason why it could not be.

—A subsidy can actually be an incentive to produce wastes if it is greater than the costs of reducing pollution. The polluter will produce more wastes in order to receive more of a subsidy and thus a higher profit. In fact, a subsidy may make marginal or unprofitable firms profitable, and encourage entrance to the polluting industry.

—Subsidies that are tied directly to reduction in pollution, rather than being for treatment or other capital expenditures, may lead the polluter to exaggerate his true discharges and could actually encourage entrance to the polluting industry.

—Because a subsidy induces entry of firms, Baumol and Oates (1975:174) exclaim, "Although a subsidy will tend to reduce the emissions of the *firm*, it is apt to *increase* the emissions of the industry beyond what they would be in the absence of fiscal incentives!" Here it is assumed that the industry is competitive. Furthermore, "the more effective the subsidy program is in inducing the individual firm to reduce its emissions, the larger is the *increase* in total industry emissions that can be expected to result from the subsidy" (Baumol and Oates 1975:184).

—Subsidies have been held to be inequitable on the grounds that they reward the receiver for doing what he has no right to do; it amounts to blackmail. But against this it has been argued, first, that the whole community is really the beneficiary of the subsidy. And, second, it has been noted that conceptions of rights have been changing. It might be unfair, for example, to suddenly disallow the rights of a polluter who has been polluting unmolested for years (Thompson 1973:167–68).

—Additional equity questions include: Why should certain firms, and not others, get government support? Why should the public pay for private waste and disregard of the "public interest," costs that should be borne by product users?

—Subsidies can have high intrinsic costs; the costs of waste treatment facilities built under federal controls have been enormous.

—Subsidies could be essentially redundant; the activity they seek to stimulate might have occurred anyway. Their intrinsic cost could make this a significant consideration.

—Like other incentive means, a subsidy program would depend on polluters for information on waste discharged and methods of reducing it. This may result in nonoptimal levels of subsidy, given pollution reduction goals. At any rate, recipients of subsidies may demand, or end up receiving, a level of subsidy higher than what they would prefer or choose if they controlled the expenditure. This is because the subsidy may be, in effect, a free good, without cost in some cases.

—Subsidies do not cause the costs of pollution in the form of environmental damage to be reflected in the costs of products whose production causes that pollution. Thus consumption of such goods is greater than it ought to be, according to some societal goals.

—To prevent a subsidy from becoming a broad subsidy of a business (rather than support, say, for pollution control), the target of the subsidy must be restrictively, even narrowly, defined, e.g., specific treatment processes for wastes. This inhibits exploration of other alternatives, such as changes in the production process, recycling, changes in consumption, and so on, that may be more efficient. The firm will of course tend to choose that method of control subject to the subsidy rather than any other.

—In practice, subsidies tend to be decentralized in administration and uncoordinated with respect to overall goals, since they may originate in many pieces of legislation and be administered by many offices of government. Of course, there is no reason why such lack of coordination is necessary.

—The administrative apparatus necessary to process and audit applications for subsidies may be costly.

4. *Enforcement Factors*

—Subsidies frequently do not cover the full cost of pollution control, and so sanctions or incentives like rules, taxes, or effluent charges must in this case accompany them. The subsidies by themselves do not provide an incentive to take action to control waste discharges; even if the industry gets paid almost the entire cost of treatment, it is still cheaper to

REGULATION BY INCENTIVE

dump directly in the river or atmosphere. Thus subsidies often require enforcement mechanisms, and thus have enforcement costs.
—Though subsidies require enforcement, the legal weapons used have been judged to be poor and ineffective. Enforcement through the legal process has been slow, with information problems leading to difficulty in establishing convincing legal cases. And the prosecution of pollution cases may be subject to political influence and, in general, to negotiation and compromise (Kneese and Schultze 1975:40–42).

5.0 Summary: Tax Incentives, Effluent Charges, and Subsidies

What do these lists of advantages and disadvantages indicate regarding choice among incentive regulatory means in a given situation? Perhaps outstanding is the fact that choice will involve trade-offs; there is no means that appears universally superior for all cases.

The "hidden" nature of tax incentives, together with the diffusely spread, revenue-forgone nature of their cost, probably makes tax incentives easiest to establish. This perhaps accounts for their widespread use, though they have many disadvantages. Effluent charges and subsidies involve costs that seem more real, and are more likely to be opposed either by those who pay the cost, or by those who would otherwise get or use the benefit (subsidies).

Effluent charges are flexible and relatively easier to adjust under changing conditions, though perhaps not so easily as some adherents claim. To some extent all three (if designed appropriately) can permit gradual accommodation by subject parties. All three means, however, are probably not very effective in crises requiring rapid action.

The situation with administration factors is somewhat more complex. Tax incentives have some convincing disadvantages, e.g., their size is often insufficient to induce the behavior desired; they tend to emphasize certain techniques such as treatment; they are regressive and of no use to those outside the tax system; they reduce revenues; they pose problems of control of government expenditure; and they complicate the tax code. Effluent charges and subsidies have mixed advantages and disadvantages. Charges can be efficient, yield revenue, be flexible in construction, and economize on information costs through experimental setting. But it is difficult to tell whether they have produced efficiency; the revenue they yield is decreasing; they are not effective in a noncompetitive market or where demand is inelastic; they may have high information requirements and costs to counter geographical variations; and they provide no basis for comprehensive planning. Subsidies are flexible and easy to include in planning, but they may be intrinsically costly; they may be ineffective because they often do not cover the full cost of the activity; they can be an incentive to produce waste (or more of whatever undesirable activity is being regulated); they depend on polluters for information; they need to be narrowly defined; and they have some administration cost of processing applications.

The indications are also mixed regarding enforcement factors, but effluent charges have several advantages that could be important in some situations. Charges permit graduated enforcement that could be useful where opposition is strong or the effects of regulation possibly disruptive. In addition, they do not rely so much on the enthusiasm of regulators for enforcement or are as much subject to bargaining as rules or subsidies. The monitoring which is so essential to experimental adjustment of the charges is difficult and costly, and a charge system relies ultimately on coercion, with some unavoidable enforcement costs. Tax incentives can rely on the enforcement experience of the tax system, and their enforcement can, in effect, be partially subsidized by its ready-made enforcement apparatus. Because subsidies often do not cover the full cost of the activity they are supposed to induce, sanctions or other incentives may be necessary with them. And like the enforcement mechanisms necessary with effluent charges and tax incentives, that with subsidies has some cost.

In conclusion, we have presented some advantages and disadvantages of tax incentives, effluent charges, and subsidies as regulatory means. The relative importance of the varying conditions under which the means is to be established and operated may indicate the relative desirability of one means or another. If political feasibility is particularly important, tax incentives may be indicated, for example; if certain kinds of information costs are high and others low, effluent charges may be the means of choice. In the end, the choice is one of trade-offs.

6.0 A Market Alternative: Auctions of Pollution Rights

A regulatory mechanism that has been offered as a substitute for the other means we have discussed earlier and those we will examine in chapter 8 is the auction of property rights or use permits in the resource to be regulated. In the context of environmental regulation, this alternative is often referred to as "pollution rights." Under this mechanism, a pollution authority or local government issues a fixed (and, consequently, scarce) quantity of transferable "rights" to consume the common property resource. This resource may be a river system; the scheme has also been advanced in the context of air pollution. The quantity of rights is fixed so that a certain socially desired level of quality in the resource is not exceeded if all "rights" are exercised. Each "right" can be viewed as a permit to issue or cause a certain amount of pollution, but can be more or less than a permit or license depending on the degree to which the "right" confers the resource as individual property to be consumed.

Parties desiring to use the resource—i.e., parties wishing to pollute—would bid at the auction for these rights. Those to whom the rights would be more valuable would of course bid higher—and thus purchase more. Firms would have the options either of reducing the pollution they emit, through whatever means they chose (presumably that which is most efficient for them), or of purchasing sufficient "rights" to cover their pollution, or of a mixture of both. The individual adaptations that make the effluent charge means so attractive would be operative for "rights" as well. Firms would be able to sell the rights to one another either directly or through a broker. Thus firms would be able to make adjustments to growth and changing technologies, with pollution rights priced as just another scarce resource used in production.

Effluent charges and pollution rights are often bracketed together as means that make use of "market incentives." Both create market-like situations where no market has existed previously. Effluent charges do this by setting prices; quantities "purchased" are then at the discretion of individual firms. Pollution rights, on the other hand, set quantities; i.e., establish the fixed pie of resources and the multiples into which it may be divided. The auction mechanism then disperses these rights among buyers who desire them, and in the process sets their prices. (See, e.g., Rose-Ackerman 1977; Weitzman 1974.)

Although both means make use of individual choice and adaptation, rather than specify individual action, as a directive means would, we prefer not to classify pollution rights as an incentive means. Effluent charges are set and manipulated by an authority in an essentially hierarchical relation; the firm is paying a pollution tax (a price for pollution) much as it would pay other taxes controlled by some authority to elicit certain behavior. Although pollution rights would also be controlled, at least initially (and probably over time, if in a somewhat distant fashion), by some authority, they would create their own institution—their own social choice process, a market in pollution rights. It is not a perfect market operating free from external constraint; after all, the total quantity of rights is artificially (and hierarchically) set, and there must be some provision for enforcement. But resultant allocations of the environmental resource are made through actual market exchanges. No incentive relation is created directly; no rewards are manipulated and no choices made directly more or less attractive. The mechanism of pollution rights is a mixed social choice process, joining hierarchy with market, but is essentially market in character. In contrast, effluent charge systems essentially involve individual adaptations to hierarchically sent incentives.

Pollution rights do, however, share many of the advantages of effluent charges since both permit individual choice and adaptation. Thus, in the discussion below, we shall highlight some of the particular advantages and disadvantages of pollution rights, and not repeat all of the relevant effluent charge arguments (for most of the arguments below, see Rose-Ackerman 1977; also Dales 1968; Rothenberg 1974; Ackerman et. al. 1974; Roberts and Stewart 1976; on auctions as substitutes for other forms of regulation, see the discussion in chapter 5). Auctions in property rights can, of course, be used as a regulatory mechanism outside the environmental context. They could conceivably be used, for example, to ration gasoline (where a market already exists), or to regulate use of congested commuter highways (where one does not).

ADVANTAGES AND DISADVANTAGES OF POLLUTION RIGHTS

1. *Establishment Factors*
   —Some directive permit systems, such as the present system of water pollution regulation, may be readily converted to a pollution rights system by allowing the sale of permits among private parties (Rose-Ackerman 1977). This could be conducive to establishment of a rights system.
   —Establishment of a pollution rights mechanism may be opposed by those who do not wish to concede a "right to pollute" in the environment. The description, and possible status, of the mechanism as "rights" may be perceived as giving symbolic—or actual—support to tolerance of environmental pollution. Because it involves "rights," the mechanism's

problem may be more severe than the similar one affecting effluent charge systems.

—In order to be workable, a pollution rights system may require establishment of a river-basin-wide authority. But cooperation and agreement among the numerous governments likely to be affected could be difficult to obtain. Governments would have to agree to yield local control to the regional authority, and such powers, if only for patronage and local favoritism reasons, could be jealously guarded.

—A pollution rights scheme may be opposed by marginal firms who either could not afford to purchase sufficient rights to continue in business (the waste treatment alternative being even more costly), or could not afford to purchase sufficient rights to keep pace with competitors who can. In addition, the cost of the minimum size of a right that can be purchased could be too large for the very smallest firms, who might then oppose the system.

Finally, firms with a temporary shortage of funds due to business reverses or cash-flow problems may not be able to participate in the initial auction at the level that they would prefer. They may then not be able to recover from their otherwise temporary setback since they would be constrained either to make more costly investments in pollution control equipment, to produce at lower levels of output, or to make other less than optimal changes. They may never be able to earn enough to buy sufficient rights from other firms. And if the holders of the other rights are competitors, they might then not be able to buy those rights at all.

On the other hand, rights auctions may give at least short-term advantages to first-mover firms in a position to purchase more rights. If the area is subject to rapid growth, purchase of rights for later sale could simply be a good investment. Thus strategic considerations regarding individual firm positions can promote opposition to the rights scheme, as well as prevent it from operating as intended.

2. *Change Factors*

—If a charge system is set too low, such that desired levels of environmental quality are not met, it can be difficult to change. "Tuning" the charge is easy only if investment in pollution control technology is either not costly or has not yet been made (based on the lower charge level). Firms that have invested in now-inappropriate technology are likely to resist the change, opposing through the legal process and delaying implementation. If change in the charge level is possible, the pollution authority, in order to get polluters to comply in the first place, may have to promise relative stability in the charge level. This would work against the charge's supposed "tuning" advantage.

But a rights scheme will set the desired environmental quality levels directly (assuming, of course, that knowledge exists to link given amounts of polluting effluent to subsequent water quality) and maintain it as the environment changes. Errors in the rights system might involve predictions of lower-than-actual prices for rights, but the important environmental quality level would already be determined. Of course, if societal preferences for environmental quality prove fickle, so that the rights themselves are altered, a similar problem would ensue.

—If the region to which an effluent charge regime applies is a growing one, upward adjustments in charges may be required to retain water quality levels. As observed above, installation of costly new technologies—and firm resistance and delay—could follow. But under a rights system, growth would simply mean a rise in prices as rights become relatively more scarce.

—As we discussed earlier, charges may not be effective in crises or emergencies; directives would be more immediately successful. The advantages of a directive system can, however, be built into a rights scheme. It has been proposed that two sets of rights be sold—one for normal, and one for emergency conditions. The scarcer emergency rights would tend, of course, to be more expensive in the rights market. Firms that cannot store waste and must continue to discharge it would be constrained to buy both types of rights. By invoking the emergency regime under previously worked out conditions (e.g., drought), the pollution rights authority could enjoy the advantages of directive controls in what is then, in essentials, a mixed system. (Rose-Ackerman 1977)

—Collusion by firms under an effluent charge system can convey false information to the pollution authority regarding the relation between the costs of control and resulting levels of environmental quality. Under a charge scheme, the authority relies on polluter responses to adjust the initial level of the charge. Thus collusion could lead the authority to make inappropriate changes. If collusion occurs under a rights scheme—the prices of rights may be collusively fixed, for example—the price, and revenue to the authority, may be lowered. But the quality level set by the rights would still be reached with efficiency.

—Firms could, however, exploit a rights system by using it as an entry barrier. By purchasing and hoarding rights, existing firms in the market could discourage entry of new firms, who would have to use more expensive methods to deal with waste. Rights schemes might therefore encourage excessive industry concentration, with undesirable antitrust implications, especially where the industry is already concentrated to some extent and can more easily collude on purchase of the rights.

—Although innovation is frequently held to be an advantage of mechanisms like effluent charges and rights that permit and promote individual choice and adaptation, it has been argued that this advantage has been overstated (for the arguments below, see Rose-Ackerman 1977). Municipalities, who are major polluters, are unlikely to do research on new control methods because of budget constraints. Research and development can be costly, and charge and rights schemes may not provide sufficient gains for individual parties to perform it. Many innovations, at any rate, come from suppliers.

Some directive systems may actually perform better in this area. A growing firm under a rights scheme may not be at all constrained to innovate; it can simply use some of its growing resources to buy more rights. But if the same firm is faced with a directed limit on its effluent, it would be under greater pressure to innovate in order to permit continued growth. Finally, if the polluter expects that any control method is likely to be made more stringent in the future, innovation could be encouraged under any method. But if the polluter expects that his demonstration of successful innovation may actually lead the authority to increase the stringency of its controls, the polluter may simply hold back in innovation.

3. *Administration Factors*
—Assuming knowledge of the tie between pollution emission and water quality is perfect, pollution rights set the level of water quality exactly as desired, no matter what the state (and cost) of information is regarding control technologies, production processes, and so on. Firms may try to cheat or evade it, of course, but the mechanism does set the quality level directly. A charge system, however, could "miss" the desired level, perhaps being set too low, and would require subsequent experimental "tuning." Since thresholds of quality (e.g., levels fit for drinking, fishing, swimming, boating) can be very important, and very sensitive to small changes in pollutants, the precision of the rights scheme can be a major administrative advantage.
—A rights scheme can sometimes produce a desirable outcome even if polluters are spread over a relatively large area with varying local conditions. Normally, this could require charges, standards or legal orders—or rights—to be tailored specially, leading to equity problems. A system of zones, rather than individual adjustments, could still suffer from equity problems. And this could encourage the piping of wastes to a cheaper zone for disposal. Piping under a charge system could potentially lead to undesirable concentrations of pollutants in some areas. But piping *could* be possible under a rights scheme, since the total pollution in any zone would be limited.
—In general, desirable localized conditions may not be met for rights schemes covering substantial regions. Thus the individually optimal choices of a few large firms could lead them to pollute heavily, for example, directly opposite the county park, while long stretches of river lined with light industry could remain relatively clean. For the whole region, of course, the quality level would be met. A directive mechanism, on the other hand, through its central planning and coordination, might avoid such undesirable outcomes of individual, uncoordinated choice.
—Where there are economies of scale in treatment, rights schemes may be less desirable than a centrally directed treatment center, perhaps in conjunction with an effluent charge system (see Rose-Ackerman 1977).
—Where prohibitions are necessary, i.e., to remove highly toxic substances, it would seem undesirable to permit any "rights." Thus prohibition through direct regulation would be indicated.
—Although rights may be initially sold by a governmental authority, they could not be relied on as a source of continuing revenue (the private

market would take over). Even if they could provide such revenue, their employment as a revenue source could distort their use in pollution control as the governmental authority made decisions based on maximizing revenue as well as pollution control.

4. *Enforcement Factors*

—Because consummate voluntary compliance is unlikely, both charges and rights will have enforcement costs; inspectors will have to monitor and police compliance. But policing could be more costly under a rights scheme. Firms may be more likely to try to evade it; rights will be scarce and costly, and firms that cannot obtain rights will not have the effluent charge option—and positive incentive—to simply pollute less and/or pay the charge on the remaining pollutant. Furthermore, while inspectors will, under both charges and rights, have to measure the amount of pollutants, penalties will have to be assessed and enforced only under rights. Under charges, the firm would simply be paying a higher total charge. Penalties associated with rights violations may have to be substantial to encourage compliance. Their imposition would be challenged, introducing the procedural due process costs (and delays) of directive systems. Thus some of the enforcement problems of directives may be associated with rights systems.

In conclusion, pollution rights are an intriguing alternative to other regulatory mechanisms. They involve resort to a basically market, rather than hierarchical choice method. Since reliance on hierarchical means in regulation has, historically, not proved satisfactory, serious consideration of alternative social choice processes seems warranted. Pollution rights enjoy many of the advantages of individual choice and adaptation that characterize means like effluent charges. They appear to have significant advantages under changing conditions, and, unlike charges, can be designed to be effective in emergencies. They have a particular advantage in setting and assuring desired levels of quality directly and precisely. On the other hand, they share with directives not only the advantage of efficacy in emergencies, but also the disadvantage of potentially significant enforcement costs.

In the next chapter, we continue our discussion of regulatory means with a closer look at two means of regulation by directive (actually, one is an extreme case) that have been widely relied upon in the past: rules or standards, and public enterprise.

VIII

Regulation by Directive: Rules and Standards, Public Enterprise

LIKE REGULATION by incentive, regulation by directive takes many forms. In this chapter, we shall consider the advantages and disadvantages of two broad means of regulation by directive: administrative rules or standards, and public enterprise.[1] Public enterprise, of course, is not formally a regulatory means according to our definition because the regulator becomes directly involved in the subject activity. But, as we have seen, the degree of interference in the subject activity varies across regulatory means, and we shall look at public enterprise as an extreme case.

1.0 Rules and Standards

Under rules and standards, we shall actually be considering a very broad class of devices—devices that go by such names as rules, regu-

---

[1] Most of the advantages and disadvantages listed in this chapter were compiled, derived, or extended from discussions in the works cited in chapter 7 and from the works listed below. On rules and standards, see especially (in addition to works cited in chapter 7): Ackerman et al. (1974); Blachly and Oatman (1940); Cornell, Noll and Weingast (1976); Davis (1975); Dubnick and Walker (1979); Friendly (1962); Gellhorn (1972); Jaffe (1965); Kaufman (1977); Kelman (1974); Kneese and Schultze (1975); Lyon, Watkins, and Abramson (1939:213–45); Rabinovitz, Pressman, and Rein (1976); Redford (1952); Shapiro (1968). See also Davis (1971); Gifford (1974); Jowell (1975); Krier and Ursin (1977); Rosenbaum (1977); and Surrey (1976). The materials in Anderson et al. (1977) were not completely reviewed for this chapter because the work was received by the author after the chapter was largely complete.

On public enterprise, see especially: Abel (1970); Dahl and Lindblom (1953); Dimock (1949:648–90); Fainsod, Gordon, and Palamountain (1959:734–65); Farris and Sampson (1973:265–306); Friedmann (1970); Gerwig (1961); Glaeser (1957:439–573); Hanson (1959); Key (1959:219–45); Koontz and Gable (1956); Mund (1960:483–503); Musolf (1972); Pegrum (1959:653–79); Seidman (1975b); Shepherd (1965, 1974, 1975); Smead (1969:461–538); United Nations (1954); Wilcox (1966:481–576); Wilcox and Shepherd (1975:515–602). See also DeAlessi (1974, 1975); Dunn (1976); Hall (1949:504–77); Rainey, Backoff and Levine (1976); Rawson (1978); Turvey (1968); and Vernon (1974). Walsh (1978) was received by the author too late for review for this chapter.

lations, standards, permits, prohibition, legal orders, directives, direct regulation, allocation systems, and the regulation/enforcement strategy. These are not all the same by any means, and, in our listing of advantages and disadvantages, we shall occasionally make distinctions regarding a particular device. In general, however, we shall be dealing with the generic type "rule," conceived of as a guide, instruction, or description for behavior or decision that is consistent in pattern and applicable at different points in time (or created at a time previous to its invocation). Although rules generally apply to a broad class, we shall allow as rules instructions that apply to specific cases—e.g., rules for control of pollution at a particular plant—as long as they are consistent in pattern and applicable over time. Rules have been distinguished from orders, where rules are the result of the legislative action of an agency, and orders are the result of judicial or adjudicatory action, i.e., decisions on cases. But their effects are often similar, and we shall treat them together under "rules."

"Rules" and "standards" are terms that are not always used in the same ways in the literature. "Standards" are frequently simple, general criteria which guide the formation or implementation of more specific "rules" or are parts of the rules themselves (cf. Ehrlich and Posner 1974; Jowell 1975:134–39). Sometimes "rules" are viewed as general formalized guides to decision, while "standards" are local or subject specific results of application of rules to a class of localized cases, e.g., local effluent standards derived from regional, state, or federal rules governing their setting. At any rate, whatever their names, criteria called "standards" and "rules" are usually arrayed in some hierarchical fashion, moving down from less to more specificity and less to more conditionality or contingency. We shall not make a consistent distinction between "standards" and "rules" in the subsequent analysis. Unless otherwise indicated, mention of one will be taken to apply to the other as well.

Rules may apply to the activity subject to regulation, or to the process by which the regulation occurs. The former may be called *substantive rules,* and the latter, *procedural rules*. Procedural rules specify, for example, the organization of an administrative agency that regulates, the method of its operation, the manner in which subjects may approach the agency and cases considered by it, and so on (e.g., Gellhorn 1972:122). Substantive rules may extend, give content to, or interpret the capability or power inherent in the delegation to the agency. Rules whose creation follows directly from the grant of power to the agency are "legislative" rules; those which prove necessary but are not determined by the legislative grant of power to the agency are called "interpretative." Interpretative rules may become necessary to interpret the statutory mandate given the agency, though that statutory mandate may say nothing about the making of such rules.[2] In the discussion of advantages and disadvantages, we shall assume for the most part that rules are administratively established, though they obviously must rest on some legislated authority. Changes in rules that go beyond that authority would of course require legislative action, with all of its constraints.

Rules may be employed by regulators in the course of regulatory decision-making, specifying, in effect, whether a given fact or condition should be determinative or relevant. Jaffe (1965:555) divides rules according to this criterion, identifying rules that "isolate a fact as determinative," rules that "provide that a fact is relevant but not conclusive," and rules that specify that a fact is irrelevant, e.g., that some state should be ignored in decision-making. The second case, that of relevance alone, is said to permit the administrators discretion in their decision in the sense of permitting them choice among alternatives (Jaffe 1965:555–56).

Dubnick and Walker (1979; cf. Lyon, Watkins, and Abramson 1939:213–45) distinguish three types of *standards*, based on the task or function each performs:

1. *Comparative standards* are used in assessing how "actions and products" compare to the fixed level or absolute value represented by the standard. An example is egg grading.

2. *Integrating* or *coordinating* standards are used in linking activities. Periods of time used to coordinate work in an assembly-line setting are examples.

3. *Control standards* set levels of quality with respect to which subject parties are policed. These are basically regulating standards in the sense we are using, since they can be used to guide regulatory interferences. An example would be an effluent standard in water pollution control.

To some extent, it seems all standards can be viewed as "comparative," since all are used in comparisons. Furthermore, although we may be interested in egg grading, for example, merely to distinguish egg quality, such a standard can also be "control" or regulatory in character. Eggs may be graded as part of regulatory consumer protec-

---

[2] For conditions under which a court will uphold such rules, see Gellhorn (1972:124–25); Davis (1975:119).

tion. Thus the purposes or uses of given standards can be multiple, even in the same application area.

Rules and standards, as we observed earlier, may be more or less specific. Greater specificity of rules has been held to be desirable by some, such as Henry Friendly, and overly constraining by others (see, e.g., Landis 1938; cf. Jaffe 1954, 1973). Friendly (1962:19–23) offers several reasons for seeking better definition of rules and standards. Ambiguous rules could permit differential treatment of those subject to regulation, raising equity questions. There is a "social value in encouraging the security of transactions" that would be provided by rules whose meaning was well-defined (Friendly 1962:20). Vague rules which do not properly represent the intent of a legislature are undemocratic rules. If rules are unclear, an agency may be more subject to political pressures to decide cases in certain ways, threatening the independence and impartiality of the agency. There are several intra-agency advantages, including the education of the staff that occurs in discussions surrounding the specification of a rule; the reduction in the volume of the agency's cases, which would grow under uncertainty; protection against incompetence on the part of appointed commissioners who would be constrained by specific rules; a decrease in the chance that decisions will be appealed or reversed; and savings in time and expense from not having to treat each case from scratch.

Friendly cautions that an emphasis on making careful and specific rules and standards may not be sufficient. The Interstate Commerce Commission, he notes, where the making of rules and standards has been most developed, has produced economic results from its regulation that have been widely criticized as far from desirable. The lawyers of the ICC, where the judicial model has been most advanced, have, like many lawyers elsewhere, not realized what the impact of their actions have been; they do not realize what is happening as long as the procedure appears good. Thus the need for better definition of rules and standards cannot really be evaluated apart from its effects.

2.0 Public Enterprise

Public enterprise may be viewed as an extreme case of the application of rules, where the rules have been made particular so as to cover all activities, as would the internal directives of an organizational management. The makers of the rules have in effect merged with the management. We have already noted Hurst's observation on the historical trend in regulation toward tighter controls and virtual management in some areas; at any point in time we can, at any rate, observe variations in the directness and completeness of regulatory controls.

Unfortunately there is no generally accepted definition of "public enterprise." This is perhaps due to the diversity of organizations under this general heading, and the fact that at the extremes of variation they may be similar in appearance to ordinary government bureaucracy and to private enterprise. Public enterprises have been described variously as government enterprises that "are financed wholly or in part by the fee or price charged for the good or service" (Koontz and Gable 1956:679), government "economic activities, businesslike in character, for which some direct payment is made" (Fainsod et al. 1959:734), and "those [government] activities that are businesslike in character, involving services that might be provided commercially" (Wilcox 1966:482).

We can, however, identify several factors which tend to reappear in definitions and discussions of public enterprise. A given public enterprise may exhibit some or all of the factors. We may divide them into factors relating to ownership and control, and factors relating to the nature of the activity and its sale:

Ownership and control:
  —There is some degree of public ownership.
  —There is some degree of public control or direct management of the organization.
Nature of activity and its sale:
  —The organization is located in government and engages in the performance of a service or the production of a product similar to that which is, or perhaps could be, performed or produced outside of government, i.e., by private enterprise.
  —The government organization sells a product or service that is also, or perhaps could also be, sold by private enterprise.
  —The government organization is financed at least partly through the sale of a product or service.

There are three generally recognized types of public enterprise, with a fourth type sometimes mentioned.[3] The *government department* form is financed by appropriations rather than through any sale of products or services, is subject to regulations similar to those of regular government departments concerning financial practices, per-

---

[3] For descriptions of these forms, see especially United Nations (1954); and Wilcox (1966).

sonnel (i.e., Civil Service), and the like, and has sovereign immunity and therefore cannot be sued without government consent. The *public corporation* is owned entirely by the state, is financed independently except for capital or losses through borrowing or through revenues from the sale of products or services, is generally not subject to regulations similar to those of regular government departments in such areas as financial practices and personnel, and is a separate legal entity without sovereign immunity and can be sued, enter contracts, and so on. It should be noted that federal acts have put restrictions similar to some of those of the department form on federal public corporations. The *mixed-ownership corporation* or *joint stock company* has stock both owned by government and in private hands. A fourth type is the *operating contract,* in which the government contracts with a private firm to manage an enterprise for it, where the private firm is guaranteed all costs and receives a fee for its efforts. In our listing of advantages and disadvantages, we shall sometimes distinguish the form to which an advantage or disadvantage is most relevant.

Public enterprise can vary in scope, from complete or near monopoly of a field (e.g., Postal Service) to segments of a market where it may or may not be competitive with private firms (e.g., public power authorities like the TVA). And public enterprise occurs on all levels of government, including, at the state level, public authorities like the Port of New York Authority.

Listed below are some advantages and disadvantages of rules and standards, and public enterprise. Because public enterprise is in a sense an extreme case of regulation by directive, including regulation by rules or standards, many of the advantages and disadvantages of rules or standards apply to public enterprise as well. Because the regulator actually performs the activity rather than regulating it at some distance, the implicit comparison in the public enterprise advantages and disadvantages will often be between public performance and regulated private performance, rather than between public performance and some specific regulatory means.

3.0 Advantages and Disadvantages of Rules and Standards

3.1 ADVANTAGES OF RULES AND STANDARDS

1. *Establishment Factors*
   —There is frequently no need for very high initial information costs regarding preferences, internal cost conditions if the subject is a firm, or

other factors, as there may be with some means of regulation by incentive. A rule may set a pollution reduction level directly, for example, with no need either to "tune" the control, or to know the adjustment mechanisms, as with an indirect method like an effluent charge. Of course, if the rule were aimed at which control technology to use, high information costs might be necessary to choose the appropriate control technology for the firm's production technology (see Anderson et al. 1977).

—Rules may be easier to establish because they require administrative, not legislative, enactment, though a legislature may have to authorize them.

—Use of a rule may gain support from certain groups, and may thus be easier to establish, because it may imply, symbolically, intent to remove entirely the undesirable feature subject to regulation. Thus rather than effectively "license" some pollution, as with an effluent charge, a rule may simply prohibit pollution of a certain level. The rule may, further, be part of a program—or in response to an avowed aim—to eliminate pollution. It is also argued, of course, that the rule and the effluent charge are equivalent in their implications.

—A rule of prohibition may gain support on equity grounds and be easier to establish. It might be considered fair to prohibit all from polluting, for example, rather than to allow a few, inequitably chosen, as might be the case under some incentive schemes. In general, rules that apply to all may in many circumstances be considered intrinsically equitable, and thus receive support and be easier to establish.

—Prohibition may gain support where uncertainty makes one unable to measure marginal benefits and costs. In this case, prohibition may be desirable to prevent irreversible damage.

—Where the subject activity is judged wholly undesirable, prohibition may be indicated and gain general support. Thus laws against littering may be easy to pass, though fail in observance and enforcement.

2. *Change Factors*

—Because rules are administratively specified and do not require legislative enactment, they may be easier to change. Legislative enactment could require time-consuming negotiation and compromises that alter the content of the rule, or prevent its alteration.

—Changes in rules may have more direct and rapid effects than changes in incentive means that require indirect, and possibly time-consuming, mechanisms of adjustment. Thus rules may be relatively more effective in crises or emergencies. They can also set desired levels more or less directly and maintain them under change.

3. *Administration Factors*

—Rules can with perfect information produce the same result as incentive methods, such as subsidies and effluent charges, including efficient allocations of resources with respect to preferences. With perfect information on the differing conditions in each firm, or if marginal cost and benefit relationships are the same for all firms and known, rules can set pollution reduction at the optimum level directly.

—Rules can differentiate among possible regulatory targets and provide for localized exemptions or variations. In the same region, one river may be protected as pristine, while another is designated as open sewer (Rothenberg 1974:208–9).

—Rules impose costs on a firm, causing it to alter its operations or raise its prices. At any rate, in the case of pollution control, the firm may, for example, use resources more efficiently or, by raising prices, cause consumption to shift to more environmentally desirable goods.

—An administrative rule system permits coordination in the present and comprehensive planning for the future. This assumes that the (easily) known rules will have the expected consequences. Of course, perfect information on the (harder to know) indirect adjustment mechanisms of incentive means would also permit such coordination and planning. Manipulation of rules is, however, frequently considered easier than manipulation of incentive means that have such indirect adjustment mechanisms.

—Rules permit predictability of regulation. Organizations that interface with the regulatory agency, or with organizations subject to regulation, can better deal with uncertainty. There are intra-agency advantages as well, since rules reduce uncertainty over organizational goals, enabling the agency to act decisively.

—Rules not only direct action; they often also supply information that would be voluntarily adopted if available. For example, administrative rules on the safety of products may supply information on risks—information that would be otherwise difficult to obtain (see, e.g., Kelman 1974; Cornell, Noll, and Weingast 1976).

—A rule of prohibition may have especially low information costs to maintain, because it requires a simple on/off measure. Effluent charges and other forms of rules may require measurements of emissions for effective pollution control.

—Whereas a firm may be tempted to avoid controlling pollutants by paying an effluent charge and passing the cost on to the consumer if it faces a noncompetitive market, it cannot under these conditions escape a rule.

4. *Enforcement Factors*

—Rules can be effective in emergencies when resources for policing are stretched thin because high penalties can be set to compensate for the low chance of catching offenders. The expected value of getting caught (probability times punishment) will then be sufficiently negative to dissuade rational prospective rule breakers. Similarly, rules can be effective whenever metering is insufficient to detect miscreants.

—If a single rule applies to all, enforcement could be made simpler than under an incentive means, where individual adjustments are allowed.

—A permit and daily fine system may be structured to approximate the effects of an effluent fee, and may then enjoy some of the same advantages. The fines may have an effect similar to the effluent tax.

—A rule system can respond accurately to conditions of the moment or recent past if there is no or little delay in gathering information to construct the rule system. The rule system may, however, be subject to lags in meeting changing conditions.

3.2 DISADVANTAGES OF RULES AND STANDARDS

1. *Establishment Factors*

—Industries subject to rules will oppose them because they may impose a cost that will either reduce profit directly, or force a raise in prices which will make their product less competitive and thus also affect profit. In general, rules will not coincide with the interests of the party subject to them, and may have to be coercively backed. Their establishment will therefore be opposed. This is to be contrasted with the situation with incentive means.

—A rule system which attempts to simulate an efficient allocation of resources, such as that under an effluent charge scheme, may produce inequities and be politically infeasible. That is, it may require different rules for each pollution source, simulating the individual adjustments of an effluent charge system.

2. *Change Factors*

—A rule system may require changes as those subject to it change, e.g., firms and their effluent grow. But stricter rules will be opposed by those who must pay for them.

—Rigidly specified and enforced rules and standards could inhibit innovative practices that require flexibility for their adoption. New processes may have break-in periods, for example, in which pollution reduction levels may have to be temporarily exceeded.

—A rules system may be costly to maintain due to the necessity of paying experts to continually set the rules. There is also the cost of interpreting feedback on the effects of rules and the cost of issuing new rules.

—The frequent shortness of deadlines in required observance of rules (e.g., automobile-exhaust standards) could prevent wide-ranging research and development, and ultimately inhibit development of new and more efficient processes or pollution control methods (see Kneese and Schultze 1975).

—Where there is an administrative requirement that a given regulatory method be used, as in pollution control, there is no incentive for the development and introduction of new technology in the area.

—Under conditions such as a regulated monopoly, where costs can be passed on to the consumer by raising prices without threatening the firm's competitive position, rules—including prohibition—provide no incentive, for example, to engage in research and development or to make process changes to reduce cost.

—A rule that requires the use of the best available technology could have perverse effects on innovation. Firms will oppose the development of new, more costly systems, since this would increase the range of what is available, and they would be forced to increase their costs (Kneese and Schultze 1975:63).

—Because rules tend over time to gain legitimacy, i.e., a prescribed status like norms, they may be difficult to change.

—Rules may be inflexible in application, especially if they are applied equally to all. A given rule may not permit individual adjustments necessary under differing circumstances according to efficiency or equity considerations. Uniform rules ignore differences in pollution effects, for example, at given times, and across time, due to the varying assimilative or absorptive capacity of the waste sink, the location of other plants, differing cleanup costs at different locations, and so on. They can therefore lead to inefficient results.

—Rules provide no incentive to lower pollution more than the standard prescribes; under an effluent charge, in comparison, gains in terms of reduced tax would be made possible by each reduction.

—Rule systems may experience problems in adopting to the entrance of new subject parties. Should new firms be required to use the latest pollution control methods while old firms are not? This is a problem of equity.

—Like effluent charges, permit systems could require seasonal variations to account for changing environmental conditions (e.g., high stream flow with good waste assimilation in the spring) and seasonal changes in industrial production and processes, perhaps due to changes in demand.

3. *Administration Factors*

—Rules often do not attack the problem directly, though of course they could be structured to do so. For example, requiring a certain sulfur content of a fuel still allows a wide variation in pollutant release.

—Rules do not produce revenue, as effluent charges do.

—It is difficult, even impossible, and at any rate very costly, to supervise every waste source, make special rules for it, and police it. So rule systems that attempt this are likely to be inefficient and ineffective.

—The imposition of separate rules for each plant could be an efficient solution from the perspective of overall resource allocation but would result in differing pollution control costs. Such a permit system could be seen as inequitable because all are not treated alike.

—The price of goods whose production is subject to rules for pollution control may increase, given certain market conditions, as with effluent charges, as additional costs are imposed by the rules. But because rules may not produce the efficient individual adjustments of an effluent charge system, the added cost, and the consequent price rises, may be higher than under a charge system. The shifting of costs to consumers may then be judged undesirable.

—Rule systems may have high information costs, especially if it is a "point-to-point" system, involving individual rules for each location. The firm may have better information than the administrative agency on the costs, for example, of given waste treatment methods. Thus the rule system may have higher information costs in administration than an effluent charge system in which such decisions are made by the firm.

—An individually set permit or rule system is more likely to be responsive to political pressures than a uniform effluent charge. In the bargaining over setting the permit, special interests may enlist allies inside and out of government and gain concessions. The overall result may be uneven and inequitable.

—If a given waste treatment method is required by a rule, there may be no incentive to utilize it fully and efficiently. Thus requirement of a given regulatory method may not mean that method is employed in a manner satisfying regulatory goals. It has been observed that waste treatment facilities are often operated in an inefficient fashion because of lack of incentive (Kneese and Schultze 1975).

—Rules must be comprehensive in consideration in order to prevent substitution effects that have undesirable impacts in areas not subject to regulation. Thus prohibitions in one area may lead to increased use in another equally or less desirable area. Patchwork regulation to correct unexpected consequences may lead to an inefficient and largely ineffective regulatory system.[4]

—A rule of prohibition may be disruptive both because of its wide-ranging impact and because it may permit no intervening adjustment period, as some incentive mechanisms do.

4. *Enforcement Factors*

—In general, rule systems, because they must be coercively backed, have high enforcement costs, including information, investigation, detection of violations, and prosecution costs.

—Rule systems are subject to administrative discretion. The zeal of a regulatory agency tends to change over time, with the agency "life cycle" (see chapter 2). But as long as it is not crippled by inflation, an effluent charge may remain effective.

—Lags between the issuance of rules cause faulty compliance as conditions change faster than the directives.

—The possible noncoincidence of the rule with the regulated interests means that the regulated party will try to escape if enforcement is lacking or faulty.

—An industry may be so important that severe fines from breach of rules—fines that could lead to shutdown—simply will not be applied. This could imply a bias against smaller industries that would not be protected in this way.

—Individually set rules or orders may be subject to lengthy and expensive court battles. Fighting compliance through the enforcement system may just be cheaper than complying. Each polluter may delay compliance until the regulatory agency marshalls effective sanctions. Note that an effluent charge applies constant pressure to comply (Ackerman et al. 1974:261).

—Individually set rules may lead to an avalanche of cases that overwhelms the regulatory agency. And enforcement in each case may be additionally complicated by the need to observe due process.

—Enforcement of a rule of prohibition may be difficult if there are many

[4] McKie (1970) calls this the "tar-baby effect."

regulated parties and the prohibited practice is widespread and in the interests of those parties.

—The outcome of enforcement where rules are individually set is likely to be political, based on negotiation, with each side getting and giving something.

—Because rules are generally on/off in nature, i.e., are or are not put into effect, they do not permit graduated enforcement (as against sporadic or uneven enforcement). In other words, the restriction cannot be applied at less than full levels to all subjects.

—The enforcement of an individually set permit or rule system is more likely to be responsive to political pressures than a uniform effluent charge. Bargaining may occur in enforcement as well as in setting the permit, and the outcome of such bargaining may favor special interests.

4.0 Advantages and Disadvantages of Public Enterprise

4.1 ADVANTAGES OF PUBLIC ENTERPRISE

1. *Establishment Factors*

—Where the returns are uncertain, the risks of investment too high, the profits too low, or the costs or capital outlay is too great, private provision may not occur. Given an expressed or demanding need, public action, perhaps through public enterprise, may thereby be encouraged.

—The state may desire to perform some task, e.g., a major public works, that cannot be performed by the private sector alone. A mixed-ownership corporation could be created to perform it.

—Where private enterprise has performed poorly or not at all, public provision may be encouraged, given the need. Thus the mixed-ownership corporation, for example, can be a method of rescuing private industry judged socially desirable when that industry is in crisis. Public enterprise can provide services that are not provided or insufficiently provided in quality or quantity by other means. It can be operated at a loss to provide service that would not be provided under private management.

—Public enterprise may escape the possibly distorting effects of special, industry-favoring orientations and relationships that have been alleged to arise in regulation.

—Where private provision is performing poorly or uncertainly, addition of some public provision may provide a "yardstick" for comparison and so may be encouraged. But, of course, if no similar private industries then remain, their possible usefulness as a yardstick to gauge *public* performance is gone.

—Where public provision is held intrinsically desirable, or private provision intrinsically undesirable, or where national public interest goals preclude private ownership (e.g., defense needs), establishment of a public enterprise is encouraged.

—The patronage and pork-barrel opportunities of public enterprise may lead politicians to support its establishment.

—Public enterprise may bring prestige to the state, as with the national airlines of certain countries. This may support establishment of the enterprise.

—Public enterprise can legitimize a control that already exists in fact, or can be a method of getting public support for such control. In either case, establishment may be encouraged.

—Public enterprise may be established incidental to other governmental functions, as when military bases run local utilities, or the government through the Government Printing Office engages in publishing.

2. *Change Factors*

—The autonomy of the public corporation may permit it to maintain a continuity of policy, free from political pressures.

—The lack of a need to check continually with a legislature on appropriations and the lack of possibly interfering legislative oversight may enable the public corporation to take faster action in response to changing conditions.

—A public enterprise may be a method for spurring innovation not provided by private enterprise in the field.

—A public enterprise, as a large special-purpose effort, can be directed at special national or regional developmental problems or goals.

3. *Administration Factors*

—Public enterprise may simplify management if regulation is already extensive, i.e., reduce what is in effect a double layer of management to a single. It may bring economies by consolidating and rationalizing other kinds of existing regulation.

—Public enterprise can alter the products or services it produces to serve national or social public interest goals not served, or insufficiently served, by private enterprise. Services can be performed, for example, at a loss, with the difference met by other public revenue, to benefit or subsidize certain segments of the population such as the poor or the elderly.

—A public enterprise can be a means to insure that internal subsidization is maintained at desired levels. Thus the postal service retains uneconomic service to rural small-town post offices—service that a private firm might terminate or a regulated firm seek to terminate. Regulated firms could conceivably also maintain such services for political or other reasons (see Posner 1971).

—Worker morale and consequently productivity under public enterprise may be better than under private enterprise because the employee could see himself as working for the country as a whole, not just private ownership. But in practice this has not generally been observed.

—Where private enterprise is insufficiently responsive to market controls or controls imposed by regulation, e.g., the natural monopolist who does not minimize costs or provide adequate service, public enterprise may be substituted.

—Government, and therefore public enterprise, has been said to have, in general, a lower cost of capital. Supported by coercion, the government power to tax backs any risks, and leads to lower interest rates on bonds.

—The large scale of government may be able to realize economies of scale not possible under private enterprise. The duplication of competing firms may also be avoided.

—A public enterprise may be a means of allowing expenditures large compared with the ordinary government department; the enterprise may, for example, float bonds to raise additional capital in addition to earning revenue. Thus an enterprise like a public corporation may not have to consider existing tax burdens.

—A public enterprise can make use of government services that a private organization would have to maintain or hire.

—Labor costs and difficulties may be less in some forms of public enterprise, e.g., the public corporation. Except for forms like some public authorities, pay for higher-level managers is generally less; in addition, strikes and labor unrest may be less.

—Because some forms of public enterprise sell goods or services, the possibility exists of government making a profit. This profit could substitute for taxation. Profit has not usually been a purpose served by public enterprise in the United States.

—Public enterprises supported through sale of products or services may be considered equitable because only users, not the ordinary taxpayer, may pay for the products or services.

—Public enterprise may be a source of expertise or a means of training personnel not provided by private enterprise.

—The autonomy of the public corporation protects it from the influence of pressure groups acting through the legislature.

—The autonomy of the public corporation may shield it from exploitation for political considerations, including application of the spoils system. But the department form may not be so isolated, as witnessed by the use of the U.S. Post Office Department over the years.

—The financial autonomy of the public corporation has advantages. The public corporation may not be required to return unexpended funds to the treasury, providing an incentive to earn more, perhaps by reducing cost and increasing efficiency. It also may not have to defend its expenditures to a Bureau of the Budget or legislative committee. This allows managers to plan more freely.

—The public corporation may be free from restrictive government regulations in areas other than financial practices, e.g., personnel (no Civil Service requirement) or purchasing (more freedom to make contracts). This may allow it added flexibility and permit it to compete with private enterprise or attain the efficiency of private enterprise.

—Public enterprises can have lower costs because they may avoid lobbying, legal costs to prepare rate and other service applications to regulatory agencies, some advertising, and taxes. Tax savings should be passed on to consumers, who will then pay increased taxes, to some extent making up the forgone revenue from taxing the enterprise directly.

—A public enterprise may be a means for the state to operate outside of its territory; or it may help cope with conflicting or overlapping jurisdictions by spanning them.

—A public enterprise may enjoy better coordination with other public agencies because the regulatory adversary relationship is missing.

—A public enterprise may be an organizational means that allows concentrated, single-purpose effort, with no diffusion of tasks with competing or conflicting goals, as in the multipurpose government department.

—The operating contract is a means of utilizing privately held technical and managerial skill for public purposes. Thus expertise outside the government may be employed. This allows the government a wider range of activities and a certain flexibility in choosing means to perform them.

4. *Enforcement Factors*

—Public enterprise may substitute for costly regulation, with consequent savings in enforcement.

4.2 DISADVANTAGES OF PUBLIC ENTERPRISE

1. *Establishment Factors*

—If the public enterprise is competitive with existing private enterprise, it is likely to be opposed by those interests.

—Establishment of the public enterprise often requires legislative action, which may be difficult to obtain.

—Public enterprise that has a monopoly or near monopoly may be ideologically undesirable because it reduces consumer choice or removes "free" enterprise. Of course, this applies to any monopoly. But public enterprise may be opposed for this reason.

2. *Change Factors*

—The department form of public enterprise may be subject to a "life cycle" of decay, like other administrative agencies, in which initial enthusiasm is replaced by emphasis on routine. And as the glamour of the agency fades, so may its attractiveness to exceptionally competent personnel.

—Centralized decision-making in the hierarchical department may lead to delays and difficulty in adjusting rapidly to change.

—Incentives to innovate may be difficult to supply in the department form of the public enterprise. National or social public interest goals may replace profit goals, so that the cost minimization that could be achieved through innovation may not be sought. This may not be true, of course, in a for-profit public corporation.

—Legislative controls in the forms of appropriations approval and oversight may retard innovative changes.

3. *Administration Factors*

—It may be difficult to supply effective managerial incentives to efficiency in the public enterprise. The profit goal may be absent or secondary to national or social public interest goals. The public enterprise with a monopoly may not have the spur, or yardstick, of private competition.

—Reimbursement of costs and a fixed fee may remove incentives to efficiency in the operating-contract situation.

—As a result of the absence of adequate managerial incentives, it may be difficult, over time, to attract and keep high-quality personnel in the public enterprise.

—Comparatively low salaries in the higher levels of some, though not all, public enterprises make it difficult to attract especially competent personnel.

—Promotion tends to be based on seniority, rather than merit, in the department form of public enterprise. Although it is better for overall morale, competence at the upper levels is not thereby guaranteed.

—The public enterprise may be restrained by national or social public interest goals from reducing costs in some areas; it may be forbidden, for example, from abandoning unprofitable services.

—The public enterprise may have a tendency to overspend on capital improvements compared to what is desirable from the point of view of efficiency or national or social public interest goals. This is because it may be used as a tool of national policy, e.g., to overcome a depression, or be subject to pork-barrel expenditures to satisfy political pressures or the interests of particular legislators.

—Public enterprises tend to pay too much for their supplies. Private suppliers rarely offer the government special prices. And government buyers are often required to purchase from certain sellers, e.g., "Buy American," or those who do not practice racial discrimination.

—Labor costs may be relatively higher in the department form of public enterprise. The enterprise may be forced to employ more to reduce unemployment, or because of political pressures be forced not to fire workers that they otherwise would. Political patronage could force the discharge of competent, trained employees in favor of the opposite. It must pay the costs of Civil Service and of security investigations. Organized public unions are powerful in some areas. And it may not be as constrained as private enterprises in setting employee wages; deficits can be made up out of the treasury so all costs need not be covered, and the ownership, the public, is an absentee one.

—Civil Service requirements in the department form of public enterprise may inhibit administrative efficiency.

—Public enterprise, especially the department form, may be subject in general to possibly detrimental political influence. Political pressure, for example, may lead to favoritism in contracts with uneconomic results, and pressure groups acting through legislators may be effective.

—The public enterprise that replaces market competition has the problem and cost of setting prices for its output, whereas price setting is, of course, costless in the competitive market. There are inherent costs of administration, involving information and other costs.

—The cost of capital for public enterprises will not vary once it is raised, since the interest rates for bonds are fixed. The cost of stocks issued by private enterprise will be lower, however, under adversity.

—The centralization of a public enterprise may lead to difficulty in adjusting to variations in local conditions it deals with.

—The public enterprise operated at a loss will have to be subsidized by other revenues. This may mean increased burdens on some or all taxpayers. Because of relatively low prices, wasteful overuse of the product or service produced by the public enterprise may result.

—Legislative controls over appropriations make long-range planning difficult for the department form of the public enterprise.

—Default by a public enterprise on its bonds would affect the credit of the relevant government.

—Public enterprise that has a monopoly or near monopoly could be considered intrinsically undesirable because, as monopoly, it constrains free choice.

—The autonomy of a public corporation may be such as to threaten the public's right to supervise its operations through its representatives.

—The public corporation may have coordination problems with other agencies because of its autonomy.

—Under an operating contract, the government has little control over the policies of the public enterprise, because its major sanction, contract termination, can only be used in extreme cases. It would also mean stopping the program until a new contractor could be found or until government could manage the enterprise itself.

4. *Enforcement Factors*

—Although performance of an activity through a public enterprise saves on the cost of the regulation it replaces, it would still be necessary to guard against abuses in the operation of the public enterprise. The consumer of the product or service produced by the public enterprise may not be protected through the controls of regulation or of competition if the enterprise is a monopoly or near monopoly. Regulatory controls to conduct reviews of prices or services may then still be necessary and have a cost.

—Control loss may occur in the large, hierarchical, centralized public enterprise, and attempts at overcoming it may have a cost.

—Policing of a public enterprise through legislative oversight is difficult, since legislators are relatively inexpert.

—The autonomy of the public corporation could promote efficient operation, but it increases distance from elected representatives and causes an accountability problem.

5.0   Contrast with Incentive Means and Conclusion

Rules or standards have establishment advantages in that, unlike some incentive means, there is frequently no need for very high initial information cost; they require administrative not the more difficult legislative action; and in the form of prohibition they can prevent what may be irreversible damage. But rules may be opposed because of the costs they impose; in general, they may not coincide with the interest of the regulated party and so be opposed. Tax incentives and subsidies, on the other hand, are positive incentives that do coincide with the regulated party's interest, and the "hidden" nature of tax incentives may compensate for the potential difficulties of their legislative origin.

Like tax incentives, public enterprise has substantial establishment advantages. It may be instituted when risk is too high, profit too low, or the resources necessary too great for private enterprise. It can provide a yardstick for comparison with private enterprise, and offer the state prestige. But public enterprise may be opposed by private interests with which it is competitive, may be ideologically undesirable and so opposed, and, unlike some rules but like the incentive means, it requires possibly difficult-to-obtain legislative action.

Rules may have a more direct and rapid effect than incentive means, and be more effective in crises or emergencies. They share this advantage with some pollution rights schemes. Also, like rights, they can set the desired level more or less directly and maintain it under change. And changes in rules can require only administrative not legislative action, unlike tax incentives and subsidies. But rigid rules may inhibit innovation; the frequently short, imposed deadlines of rules prevent research and development; a uniformly applied rule may not permit the individual adjustments that are an advantage of effluent charges and pollution rights; there is no incentive for compliance beyond the level of the standard, again unlike effluent charges; and rules may gain legitimacy and thus be hard to change.

The public enterprise may be a means of spurring innovation. Further indications of change factors depend on whether the public enterprise is a public corporation or has department form. The autonomy of the public corporation may permit it to take faster action and exhibit continuity of policy. The department form, however, may be subject to decay in a life cycle characteristic of some administrative agencies, may be unable to adjust to change because of its centralization, and may possess no incentives to innovate.

Directive means in general have the administration advantages of easier coordination and planning, and that of permitting predictability. Public enterprise, in addition, may be a means of simplifying management, eliminating the possibly redundant level of regulation; may be single rather than multipurpose; can permit operation on a large scale and realize any economies of scale; and can perform the activity at a loss. In the case of the public corporation, it may have an autonomy that protects it from politics, provides incentives to its managers, and gives it freedom in administrative practices in such areas as financial operations, personnel, and purchasing. Recall, of course, that public enterprise is not a means of regulation to be compared directly with other means; it is an extreme case that effectively substitutes for regulation. Comparisons are therefore chiefly made implicitly between public enterprise and regulated private enterprise, rather than the means of regulation per se.

Directive means may have relatively higher administration costs, however, and some forms may be more responsive to political pressures (administrative rules; department form). Rules and some varieties of public enterprise do not produce revenue, like tax incentives and subsidies, though perhaps most public enterprises do, as do effluent charges and, at least initially, pollution rights. Rules may have unforeseen consequences as regulated parties make adjustments to them, often by taking new action in unregulated areas. There are a number of administration disadvantages to public enterprise, including lack of incentives for efficiency, because the profit goal may be absent or secondary; possible restraint from reducing costs due to public interest considerations; a tendency to overspending on capital improvements; high labor costs; poor adjustment to local conditions due to centralization; and, if operated at a loss, the requirement of subsidization from tax revenues. If the public enterprise form is highly autonomous, like some public corporations, it may experience coordination problems with other agencies. And legislative controls over appropriations may cause long-range planning problems for the department form of public enterprise.

Directive means in general have greater enforcement problems than incentive means because directives may not coincide with the interests of the regulated party. They do have some advantages; rules may be effective in emergencies (like some pollution rights schemes) or where enforcement resources are thin (because of high penalties), and public enterprise is of course a substitute for costly regulation, including its enforcement system. But if rules are coercively backed, they may have high enforcement costs. A rule system is subject to administrative discretion and decaying enforcement with the life cycle of the agency. Lags between rules cause faulty compliance as conditions change faster than the rules. Rules do not permit graduated enforcement, unlike effluent charges. And if rules are individually set for each party, they may be subject to political negotiation and lengthy litigation. In the case of public enterprise, it is still necessary to guard against abuses, so some monitoring or other regulatory mechanism may be necessary. Autonomy in the case of the public corporation presents accountability problems, and in any large hierarchical organization like the public enterprise there are problems of control loss.

In conclusion, we have presented some advantages and disadvantages of one regulatory means—rules or standards, and an extreme type that may effectively substitute for regulation—public enterprise. The major advantages and disadvantages were then contrasted with those of the incentive means presented in the previous chapter. As we noted earlier, choice among these claims, tendencies, and propositions may depend on specified goals and the conditions of the particular case. At any rate, it will likely consist of trade-offs. This concludes our discussion of general regulatory means.

IX

Deregulation as a Process of Organizational Reduction

UNLIKE OLD SOLDIERS, regulatory agencies seem not only never to die, but never to fade away. In this, they are not unlike public organizations in general. Herbert Kaufman (1976:34) found that of a sample of 175 federal organizations in 1923, 85 percent were still around in 1973. The average rate seemed to be below that of business failures (Kaufman 1976:54). Public organizations are not only persistent; they are also prolific. Enough new units appeared over time in Kaufman's study so that the median age (twenty-seven years) was the same at the end of the period (on growth of government see also, e.g., Freeman 1975). Between 1970 and 1975 the number of major "economic" regulatory agencies increased by 25 percent, and the number of major "social" regulatory agencies, by 42 percent (Lilley and Miller 1977).

In 1938, James Landis wrote that "efficiency in the processes of governmental regulation is best served by the creation of more rather than less agencies" (Landis 1938:24). Furthermore, "the existence of a number of specialized administrative agencies need not disturb us. Instead, if appropriate coordination of their policies can be effected, number affords assurance of expertness in the performance of duties and results in a desirable focusing of responsibility" (Landis 1938:30).

It certainly appears as if Landis's dictum has been followed, at least as to number if not effects. As we have noted several times in this work, the history of regulation is littered with critical reform proposals. In chapters 2 and 3 several models of how regulation ends up serving the interests of the regulated parties were presented. Many regulatory agencies at all levels of government have been charged with having either undesirable or no impacts. What accounts for the

persistence of regulatory agencies that by some goals seem to perform poorly? How can we understand the processes of regulatory
ending (or nonending)?

Thus the logic of this work has come full circle. We began by considering the concept of regulation and regulatory creation and evolution. We shall begin below by considering the concept of *deregulation*. In chapters 4 and 5 we examined the rationales for regulation
and then contrasted alternative means of regulation in chapters 6
through 8 (on the rationale for deregulation, see, e.g., Sichel 1976;
Martin and Schwartz 1977). We wished to begin building a capability
for regulatory design. Our knowledge—and the knowledge of those
who designed existing agencies—is, and was, rudimentary and lacking a systematic basis. At any rate, given uncertainty and the complexity of societal operation and change, organizational "failures"
are hardly surprising. We should then also seek to begin building a
capability to understand and perhaps design regulatory endings.

Of course, "failure" may lie in the eye (and objective function) of
the beholder. Industries who enjoy protective regulation may deem
that regulation successful indeed. Furthermore, we make no a priori
normative assertion regarding the general desirability of regulation.
With given goals and a knowledge of alternatives, judgments of desirability must be made for individual cases. The limits on public action may be such that we must sometimes, in the light of alternative
possibilities, grow tolerant of the motes that seem inevitably to float
in one's eyes as public beholder (see, e.g., Mitnick 1975b).

One research approach for analyzing the persistence of regulatory
agencies involves examining the strategies that participants, e.g., re-
formers, agency personnel, regulated industry, might follow in cases
of (potential) deregulation. Deregulation can thus be viewed as a *process* of organizational reduction, i.e., as a special case of more general reduction or decline processes in organizations. Because the
study of organizational or programmatic termination is relatively recent and rare in the literature, and the study of processes of decline,
reduction, or termination perhaps rarer still, much of the analysis
may also inform more general studies of decline or termination.

Before discussing the *processes* of deregulation, we consider the
concept of "deregulation"—a concept that has been used in various
ways in the literature. Arguments regarding regulation, environmental control, and the collective action dilemma are then reviewed.
These help identify the parties seeking deregulation and aid consider-

ation of the strategies adopted by parties in deregulatory controversy. We continue by considering some types of support loss that can affect environmental control and some reasons for such loss. Next, we describe several characteristic forms of deregulation. Finally, the emphasis on process leads to a discussion of the tactics and strategies likely to be employed by agencies and by the regulated parties.

1.0 The Concept of Deregulation

Regulation in the most general sense (see chapter 1) may be considered the intentional restriction of a subject's choice of activity by an entity not directly involved in performance of the activity. Consequently, a broad definition of *deregulation* may be simply the removal of such a choice restriction.

The concept of deregulation has been given many meanings. Deregulation has been defined with respect to: 1) the goal of the removal; 2) the nature of the activity which is deregulated; 3) the thing which is actually removed; and 4) factors affecting changes in response to, or compliance with, the regulation.

Herman (1976), for example, distinguishes deregulation according to the goal of the removal. He contrasts deregulation as the removal of government obstacles to profit making with deregulation as removal of governmental and other obstacles to price competition. In the first category, he is talking about regulations pertaining to the "social responsibility of business," e.g., pollution control, affirmative action, health and safety standards. The second category deals with regulations that protect monopolies, cartels, franchises, and the like, and that therefore interfere with competition. A related usage of the term takes deregulation as implicitly meaning restoration to market control.

A second basic distinction relates to the nature of the activity being regulated. Thus "deregulation" is here often taken to mean implicitly the removal of governmental restrictions on *economic* activity. Restrictions on social behavior, for example, are then ignored or treated under some other classification.

The third basic distinction, deregulation according to the thing being removed, has many possible categories. "Deregulation" can be used to refer to (among other meanings) removing a regulatory organization or agency, removing a program, or removing specific regulations (without necessarily ending a program involving regulatory control). For the most part, this chapter is concerned with regulation by administrative agency.

Finally, the fourth basic distinction—deregulation defined with respect to factors affecting changes in the response of the regulated party to the regulation—includes reducing the "effectiveness" of, or expected compliance to, a program, whether by formal or informal means. This can involve, for example, manipulating the coerciveness with which a regulatory program is enforced.

If deregulation is conceptualized in the broad sense of removal of choice restriction (which will be our selection here), the choice area must be identified carefully (and, probably, who cares about the choice) in order to study cases of deregulation. Similarly, if deregulation is considered in the context of reducing a program's effectiveness or the compliance expected under it, we must consider with respect to which and whose goals "effectiveness" is determined, and with respect to which and whose preferences compliance expectations are established.

2.0   Regulatory Organizations and Environmental Control

Perhaps a major factor in the persistence of regulatory organizations is their ability to manage their environment. In chapter 3, we argued that such factors as coercive backing, legitimacy, size, and so on contributed to the ability of public organizations (including regulatory ones) to manage their environment. But such organizations also must face such restrictions on program implementation as reliance on external constituencies, the central allocation process through the legislature, legislative and public oversight, and so on. Thus, public (including regulatory) organizations may manage their environments most effectively in the areas of insuring survival and persistence of the organization, and realization of the goals of organizational members through it, rather than in achieving given programmatic or formal organizational goals.

A major factor in the deregulation process will therefore be the power of regulatory agencies to defend themselves through controlling their environment. Recall that, in the area of economic regulation, agencies often have the ability to structure their environment through such regulations as entry restrictions and merger controls, can reward and punish subject firms through various services, the impact of regulation, and its penalties, and can absorb uncertainty in the environments of regulated parties by guaranteeing the stability and maintenance of exchange relationships.

Private parties can seek regulation in order to use the agency's environmental control capabilities. These parties may be facing "collective action dilemmas" in which organized action fails to develop or to maintain itself because parties in the group can find it in their self-interest to be "free riders" on the efforts or contributions of others in the group. As a result, group action, which is necessary to achieve the common goal, either does not form or disintegrates.

The (to be) regulated parties or other clients of the regulation (e.g., consumers) can then be viewed as seeking the creation of regulatory bodies as *agents* administering collective agreements that resolve their collective action dilemmas and thereby manage their environments. The governmentally administered collective agreements replace, for example, private ones that failed to prevent cutthroat competition among firms. Alternatively, consumers unable to collectively supply information on product quality or consumption risk, perhaps due to free-rider effects, obtain the governmental agent. In effect, they agree to be collectively coerced through taxation to support supply of the information. Or they may arrange to have the agent coerce a third party into supplying it (e.g., drug firms compelled to pay the costs of research on new drugs). It follows that if the regulatory agency has been established to mediate the environments of the regulated parties or other clients, it may, through the same powers, control its own environment to some extent (see chapter 3 citations).

We can now identify the kinds of actors who are likely to consistently propose or oppose deregulation. In general, those who may benefit from breach of the collective agreement (and removal of the collective coercion) may obviously seek deregulation. Those who, as third parties, are coerced by the governmental agent will seek deregulation. Potential free riders who expect to be able to shift the cost of provision of the good or service to others may seek deregulation. On the other hand, those parties who benefit from the collective agreement, and who may be less able to exploit the absence of the collective agreement (or less able to supply by themselves the good or service that was previously subject to collective provision), may oppose the deregulation.

In particular, industries who may have secured regulation as a means of managing their environments may be expected to oppose deregulation; those who have, in turn, been coerced by the governmental agent to pay part of the cost for the collectivity (e.g., pay costs of researching safety) will support deregulation. Firms which may be in a better position than others in the market to capitalize on an easing of restrictions may support deregulation (or at least oppose it much less strongly). For example, an airline whose existing, regulated route system, resources, and operations structure would give it a chance to capture lucrative market shares on new routes made available by removal of route restrictions may support such deregulation. Weaker airlines would oppose it.

Consumers exploited by the industry's success in managing its environment may support deregulation, though there is some evidence that the collective agreement secured by industry for itself may have some benefits for consumers as well (see chapter 3). Consumers whose own collective action dilemma is solved through governmental agency may oppose deregulation.

The bureaucrats who administer the existing regulation, however, will probably almost always oppose deregulation. They are the beneficiaries of the resolution of collective action dilemmas through governmental action. Attainment of such self-interest goals as maintaining and/or increasing salary and status may rely on survival (and, if possible, expansion) of the regulatory organization. And, of course, survival and expansion could serve any motives of service to a given program, to the organization, or to society as a whole. Regulators may simply gain satisfaction from the job of regulating or wish to retain or increase their convenience in performing that job. Regulators may structure the regulation they administer, i.e., manage their environment, to serve their own interests, as well as play an active role in resisting deregulation (see chapter 3).

3.0 Support and Environmental Control

A regulatory agency's control of its environment may be affected by loss of support for the regulation (cf. Huntington 1952; Rourke 1976:42–80). Such losses can affect the factors discussed earlier that contribute to environmental control capabilities. Consider, for example, several types of loss of support that may be suffered by such an agency.

1. The agency may simply lose resources that may have contributed to the regulatory function. This may lessen the agency's capability to influence or manage its environment. These resources include funding, expertise as embodied in key staff, physical facilities, and so on. If success in environmental control depends on the costly monitoring and policing of other organizations, for example, lack of funds and trained personnel can lead to less control. The agency with fewer resources may be less able to implement its powers to structure its environment, less able to reward or punish the regulated industry and guarantee those rewards or punishments, and less able to provide stability and reduce uncertainty in that environment.

2. The agency may lose what could be called coordinative/linkage support. The agency's actions may be interdependent with, or complementary to, those of other agencies, so that a failure to act by such a linked agency may have the effect of a loss of support for the given agency's action. For example, antitrust regulation may be complementary to regulation of certain trade practices; firms in certain situations could conceivably get around trade practice regulation through collusive activities in the absence of antitrust enforcement. Regulatory agencies that depend on Department of Justice prosecutors may fail in managing their environment if Justice is unsympathetic to their case (cf. Horowitz 1977).

3. The agency may lose political support from elected politicians, appointed officials, and/or legislators. This may hinder implementation of regulatory policies and even threaten their existence. Regulators subject to reappointment value such support and may curtail or compromise regulatory activity in order to maintain it.

4. The agency may lose public support. Such support loss may be manifested in formal interventions in agency proceedings by interested parties, including public interest groups and industry associations; letters to legislators and consequent oversight hearings, with the threat of loss of political support as well; lack of compliance with regulatory directives; and so on.

Possible causes for loss of support are, of course, large in number. Consider, however, some reasons for political and/or public support loss. These can be related to the regulatory function expected of the agency by the unhappy party who withholds support:

1. The job (the job *expected* by the group in question) is done not at all. Paul MacAvoy has written what is essentially a book review of the Annual Report (Volume 42) of the Federal Power Commission

for 1969. He concluded that "there would seem to have been very little substance to the more than 240 certificate, license, and stock issuance cases reported in 1969" (MacAvoy 1971:394). Those who expect certain types of activity from the FPC might be expected to withhold support if they come to share Professor MacAvoy's opinion. Of course, environmental management aside, the regulated industry might sometimes prefer actions of little substance (and give support to regulation with this character).

2. The job is done poorly. Criticisms of the performance of regulatory agencies have a long history, stretching in the last forty years from the Brownlow Committee, through the Hoover Commissions, to the Landis report, the Ash Council, and recent reform studies. James Landis, for example, in his report to President-elect John Kennedy in 1960, called the Federal Power Commission of that period "the outstanding example in the federal government of the breakdown of the administrative process. The complexity of its problems is no answer to its more than patent failures" (Landis 1960:54).

With respect to the interests of those judging it, the performance of the FPC (like that of many other regulatory agencies) has thus been held to be at various times poor or simply lacking in substance. Waves of criticism of regulatory performance have historically been followed by at least some structural tinkering. Loss in political and public support for the regulatory organization in its present form as a consequence of the criticism may contribute to such changes.

3. The job is done too well. An example of this may be enforcement of the Delaney clause by the Food and Drug Administration in the saccharin controversy. That clause prohibited approval of any food additive for safety that "is found to induce cancer when ingested by man or animal, or . . . if found, after tests which are appropriate for the evaluation of the safety of food additives, to induce cancer in man or animal" (Link 1977:539). Critics charged, among other things, that the wording and interpretation of the Delaney clause was too rigid; few people ingested the human-equivalent dosage administered in the rat studies on which the proposed ban was based, e.g., eight hundred cans of diet soda per day (Link 1977). Another example is the enforcement of the Endangered Species Act of 1973. The U.S. Court of Appeals for the Sixth Circuit halted a nearly completed TVA dam project in January 1977 due to danger to the habitat of the snail darter, a minnow. The Endangered Species Act had received wide support when passed in 1973. That consensus

evaporated as implementation of the Act by the Department of Interior greatly expanded the list of species, from 109 to 172, setting the stage for traditional conflicts between environmentalists and advocates of regional development projects (Wagner 1977). Thus loss of political and public support as a result of effective implementation may lead to new legislation weakening the existing laws—or to *deregulation*.

These reasons for loss of support deal essentially with questions of performance. The success (or simply lack of notable and/or extensive failure) in efforts in government intervention since the Depression has been offered as one reason for the substantial expansion in regulation (Leone 1977). Demonstrated "failures," whether in massive "Great Society" programs or in the performance of regulation, may have then contributed to the loss of support that can lead to deregulation.

Similarly, other factors that may have contributed to the expansion of regulation may have changed, contributing to deregulation. Rising affluence may have made pursuit of other goals, such as those now represented by social regulation, affordable. Scientific advances contributed to an awareness of environmental harms, e.g., certain food additives, pesticides, workplace contaminants, that were not perceived previously. And government and business had had common interests in supporting economic development; we have already considered, for example, the promotional character of regulation such as that which first made its appearance in the Transportation Act of 1920. (On these points, see Leone 1977.)

But the rising costs of regulation have collided with incomes that may have become stationary under inflation; scientific advances have been sufficient to identify many potential dangers but not able to establish exact effects and levels of danger (e.g., saccharin); and the common interests of government and business in economic development have diverged over the costliness of some of the social regulation. A fall in support for regulation may have therefore followed these changes.

There are many other factors that could contribute to fall in support for regulation. Regulation may be poorly designed; knowledge to design efficient and effective regulation may simply be lacking. Conflicts among regulatory programs administered in different parts of government can affect support. Alternatives to existing methods of regulation, or better methods of regulation, may receive increased attention (e.g., market or incentive solutions). Some regulatory programs may experience poor implementation or administration; these may be sufficient to lead to loss in support even if the programs are designed well in principle.

Expansion in social regulation may extend the undesirable impacts of such regulation to more (or most) people. Some regulatory programs may impose very high costs on certain parties, perhaps inequitably compared with others. The costs may mean difficulty in compliance for affected parties, and/or undesirable impacts that may not be less than societal benefits. Societal benefits are, of course, rarely compared to costs, even in those few cases where such a calculation can be reliably made.

The level of trust in government may affect attitudes of support for regulation as part of government; the era that follows a Watergate may see a fall in support for any government activity—or official. Highly visible regulation may be blamed for economic ills, e.g., inflation, stemming mostly from other, perhaps more subtle, sources. And basic values, such as free choice or individual liberties, can oppose imposition of social controls through government regulation.

Thus, although regulatory agencies may often be relatively better able than many other organizations to manage their environments, and could survive for longer periods as a result, losses in support in any or all of a number of areas, and for any or all of a number of reasons, can leave them vulnerable to change. That change could even include deregulation.

4.0 Forms of Deregulation

Both formal (and frequently planned) structural forms and informal (and/or evolutionary) forms of deregulation may be distinguished. Informal forms include: 1) life cycle effects, and 2) non- or selective enforcement. Assuming an organizational administration of the regulation, four types of relatively formal methods for deregulation may be identified: 1) catastrophic ending, 2) guided/unguided wind-down, 3) stripping, and 4) disintegration with transfer of programs. These types are not limited to the deregulation case; they may characterize as well other instances of organizational reduction. Also, they are not exclusive in operation; any given case of deregulation (or organizational reduction, for that matter) may evidence any or all of these forms.

4.1 INFORMAL DEREGULATION

4.1.1 Deregulation and the "Life Cycle" of Regulatory Agencies

Life cycle theories of agency evolution typically assume that agencies evolve from active and flexible defenders of consumer or public interests (the *formal* goals of the regulation) through various stages to a senescence in which procedures are rigidified and the agency passively serves the interests of the industry subject to regulation (Bernstein 1955; see chapter 2). This is in the context of economic regulation, of course. If these theories are assumed correct, then with respect to the *formal* goals of regulatory establishment (e.g., certain alleged public interest goals), deregulation tends to occur "naturally" over the life cycle: regulation that serves the public interest goals gradually disappears. If, on the other hand, industry protection is the real goal behind most cases of regulatory establishment (see chapter 3), then deregulation with respect to the formally stated public interest goals was there all along.

With respect to the interests of the regulated industry, of course, the situation is different. Over time, favorable regulation controlling the environment of the industry (and the agency) will increase. The industry may in effect shift many of its collective management problems to the agency, which will respond with protective regulation. Thus, with respect to industry interests, there is a trend away from the initial deregulated state as the industry obtains better and better management of its environment, and increased regulation.

At any rate, due to life cycle effects, it may be emphasized that the agency may have already performed the deregulation task *in effect,* with respect to the *formal* goals of regulation.

Thus, as noted above, one should choose whose interest, out of the vast range of arguably "public" interests, one wishes to protect before considering deregulation. It may be that the formally stated reasons for regulation are now considered undesirable or would not have net beneficial effects if enforced. And we should therefore deregulate. But perhaps because of the costs of changing (e.g., political, real economic dislocation) or perhaps because the present situation of whose interests are served (in actuality, not formalistically) is held desirable, maybe the best thing would be to do nothing. Opponents of deregulation of the functions of the Interstate Commerce Commission have claimed that the changeover would have huge dislocation costs. Perhaps full information on the costs and benefits of deregulation and their distribution would indicate that it does not pay to do away with even a poorly performing regulatory agency, as the ICC has been characterized by its critics. One would keep the regulation and/or regulatory agency even if its actions are basically ritualistic with respect to the formal public interest goals it is supposed to serve.

4.1.2   Deregulation vs. Nonenforcement

Sometimes, due to the costs associated with altering regulatory mechanisms, nonenforcement may be a better alternative than deregulation. Nonenforcement, after all, leaves the regulation formally in place should it be needed, for example, in a future crisis or in response to temporary needs. Of course, nonenforcement may have questionable legality and may raise equity problems of equal treatment before the law.

A form of deregulation through nonenforcement can occur if a regulatory unit's budgetary or other support is cut, so that the unit is simply unable to enforce the regulation (cf. Jaffe 1954:1118–19). Such a tactic could successfully elude the difficulties of getting deregulation through the legislative process. Selective cuts in support, with consequently selective nonenforcement, or shift in enforcement priority, can therefore be a way to control regulatory performance and, possibly, to avoid major attacks from the regulation's supportive clientele.

The utility of nonenforcement is evident in the following illustration. Graft in the building industry in New York has been said to be commonplace; nearly two-thirds of the construction inspectors in the Manhattan Buildings Department were indicted in 1975. Builders allegedly bribe the inspectors to overlook violations of an extraordinarily complex building code and to expedite approval of projects. Loss of time, of course, means idle construction crews, and loss of money. One partial solution would simply be a policy of nonenforcement of many of the lesser code restrictions; police have in fact been directed to cease enforcing construction-site laws unless danger or interference with traffic exists (Darnton 1975). Another solution, of course, would simply be deregulation of much of the building code. This, however, would not permit action in circumstances in which the public is inconvenienced or threatened.

4.2 FORMAL DEREGULATION

4.2.1 Catastrophic Ending

In this form, the program or agency ceases on a certain date without appreciable wind-down, i.e., catastrophically. Not often proposed in the extreme form because of the sometimes catastrophic effects that may result, it has, however, been said to be not uncommon (cf. Bardach 1976). Termination without wind-down could create a large number of unemployed at once, who may not be able to find substitute employment quickly. They may even be in partial competition with one another for jobs. Organizations or units in the program's or agency's environment who are dependent on it in some way must suddenly be able to do without the program or agency. This includes parties who depend on the regulation to control their environments, providing stability and reducing uncertainty.

Catastrophic ending need not, of course, be catastrophic in effect as well as in form. Knowledge of the termination is likely to precede its actual occurrence, so that adjustment or cutback planning among organizational members and environmental parties can occur. Organizational members who know of the event in advance, however, may lack incentives to continue high performance and, in fact, may experience low work demands as environmental units who know of the coming event create substitute relations elsewhere. The ending of regulation administered as a supplement to other more primary regulatory duties (e.g., administration of the so-called Blue Laws by the police) may cause few administrative headaches, though the external impacts may still be considerable. Major programs whose termination is widely supported can provide fewer problems of this type, because of the possible willingness of supporters of the deregulation to compensate others for any dislocation, or to suffer short-term losses themselves, in order to reap considerable future benefits from the change.

Proposals for sunset legislation may feature aspects of catastrophic ending, though usually a phaseout period of perhaps a year is permitted.[1] If the time for phase out is relatively long, e.g., a year or more, we may have in effect the next type: wind-down.

---

[1] See, e.g., Kopel (1976); Gardner (1976); Shimberg (1976a). An early proposal for sunset as a major feature of design of a regulatory agency appeared in Mitnick and Weiss (1970, 1974). For arguments for and against sunset legislation, see Behn (1977).

4.2.2 Wind-Down: Guided/Unguided

In the wind-down form, all functions are at least nominally retained, but at continually lower levels of activity. The wind-down may be guided according to some established plan, or unguided, perhaps being managed in response to external demands for service that are decreasing, and that cannot be perfectly predicted.

Wind-down may escape some of the "catastrophic" effects mentioned above, potentially permitting gradual adjustments both within and without the organization. But such factors as lack of worker commitment; exits of key, able personnel who may find new jobs more quickly than other employees; economies of scale and reduction below threshold sizes needed to operate subunits efficiently; and inability to train remaining specialists with differing abilities to perform the jobs of departing specialists as well as they did, in a relatively short time (and without expectation of continued work by the substitutes in the added specialty area), may lead to seriously degraded performance. Organizations in the agency's environment dependent on it may consequently suffer.

A major problem is to provide incentives to key, able personnel to remain with the organization. Managers of a wind-down in a private firm typically face an agonizing notification problem, in which their perceived obligation to workers to give them time to find new jobs conflicts with factors such as those we have listed (see, e.g., Slote 1969). If deregulation is legislatively authorized, however, the notification decision is taken out of the hands of higher agency or executive branch officials. Agency workers will of course follow legislative action in this area closely. Note that advance notice of endings to be carried out by any of the other means may lead to some of the same adverse effects. These effects would only be exacerbated under wind-down.

4.2.3 Stripping

In this form, functions, activities, and/or subprograms are dropped, one by one. Remaining subprograms or activities may continue at the same effort level, or be reduced or removed at a later date by this or other means. The subprograms or activities dropped may be subject to catastrophic or wind-down endings, with the effects discussed above. Some of the proposals to change airline regulation, e.g., drop entry restrictions, might fall into this category.

4.2.4   Disintegration with Transfer of Programs

In this form, the program or agency is disintegrated, with parts transferred to a new or different agency, or recombined into a new form with parts taken from other agencies. This can mean de-emphasis, change in emphasis, or net loss of some regulatory functions after transfer. It can also precede new emphasis in regulation, as with the creation of the Consumer Product Safety Commission. In the context of deregulation, the process of disintegration with transfer and/or recombination may have a "lost-in-the-cracks" effect: Some activities or subprograms are weakened as a result of the change to a new formal mandate, while others simply fall between and do not really reappear. The transfer can also be to an agency at another level of government.[2] This can be done explicitly or implicitly, with governments at other levels stepping in to replace deregulation at a given level.

The effects of disintegration and transfer are discussed later, when we consider strategies against deregulation.

4.3   WHY ANY OF THESE FORMS IS HARD TO GET EVEN FOR PROGRAMS WITH DEMONSTRABLE PERVERSITIES

Even given demonstrably poor performance, it is notoriously difficult to adopt and to implement any of the formal reducing methods noted above. Before we consider deregulation as a process and describe the strategies of participants that exacerbate this difficulty, we shall list some basic contributing conditions. Note that these are mostly generalizable to public organizations at large.

1.   Information Effects

The process of change is often inherently cumbersome and can take considerable time, e.g., the legislative process. Thus it may appear to others that perversities are being irrationally tolerated.

Perversities may not be recognized by those who have the power to change the regulation to remove the perversity.

Perversities may not be measurable; they may be hard to demonstrate, though their existence may be suspected. The effects of regulation may be diffusely distributed and therefore hard to observe and aggregate.

---

[2] This was suggested to the author by Douglas Jones, personal communication.

2. Cost of Change

It may be that the costs of changing—i.e., of correcting—the perversities are too high, so that, from a comprehensive viewpoint, eliminating the perversities is just not rational.

Because the costs of change may be differentially imposed, some people may have to take relatively high short-term losses. If these people are key decision-makers, they may take extra effort to oppose the change, and be successful. For example, Mansfield (1969:339) suggests that reorganization plans have not been proposed for agencies with strong Congressional protectors, e.g. Senator McClellan of the Rivers and Harbors Committee and the Corps of Engineers between 1939 and 1963.

Change itself may be too costly in the short run to be borne at that time, though there may be long-run net benefits.

3. Opposition Factors

Our arguments here overlap to some extent with the preceding category.

In general, parties unintentionally (or intentionally) favored by the regulation can be expected to support it and oppose change. As above, if key decision-makers are the ones affected, success—or failure—depending on the effect on them, is consequently more likely. In addition, those who are not strongly favored by the regulation now directly, but would suffer longtime losses either from removal of the regulation or from what may substitute for it, may oppose change.

5.0 Proposing and Opposing Deregulation: Tactics and Strategies

5.1 DEREGULATION AS A POLICY PROCESS

Deregulation of a policy, program, agency, and so on, is itself a policy that must reach an institutional agenda, be subject to decision on that agenda, and experience implementation (on the agenda-building process, see Cobb and Elder 1972). The characteristics of the policy formulation and implementation process for deregulation are therefore similar in many major respects to that of the process for regulation. But there now exists a set of interested parties to the regulation with a history of receiving positive (or negative) rewards as a result of it. In addition, there are structural and other problems of managing organizational (or programmatic) reduction that do not necessarily parallel the problems of organizational creation or building. During implementation of deregulation, for example, individuals in regulatory agencies (or any other agencies) subject to cutting down will often take every opportunity to delay, divert, or avoid the reduction entirely. If it occurs over time, unexpected opportunities for doing this will occur. In regulatory creation, "vested" interests of this type may not exist (although we may of course expect opposition from those hurt by the regulation).

5.2 POLITICS AND ADVOCACY OF DEREGULATION PROPOSING

Several notable aspects of the controversy that often surrounds deregulation can be identified.

Argumentation frequently involves ignoring intangible and/or diffuse benefits and costs, sometimes deliberately. For example, safety regulations involve relatively easily measurable impacts on specific manufacturers, while the costs to consumers to get information on risk and then protect themselves in the absence of such regulations are diffusely spread and hard to measure. Not surprisingly, industry opponents will emphasize the more easily measurable costs they would pay. Similarly, in air pollution control controversies, the health or discomfort costs of the pollution are hard to measure and diffusely spread. The costs to given polluters to clean their emissions, on the other hand, may be substantial and easily dramatized for the rhetoric of public debate. Intangible benefits from regulation, e.g., preservation of aesthetic beauty, are similarly hard to advocate, while the economic benefits from development projects that affect that beauty are more calculable. Consequently, in such controversy, decisions are often made on the basis of comparisons among the measures that can be given concrete values.[3]

A relevant tactic, common in agenda-building conflict, is that of redefining the issue (see, e.g., Cobb and Elder 1972; Schattschneider 1960). The issue may be deliberately blurred in advocacy: all regulation is opposed, including safety and health regulation (which may be costly to business), but the chief examples attacked are those with more easily demonstrable perversities, e.g., transport regulation.

---

[3] For a discussion of the distribution of costs and benefits and the occurrence of regulation, see J. Q. Wilson (1974).

Ralph Nader and other consumer advocates, for example, have criticized publicity "aimed at confusing wasteful cartel regulation with
life-saving consumer protection regulation." They note that "business proponents invariably confuse the two and invariably conclude
that it is consumer regulation which must be curtailed" (Nader and
Green 1975; see also Crewdson 1975:989).

Because of the distribution of costs and benefits, deregulation controversy sometimes creates allies and enemies that seem strange in
the context of traditional conflicts. Thus one group of businessmen,
presumably Republican, who head a chain of retail stores, planned to
form a Washington lobby to secure changes in the Interstate Commerce Commission and the Federal Maritime Commission. They
were opposed by the businessmen, also presumably Republican, who
run the railroads and shipping lines. In this situation, of course, the
retail stores are in effect consumers since they ship their goods on the
railroads and shipping lines.[4]

Traditionally Democratic railroad and maritime unions, on the
other hand, were united with their Republican management in opposing change in those regulatory agencies. Change could bring both
lower prices for the workers as consumers and, it is feared, loss of
jobs in the respective industries.

Similarly, the teamsters and truck company managements have
united against threats of ICC deregulation (Vaden 1976; R. J.
Samuelson 1979).

There may be disagreement among the regulators or potential regulators as well. A rival bureau may propose deregulation, or disman-
tling or reorganization of the existing regulatory apparatus. This may
permit it to acquire those regulatory activities or enhance its own
position in the functional area. During the Ford administration, part
of the drive for deregulating the areas covered by the Interstate Commerce Commission, for example, came from professionals in the potentially rival Department of Transportation.[5] Vaden (1976:3254)
quotes a staffer in the House of Representatives as saying that "I do
think there is an institutional bias in the department for deregulation.
Even if you rearrange the top people, people up to the GS 15 level
would be still churning the deregulation stuff out." The Department
of Transportation also provided estimates of the excess costs said to

---

[4] For this and the following example, see Burnham (1976:39).
[5] Vaden (1976). But President Carter's Secretary of Transportation, Brock Adams, personally
appeared to oppose major change. See R. E. Cohen (1977).

be due to airline regulation by the Civil Aeronautics Board, and contributed to Ford administration proposals to deregulate some of that agency's functions (Lowe 1975).

The technology of the regulated area or of the feasible means of regulation may be a factor in deregulation. The greater the technical obscurity of the area to be regulated, the less likely it will cause controversy, and the more likely that regulated industries can thus avoid public oversight. This may permit them to influence or "capture" the regulatory agency (cf. Sabatier 1975). Technical obscurity or complexity may structure what controversy that does occur, since the public arguments cannot easily express the true differences. This implies that in such cases some easily understood facet or symbolic aspect can come to dominate the deregulation controversy and, seemingly irrationally with respect to formally expressed goals, determine the outcome. Arguing that issues of implementation are in general far more technical than those relating to basic program goals, Paul Sabatier describes how this complexity contributed to the end of a compliance-monitoring program in air pollution control (Sabatier 1975).

5.3 STRATEGIES OF REGULATED INDUSTRY

Industries which enjoy regulatory protection (i.e., for which the regulatory body has supplied environmental control) may adopt a number of strategies in the face of threats of deregulation. It is expected, of course, that the industry (and any other parties benefited by the regulation) will resist deregulation. In general, those benefited by regulation may: (*a*) attempt 1) reconsideration and reversal of a deregulatory policy intention; and 2) reconsideration with alteration, compromise, or watering down of the deregulation proposal in order to retain at least some of the advantages enjoyed by the industry. Failing this, they (*b*) attempt to guide, or affect in favorable ways, the implementation of the deregulation. We posit that the industry may prefer, in order, the following conditions:

1. To retain the existing regulatory bureaucracy.

The industry has an "investment" in the creation over time of the existing administrative rules and interpersonal ties. These rules presumably aid the industry in managing its environment and at any rate reduce uncertainty for the operations of the industry. As we discussed in chapter 3, many of the rewards received by agency personnel can be manipulated by the industry: the industry can offer the promise of future lucrative employment in the regulated industry or dealing with it (which may be limited under recently adopted "ethics" policies); can help reduce the regulators' work load by offering advice and information; can offer the regulator the prestige and status rewards he usually gets from nowhere else due to his position in an essentially backwater agency dealing with relatively esoteric matters; and, occasionally, although perhaps less so now, can offer more material inducements, such as meals, airplane trips, and vacations. This creates a reservoir of good feeling between agency members and their industry counterparts, which may supplement in important ways the role expectations acquired by regulators after they join the agency. These expectations may be created as new regulators are exposed to the activities and expectations of others in an agency that can have important protective functions for the regulated industry.

Industry personnel, like the regulators, have had to make an investment in *idiosyncratic* aspects of the regulatory process. If the structure of the regulatory agency, its personnel, and/or the content of the regulation is changed, the industry will have to pay the costs of learning or developing needed adaptations to idiosyncracies in new equipment or technology and in regulatory compliance procedures that are required under the new regulatory regime (whether to meet new regulations, new interpretations of old regulations, or merely to respond to new monitoring, inspecting, reporting, or other regulatory stipulations). These adaptations are in addition to the development of new idiosyncratic social relationships with the regulators, and of new communication patterns among themselves and with the regulators. These idiosyncracies are special to the particular regulatory and interpersonal relationships established under the new system and cannot be carried over from the previous system (see Williamson 1976:88; Williamson, Wachter, and Harris 1975).

The industry thus has an investment in the existing network of regulatory and interpersonal relationships that would be destroyed through reorganization, or, of course, deregulation, and so it will oppose change. Note that stable expectation of the behavior of individuals, based on interpersonal ties, may contribute importantly to the stable and therefore predictable environment the industry seeks.

2. To transfer functions (and personnel) intact to another agency.

It follows from the above discussion that the industry, if unsuccessfull in retaining the existing agency, will seek to transfer all relevant functions and the personnel who administer them intact. For example, they may seek to move the functions (and personnel) under the administrative umbrella of a department or bureau judged friendly to the functions performed, or create a "new" agency with a new name in a different setting as a "cover" for the old functions and personnel.

3. To retain the regulation, but allow splitting up and transfer of functions (and personnel).

Again, it follows that if the regulatory apparatus cannot be transferred in a lump-sum manner, permitting retention of both the regulation and the social system that administers it, the industry may seek to keep the elements of the regulation and whatever parts of the administering social system, including personnel, it can salvage. Splitting up and transfer of functions and personnel may require establishment of a new set of coordinative mechanisms to deal with the regulatory apparatus, and of a new system of interpersonal relationships with some of the uninitiated, as it were, members of the agency that is the new home for the regulation. All of this, of course, is costly for the industry and may lead to at least short-term decrement in the environmental-management functions served by the regulation.

4. To retain a few key functions in the same or, failing that, a different bureaucracy, if some functions are to be completely deregulated.

The rationale would once more proceed from consideration of the functions served by the regulation for the industry, and the "investment" the industry has made in its regulation and would have to make again.

5. To transfer control to the industry via establishment of self-regulation.

Models for this include the largely self-regulating profession (preferably government backed) and the railroad "pools" of the nineteenth century or other cartel-like structures. But self-regulation without government backing has historically not worked well in some industries. Some have argued, as we noted earlier, that failure of self-regulation, in effect, led to the founding of the ICC. It may therefore be predicted that industries will first push for self-regulation with governmental backing or legitimation (as with certain professional groups— e.g., lawyers, physicians) and only when failing that will push to be allowed to practice purely private self-regulation.

Cases where the industry opposes deregulation are common. For example, President Ford's 1976 proposals to reduce regulation by the ICC were strongly opposed by the relevant industries. The trucking proposal, in particular, "was greeted with cries of outrage from the trucking industry and related unions." The American Trucking Association asserted that "America's surface freight transportation system, the finest man has ever devised, is under attack." The International Brotherhood of Teamsters called it "the most destructive legislative proposal in the last 40 years" (Vaden 1976:3250). The ATA and Teamsters feared the loss of protection against competition offered by entry controls, rate-setting functions, and other regulation threatened by such proposals.

State trucking deregulation has been opposed no less strongly. Elimination of minimum rates and a rollback of an 11 percent rate increase by the California Public Utilities Commission was met with anger. An official of the California Trucking Association said the decision "will throw (the industry) back to the law of the jungle. Big shippers will charge lower rates, smaller shippers will charge higher rates. I wonder why the PUC did this." One trucker said, "it's going to be chaos" (Taylor 1975). The role of regulation as environmental manager and bringer of stability is vividly highlighted here.

The parties involved are also capable of a turnaround on regulation as conditions change and regulation, or the deregulated state, no longer favors the party in question. Urban and Mancke (1972) discuss how labeling regulations originating in the late thirties that were favorable to the makers of whiskey barrels and heavy-bodied American whiskey apparently drove out production of domestic "light whiskey." They infer from other evidence that these regulations were in fact sought to serve the protective purpose. The rising popularity of imported "light whiskey" in the 1960s led to a desire by the American industry to tap this market. In 1968 new regulations repealing the earlier ones were issued, effective in 1972, again issued at the behest of the industry.

Sometimes only part of the industry will oppose deregulation because of the differential benefits expected. United Airlines, for example, supported some deregulation, being in a better position than some of its competitors to exploit eased route restrictions (see, e.g., A. Cooper 1977).

5.4 STRATEGIES OF AGENCIES IN RESPONSE TO THE THREAT OF DEREGULATION

Regulators will be reluctant to change the structure of the agency and the form and content of the regulation, because such changes could threaten both the rewards they receive from external sources, and those that are generated as a normal concomitant of intraorganizational activities. These intraorganizational factors may be derived from such aspects of organizational activity as the network of interpersonal friendships, promotion patterns and possibilities, sunk costs of the establishment of organizational procedures and individual response patterns to them, informal norms and role expectations, and so on (cf. Kaufman 1960, 1970; McGregor 1974). In particular, if the structure of the agency and/or its regulation is altered, regulators may have to pay the costs of learning or developing needed adaptations to new idiosyncracies in necessary equipment or technology, regulating procedures, informal social and task adaptations with co-workers, and communication among themselves and with parties in the regulatory environment, e.g., industry personnel and public interest groups (Williamson 1976:88; Williamson, Wachter and Harris 1975). Such factors constitute disincentives to change in any organization, though perhaps not all to the same degree in all organizations (see, e.g., Downs 1967, ch. 16). Resistance to change in regulatory agencies may thus be seen as a special case of resistance to change in organizations in general (see, e.g., Kaufman 1971), where organizational members receive incentives to resist the change both from clients of the organization and from intraorganizational sources.

There are several strategies that may be adopted in response to the threat of deregulation. It is argued that agency members will first try to prevent change. Failing that, or with the prospect of failing that, they will seek to control the change to safeguard their externally and internally sent rewards as much as possible, i.e., try to protect the extant incentive system. In general, if the regulated industry controls important agency member rewards, the agency will also prefer the order of and types of changes preferred by the industry.

1. Change personnel titles and/or bureau names, make fairly limited shifts of personnel within the agency who have externally meaningful and/or impressive credentials relevant to some external demand, and publicize externally all changes made.

Sometimes relatively small amounts of funds can be diverted to the "new" areas or personnel or to hire a few new personnel to give the appearance of work in the area. A typical response of this kind would be for a public utilities commission that had been involved in controversy over the environmental impacts of power projects to designate a division of its existing technical staff "Environmental Analysis Division" and/or appoint some longtime engineering employee "Chief Environmental Engineer." This is an essentially *symbolic response* designed to placate external critics without disturbing in any significant way the extant incentive system, and is not particular to regulatory agencies; organizations like public utilities faced with client demands do this too.

David T. Stanley suggests that another tactic of this type is to "freeze" money that at any rate was not going to be spent, positions that really were not going to be filled, and other such expenditures.[6] This is a tactic that bureaucracies in general may adopt when required to cut down. Regulatory agencies, when faced with threats of deregulation in areas in which they wish to resist real cuts, could select this technique, among others. Note that the agency may be able to give the appearance of, or delay the actual implementation of, a winddown by choosing this method.

2. Offer (and then voluntarily make) small concessions in the form of essentially minor new administrative regulations and, failing that, legislation.

The agency, of course, is better able to control the final content of administrative regulations than of legislation. The minor changes may receive more than commensurate publicity, however, and the agency may even seem to be taking the offensive in proposing change. This will be done only if the more tentative proposals and then implementation of small changes prove insufficient; the agency does not itself wish to publicize and add fuel to a deregulation push. The agency may try to wrest control of any deregulation movement to insure that the changes will be relatively small.

[6] David T. Stanley, personal letter, August 17, 1977. See also Stanley (1977).

3. Offer relatively larger changes; these may include co-opting one or a few
of the relatively major changes proposed by deregulation proponents.

But only a few, not all of such changes, are proposed. And the agency will typically propose that it be allowed to determine the exact form of the changes, and to plan and manage the implementation of the changes. The agency may again try to depict itself as being in the forefront of the deregulation effort.

Consider some examples of strategies (2) and (3). In 1976, in the earlier stages of the transport deregulation controversy, the ICC opposed reform legislation, favoring administrative action. Significantly, it was supported in this by the trucking industry. The ICC took several relatively minor administrative actions, e.g., restricted the right of rate bureaus to interfere with independent rate actions, and began studies of others. A lawyer in the Department of Transportation (which favored deregulation) commented that "they've done maybe 10 per cent of the stuff [in the Ford Administration's bill], and it just comes out perverse" (Vaden 1976:3252–53).

President Carter's new ICC Chairman, Daniel O'Neal, when mentioned among possible candidates for the chairmanship, was characterized as "presumably . . . less interested in paring the agency's powers" because he had been a member of the Commission (Karr 1977). The *Wall Street Journal* reported that after his appointment O'Neal sought "to head off legislative deregulation by making the commission more progressive and vigorous. He promises to remove restrictions on entry into the trucking business, acts to protect customers of household movers, cracks down on illegal trucking. O'Neal hopes to convince Carter and Congress that he can make all necessary changes himself" (*Wall Street Journal*, June 3, 1977, p. 1; see also, e.g., R. J. Samuelson 1979). These changes are more major ones, but O'Neal is still trying to permit the ICC to determine and manage whatever change is to be made.

Another example of an agency seeking, through open support of relatively small change and/or self-implementation of the change, to control the changes imposed upon it is, possibly, the strategy of the Civil Aeronautics Board during the same wave of deregulation controversy. The CAB supported the Republican reform bill, submitted by Senators Pearson and Baker, which called for less radical changes than the bill introduced by Senators Cannon and Kennedy. Leaving more of the existing regulatory apparatus intact, the Pearson-Baker bill even received support for some of its "less drastic reforms" from several airlines (A. Cooper 1977).

Once basic rules or legislation is passed, the agency may try to control implementation in such a way as to guarantee that the actual change is as "small" as possible. The agency may even take formal actions that make implementation difficult. Thus the ICC's proposed and final rules for implementing the deregulation provisions of the Railroad Revitalization and Regulatory Reform Act of 1976 were characterized as being "considered by many to be so restrictive as to sabotage the provisions' aims." The ICC and the Ford administration allegedly did "everything they can to see that [the new legislation] doesn't work" (Karr 1977; see also T. G. Moore 1978:38–39).

There follow two strategies which, depending on the nature or magnitude of the change in functions, and the shift in administrative locus, respectively, may involve major or minor change. In order to be effective as opposition strategies, however, the changes are likely to be relatively major, and could result in disruption of the existing incentive system.

4. Try to be transferred with as little disruption as possible into a new organization or organizations.

Transfer may be used as a tactic to yield symbolically to the reform or deregulation demand, and, if it can be done so that the agency remains relatively intact, may be a preferred strategy. If the interests of industry and agency coincide, the agency may be able to, in effect, enlist components of its environment in support of a threat coming from other components. An example may be the recent re-creation of the Federal Power Commission as the Federal Energy Regulatory Commission inside the new Department of Energy (Rankin 1977). The transformation of the ICC in 1889 into an "independent" agency, the model for subsequent "independent" agencies, was described in chapter 3 as essentially an attempt by agency proponents to prevent deregulation or deregulating-like influences. Senator Reagan of Texas (raised from the House to the Senate in 1887) supposedly created the independent commission, removing the ICC from the Department of Interior, because he thought the new President, Harrison, was sympathetic to the railroads (Bernstein 1955:23; but see ibid. n. 13).

Breakup or modification of the essential form or functions of the agency, together with the effects of its new environment, could, of course, disrupt the incentive system faced by agency members. Thus, although the FPC may have successfully made the transfer, the tactic can be very risky.

5. *Propose new duties to increase the importance of, or need for, the agency.*

In effect this may involve substitution of new functions for those considered outdated or newly undesirable. This is the frequently described succession-of-goals strategy, exemplified for private organizations by the change in goals of the March of Dimes after its success with polio. But organizations like regulatory agencies can also use this as a strategy of survival in a hostile environment, whether that environment results from success or from externally judged failure. Note that extension or expansion of functions, or shift of functions to a new area, could disrupt the extant incentive system. It may change, for example, the regulated parties and/or their relationship to the agency and its members.

James McKie (1970) has described what he calls the "tar-baby effect" in which regulatory agencies continually seek additional controls, supposedly in a public-spirited effort to correct for the defects of existing controls. Based on the previous analysis, we can offer an alternative explanation: Regulators may seek additional powers or duties, i.e., environmental controls, in order to insure survival of the regulatory agency. In this way potential threats to the regulators from publicly manifest regulatory failures can be avoided.

5.5 REACTIONS OF BUREAUCRATS TO DEREGULATION

Agency members are not identical; they have differing preferences and may be expected to react in somewhat different ways to deregulation or the threat of deregulation. We do expect some strong overall uniformities, as indicated above, based on the nature of the incentive system and the relatively common preferences satisfied by that incentive system. A suggestion of the uniformities and differences is in the following quote concerning the ICC from the Transportation Department lawyer cited earlier: "First of all, their jobs depend upon the system. And second, the ambitious ones want to go into the industry.

DEREGULATION 443

If you're a lawyer at the ICC and you deregulate, all of a sudden all your knowledge is useless'' (Vaden 1976:3253).

Opposition to change stemming from desires to retain basic job rewards and to not have to repay the sunk costs of specialized expertise are evident here, i.e., desires to retain the benefits of the status quo. In addition, the "ambitious ones" seek the promise of future rewards in jobs with the industry. Might not those whose chief rewards are tied to the agency behave differently under threat of deregulation than those who, for example, foresee a chief reward in the future outside the agency?

Anthony Downs's (1967) typology of bureaucrats, which we generalized in chapter 2, permits us to discuss—or at least speculate on—likely behavioral differences. Recall that in Downs's typology, *climbers* seek only their own self-interest goals of power, income, and prestige; *conservers* seek only their own self-interest goals of convenience and security, seeking to retain what power, income, and prestige they have; *zealots* are mixed-motive in that they possess similar self-interest goals, but also strongly desire to achieve or implement a relatively narrow policy, program, or concept; *advocates* are mixed-motive and value in addition to self-interest goals the broader goals or functions of the organization; and *statesmen* are mixed-motive and desire in addition to self-interest to achieve goals relating to the benefit of society as a whole. To this list we added the *loyalists,* who are mixed-motive and value in addition to self-interest goals the goals of another individual, e.g., a charismatic leader or chief executive.

Consider now how these types are likely to behave in a situation of real or potential deregulation.

Climbers may "jump" out of the agency into other, promising, agencies or into the regulated industry. Deregulation could mean, of course, that they may not have the future chance to gain a lucrative position in the industry. In addition, the agency, if it survives, may have a reduced potential for growth. This would limit the climber's promotion opportunities. For these reasons, then, the climber jumps. Since the climber will normally seek to perform well according to objective criteria (or to please his superior) in order to gain promotion, loss of climbers may mean that the quality of agency service or performance if measured by the same tests, or tests interdependent with them, may fall. This implies the possibility of a downward spiral: an agency under attack for poor performance according to set criteria may lose some of its "better" performers, and so perform even more poorly. Note of course that climbers seek only to appear to perform well according to whatever tests are used to determine promotion, not actually to offer good performance.

Conservers will strongly resist deregulation because of the threat it poses to continued receipt of the rewards they get from both within and without the agency. In their resistance they are linked to the advocates, who defend the organization. But conservers would probably not oppose transfer of the agency, change in function, or reorganization as long as their own positions, i.e., rewards, were protected. Thus conservers may favor those concession tactics noted above that involve minimum violence to the incentive system (e.g., transfers intact).

Advocates, however, would resist the threat to the organization and its identifying functions, though they may be willing to offer or concede relatively small changes if this permits the organization to survive.

Zealots (who seek pet projects) would strongly resist any programmatic changes (e.g., changes in organizational functions) unless they favored their pet projects. This inflexibility, of course, could work to the advantage of deregulation proponents.

Statesmen may take the other side if they perceive deregulation is best with respect to societal goals. Statesmen, however, are probably as uncommon in regulatory agencies as they are elsewhere.

Loyalists will take the side of their leader, assuming (as is the case with the other mixed-motive agents) that their self-interest is suitably safeguarded. Loyalists may be inserted in agencies to assert political control or achieve new policy directives which may be counter to prevalent agency views. Thus loyalists could be used to counter the agency protective strategies enumerated earlier. Loyalists may therefore be "hatchet men" or expediters; they are at any rate one of the tools by which executives as principals can insure realization of their preferences by agent-workers in subject organizations.

Young agencies have relatively more climbers and zealots; in part this is due to the increased opportunities for promotion in a new agency (climbers) and the at least partial realization of someone's desired program represented in the new agency (zealots). The above discussion implies that such agencies, because they have proportionately more climbers (who may leave) and zealots (who are inflexible), may be easier to "kill off," i.e., deregulate. In addition, of course, a young agency may suffer from a lack of established allies and a general dearth of public or political support if the enthusiasm attending its founding has waned. (Cf. Downs 1967.)

6.0 Conclusion

The discussion in this chapter has proceeded on the assumption that the regulation subject to removal is a regulatory program or organization. Of interest (and not pursued here) would be a consideration of deregulatory processes according to type or regulatory means, incentive or directive. If we make a mistake by, say, establishing an effluent charge system, how hard will it be to remove it? How hard to substitute another means? Given the likelihood of design failure in an uncertain world, choice of means should consider the costs not only of establishment, but of termination or conversion to another means. These costs include both ending or changing the mechanism itself, and transition costs imposed on or affecting parties subject to or affected by the regulation.

Some alternatives that look ''good'' on paper may be riskier than we realize if termination costs reveal themselves to be substantial. Subsidies, in so far as they are tied to lumpy investments in single items, can turn out to have irreversibly lost opportunity costs. The resources devoted to them may be lost and not convertible to other uses relevant to another form of regulation (or not convertible to uses outside regulation in the event of termination). Before we create subsidies to support railroads, for example, we should be clear about the risks involved in acquiring thousands of miles of limited use, nonconvertible right-of-way lined with steel rails.

In general, deregulation of incentive means should be more difficult than deregulation of directive means because they involve positive rather than negative incentives. There can be a community of interest with incentive means that is only reluctantly broken. But of course the situation is much more complex than this. Redundant incentive mechanisms, in which the subject can retain a positive reward for doing something that would have been done anyway, should be hardest to remove. Incentive means that do not cover the cost of designated action may not enjoy persistent supporters. Incentive mechanisms like effluent charges that are really mixed in character, e.g., involve reductions in penalty with directives at the ''boundary," would hardly be preferred to no regulation by parties subject to them (unless they thereby gain competitive market advantage, a possibility).

The standard of comparison is of course crucial; in choosing whether to support or oppose deregulation, parties must make some comparison to a substitute state. The available alternatives or substitutes may or may not include "no regulation" and may or may not be preferable to an existing regulation that the subject party finds distasteful, but less so.

Directive regulation, as we have seen, can be (and apparently has often been) sought. The costs and benefits of regulation to an individual party are not always properly calculated by reference to direct impacts on the party. Regulation is often a *collective good;* directive coercion may be necessary that all may benefit. In such a situation there may be some who would like to benefit as free riders or whose particular gains would persist after deregulation. For example, some firms, such as United Airlines in the controversy over deregulation of airline regulation, might stand to better their market share under deregulation. Deregulatory design is no more simple than regulatory design.

Work on understanding the decline or reduction of public organizations, including regulatory agencies, is in its infancy. In this chapter, deregulation was discussed as a process of organizational reduction. Noting the relatively stronger ability of regulatory agencies to control their environment, we discussed the concept, forms, and process of deregulation, including strategies adopted by parties opposing it. Much of the discussion of strategies is generalizable to the reduction of all public organizations.

Although deregulation is viewed as a case of organizational reduction, it is important to recall aspects of deregulation that make it a special case. Regulation provides environmental control and thus can help solve collective action dilemmas. This leads groups/industries to seek it, assuring a strong, continuing interest in the regulation. Note that groups strong enough to get government action to help themselves are likely to be strong enough to play a major role in preserving the regulation against threats from those who wish to remove it. Unlike some models of regulatory capture that depict the regulators solely as passive responders to industry initiative, we argue that regulators can play an active role in managing their own environment and opposing deregulation. As a consequence of these factors, reduction in regulatory organizations may be particularly difficult to obtain.

Reduction in other types of public organizations in similar contexts, e.g., with strong constituency support, may therefore also be difficult.

An understanding of the processes of organizational reduction in regulation may have prescriptive utility. For example, it could enable those formally imposing the deregulation to recognize and perhaps forestall deregulation that is merely symbolic, predict and possibly overcome resistance to deregulation, and anticipate and perhaps control performance degradation during the deregulatory process. Thus, if operative conceptions of the public interest indicate that removal of some regulation would be desirable, an understanding of its processes may assure that the old soldiers of regulation will finally fade away.

References

Aaron, Henry. "Inventory of Existing Tax Incentives—Federal." In *Tax Incentives*, Symposium conducted by the Tax Institute of America (November 20–21, 1969). Lexington, Mass.: Heath Lexington Books, 1971.

Abel, Albert S. "The Public Corporation in the United States." In W. Friedmann and J. F. Garner, eds., *Government Enterprise*, pp. 181–99. London: Stevens, 1970.

Aberbach, Joel D. "The Development of Oversight in the United States Congress: Concepts and Analysis." Paper presented at the 1977 Annual Meeting of the American Political Science Association, Washington, D.C.

Abrams, Burton A. and Russell F. Settle. "The Economic Theory of Regulation and Public Financing of Presidential Elections." *Journal of Political Economy*, Part 1 (April 1978), 86(2):245–57.

Ackerman, Bruce A., with Susan Rose-Ackerman, James W. Sawyer, Jr., and Dale W. Henderson. *The Uncertain Search for Environmental Quality*. New York: Free Press, 1974.

Adams, Bruce. "Money, Secrecy, and State Utility Regulation: A Common Cause Report on the Accountability (or Lack Thereof) of State Public Utility Commissions." Washington, D.C.: Common Cause, August 1976.

Adams, Charles Francis, Jr. *Railroads: Their Origin and Problems*, rev. ed. New York: Putnam, 1887; reprinted, Harper and Row, 1969.

Adams, Henry C. "A Decade of Federal Railway Regulation." *Atlantic Monthly* (April 1898), 81(486):433–43.

Alchian, Armen A. and Harold Demsetz. "Production, Information Costs, and Economic Organization." *American Economic Review* (December 1972), 62(5):777–95.

Aldrich, Howard E. and Jeffrey Pfeffer. "Environments of Organizations." In Alex Inkeles, ed., *Annual Review of Sociology*, vol. 2. Palo Alto, Calif: Annual Review, 1976.

Allison, Graham. *The Essence of Decision: Explaining the Cuban Missile Crisis*. Boston: Little, Brown, 1971.

Altman, Irwin. "Choicepoints in the Classification of Scientific Knowledge." In B. P. Indik and F. K. Berrien, eds., *People, Groups, and Organizations*, pp. 3–26. New York: Teachers College Press, 1968.

Anderson, Frederick R. et al. *Environmental Improvement Through Eco-*

nomic Incentives. Baltimore, Md.: Johns Hopkins University Press, for Resources for the Future, 1977.

Anderson, James E. *The Emergence of the Modern Regulatory State*. Washington, D.C.: Public Affairs Press, 1962.

—— *Public Policy-Making*. New York: Praeger, 1975.

Arrow, Kenneth J. "Political and Economic Evaluation of Social Effects and Externalities." In Julius Margolis, ed., *The Analysis of Public Output*, pp. 1–30. New York: Columbia University Press, 1970.

Ashby, W. R. *Introduction to Cybernetics*. New York: Wiley, 1956.

Backoff, Robert W. 1974a. "Operationalizing Administrative Reform for Improved Governmental Performance." *Administration and Society* (May 1974), 6(1):73–106.

—— 1974b. "Organizational Innovation Theory: Integration, Evaluation, and Prescription." Ph.D. dissertation, Department of Political Science, Indiana University, 1974.

Backoff, Robert W. and Barry M. Mitnick. "The Incentive Systems Approach to the Study of Innovation Productivity in Organizations." Paper presented at the 1978 Annual Meeting of the Midwest Political Science Association, Chicago, Ill.

Bailey, Kenneth D. "Monothetic and Polythetic Typologies and Their Relation to Conceptualization, Measurement and Scaling." *American Sociological Review* (February 1973), 38(1):18–33.

—— "Systematics and Taxonomy in Organization Science." Human Systems Development Study Center Working Paper No. 75-10. Los Angeles, Calif.: Graduate School of Management, U.C.L.A., November 1975.

Baldwin, John R. *The Regulatory Agency and the Public Corporation: The Canadian Air Transport Industry*. Cambridge, Mass.: Ballinger, 1975.

Banfield, Edward C. "Note on Conceptual Scheme." In M. Meyerson and E. C. Banfield, *Politics, Planning and the Public Interest*. New York: Free Press, 1955.

—— *Political Influence*. New York: Free Press of Glencoe, 1961.

—— "Corruption as a Feature of Governmental Organization." *Journal of Law and Economics* (December 1975), 18(3):587–605.

Barber, Sotirios. *The Constitution and the Delegation of Congressional Power*. Chicago: University of Chicago Press, 1975.

Bardach, Eugene. "Policy Termination as a Political Process." *Policy Sciences* (June 1976), 7(2):123–31.

Barnard, Chester I. *The Functions of the Executive*. Cambridge, Mass.: Harvard University Press, 1938.

Barnes, Irston R. *The Economics of Public Utility Regulation*. New York: F. S. Crofts, 1942.

Barrett, Jon. *Individual Goals and Organizational Objectives*. Ann Arbor, Mich.: Institute for Social Research, 1970.

Barry, Brian. *Political Argument*. London: Routledge and Kegan Paul, 1965.

Baumol, William J. *Welfare Economics and the Theory of the State*. Cambridge, Mass.: Harvard University Press, 1965.

Baumol, William J. and Wallace E. Oates. *The Theory of Environmental Policy: Externalities, Public Outlays, and the Quality of Life*. Englewood Cliffs, N.J.: Prentice-Hall, 1975.

Bauer, Raymond A., Ithiel de Sola Pool, and Lewis Anthony Dexter. *American Business and Public Policy*. New York: Atherton, 1963.

Behn, Robert D. "The False Dawn of the Sunset Laws." *The Public Interest* (Fall 1977), 49:103–18.

—— "How the Differences Between Private and Public Organizations Affect Their Abilities to Terminate Their Activities." Paper presented at the 1978 National Conference of the American Society for Public Administration, Phoenix, Arizona.

Belonzi, Arthur, Arthur D'Antonio, and Gary Helfand. *The Weary Watchdogs: Governmental Regulators in the Political Process*. Wayne, N.J.: Avery Publishing Group, 1977.

Benditt, Theodore M. "The Public Interest." *Philosophy and Public Affairs* (Spring 1973), 2(3):291–311.

Bendix, Reinhard. *Higher Civil Servants in American Society: A Study of the Social Origins, the Careers, and the Power-Position of Higher Federal Administrators*. Boulder: University of Colorado Studies, Series in Sociology No. 1; University of Colorado Press, July 1949.

Benham, Lee and Alexandra Benham. "Regulating through the Professions: A Perspective on Information Control." *Journal of Law and Economics* (October 1975), 18(2):421–47.

Benson, Lee. *Merchants, Farmers, and Railroads: Railroad Regulation and New York Politics, 1850–1887*. New York: Russell and Russell, 1955, 1969.

Bentley, Arthur F. *The Process of Government*. Cambridge, Mass.: Belknap Press of Harvard University Press, 1967; first published 1908.

Bernstein, Marver H. *Regulating Business by Independent Commission*. Princeton, N.J.: Princeton University Press, 1955.

—— "Independent Regulatory Agencies: A Perspective on Their Reform." *The Annals of the American Academy of Political and Social Science* (March 1972), 400:14–26.

Berry, Jeffrey M. *Lobbying for the People: The Political Behavior of Public Interest Groups*. Princeton, N.J.: Princeton University Press, 1977.

Bibby, John F. "Committee Characteristics and Legislative Oversight of Administration." *Midwest Journal of Political Science* (1966), 10:78–98.

Bird, Richard M. and Leonard Waverman. "Some Fiscal Aspects of Controlling Industrial Water Pollution." In D. A. L. Auld, ed., *Economic*

Thinking and Pollution Problems, pp. 75–102. Toronto: University of Toronto Press, 1972.

Bish, Robert L. *The Public Economy of Metropolitan Areas*. Chicago: Markham, 1971.

Blachly, Frederick F. and Miriam E. Oatman. *Federal Regulatory Action and Control*. Washington, D.C.: Brookings Institution, 1940.

Black, Duncan. *The Theory of Committees and Elections*. Cambridge: Cambridge University Press, 1958, 1963.

Bonbright, James C. *Principles of Public Utility Rates*. New York: Columbia University Press, 1961.

Borcherding, Thomas E., ed. *Budgets and Bureaucrats: The Sources of Government Growth*. Durham, N.C.: Duke University Press, 1977.

Boyes, William J. "An Empirical Examination of the Averch-Johnson Effect." *Economic Inquiry* (March 1976), 14(1):25–35.

Braybrooke, David and Charles E. Lindblom. *A Strategy of Decision*. New York: Free Press, 1963.

Brenner, Michael J. *The Political Economy of America's Environmental Dilemma*. Lexington, Mass: Lexington Books, D.C. Heath, 1973.

Brewer, W. D. "Regulation—The Balance Point." *Pepperdine Law Review* (1974), 1:355–71.

Brumm, Harold J., Jr., and Daniel T. Dick. "Federal Environmental Policy and R & D on Water Pollution Abatement." *American Economic Review* (May 1976), 66(2):448–53.

Buchanan, James M. *The Demand and Supply of Public Goods*. Chicago: Rand McNally, 1968.

Buchanan, James M. and William Craig Stubblebine. "Externality." *Economica* (November 1962), 29:371–84.

Buchanan, James M. and Gordon Tullock. *The Calculus of Consent*. Ann Arbor: University of Michigan Press, 1962.

—— "Polluters' Profits and Political Response: Direct Controls Versus Taxes." *American Economic Review* (March 1975), 65(1):139–47.

Buck, Solon Justus. *The Granger Movement: A Study of Agricultural Organization and Its Political, Economic and Social Manifestations, 1870–1880*. Cambridge, Mass.: Harvard University Press, 1913, 1933.

Burby, John. *The Great American Motion Sickness or Why You Can't Get There from Here*. Boston: Little, Brown, 1971.

Burnham, David. "Regulatory Agencies and Competition." *New York Times* (September 20, 1976), pp. 37, 39.

Canon, Bradley C. "Voting Behavior on the FCC." *Midwest Journal of Political Science* (November 1969), 13(4):587–612.

Capron, William M., ed. *Technological Change in Regulated Industries*. Washington, D.C.: Brookings Institution, 1971.

Carbone, R. and J. R. Sweigart. "Equity and Selective Pollution Abatement Procedures." Paper in the Series in Numerical Optimization and Pollution

Abatement, School of Urban and Public Affairs, Carnegie-Mellon University, June 1974.

Cary, William L. *Politics and the Regulatory Agencies*. New York: McGraw-Hill, 1967.

Chalmers, David M. *Neither Socialism nor Monopoly: Theodore Roosevelt and the Decision to Regulate the Railroads*. Philadelphia: Lippincott, 1976.

Chamberlin, John. "Provision of Collective Goods As a Function of Group Size." *American Political Science Review* (June 1974), 68(2):707–16.

Clark, Peter B. and James Q. Wilson. "Incentive Systems: A Theory of Organizations." *Administrative Science Quarterly* (September 1961), 6:129–66.

Cobb, Roger W. and Charles D. Elder. *Participation in American Politics: The Dynamics of Agenda-Building*. Boston: Allyn and Bacon, 1972.

Cobb, Roger W., Jennie-Keith Ross, and Marc Howard Ross. "Agenda Building as a Comparative Political Process." *American Political Science Review* (March 1976), 70(1):126–38.

Cochran, Clarke E. "Political Science and 'The Public Interest'." *Journal of Politics* (May 1974), 36(2):327–55.

Cochran, Thomas C. *Railroad Leaders, 1845–1890: The Business Mind in Action*. Cambridge, Mass.: Harvard University Press, 1953; reprinted New York: Russell and Russell, 1965.

Cohen, Harris S. "Professional Licensure, Organizational Behavior, and the Public Interest." *Milbank Memorial Fund Quarterly* (Winter 1973), 51(1):73–88.

—— "Regulatory Politics and American Medicine." *American Behavioral Scientist* (September/October 1975), 19(1):122–36.

Cohen, Richard E. "Will Carter Be Able to Apply the Brakes to Trucking Regulation?" *National Journal* (May 14, 1977), 9(20):748–53.

Coleman, James S. "Foundations for a Theory of Collective Decisions." *American Journal of Sociology* (May 1966), 71(6):615–27.

Comanor, William S. and Bridger M. Mitchell. "The Costs of Planning: The FCC and Cable Television." *Journal of Law and Economics* (April 1972), 15(1):177–206.

Commission on Organization of the Executive Branch of the Government. *Task Force Report on Regulatory Commissions (Appendix N)*. Washington, D.C.: U.S. Government Printing Office, January 1949.

Comptroller General of the United States, United States General Accounting Office. *Government Regulatory Activity: Justifications, Processes, Impacts, and Alternatives*. PAD-77-34. Washington, D.C.: June 3, 1977.

—— *Federal Regulatory Programs and Activities*. PAD-78-33. Washington, D.C.: March 16, 1978.

Conant, Michael. *The Constitution and Capitalism*. St. Paul, Minn.: West, 1974.

Congressional Budget Office. "The Number of Federal Employees Engaged in Regulatory Activities." Staff paper prepared for the Subcommittee on Oversight and Investigations of the Committee on Interstate and Foreign Commerce, U.S. House of Representatives. Washington, D.C.: U.S. Government Printing Office, 1976.

Connolly, William E. "On 'Interests' in Politics." *Politics and Society* (Summer 1972), 2:459–77.

Cooper, Ann. "Sen. Cannon Undecided On How Far to Deregulate Nation's Airlines Industry." *Congressional Quarterly* (April 9, 1977), 35(15):656.

Cooper, Joseph. "Strengthening the Congress: An Organizational Analysis." *Harvard Journal on Legislation* (April 1975), 12(3):307–68.

—— "Congress in Organizational Perspective." In L. C. Dodd and B. I. Oppenheimer, eds., *Congress Reconsidered*, pp. 140–59. New York: Praeger, 1977.

Corley, Robert N. and Robert L. Black. *The Legal Environment of Business.* 2d ed. New York: McGraw-Hill, 1963, 1968.

Cornell, Nina W., Roger G. Noll, and Barry Weingast. "Safety Regulation." In Henry Owen and Charles L. Schultze, eds., *Setting National Priorities: The Next Ten Years*, pp. 457–504. Washington, D.C.: Brookings Institution, 1976.

Corson, John J. and R. Shale Paul. *Men Near the Top: Filling Key Posts in the Federal Service.* Baltimore, Md.: Johns Hopkins University Press, 1966.

Council of State Governments. *Occupational Licensing Legislation in the States.* Chicago: Council of State Governments, 1952.

—— *Occupations and Professions Licensed by the States, Puerto Rico, and the Virgin Islands.* RM-422. Chicago: Council of State Governments, December 1968.

Courville, Leon. "Regulation and Efficiency in the Electric Utility Industry." *Bell Journal of Economics and Management Science* (Spring 1974), 5(1):53–74.

Cowhey, Peter F. and Jeffrey A. Hart. "The Theory of Collective Goods Reexamined." Revised version of paper presented at the 1973 Annual Meeting of the International Studies Association, New York, N.Y.

Crewdson, Prudence. "Ford Presses Deregulation as Alternative to Proposed Consumer Advocacy Agency." *Congressional Quarterly* (May 10, 1975), 38(19):988–89.

Crumbaker, Calvin. *Transportation and Politics: A Study of the Long-and-Short-Haul Policies of Congress and the Interstate Commerce Commission.* Eugene: University of Oregon, 1940.

Curry, R. L., Jr. and L. L. Wade. *A Theory of Political Exchange.* Englewood Cliffs, N.J.: Prentice-Hall, 1968.

Cushman, Robert E. *The Independent Regulatory Commissions.* New York:

Oxford University Press, 1941; reprinted by Octagon Books, 1972.

Cutler, Lloyd N. and David R. Johnson. "Regulation and the Political Process." *Yale Law Journal* (June 1975), 84(7):1359–1418.

Cyert, Richard M. and James G. March. *A Behavioral Theory of the Firm.* Englewood Cliffs, N.J.: Prentice-Hall, 1963.

Dahl, Robert and Charles E. Lindblom. *Politics, Economics and Welfare.* New York: Harper and Row, 1953.

Dales, J. H. *Pollution, Property and Prices.* Toronto: University of Toronto Press, 1968.

Darnton, John. "Construction Industry: The Graft Is Built In." *New York Times* (July 13, 1975), section 4, p. 5.

Davis, J. Ronnie and Joe R. Hulett. *An Analysis of Market Failure: Externalities, Public Goods, and Mixed Goods.* Gainesville: The University Presses of Florida, 1977.

Davis, Kenneth Culp. *Administrative Law Treatise.* St. Paul, Minn.: West, 1958.

——*Administrative Law Treatise, 1970 Supplement.* St. Paul, Minn.: West, 1970.

——*Discretionary Justice: A Preliminary Inquiry.* Urbana: University of Illinois Press, 1971.

——*Administrative Law Text.* 3d ed. St. Paul, Minn.: West, 1972.

——*Administrative Law and Government.* 2d ed. St. Paul, Minn.: West, 1975.

Davis, Otto A. and Morton I. Kamien. "Externalities, Information and Alternative Collective Action." In Robert H. Haveman and Julius Margolis, eds., *Public Expenditures and Policy Analysis,* pp. 74–95. Chicago: Markham, 1970.

Davis, Lance E. and Douglass C. North. *Institutional Change and American Economic Growth.* Cambridge: Cambridge University Press, 1971.

DeAlessi, Louis. "An Economic Analysis of Government Ownership and Regulation: Theory and the Evidence from the Electric Power Industry." *Public Choice* (Fall 1974), 19:1–42.

—— "Some Effects of Ownership on the Wholesale Prices of Electric Power." *Economic Inquiry* (December 1975), 13(4):526–38.

DeFina, Robert. "Public and Private Expenditures for Federal Regulation of Business." Working Paper No. 22. St. Louis: Center for the Study of American Business, Washington University, November 1977.

Demsetz, Harold. "Why Regulate Utilities?" *Journal of Law and Economics* (April 1968), 11:55–65.

Deutsch, Karl W. "On Theories, Taxonomies, and Models as Communication Codes for Organizing Information." *Behavioral Science* (1966), 11:1–17.

Dewees, D. N., C. K. Everson, and W. A. Sims. *Economic Analysis of En-*

vironmental Policies. Toronto: Published for the Ontario Economic Council by the University of Toronto Press, 1975.

Dexter, Lewis Anthony. *How Organizations Are Represented in Washington.* Indianapolis, Ind.: Bobbs-Merrill, 1969.

Dimock, Marshall Edward. *Business and Government.* New York: Henry Holt, 1949.

Domestic Council Review Group on Regulatory Reform. *The Challenge of Regulatory Reform: A Report to the President.* Washington, D.C.: January 1977.

Dominguez, George S. *Marketing in a Regulated Environment.* New York: Wiley, 1978.

Downs, Anthony. *An Economic Theory of Democracy.* New York: Harper and Row, 1957.

—— "The Public Interest: Its Meaning in a Democracy." *Social Research* (Spring 1962), 29(1):1–36.

—— *Inside Bureaucracy.* Boston: Little, Brown, 1967.

Dubnick, Mel. "Making Regulators Regulate." Paper presented at the 1979 National Conference of the American Society for Public Administration, Baltimore, Md.

Dubnick, Melvin J. and Lafayette Walker. "Problems in U.S. Standard-Setting." *Midwest Review of Public Administration* (March 1979).

Dunn, James A., Jr. "The Debate on Public Ownership of U.S. Railroads: A Comparative Perspective." In James E. Anderson, ed., *Economic Regulatory Policies,* pp. 149–58. Carbondale: Southern Illinois University Press, 1976.

Eastman, Joseph B. "The Place of the Independent Commission." *The Constitutional Review* (1928), 12:95–102.

Eckert, Ross D. "On the Incentives of Regulators: The Case of Taxicabs." *Public Choice* (Spring 1973), 14:83–99.

Edelman, Murray. *The Symbolic Uses of Politics.* Urbana: University of Illinois Press, 1967.

Ehrlich, Isaac and Richard A. Posner. "An Economic Analysis of Legal Rulemaking." *Journal of Legal Studies* (January 1974), 3(1):257–86.

Elazar, Daniel J. "The New Federalism: Can the States Be Trusted?" *The Public Interest* (Spring), 35:89–102.

Elkin, Stephen. "Political Science and the Analysis of Public Policy." *Public Policy* (Summer 1974), 22:399–422.

Eulau, Heinz and John D. Sprague. *Lawyers in Politics.* Indianapolis: Bobbs-Merrill, 1964.

Evan, William M. "The Organization Set: Toward a Theory of Interorganizational Relations." In James D. Thompson, ed., *Approaches to Organizational Design.* Pittsburgh: University of Pittsburgh Press, 1966.

—— "An Organization-Set Model of Interorganizational Relations." In M. Tuite, R. Chisholm, and M. Radnor, eds., *Interorganizational Decision Making*, pp. 181–200. Chicago: Aldine, 1972.

—— *Organization Theory*. New York: Wiley, 1976.

Evans, John H., III. "Economic Models of Auditors' Responsibilities in the Accountability Environment." Unpublished paper (January 1978).

Fainsod, Merle. "Some Reflections on the Nature of the Regulatory Process." *Public Policy*, C. J. Friedrich and Edward S. Mason, eds. (Cambridge, Mass.: Harvard University Press, 1940), 1:297–323.

Fainsod, Merle and Lincoln Gordon. *Government and the American Economy*. New York: Norton, 1941.

Fainsod, Merle, Lincoln Gordon, and Joseph C. Palamountain, Jr. *Government and the American Economy*. 3d ed. New York: Norton, 1941, 1948, 1959.

Farris, Martin T. and Roy J. Sampson. *Public Utilities: Regulation, Management and Ownership*. Boston: Houghton Mifflin, 1973.

Fellmeth, Robert C. *The Interstate Commerce Omission: The Public Interest and the ICC*. New York: Grossman, 1970.

Ferrar, Terry A. and Robert L. Horst. "Effluent Charges—A Price on Pollution." *Atmospheric Environment* (1974), 8:657–67; see also exchange between James P. Lodge, Jr., and Ferrar and Horst in *Atmospheric Environment* (December 1974), 8:1343; and (1975), 9:460.

Fesler, James W. *The Independence of State Regulatory Agencies*. Chicago: Public Administration Service, 1942.

—— "Independent Regulatory Establishments." In Fritz Morstein Marx, ed., *Elements of Public Administration*, pp. 207–35. New York: Prentice-Hall, 1946.

"The Financial Situation." *Commercial and Financial Chronicle* (April 9, 1898), 66(1711):682–84.

Finch, Charles Edgar. *Everyday Civics: Community, State, and Nation*. New York: American Book Co., 1934.

Fiorina, Morris P. *Congress: Keystone of the Washington Establishment*. New Haven, Conn.: Yale University Press, 1977.

Fiorino, Daniel and Daniel S. Metlay. "Theories of Agency Failure, or, Why Regulatory Agencies Continue to Be Unreliable When the Solutions Seem So Obvious." Paper presented at the 1977 Annual Meeting of the American Political Science Association, Washington, D.C.

Fishburn, Peter C. *Theory of Social Choice*. Princeton, N. J.: Princeton University Press, 1973.

Flathman, Richard. *The Public Interest*. New York: Wiley, 1966.

Freedman, James O. "Crisis and Legitimacy in the Administrative Process." *Stanford Law Review* (April 1975), 27:1041–76.

Freeman, A. Myrick, III and Robert H. Haveman. "Water Pollution Control, River Basin Authorities, and Economic Incentives: Some Current Policy Issues.'' *Public Policy* (Winter 1971), 19(1):53–74.

—— ''Residuals Charges for Pollution Control: A Policy Evaluation.'' *Science* (July 28, 1972), 177(4046):322–29.

Freeman, A. Myrick III, Robert H. Haveman, and Allen V. Kneese. *The Economics of Environmental Policy.* New York: Wiley, 1973.

Freeman, Roger A. *The Growth of American Government: A Morphology of the Welfare State.* Stanford, Calif.: Hoover Institution Press, 1975.

Friedlaender, Ann F. *The Dilemma of Freight Transport Regulation.* Washington, D.C.: Brookings Institution, 1969.

Friedman, Milton. *Capitalism and Freedom.* Chicago: University of Chicago Press, 1963.

Friedmann, W. ''Government Enterprise: A Comparative Analysis.'' In W. Friedmann and J. F. Garner, eds., *Government Enterprise,* pp. 303–36. London: Stevens, 1970.

Friendly, Henry J. *The Federal Administrative Agencies: The Need for Better Definition of Standards.* Cambridge, Mass.: Harvard University Press, 1962.

Frohlich, Norman, Joe A. Oppenheimer, and Oran Young. *Political Leadership and Collective Goods.* Princeton: Princeton University Press, 1971.

Funigiello, Philip J. *Toward a National Power Policy: The New Deal and the Electric Utility Industry, 1933–1941.* Pittsburgh: University of Pittsburgh Press, 1973.

Galbraith, Jay R. *Designing Complex Organizations.* Reading, Mass.: Addison-Wesley, 1973.

—— *Organization Design.* Reading, Mass.: Addison-Wesley, 1977.

Gardner, Judy. ''Doubts Over 'Sunset' Bill Fail to Deter Backers of Concept.'' *Congressional Quarterly* (November 27, 1976), 34(48):3255–58.

Garraty, John A. *The New Commonwealth, 1877–1890.* New York: Harper and Row, 1968.

Gellhorn, Ernest. *Administrative Law and Process in a Nutshell.* St. Paul, Minn.: West, 1972.

Gellhorn, Walter. *Individual Freedom and Governmental Restraints.* Baton Rouge: Louisiana State University Press, 1956.

Georgiou, Petro. ''The Goal Paradigm and Notes Towards a Counter Paradigm.'' *Administrative Science Quarterly* (1973), 18:291–310.

Gerhardt, Paul H. ''Air Pollution Control: Benefits, Costs, and Inducements.'' In Selma Mushkin, ed., *Public Prices for Public Products,* pp. 153–71. Washington, D.C.: Urban Institute, 1972.

Gerwig, Robert. ''Public Authorities in the United States.'' *Law and Contemporary Problems* (Autumn 1961), 26(4):591–618.

Gifford, Daniel J. ''Decisions, Decisional Referents, and Administrative Justice.'' In Clark C. Havighurst, ed., *Administrative Discretion: Prob-*

lems of Decision-Making by Governmental Agencies. Dobbs Ferry, N.Y.: Oceana Publications, 1974. Reprinted from *Law and Contemporary Problems* (Winter 1972).

Glaeser, Martin G. *Public Utilities in American Capitalism.* New York: Macmillan, 1957.

Goldberg, Victor P. "Consumer Choice, Imperfect Information and Public Policy." IGA Research Report No. 26. Davis: University of California, Institute of Governmental Affairs, August 1973.

—— "Institutional Change and the Quasi-Invisible Hand." *Journal of Law and Economics* (October 1974), 17(2):461–92.

—— "Regulation and Administered Contracts." *Bell Journal of Economics* (Autumn 1976), 7(2):426–48.

Goodrich, Carter. *Government Promotion of American Canals and Railroads, 1800–1890.* New York: Columbia University Press, 1960.

Gorr, W. L., R. Carbone, K. O. Kortanek, J. R. Sweigart, and S. A. Gustafson. "Environmental-Energy-Equity Models for Resource Management in an Airshed." Paper presented at the 1975 ORSA/TIMS National Meeting; College of Administrative Science, Ohio State University, Working Paper No. 75–16, June 1975.

Graham, James M. and Victor H. Kramer. *Appointments to the Regulatory Agencies: The Federal Communications Commission and the Federal Trade Commission (1949–1974).* Committee print, Committee on Commerce, U.S. Senate, 94th Congress, 2d session. Washington, D.C.: U.S. Government Printing Office, April 1976.

Gray, Horace M. "The Passing of the Public Utility Concept." *Journal of Land and Public Utility Economics* (February 1940), 16(1):8–20. Reprinted in American Economic Association, ed., *Readings in the Social Control of Industry,* pp. 280–303. Philadelphia: Blakiston, 1949.

Green, Mark and Ralph Nader. "Economic Regulation vs. Competition: Uncle Sam the Monopoly Man." *Yale Law Journal* (April 1973), 82(5):871–89.

Guggenheimer, Jay Caesar. "The Development of the Executive Departments, 1775–1789." In J. Franklin Jameson, ed., *Essays in the Constitutional History of the United States in the Formative Period, 1775–1789,* pp. 116–85. Boston: Houghton Mifflin, 1889; reprinted New York: Da Capo Press, 1970.

Haefele, Edwin T. 1973a. "General Purpose Representatives at the Local Level." *Public Administration Review* (March/April 1973), 33(2):177–79.

—— 1973b. *Representative Government and Environmental Management.* Baltimore, Md.: Johns Hopkins University Press, 1973.

Hall, Ford P. *Government and Business.* 3d ed. New York: McGraw-Hill, 1949.

Hanson, A. H. *Public Enterprise and Economic Development*. London: Routledge and Kegan Paul, 1959.

Harbeson, Robert W. "Railroads and Regulation, 1877–1916: Conspiracy or Public Interest?" *Journal of Economic History* (June 1967), 27(2):230–42.

—— "Transport Regulation: A Centennial Evaluation." *ICC Practitioners Journal* (July/August 1972), 39:628–37.

Hardin, Russell. "The Economics and Politics of Collective Action." Paper presented at the Foundations of Political Economy Conference, University of Texas, Austin (1975). Fels Discussion Paper No. 66, School of Public and Urban Policy, University of Pennsylvania.

Harris, Milton and Artur Raviv. "Some Results on Incentive Contracts with Applications to Education and Employment, Health Insurance, and Law Enforcement." *American Economic Review* (March 1978), 68(1):20–30.

Hayashi, Paul M. and John M. Trapani. "Rate of Return Regulation and the Regulated Firm's Choice of Capital-Labor Ratio: Further Empirical Evidence on the Averch-Johnson Model." *Southern Economic Journal* (January 1976), 42(3):384–98.

Hayes, Michael T. "The Semi-Sovereign Pressure Groups: A Critique of Current Theory and an Alternative Typology." *Journal of Politics* (February 1978), 40(1):134–61.

Head, John G. "Public Goods and Public Policy." *Public Finance* (1962), 17:197–219.

Healy, Kent T. *The Economics of Transportation in America*. New York: Ronald Press, 1940.

Held, Virginia. *The Public Interest and Individual Interests*. New York: Basic Books, 1970.

Henderson, James M. and Richard E. Quandt. *Microeconomic Theory*. 2d ed. New York: McGraw-Hill, 1958, 1971.

Herman, William R. "Deregulation: Now or Never! (Or Maybe Someday?)" *Public Administration Review* (March/April 1976), 36(2):223–28.

Herring, E. Pendleton. 1936a. *Public Administration and the Public Interest*. New York: McGraw-Hill, 1936; reissued by Russell and Russell, 1967.

—— 1936b. *Federal Commissioners: A Study of Their Careers and Qualifications*. Cambridge, Mass.: Harvard University Press, 1936.

—— "The Experts on Five Federal Commissions." *American Political Science Review* (1938), 32:86–93.

Hillman, Jordan Jay. *Competition and Railroad Price Discrimination: Legal Precedent and Economic Policy*. Evanston, Ill.: The Transportation Center at Northwestern University, 1968.

Hilton, George W. "The Consistency of the Interstate Commerce Act." *Journal of Law and Economics* (October 1966), 9:87–113.

—— *The Transportation Act of 1958: A Decade of Experience*. Blooming-
ton: Indiana University Press, 1969.

—— 1972a. "The Basic Behavior of Regulatory Commissions." *American
Economic Review* (May 1972), 62(2):47–54.

—— 1972b. "Albro Martin's *Enterprise Denied.*" *Bell Journal of Economics and Management Science* (Autumn 1972), 3(2):628–31.

Hines, Lawrence G. *Environmental Issues: Population, Pollution, and Economics*. New York: Norton, 1973.

Holden, Matthew, Jr. " 'Imperialism' in Bureaucracy." *American Political
Science Review* (December 1966), 60(4):943–51.

Hoogenboom, Ari and Olive Hoogenboom. *A History of the ICC: From
Panacea to Palliative*. New York: Norton, 1976.

Horowitz, Donald L. *The Jurocracy: Government Lawyers, Agency Programs, and Activist Courts*. Lexington, Mass.: Lexington Books, Heath,
1977.

Huntington, Samuel P. "The Marasmus of the ICC: The Commission, the
Railroads, and the Public Interest." *Yale Law Journal* (April 1952),
61(4):467–509.

Huntington, Samuel P., G. Dickerman Williams, and Charles S. Morgan.
"The ICC Re-Examined: A Colloquy." *Yale Law Journal* (1953),
63:44–63.

Hurst, James Willard. *The Growth of American Law: The Law Makers*. Boston: Little, Brown, 1950.

Ilchman, Warren F. and Norman Thomas Uphoff. *The Political Economy of
Change*. Berkeley: University of California Press, 1969.

Jaffe, Louis L. "The Effective Limits of the Administrative Process: A
Reevaluation." *Harvard Law Review* (May 1954), 67(7):1105–35.

—— "James Landis and the Administrative Process." *Harvard Law Review*
(1964), 78:319–28.

—— *Judicial Control of Administrative Action*. Boston: Little, Brown,
1965.

—— "The Illusion of the Ideal Administration." *Harvard Law Review*
(May 1973), 86(7):1183–99.

Jensen, Michael C. and William H. Meckling. "Theory of the Firm: Managerial Behavior, Agency Costs and Ownership Structure." *Journal of Financial Economics* (October 1976), 3(4):305–60.

Johns, C. H. W., trans. *The Oldest Code of Laws in the World*. Edinburgh:
T. and T. Clark, 1903.

Jones, Charles O. *Clean Air: The Policies and Politics of Pollution Control*.
Pittsburgh: University of Pittsburgh Press, 1975.

—— *An Introduction to the Study of Public Policy*. 2d ed. North Scituate,
Mass.: Duxbury Press, 1977.

Jones, William H. "ICC Collision: Regulation Debate May Produce Challenge to Agency Survival.'' *Washington Post* (January 26, 1975), p. C-1.

Jordan, William A. ''Producer Protection, Prior Market Structure and the Effects of Government Regulation.'' *Journal of Law and Economics* (April 1972), 15(1):151–76.

Josephson, Matthew. *The Politicos, 1865–1896*. New York: Harcourt, Brace, and World, 1964.

Joskow, Paul L. ''The Determination of the Allowed Rate of Return in a Formal Regulatory Hearing.'' *Bell Journal of Economics and Management Science* (Autumn 1972), 3(2):632–44.

—— ''Pricing Decisions of Regulated Firms: A Behavioral Approach.'' *Bell Journal of Economics and Management Science* (Spring 1973), 4(1):118–40.

—— ''Inflation and Environmental Concern: Structural Change in the Process of Public Utility Price Regulation.'' *Journal of Law and Economics* (October 1974), 17(2):291–327.

Jowell, Jeffrey L. *Law and Bureaucracy: Administrative Discretion and the Limits of Legal Action*. Port Washington, N.Y.: Dunellen, Kennikat, 1975.

Kahn, Alfred. *The Economics of Regulation: Principles and Institutions*. 2 vols. New York: Wiley, 1971.

Karr, Albert. ''Aid to Railroads, Deregulation by ICC, Are Expected to Get Push From Carter.'' *Wall Street Journal* (January 6, 1977), p. 3.

Kaufman, Herbert. *The Forest Ranger: A Study in Administrative Behavior*. Baltimore: John Hopkins University Press, 1960.

—— *The Limits of Organizational Change*. University: University of Alabama Press, 1971.

—— ''The Direction of Organizational Evolution.'' *Public Administration Review* (July/August 1973), 33(4):300–7.

—— ''The Natural History of Human Organizations.'' *Administration and Society* (August 1975), 7(2):131–49.

—— *Are Government Organizations Immortal?* Washington, D.C.: Brookings Institution, 1976.

—— *Red Tape: Its Origins, Uses, and Abuses*. Washington, D.C.: Brookings Institution, 1977.

Kaysen, Carl and Donald F. Turner. *Antitrust Policy*. Cambridge, Mass.: Harvard University Press, 1959, 1965.

Kelman, Steven. ''Regulation by the Numbers—A Report on the Consumer Product Safety Commission.'' *The Public Interest* (Summer 1974), 36:83–102.

Kemmerer, Donald L. and C. Clyde Jones. *American Economic History*. New York: McGraw-Hill, 1959.

Key, V. O., Jr. ''Government Corporations.'' In Fritz Morstein Marx, ed.,

Elements of Public Administration, pp. 219–45. 2d. ed. Englewood Cliffs, N.J.: Prentice-Hall, 1946, 1959.

Keyes, Lucile Sheppard. "The Protective Functions of Commission Regulation." *American Economic Review Papers and Proceedings* (May 1958), 48(2):544–52.

Khandwalla, Pradip N. *The Design of Organizations.* New York: Harcourt Brace Jovanovich, 1977.

Kilmann, Ralph H., Louis R. Pondy, and Dennis P. Slevin, eds. *The Management of Organization Design.* Vol. I: *Strategies and Implementation.* Vol. II: *Research and Methodology.* New York: North-Holland, 1976.

Kilpatrick, Franklin P., Milton C. Cummings, Jr. and M. Kent Jennings. *The Image of the Federal Service.* Also, *Source Book of a Study of Occupational Values and the Image of the Federal Service.* Washington, D.C.: Brookings Institution, 1964.

Kirkland, Edward C. *Industry Comes of Age: Business, Labor, and Public Policy, 1860–1897.* Vol. VI of *The Economic History of the United States.* New York: Holt, Rinehart and Winston, 1961.

Kneese, Allen V. "Strategies for Environmental Management." *Public Policy* (Winter 1971), 19(1):37–52.

—— "Discharge Capacity of Waterways and Effluent Charges." In Selma Mushkin, ed., *Public Prices for Public Products,* pp. 133–51. Washington, D.C.: Urban Institute, 1972.

—— *Economics and the Environment.* New York: Penguin Books, 1977.

Kneese, Allen V. and Blair T. Bower. *Managing Water Quality: Economics, Technology, Institutions.* Baltimore, Md.: Johns Hopkins University Press, for Resources for the Future, 1968.

Kneese, Allen V. and Charles L. Schultze. *Pollution, Prices, and Public Policy.* Washington, D.C.: Brookings Institution, 1975.

Kochen, M. and K. W. Deutsch. "Delegation and Control in Organizations with Varying Degrees of Decentralization." *Behavioral Science* (July 1977), 22(4):258–69.

Kohlmeier, Louis M., Jr. *The Regulators: Watchdog Agencies and the Public Interest.* New York: Harper and Row, 1969.

Kolko, Gabriel. *Railroads and Regulation, 1877–1916.* Princeton, N.J.: Princeton University Press, 1965.

Koontz, Harold and Richard W. Gable. *Public Control of Economic Enterprise.* New York: McGraw-Hill, 1956.

Kopel, Gerald H. "Sunset in the West." *State Government* (Summer 1976), 49(3):135–38.

Krasnow, Erwin G. and Lawrence D. Longley. *The Politics of Broadcast Regulation.* 2d ed. New York: St. Martin's Press, 1973, 1978.

Krier, James E. and Edmund Ursin. *Pollution and Policy: A Case Essay on*

California and Federal Experience with Motor Vehicle Air Pollution 1940–1975. Berkeley: University of California Press, 1977.

Landis, James M. *The Administrative Process.* New Haven, Conn.: Yale University Press, 1938.

—— *Report on Regulatory Agencies to the President-Elect.* Subcommittee on Administrative Practice and Procedure, Committee on the Judiciary, United States Senate, 86th Congress, 2d Session. Washington, D.C.: U. S. Government Printing Office, December 1960.

Lane, Anne Wintermute and Louise Herrick Wall. *The Letters of Franklin K. Lane: Personal and Political.* Boston: Houghton Mifflin, 1922.

Larrabee, William. *The Railroad Question: A Historical and Practical Treatise on Railroads, and Remedies for Their Abuses.* 10th ed. Chicago: Schulte Publishing Co., 1893, 1898.

Learned, Henry Barrett. *The President's Cabinet.* New Haven, Conn.: Yale University Press, 1912.

Lee, R. Alton. *A History of Regulatory Taxation.* Lexington: University Press of Kentucky, 1973.

Leiserson, Avery. *Administrative Regulation: A Study in Representation of Interests.* Chicago: University of Chicago Press, 1942; Midway Reprint 1975.

Leone, Robert. "The Real Costs of Regulation." *Harvard Business Review* (November/December 1977):57–66.

Levine, Charles H., Robert W. Backoff, Allan R. Cahoon, and William J. Siffin. "Organizational Design: A Post Minnowbrook Perspective for the 'New' Public Administration." *Public Administration Review* (July/August 1975), 35(4):425–35.

Levy, Lester S. and Roy J. Sampson. *American Economic Development.* Boston: Allyn and Bacon, 1962.

Leys, W. A. R. and C. M. Perry. *Philosophy and The Public Interest.* Chicago: Committee to Advance Original Work in Philosophy, 1959.

Lichty, Lawrence W. "Members of the Federal Radio Commission and Federal Communications Commission 1927–1961." *Journal of Broadcasting* (Winter 1961–62), 6(1):23–34.

—— "The Impact of FRC and FCC Commissioners' Backgrounds on the Regulation of Broadcasting." *Journal of Broadcasting* (Spring 1962), 6(2):97–110.

Liebhafsky, H. H. *American Government and Business.* New York: Wiley, 1971.

Lilley, William, III and James C. Miller, III. "The New 'Social Regulation'." *The Public Interest* (Spring 1977), 47:49–61.

Lin, Steven A., ed. *Theory and Measurement of Economic Externalities.* New York: Academic Press, 1976.

Link, Mary. "Proposed Saccharin Ban Causes Controversy." *Congressional Quarterly* (March 26, 1977), 35(13):539–41.

Litwak, Eugene, with collaboration of Jack Rothman. "Towards the Theory and Practice of Coordination Between Formal Organizations." In William R. Rosengren and Mark Lefton, eds., *Organizations and Clients: Essays in the Sociology of Service,* pp. 137–86. Columbus, Ohio: Charles E. Merrill, 1970.

Locklin, D. Philip. *Railroad Regulation Since 1920.* New York: McGraw-Hill, 1928.

—— *Economics of Transportation.* 6th ed. Homewood, Ill.: Richard D. Irwin, 1966.

Loevinger, Lee. *The Law of Free Enterprise.* New York: Funk and Wagnalls in association with Modern Industry Magazine, 1949.

—— "Regulation and Competition as Alternatives." *The Antitrust Bulletin* (January/April 1966), 11(1/2):101–40.

—— "The Sociology of Bureaucracy." *The Business Lawyer* (November 1968), 24:7–18.

Lowe, Margaret. "Pro-Con: Deregulation of the Airline Industry." *Congressional Quarterly* (May 10, 1975), 33(19):977–80.

Lowi, Theodore J. *The End of Liberalism.* New York: Norton, 1969.

Lyon, Leverett S., Myron W. Watkins, and Victor Abramson. *Government and Economic Life: Development and Current Issues of American Public Policy,* vol. I. Washington, D.C.: Brookings Institution, 1939.

Macaulay, Hugh H. and Bruce Yandle. *Environmental Use and the Market.* Lexington, Mass.: Lexington Books, 1977.

MacAvoy, Paul W. *The Economic Effects of Regulation: The Trunk-Line Railroad Cartels and the Interstate Commerce Commission Before 1900.* Cambridge, Mass.: M.I.T. Press, 1965.

—— "The Formal Work-Product of the Federal Power Commissioners." *Bell Journal of Economics and Management Science* (Spring 1971), 2(1):379–95.

McClintock, Charles G. "Social Motivation—A Set of Propositions." *Behavioral Science* (September 1972), 17:438–54.

McConnell, Grant. *Private Power and American Democracy.* New York: Vintage Books, Alfred A. Knopf, 1966.

McCraw, Thomas K. "Regulation in America: A Review Article." *Business History Review* (Summer 1975), 49(2):159–83.

McGregor, Eugene B., Jr. "Politics and the Career Mobility of Bureaucrats." *American Political Science Review* (March 1974), 68(1):18–26.

McKie, James W. "Regulation and the Free Market: The Problem of Boundaries." *Bell Journal of Economics and Management Science* (Spring 1970), 1(1): 6–26.

—— "The Ends and Means of Regulation." In Charles F. Phillips, Jr., ed., *Competition and Monopoly in the Domestic Telecommunications Industry*. Lexington, Va.: Washington and Lee University Press, 1974.

MacRae, Duncan, Jr. and James A. Wilde. *Policy Analysis for Public Decisions*. North Scituate, Mass.: Duxbury Press, 1979.

Madden, Carl H. and James R. Morris. "Tax Incentives: Employment and Training of the Disadvantaged." In *Tax Incentives, Symposium conducted by the Tax Institute of America* (November 20–21, 1969). Lexington, Mass.: Heath Lexington Books, 1971.

Magee, Robert P. "Accounting Measurement and Employment Contracts: Current Value Reporting." *Bell Journal of Economics* (Spring 1978), 9(1):145–58.

Majone, Giandomenico. "Standard Setting and the Theory of Institutional Choice: The Case of Pollution Control." *Policy and Politics* (December 1975), 4:35–51.

—— "Choice among Policy Instruments for Pollution Control." *Policy Analysis* (Fall 1976), 2(4):589–613.

Mäler, Karl-Göran. *Environmental Economics: A Theoretical Inquiry*. Baltimore, Md.: Johns Hopkins University Press, 1974.

Manne, Henry G. "Mergers and the Market for Corporate Control." *Journal of Political Economy* (April 1965), 73:110–20.

Mansfield, Edwin. *Microeconomics: Theory and Applications*. New York: Norton, 1970.

Mansfield, Harvey C. "Federal Executive Reorganization: Thirty Years of Experience." *Public Administration Review* (July/August 1969), 29(4): 332–45.

March, James G. and Herbert A. Simon. *Organizations*. New York: Wiley, 1958.

Marcus, Alfred. " 'Command and Control': An Assessment of Smokestack Emission Regulation." Working Paper No. 308, Graduate School of Business, University of Pittsburgh, Pittsburgh, PA (1978).

Martin, Albro. *Enterprise Denied: Origins of the Decline of American Railroads, 1897–1917*. New York: Columbia University Press, 1971.

—— "The Troubled Subject of Railroad Regulation in the Gilded Age—A Reappraisal." *Journal of American History* (September 1974), 61(2):339–371.

Martin, Donald L. and Warren F. Schwartz, eds. *Deregulating American Industry*. Lexington, Mass.: Lexington Books, D.C. Heath, 1977.

Meade, James W. *The Theory of Economic Externalities: The Control of Environmental Pollution and Similar Social Costs*. Leiden: A. W. Sijthoff; Institut Universitaire de Hautes Etudes Internationales, Geneve, 1973.

Meier, Kenneth J. and John P. Plumlee. "Capture and Rigidity in Regulatory Administration.'' Paper presented at the 1977 Annual Meeting of the American Political Science Association, Washington, D.C.

—— "Regulatory Administration and Organizational Rigidity.'' *Western Political Quarterly* (March 1978), 31(1):80–95.

Meyer, Balthasar Henry. *Railway Legislation in the United States.* New York: Macmillan, 1903, 1909.

Meyer, Marshall W. and M. Craig Brown. "The Process of Bureaucratization.'' *American Journal of Sociology* (September 1977), 83(2):364–85.

Migue, Jean-Luc and Gerard Belanger. "Toward A General Theory of Managerial Discretion.'' *Public Choice* (Spring 1974), 17:27–47.

Milgram, Stanley. *Obedience to Authority.* New York: Harper and Row, 1974.

Miller, Clarence Altha. *The Lives of the Interstate Commerce Commissioners and the Commission's Secretaries.* Washington, D.C.: Association of Interstate Commerce Commission Practitioners, 1946.

Miller, George H. *Railroads and the Granger Laws.* Madison: University of Wisconsin Press, 1971.

Miller, Sidney L. *Railway Transportation: Principles and Point of View.* Chicago: A. W. Shaw, 1924.

—— *Inland Transportation: Principles and Policies.* 2d ed. New York: McGraw-Hill, 1933.

Mills, Edwin S. "Economic Incentives in Air Pollution Control.'' Reprinted from H. Wolozin, ed., *The Economics of Air Pollution.* New York: Norton, 1966; in D. A. L. Auld, ed., *Economic Thinking and Pollution Problems,* pp. 67–74. Toronto: University of Toronto Press, 1972. Also reprinted in Marshall I. Goldman, *Ecology and Economics: Controlling Pollution in the 70s,* pp. 142–48. Englewood Cliffs, N.J.: Prentice-Hall, 1967, 1972.

Mirrlees, James. "The Optimal Structure of Incentives and Authority within an Organization.'' *Bell Journal of Economics* (Spring 1976), 7(1):105–31.

Mishan, E. J. "The Postwar Literature on Externalities: An Interpretative Essay.'' *Journal of Economic Literature* (March 1971), 9(1):1–28.

Mitnick, Barry M. 1973a. "The Limits to Prediction.'' *Orbis* (Winter 1973), 16(4):1073–79.

—— 1973b. "Fiduciary Rationality and Public Policy: The Theory of Agency and Some Consequences.'' Paper presented at the 1973 Annual Meeting of the American Political Science Association, New Orleans, La.

—— "The Theory of Agency: The Concept of Fiduciary Rationality and Some Consequences.'' Ph.D. dissertation, Department of Political Science, University of Pennsylvania, 1974.

—— 1975a. "The Theory of Agency: The Fiduciary Norm.'' Paper presented at the 1975 Annual Meeting of the American Sociological Association, San Francisco, Calif.

—— 1975b. "The Theory of Agency: The Policing 'Paradox' and Regulatory Behavior." *Public Choice* (Winter 1975), 24:27–42.

—— "The Theory of Agency: A Framework." Paper presented at the 1976 Annual Meeting of the American Sociological Association, New York, N.Y.

—— "Government Self-Regulation." Paper presented at the 1978 National Conference of the American Society for Public Administration, Phoenix, Ariz.

—— "An Incentive Systems Theory of Regulatory 'Capture': Career Patterns and the Implementation of Regulation." Paper presented at the 1979 National Conference of the American Society for Public Administration, Baltimore, Md.

Mitnick, Barry M., Robert W. Backoff, and Hal G. Rainey. "The Incentive Systems Approach to the Study of Public Organizations." Paper presented at the 1977 Annual Meeting of the American Political Science Association, Washington, D.C.

Mitnick, Barry M. and Charles Weiss, Jr. "An Agency for Power Plant Siting." Unpublished paper. Salk Institute-Columbia University Urban Ecology Program, October 1970.

—— "The Siting Impasse and a Rational Choice Model of Regulatory Behavior: An Agency for Power Plant Siting." *Journal of Environmental Economics and Management* (1974), 1:150–171.

Moore, John E. "Recycling the Regulatory Agencies." *Public Administration Review* (July/August 1972), 32(4):291–98.

Moore, Thomas G. "The Purpose of Licensing." *Journal of Law and Economics* (October 1961), 4:93–117.

—— *Freight Transportation Regulation: Surface Freight and the Interstate Commerce Commission.* Washington, D.C.: American Enterprise Institute, 1972.

—— "Deregulating Transportation: Tracking the Progress." *Regulation* (March/April 1978), 2(2):37–44.

Morgan, Charles S. "A Critique of 'The Marasmus of the ICC: The Commission, the Railroads, and the Public Interest.'" *Yale Law Journal* (1953), 62:171–225.

Mund, Vernon A. *Government and Business.* 3d ed. New York: Harper, 1960.

Musgrave, Richard A. and Peggy B. Musgrave. *Public Finance in Theory and Practice.* New York: McGraw-Hill, 1973.

Mushkin, Selma J. and Charles L. Vehorn. "User Fees and Charges." *Governmental Finance* (November 1977), 6(4):42–48.

Musolf, Lloyd D. *Mixed Enterprise*. Lexington, Mass.: Lexington Books, Heath, 1972.

Nader, Ralph and Mark Green. "Nader: Deregulation is Another Consumer Fraud." *New York Times* (June 29, 1975), section 3, p. 14.

Nagel, Jack. *The Descriptive Analysis of Power*. New Haven, Conn.: Yale University Press, 1975.

Nagel, Stuart S. "Regulatory Commissioners and Party Politics." In Nagel, *The Legal Process from a Behavioral Perspective*, pp. 237–44. Homewood, Ill.: Dorsey, 1969.

—— "Incentives for Compliance with Environmental Law." *American Behavioral Scientist* (May/June 1974), 17(5):690–710.

Nash, Gerald D. "Origins of the Interstate Commerce Act of 1887." *Pennsylvania History* (1957), 24:181–90.

Niskanen, William. *Bureaucracy and Representative Government*. Chicago: Aldine-Atherton, 1971.

—— "Bureaucrats and Politicians." *Journal of Law and Economics* (December 1975), 18(3):617–43; "Comment" by Julius Margolis, pp. 645–59.

Noll, Roger G. 1971a. *Reforming Regulation: An Evaluation of the Ash Council Proposals*. Washington, D.C.: Brookings Institution.

—— 1971b. "The Economics and Politics of Regulation." *Virginia Law Review* (1971), 57:1016–1032.

—— 1971c. "The Behavior of Regulatory Agencies." *Review of Social Economy* (March 1971), 29:15–19.

Noll, R., M. J. Peck, and J. J. McGowan. *Economic Aspects of Television Regulation*. Washington, D.C.: Brookings Institution, 1973.

Ogul, Morris S. *Congress Oversees the Bureaucracy: Studies in Legislative Supervision*. Pittsburgh: University of Pittsburgh Press, 1976.

Ohio Legislative Service Commission. "Aspects of Public Utility Regulation." Columbus, Ohio: June 1977.

Olson, Mancur, Jr. *The Logic of Collective Action: Public Goods and the Theory of Groups*. New York: Harvard University Press and Schocken Books, 1965.

Olson, Mancur, Jr. and Richard Zeckhauser. "An Economic Theory of Alliances." *Review of Economics and Statistics* (August 1966), 48(3):266–79.

Orr, Lloyd. "Incentive for Innovation as the Basis for Effluent Charge Strategy." *American Economic Review* (May 1976), 66(2):441–447.

Orton, William. "Culture and Laissez-Faire." *Atlantic Monthly* (June 1935), 155:46.

Ostrom, Vincent. *The Intellectual Crisis in American Public Administration*. Revised ed. University: University of Alabama Press, 1973, 1974.

Owen, Bruce M. and Ronald Braeutigam. *The Regulation Game.* Cambridge, Mass.: Ballinger, 1978.

Pegrum, Dudley F. *Public Regulation of Business.* Homewood, Ill.: Irwin, 1959.

Pelsoci, Thomas M. "Commission Attributes and Regulatory Discretion: A Longitudinal Study of State Public Utility Commissions." Paper presented at the 1978 Annual Meeting of the American Political Science Association, New York, N.Y.

Peltzman, Sam. "Toward a More General Theory of Regulation." *Journal of Law and Economics* (August 1976), 19(2):211–40; see also comments by Jack Hirshleifer and Gary Becker, pp. 241–44 and 245–48.

Petersen, H. Craig. "An Empirical Test of Regulatory Effects." *Bell Journal of Economics* (Spring 1975), 6(1):111–26.

Pfeffer, Jeffrey. "Administrative Regulation and Licensing: Social Problem or Solution?" *Social Problems* (April 1974), 21(4):468–79.

—— *Organizational Design.* Arlington Heights, Ill.: AHM Publishing, 1978.

Pfeffer, Jeffrey and Gerald R. Salancik. *The External Control of Organizations: A Resource Dependence Perspective.* New York: Harper and Row, 1978.

Phillips, Charles F., Jr. *The Economics of Regulation: Theory and Practice in the Transportation and Public Utility Industries.* Homewood, Ill. Richard D. Irwin, 1965.

Pitkin, Hanna Fenichel. *The Concept of Representation.* Berkeley: University of California Press, 1967.

Plott, Charles R. "Occupational Self-Regulation: A Case Study of the Oklahoma Dry Cleaners." *Journal of Law and Economics* (October 1965), 8:195–222.

Plott, Charles and Robert Meyer. "The Technology of Public Goods, Externalities, and the Exclusion Principle." "Comment" by Robert H. Haveman. In Edwin S. Mills, ed., *Economic Analysis of Environmental Problems,* pp. 65–94. New York: National Bureau of Economic Research; Columbia University Press, 1975.

Porter, Michael E. and Jeffrey F. Sagansky. "Information, Politics, and Economic Analysis: The Regulatory Decision Process in the Air Freight Cases." *Public Policy* (Spring 1976), 24(2):263–307.

Posner, Richard A. "Natural Monopoly and Its Regulation." *Stanford Law Review* (February 1969), 21:548–643.

—— "Taxation by Regulation." *Bell Journal of Economics and Management Science* (Spring 1971), 2(1):22–50.

—— "Theories of Economic Regulation." *Bell Journal of Economics and Management Science* (Autumn 1974), 5(2):335–58.

President's Advisory Council on Executive Organization. *A New Regulatory*

Framework: Report on Selected Independent Regulatory Agencies. Washington, D.C.: U.S. Government Printing Office, January 1971.

Pressman, Jeffrey L. and Aaron Wildavsky. *Implementation.* Berkeley: University of California Press, 1973.

Price, James L. *The Study of Turnover.* Ames, Iowa: Iowa State University Press, 1977.

Purcell, Edward A., Jr. "Ideas and Interests: Businessmen and the Interstate Commerce Act." *Journal of American History* (December 1967), 54:561–78.

Rabinovitz, Francine, Jeffrey Pressman, and Martin Rein. "Guidelines: A Plethora of Forms, Authors, and Functions." *Policy Sciences* (December 1976), 7(4):399–416.

Rainey, Hal G. "Comparing Public and Private: Conceptual and Empirical Analysis of Incentives and Motivation Among Government and Business Managers." Ph.D. dissertation, School of Public Administration, Ohio State University, 1977.

Rainey, Hal G., Robert W. Backoff, and Charles H. Levine. "Comparing Public and Private Organizations." *Public Administration Review* (March/April 1976), 36(2):233–44.

Rankin, Bob. "New Department Given Wide Energy Powers." *Congressional Quarterly* (July 30, 1977), 35(31):1581–84.

Rawson, George E. "The Implementation of Public Policy by Third-Sector Organizations." Paper presented at the 1978 Annual Meeting of the American Political Science Association, New York, N.Y.

Redford, Emmette S. *Administration of National Economic Control.* New York: Macmillan, 1952.

—— *The Regulatory Process: With Illustrations from Commercial Aviation.* Austin: University of Texas Press, 1969.

Rickson, Roy E. "Dimensions of Environmental Management: Legitimation of Government Regulation by Industrial Managers." *Environment and Behavior* (March 1977), 9(1):15–40.

Riker, William. *The Theory of Political Coalitions.* New Haven: Yale University Press, 1962.

Riker, William and Peter C. Ordeshook. *An Introduction to Positive Political Theory.* Englewood Cliffs, N.J.: Prentice-Hall, 1973.

Ripley, William Z. *Railroads: Rates and Regulation.* 2d ed. New York: Longmans, Green, 1912, 1913.

Roberts, Marc J. "River Basin Authorities: A National Solution to Water Pollution." *Harvard Law Review* (May 1970), 83(7):1527–56.

—— "Organizing Water Pollution Control: The Scope and Structure of River Basin Authorities." *Public Policy* (Winter 1971), 19(1):75–141.

Roberts, Marc J. and Richard B. Stewart. "Energy and the Environment." In Henry Owen and Charles L. Schultze, eds., *Setting National Priorities:*

The Next Ten Years, pp. 411–56. Washington, D.C.: Brookings Institution, 1976.

Rohlfing, Charles C., et al. *Business and Government.* 4th ed. Chicago: Foundation Press, 1941.

Ronen, Joshua. "The Dual Role of Accounting: A Financial Economic Perspective." In Bicksler, ed., *Handbook of Financial Economics,* ch. 20:415–54. North-Holland, 1979.

Roos, Leslie L., Jr. and Noralou P. Roos. "Pollution, Regulation, and Evaluation." *Law and Society Review* (May 1972), 6(4):509–29.

Rose-Ackerman, Susan. "Effluent Charges: A Critique." *Canadian Journal of Economics* (1973), 6(4):512–28; reprinted in R. Zeckhauser et al., eds., *Benefit-Cost and Policy Analysis 1974,* pp. 308–24. Chicago: Aldine, 1975.

—— "Market Models for Water Pollution Control: Their Strengths and Weaknesses." *Public Policy* (Summer 1977), 25(3): 383–406.

Rosenbaum, Walter A. *The Politics of Environmental Concern.* 2d ed. New York: Praeger, 1977.

Rosengren, William R. "The Careers of Clients and Organizations." In William R. Rosengren and Mark Lefton, ed., *Organizations and Clients: Essays in the Sociology of Service,* pp. 117–35. Columbus, Ohio: Charles E. Merrill, 1970.

Rosenthal, Albert J. "The Federal Power to Protect the Environment: Available Devices to Compel or Induce Desired Conduct." *Southern California Law Review* (Spring 1972), 45(2):397–449.

Ross, Stephen A. "The Economic Theory of Agency: The Principal's Problem." *American Economic Review* (May 1973), 63(2):134–39.

—— "On the Economic Theory of Agency and the Principle of Similarity." In M. Balch, D. McFadden, and S. Wu, eds., *Essays on Economic Behavior Under Uncertainty,* ch. 8. North-Holland, 1974.

Rothenberg, Jerome. "The Physical Environment." In James W. McKie, ed., *Social Responsibility and the Business Predicament,* pp. 191–215. Washington, D.C.: Brookings Institution, 1974.

Rourke, Francis E. *Bureaucracy, Politics, and Public Policy.* 2d ed. Boston: Little, Brown, 1969, 1976.

Ruff, Larry E. "The Economic Common Sense of Pollution." *The Public Interest* (Spring 1970), 19:69–85.

Russell, Milton and Robert B. Shelton. "A Model of Regulatory Agency Behavior." *Public Choice* (Winter 1974), 20:47–62.

Sabatier, Paul A. "Social Movements and Regulatory Agencies: Toward a More Adequate—and Less Pessimistic—Theory of 'Clientele Capture.' " *Policy Sciences* (September 1975), 6(3):301–42.

—— "Regulatory Policy-Making: Toward a Framework of Analysis." *Natural Resources Journal* (July 1977), 17(3):415–60.

Samuels, Warren J. "Public Utilities and the Theory of Power." In Milton

Russell, ed., *Perspectives in Public Regulation: Essays on Political Economy,* pp. 1–27; "Comments" by Mark V. Pauly, pp. 27–33. Carbondale and Edwardsville, Ill.: Southern Illinois University Press, 1973.

Samuels, Warren J. and A. Allan Schmid. "Polluters' Profit and Political Response: The Dynamics of Rights Creation." *Public Choice* (Winter 1976) 28:99–105.

Samuelson, Paul. "The Pure Theory of Public Expenditure." *Review of Economics and Statistics* (November 1954), 36:387–89.

—— "Diagrammatic Exposition of a Theory of Public Expenditure." *Review of Economics and Statistics* (November 1955), 37:350–56.

Samuelson, Robert J. "The Truckers and the Feds—A Tangled Relationship." *National Journal* (January 6, 1979), 11(1):4–8.

Sanborn, John Bell. *Congressional Grants of Land in Aid of Railways.* Ph.D. dissertation, University of Wisconsin, 1899. *Bulletin of the University of Wisconsin,* Economics, Political Science, and History Series, 2(3):263–392.

Schattschneider, E. E. *The Semi-Sovereign People.* New York: Holt, Rinehart and Winston, 1960.

Scheiber, Harry N. "The Road to *Munn:* Eminent Domain and the Concept of Public Purpose in the State Courts." In Donald Fleming and Bernard Bailyn, eds., *Perspectives in American History,* vol. 5, pp. 329–402. Cambridge, Mass.: Charles Warren Center for Studies in American History, Harvard University, 1971.

Schelling, Thomas C. *The Strategy of Conflict.* New York: Oxford University Press, 1960.

—— "On the Ecology of Micromotives." *The Public Interest* (Fall 1971), 7(25):61–98.

—— "Command and Control." In James W. McKie, ed., *Social Responsibility and the Business Predicament,* pp. 79–108. Washington, D.C.: Brookings Institution, 1974.

—— *Micromotives and Macrobehavior.* New York: Norton, 1978.

Scher, Seymour. "Regulatory Agency Control through Appointment: The Case of the Eisenhower Administration and the NLRB." *Journal of Politics* (November 1961), 23(4):667–688.

Schubert, Glendon. *The Public Interest.* Glencoe, Ill.: Free Press, 1960.

Schultze, Charles L. "The Role of Incentives, Penalties, and Rewards in Attaining Public Policy." In R. H. Haveman and J. Margolis, eds., *Public Expenditures and Policy Analysis,* ch. 6, pp. 145–72. Chicago: Markham, 1970.

—— *The Public Use of Private Interest.* Washington, D.C.: Brookings Institution, 1977.

Schwartz, Bernard. *The Professor and the Commissions.* New York: Alfred A. Knopf, 1959.

—— *Administrative Law.* Boston: Little, Brown, 1976.

Schwartz, Michael. *Radical Protest and Social Structure: The Southern Farmers' Alliance and Cotton Tenancy, 1880–1890*. New York: Academic Press, 1976.

Seavoy, Ronald E. "The Public Service Origins of the American Business Corporation." *Business History Review* (Spring 1978), 52(1):30–60.

Seidman, Harold. 1975a. *Politics, Position, and Power*. 2d ed. New York: Oxford University Press, 1970, 1975.

—— 1975b. "Government-Sponsored Enterprise in the United States." In Bruce L. R. Smith, ed., *The New Political Economy: The Public Use of the Private Sector*, pp. 83–108. New York: Halsted, Wiley, 1975.

Selznick, Philip. *TVA and the Grass Roots*. Berkeley: University of California Press, 1949.

Seneca, Joseph J. and Michael K. Taussig. *Environmental Economics*. Englewood Cliffs, N.J.: Prentice-Hall, 1974.

Shapiro, Martin. *The Supreme Court and Administrative Agencies*. New York: Free Press, 1968.

Sharfman, I. L. *The Interstate Commerce Commission: A Study in Administrative Law and Procedure*. Parts 1–4. New York: Commonwealth Fund, 1931–37.

Sharp, Margaret. *The State, the Enterprise and the Individual*. London: London School of Economics and Political Science, Weidenfeld and Nicolson, 1973.

Shepherd, William G. *Economic Performance Under Public Ownership: British Fuel and Power*. New Haven, Conn.: Yale University Press, 1965.

—— "Entry as a Substitute for Regulation." *American Economic Review* (May 1973), 63(2):98–105.

—— "Regulation, Entry and Public Enterprise." In William G. Shepherd and Thomas G. Gies, eds., *Regulation in Further Perspective: The Little Engine That Might*, pp. 5–25. Cambridge, Mass.: Ballinger, 1974.

—— *The Treatment of Market Power: Antitrust, Regulation, and Public Enterprise*. New York: Columbia University Press, 1975.

Shimberg, Benjamin. 1976a. "The Sunset Approach: The Key to Regulatory Reform?" *State Government* (Summer 1976), 49(3):140–47.

—— 1976b. *Improving Occupational Regulation*. Final Report to Employment and Training Administration, U.S. Department of Labor, under Grant No. 21-34-75-12, "Cooperative Planning to Improve Occupational Regulation." Princeton, N.J.: Educational Testing Service, July 1976.

Shimberg, B., B. F. Esser, and D. H. Kruger. *Occupational Licensing: Practices and Policies*. Washington, D.C.: Public Affairs Press, 1972, 1973.

Short, Lloyd M. *The Development of National Administrative Organization in the United States*. Baltimore, Md.: Johns Hopkins University Press, 1923.

Sichel, Werner, ed. *Salvaging Public Utility Regulation*. Lexington, Mass.: Lexington Books, D.C. Heath, 1976.

Slesinger, Reuben E. and Asher Isaacs. *Business, Government and Public Policy*. 2d ed. Princeton, N. J.: D. Van Nostrand, 1968.

Slote, Alfred. *Termination: The Closing at Baker Plant*. Ann Arbor, Mich.: Institute for Social Research, 1977.

Smead, Elmer E. *Governmental Promotion and Regulation of Business*. New York: Appleton-Century-Crofts, Meredith Corporation, 1969.

Smith, Adam. *An Inquiry into the Nature and Causes of the Wealth of Nations*. Edited by C. J. Bullock. Vol. 10. Harvard Classics. New York: P. F. Collier, 1909.

Smith, Bruce L. R., ed. *The New Political Economy: The Public Use of the Private Sector*. New York: Halsted, Wiley, 1975.

Smith, Lincoln. "Recent Trends in the Appointment of Commissioners." *Ohio State Law Journal* (Autumn 1952), 13(4):479–502.

—— "Lawyers as Regulatory Commissioners." *George Washington Law Review* (March 1955), 23(4):375–428.

—— 1957a. "Accountants as Regulatory Commissioners." *Public Utilities Fortnightly* (January 17, 1957), 59(2):93–104.

—— 1957b. "Engineers as Regulatory Commissioners," Parts I and II. Public Utilities Fortnightly (November 7 and 21, 1957), 60(10,11): 718–27 and 846–54.

—— "Businessmen as Regulatory Commissioners." *Journal of Business* (April 1958), 31(2):132–44.

—— "Laymen as Regulatory Commissioners," Parts I and II. *Public Utilities Fortnightly* (May 7 and 21, 1959), 63(10,11):673–82 and 750–59.

—— "State Utility Commissioners—1978." *Public Utilities Fortnightly* (February 16, 1978), 101(4):9–15.

Sokal, Robert R. "Classification: Purposes, Principles, Progress, Prospects." *Science* (September 27, 1974), 185(4157):1115–23.

Sorauf, Frank. "The Public Interest Reconsidered." *Journal of Politics* (November 1957), 19:616–39.

Sorg, James D. "A Theory of Individual Behavior in the Implementation of Policy Innovations." Ph.D. dissertation, School of Public Administration, Ohio State University, 1978.

Spann, Robert M. "Rate of Return Regulation and Efficiency in Production: An Empirical Test of the Averch-Johnson Thesis." *Bell Journal of Economics and Management Science* (Spring 1974), 5(1):38–52.

Spann, Robert M. and Edward W. Erickson. "The Economics of Railroading: The Beginning of Cartelization and Regulation." *Bell Journal of Economics and Management Science* (Autumn 1970), 1(2):227–44.

Staaf, Robert and Francis Tannian, eds. *Externalities: Theoretical Dimensions of Political Economy*. New York: Dunellen, 1972.

Stanley, David T. *The Higher Civil Service*. Washington, D.C.: Brookings Institution, 1964.

——— "Trying to Avoid Layoffs." *Public Administration Review* (September/October 1977), 37(5):515–17.

Stanley, David T., Dean E. Mann, and Jameson W. Doig. *Men Who Govern*. Washington, D.C.: Brookings Institution, 1967.

Starbuck, William H. "Organizational Growth and Development." In James G. March, ed., *Handbook of Organizations,* pp. 451–533. Chicago: Rand McNally, 1965.

——— "Organizations and Their Environments." In Marvin D. Dunnette, ed., *Handbook of Industrial and Organizational Psychology,* pp. 1069–1123. Chicago: Rand McNally, 1976.

Steiner, George A. *Government's Role in Economic Life*. New York: McGraw-Hill, 1953.

Steiner, Peter O. "The Public Sector and the Public Interest." In R. H. Haveman and J. Margolis, eds., *Public Expenditures and Policy Analysis,* pp. 21–58. Chicago: Markham, 1970.

Stickney, A. B. *The Railway Problem*. St. Paul, Minn.: D. D. Merrill, 1891.

Stigler, George J. "The Theory of Economic Regulation." *Bell Journal of Economics and Management Science* (Spring 1971), 2(1):3–21.

——— "Free Riders and Collective Action: An Appendix to Theories of Economic Regulation." *Bell Journal of Economics and Management Science* (Autumn 1974), 5(2):359–65.

——— *The Citizen and the State: Essays on Regulation*. Chicago: University of Chicago Press, 1975.

Stigler, George J. and Claire Friedland. "What Can Regulators Regulate?: The Case of Electricity." *Journal of Law and Economics* (October 1962), 5:1–16.

Stiglitz, Joseph E. "Incentives, Risk, and Information: Notes towards a Theory of Hierarchy." *Bell Journal of Economics* (Autumn 1975), 6(2):552–79.

Stinchcombe, Arthur L. "Social Structure and Organizations." In James G. March, ed., *Handbook of Organizations,* pp. 412–93. Chicago: Rand McNally, 1965.

Stone, Alan. *Economic Regulation and the Public Interest: The Federal Trade Commission in Theory and Practice*. Ithaca: Cornell University Press, 1977.

Stover, John F. *American Railroads*. Chicago: University of Chicago Press, 1961.

Surrey, Stanley S. "The Congress and the Tax Lobbyist—How Special Tax Provisions Get Enacted." *Harvard Law Review* (May 1957), 70(7):1145–82.

—— "Tax Incentives as a Device for Implementing Government Policy: A Comparison with Direct Government Expenditures." *Harvard Law Review* (February 1970), 83(4):705–38. Reprinted in *Tax Incentives,* Symposium conducted by the Tax Institute of America (November 20–21, 1969). Lexington, Mass.: Heath Lexington Books, 1971.

—— "Treasury Department Regulatory Material Under the Tax Code." *Policy Sciences* (December 1976), 7(4):505–18.

Swenson, Rinehart John. *The National Government and Business.* New York: Century, 1924.

Tansik, David A. and Michael Radnor. "An Organization Theory Perspective On the Development of New Organizational Functions." *Public Administration Review* (November/December 1971), 31(6):644–52.

Tax Incentives, Symposium conducted by the Tax Institute of America (November 20–21, 1969). Lexington, Mass.: Heath Lexington Books, 1971.

Taylor, Michael. "Minimum Rates for Trucking May End." *San Francisco Chronicle* (September 4, 1975), p. 17.

Thompson, Donald N. *The Economics of Environmental Protection.* Cambridge, Mass.: Winthrop, 1973.

Thompson, James D. *Organizations in Action.* New York: McGraw-Hill, 1967.

Trebing, Harry M. "The Chicago School versus Public Utility Regulation." *Journal of Economic Issues* (March 1976), 10(1):97–126.

Truman, David B. *The Governmental Process: Political Interests and Public Opinion.* 2d ed. New York: Alfred A. Knopf, 1951, 1971.

Tullock, Gordon. *The Politics of Bureaucracy.* Washington, D.C.: Public Affairs Press, 1965.

Turvey, R., ed. *Public Enterprise.* Baltimore, Md.: Penguin Books, 1968.

Tussman, Joseph. *Obligation and the Body Politic.* New York: Oxford University Press, 1960.

United Nations Technical Assistance Administration. *Some Problems in the Organization and Administration of Public Enterprise in the Industrial Field.* New York: United Nations, 1954.

U.S. Bureau of the Census, United States Department of Commerce. *Statistical Abstract of the United States, 1978.* 99th ed. Washington, D.C.: U.S. Government Printing Office, 1978.

U.S. Department of Commerce. *State Occupational Legislation,* A Marketing Laws Survey Publication, vol. 6. Washington, D.C.: Marketing Laws Survey, Bureau of Foreign and Domestic Commerce, U.S. Department of Commerce, March 1942.

United States George Washington Bicentennial Commission. *The Writings of George Washington from the Original Manuscript Sources, 1745–1799,* John C. Fitzpatrick, ed., vol. 14. Washington, D.C.: U. S. Government Printing Office, August 1936.

U.S. House of Representatives, Subcommittee on Oversight and Investigations, Committee on Interstate and Foreign Commerce. *Regulatory Reform–Volume I: Quality of Regulators.* 94th Congress, 1st Session. Washington, D.C.: U.S. Government Printing Office, November 6 and 7, 1975.

—— *Federal Regulation and Regulatory Reform.* 94th Congress, 2d Session. Washington, D.C.: U.S. Government Printing Office, October 1976.

U.S. Senate, Committee on Governmental Affairs. *Study on Federal Regulation,* 6 vols. Vol. 1: *The Regulatory Appointments Process,* by James M. Graham (January 1977). Vol. 3: *Congressional Oversight of Regulatory Agencies,* by Paul Rosenthal and Mark Nadel (February 1977). Vol. 4: *Delay in the Regulatory Process,* by Lawrence B. Novey, William F. Pedersen, Jr., Paul Rosenthal, and others (July 1977). Vol. 5: *Regulatory Organization,* by Ethel Z. Geisinger, James M. Graham and Theodore J. Jacobs (December 1977). 95th Congress, 1st and 2d Sessions. Washington, D.C.: U.S. Government Printing Office, 1977–78.

U.S. Senate, Subcommittee on Intergovernmental Relations, Committee on Government Operations. *State Utility Commissions.* 90th Congress, 1st Session. Washington, D.C.: U.S. Government Printing Office, September 11, 1967.

Uphoff, Norman T. and Warren F. Ilchman. *The Political Economy of Development: Theoretical and Empirical Contributions.* Berkeley: University of California Press, 1972.

Urban, Raymond and Richard Mancke. "Federal Regulation of Whiskey Labelling: From the Repeal of Prohibition to the Present." *Journal of Law and Economics* (October 1972), 15(2):411–26.

Vaden, Ted. "Truckers Fear Continued Deregulation Drive." *Congressional Quarterly* (November 27, 1976), 34(48):3249–54.

Vernon, Raymond, ed. *Big Business and the State: Changing Relations in Western Europe.* Cambridge, Mass.: Harvard University Press, 1974.

Vladeck, Bruce C. "The Limits of Regulation: Implications of Alternative Models for the Health Sector." Paper presented at the Committee on Health Politics meeting, 1975 Annual Meeting of the American Political Science Association, San Francisco, Calif.

Wagner, James R. "Endangered Species Law Threatens Federal Project; Amendments Contemplated." *Congressional Quarterly* (March 12, 1977), 35(11):453–54.

Wallace, Walter L. "Overview of Contemporary Sociological Theory." In Wallace, ed., *Sociological Theory: An Introduction,* pp. 1–59. Chicago: Aldine, 1969.

Walsh, Annmarie Hauck. *The Public's Business: The Politics and Practices of Government Corporations.* Cambridge, Mass.: M.I.T. Press, 1978.

Walters, A. A. *The Economics of Road User Charges*. World Bank Staff Occasional Papers Number Five. Baltimore, Md.: Distributed by Johns Hopkins Press for the International Bank for Reconstruction and Development, 1968.

"Wanting More Power." *Commercial and Financial Chronicle* (December 18, 1897), 65(1695):1148–49.

Warner, W. Lloyd, Darab B. Unwalla, and John H. Trimm. *The Emergent American Society: Large-Scale Organizations*, vol. 1. New Haven: Yale University Press, 1967.

Warner, W. Lloyd, Paul P. Van Riper, Norman H. Martin, and Orvis F. Collins. *The American Federal Executive*. New Haven: Yale University Press, 1963.

Weaver, Paul H. "Regulation, Social Policy, and Class Conflict." *The Public Interest* (Winter 1978), 50:45–63.

Weidenbaum, Murray L. *Business, Government, and the Public*. Englewood Cliffs, N.J.: Prentice-Hall, 1977.

Weingast, Barry R. "A Positive Model of Public Policy Formation: The Case of Regulatory Agency Behavior." Working Paper No. 25. Washington University, St. Louis: Center for the Study of American Business, January 1978.

Weitzman, Martin L. "Prices vs. Quantities." *Review of Economic Studies* (October 1974), 61(4) No. 128:477–91.

Welborn, David M. "Presidents, Regulatory Commissioners and Regulatory Policy." *Journal of Public Law* (1966), 15(1):3–39.

—— *Governance of Federal Regulatory Agencies*. Knoxville: University of Tennessee Press, 1977.

Wenner, Lettie McSpadden. "Enforcement of Water Pollution Control Law." *Law and Society Review* (May 1972), 6(4):481–507.

—— "Pollution Control: Implementation Alternatives." *Policy Analysis* (Winter 1978), 4(1):47–65.

White, Lawrence J. "Effluent Charges as a Faster Means of Achieving Pollution Abatement." *Public Policy* (Winter 1976), 24(1):111–25.

White, Leonard D. *The Federalists*. New York: Macmillan, 1948.

White, Ron D. "The Anatomy of Nonmarket Failure: An Examination of Environmental Policies." *American Economic Review* (May 1976), 66(2):454–58.

Wilcox, Clair. *Public Policies Toward Business*. 3d ed. Homewood, Ill.: Richard D. Irwin, 1966.

Wilcox, Clair and William G. Shepherd. *Public Policies Toward Business*. 5th ed. Homewood, Ill: Richard D. Irwin, 1975.

Williams, Wenmouth, Jr. "Impact of Commissioner Background on FCC Decisions: 1962–1975." *Journal of Broadcasting* (Spring 1976), 20(2):239–60.

Williamson, Oliver E. *The Economics of Discretionary Behavior: Managerial Objectives in a Theory of the Firm.* Englewood Cliffs, N.J.: Prentice-Hall, 1964.

—— "Administrative Controls and Regulatory Behavior." In Harry M. Trebing, ed., *Essays on Public Utility Pricing and Regulation,* pp. 411–52. East Lansing, Mich.: Institute of Public Utilities, Graduate School of Business Administration, Michigan State University, 1971.

—— *Markets and Hierarchies: Analysis and Antitrust Implications.* New York: Free Press, 1975.

—— "Franchise Bidding for Natural Monopoly—in General and with Respect to CATV." *Bell Journal of Economics* (Spring 1976), 7(1):73–104.

Williamson, Oliver E., Michael L. Wachter, and Jeffrey E. Harris. "Understanding the Employment Relation: The Analysis of Idiosyncratic Exchange." *Bell Journal of Economics* (Spring 1975), 6(1):250–78.

Wilson, George W. "Deregulation: How Far Should It Go?" *Indiana Law Journal* (Spring 1976), 51:700–717.

Wilson, James Q. "The Dead Hand of Regulation." *The Public Interest* (Fall 1971), 7(25):39–58.

—— *Political Organizations.* New York: Basic Books, 1973.

—— "The Politics of Regulation." In James W. McKie, ed., *Social Responsibility and the Business Predicament,* pp. 135–68. Washington, D.C.: Brookings Institution, 1974.

Wilson, James Q. and Edward C. Banfield. "Public-Regardingness as a Value Premise in Voting Behavior." *American Political Science Review* (December 1964), 58(4):876–87.

—— "Political Ethos Revisited." *American Political Science Review* (December 1971), 65(4):1048–62.

Wilson, James Q. and Patricia Rachal. "Can the Government Regulate Itself?" *The Public Interest* (Winter 1977), 46:3–14.

Wright, Deil S. *Understanding Intergovernmental Relations: Public Policy and Participants' Perspectives in Local, State, and National Governments.* North Scituate, Mass.: Duxbury Press, 1978.

Index